GEORGE ELIOT

A BIOGRAPHY

GEORGE ELIOT 1860
From a drawing in chalks by Samuel Laurence

GEORGE ELIOT

A BIOGRAPHY

❄

GORDON S. HAIGHT

OXFORD UNIVERSITY PRESS
NEW YORK AND OXFORD

TO

ELINOR SOUTHWOOD LEWES OUVRY

ACKNOWLEDGEMENTS

✳

In 1933 I came upon a group of George Eliot's letters in the Yale University Library. It was apparent that much of interest had been omitted from the portions included by John Walter Cross in *George Eliot's Life* (1885), and I decided to spend the summer reading them and gathering material for a new biography. I quickly saw that it would be more than a holiday task. Many other manuscripts were soon added to the collection, which is still growing after thirty-five years. Among them were two diaries of John Chapman, at whose house in the Strand George Eliot lived while editing the *Westminster Review*. They threw so revealing a light on this little-known period of her life that I published them separately in *George Eliot and John Chapman* (1940), of which a second edition is soon to appear. In 1941 Mrs. E. Carrington Ouvry, a grand-daughter of George Henry Lewes, consigned to the Yale Library her great collection of his papers, including the journals and diaries, which with those of George Eliot form the essential framework of this biography. In 1947 when a Guggenheim Fellowship enabled me to spend part of the year in Great Britain, I made the acquaintance of Mrs. Ouvry, whose friendship has been one of the pleasantest of many that the study of George Eliot has brought. As owner of the copyright she generously gave me permission to publish for the first time any letters or other writings of George Eliot and George Henry Lewes.

The members of the Evans family, George Eliot's great-nephews and nieces, also kindly made their manuscripts available. In Edinburgh George Eliot's publisher William Blackwood & Sons allowed me to examine her correspondence (now in the National Library of Scotland) as well as the business records at 45 George Street. Many librarians and collectors of manuscripts all over the world have helped with my work. I might properly repeat here the long lists of acknowledgements in Volumes I and VII of *The George Eliot Letters*, published in 1954–5 by the Yale University Press, to which I am grateful for permission to reprint both my text and notes. The John Simon Guggenheim Foundation renewed my appointment in 1953 and again in 1960, when Yale University granted me a Senior Faculty Fellowship.

I offer my warmest thanks to the Yale University Library and its staff, in particular to Mr. H. W. Liebert, Librarian of the Beinecke Rare Book Room and Manuscript Library, and Miss Marjorie G. Wynne, Research Librarian, who have nobly fostered the collection of George Eliot and Lewes manuscripts begun by Yale's first Keeper of Rare Books, Chauncey Brewster Tinker. For permission to quote from additional manuscripts I am especially obliged to Dr. John D. Gordan of the Henry W. and Albert A. Berg Collection at the New York Public Library; Mr. Rodney G. Dennis III, Curator of Manuscripts at the Houghton Library, Harvard University; Mr. William Park and Mr. James S. Ritchie of the Department of Manuscripts, National Library of Scotland; Mr. John H. P. Pafford, Goldsmiths' Librarian of the University of London; Mr. S. H. Barlow, Librarian of the Nuneaton Public Library; Mr. Ernest Simpson, Librarian of the Coventry City Libraries; and Mr. Robert Mackworth Young, Librarian of the Royal Library, Windsor Castle. To the authorities of the following I would record my thanks for permission to quote from manuscripts in their possession: Balliol College; Bodleian; British Museum; Brotherton Library, Leeds; Cambridge University Library; Edinburgh Public Library; Fales Collection, New York University; Folger Shakespeare Library; General Register Office, Somerset House; Girton College; J. Pierpont Morgan Library; Hughenden Manor; Parrish Collection, Princeton University Library; Carl and Lily Pforzheimer Foundation, Inc.; Public Record Office, London; John Rylands Library, Manchester; L. W. Smith Collection, Morristown, New Jersey; Dr. Williams's Library.

To Professor K. A. McKenzie of the University of New England, Armidale, New South Wales, author of *Edith Simcox and George Eliot* (1961) I owe particular thanks for his transcript of Edith Simcox's 'Autobiography', which provides some startling new information about George Eliot's last years. Mrs. Norman Dodds has continued to give me the benefit of her genealogical and topographical researches in Warwickshire. For other help too varied to specify I wish to thank the Reverend William C. Abrahams; Mr. Reginald Allen; Mr. John Bakeless; Professor James D. Barry; Mr. R. M. Bennett; Wing-Commander G. D. Blackwood; Professor Heinz Bluhm; Mrs. Vernon L. Bobbitt; Lady Browning (Daphne du Maurier); Mr. John Buxton; Mr. Antony Chambers;

Mrs. Douglas Delanoy; Miss Inez R. Elliott; Lord Evans of Hungershall; Mr. David Fletcher; Mrs. Harold Hochschild; Professor Walter E. Houghton; Mrs. Humphry House; Miss Alice Lynes; Mrs. Ian Maclean; Miss Helen I. McMorran; Mr. John Martineau; Mr. David I. Masson; Miss Sondra Miley; Mrs. Conwy Morgan; Mr. Dermot Morrah; Miss Diana Nelson; the Honourable Mrs. John FitzRoy Newdegate, O.B.E.; Mr. Simon Nowell-Smith; Mrs. Joan Osiakovski; Mr. Norman Delamain Ouvry; Mr. Romilly Southwood Ouvry; the late Mrs. Katherine M. Portlock; Mr. Vincent Quinn; Mrs. Sheila K. Rosenberg; Mr. William E. Stockhausen; Mrs. James Sutherland; Mrs. Gilbert McCoy Troxell; Mr. J. R. Tye; Lady Vaughan-Morgan; Dame Rebecca West, D.B.E.; Mrs. Michael Womersley.

To Mr. Frank Miles I am indebted for several of the illustrations and for many extraordinary kindnesses. Four other friends have read the manuscript. After it was completed Professor H. TenEyck Perry tested it for narrative interest. During its progress Professors Gordon N. Ray, Geoffrey Tillotson, and Kathleen Tillotson followed it almost chapter by chapter and made suggestions of the highest value. For their advice I would offer more than gratitude. My greatest debt is to my dear wife, who with patience and rare good humour suffered the rivalry of George Eliot for more than thirty years and in the most practical ways helped in the writing of this book.

CONTENTS

❃

LIST OF PLATES

ABBREVIATIONS

※

[ ]	Matter supplied by the author.
⟨ ⟩	Overscored but recoverable.

Bray–Hennell Extracts   Passages concerning George Eliot copied by Sara Hennell from letters between Mrs. Bray and members of the Hennell family (Yale).

CLL   Charles Lee Lewes.

Cross   *George Eliot's Life as Related in Her Letters and Journals.* Arranged and Edited by Her Husband, J. W. Cross (3 vols., Edinburgh and London), W. Blackwood & Sons. 1885.

Cross, New ed.   —— (1 vol., Edinburgh and London) [1887]. This ed. has been much revised by the addition of new matter and the deletion of many pages.

DNB   *Dictionary of National Biography.*

GE   George Eliot. Mary Anne (as she was christened) also spelt her name Mary Ann and Marian. Polly and Pollian were usual nicknames. In the notes she is referred to as GE.

GE Journal   MS. journal [1849]–61. The first forty-six pages were removed, probably by Cross; the extant portion begins 20 July 1854 (Yale).
MS. journal, Germany 1858 and Italy 1860 (Yale).
MS. journal, 1861–77 (Yale).
MS. journal, Italy 1864 and France 1865 (Yale).
MS. journal, Spain 1867 (not traced).

GE Diary   MS. diary for 1879 (Berg Collection, NYPL).
MS. diary for 1880 (Yale).

GHL   George Henry Lewes (pronounced Lewis).

GHL Journal   MS. journals numbered
X 24 July 1856–31 Mar. 1859,
XI 1 Apr. 1859–1 Jan. 1866, and
XII 1 June 1866–6 May 1870 (Yale).

GHL Diary   MS. diaries for 1869–76 (Yale).
MS. diary for 1877 (Mrs. E. Carrington Ouvry).
MS. diary for 1878 (Mrs. Robert Nuttall).

JB   John Blackwood

Letters	*The George Eliot Letters*, ed. Gordon S. Haight (7 vols., New Haven), Yale University Press, 1954–55; (London), Oxford University Press, 1954–56.
Maga	*Blackwood's Edinburgh Magazine.*
NLS	National Library of Scotland.
NYPL	New York Public Library.
'Occurrences at Nuneaton'	MS. journal by an unidentified writer of 'Occurrences at Nuneaton' 1810–45 (Nuneaton Public Library).
Robert Evans Journal	MS. journals for 1823, 1826, 1835–7, 1839–42 (Mr. Charles F. H. Evans); for 1831–2 (Mrs. Michael Womersley).
Simcox Autobiography	'Autobiography of a Shirt Maker', MS. journal kept by Edith Simcox, 1876–1900 (Bodleian: Eng. misc. d. 494).
TLS	*Times Literary Supplement.*
WB	William Blackwood
WR	*Westminster Review.*

GEORGE ELIOT

A BIOGRAPHY

CHAPTER I

A LITTLE SISTER

※

ARBURY HALL, the seat since 1586 of the Newdigate-Newdegate family in Warwickshire, stands squarely in the middle of the great park, reflected in two pools—the ancient fishponds of the twelfth-century monastery. Under old oaks and beech trees the drive stretches for nearly a mile from the round twin towers of North Lodge before turning through the gate at the imposing brick stables, built in the 1670s by Sir Richard Newdigate, partly from designs of his friend Sir Christopher Wren, who may have advised in the rebuilding of the chapel at the north-east corner of the house. Beginning in 1750 (three years before Horace Walpole embarked on Strawberry Hill), Sir Roger Newdigate, fifth baronet, the founder of the Newdigate Prize at Oxford, rebuilt the huge hollow square of the Tudor house, vaulted the cloister in the inner court, added oriel windows, turrets, pinnacles, and castellated battlements in Gothic style, and the exquisite fan-vaulted plaster ceilings exactly as they remain to this day. When he died childless in 1806, a year after the work was finished, the Arbury estates passed for life use to his cousin Francis Parker of Kirk Hallam, Derbyshire, who assumed the name and arms of Newdigate. He brought with him to Arbury his agent Robert Evans, a man of thirty-three, who with his wife and two children was installed at South Farm on Arbury Lane, midway between the South Lodge and Astley Castle, where Francis Parker Newdigate's eldest son was living.

Though he had little schooling, Robert Evans by his own efforts had made himself a thoroughly competent and versatile man of business. Bred to his father's trade of carpenter, he found good use for his experience in overseeing the buildings on the 7,000 acres of the Arbury lands. He could estimate within a few feet the amount of timber a given tree would provide. He surveyed and built roads in many parts of Chilvers Coton parish. He was a shrewd judge of land values. Beneath Arbury lay the richest coal deposits in Warwickshire, and part of his responsibility involved its mining and transportation on the Griff arm of the Coventry Canal. His practical knowledge and strict honesty won him the respect of every one so that he was in great demand as a valuer and arbitrator, sometimes being chosen independently by both sides in a dispute. His own farm on the estate he managed easily. His physical strength was legendary. Once when two labourers were waiting for a third to help them move a heavy rick-ladder, he lifted it and carried it to the next rick unaided.

Robert Evans's wife Harriet Poynton, whom he married in 1801 at Ellastone, Staffordshire, died in 1809 soon after the birth of a third child, which did not long survive her. She is described on a tablet in Astley Church as 'for many years the faithful friend and servant of the family of Arbury'. In 1813 Robert Evans married again. His second wife Christiana Pearson was the youngest daughter of Isaac Pearson, a well-established yeoman and a church warden, living at Old Castle Farm, Astley. She had a brother, also named Isaac, a prosperous farmer at Fillongley, and three sisters, who are immortalized as the Dodsons in *The Mill on the Floss*: Mary (Aunt Glegg), second wife of John Evarard of Attleborough; Ann (Aunt Deane), wife of George Garner of Sole End, Astley; and Elizabeth (Aunt Pullet), wife of Richard Johnson of Marston Jabbett. There is little doubt that Robert Evans was made aware that he had raised himself socially by this match. The Pearsons practised that 'variation of Protestantism unknown to Bossuet', which George Eliot described so brilliantly in the Dodsons: they revered

whatever was customary and respectable: it was necessary to be baptised, else one could not be buried in the churchyard, and to take the sacrament before death as a security against more dimly understood perils; but it was of equal necessity to have the proper pall-bearers and well-cured hams at one's funeral, and to leave an unimpeachable will.[1]

Many of the brief references to the family in Robert Evans's Journal mention funerals at which they all assembled. After Mr. Evarard was buried, for example, the lawyer came and read the will, 'and it seemed to give satisfaction'. But when Isaac Pearson died there was some displeasure with his will 'as he left all the stock to his Wife'.

While the Pearson aunts are easily recognized in the Dodsons, there was nothing of Mr. Tulliver in Robert Evans: he never failed

---

[1] *Mill on the Floss*, Bk. IV, ch. I.

at anything, never found the world too much for him. Nor did Mrs. Evans resemble the scatter-brained Mrs. Tulliver. From all one can learn about her she was an intelligent, thoughtful woman, efficient in her household and dairy, well known in the neighbour-hood for her keen sense of humour and that epigrammatic turn of phrase made famous by Mrs. Poyser, whose tongue was 'like a new-set razor'.

Besides her stepchildren, Robert (born 1802) and Frances Lucy (born 1805), Mrs. Evans soon had babies of her own to look after: Christiana, or Chrissey, as she was always called (born 1814), Isaac Pearson (born 1816), and Mary Anne, the subject of this book, who was born at South Farm, Arbury, 22 November 1819. The choice of names reflects the dominance of the Pearson side of the family; Chrissey was named for her mother, Isaac for his grandfather and uncle, while Mary Anne[1] shared the names of two Pearson aunts. Twin sons, born 16 March 1821 and named William and Thomas after Mr. Evans's brothers, lived only ten days.

When Mary Anne was four or five months old the family moved to a delightful, roomy, red-brick farm-house facing the Coventry Road at Griff where Arbury Lane joins it. It was set well back on a pleasant lawn with two tall Norway firs flanking the gate and the broad sweeping branches of a sombre old yew almost touching some of the upper windows. Beyond the house lay the farmyard with low rambling stables and out-buildings. In the garden flowers and fruit trees jostled each other in profusion. A gate opened into green fields, where not far from the road lay the Round Pool, recalled like so many other features of the Griff neighbourhood in *The Mill on the Floss* and *Adam Bede*. Early memories of the country were stamped indelibly on Mary Anne's mind. 'A human life', she said in *Daniel Deronda*,[2] 'should be well rooted in some spot of a native land, . . . a spot where the definiteness of early memories may be inwrought with affection.' Throughout thirty years in London her yearning for blue sky, orchards full of old trees and rough grass, hedgerow paths among endless fields, haunted her always. Where-ever she travelled she would notice the slope of the land, the quality of the soil, the harvest. 'I am always made happier by seeing well-cultivated land', she wrote; in fact, she seldom saw

---

[1] The Chilvers Coton Parish Register records her baptism as *Mary Anne*, and her earliest letter is so signed. In 1837 she began to write *Mary Ann*, in 1850 it became *Marian*, and in 1880 she reverted to *Mary Ann*. I use the spelling favoured at the time. Robert Evan's youngest sister was also named Ann.   [2] Ch. 3.

beauty in any terrain that was unsuitable for farming. Romantic views of mountain or sea attracted her less than the meadows with long grass in the luxuriance of June, and, everywhere, the 'tethered cows, looking at you with meek faces—mild eyed, sleek, fawn-coloured creatures, with delicate downy udders'.[1] Her comments on the weather usually considered its possible effect on the crops. When the rain poured down, her first thought was not of muddy London pavements, but of the wet hay and laid corn in the fields of Warwickshire. Of the scene so lovingly described in *Middlemarch* with little details that give each field a particular physiognomy, she wrote: 'These are the things that make the gamut of joy in landscape to midland-bred souls—the things they toddled among, or perhaps learned by heart, standing between their father's knees, while he drove leisurely.'[2] Almost every day Robert Evans went about the country looking after Mr. Newdigate's business, collecting rents, inspecting buildings, giving orders for repairs, valuing crops or cattle, arranging for the cutting and sale of timber. Often little Mary Anne was taken with him, to be left prattling with the servants in the kitchen at Astley Castle or Packington Hall or in the housekeeper's room at Arbury till her father was ready to go. She was only six years old when he took her and Mrs. Evans on a week's drive through Derbyshire and Staffordshire to visit his relations, returning through Lichfield, where they slept at the Swan.

The younger Robert Evans, still in his teens, soon returned to Kirk Hallam to act as subagent under his father, taking his sister Frances (or Fanny) with him as housekeeper and, later, governess to Mr. Parker's children. The Parker–Newdigate affairs were important in both places, and the Evans family ties were not weakened by distance. In 1864 after Robert's death Mary Anne wrote that 'in all the years I have lived I remember nothing that is much earlier than the knowledge that I had a brother Robert, and I have always thought of him, throughout the years we have been separated, as one whose heart had on every opportunity shown its ready kindness towards me'.[3] Her own sister Chrissey was sent off early to boarding school at Miss Lathom's in Attleborough, two or three miles from Griff, but close to her Aunt Evarard, whose favourite she was.

Isaac and Mary Anne spent part of each day at a dame's school kept by a Mrs. Moore just across the road from Griff House. They

[1] *Letters*, II. 368.   [2] Ch. 12.   [3] *Letters*, IV. 134.

PLATE I

ARBURY HALL

GRIFF HOUSE, CHILVERS COTON

BIRD GROVE, FOLESHILL

became inseparable playmates. There is good reason for reading autobiography in the childhood of Tom and Maggie Tulliver, who were born in the same years as they. Perhaps the earliest reminiscence is of the spring flowers 'that we used to gather with our tiny fingers as we sat lisping to ourselves on the grass',[1] and there are others in the childish daydream of a passage deleted from the manuscript of *The Mill on the Floss*, telling how Maggie,

down by the holly made her little world just what she would like it to be: ... Tom never went to school, and liked no one to play with him but Maggie; they went out together somewhere every day, and carried either hot buttered cakes with them because it was baking day, or apple puffs well sugared; Tom was never angry with her for forgetting things, and liked her to tell him tales; there were no bulls to run at her, or fierce dogs chained up and leaping out unexpectedly; her mother never wanted her hair to curl or to have her wear frills that pricked her, and the patch-work was mislaid somewhere, where it could never be found again. ... Above all, Tom loved her—oh, so much,—more, even than she loved him, so that he would always want to have her with him and be afraid of vexing her; and he as well as every one else, thought her very clever.[2]

This yearning for admiration appears again in Maggie's attempt to impress the gypsies, by one of whom little Mary Anne had been startled in what is still called Gypsy Lane near Griff. And she recalled that once, when only four years old, 'in order to impress the servant with a proper notion of her acquirements and generally distinguished position', she had played on the piano, of which she did not know a note.[3]

The dominating passion of her childhood was love for her brother Isaac. The 'Brother and Sister' sonnets recall how she followed him about everywhere, 'puppy-like', on little expeditions to the Round Pool or the rookery oaks (they become elms only for the rhyme) beyond the garden, or along the brown canal, where the barges floated past from the Griff colliery. Here she was once entrusted with the fishpole while he went off to hunt bait and was praised for getting a fish she did not know she had caught. No doll or childish toy could hold her interest if Isaac was near. He is the first example of what Cross called her 'absolute need of some one person who should be all in all to her, and to whom she should be all in all'.[4]

---

[1] *Mill on the Floss*, Bk. I, ch. 5.
[2] *Mill on the Floss*, ed. G. S. Haight (Boston, 1961), p. 44.
[3] Cross, I. 14.
[4] Cross, I. 15.

School parted them, ending these blissful days. Since the twins died Mrs. Evans had not been well. In 1824, when Isaac was eight years old, he was sent off to a school at Foleshill, near Coventry, while Mary Anne joined her sister Chrissey at Miss Lathom's. Five seems to us a tender age to be turned out to boarding school, even three miles from home. Mary Anne never forgot her suffering from cold in the circle of bigger girls around the too-narrow fireplace and her fears at night, which were something like the 'susceptibility to terror' later to haunt Gwendolen Harleth. Mr. Evans would come by frequently to see his 'little wench', and he brought the girls home for week-ends and holidays or when they were ill. He rather than her mother held Mary Anne's affection. Of her feeling for her mother one can gather little. Inferences drawn from the mothers in her novels are dangerous. In the solicitous ones—Milly Barton, Mrs. Poyser, Mrs. Moss, Dolly Winthrop, and Mrs. Davilow—the maternal is probably idealized for functional contrast. Of the others Mrs. Tulliver is most convincing when criticizing Maggie's dirty pinafore and untidy hair; we rarely see her soothing or consoling, and at the end of the novel, when Maggie needs her desperately, she has dwindled to a cipher; in Mrs. Tulliver most often we seem to see the eyes of the Pearsons, looking with silent reproach at George Eliot's misunderstood heroine.

Whatever traumatic effect the early separation from her mother may have had on Mary Anne, the separation from Isaac hurt her most keenly. Her delight at seeing him again when he came home from Foleshill for the holidays, is clearly reflected in *The Mill on the Floss*:

> Mrs. Tulliver stood with her arms open; Maggie jumped first on one leg and then on the other; while Tom descended from the gig, and said, with a masculine reticence as to the tender emotions, 'Hallo! Yap— what! are you there?'
> Nevertheless he submitted to be kissed willingly enough, though Maggie hung on his neck in rather a strangling fashion, while his blue-grey eyes wandered towards the croft and the lambs and the river, where he promised himself that he would begin to fish the first thing to-morrow morning.[1]

Isaac was already growing away from his little sister. When he was given a pony of his own, riding absorbed him completely, and he found no time to play with the disconsolate Mary Anne.

[1] Bk. I, ch. 5.

She was forced to turn for amusement to books. She was not at all precocious; her half-sister Fanny declared that, because she liked playing with Isaac so much better, Mary Anne had learnt to read with some difficulty. Her first book—the first present she remembered receiving from her father—was *The Linnet's Life*, which she kept until her death. 'It made me very happy when I held it in my little hands', she told Cross, 'and read it over and over again; and thought the pictures beautiful, especially the one where the linnet is feeding her young.'[1] There were then few books for children, in the Evans household, at least, but she had *The Pilgrim's Progress*, *The Vicar of Wakefield*, *Aesop's Fables* with pictures, and less likely favourites in Defoe's *History of the Devil* and *Joe Miller's Jest Book*, from which she sometimes recounted stories that astonished her family. Sir Walter Scott first introduced her to the writing of fiction. About 1827 a neighbour lent her sister a copy of *Waverley*, which had to be returned before the slow-reading Mary Anne had finished it. In her distress she began to write out the story herself. The episode is described in the epigraph to Chapter 57 of *Middlemarch*:

> They numbered scarce eight summers when a name
>   Rose on their souls and stirred such motions there
> As thrill the buds and shape their hidden frame
>   At penetration of the quickening air:
> His name who told of loyal Evan Dhu,
>   Of quaint Bradwardine, and Vich Ian Vor,
> Making the little world their childhood knew
>   Large with a land of mountain, lake, and scaur,
> And larger yet with wonder, love, belief
>   Toward Walter Scott, who living far away
> Sent them this wealth of joy and noble grief.
>   The book and they must part, but day by day,
> In lines that thwart like portly spiders ran,
>   They wrote the tale, from Tully Veolan.

The talent of the future novelist may perhaps be traced here in its earliest form. There is a parallel reference to Scott by Maggie Tulliver, who says of *The Pirate*:

> O, I began that once; I read to where Minna is walking with Cleveland, and I could never get to read the rest. I went on with it in my own head, and I made several endings; but they were all unhappy. . . . For a long while I couldn't get my mind away from the Shetland Isles—I used to feel the wind blowing on me from the rough sea.[2]

[1] Cross, I. 19.   [2] Bk. v, ch. I.

She seems to have been a very serious child, even at this period.
It may have been her unusual gravity that prompted the girls at
Miss Lathom's, who were much older than she, 'to call her "little
Mamma" and swoop down upon her; "I want to kiss you, little
Mamma", they would say, "but I mustn't tumble your collar"—
alluding to a phrase of hers, for she did not like to be ruffled or
made untidy'.[1] But they made a great pet of her and did as much
as thoughtless youngsters could to calm her night terrors. Though
affectionate, she was sensitive and easily reduced to passionate
tears. Her gravity at the age of nine or ten is illustrated by an
authentic anecdote recalled by Mrs. Shaw, who at a children's party
noticed Mary Anne sitting alone. Going up to her, Mrs. Shaw
said,
'My dear, you do not seem happy; are you enjoying yourself?'
'No, I am not,' said Mary Anne. 'I don't like to play with children. I like to talk to grown-up people.'[2]
She found what she liked in 1828, when she was sent to Mrs.
Wallington's Boarding School in Church Lane, Nuneaton. Born
Nancy Parnell in Cork, Mrs. John Wallington had been left with
four children when her husband died in 1805. With the help of her
eldest daughter Nancy she started the school, partly to educate her
own children, and it succeeded so well that by the time Mary Anne
came there were about thirty boarders. The principal governess
was another Irishwoman, Miss Maria Lewis, still in her twenties,
with an ugly squint in one eye, but with a kind heart and good
sense of humour about everything except religion. She was so
deeply imbued with evangelical earnestness that she would teach
only in Church of England schools or families. She took an immediate interest in unprepossessing little Mary Anne Evans, and the
affectionate relation between them continued for more than fourteen years. Miss Lewis was the most important early influence on
the child.

Religion in the Evans family had been of the old-fashioned
high-and-dry sort. Robert Evans, suspicious of all forms of
'enthusiasm', took both his politics and his religion from Arbury
Hall, never troubling his head with questions of doctrine. To be
sure, his younger brother Samuel and his wife had been converted
to Methodism in their youth, the wife causing something of a stir
by her public preaching—but that was in another county and long
ago. Miss Lewis's serious evangelicalism rested on diligent study

---

[1] Simcox Autobiography, 20 Feb. 1881, fol. 133 (Bodleian).
[2] *Letters*, I. 41.

of the Scriptures; following her example, Mary Anne read the Bible over and over again during her four years at Mrs. Wallington's. The vigorous prose of George Eliot is based on a thorough familiarity with the King James version. To those days can also be traced the habit of introspection, which led to the psychological analysis for which her novels are notable, and a profound concern with religion.[1]

Evangelicalism came rather late to Nuneaton. Only after 1824, when Henry Ryder, the first Evangelical to be made a bishop, was translated to the diocese of Lichfield and Coventry, did the parishes thereabout begin to feel the new influence. Ryder, a brother of the first Earl of Harrowby (the 'great Whig lord' referred to in 'Janet's Repentance') and a friend of Wilberforce and Hannah More, took pains to recommend for places in the diocese only men of suitable evangelical 'seriousness'. Among these was John Edmund Jones, made in 1828 Perpetual Curate of the Chapel of Ease at Stockingford, Nuneaton, which his earnest eloquence soon filled to overflowing. Bishop Ryder then licensed Mr. Jones to give a series of evening lectures in Nuneaton Parish Church, where for nearly half a century the kindly but ineffectual Reverend Hugh Hughes had been preaching totally inaudible sermons to a handful of indifferent church-goers. Mr. Jones's stirring talks at once crowded the old church with serious listeners, both Churchmen and Dissenters, and set off a great religious awakening in Nuneaton. But they also roused vociferous opposition from the conservatives, who resented any innovation. A stone was thrown through one of the upper windows during a lecture; Mr. Jones was threatened with mob action, and the violence and slanders directed at him ended only with his death in 1831. One contemporary observer, obviously hostile to the Evangelicals, declared that Mr. Jones 'had caused more divisions and quarrels on a religious score in the Town among the Church people and Dissenters than had taken place during the last quarter century'.[2]

Among Mr. Jones's ardent disciples was Maria Lewis, whose enthusiasm was imparted to her impressible young pupil Mary Anne Evans. Another was Miss Lewis's friend Nancy Wallington, who had become the wife of the Nuneaton lawyer J. W. Buchanan, leader of the opposition to Mr. Jones. The Buchanans appear as

[1] For the relation between religious introspection and the novel see Kathleen Tillotson, *Novels of the Eighteen-Forties* (Oxford, 1954), pp. 131–7.
[2] 'Occurrences at Nuneaton', Dec. 1831 (Nuneaton Public Library).

the Dempsters in all the 'keys' to the originals of 'Janet's Repentance' circulated in Warwickshire after its publication in 1857. George Eliot's assurance to her publisher that the 'real town was more vicious than my Milby; the real Dempster was far more disgusting than mine; the real Janet alas! had a far sadder end than mine',[1] probably reflects some of the partisan prejudice of her friend and teacher.

More like an elder sister than a governess, Miss Lewis gave the bright, eager little girl the sympathetic support and affection that she needed. Except from her father, she did not find it at home. There, her mother's favourites were Isaac and Chrissey. Chrissey's blond curls were always neat, while Mary Anne's straight light-brown hair defied all measures of control. Chrissey's clothes were always tidy, delighting her critical Pearson aunts, and she had that 'habitual care of whatever she held in her hands' that was to be seen in Celia Brooke. Mary Anne is described at this time as 'a queer, three-cornered, awkward girl, who sat in corners and shyly watched her elders'.[2] We must be grateful to Miss Lewis for being the first to perceive the remarkable quality of her mind and fostering it. The child developed rapidly; no stimulus to learn is stronger than admiration for the teacher. By the age of thirteen Mary Anne had mastered everything offered at Nuneaton, and her father was advised to send her to the Miss Franklins' School in Coventry. Miss Lewis continued to follow her progress there with the same affectionate interest. She came often to Griff to visit her pupil during holidays. Most of the early letters that survive are those Mary Anne wrote to Maria Lewis.

Mary and Rebecca Franklin, daughters of Francis Franklin, minister of the Cow Lane Baptist Chapel in Coventry, were not yet in their thirties. Mary had been sent to school at Bocking, Essex, where she served as pupil-teacher before she began to take pupils of her own in Mr. Franklin's little parlour in Cow Lane. Rebecca, her younger sister, after a year at school in Paris, returned to Coventry with a passable French accent and elegant manners to preside as the unimpeachable authority in all questions of language, literature, or etiquette. According to her niece, 'Mary was motherly, warm-hearted, businesslike, bustling, and self-sacrificing in the extreme, rendering to the last day the utmost homage to her sister's superiority.' Rebecca lived in a loftier atmosphere, expres-

---

[1] *Letters*, II. 347.
[2] Mathilde Blind, *George Eliot* (1883), p. 16.

sing her thoughts with exquisite elaboration; her 'conversational and epistolary powers' were considered the best in the country. Now large and flourishing, the school had moved into fine new quarters in Warwick Row. To Mary Anne Evans it opened glimpses of a great world undreamt of at Nuneaton. One student came all the way from India; another, a niece of Miss Franklin, had been sent from New York to finish her education; many were from London. The diffidence that afflicted little Mary Anne had declined under Miss Lewis's gentle sympathy, and she made an immediate impression on her schoolmates; some of them became warm friends. They envied her 'the weekly cart which brought her new-laid eggs and other delightful produce of her father's farm'.[1] He himself probably stopped often to see his little wench when he had business in Coventry.

One of the first things Mary Anne learnt was a new pronunciation of the English language. The broad Midland dialect that she had spoken all her life with many north Staffordshire phrases used by her father had been softened somewhat by Miss Lewis. Now it was banished quickly in favour of Miss Rebecca's precise, cultivated speech. Unfortunately, Mary Anne's 'chameleon-like nature', as Cross calls it, led her also to imitate the pompous Johnsonian diction, which was probably less vigorous than her own homely country talk. One of the things modelled on Miss Rebecca's example was entirely good: the low, well-modulated, musical voice, which impressed every one who knew George Eliot in later years.

The formal course of study included music, drawing, English, French, history, and arithmetic. Mary Anne's performance on the piano reached such perfection, according to a fellow student, that when visitors came to the school she was 'sometimes summoned to the parlour to play for their amusement, and, though suffering agonies from shyness and reluctance, she obeyed with all readiness'. But on being released, she was known to 'rush to her room and throw herself on the floor in an agony of tears'[2]—a repetition of the old pattern of her childhood, the bursts of tears now, perhaps, infused with adolescent sensibility. A book of her musical studies is extant, dated 1 April 1835, containing scales, chords, exercises of various kinds, with a number of songs, of which she has copied both words and music. As evidence of her proficiency in painting there are two large water-colours, dating from about the same time, of floral arrangements—honeysuckle, moss rose,

[1] Cross, I. 26.　　　[2] Cross, I. 25–6.

auricula, and so on, the stems lightly caught in a bow of blue ribbon—exercises meticulously copied. One is signed 'M. A. E. delint.', the other 'M. A. Evans delint'. Her study of French was begun at once, Miss Rebecca setting her to translate pages of Maria Edgeworth. We know that her progress must have been rapid, since she won the first-year prize, a copy of Pascal's *Pensées*. Arithmetic, too, she began in her first year under Miss Mary Franklin. Her school notebook opens with 'The Single Rule of Three. If a gallon of beer cost 10d what is that per barrel?' The problem is carefully worked out to the answer, £1. 10. 0. More than twenty pages are filled with rules and problems.

On the first page of this Notebook,[1] the earliest George Eliot manuscript, she wrote in large ornate script 'Marianne Evans', a spelling of her name that probably reflects her recent introduction to French. After the arithmetic there is an essay of more than a thousand words headed: 'A small very small portion of the many reasons why affectation is not only a folly distressing to the more sensible and humble part of mankind, but one of the most contemptible weaknesses of the human species.' Beginning with the distinction between affectation and conceit, the essay gives in long, rolling sentences satirical examples of these vices.

Thus women guilty of this foible, are those who set great store by their personal charms these in their youth they consider sufficient to secure the admiration and worship of the whole world and safe in this belief they flutter, on the flattered of the one sex, the envy of the other; and they are happy while thus admired and envied, their whole minds being in one confusion and whirl of excitement and vanity; They study no graces of mind or intellect their whole thoughts are how they shall best maintain their empire over their surrounding inferiors, and the right fit of a dress or bonnet will occupy their minds for hours together. . . . They are conceited not affected but when that youth departs alas how often do we find the conceited woman one mass of nothing but affectation, real genuine affectation—She is so used to admiration that she finds it impossible to live without it, and as the drunkard turns to his wine to drown his cares, she the former beauty, finding all that before naturally attracted gone, flies to artificial means, in order she vainly hopes and believes to secure still her usual meed of adulation—She affects a youthful walk, and a youthful manner, upon all occasions, and at the age of fifty may often be seen clothed in the girlish fashion of sixteen totally forgetting that her once rounded neck and shoulders which at the latter age were properly uncovered, are now pointed and scraggy and would be much better hidden from sight by a more matronly habiliment.

---

[1] For an account of GE's Notebook see Appendix I.

Mary Anne was especially remembered at Miss Franklins' for English composition. A fellow pupil recalled that she was 'from her first entering the school, far in advance of the rest; and while the themes of the other children were read, criticised, and corrected in class, hers were reserved for the private perusal and enjoyment of the teacher, who rarely found anything to correct'.[1] The tone of hyperbole at least shows that Mary Anne won the envy and admiration of her schoolmates. Her essay on 'Affectation and Conceit', which may well be one of the themes reserved for private perusal, provides ample evidence of how thoroughly she had caught Miss Rebecca Franklin's diction. The eighteenth-century moral essay has been carefully studied as a model, whose limitations the fourteen-year-old critic, with some danger of conceit, is happy to exhibit. In her description of women who 'set great store by their personal charms' there is perhaps a glimpse into the sensitive feelings of the plain little girl, already aware that her strength must lie in the graces of mind and intellect. The essay is published for the first time in Appendix I.

Miss Rebecca encouraged the girls to read widely. Under her guidance Mary Anne made her first acquaintance with many English authors. Shakespeare, Milton, Isaac Watts, Pope, Young, Cowper, Southey, Moore, and Byron are a few that we know she read during her years at school, along with a good deal of trashy verse. The girls admired annuals and gift-books like the *Keepsake* with its preposterous engraving of a bride and groom leaving church that Lydgate ridicules so mercilessly in *Middlemarch*.[2] Many favourite sentimental poems Mary Anne copied into her Notebook. One is entitled 'The Forsaken':

> Oh! does he think when I assume
>   This cold unmeaning smile
> That I forget his vows of love?
>   That I forget his guile?
> T'was he, that left remorse to pine
>   Where peace was wont to dwell:
> And shall the trampled foot forget?
>   Oh! I remember well.

Succeeding stanzas tell how the false one, coming to buy the simple wreaths her mother used to sell, paused to whisper praises of her

---

[1] Cross, I. 25.   [2] Ch. 27.

beauty, danced with her at harvest home, and put a ring upon her finger.

> The summer passed, he came no more
> I thought I should have died;
> When next we met, a lovely girl
> Was smiling at his side.
> He saw me, but his guilty eye
> Abashed before me fell.
> The lady soothed him, and he smiled,
> Ah! I remember well!
>
> .   .   .   .   .
>
> And I have met him in the world,
> And I have heard him speak,
> And madly forced a smile to light
> My flushed and feverish cheek;
> Do I forget?—No!; let him wait
> Until he hears my knell,
> For till I rest beneath the turf
> I shall remember well!

This unsigned poem is found in Alaric Alexander Watts's *Poetical Album* (1829), p. 364. Next, Mary Anne copied an even more melodramatic piece, 'The Unwilling Bride':

> The joy bells are ringing—oh! come to the church
> We shall see the bride pass if we stand in the porch;
> The bridegroom is wealthy; how brightly arrayed
> Are the menials who wait on the gay cavalcade,
> The steeds with the chariots prancing along
> And the peasants advancing with music and song—
>
> Now comes the procession, the bridesmaids are there
> With white robes and ribbons, and wreaths in their hair;
> Yon feeble old knight the bride's father must be
> And now walking proudly, her mother we see;
> A pale girl in tears, slowly moves by her side;
> But where is the bridegroom, and where is the bride?

The answer is given in the next stanza:

> A Bridal like *this* is a sorrowful sight
> For *that* pale girl is bride, to the feeble old knight.

Out of the church she comes, drawing the rich veil over her eyes, while

> her pale lips inaudibly move.
> Her equipage waits—she is placed by the side
> Of her aged companion, a sorrowing bride!

This piece, also unsigned, is by Thomas Haynes Bayly, author of 'I'd be a Butterfly', who then divided Mary Anne's admiration with Alaric Watts. It is worth noting that in the plot of 'The Forsaken' there is a crude parallel to the seduction of Hetty Sorrel in *Adam Bede* and that the marriage of a young girl to an old man recurs in *Middlemarch*. It is curious to see the rudiments of those situations attracting George Eliot's imagination so early.

Miss Franklin was surprisingly liberal about the girls' reading and did not forbid novels. During her first year at the school, when she was thirteen years old, Mary Anne read Bulwer Lytton's *Devereux*, and, we may be sure, most of Scott, who was producing novels until his death in 1832. With none of Scott's genius G. P. R. James succeeded to his market, and the hungry public gobbled avidly whatever he put before them. Mary Anne read his *Richelieu* (1829), *Darnley* (1830), and *Mary of Burgundy* (1831) during her school years; some of his semi-fictitious historical works like *The Life and Times of Louis XIV* (1838) are later referred to in letters. But the clearest evidence of her fondness for James is found in her Notebook in an original story, which opens with the same solitary horseman on his fine black steed who rides through the clear autumn air in the first pages of at least six of James's romances.

'Edward Neville', as the story may be called, is the earliest extant fiction from the pen of George Eliot. It begins 'on a bright and sunny morning' towards the end of 1650, when the young stranger approaches the bridge over the Wye at the entrance of the town of Chepstow. He 'seemed as he gazed on the beautiful prospect before him to unbend the stern rigidity of his fine features, and a tear started to his eye', which roved over the scene from 'the majestic walls of the Castle, then in its prime (though now still more beautiful in its ruins)', to stately Piercefield House, embosomed in the rich foliage of the woods. While his proud eye was fixed on the latter, the 'ferocity and sternness vanished from his countenance and a deep sigh burst from his heart' as he uttered his first words:

"Well done, my brave and trusty Ronald", said he, addressing his horse and patting him. "Thou hast served me this day better than thou hast ever done before, though never yet hast thou been lacking in thy service to thy master—but I will urge thee no more. Now thy trusty feet have brought me where I had scarcely ever dared hope I might again come. Welcome welcome to my eyes the scene of my happiest days." But his return (as he confided to

Ronald) was dimmed by his unhappy position as an outcast from society, an alien from his family, a deserter, and a regicide. At this word a bitter smile curled his lip, and, dashing another tear from his eye, he resumed his former reckless demeanour, crossed the bridge, and went at once to the Castle, where he asked to see Henry Marten, at that time a prisoner confined to the Eastern Tower.

Henry Marten's character is then described. Originally intended for the Church, he had been sent to college. But his 'character was licentious in the extreme and, hating the profession he was intended for, he early in life married a rich widow and gave up his gown. From being careless on the religious subject, he soon began to grow opposed to them and joined with several public characters of the time in openly denying the truths of revelation.' Soon Marten 'added disdain and insult to dislike of the King, and eventually with his own hand signed the death warrant for that unhappy monarch's execution'. Of this crime he was 'found guilty and confined for life in the Castle of Chepstow, to which I have now introduced my reader'.

When the stranger addressed Marten by the name of Uncle, he started, and rising hurriedly from his seat, exclaimed:

'Edward, is it possible? What evil genius brings you here *now*? . . .'

'My horse and my *will* have brought me here,' said the young man. '. . . I am come to you for shelter. . . .'

'And how am I, a prisoner, to afford you shelter, Edward Neville? . . . I hope', said he, bending on his nephew [Mary Anne spells it *newphew* throughout] a keen and searching look, 'that you are not such a boy as to be drawn hither by a fair form and a bright eye.'

'Uncle,' said the young man, 'from you only would I brook such questions, but do not provoke me too far. I have served you through many dangers; I would serve you through more if you needed them, for you are my nearest living relative. But breathe not one word of *her* in my presence—no, stay', he rejoined, as the old man was about to interrupt him, 'I will tell you all that has befallen me since we last parted, but not another word on the subject you have broached, or we part forever.'

Edward proceeds to describe the defeat of Cromwell's troops, who are scattered 'far and wide over the country, fugitives they themselves know not where'. Their commander Saltmarsh had been rebuked by Cromwell for impetuosity in attacking at Faldon Hill. Edward himself bore the letter from the Protector.

'How,' said Marten, interrupting him, 'how did Saltmarsh receive the Protector's letter? How did his impatient temper brook his general's resentment?'

'I can tell you in few words. He tore the paper in a thousand fragments, stamped on it in his rage, and ordering his horse, without one
moment's reflection galloped away he knew not where, for he was absent
two whole days.'

Saltmarsh had not fallen into the enemy's hands, but had betrayed his own troops to the King's commander, who took
many prisoners and compelled the rest 'to fly they knew not
where'.

Edward Neville, the only son of Marten's favourite sister, was
adopted by his uncle, 'who having no children of his own and
possessing but little love for his wife, whom fortune alone had
induced him to marry, lavished all the love his stern heart could
hold upon his nephew'. When the lad was eight years old he
accompanied Marten to Chepstow, and was imbued with all his
hatred of kingly power. The one family in the neighbourhood that
they were allowed to visit was that of Sir Verner Mordaunt of
Piercefield House; he had a daughter Mary, to whom Edward,
though stern and harsh to others, was 'gentle, tender, and kind'.
Mary was three years younger than Edward, and 'a mutual intimacy had sprung up between them, which as they grew up ripened
into a much warmer sentiment'. In their childhood it was not
objected to by her parents; 'but when Edward reached his eighteenth year and Mary her fifteenth, it was deemed advisable they
should be separated'.

Though Sir Verner was a firm Loyalist, directly opposed to
Marten's principles, out of humanity he used to invite him to
dinner as much as possible to soften the rigour of his confinement.
One day he unfortunately asked Marten how he would behave if
the whole scene of the condemnation of King Charles could be
acted over again. Marten immediately replied that he would do
again 'exactly as he *had* done before'. Sir Verner was so indignant
at this that he would never see him after. Edward Neville, of
course, was included in the dismissal, 'for the parents of Mary were
glad of some pretext for removing him from her society'.

Here, without even a period, the story breaks off, though twelve
blank pages follow in the Notebook. Perhaps the young author's
invention faltered. Her principal source, Coxe's *Historical Tour
of Monmouthshire*, explains some of the anachronisms, which the
author of *Romola* would never have tolerated. But to set her tale
in 1650, fourteen years before Marten had been condemned as a
regicide, shows a surprising ignorance of history. He was not confined at Chepstow till 1665. Chronology did not much trouble

Mary Anne in this romance. The complete text and a discussion of its source will be found in Appendix I.

Towards the end of her anthology of poems in the Notebook Mary Anne's taste seems to shift from romantic melancholy to a more sombre note. In lines 'To a Sister', for example, the young brother, far away, begs her to remember him:

> But not in Fashion's brilliant hall
> Surrounded by the gay and fair
> And thou the fairest of them all
> Ah! think not, think not of me there,
> But when the thoughtless crowd is gone
> And hushed the voice of senseless glee
> And all is silent, still and lone,
> And thou art sad, remember me.
>
> .   .   .   .   .
>
> Remember me, not I entreat
> In scenes of festal week-day joy. . . .
> But on the sacred solemn day
> And dearest on thy bended knee
> When thou for those thou lov'st dost pray,
> Sweet spirit, *then* remember me.

Of the seven stanzas, copied from some evangelical magazine, these are enough to indicate the change that came over Mary Anne about the time of her fifteenth birthday. No letters remain to document it; the experience of George Eliot's heroines provides not even hypothetical parallels. Maggie Tulliver, who matches Mary Anne closely in childhood, betrays no interest in the Evangelical Movement. The vicar of the Tullivers' 'pleasant rural parish was not a controversialist, but a good hand at whist', and kind Dr. Kenn, who is said to have upset St. Ogg's by putting candlesticks on the altar, touches Maggie with no doctrines. When trouble came to her it was economic, not spiritual; she found her solace not in evangelical tracts but in Thomas à Kempis's *Imitation of Christ* and in *The Christian Year* of John Keble, the 'true and primary author' of the Oxford Movement. Though little is said of Maggie's life at Miss Firniss's school at Laceham, she certainly underwent no such conversion as befell Mary Anne at Coventry.

Miss Lewis's religion was mild and sentimental, emphasizing love and salvation rather than hell fire. She read her Bible constantly and taught its moral examples to her pupils; she visited the sick, comforted the mourner, and embroidered slippers for the curate. The Evangelicalism she inculcated in Mary Anne was a gentle benevolence, more like the teaching of the early Wesleyans than the harshness of Amos Barton, who talked of nothing but sin and the need of an unobtainable mercy. If, as we are told, Mary Anne taught Sunday School near Griff before she was twelve years old, she was probably impelled as much by desire to exhibit her learning as by spiritual zeal.

In her first years at the Miss Franklins' her thirst for knowledge was still dominant. The religious life of the School was always serious. Mrs. Franklin's brother was Secretary of the Baptist Missionary Society; one of her daughters had gone as a missionary to India, and a son had died in training for a missionary career. It is surprising that the School was not more limited in view than it was. Moderation and good sense seem to have animated the place with a tone that held adolescent religious yearnings within reasonable bounds. On Sundays all the girls went to the Cow Lane Chapel to hear Mr. Franklin preach. During the week they organized prayer meetings among themselves, in which, we are told, Mary Anne was one of the leaders—by no means the least eloquent. Mr. Franklin held, not the stricter doctrines of the Particular Baptists, but the more liberal tenets of the General Baptists, which in spirit were close to those of the stricter Evangelicals in the Established Church. Yet conversion, the conviction that one was utterly sinful and could be saved from hell only by accepting the atonement of Christ, was the conventional beginning of the religious life. One feels certain that it struck Mary Anne suddenly and hard. Though she had never cared much about dress and had no beauty to be proud of, she now began to neglect her personal appearance in order to show concern for the state of her soul. Her acts of charity were performed with greater fervour, and she practised mild abstinences from innocent pleasures.

Her brother Isaac had gone from the Foleshill school to a private tutor named Docker at Birmingham, where along with a comfortable worldliness he imbibed High Church views. At home during the holidays the sincere but misguided efforts of his young sister, immersed in gloomy Calvinism, to show him the error of his ways could only have widened the gap between them. 'I used to go about like an owl', she confessed, 'to the great disgust of my brother, and I would have denied him what I now see to have been quite lawful amusements.'[1] Her conversion is reflected in the

[1] Mrs. John Cash in Cross, I. 157.

poems copied into her Notebook. Instead of 'The Indian Girl's
Song' or 'The Corsair' there are pieces from *The Sabbath Harp*
by notable Evangelicals like Thomas Dale and Henry Hart
Milman:

> Lord have mercy, and remove us
> Early to thy place of rest.

There is an imitation of Anna Walther's 'Work, for the Night is
Coming' that begins:

> Go when the evening shineth
> Go when the moon is bright,
> Go when the eve declineth
> Go in the hush of night.
> Go with June wind and feeling,
> Fling earthly thoughts away,
> And in thy chamber kneeling
> Do thou in secret pray.

Some notice was apparently attracted by her new ascetic way of
life. The last poem in the Notebook, probably written by Mary
Anne herself, is entitled 'On Being Called a Saint':

> A Saint! Oh would that I could claim
> The privileg'd, the honor'd name
> And confidently take my stand
> Though lowest in the saintly band!
>
> .   .   .   .   .
>
> Oh for an interest in that name
> When hell shall ope its jaws of flame
> And sinners to their doom be hurl'd
> While scorned saints 'shall judge the world.'
>
> How shall the name of Saint be prized
> Tho' now neglected and despised
> When truth

With this ominous aposiopesis the Notebook ends. 'What is
truth?' said jesting Pilate. It was no question for an earnest young
convert to answer in laboured rhymes.

Though profoundly affected by her religious experience at
Coventry, Mary Anne showed no interest in specifically Baptist
doctrines. She always regarded herself as belonging to the Church
of England, of which the Evangelical party was then not far in
feeling from many groups of Dissenters. No record can be found

of her confirmation, a sacrament much neglected at this time in Warwickshire.[1] On Christmas Day in 1836 her father records in his Journal: 'Went to Coton Church in the forenoon there were a sacriment I and Crissey stoped and received it, and Mary Ann stopd. This is her first time she has received the sacriment.'

Much had happened during that year. For a long time Mrs. Evans had been growing steadily weaker, suffering from what was probably cancer. In July 1835 Mr. Evans was taking her about 'in the little 4 wheel carriage as she is so unwell that she does not ride in the Gig'. Driving about on business, 31 December, he suffered an acute attack of kidney stone and in great pain reached Griff House with difficulty.[2] Mr. Bucknill, the Nuneaton surgeon, stayed with him day and night. In his Journal for 3 January 1836 he wrote: 'this was a terable day and night I thought I could not live this day and night—I was blooded several times in the arm and six or seven dozen of leeches set on about my kidneys Dr. Mellor attended me as well as Mr Bucknill three days'. After further severe attacks he began to recover. But Mrs. Evans was now growing rapidly worse. By the 25th of January her legs were paralysed and her pain intense. Soon Mr. Bucknill was back in the house, staying by her day and night, warning the family that she might die at any time. 'We look for her death every hour', Mr. Evans wrote; 'no ease can be given her.' The end came on 3 February 1836: 'My dear Wife Christiana died this morning about 5 o'clock after a Dreadfull night of pain but I was happy to see her go off at last without a Struggle her Breath stopd.' All three of her children were at home with him during these sad days.

Her mother had never been very close to Mary Anne; her father was 'the one deep strong love I have ever known',[3] and she resolved to fill the empty place for him as well as she could. Chrissey was the elder, to be sure, but not the more helpful. It was Mary Anne whom Mr. Evans took with him to Coventry to buy wallpaper and to choose a new sideboard; Mary Anne mended his clothes, looked after the servants, and in the evenings read him his favourite novels of Walter Scott. Chrissey was instinctive, with no strong intellectual interests, and though Mary Anne loved her dearly, their minds moved on different planes. Their half-sister

[1] 'Occurrences at Nuneaton' records a confirmation at Nuneaton by Bishop Ryder, 14 Aug. 1829, 'to the number of 606'.
[2] His Journal records an earlier attack in Apr. 1831.
[3] *Letters*, I. 284.

Fanny, who came with her husband Henry Houghton to visit, understood her best.

Chrissey was married at Chilvers Coton 30 May 1837 to Edward Clarke, son of Robert Clarke, Esq., of Brooksby Hall, now the County Agricultural College near Leicester. In the register Mary Ann, as bridesmaid, signed her name for the first time without the final *e*. Mr. Clarke, a member of the Royal College of Surgeons and a licentiate of the Society of Apothecaries, had a small practice at Meriden, a pleasant village five miles northwest of Coventry, and served as medical officer of the Union or Workhouse. On returning from their wedding journey the Clarkes presented Mary Ann with a pocket Prayer Book and Book of Sunday Lessons, an appropriate gift.

Her religious zeal, far from wavering, had increased markedly since her return to Griff. If this kind of evangelical severity had not been endemic and increasing, one might be tempted to look for psychological explanations—a feeling of guilt over the death of her mother that demanded punishment, and so on; the very paucity of comment about her mother is suspicious, and the period of renunciation and asceticism was prolonged till she was past twenty. But such speculations are futile; one can tell only the facts. We know that she relieved the poor and visited the sick, praying with them as if she were 'living in the time of the Apostles'.[1] We know that during a week in London with Isaac in 1838 she refused to go to the theatre and spent her evenings reading Josephus's *History of the Jews*. On the Sunday morning they heard a sermon at St. Bride's by the Reverend Thomas Dale, whose poems she had long admired, and in the afternoon went to St. Paul's, where her 'strongest feeling was that of indignation (I mean during the sermon) towards the surpliced personages, chapters I think they are, who performed the chanting, for it appears with them a mere performance, their behaviour being that of schoolboys, glad of an opportunity to titter unreproved'.[2] The same Puritanical sternness appears at Coventry, during a return visit to the Miss Franklins, who had stayed with her successively at Griff. On the last day she went with Miss Rebecca to a concert at St. Michael's, arranged in honour of her old music teacher, the organist Edward Simms, the programme including Haydn's *Creation*, Handel's *Jephtha*, and Mendelssohn's new oratorio *Paul*, sung by John Braham and other noted singers. 'I think', she wrote to her schoolmate Martha Jackson, who shared her serious evangelical views,

---

[1] *Middlemarch*, Ch. 1. [2] *Letters*, 1. 7.

'nothing can justify the using of an intensely interesting and solemn passage of Scripture as a rope dancer uses her rope'; it seems 'not consistent with millennial holiness'.[1] And to Maria Lewis she announced a determination to attend no more oratorios; 'for my part I humbly conceive it to be little less than blasphemy for such words as "Now then we are ambassadors for Christ" to be taken on the lips of such a man as Braham (a Jew too!)'.[2]

In these austerities Mary Ann far surpassed her teachers. Miss Rebecca, arbitress of the arts for Coventry, had no intention of abandoning Haydn or Handel. Miss Lewis lent her a novel soon after receiving the much-quoted letter in which Mary Ann makes her most uncompromising comments on fiction. At the start she excepts 'omnivorous' readers, of whom she was certainly one ('For such persons we cannot legislate.'), and puts out of question 'standard works whose contents are matter of constant reference' like *Don Quixote*, *Hudibras*, *Robinson Crusoe*, *Gil Blas*, Byron's and Southey's poems, Scott's novels, and the plays of Shakespeare, though we need 'as nice a power of distillation as the bee to suck nothing but honey from his pages'. In examining novels read merely for entertainment, she speaks from her own experience:

I am I confess not an impartial member of a jury in this case for I owe the culprits a grudge for injuries inflicted on myself. I shall carry to my grave the mental diseases with which they have contaminated me. When I was quite a little child I could not be satisfied with the things around me; I was constantly living in a world of my own creation, and was quite contented to have no companions that I might be left to my own musings and imagine scenes in which I was chief actress. Conceive what a character novels would give to these Utopias. I was early supplied with them by those who kindly sought to gratify my appetite for reading and of course I made use of the materials they supplied for building my castles in the air. . . . Religious novels [like James's *Huguenot*] are more hateful to me than merely worldly ones. . . . The weapons of the Christian warfare were never sharpened at the forge of romance.[3]

Of course, this long effusion was something of a show-piece, an improvisation on a set moral theme like her essay on 'Affectation and Conceit', designed to dazzle her teacher. No one needed less than Maria Lewis to be told about Mary Ann's childhood; we must not take the statement too seriously.

During the years at Griff her reading was certainly omnivorous. The Bible, of course, she read every day, studying the text with

[1] *Letters*, I. 9.   [2] *Letters*, I. 13.   [3] *Letters*, I. 21–3.

ever closer scrutiny. She acquired a polyglot version edited by Samuel Lee (1831) and a copy of Cruden's *Concordance*. Her letters, particularly those to the Samuel Evanses, are tissues of biblical quotation, sometimes a bit too proudly displaying her humility. Among her favourite authors were Milton, Shakespeare, and Young, whose *Night Thoughts* she knew almost by heart; Isaac Watts, John Ryland, and Cowper followed. Most of the books she mentioned in 1838 and 1839 are religious. On the lighter side were the letters of Hannah More and biographies of other eminent Evangelicals like Wilberforce, Sir Richard Hill, and Mrs. Mary Fletcher of Madeley, or narratives of missionaries like John Williams, who had just died in the South Sea Islands. The more solid fare consisted of works like *A Practical Commentary upon the Two First Chapters of the First Epistle of Peter* (1693) by Archbishop Leighton, and his *Theological Lectures*, which Mary Ann read in Ward's Library of Standard Divinity and the Christian Family Library, to both of which precursors of the Religious Book-of-the-Month Club she subscribed. Joseph Milner's *History of the Church of Christ* (1794–7) and Joseph Hoppus's *Schism as Opposed to Unity of the Church* (1839) also came to her hand.

Her reputation as a learned young lady was spreading in the neighbourhood. The squire of Chilvers Coton, Henry Harpur, tried to mollify her evangelical rigour by lending her books by William Gresley and some of the Oxford *Tracts for the Times*. Kind Mrs. Charles Newdegate, mistress of Arbury Hall since the death of Francis Newdigate in 1835, invited her to borrow freely any books she liked from the great library there, which had been growing steadily since Queen Elizabeth's day. This offer proved useful for a plan Mary Ann conceived in 1839 of compiling a Chart of Ecclesiastical History, which would show on one sheet in perpendicular columns the Roman emperors with their dates, the political and religious state of the Jews, the bishops and remarkable men of the several Christian churches, the chronology of apostolical and patristic writings, the schisms and heresies, and much, much more, from the birth of Christ to the Reformation. Profits were destined partly for the new church to be built at Attleborough. Mary Ann worked hard on the project for some six months before the publication of a similar chart brought her labour to an end. Robert Evans, a self-educated man, who spelled all his life like Mr. Tulliver 'on an impromptu phonetic system', was naturally proud of his daughter's achievements and gave her every means to continue them. He let her buy whatever books she wanted, and arranged to have Joseph Brezzi, the language teacher at Coventry, come once a week to give her lessons in Italian and (beginning in March 1840) in German. Soon she was reading Botta's *Storia d'Italia*, Silvio Pellico's *Le mie Prigioni*, and Schiller's *Wallenstein*. But it is wrong to think of Mary Ann as a recluse, burying herself in tomes of theology. Several young friends of her school-days corresponded with her and visited her sometimes at Griff. One was Jessie Barclay, daughter of a prosperous manufacturer of patent medicines, who came in July 1839. In November Mary Ann went with her father to London, travelling for the first time by the railway, and stayed five days with Jessie while he saw to his employers' business at Maidstone, Uxbridge, and Harefield. Another friend was Martha (or Patty) Jackson, with whom Mary Ann corresponded for years. Though Patty too was 'serious' in the evangelical sense, their correspondence is much lighter than that with Miss Lewis; one regrets that more of it has not survived. Even with Patty, however, the didactic note is heard. Mary Ann proposed that they take assigned subjects for their letters, bones 'to pick together without contention'.[1] Though she encouraged her friend to follow her example of studying Latin by Locke's System of Classical Instruction, in which Mary Ann was reading Aesop with the help of Taylor's interlineal literal translation, Patty was not up to such heroic measures. The Language of Flowers seems to have marked the height of Patty's linguistic power. She signed her letters Ivy, signifying Constancy, and chose the name Clematis or Mental Beauty for Mary Ann, who in turn christened Maria Lewis Veronica, Fidelity in Friendship.

Mary Ann's literary urge was not extinguished by the 'too varied and laborious set of studies' she had adopted. She continued to write verse as she had at Miss Franklins'. In July 1839 she sent Miss Lewis some carefully polished lines, 'the crude fruit of a lonely walk last evening, when the words of one of our martyrs occurred to me'.[2] Urged on by her former teacher, she sent the piece to the *Christian Observer*, where it appeared in January 1840, signed M. A. E., George Eliot's first published work.

> As o'er the fields by evening's light I stray,
> I hear a still, small whisper—'Come away!
> Thou must to this bright, lovely world soon say
> Farewell!'

[1] *Letters*, I. 48.　　[2] *Letters*, I. 27.

> The mandate I'd obey, my lamp prepare,
> Gird up my garments, give my soul to pray'r
> And say to earth and all that breathe earth's air
> Farewell!

In succeeding stanzas farewells are extended to the sun, moon, stars, meadows and trees, animals and birds, insects and fishes, until

> Books that have been to me as chests of gold,
> Which miser like, I secretly have told,
> And for them love, health, friendship, peace have sold,
> Farewell!

But to the Bible, 'of earth's gifts alone', she will not say farewell; and with her 'dear kindred' she parts 'only till we meet in heaven'. The editor could not resist a note reminding M. A. E. that there would be no need of a Bible in the New Jerusalem. Another poem sent to Miss Lewis, a sonnet beginning characteristically,

> Oft, when a child, while wand'ring far alone,
> That none might rouse me from my waking dream,

restates rather mechanically the vanity of human wishes. Later, 'What do you think of the Progress of Architecture as a subject for Poetry?'[1] she asked Miss Lewis. Happily, no more is heard of it.

Social life at Griff centred naturally about her 'dear kindred'. Robert, who lived at Kirk Hallam, they saw least often, but they followed the news of his family closely, noting how his first son was named Isaac, the second Robert, and the second daughter Mary. Fanny Houghton, who now lived at Baginton, Mary Ann saw frequently. But her own sister Chrissey Clarke at Meriden was dearest to her, and she followed the fast-growing family with affectionate concern. Of her nine children Chrissey Clarke too named her second son Robert and her first daughter Mary Louisa, 'owing partly to my denunciation of everyday names [like Ann] before the plebeian monosyllabic surname to which her star has made her inheritor'.[2] Of wider social relations Church bazaars and charity sermons seem to fill the genteel side. But Mary Ann was energetically engaged in private benevolence among the poor of Griff and Chilvers Coton. She organized a clothing club for the families of unemployed ribbon weavers, left idle for long periods

---

[1] *Letters*, I. 37.   [2] *Letters*, I, 79.

by the vagaries of fashion. Years later, it was recalled, one of these poor people had said when she had left Griff, 'We shall never have another Mary Ann Evans.'[1]

Her friends were not all of her own sex. There is a hint in the spring of 1840 that her heart may have been caught by a young man who, not holding her evangelical views, was (on the advice of Miss Lewis) removed from her thoughts, perhaps without ever having realized that he occupied them.

I feel that a sight of one being whom I have not beheld except passingly since the interview I last described to you would *probably* upset *all*; but as it is, the image now seldom arises in consequence of entire occupation and, I trust in some degree, desire and prayer to be free from rebelling against Him whose I am by right, whose I would be by adoption. I endeavoured to pray for the beloved object to whom I have alluded, I must still a little while say *beloved*, last night and felt soothingly melted in thinking that if mine be really prayers my acquaintance with him has probably caused the *first* to be offered up specially in his behalf. But all this I ought not to have permitted to slip from my pen.[2]

'Cupid', she told Patty Jackson, 'listens to no entreaties; we must deal with him as an enemy, either boldly parry his shafts or flee.'[3] Like any adolescent Mary Ann was susceptible. There was Joseph Brezzi, for example, her language teacher, whom she found

anything but uninteresting, all external grace and mental power, but 'Cease ye from man' is engraven on my amulet. And to tell you the truth [she writes to Maria Lewis] I begin to feel involuntarily isolated, and without being humble, to have such a consciousness that I am a negation of all that finds love and esteem as makes me anticipate for myself—no matter what; I shall have countless undeserved enemies if my life be prolonged, wherever my lot may be cast, and I need rigid discipline, which I have never yet had.[4]

It was a prophetic remark. As time passed, the prospect of a lover seemed more remote. In a letter to Patty, 20 October 1840, she said:

Every day's experience seems to deepen the voice of foreboding that has long been telling me, 'The bliss of reciprocated affection is not allotted to you under any form. Your heart must be widowed in this manner from the world, or you will never seek a better portion; a consciousness of possessing the fervent love of any human being would soon become your heaven, therefore it would be your curse.'[5]

[1] Cross, I. 156.   [2] *Letters*, I. 46–7.   [3] *Letters*, I. 49.
[4] *Letters*, I. 51.   [5] *Letters*, I. 70.

One day in her twentieth year she went to a dance at Mrs. Thomas Bull's;

> when I had been there some time the conviction that I was not in a situation to maintain the *Protestant* character of the true Christian, together with the oppressive noise that formed the accompaniment to the dancing, the sole amusement, produced first headache and then that most wretched and unpitied of afflictions, hysteria, so that I regularly disgraced myself. Mrs. Bull was extremely kind. One good effect of a temporary annoyance and indisposition will be to render me more decided in rejecting all invitations of a dubious character.[1]

One is reminded of the ten-year-old Mary Ann, who would rather talk to grown-up people than play with children.

Her household duties at Griff included supervising the kitchen, making the mince pies, damson cheese, and currant jelly, as well as overseeing the dairy. She had large, finely shaped hands such as she gives several of her heroines; she once pointed out to a friend that one hand was broader across than the other because, she thought, of making so much butter and cheese during those years at Griff. The housekeeping was particularly irksome during the times of traditional hospitality like the harvest home feast described in *Adam Bede* (Chapter 53), which her evangelical strictness found repugnant for its pagan jollity. Isaac's birthday was always an occasion for gaiety, when the disapproving young housekeeper had to provide the fare. Robert Evans's Journal for Monday, 20 May 1839 notes that 'Isaac had a party Shooting Rooks at Arbury and dined with him as it was his [23rd] Birthday yesterday the 19th so he kept it today', a concession to Sabbath observance one might not have seen at Griff a decade before. In March 1840 Mary Ann was pleased to report 'that Isaac is determinedly busy, and altogether improving'.

But it was not Isaac alone who was changing; there were faint signs that her own Evangelicalism was cooling. Early in 1839 when her Methodist aunt Mrs. Samuel Evans first visited Griff, Mary Ann used to have little debates with her about predestination, upholding the Calvinist position against her aunt's mild Arminianism.

When my uncle came to fetch her, after she had been with us a fortnight or three weeks, he was speaking of a deceased minister, once

---

[1] *Letters*, I. 41. In 1815 Jane Porter wrote: '(then a very young person) I burst into tears at a large table after dinner from horror and pity of some persons present, who were scoffing at religion without reprimand from any one.'

PLATE II

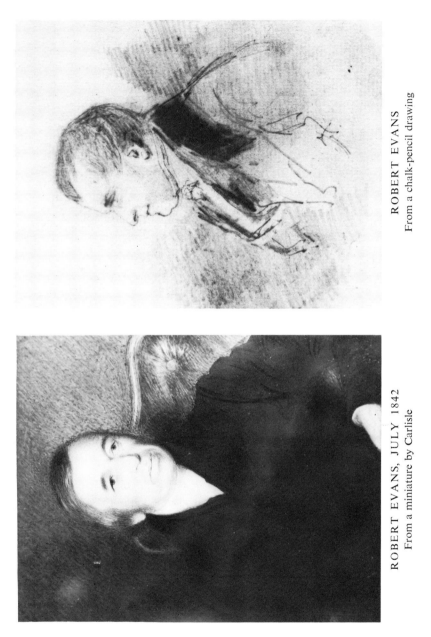

ROBERT EVANS
From a chalk-pencil drawing

ROBERT EVANS, JULY 1842
From a miniature by Carlisle

greatly respected, who from the action of trouble upon him had taken to small tippling, though otherwise not culpable. 'But I hope the good man's in heaven for all that,' said my uncle. 'Oh yes,' said my aunt, with a deep inward groan of joyful conviction. 'Mr. A's in heaven—that's sure.' This was at the time an offence to my stern, ascetic hard views—how beautiful it is to me now![1]

she added when recalling it in 1859. During this visit Mrs. Evans told her about going to prison to talk to a young girl condemned to death for child murder and softening her heart so that she died penitent—a story that was to form the germ of *Adam Bede*. In June 1840 Mary Ann went with her father to visit his Staffordshire relatives, staying overnight with the Samuel Evanses. On this occasion she found the interview less interesting, because 'I think I was less simply devoted to religious ideas'.[2]

The pattern of her reading was changing, too. She now revels in the Romantics, some of whom she had not looked into since her conversion. Byron, Shelley, Coleridge, Southey, and particularly Wordsworth, whose poems in her six-volume Moxon edition she read steadily all the rest of her life. 'I never before met with so many of my own feelings, expressed just as I could like them', she wrote on her twentieth birthday. In March 1840 she bought *The Christian Year*, in which, despite Keble's position among the Anglo-Catholics, she found the 'fields of poesy' lovelier than ever. She read both the *Lyra Apostolica* and the *Tracts for the Times*, and subscribed to Isaac Taylor's *Ancient Christianity*, which showed that the Church of the fourth century, from which the Tractarians tried to derive Anglo-Catholic institutions, was already corrupted with superstition. Science had always interested her, and she read widely in mathematics, astronomy, chemistry, geology, entomology, phrenology—whatever she could lay hands on. Books like L. Vernon Harcourt's *Doctrine of the Deluge*, which aimed to vindicate the scriptural account from the doubts being cast on it by geology, seemed 'to shake a weak position by weak arguments'.[3] Her intensive study of the Bible had laid a foundation for the rational textual criticism that was to come. Her gradual emergence from the long dominance of evangelical belief is obscured by the fact that all her letters are written to earnest Evangelicals and conceal as long as possible the change in her view.

Isaac, under his father's watchful eye, was making his way in the world. He was only sixteen when his father noted with

---

[1] *Letters*, III. 175.   [2] *Letters*, III. 176.   [3] *Letters*, I. 34.

satisfaction that he had sold his pony for £22.[1] He would soon be ready to carry on as agent for the Newdegate family. Robert Evans, having raised himself by his own efforts from the artisan class, wrote with pride in his Journal, 16 May 1836: 'Isaac entered into the yeomanry today at Warwick.' In 1840 at the age of twenty-four, home from a holiday in Paris, Isaac was making plans for his marriage to Sarah Rawlins. She was the daughter of Samuel Rawlins, a hide and leather merchant of Birmingham, who lived at Rotton Park, Edgbaston. Rawlins was an old friend of Robert Evans. In 1832 he drove over with his wife, his son Samuel, Jr., and his daughter-in-law to have tea at Griff and go to see the house and gardens at Arbury. At Mrs. Evans's funeral he was one of the pallbearers. Isaac had probably known Sarah during his stay with the tutor at Birmingham after the Foleshill school. She was ten years older than he.

Mary Ann, always shy about social functions, was prevailed on to go with Isaac to visit at Edgbaston in September 1840—'to gratify another's feelings', she wrote, though she confessed to enjoying the *Messiah* on one day and some selections from other oratorios of Handel and Haydn the next.[2] She felt some uncertainty about her position at Griff when the new matron should arrive as mistress. Robert Evans, now sixty-seven, could no longer work as hard as he had, and was well able to retire. He finally decided to leave Isaac and Sarah at Griff while he and Mary Ann would go to a new house at Foleshill. They looked it over approvingly 15 January 1841, with Maria Lewes, who was spending her Christmas vacation with them, and Mr. Evans took it with 'the window curtains, Blinds, and the Carpiting on the Dining-room and Drawing-room floors'. In February at the sale of the previous tenant's furniture he and Mary Ann bought nearly £100 worth. They brought kitchen things and a load of coals from Griff, leaving a servant as caretaker till they were ready to move. On 17 March Isaac drove Mary Ann to Foleshill in the gig to get everything in order before her father came. 'It was a rough day for them but they got in just before the storm and had unloaded the Furniture', Mr. Evans wrote in his Journal. When he told Lord Aylesford that 'I was going to my new residence this evening for the first night, on the Foleshill road in Coventry parish, he Laphd and said they would make me Mayor.'[3]

[1] Robert Evans Journal, 25 Sept. 1832.
[2] *Letters*, I. 68.
[3] Robert Evans Journal, 19 Mar. 1841.

Mr. Evans did not go to Edgbaston for Isaac's wedding 8 June 1841; he lent his carriage to take Chrissey and Edward Clarke, while he rode to Packington to look over 'different things'. Mary Ann, who was a bridesmaid, went with Isaac early the day before. The ceremony was performed by the Reverend Richard Rawlins, of Kneeton, Nottinghamshire, a brother of Sarah. After a brief journey to Scotland and the Lakes, Isaac and Sarah settled at Griff for the rest of their days. It proved a happy match. Before long, four nephews and nieces were playing about the fields where Mary Ann had roamed hand in hand with her brother twenty years before.

CHAPTER II

THE HOLY WAR

✴

Rᴏʙᴇʀᴛ Eᴠᴀɴs's new home was a large, semi-detached house known as Bird Grove, set well back from the Foleshill Road, surrounded by fine trees, among which a silver birch was conspicuous. To the right of the front door was his office; the drawing-room, dining-room, and kitchen occupied the rest of the ground floor. Above, over the south entrance, Mary Ann had her study, a tiny room with a window looking down across meadows and gardens to the twin spires of Coventry less than a mile away. A door opened from the study into her bedroom, which like her father's faced west towards the Foleshill road. Though the neighbourhood was not then heavily populated, Mary Ann at first missed the 'free range for walking' she had enjoyed at Griff and what she had learned from Cowper to call the 'prolixity of shade'. But Griff was only five miles off, and they saw the Isaac Evanses fairly often. Fanny and her husband Henry Houghton lived at Baginton, two miles south. Chrissey and Edward Clarke at Meriden, five miles west, had three children, and when Mary Ann visited them she occasionally brought little Edward and Robert home with her to stay for a week or two. Chrissey herself sometimes came with the baby. Mary Ann loved the children, especially Mary Louisa, who had been named for her; every night, long before bedtime, she told Edith Simcox, she 'used to undress this child and rock her to sleep in her arms, feeling a sort of rapture in the mere presence, even though she might want the time for reading'.[1]

Chrissey's visits this first summer were related to domestic problems in Meriden. Her brother-in-law Charles Clarke, an attorney only twenty-six years old, had come down with 'galloping consumption' and was cared for by Edward in their house till he died 13 July 1841. Edward himself was neither well nor prosperous. The practice of a country surgeon, a newcomer, competing for

---

[1] Simcox Autobiography, 29 Apr. 1879.

patients with old Dr. Kittermaster, was far from lucrative. His experience recalls some of Lydgate's troubles in *Middlemarch*. Robert Evans noted in his Journal on 24 January 1842 that he paid Mr. Clarke £250 to purchase the house at Attleborough that Chrissey's uncle John Evarard had left her; in September he advanced £800 more, and Mr. Clarke 'give me a Bond for it, and if he does not pay it to me in my Life time it must be stopd out of my Daughters fortune after my Death.' These were ominous notes for the future. But Mary Ann loved to have her sister and the children, who made Bird Grove ring with happy laughter.

The transition from Griff was easier for Mary Ann than for her father. During the last five or six years his strength had been declining. Though the severe illness suffered at the time of his wife's death had not recurred, he never recovered completely. A hot walk over the Packington estate, he told Francis Newdigate, 'nearly nocked me up, and have been unwell since, but am now getting well I hope'.[1] Settled in Foleshill at the age of sixty-eight, he found unaccustomed leisure hanging heavy on him. He was not used to being idle. For many years he had managed affairs, conferring almost daily with the Squire at Arbury, planning and directing important works—building, coal-mining, surveying roads, valuing timber, draining fields. In 1832 in preparation for the first election after the Reform Bill he arranged at Lord Aylesford's order to have tenants qualify to vote for the conservative incumbent W. S. Dugdale against the more popular candidates.[2] When the dowager Queen Adelaide passed through Griff in 1839 it was Robert Evans who assembled Mr. Newdegate's tenants on horseback to escort her beyond Nuneaton, riding 'very fast, faster than I like to ride'.[3] Lord Lifford, who had leased Astley Castle, and other great landowners consulted him. He had grown prosperous serving the aristocracy, and he accepted their views without question. In politics he was a staunch conservative with that genuine fear of democracy ingrained in so many who grew up during the French Revolution. Now he had little to occupy his time. His Coventry acquaintances were mostly from business connections. Except for his children and grandchildren who visited him, he saw few people. On Saturdays he would balance his week's accounts, sitting near the door of his office, whence his gruff but kindly question, 'Come to see Mary Ann?' sometimes startled her callers.[4] In the evenings

---

[1] Robert Evans to Francis Newdigate, 8 July 1839 (Warwick).
[2] Robert Evans Journal, 18 Aug., 12, 14 Dec. 1832.   [3] Ibid. 5 Nov. 1839.
[4] Coventry *Herald*, Supplement, 7–8 Nov. 1919, p. 3.

after he laid his papers aside, she would read aloud to him in her rich low voice, usually one of the Waverley novels, which he never tired of hearing.

His principal social link in Coventry was the Church. His old-fashioned high-and-dry religion, taken for granted, had been immune to the Methodist enthusiasm of his brother Samuel. But in the 1830s it had felt the constant, pervasive pressure of the Evangelicals, exerted systematically on 'the better sort of people' everywhere. He had been drawn to Mr. Jones's evening lectures at Nuneaton, had heard him preach 'exelent' sermons, and noted more than one 'Beautifull Sermon' by his successor Mr. King. Though less fervid than Mary Ann, he too was touched by the evangelical spirit. The nearest church was Trinity, in the centre of Coventry, only a mile down the hill. They went there nearly every Sunday. The Vicar, the Reverend John Howells, who had owned the lease of Bird Grove, welcomed them into the parish. On Easter Day, Mr. Evans noted, they 'received the sacriment' and went back again in the evening to hear a charity sermon. 'I held a plate and give £1. The Hon^le and Rev^d Mr. Villers Preached a good sermon it was 9 oclock when we got home.'[1] The Honourable Henry Montagu Villiers, a brother of the Earl of Clarendon, only twenty-eight years old, was about to leave Kenilworth to become Rector of St. George's, Bloomsbury, where his earnest Evangelicalism, appealing to Churchmen and Dissenters alike, would soon make him a bishop. In June the Evanses drove over to Kenilworth to hear him for the last time.[2] When the new church of St. Peter's, Coventry, was dedicated, Robert Evans again 'held a plate for a collection and I give £1 we collected upwards of £40'.[3]

For Mary Ann there were no such minor dignities to give her a sense of importance. Returning from the consecration of another of the new churches, St. Paul's, Foleshill, she meditated sadly on the gaily dressed people attending the ceremony; she 'could not help thinking how much easier life would be to her, and how much better she would stand in the estimation of her neighbours, if only she could take things as they did, be satisfied with outside pleasures, and conform to popular beliefs without any reflection or examination'.[4] Religious seriousness did little to recommend the

[1] Robert Evans Journal, 11 Apr. 1841.
[2] *Letters*, i. 98; Robert Evans Journal, 20 June 1841.
[3] Robert Evans Journal, 31 Oct. 1841.
[4] 30 July 1841. Cross, New ed., p. 54.

quiet Miss Evans, with her pale face and pensive look, to the young people of Coventry. Miss Lewis had asked her friends the Stephensons to be kind to her; though they spoke to her on their way to church and expressed the hope of seeing her often, they never called. Mary Ann thought that she might like Mr. Stephenson, a ribbon manufacturer, and his wife, but, she added characteristically, the two young ladies of the family 'possess the minimum of attraction for me'.[1] It was doubtless mutual.

Her oldest Coventry friends were the Miss Franklins. Miss Rebecca soon spread news of the arrival of her most distinguished pupil through the circle of her friends, among others to the family of Mr. John Sibree, minister of the Independent Chapel in Vicar Lane, who lived at Foleshill on the Heath, not far from Bird Grove. Praising Mary Anne's intellectual power, her skill in music, and so on, she told of the remarkable piety, which during her school-days 'had induced the girls to come together for prayer and which had led her to visit the poor most diligently in the cottages round her own home'.[2] The Sibrees had two children, John, aged eighteen, who was planning to follow his father in the ministry, and Mary, a girl of sixteen, who became an immediate admirer of Miss Evans. Her seriousness recommended her also to her nearest neighbours, Mr. and Mrs. Abijah Hill Pears, whose house adjoined Bird Grove. Mr. Pears, who had known Robert Evans in business affairs, was a prosperous ribbon manufacturer; he had been active in the Liberal Party before the Reform Bill, and was to serve as Mayor of Coventry 1842-3. His wife Elizabeth Bray, who came from another old family of ribbon manufacturers, held earnest evangelical views. She was soon helping manage a clothing club for the miners' families at the Pudding Pits got up by Mary Ann, who referred to Mrs. Pears as 'my neighbour who is growing into the more precious character of a friend'.[3]

If Mary Ann's social distractions were limited, they left her the more time for her own studies. She attended some lectures on chemistry; she continued Italian and German lessons with the appealing Mr. Brezzi, and got help with her Latin from the Reverend Thomas Sheepshanks, Rector of St. John's Church, Coventry, and Headmaster of the Free Grammar School. The Coventry book shops supplied some of her needs, though her interests ranged far, and Miss Lewis sometimes ordered books for her in London. Isaac Taylor's writings continued to fascinate her; she confessed that his *Physical Theory of Another Life* (1836),

[1] *Letters*, I. 91.   [2] Cross, New ed., p. 46.   [3] *Letters*, I. 90.

an imaginative anticipation of a world after death in which our duties would be suited to the assumed expansion of our powers, led speculation further than Taylor would have desired. She 'revelled' in astronomy, winging her flight 'from system to system, from universe to universe' through the books of John Pringle Nichol, *The Phenomena and Order of the Solar System* and *View of the Architecture of the Heavens* (1838). Nichol had withdrawn from the ministry because of his changed religious belief and had become Professor of Astronomy at Glasgow. She pored over John Pye Smith's *Relation between the Holy Scriptures and Some Parts of Geological Science* (1839), the work of a Nonconformist, which also encouraged speculation about the very doubts it was meant to dispel. Her letters speak largely of pious little books like *The Test of Truth* (a book for the use of Spanish refugees 'in the dreary plains of infidelity') and *Thoughts Preparative or Persuasive to Private Devotion,* 'a sweet booklet of pious meditation adapted to accompany the Christian in all the windings of his experience'.[1] But they hardly mention the more significant books she was reading, such as Carlyle's *Sartor Resartus,* just reprinted with Emerson's preface, which were soon to lead her into some very sharp windings. The evangelical tone naturally persists in the letters to Miss Lewis, but the style shows greater freedom. Even in conventional phrases—'the desolating effects of back-sliding on my heart', or 'Alas, I need monitors and I need chastisement'[2]— one hears a note of urgency that hints new conflict. She begins to drop the schoolgirl affectations; she abandons the Language of Flowers, asking her Veronica in October 1841, 'May I call you Maria? I feel our friendship too serious a thing to endure an artificial name. And restore to me Mary Ann.' In November she writes: 'Why may we not talk without so much circumlocution; 'tis a very great compliment to the understanding of one's hearers to speak elliptically.' In the same letter she asks Miss Lewis a curious question: 'Think—is there any *conceivable* alteration in me that would prevent your coming to me at Christmas? I long to have a friend such as you are, I think I may say, alone to me, to unburthen every thought and difficulty—for I am still a solitary, though near a city.'[3]

She had, however, already made the acquaintance of two persons who were to be her most intimate friends during the next thirteen years, Mr. and Mrs. Charles Bray. Charles, born in 1811,

[1] *Letters,* I. 98, 101.   [2] *Letters,* I. 114, 100.   [3] *Letters,* I. 121.

the son of a ribbon manufacturer, had got an indifferent education, resisting even the efforts of Miss Franklin. Sent off to a boarding school at Isleworth, he picked up smatterings of mathematics, a little French, and less Latin. Then, having been articled for three years to learn the ribbon trade in one of the large London warehouses, he returned to Coventry at the age of twenty to be installed in the Bray firm. Ribbons were booming, and with the benefit of his London experience the firm prospered. On his father's death in 1835 Charles inherited control, and when he married in 1836 he set up housekeeping with the very handsome income of £1,200 a year. During his London years he had been converted by 'a highly intelligent Evangelical Dissenter', a medical man, conviction of sin being followed by the usual state of depression and the practice of austerities, combined with the intensive study of religious writings. His experience was thus somewhat like Mary Ann Evans's, though of shorter duration. In undertaking to convert the Unitarian minister at Coventry to his own view of the Trinity, young Bray found himself quite out of his depth. He soon abandoned Christianity entirely in favour of a sort of philosophical necessity. To him the mind seemed subject to the same invariable rules as matter; one had only to discover the rules and act on them to be happy. Stumbling by accident on the 'science' of phrenology as expounded by George Combe, Bray accepted it eagerly as 'the machinery by and through which the "Soul of each and God of All" worked such wonderfully varied but invariable effects'. He had a plaster cast made of his head in order to examine the 'skull of the man whose character I knew best', and bought more than a hundred other casts with which to study 'the Natural Laws of Mind'.[1]

In the summer of 1835 Bray fell in love with Caroline Hennell, who was visiting her uncle Samuel Hennell, another Coventry ribbon manufacturer, and married her the following April. Like her husband, Cara (as she was always called) was a philanthropist. At Hackney, where she was brought up, her family were pillars of the cultivated, intelligent Unitarian congregation of the Gravel Pit Chapel under Robert Aspland. Mary Ann once called Cara 'the most religious person I know'.[2] Her mind was of a much finer grain than her husband's. When, during their honeymoon, Charles broached his rather crude, free-thinking views by reading her Holbach's *System of Nature* and Volney's *Ruins of Empire*, he

---

[1] Charles Bray, *Phases of Opinion and Experience during a Long Life: An Autobiography* [1885], pp. 23, 22.   [2] Cross, I. 158.

made her exceedingly uncomfortable,[1] for her religion was based, not on philosophical theory but on deep reverence and long-cherished family associations. In perplexity she appealed for support to her elder brother Charles Christian Hennell, a London merchant, who by careful study had satisfied himself of the validity of the Unitarian position. Reluctantly he agreed to re-examine the biblical evidence. After two years of hard work he published in December 1838 *An Inquiry into the Origins of Christianity*, in which he conceded that 'the true account of the life of Jesus Christ, and of the spread of his religion, would be found to contain no deviation from the known laws of nature'. Though, as Basil Willey observes, to embark upon such a scrutiny of the Gospels at all, 'a man must have abandoned all notion of Scriptural infallibility',[2] the *Inquiry* contains no iconoclasm. To Hennell the Gospels, critically analysed like any other documents, present striking variations in their reports of the same episodes; the miracles are like the legendary wonders seen in all mythologies, but reflect the sincere faith of the early Christians without wilful imposture. Though Christianity could no longer be accepted as a divine revelation, it was certainly 'the purest form yet existing of natural religion'.[3]

The Brays lived at Rosehill, a fine house they had bought in 1840, on the Radford Road about a mile from the centre of Coventry and the same distance from Bird Grove by a pleasant walk through fields and rustic lanes, now covered by the Daimler works. When Mary Ann was taken there by Bray's sister Mrs. Pears to make a morning call, 2 November 1841, she was suffering from her usual diffidence. 'I am going I hope today to effect a breach in the thick wall of indifference behind which the denizens of Coventry seem inclined to entrench themselves,' she wrote to Maria Lewis, 'but I fear I shall fail.'[4] Bray described his impressions of the visit in his *Autobiography*: 'I can well recollect her appearance and modest demeanour as she sat down on a low ottoman by the window, and I had a sort of surprised feeling when she first spoke, at the measured, highly cultivated mode of expression, so different from the usual tones of young persons from the country. We became friends at once.'[5] One of Mrs. Pears's reasons for introducing Mary Ann, Bray added in his bantering style, was

[1] C. Bray, *Autobiography*, p. 48.
[2] Basil Willey, *Nineteenth Century Studies* (1949), p. 211.
[3] C. C. Hennell, *An Inquiry* (1838), p. viii.
[4] *Letters*, I. 120.
[5] C. Bray, *Autobiography*, p. 76.

the hope that 'the influence of this superior young lady of
Evangelical principles might be beneficial to our heretical minds.'
Like many a well-laid plot it turned out differently. Before they
had talked very long, Mary Ann must have discovered that the
doubts secretly gnawing at her own religious belief had long since
been dismissed with equanimity by the Brays. The first volume of
his *Philosophy of Necessity* had just appeared and the second was
due shortly, so he doubtless described to her the wonderfully
tranquillizing effect that acceptance of the inevitable had had on
his troubled mind. No doubt they also talked about Cara's brother's
Inquiry, the second edition of which had been published in August.
It is impossible to say whether Mary Ann had read it before meeting the Brays. The title alone was enough to attract her to it, and
the Coventry book shop probably displayed it. As Bray says, they
'soon found that her mind was already turning towards greater
freedom of thought in religious opinion, and that she had even
bought for herself Hennell's *Inquiry*'.[1] Ten days after this meeting
she wrote to Miss Lewis: 'My whole soul has been engrossed in
the most interesting of all enquiries for the last few days, and to
what result my thoughts may lead I know not—possibly to one
that will startle you.'

To attribute the change in her religious view solely to the Brays'
influence oversimplifies. It would have come in any case. Its roots
go far back. When only thirteen Mary Ann read Bulwer Lytton's
Devereux, in which there is an 'amiable atheist', an Italian named
Bezoni, 'a believer in the dark doctrine which teaches that man is
dust', but who nevertheless lived virtuously and 'lost his life in
attending the victims of a fearful and contagious disease'.[2] Mary
Ann recalled being then 'considerably shaken by the impression
that religion was not a requisite to moral excellence'.[3] When Mrs.
Congreve asked her to what influence she attributed the first
unsettlement of her orthodox views, she answered quickly, 'Oh,
Walter Scott's.'[4] He was healthy and historical; it would not fit
on to her creed.[5] In her calls on the miners near Foleshill, who
were mostly Methodists, she was shocked at the apparent union
of religious feeling with a low sense of morality. While the Brays
certainly crystallized her rejection of orthodoxy, it was long in

---

[1] GE's copy of Hennell's *Inquiry*, now in Dr. Williams's Library, is inscribed
'Mary Ann Evans. Jany 1st, 1842'.   [2] *Devereux*, Bk. v, ch. 6.
[3] *Letters*, I. 45.   [4] Cross, New ed., p. 48.
[5] Simcox Autobiography, 16 Feb. 1885, fol. 132.

suspense and inevitable. The surprising thing is that her Evangelicalism persisted until she was twenty-two.

When Miss Lewis arrived before Christmas we may be sure that the change startled her. But her earnest pupil, who despite ridicule and opposition had long clung to evangelical austerities, was not now to be swayed by sentimental piety. She did not tell her father immediately. With the whole family gathered in the house for Christmas dinner—the Houghtons, the Clarkes, and the Isaac Evanses—it would have been rash to proclaim her new opinions. Her father set out for Kirk Hallam on the 27th, and Miss Lewis, too, left for a few days to see about her new school at Nuneaton, promising to return. 'Come when it suits you best', wrote Mary Ann on New Year's Day, ending her letter: 'Goodbye, and may Heaven bless you as it does by the sure laws of consequence bless every one who does his work faithfully and lives in loving activity.' The phrases suggest that she had followed her study of Hennell's *Inquiry* with Charles Bray's *The Philosophy of Necessity; or, the Law of Consequences as Applicable to Mental, Moral, and Social Science.* Miss Lewis was back at Foleshill the same evening. The next morning, Sunday, 2 January 1842, the storm broke: 'Went to Trinity Church in the forenoon', wrote Robert Evans in his Journal. 'Miss Lewis went with me. Mary Ann did not go. I stopd the sacriment and Miss Lewis stopd also.' Two weeks later there is a similar laconic entry: 'Went to Church in the forenoon Mary Ann did not go to Church.' Miss Lewis had departed. Unsuccessful in altering Mary Ann's opinion, she did not break completely with her, though their correspondence dwindled away.

Mr. Evans, after a fruitless outburst of parental authority, lapsed into stony silence, refusing to discuss the question of religion with his disobedient child. How was he to hold a plate on Sunday mornings at Trinity, the father of an avowed free-thinker? He could see nothing but impropriety and rebellion, which he blamed entirely on the Brays' influence. Having failed to bring Mary Ann to her senses, he got her brother and sisters to try. Fanny Houghton, the most intelligent of them, who shared her scepticism but was too wise to publish it, urged outward compliance, a course too devious for honest Mary Ann. Chrissey, whom she saw often, had no argument but that of affection. Isaac, conventional as Tom Tulliver, feared most that his sister's singularity might prevent her from catching a husband; egged on by his father, he called at Meriden while she was staying there and '*schooled* Mary Ann'.[1]

---

[1] Robert Evans Journal, 25 Feb. 1842.

All these efforts having failed, other friends were enlisted to reason with her. Mrs. Pears pleaded in fervid evangelical terms without effect. Miss Rebecca Franklin, unable to swerve the mind she had done so much to fashion, introduced a Baptist minister of her acquaintance, a man well read in divinity, who after a single interview said: 'That young lady must have had the devil at her elbow to suggest her doubts, for there was not a book that I recommended to her in support of Christian evidences that she had not read.'[1] The Sibree family learned of her defection with unfeigned grief; in a long evening of discussion Mr. Sibree vainly marshalled every argument he could find to convince her of the truth of the Gospels. His young daughter Mary remembered 'how deeply Miss Evans was moved, and how, as she stood against the mantelpiece during the last part of the time, her delicate fingers, in which she held a small piece of muslin on which she was at work, trembled with her agitation. To her affectionate and pathetic speech to my mother, "Now, Mrs. Sibree, you won't care to have anything more to do with me", my mother rejoined: "On the contrary, I shall feel more interested in you than ever".'[2] The Sibrees called in their friend the Reverend Francis Watts, Professor of Theology at Spring Hill College, Birmingham, who had studied at Halle with Tholuck, the great apologist for Evangelicalism. He too reported after his first interview: 'She has gone into the question.' She wrote to Mr. Watts: 'It is no small sacrifice to part with the assurance that life and immortality have been brought to light, and to be reduced to the condition of the great spirits of old who looked yearningly to the horizon of their earthly career, wondering what lay beyond; but I cannot think the conviction that immortality is man's destiny indispensable to the production of elevated and heroic virtue and the sublimest resignation.'[3]

Nine weeks had passed since she refused to go to church. Though living in the same house with her father, driving about with him to visit the family, she could get no understanding of her position, no discussion of it. Finally, in desperation, she wrote him a letter:

Foleshill Monday Morning. [28 Feb. 1842]
My dear Father,

As all my efforts in conversation have hitherto failed in making you aware of the real nature of my sentiments, I am induced to try if I can express myself more clearly on paper so that both I in writing and you

[1] Cross, New ed., p. 50.   [2] Ibid., p. 49.   [3] Letters, I. 136.

in reading may have our judgements unobstructed by feeling, which they can hardly be when we are together. I wish entirely to remove from your mind the false notion that I am inclined visibly to unite myself with any Christian community, or that I have any affinity in opinion with Unitarians more than with other classes of believers in the Divine authority of the books comprising the Jewish and Christian Scriptures. I regard these writings as histories consisting of mingled truth and fiction, and while I admire and cherish much of what I believe to have been the moral teaching of Jesus himself, I consider the system of doctrines built upon the facts of his life and drawn as to its materials from Jewish notions to be most dishonourable to God and most pernicious in its influence on individual and social happiness. In thus viewing this important subject I am in unison with some of the finest minds in Christendom in past ages, and with the majority of such in the present (as an instance more familiar to you than any I could name I may mention Dr. [Benjamin] Franklin). Such being my very strong convictions, it cannot be a question with any mind of strict integrity, whatever judgement may be passed on their truth, that I could not without vile hypocrisy and a miserable truckling to the smile of the world for the sake of my supposed interests, profess to join in worship which I wholly disapprove. This and *this alone* I will not do even for your sake—anything else however painful I would cheerfully brave to give you a moment's joy.

I do not hope to convince any other member of our family and probably not yourself that I am really sincere, that my only desire is to walk in that path of rectitude which however rugged is the only path to peace, but the prospect of contempt and rejection shall not make me swerve from my determination so much as a hair's breath until I feel that I *ought* to do so. From what my Brother more than insinuated and from what you have yourself intimated I perceive that your establishment at Foleshill is regarded as an unnecessary expence having no other object than to give me a centre in society—that since you now consider me to have placed an insurmountable barrier to my prosperity in life this one object of an expenditure held by the rest of the family to be disadvantageous to them is frustrated—I am glad at any rate this is made clear to me, for I could not be happy to remain as an incubus or an unjust absorber of your hardly earned gains which might be better applied among my Brothers and Sisters with their children.

I should be just as happy living with you at your cottage at Packington or any where else if I can thereby minister in the least to your comfort—of course unless that were the case I must prefer to rely on my own energies and resources feeble as they are—I fear nothing but voluntarily leaving you. I can cheerfully do it if you desire it and shall go with deep gratitude for all the tenderness and rich kindness you have never been tired of shewing me. So far from complaining I shall joyfully submit if as a proper punishment for the pain I have most unintentionally given you, you determine to appropriate any provision you may have intended to make for my future support to your other children whom you may consider more deserving. As a last vindication of herself from one who has no one to speak for her I may be permitted to say that if ever I loved you I do so now, if ever I sought to obey the laws of my Creator and to follow duty wherever it may lead me I have that determination now and the consciousness of this will support me though every being on earth were to frown upon me.

Your affectionate Daughter
Mary Ann.[1]

Even this heart-felt appeal failed to break his stony silence. He was resolved to send Mary Ann away, not to see her again till she had abandoned her stubborn disobedience. He ordered the house agent to find a purchaser or tenant for Bird Grove, and told Lord Aylesford that 'I should leave Coventry and come to my cottage at Packington and I give him the reasons for it.'[2] Mary Ann considered taking lodgings at Leamington, where she hoped to earn a living by teaching. Her only woe, she told Cara, was 'that of leaving my dear Father. All else, doleful lodgings, scanty meals, and *gazing-stockism* are quite indifferent to me.'[3] Clarissa Harlowe could not have been more sincere. At this point Isaac proved more reasonable than his father. In reply to Mary Ann's letter, he admitted that she was being treated very harshly; the sending her away, he said, was entirely their father's doing, not from economy, but because he could not bear Foleshill after what had happened; and ended by urging her to come stay with him at Griff until their father was willing to have her back. Both Mrs. Pears and Miss Rebecca Franklin discussed the case with Mr. Evans, impressing on him how much the world would condemn his severity; both of them defended Mrs. Bray against any disposition to proselytize. In consequence of their arguments he cancelled the order to let the house, and on 23 March sent Mary Ann off to join Isaac.

At Griff she had her favourite country walks again in all the beauty of spring. Isaac and Sarah were as kind as could be, and old acquaintances smiled on her in spite of heresy. But no word came from her father except that the alterations on the cottage at Packington had begun. She appealed to Mrs. Pears to try to discover his intentions. 'I must have a *home*, not a visiting place.'[4] When she had been about a month at Griff, Mrs. Isaac Evans got an interview with Mr. Evans and convinced him that by making

---

[1] *Letters*, I. 128–30. [2] Robert Evans Journal, 3 Mar. 1842.
[3] *Letters*, I. 131. [4] *Letters*, I. 134.

Mary Ann's worldly interests dependent on a change in her opinion he was setting up the most effective barrier to her reversion to orthodoxy. He agreed reluctantly that she might return to him after a time, though he was more determined than ever to leave Foleshill and was considering a 'most lugubrious looking place at Fillongley (!)' as more desirable.[1] But he missed her more than he would admit. A week or two later the 'Holy War' ended in a truce. Mary Ann agreed to attend church with him as usual, and he tacitly conceded her the right to think what she liked during service.

When she returned to Foleshill on Saturday, 30 April, she found three visitors: her uncle William and Mr. and Mrs. Samuel Evans. It is easy to believe that her intercourse with them was 'constrained and painful'. But Robert Evans, probably not eager to appear at Trinity with his humble relatives, drove away in the morning to take them to Chilvers Coton Church and dine with Isaac at Griff, leaving the recalcitrant Mary Ann behind. She 'opened the day' at Rosehill, where Cara delighted her by letting her read some of the letters Charles Hennell had written while working on the *Inquiry*. Two weeks later Robert Evans noted in his Journal without comment: 'Went to Trinity Church Mary Ann went with me today.' The same entry appears the following Sunday. Conformity was what he cared for most. Mary Ann, secure in her emancipated belief, could now yield easily. She felt 'inexpressible relief' at being freed from the appalling apprehension of eternal damnation and the heavy burden of evangelical dogmas, which so long disturbed 'that choice of the good for its own sake that answers my ideal'.[2] Yet she never ceased to regret the impetuosity that had caused the conflict. Years later, in 1869, she told Emily Davies of 'having come into collision with her father and being on the brink of being turned out of his house. And she dwelt a little on how much fault there is on the side of the young in such cases, of their ignorance of life, and the narrowness of their intellectual superiority.'[3]

It is impossible to overestimate the importance of Mary Ann's introduction to the Brays, which led quickly to a warm, life-long friendship. Charles Bray was a kind-hearted, generous, impulsive man with a consuming thirst for reform. Every philanthropy found him on its side. Education, labour relations, co-operatives, freedom of religion, freedom of speech, public health, extension of the ballot—these were only a few of the causes he supported in the most

[1] *Letters*, I. 137.   [2] *Letters*, I. 144.
[3] Barbara Stephen, *Emily Davies and Girton College* (1927), p. 183.

practical way. Intellectually he was bold rather than profound. Enthusiasm out-weighed judgement in his acceptance of Robert Owen's socialism or in his devotion to phrenology. He had a naturally optimistic disposition and a keen but boisterous sense of humour, which at once livened the over-solemn Mary Ann Evans, reviving the old strain that in childhood revelled in *Joe Miller's Jests*.

Cara Bray, a gentle, pretty little woman, only six years older than Mary Ann, had most of the qualities Charles lacked. She had been a governess for a brief time before her marriage, and continued to work for education of the poor, teaching in the infant school he organized, writing books for children on physiology and morality, and founding a society to inculcate kindness to animals. She was an independent thinker, reflective, considerate of others' opinions; without openly expressing disapproval she could let her own refinement be felt. Intelligent, accomplished, candid, unaffected, she was the perfect friend, and her good-natured geniality and quiet dignity were soon reflected by the 'chameleon-like' Mary Ann. Cara was an excellent pianist, and soon drew her in to play duets or to take her place in the musical evenings at Rosehill. In 1842 she painted a revealing water-colour portrait of Mary Ann, now in the National Portrait Gallery, the earliest likeness we have. Dressed in a rather too-elaborately frilled heliotrope gown with a lace collar fastened at the throat by a brooch, Mary Ann sits with head tilted a little towards the right; her light-brown hair, tightly drawn from the parting in the centre, ends in a bundle of curls gathered over each ear. Her forehead is high and broad, the blue eyes pensive and somewhat larger than in most of the other portraits. Her nose is long and prominent above the short upper lip, the mouth wide, with full, well-formed lips. The arms are crossed, clasping each other in the gesture which Henry James was to object to in her Mirah.

Rosehill was a delightful gabled house,'far enough from the town for country quiet, and yet near enough to hear the sweet church bells and the chimes of St. Michael's, with the distant hum of the city'. On the broad lawn, shaded by groups of noble trees, stood an especially fine old acacia, the sloping turf about whose roots made a delightful seat in summertime. On it they would spread a great bear skin and sit for long afternoons of unrestrained talk. Many notable men who came to Coventry were entertained there, and any one who had 'a queer mission or a crochet, or was supposed be a "little cracked" was sent up to Rosehill'.[1] Robert Owen,

---

[1] C. Bray, *Autobiography*, pp. 69–70.

whose opening of the Millennium at Harmony Hall, Queenwood, Hampshire, Bray had attended in May 1842; Dr. John Conolly, the pioneer in humane treatment of the insane; James Simpson, the old friend of Walter Scott, a champion of free elementary education; George Dawson, the heterodox lecturer, a friend of Carlyle; William Johnson Fox, the Unitarian preacher and writer for the *Westminster Review*; George Combe, the phrenologist, and his wife, daughter of the great Sarah Siddons; Ralph Waldo Emerson—these were a few of the interesting people to whom the Brays introduced Mary Ann. She was quickly brought from provincial isolation into touch with the world of ideas.

The ideas were not those of Robert Evans. Since he was still suspicious of the influence of Mary Ann's new friends, she could go to them at first only when he was away from home. She began to help Cara with the teaching at the infant school and with some of her other charitable works. One Sunday afternoon she came to Rosehill to tea and went afterwards to the Unitarian Chapel to hear James Martineau, whose wife was a cousin of Cara. The Brays were completely eclectic in religion. They were good friends of Dr. W. B. Ullathorne, who after his return from Australia and his exposure of the horror and immorality of transporation, had just been assigned to the Roman Catholic mission in Coventry. Before the restoration of the hierarchy in 1850, when he became the first Bishop of Birmingham, Cara went several times to hear him, and he was a welcome visitor at Rosehill. In September 1842 Cara wrote to her sister Sara Hennell that she had sent for Mary Ann 'to come and be enlightened with us' by Dr. Ullathorne.

Sara Sophia Hennell, who completes the trio of Mary Ann's close Coventry friends, spent six weeks at Rosehill in the summer of 1842. She was a handsome, animated woman, nearly thirty. For ten years she had been a governess, during the last five to the daughters of John Bonham Carter, M.P. Her pupils were first cousins of the not-yet-famous Florence Nightingale; Hilary, the eldest, whom Sara long continued to visit, was Florence's most intimate friend. Sara had lived all her life among people who knew and cared for the best in music, art, and literature; she knew German and some Latin, and was expert in matters of philosophy and theology, on which she wrote sedulously all her life. Many things the Brays had told her about Mary Ann's 'Holy War' made her eager to meet their new friend. To Mary Ann's limited social experience Sara brought a knowledge of life in great houses like

Ravensbourne and Lea Hurst and Waverley, of manners more
sophisticated than Miss Rebecca Franklin's old-fashioned etiquette. They took to each other immediately, and were soon singing duets with mutual delight, accompanied by Cara on the piano;
they talked of everything under the sun. When Sara had to leave
on 12 August, she soon became Mary Ann's most important
correspondent.

In October another learned young lady, Elizabeth Rebecca
Brabant, came to Rosehill. She was the only daughter of Robert
Herbert Brabant (M.D. Edinburgh, 1821) of Devizes, who once
numbered among his patients Thomas Moore and Samuel Taylor
Coleridge. The name Rufa, given to her as a child in some verses
by Coleridge because of her red-gold hair, stayed with her always.
Dr. Brabant had studied German in order 'to sound the perilous
depths of theological science under the guidance of fearless and
learned interpreters',[1] and knew both Paulus and David Friedrich
Strauss. In 1839 after Charles Hennell had published the *Inquiry*,
Dr. Brabant called at his office in London to make his acquaintance and invite him to come visit at Devizes. Within a week
Charles proposed to Rufa. But Dr. Brabant, finding his lungs un-
sound, opposed the match, and they agreed not to see each other
for a time. Rufa did not forget him. In July Emerson received from
'a person in London signing himself E. R. Brabant a translation
of a Review of Hennell from the German of Dr. Schmitzer'.[2] At
Charles's request she had begun to translate the *Leben Jesu*. It was
not by chance that Charles reached Rosehill the day after Rufa
arrived and stayed until she left three weeks later.

Rufa too had been following the story of her trials and was
delighted to make Mary Ann's acquaintance. She came over to
Rosehill one evening, read Southey's *Thalaba* aloud, and perhaps
discussed Tholuck's *Die Glaubwürdigkeit der evangelischen Geschichte* and Carl Ullmann's *Historisch oder Mythisch?*, which Mary
Ann had been reading. When Rufa and Charles Hennell had both
left Coventry, Mary Ann wrote to Sara that her first impression
of Rufa was 'unfavourable and unjust, for in spite of what some
caustic people say, I fall not in love with every one, but I can now
satisfy your affection by telling you that I admire your friend exceedingly; there is a tender seriousness about her that is very much
to my taste, and thorough amiability and retiredness, all which

[1] *WR*, 93 (Apr. 1870), 346.
[2] *The Letters of Ralph Waldo Emerson*, ed. R. L. Rusk (6 vols., 1939), III. 70–1.

qualities make her almost worthy of Mr. Hennell'.[1] Stimulated perhaps by Rufa's visit, Cara now began to study German seriously with Mary Ann, working in her quiet, steady way on Schiller.

Mary Ann kept her bargain with her father scrupulously, going to church with him on Sundays and saying nothing about her changed belief. But her family was still dissatisfied with her. When they gathered at Bird Grove for Christmas dinner—the Houghtons, the Clarkes, and the Isaac Evanses—the problem of her intimacy with the Brays was canvassed again. Once more the threat of parental discipline loomed up as a way of removing her from their influence. Again Mrs. Pears, who was a great favourite with old Mr. Evans, took Mary Ann's part; she called and talked to him for two hours on the absurdity of such interference. Mr. Evans insisted that it was not of his doing, but Isaac's. As Cara described it to Sara, 22 February 1843:

It seems that brother Isaac with real fraternal kindness thinks that his sister has no chance of getting the one thing needful—i.e. a husband and a settlement—unless she mixes more in society, and complains that since she has known us she has hardly been anywhere else; that Mr. Bray, being only a leader of mobs, can only introduce her to Chartists and Radicals, and that such only will ever fall in love with her if she does not belong to the church. So his plan is to induce his father to remove to Meriden where, being away from us under the guardianship of her sister, she may be brought back to her senses. Mary Ann is sure there is no interested motive in it, but a pure zeal for her welfare. But Mr. Evans says he does not wish to leave Coventry, and does not mind her coming here, so Isaac must be quiet for the present.

Charles Hennell was back at Rosehill, having come in January 1843 for the country air. His lungs were still weak. His sister Mary was dying of tuberculosis at Hackney, and it seemed wiser to remove him from the proximity. The musical evenings were resumed, Charles playing the old bass viol, others the violin and flute, while Cara and Mary Ann took turns at the piano. She had grown more circumspect about discussing her heresy—possibly at the suggestion of her sister Fanny Houghton, who read the *Inquiry* and agreed with its view of the miraculous aspects of Christianity, but prudently said nothing about it. Mary Ann, leaning more toward the doctrines of Carlyle and Emerson, no longer wanted controversy. In mid May her father allowed her to go with the Brays and

[1] *Letters*, I. 150.

Sara and Charles Hennell on a five-day trip to Malvern and Worcester, spending a night each way at Stratford on Avon, where the Bray's friend, Edward Fordham Flower, the Unitarian brewer, lived. In July they made a longer excursion to Wales, staying ten days at Tenby and returning home by way of Pembroke and Swansea, spending several days at each. With Sara in high spirits Mary Ann clambered over the rocks and 'pawed the sand'. On this trip Rufa Brabant accompanied them. She too was in a buoyant mood. At Tenby she insisted on Mary Ann's going to a public ball, where, however, they found no partner for her. Rufa had one for herself: before many days had passed she and Charles Hennell renewed their engagement. This time Dr. Brabant, who joined them at Swansea, did not oppose the match. The wedding was planned for 1 November. Mary Ann was invited to be a bridesmaid. She went to London with Mr. Bray a few days before, staying with Sara at Hackney, enjoying some sightseeing and the theatre. After the Unitarian ceremony, performed at Finsbury Chapel by William Johnson Fox, she spent another week of pleasure—in marked contrast to her gloomy visit with Isaac five years before.

When the Brays returned to Coventry, 7 November, Mary Ann was carried off to Devizes by Dr. Brabant, 'to fill the place of his daughter'. According to Cara, she was much pleased 'that the Doctor seemed to like her, as he has quite captivated her heart—she considers him a model of all that is charming'. Cara obviously did not; she saw him as a silly, vain little man of sixty-two, and was no more deceived by his pretence to learning than Tom Moore, who had once tried to help him write an article. At Devizes Dr. Brabant insisted that Mary Ann must consider the library *her* room and punningly baptized her *Deutera* because she was to be a second daughter to him. Mary Ann liked Mrs. Brabant, too, who had been blind for some years; she talked 'very *neatly*', and was perhaps a little too perfectly polite to the new Deutera. But, wrote Mary Ann, a 'dose of precision, *not* preciseness, will be the best thing in the world for me'. After two weeks she wrote to Cara: 'I am in a little heaven here, Dr. Brabant being its archangel . . . time would fail me to tell of all his charming qualities. We read and walk and talk together, and I am never weary of his company. I have just written to Father to beg for a longer leave of absence than I had thought of when I came.' She hoped to stay until 13 December. 'I am petted and fed with nice morsels and pretty speeches until I am in danger of becoming even more conceited than ever.' Though the air of Devizes was wonderfully invigorating after reading German to the Doctor for two hours, Mary Ann, the healthy country girl who not two years before was making butter and currant jelly and damson cheese in the old kitchen at Griff, 'often felt so faint as to be obliged to lie on the sofa until walking time'. They read a little Greek, 'read de omnibus rebus et quibusdam aliis, but the genius of sloth has possessed us, and we have sent much new pavement to our future abode'. (Cara must have frowned a little in reading this.) They made a few visits in the neighbourhood; 'Dr. Brabant spoils me for every one else, and the Trennung from such a companion will be very painful.'[1]

The parting was painful indeed, and came sooner than she expected. For Mrs. Brabant, though blind, knew quite well what was going on. In this little heaven there was also her rather formidable sister Miss Susan Hughes, who within two weeks of Mary Ann's arrival had begun to offer gratuitous advice about the best way to go back to Coventry. And Rufa, who came for a week's visit after her wedding journey, also saw the situation clearly. As she reported it to John Chapman in 1851, Mary Ann

in the simplicity of her heart and her ignorance of (or incapability of practising) the required conventionalisms, gave the Doctor the utmost attention; they became very intimate; his Sister-in-law, Miss S. Hughes, became alarmed, made a great stir, excited the jealousy of Mrs. Brabant. Miss Evans left. Mrs. B. vowed she should never enter the house again, or that if she did, she, Mrs. Brabant, would instantly leave it. Mrs. Hennell says Dr. B. acted ungenerously and worse towards Miss E., for though he was the chief cause of all that passed, he acted towards her as though the fault lay with her alone. His unmanliness in the affair was condemned more by Mrs. Hennell than by Miss E. herself when she (a year ago) related the circumstances to me.[2]

She returned to Coventry 4 December, somewhat wiser about human nature, but rankling under the sense of injustice and indignant at Dr. Brabant's contemptible behaviour.

Eliza Lynn, who visited Dr. Brabant in 1847 under much the same circumstances, was convinced that he was the original of Mr. Casaubon in *Middlemarch*. She describes him as

a learned man who used up his literary energies in thought and desire to do rather than in actual doing, and whose fastidiousness made his

[1] *Letters*, I. 163–8.
[2] G. S. Haight, *George Eliot and John Chapman* (New Haven, 1940), p. 186.

work something like Penelope's web. Ever writing and rewriting, correcting and destroying, he never got farther than the introductory chapter of a book which he intended to be epoch-making, and the final destroyer of superstition and theological dogma.[1]

There are interesting parallels here with Casaubon, whose soul 'went on fluttering in the swampy ground where it was hatched, thinking of its wings and never flying' while he strove to make his Key to All Mythologies unimpeachable. Dorothea, like Mary Ann, found him 'as instructive as Milton's "affable archangel"'; and with something of the archangelic manner 'he told her about his great work that would show all mythical systems to be corruptions of a tradition originally revealed'.[2]

Since it comes from those who knew her intimately, Chapman's (or Rufa's) phrase 'in the simplicity of her heart and her ignorance of (or incapability of practising) the required conventionalisms', should be weighed carefully. While staying at Devizes Mary Ann missed a chance to hear Cornelius Donovan, a phrenologist, who was lecturing at Coventry. 'Never mind,' she wrote to Cara, 'I shall miss, too, being told that I have some very bad propensities and that my moral and animal regions are unfortunately balanced, all which is too true to be heard with calmness.'[3] The following July Charles Bray took her to London to have a cast made of her head. Whatever we may think of phrenology as a 'science', the opinion of one who was her friend for so long is of unusual interest. 'Miss Evans's head is a very large one,' he wrote in his *Autobiography* '$22\frac{1}{4}$ inches round;[4] George Combe, on first seeing the cast, took it for a man's.'

In her brain-development the Intellect greatly predominates; it is very large, more in length than in its peripheral surface. In the Feelings, the Animal and Moral regions are about equal; the moral being quite sufficient to keep the animal in order and in due subservience, but would not be spontaneously active. The social feelings were very active, particularly the adhesiveness. She was of a most affectionate disposition, always requiring some one to lean upon, preferring what has hitherto been considered the stronger sex, to the other and more impressible. She was not fitted to stand alone.[5]

[1] Eliza Lynn Linton, *My Literary Life* (1899), p. 43.
[2] *Middlemarch*, ch. 29.
[3] *Letters*, I. 167.
[4] This is not very large today.
[5] C. Bray, *Autobiography*, pp. 74–5.

Sara Hennell admitted to Edith Simcox that she had always disapproved of Mary Ann for 'depending so much on the arm of man', and Miss Lewis, not without some jealousy at having been displaced, spoke of Mary Ann's walking about with Charles Bray 'like lovers'.[1] If the annoyance provoked by her behaviour with Dr. Brabant were unique, it might be attributed to provincial simplicity or ignorance, even at the age of twenty-four. But the same pattern—an intellectual friendship drawn by over-ready expansiveness into feelings misunderstood—reappears often enough to recall that phrenological cast with its moral regions sufficient to keep the animal in due subservience, but not spontaneously active. Even with a man she knew as slightly as the Reverend Francis Watts one may discern a trace of the pattern between the lines of a letter she wrote to him in July 1842:

A friend has given some admonitions that led me to fear I have misrepresented myself by my manner, and while conscious of no sentiments towards those who condescend to interest themselves on my behalf but those of admiration and thankfulness I have appeared too self-confident and indifferent to undeserved kindness. It gives me much pain to think that you should have received such an impression, and I entreat you to believe that the remembrance of you, your words and looks calls up, I will not say humble, but self-depreciating reflections and lively gratitude. I am always inclined to make a father-confessor of you, perhaps because I augur that you have no heart for inflicting heavy penances, though I fear even you will say that I deserve them when I tell you that my affections have been disturbing forces which have shaken my intellect from a steady direction to the object you and my better self would make my polestar, but this will not I trust shall not be so again.[2]

They were discussing her offer to translate Vinet's *Mémoire* to be published as Watts's work, her compensation to be 'the pleasure of being linked to your remembrance'. His interest for some reason flagged. When she sent the book back to him, she explained that she was now 'engaged in a translation of a part of Spinoza's works for a friend'.[3] This was Charles Bray, who used in his *Autobiography* (p. 18) a few sentences from Part I of the *Ethics*. She did not go far with Spinoza at that time.

Mary Ann's attention was soon turned to translating David Friedrich Strauss's *Das Leben Jesu*. The initiator of this project

---

[1] Simcox Autobiography, 12 June 1885, fol. 136.
[2] *Letters*, I. 142.
[3] Ibid. 158. Lord Acton in his review of Cross mistakenly lists Vinet as one of the eminent minds of her age whom GE disregarded.

PLATE III

MARY ANN EVANS *c.* 1846
Drawing by Sara Hennell from the shadow of a phrenological cast

was Joseph Parkes, the Radical politician, a leader in the agitation for the Reform Bill, who was married to a granddaughter of Joseph Priestley. In August 1841, the day after the second edition of the *Inquiry* had come out, Parkes asked Charles Hennell to arrange for a translation of *Das Leben Jesu*, promising to contribute generously to the cost of publishing it. Charles turned first to his sister Sara, who declared the task too difficult for her. Then he asked Rufa Brabant. Being a fairly good German scholar and having her father by for recourse in difficulty, Rufa took it up at once, Sara agreeing to revise the manuscript and compare it with the original. But after two or three months of matrimony Rufa decided that the work was beyond her, too, and early in 1844 she suggested to Sara, who was visiting at Rosehill, that Mary Ann be invited to take it over.

Your proposition to deliver up the Strauss to Mary Ann has been very cordially received, [Sara wrote] and I am sure will be a great benefit. I think she will do it admirably. She will require correcting in a few words and minor matters, but she will give the meaning faithfully and spiritedly. I have been much pleased with some specimens she has shown me. And she will get on fast—which is a great thing. I see this *is* the 4th Edition; therefore I should think we may manage without getting another. Mary Ann has such a dislike to writing on that large blue paper that I have thought it expedient to indulge her in getting her own—she has just said that as you have the paper she will not mind to use it—telling her that all expenses are to be repaid her and that she is to keep an exact account of every thing she spends. I should like to read with her all the manuscript already completed—indeed to let her see all that has been done and therefore would like it to be sent while I am here. But we do not want it immediately. . . . I have finished the 14 § in the first rough copy, and am now going over it again with Mary Ann, and copying it over. It is remarkably difficult, but we both think it very interesting.[1]

For two years Mary Ann laboured, translating the fifteen hundred pages of German, with quotations in Latin, Greek, and Hebrew. As parts of it were finished, she sent them to Sara, who had now moved with her mother to Clapton, leaving Charles and Rufa in the old house at Hackney. Most of Mary Ann's letters discuss problems of interpretation; but they are not numerous, all her energy for writing going into translation. Occasionally she argued with Sara over details—like the proper rendering of *Materielle* and *Formelle* or whether *Sacrament* or *the Sacrament*

---

[1] *Letters*, I. 171–2.

was best for *Abendmahl*. The corrections Sara promised of her English usage proved nugatory. 'I do not mind about alterations that will satisfy your taste,' Mary Ann wrote, 'though I am at a loss to know the rationale of some. According to dictionaries and grammars, *"as though"* is good gentlemanly English as well as *"as if,"* and if you heard more evangelical sermons, dear, you would find that it is invariably 1stly, 2dly, 3dly, 4thly, and *lastly*, not *finally*.'[1] Dr. Brabant was said to have translated a part of Strauss's Conclusion. When Rufa sent it to her it proved, like everything else of the Doctor's, to be only unfinished notes. If he would supply an English version for some of the Greek of Josephus, Mary Ann told Sara, 'I shall be much obliged to him, but do not urge it if there be any symptoms of the *reputation ague*.' Sara went with the Doctor and Miss Hughes to Germany in the summer of 1844, where they saw Strauss at Heilbronn. Mary Ann wrote to Sara: 'I do not think it was kind to Strauss (I knew he was handsome) to tell him that a *young lady* was translating his book.'

In July Mary Ann too had a holiday. The Brays took her off to Lake Windermere for two weeks, staying at Bowness. On the return journey they stayed overnight at Manchester to call on Cara's cousins the Hollands, who were away; but the two young bachelor sons Philip and Frank received them with most cordial hospitality.

After tea [Cara wrote] we made them take us to all the very worst places about the town that we might convince ourselves that the statisticians do not make a case: indeed they do not—the streets and houses where humans do actually live and breathe there are worse than a book can tell. Horrid place! we were rather glad to leave it the next day, though we had only seen one factory, and there *were* others to be seen.[3]

Mary Ann, tired and unwell, looked her very worst, her old diffidence naturally reasserting itself in the presence of two attractive, eligible young men. 'I wish friend Philip would fall in love with her,' Cara wrote to her mother, 'but there were certainly no symptoms of it.' At Liverpool they spent the next nights at Richard Rathbone's and called on another cousin of Cara's, Mrs. James Martineau, and her young family. Mr. Rathbone took them to see the launching of the ship *Cobden*, and in the evening had two

agreeable gentlemen to dine with us: both firm believers in mesmerism and clairvoyance, though one of them seemed much too shrewd to

---

[1] *Letters*, I. 185.   [2] *Letters*, I. 181.   [3] *Letters*, I. 178-9.

believe in anything else: he nearly succeeded in mesmerising Mary
Ann to the degree that she could not open her eyes, and begged him
most piteously to do it for her, which he did immediately by passes.[1]

This was William Ballantyne Hodgson, Principal of the Liverpool
Mechanics Institute and later an important figure in English education. Writing to his friend Alexander Ireland about the episode,
he added that Miss Evans 'reads Greek, Latin, French, Italian,
German (Richter in the original). Altogether a delightful party'.

Mary Sibree, daughter of the Independent minister at Coventry,
then nineteen years old, began to come to Bird Grove on Saturdays for German lessons. When the offer to teach her had first
been made some time before, it was refused for fear that Mary
Ann's 'dangerous' religious sentiments might harm her; and when
she offered a second time, Mrs. Sibree, who was originally a
Churchwoman, spoke candidly of her fear. 'But', she went on to
say, looking affectionately at Mary Ann, 'her father does not
agree with me; he does not see any danger, and thinks we ought
not to refuse, as it is so kind of you to take the trouble.'[2] In
October 1844 they began with *Don Carlos*, meeting pretty regularly for nearly two years, when lessons were no longer necessary.
Mary Ann never urged her heterodoxy on others. When Mary
Sibree poured out her doubts, she recalled, her teacher would
steadily turn attention 'to a confession of my own want of
thoroughness in arithmetic'; and the lessons of accuracy, tolerance,
and 'the positive immorality of frittering time away in ill-natured
or in poor profitless talk' were deeply impressed. Questions of
Calvinism and Arminianism were turned 'towards manifestations
of nobility of character and sympathy with human struggles and
sufferings.' One day Mary declared that she was sure there could
be no true morality without evangelical belief. 'Oh, it is so, is it?'
said Miss Evans with the kindest smile, and nothing further passed.
Her teaching was imaginative and vigorous. When they were
reading *Wallenstein*, she pointed out that the talk of the soldiers in
the 'Lager' was 'just what it would be'. When Mary acceded
faintly, 'I suppose it is', she returned, 'No, you do not *suppose*,—
we *know* these things', and proceeded to give a specimen of what
might be a navvy's talk: 'The sort of thing such people say is,
"I'll break off your arm, and bloody your face with the stump"'[3]
In speaking of marriage one day she said: 'How terrible it must

[1] *Letters*, I. 180.   [2] Cross, New ed., pp. 52–3.
[3] Ibid. p. 55.

be to find one's self tied to a being whose limitations you could
see, and must know were such as to prevent your ever being
understood!' Even in England, she thought, marriages were practically arranged; young people, 'being brought together and receiving intimations that mutual interest was desired and expected,
were apt to drift into connections on grounds not strong enough
for the wear and tear of life'.[1]

Mary Ann was not speaking from inexperience. In 1845 a young
painter had proposed to her. His name has never been discovered,
and all we know of the affair comes from the copy of a letter that
Cara Bray wrote to Sara 30 March:

> I must give you some account of a matter which has been much in
> our thoughts this last week relating to Mary Ann: she wished me to tell
> you and has often said 'How I wish Sara were here, for she knows
> what would be for my good!' I may as well say at the beginning though
> that it has all come to nothing. She says she was talking to you about
> a young artist she was going to meet at Baginton. Well, they did meet
> and passed two days in each other's company, and she thought him the
> most interesting young man she had seen and superior to all the rest
> of mankind; the third morning he made proposals through her brother
> in law Mr. Hooton [Houghton]—saying, 'she was the most fascinating
> creature he had ever beheld, that if it were not too presumptuous to
> hope etc. etc., a person of such superior excellence and powers of mind,'
> etc., in short, he seemed desperately smitten and begged permission to
> write to her. She granted this, and came to us so brimful of happiness;—
> though she said she had not fallen in love with him yet, but admired his
> character so much that she was sure she should: the only objections
> seemed to be that his profession—a picture-restorer—is not lucrative
> or over-honourable. We liked his letters to her very much—simple,
> earnest, unstudied. She refused anything like an engagement on so short
> an acquaintance, but would have much pleasure to see him as a friend
> etc.
>
> So he came to see her last Wednesday evening, and owing to his
> great agitation, from youth—or something or other, did not seem to
> her half so interesting as before, and the next day she made up her
> mind that she could never love or respect him enough to marry him
> and that it would involve too great a sacrifice of her mind and pursuits.
> So she wrote to him to break it off—and there it stands now. Poor girl,
> it has been a trying, exciting week to her and she seemed quite spiritless
> this morning: and we cannot help feeling that she has been over-hasty
> in giving it up. And yet—and yet—one does not know what to advise.[2]

Commenting on it a week later in a letter to Sara, Mary Ann
said:

[1] Cross, New ed., p. 58.   [2] *Letters*, I. 183–4.

I have never yet half thanked you for taking an interest in my little personal matters. My unfortunate 'affaire' did not become one 'du coeur,' but it has been anything but a comfortable one for my conscience. If the circumstances could be repeated with the added condition of my experience I should act very differently. As it is I have now dismissed it from my mind, and only keep it recorded in my book of reference, article 'Precipitancy, ill effects of.' So now dear Sara, I am once more your true Gemahlinn, which being interpreted, means that I have no loves but those that you can share with me—intellectual and religious loves.[1]

And a little later she wrote to Patty Jackson:

What should you say to my becoming a wife? Should you think it a duty to ascertain the name of the rash man that you might warn him from putting on such a matrimonial hair-shirt as he would have with me? I did meditate an engagement, but I have determined, whether wisely or not I cannot tell, to defer it, at least for the present.[2]

Despite this brave front, Mary Ann was troubled about her rejection of the painter. Mrs. Bray told Sara that

although it is given up irrevocably, she is so extremely wretched about it, and we know, wants it to come on again—not that she cares much for him, but she is so grieved to have wounded his feelings, and he has behaved so well and unselfishly that he deserves pity, if not more. But we can do nothing in the matter—indeed she entreats us not to meddle, and the Hootons are the only parties who could—they being the friends of both. She says it shall not interfere with the M.S., but poor girl, everything seems against the grain with her.[3]

Her anxiety showed itself in fierce headaches, for which she could 'find no relief but in leeches—sweet little creatures, as she calls them'. But she had a better anodyne in the mountainous task of the Strauss translation, which went steadily forward. The word that Mr. Parkes had delivered his £300 to pay for the publication was cheering. The Brays gave her what diversion they could. After two days with them in London in June 1845 she came home much better; 'I never saw her so blooming and buoyant', said Cara. A few days later they bore her off to Birmingham to see Macready play Brutus, 'a real treat, notwithstanding a ranting Cassius and a fat, stumpy Caesar and a screeching Calpurnia'.[4]

Their longest expedition took them to Scotland in October. For a while it seemed as if Mary Ann would not be able to go, for her brother-in-law Edward Clarke was finally bankrupt, and Chrissey with her four children had descended on Bird Grove. But Mary Ann looked so miserably disappointed at missing this chance to visit the scenes of the Waverley novels that Charles Bray 'persuaded her father it was most desirable for the good of her health'.[1] They set out by train to Liverpool (where again they met the Rathbones and the Martineaus), and thence by steam packet to Greenock and Glasgow. Here they spent two days, seeing the Cathedral, where Rob Roy delivered his warning, and the other spots she knew so well in imagination. After a night at Dumbarton, they had four wonderful days on Loch Lomond and another on Loch Katrine before going through Callander and Stirling to Edinburgh, where they arrived 24 October. Mrs. Bray describes the end of the trip:

We were all in ecstasies, but Mary Ann's were beyond everything—but here we met with a sad damper to all our pleasure—there was a letter from her brother which had been following her from Glasgow, saying that her father had broken his leg the very night she set out, and begging her to come home as soon as possible. We could not let her travel 300 miles alone, as she wished, and after much difficulty in contriving, CB. persuaded her to be easy and stay with us over another day, as the letter said her father was going on well.[2]

So they went to Melrose and Abbotsford, the very house where Scott created the novels. Taking the train next day to Birmingham, they reached home 28 October.

While Mr. Evans's leg was mending, Mary Ann was called on more than ever to read to him and amuse him. His health was failing, and he had some acute attacks that worried her greatly. But she kept on with the Strauss through it all. She had a cast about 20 inches high of Thorwaldsen's *Risen Christ* standing in her study, and on the wall an engraving of Delaroche's *Christ*, which she had once thought of using for a frontispiece.[3] She told the Brays that

she was Strauss-sick—it made her ill dissecting the beautiful story of the crucifixion, and only the sight of her Christ-image and picture made her endure it. Moreover as her work advances nearer its public appearance, she grows dreadfully nervous. Poor thing, I do pity her sometimes with her pale sickly face and dreadful headaches, and anxiety too about her

[1] *Letters*, I. 200.   [2] *Letters*, I. 201.
[3] Both the engraving, which GE gave to John Sibree, and the cast are now in the GE Collection at the Coventry Public Library.

father. This illness of his [has] tried her so much, for all the time she had for rest and fresh air, she had to read to him. Nevertheless she looks very happy and satisfied at times with her work.[1]

The sight of the first proofs was a comfort. After she read them, she sent them to Sara and Charles Hennell for vetting; by now they had conceived a genuine respect for her rendering of the text and suggested few changes. In April a specimen was sent to Strauss, who contributed a preface in Latin, praising the translation as being, so far as he could tell, 'et accurata et perspicua'. By the end of May the prefatory matter was finished. The book was published 15 June 1846 as *The Life of Jesus, Critically Examined* by David Friedrich Strauss. Translated from the Fourth German Edition. In Three Volumes. London: Chapman, Brothers, 121, Newgate Street, MDCCCXLVI. Mary Ann's name did not appear. For her work she was paid £20. Few books of the nineteenth century have had a profounder influence on religious thought in England.

With the last proof returned, Mary Ann found time again for her own reading. She 'is as happy as you may imagine at her work being done', Cara wrote to Sara. 'She means to come and read Shakespeare through to us as her first enjoyment.'[2] She was reading everything that came to hand. Though no list is available, casual references show the spread of her interests: Milton, Wordsworth, Dickens, Thackeray, *Sir Charles Grandison* ('I had no idea that Richardson was worth so much'), Carlyle, Goethe, Fredrika Bremer, St. Simon, Lamartine, Disraeli—once more she is the omnivorous reader, devouring everything. She has 'been *guanoing* her mind with French novels', she wrote to Mary Sibree. 'This is the impertinent expression of d'Israeli, who, writing himself much more detestable stuff than ever came from a French pen, can do nothing better to bamboozle the unfortunates who are seduced into reading his Tancred than speak superciliously of all other men and things.'[3] Her guano was chiefly George Sand; *Lélia*, *Spiridion*, *Jacques*, and the *Lettres d'un voyageur* are mentioned about this time, but we know that she also read *François le Champi*, *La Petite Fadette*, *Le Meunier d'Angibault*, *Consuelo*, *Mauprat*, and *Indiana*. Rousseau was the other great passion. She read *Émile* and *La Nouvelle Héloïse*. *Les Confessions* affected her most strongly. It would be interesting to know whether she was

[1] *Letters*, I. 206.   [2] Bray–Hennell Extracts, 19 Apr. 1846 (Yale).
[3] *Letters*, I. 234–5.

aware that it was written for the most part at Wooton Hall in Derbyshire, later the seat of Francis Parker Newdigate, her father's first employer. Cara and Sara both disapproved somewhat of George Sand and Rousseau, while Mary Ann defended them. Apropos of *Jacques* she wrote to Sara:

I wish you thoroughly to understand that the writers who have most profoundly influenced me . . . are not in the least oracles to me. It is just possible that I may not embrace one of their opinions, that I may wish my life to be shaped quite differently from theirs. For instance it would signify nothing to me if a very wise person were to stun me with proofs that Rousseau's views of life, religion, and government are miserably erroneous—that he was guilty of some of the worst bassesses that have degraded civilized man. I might admit all this—and it would be not the less true that Rousseau's genius has sent that electric thrill through my intellectual and moral frame which has awakened me to new perceptions, which has made man and nature a fresh world of thought and feeling to me—and this not by teaching me any new belief. It is simply that the rushing mighty wind of his inspiration has so quickened my faculties that I have been able to shape more definitely for myself ideas which had previously dwelt as dim 'ahnungen' in my soul —the fire of his genius has so fused together old thoughts and prejudices that I have been ready to make new combinations.

It is thus with G. Sand. I should never dream of going to her writings as a moral code or text-book. I don't care whether I agree with her about marriage or not—whether I think the design of her plot correct or that she had no precise design at all but began to write as the spirit moved her and trusted to Providence for the catastrophe, which I think the more probable case—it is sufficient for me as a reason for bowing before her in eternal gratitude to that 'great power of God' manifested in her—that I cannot read six pages of hers without feeling that it is given to her to delineate human passion and its results—(and I must say in spite of your judgement) some of the moral instincts and their tendencies—with such truthfulness such nicety of discrimination such tragic power and withal such loving gentle humour that one might live a century with nothing but one's own dull faculties and not know so much as those six pages will suggest.[1]

At the end of May 1846, Mary Ann went to London to spend ten days with Sara, who returned the visit at Bird Grove later in the summer. 'Tell Mary Ann it has been like a death in the family the non-possibility of seeing her all this week', Cara wrote. In the atmosphere of Rosehill she had matured extraordinarily from the quiet, gentle-mannered, grave-faced girl who first came there five

[1] *Letters*, I. 277–8.

years before. Though her opinions were not uttered till they had
been well considered, her painful shyness had disappeared. At
parties Cara could count on her to sing gaily and play the piano
to keep the thing from flagging, no matter how sticky the company.
Sara wrote to her mother, 'It is the greatest treat to be with
her and talk about all the things I have been thinking about
for the last six months, for she grows better and wiser every time
I see her.' In September she remarked, 'Mary Ann looks very
brilliant just now—we fancy she must be writing her novel.'[1]
Sara does not explain this interesting speculation.

It could hardly have referred to her contributions to the
Coventry *Herald*, the weekly newspaper which Charles Bray purchased in June 1846 to fight the opposition of the Coventry *Standard* to his projects for reform. Mary Ann wrote a number of
anonymous articles for the *Herald*. The earliest I have identified
is a review of three books: *Christianity in Its Various Aspects* and
The Jesuits, both by Quinet and Michelet, and *Priests, Women, and
Families* by Michelet alone, which appeared 30 October 1846.
A brief notice of Gilbert à Beckett's *Comic History of England*
with Leech's illustrations followed, 4 November. In December she
began a series of five loosely connected essays under the title
'Poetry and Prose from the Notebook of an Eccentric', which, as
Thomas Pinney remarks in reprinting them in *Essays of George
Eliot* (1963), anticipates the form she returned to in her last book,
Impressions of Theophrastus Such. 'Vice and Sausages', published
26 February 1847, is a satirical squib on the Coventry police
inspector John Vice.

As a friend Maria Lewis had now been quite displaced by Sara
and Cara. Though disagreeing radically with her old pupil's new
life, Miss Lewis still came for long visits in her holidays. During
her stay at Christmas 1846 relations between them were finally
broken off. 'Mary Ann is going to have a stupid Miss Lewis visitor
for a fortnight,' Cara wrote, 'which will keep her at home.'[2] Just
after George Eliot's death Edith Simcox inquired about the ending
of the old friendship. Sara

thought it was gradual, incompatibility of opinions etc.—'it had long
been a tax'—thought that the quarrel was by word of mouth, that Miss
Lewis had been finding fault, governess fashion, with what was impru-
dent or unusual in Marian's manners and that Marian always resented

[1] Bray–Hennell Extracts (Yale).
[2] *Letters*, I. 230; Bray–Hennell Extracts (Yale).

this and that it was some verbal *tu quoque* leading to a misunderstanding, as if Miss Lewis had reproached her with seeming to take too much interest in somebody—of the opposite sex: whereto she angrily: 'It might as well be said that *you* have an "interest" or are interested in your friendship for me.'[1]

When Mary Ann asked to have her letters back, Miss Lewis said that she would *lend* them; but Mr. Bray declared that letters were the property of the writer, and Mary Ann refused to return them, giving them instead to Sara, who delivered them to Cross after Mary Ann's death.

Increased maturity and confidence are seen in Mary Ann's revised opinion of Dr. Brabant; she wrote to Sara 5 November 1846:

I begin to be of your and Cara's opinion anent Dr. B. You are my own best plainspoken friend and generally judge better for me than I can judge for myself. I hope Rufa knows the contents of my letter to you. Pray convince her and every one concerned in the matter that I am too inflatedly conceited to think it worth my while to run after Dr. Brabant or his correspondence. If I ever offered incense to him it was because there was no other deity at hand and because I wanted some kind of worship pour passer le temps. I always knew that I could belabour my fetisch if I chose, and laughed at him in my sleeve. Even that degree of inclination towards mock reverence has long since passed away and ridiculous as it may seem to every one else, I looked on my renewal of a correspondence with him as a favour *conferred* by me rather than *received*. I shall certainly take an opportunity of certifying him on which leg the boot was. You see I am getting horridly vulgar as well as proud.[2]

But the fatuous man was hard to discourage. The following August he sent her 'a most affectionate invitation to go to Germany with him! Mr. and Mrs. Murch of Bath and a Miss Taylor being of the party. It would have been the most delightful thing in the world for her', Cara added in telling her mother about it, 'and just now she could conveniently leave her father; but she wrote back simply thanking him and saying it was impossible to accept.'[3]

She had a new correspondent now, young John Sibree, who after a year at Halle University had returned at the age of twenty-four to study at Spring Hill College, Birmingham, for the Independent ministry. During his holidays he helped Mary Ann with her Greek, reading Xenophon with her. In a note to Mary Sibree she wrote: 'I shall be quite disengaged this afternoon. Will you ask your

---

[1] Simcox Autobiography, 12 June 1885, fol. 135.
[2] *Letters*, I. 225.   [3] *Letters*, I. 236.

brother if it will be convenient to him to come to me? and will you join us when we have done our Greek and have tea with me on your way to chapel?[1] Late in 1847, having read Mary Ann's translation of Strauss, John began a correspondence that elicited some of her most spirited letters, sometimes slangy and impudent, but always full of wit and shrewd good sense. Like a child let out to play she tosses iconoclastic gibes at her old idols.

I am glad you detest Mrs. Hannah More's letters. I like neither her letters, nor her books, nor her character. She was that most disagreeable of all monsters, a blue-stocking—a monster that can only exist in a miserably false state of society, in which a woman with but a smattering of learning or philosophy is classed along with singing mice and card playing pigs.[2]

Disraeli's theory of 'pure' race Mary Ann dismisses as without a leg to stand on. She foresees an eventual extermination or fusion of all races, not even excepting Disraeli's 'Hebrew-Caucasian', though the Negroes 'are too important physiologically and geographically for one to think of their extermination, while the repulsion between them and the other races seems too strong for fusion to take place to any great extent'.[3] An observation of Hegel's leads to a discussion of the relative values of music and the plastic arts. Politics are discussed. In March 1848, when the French Revolution breaks out, she is delighted to find him sharing her contempt for Louis Philippe; she refuses to sentimentalize over 'a pampered old man when the earth has its millions of unfed souls and bodies'. But she has no hope for any English revolution. Here

a revolutionary movement would be simply destructive—not constructive. Besides, it would be put down. Our military have no notion of 'fraternizing', and the aristocracy have got firm hold of them. Our little humbug of a queen is more endurable than the rest of her race because she calls forth a chivalrous feeling, and there is nothing in our constitution to obstruct the slow progress of *political* reform. This is all we are fit for at present. The social reform which may prepare us for great changes is more and more the object of effort both in Parliament and out of it. But we English are slow crawlers.[4]

Soon Mary Ann was complaining that John's letters are too impersonal 'Every one talks of himself or herself to me',[5] she said.

[1] Undated, signature cut away (Nuneaton).
[2] *Letters*, I. 245.   [3] *Letters*, I. 246.
[4] *Letters*, I. 254.   [5] *Letters*, I. 251.

'I want you to write me a Confession of Faith—not merely *what* you believe but why you believe it. . . . I shall be a safety-valve for your communicativeness . . . and it will be fraught with ghostly comfort to me.'[1] John apparently complied; but in attempting to formulate his reasons, he found them inadequate and abandoned the ministry. 'You have my hearty and not inexperienced sympathy', Mary Ann told him, rejoicing in his honest doubt.[2] But his father and mother blamed her for having influenced their children, and relations were broken off; John went back to Germany. Mary Ann could only envy him: 'O the bliss of having a very high attic in a romantic continental town, such as Geneva—far away from morning callers, dinners, and decencies; and then to pause for a year and think de omnibus et quibusdam aliis, and then to return to life, and work for poor stricken humanity and never think of self again.'[3] It was more than a year before the high attic became a reality.

Her father's increasing infirmities demanded more and more time for entertaining him and managing the household. Sea air was prescribed. She took him to Dover for a fortnight in the summer of 1846, and to the Isle of Wight in September 1847, pausing for a few days at Brighton on the way home. In February 1848 he was able to make a last visit to Derbyshire. He continued to attend Trinity Church with Mary Ann beside him as usual, who survived Mr. Davies's sermons by making herself deaf and looking up at the fine old painted roof and arches.[4] She herself was far from well. Apart from the anxiety over her father, she was suffering from severe toothache. Two large molars had to be extracted. For the second operation the dentist insisted on having the surgeon Mr. Bury in attendance before he would give her chloroform again, and she would not have it out otherwise. Mrs. Bray describes it:

So she began to sniff the chloroform, but it brought on again the violent screaming, and it was only by giving her a second extra-strong dose that perfect unconsciousness could be produced. The tooth was dragged out with a tremendous pull, and then she opened her eyes, and told us she had been listening to 'such strains of eloquence.' Her head has felt very queer ever since, and yesterday I found her in bed with a violent headache—so I fear the chloroform did some little mischief.[5]

By April Mr. Evans had developed alarming cardiac symptoms; their plan of a journey to St. Leonard's had to be postponed for

---

[1] *Letters*, I. 255.   [2] *Letters*, I. 260.
[3] *Letters*, I. 261.   [4] *Letters*, I. 229.   [5] *Letters*, I. 257.

six weeks. Mr. Bury forbade him to climb the stair and put him on a new diet without meat or wine. A bed was set up for him in the dining room. Mary Ann stayed with him constantly, sleeping on the sofa in his room till he was better. Under the new regime he rallied somewhat. The anxiety had been hard on Mary Ann; 'the poor thing looks as thin as a poker', said Cara.[1] They found St. Leonard's cold and rainy. Much of the time she spent reading to him—*The Fair Maid of Perth* was one of the books. But she also found time to read *Jane Eyre*, and she wrote to Charles Bray that she would be glad to know 'what you admire in it. All self-sacrifice is good—but one would like it to be in a somewhat nobler cause than that of a diabolical law which chains a man soul and body to a putrefying carcase. However the book *is* interesting—only I wish the characters would talk a little less like the heroes and heroines of police reports.'[2]

Soon after her return to Foleshill she had one of the momentous experiences of her life, her meeting with Emerson—'the first *man* I have ever seen'.[3] He had been in Britain and France for eight months lecturing. The Brays heard him once in Birmingham and in June 1848 attended three of his final series of lectures in London, where he was living in the house of his publisher John Chapman. Sara Hennell had met him there, and when Mr. Bray was introduced, he invited him to stop off at Rosehill on the way to his ship at Liverpool. Emerson arrived at the Coventry station a little before midnight, 12 July. Next day at breakfast they presented Miss Evans, who fell into earnest conversation with him. Suddenly they saw Emerson start. Something she said had given him a shock of surprise: he 'asked her what had first awakened her to deep reflection, and when she answered "Rousseau's *Confessions*", he remarked that this was very interesting, inasmuch as Carlyle had told him that very book had had the same effect upon his mind'.[4] After breakfast they all went with the Brays' friend Edward Flower to 'see Shakespeare' at Stratford on Avon. Leaving Mr. Flower there, the four of them drove back from Stratford in an open carriage. 'This was the pleasantest part of the day to us', Cara wrote, 'and he talked as if we had been old friends. He was much struck with Mary Ann; expressed his admiration many times to

[1] *Letters*, I. 259. [2] *Letters*, I. 268. [3] *Letters*, I. 270–1.
[4] In 1853 GE told William Hale White that it was 'worthwhile to undertake all the labour of learning French if it resulted in nothing more than reading one book —Rousseau's Confessions'. *Athenæum*, 28 Nov. 1885, p. 702.

Charles—"That young lady has a calm, serious soul",—and regretted very much that he had no more time to stay amongst us. He came home to tea with us—and oh how stupid did those committeemen look. Well for us a great benign soul does not often come to disgust us with common life.'

By September Mr. Evans was getting rapidly worse, and the end seemed near. Mrs. Bray wrote to Sara:

The doctors expect his death to take place suddenly, by a suffusion of water on the chest; and poor Mary Ann, alone with him, has the whole care and fatigue of nursing him night and day with this constant nervous expectation. She keeps up wonderfully mentally, but looks like a ghost. It is a great comfort that he is now quite aware of his situation, and was not in the least discomposed when Isaac told him he might die suddenly. It was quite a pleasure to see him sitting in his chair looking so calm just after he had known this; and he takes opportunities now of saying kind things to Mary Ann, contrary to his wont. Poor girl, it shows how rare they are by the gratitude with which she repeats the commonest expressions of kindness.[1]

Two weeks later Mr. Evans made his will. The Derbyshire properties were left to Robert, those about Nuneaton to Isaac. Fanny and Chrissey, who had each received £1,000 when they married, were each left another thousand and certain items of the furniture. To Mary Ann he left £2,000 in trust and household goods not already disposed of to the amount of £100; but, at the suggestion of the lawyer Mr. Holbeche, £100 in cash was substituted for the household goods. Robert was to have Hume's *History of England*, Chrissey, her mother's Bible, and Fanny, the silver forks and that set of Sir Walter Scott's novels which Mary Ann had spent so many long hours reading aloud to him. Was this an intentional snub of his youngest child?

He lingered on five months longer with Mary Ann watching over him constantly, writing hurried little reports on every variation in his condition to her brothers and sisters. None of them cared for him as she did. It was no matter to her that the Waverley novels or her mother's silver forks would go to another. She now had spiritual resources that ignored such trifles. She had bought a copy of *De Imitatione Christi* by Thomas à Kempis, a new edition with quaint little woodcuts, which taught her—as it did Maggie Tulliver—that true peace lay in resignation, in renunciation of self, an inner peace far deeper than any she had known at the height of her evangelical fervour, when she enjoyed being taunted with the name of 'saint'.

As her father's feeble strength ebbed slowly away, she told Charles Bray: 'Strange to say I feel that these will ever be the happiest days of life to me. The one deep strong love I have ever known has now its highest exercise and fullest reward—the worship of sorrow is *the* worship for mortals.'[1] On 30 May she wrote:

Mr. Bury told us last night that he thought Father would not last till morning. I sat by him with my hand in his till four o'clock, and he then became quieter and has had some comfortable sleep. He is obviously weaker this morning and has been for the last two or three days so painfully reduced that I dread to think what his dear frame may become before life gives way. My Brother slept here last night and will be here again tonight. What shall I be without my Father? It will seem as if a part of my moral nature were gone. I had a horrid vision of myself last night becoming earthly sensual and devilish for want of that purifying restraining influence.[2]

Before the next day dawned Robert Evans breathed his last. He was buried 6 June 1849 beside his wife in Chilvers Coton churchyard.

[1] *Letters*, I. 283–4.   [2] *Letters*, I. 284.

CHAPTER III

HIGH ATTICS

※

F OR some time before Mr. Evans's death the Brays had been contemplating a continental tour to rest and divert Mary Ann. Within five days of the funeral they set out. Various travelling companions had been suggested—Edward Noel, George Dawson, and, a very recent acquaintance, James Anthony Froude, the author of *The Nemesis of Faith* (1849). This tale of a young man who, having been persuaded against his true feelings to take orders, admits his disbelief in Revelation, and falls into an adulterous love with the wife of a friend, had been denounced and burned in February at Exeter College, Oxford, of which Froude was a Fellow—with the usual result of making it widely read and its author a hero of heterodoxy. John Chapman, its publisher, sent a copy to Mary Ann, whose enthusiasm impelled her to write Froude a note of thanks signed 'The Translator of Strauss'. In a review for the Coventry *Herald*, she described it as one of those rare books 'among the *spawn* of the press' that makes us feel

in companionship with a spirit who is transfusing himself into our souls and so vitalizing them by his superior energy, that life, both outward and inward, presents itself to us in higher relief, in colours brightened and deepened. . . . The books which carry this magic in them are the true products of genius. . . . We are sure that its author is a bright particular star, though he sometimes leaves us in doubt whether he be not a fallen 'son of the morning'. Much there is in the work of a questionable character; . . . but its trenchant remarks on some of our English conventions, its striking sketches of the dubious aspects which many chartered respectabilities are beginning to wear under the light of this nineteenth century, its suggestive hints as to the necessity of re-casting the currency of our religion and virtue that it may carry fresh and bright the stamp of the age's highest and best ideas—these have a practical bearing which may well excite the grave, perhaps the alarmed attention of some important classes among us.[1]

[1] 16 Mar. 1849.

Chapman discreetly refused to give Froude the name of 'The Translator' but offered to forward a reply. Cara wrote 23 March to Sara:

Last night at dusk she came running in high glee with a charming note from Froude, naively and prettily requesting her to reveal herself. He says he recognized her review in the Coventry Herald, and if she thinks him a fallen star, she might help him to rise, 'but he believes he has only been dipped in the Styx, and is not much the worse for the bathing.' Poor girl! I am so pleased she should have this little episode in her dull life, but I suppose she won't continue the correspondence.[1]

Mary Ann did not reply; 'but I do hope', Cara added, 'he will come as he says and see the fair mystery'. Meanwhile, Mary Ann read his *Shadows of the Clouds* (1847), which gave her 'a sort of palpitation that one hardly knows whether to call wretched or delightful'.[2] She was trying to forget her father's hopeless condition by translating Spinoza's *Tractatus Theologico-Politicus*, which Bray wanted to have published; she found it 'such a rest to her mind'.

We have no account of her meeting with Froude 7 June 1849, the day after her father's funeral. Cara was in London, making farewell visits to her family; Sara had come to Rosehill to keep the household in order while the Brays were abroad. After the interview, which certainly included a discussion of *The Nemesis of Faith*, Charles proposed that Froude go with them to France, and he agreed. Was there a faint hope of a match between these two fallen angels? Charles took Mary Ann to join Cara in London 11 June, and the next day they set out for Folkestone. At the station John Chapman appeared with a note from Froude explaining that he could not accompany them because he was planning to be married.[3]

After two days in Paris they left at midnight by rail for Tonnerre and then by diligence to Lyons and by boat down the Rhône to Avignon. Mary Ann was by no means the cheerful companion of their trips to Wales and the Highlands. Physically exhausted by the long ordeal of her father's illness, she was in such low spirits that Cara almost regretted their having taken her away so soon. Something of her dejection is reflected in the opening of Book IV of *The Mill on the Floss*, 'The Valley of Humiliation':

Journeying down the Rhone on a summer's day, you have perhaps felt the sunshine made dreary by those ruined villages which stud the banks in

[1] Bray–Hennell Extracts (Yale).   [2] *Letters*, I. 280.
[3] C. Bray, *Autobiography*, p. 75.

certain parts of its course . . ., dismal remnants of commonplace houses, which in their best days were but the sign of a sordid life, belonging in all its detail to our own vulgar era; . . . these dead-tinted, hollow-eyed, angular skeletons of villages on the Rhone oppress me with the feeling that human life—very much of it—is a narrow, ugly, grovelling existence, which even calamity does not elevate.

After resting a day or two at Avignon, which she had 'set her heart on', they went by rail to Marseilles, and then again on the old road through Nice and along the Grande Corniche to Genoa. There they stayed a week before going through Milan to Lake Como (site of the tragic denouement of *The Nemesis of Faith*) and Lake Maggiore. Even in these lovely scenes Mary Ann did not improve. When she revisited them eleven years later, Cara's kindness came back to her with keen remembrance: 'How wretched I was then—how peevish, how utterly morbid! And how kind and forbearing you were under the oppression of my company!'[1] They rode over the Simplon Pass to Martigny and over the Col de Balme to Chamonix; the ladies were on side-saddles, Mary Ann's with an alarming tendency to turn, and her terror of being dropped over a precipice somewhat subdued her expected awe at the sublimity of snow-clad Alps. Four days later, sunburnt and exhausted, they arrived in Geneva. They spent a leisurely week along the Lake at Ouchy and Vevey. There her mind was made up; she determined to stay abroad alone all winter. Charles took her back to Geneva 25 July, establishing her in a good pension, said goodbye (probably with some feeling of relief), and rejoined Cara at Lausanne to make their way back to Coventry.[2]

Alone, in the romantic town of her dream, Mary Ann could now rest her frayed nerves and take stock of her life. What was she to do? The £100 in cash her father bequeathed would last her through the year, but the income from the £2,000 left in trust would never bring more than £90 a year; even a country curate could no longer support himself on that. She was determined not to be dependent on her family. Poor Chrissey and her bankrupt husband needed help more than she; their seven-year-old Clara had just died of scarlet fever, and the six other children, the baby only a month old, were more than they could manage. Isaac had no sympathy with Mary Ann's ideas or her feelings; if he were to help, she would have to do things his way; he was certainly not a man she

[1] *Letters*, III. 321.
[2] Details from Cara Bray's Commonplace Book (Coventry).

could lean upon. But no other had appeared ready to take the responsibility. She would be thirty in November. She had never been good looking, had none of the superficial charms that attract young men. The Language of Flowers had rightly named her Clematis—*Mental* Beauty. No, she must find work to support herself. But what? Translation? The three volumes of Strauss brought her only £20; Spinoza, if she finished it, would hardly bring more. She was reduced to the only career open to respectable women, teaching. She had once contemplated it during the conflict with her father. At best it was a dreary life for bare subsistence.[1] If she prepared herself with special lessons, she might find a place in some school where her irregular religious opinions would make less difficulty. Or could she earn her living as a writer? She had been thinking about a book on the idea of a future life. And there was that novel the Brays were expecting her to write some day; Eliza Lynn, who was not half so clever, had already published two novels. In Geneva she began to keep her Journal, a little black book of about 200 pages in which for the next eleven years she wrote down her impressions of everything, her hopes and her fears. Cross, after using it for the *Life*, cut out and destroyed the first forty-six pages, the intimate record of her life from 1849 to 1854. Only a few letters are left to help reconstruct her eight months in Geneva.

Her pension, the Campagne Plongeon, stood near the Lake a little outside the city on the site of the present Parc des Eaux-Vives. It was run with true Swiss regard for comfort and respectability by Mme de Vallière, a woman of reading and talent, whom the Radical revolution of 1845 had forced to leave her pension in Lausanne, though her husband stayed on there. Some of her guests were refugees, too. The Marquis de St. Germain, a tall, squinting man, had fled from his home in the Piedmont, accused of harbouring his brother-in-law, the proscribed Duc de Visconti. The Marquise, a good-natured person, though with 'the voice almost of a market woman', her three children, six servants, her uncle the Duc de Berray, and a young friend Signor Goldrini completed this family group. Soon the Marquise was having long talks with Mary Ann, telling her

of the comfort she has in the confessional—for our têtes-a-tête have lately turned on religious matters. She says, I am in a 'mauvaise voie

---

[1] Cf. Gwendolen Harleth's horror of the prospect, even in a bishop's family. Maggie Tulliver's two years of servitude are passed over in silence.

sans le rapport de la religion. Peut-être vous marierez—et le mariage, chère amie, sans la foi religieuse——' She says I have isolated myself by my studies—that I am too cold and have too little confidence in the feelings of others towards me—that I do not believe how deep an interest she has conceived in my lot. She says Signor Goldrini (the young Italian who was here for a week) told her when he had been talking to me one evening—Vous aimerez cette demoiselle, j'en suis sûr—and she has found his prediction true.[1]

One day she devised a new way to dress Mary Ann's hair. 'You would not know me if you saw me. The Marquise . . . has abolished all my curls and made two things stick out on each side of my head like those on the head of the Sphinx. All the world says I look infinitely better, so I comply, though to myself I seem uglier than ever—if possible.'[2] At the end of August, when an amnesty was declared in Piedmont, Mary Ann composed a dozen lines of bad French verse for the Marquise's album, and the St. Germains departed.

Another guest who interested herself in Mary Ann was known as the Baronne de Ludwigsdorf. English by birth, she had lived most of her life on the Continent, at Vienna chiefly. She

is so good to me—a charming creature—so anxious to see me comfortably settled—petting me in all sorts of ways. She sends me tea when I wake in the morning, orangeflower water when I go to bed, grapes, and her maid to wait on me. She says if I like she will spend the winter after this at Paris with me and introduce me to her friends there—but she does not mean to attach herself to me, because I shall never like her long. I shall be tired of her when I have sifted her etc. She says I have more intellect than morale—and other things more true than agreeable —however she 'is greatly interested in me'—has told me her troubles and her feelings, she says, in spite of herself—for she has never been able before in her life to say so much even to her old friends—it is a mystery she cannot unravel. She is a person of high culture according to the ordinary notions of what feminine culture should be. She speaks French and German perfectly, plays well, and has the most perfect polish of manner, the most thorough refinement both socially and morally. She reminds me of Cara in one thing, though not like her generally. Her character is really remarkably destitute of animalism and she has just that sort of antipathy towards people who offend her refined instincts which we know so well in another person. She is tall and handsome—a striking looking person but with a sweet feminine expression when she is with those she likes—dresses exquisitely—in fine is all that I am not.[3]

[1] *Letters*, I. 296.   [2] *Letters*, I. 298.   [3] *Letters*, I. 308.

PLATE IV

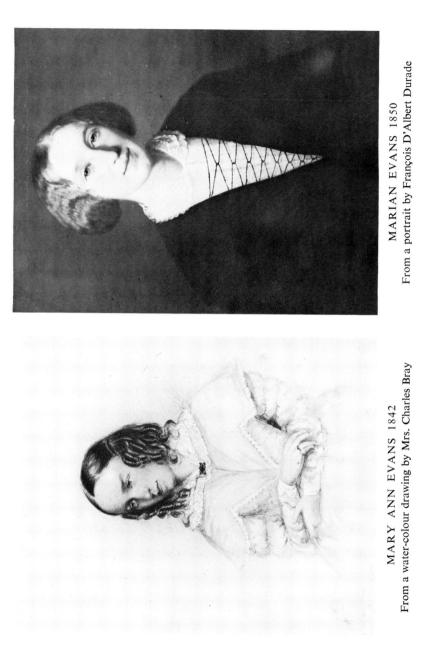

MARIAN EVANS 1850
From a portrait by François D'Albert Durade

MARY ANN EVANS 1842
From a water-colour drawing by Mrs. Charles Bray

The letters from Plongeon to Rosehill are studded with such vignettes of the guests who came and went. Mademoiselle Faisan, a dear little old maid, had spent several summers there. Prosy, full of tiny details, a sample of 'those happy souls who ask for nothing but the work of the hour, however trivial', she was never bored.[1] 'Ah!' she would say, 'nous avons un beau pays si nous n'avions pas ces Radicaux!'[2] Two Americans came under Mary Ann's sharp eye: the mother

kind but silly, the daughter silly, but not kind, and they both of them chatter the most execrable French with amazing volubility and self-complacency. They are very rich, very smart, and very vulgar—just a specimen of Americanism according to the Tories. The daughter has been presented at Court and this was the way in which she contrived to convey the fact to Mrs. Lock (my nice elderly lady). Mrs. Lock observed that she thought the health of young ladies in England was deteriorated by their habits. Miss America replied, 'I have been to court and the young ladies looked very healthy there!!' Oh, said Mrs. Lock, I belong to the gentry—I know nothing about the nobility.[3]

Mrs. Lock, widow of Captain Nagle Lock, was 'quite a mother' to Mary Ann—'helps me to buy my candles and do all my shopping—takes care of me at dinner and quite rejoices when she sees me enjoy conversation or anything else.'[4] She

is a thorough Englishwoman and can only speak French negro-fashion, and begins to tire sadly of the bows and 'Bonjours' and 'Pardons.' Yet she has no intention of returning to England. She has had very bitter trials which seem to be driving her more and more aloof from society. She has not yet had courage to tell me herself what these trials are, but I have heard from Mlle. Rosa that her daughter married one of the French noblesse. The match was in every way highly advantageous —the husband excellent, fortune considerable. They lived happily for some time—she had two little girls—when an accursed cousin of the husband's came in the way and caused a separation within the last year. Mrs. Lock is one of the Heads—the same family as that of Sir Francis Head. Her brother Major [Charles Franklin] Head wrote an 'Overland Journey from India' which you may have seen. She has multitudes of relations in England, but I suppose shame at her daughter's disgrace makes all her old associations painful. No one likes her here —simply because her manners are brusque and her French incomprehensible. She means to go to Bex for economy.[5]

[1] *Letters*, I. 313.   [2] *Letters*, I. 319.   [3] *Letters*, I. 290-1.
[4] *Letters*, I. 292.   [5] *Letters*, I. 297-8.

The day she left there is one last glimpse of her:

Poor Mrs. Lock is to write to me—has given me a little ring—says 'take care of yourself, my child—have some tea of your own—you'll be quite another person if you get some introductions to clever people—you'll get on well among a certain set, that's true'—it is her way to say 'that's true' after all her affirmations. She says, 'You won't find any kindred spirits at Plongeon, my dear.'[1]

We may be sure that notes like these were carefully entered in the little black journal. Latimer, the hero of George Eliot's story 'The Lifted Veil' (1859), was educated at Geneva, and many of the things he recalls are found also in her letters. He speaks of his first sight of the Alps as he descended the Jura, and of how, when he would go out on the Lake at evening, 'I used to do as Jean Jacques did—lie down in my boat and let it glide where it would, while I looked up at the departing glow leaving one mountain-top after another.' Latimer and his friend Meunier (named for a celebrated preacher Mary Ann used to hear at Geneva) on holidays would take the steamboat to Vevey or go up the Salève as she did. On the back of a calendar for 1876 she jotted down Mrs. Lock's name with those of the Baronne de Ludwigsdorf, Cousin Rosa, and Plongeon among a score of miscellaneous notes of characters and situations for fiction.

A dearth of young men is usual in places like Plongeon. Young students occasionally drifted through the pension, shy or boorish, and sat opposite her at table long enough to be impaled unforget-tably in a sentence or two of her letters to the Brays. There was one pleasant young German of twenty-three, with a 'bright, intelli-gent, refined face', Alexander von Herder, a grandson of Goethe's friend, the philosopher and poet. He was 'very good-natured, but a most determined enemy to all gallantry', though he took Mary Ann with some other ladies in his boat one night to the Fête de Navigation. 'I fancy he is a Communist', she wrote; he was read-ing Louis Blanc's *Histoire de dix ans, 1830–1840*, which she 'stole' to read when he went off to climb Mount Rosa. After another week or two he left for the Pyrenees and was seen no more.[2]

She too was thinking of leaving Plongeon before the severe weather set in. Having come away from England in haste, intend-ing to stay no later than July, she was quite unprepared for the cold, from which she always suffered inordinately. Charles Bray

---

[1] *Letters*, I. 307.   [2] *Letters*, I. 293, 296, 306.

was to send her box with some books, a muff, a tippet, and other warm clothes. 'I hope you managed to get in the black velvet dress', she wrote. 'The people dress and think about dressing here more even than in England.'[1] She considered the possibility of Paris for the winter, but the greater expense and the absence of a companion of any kind dissuaded her:

people do not seem to think me quite old enough yet to ramble about at will. . . . I confess I am more sensitive than I thought I should be to the idea that my being alone is odd. I thought my old appearance would have been a sufficient sanction and that the very idea of impropriety was ridiculous. Here however I am as sagely settled as possible, for Mde. de Vallière is quite a sufficient mother and the Swiss ideas of propriety are rigid to excess. Mde. de Vallière would not receive Mrs. Lock's daughter if she were to come, because she is separated from her husband. You may console the Mrs. T. Carters etc. therewith and assure them that I dare not look or say or do half what one does in England. As long as people carry a Mademoiselle before their name, there is far less liberty for them on the Continent than in England.[2]

Plongeon would be remote and uncomfortable in winter; it 'is like a bird-cage set down in a garden', she wrote. After several inquiries she found a comfortable lodging in the apartment of François D'Albert Durade, a painter forty-five years old, in the Rue des Chanoines (now de la Pélisserie) at the foot of the Rue Calvin, and moved in 9 October. Describing the arrangements, she dwelt with gusto on the excellent cooking.

Everything is on a generous scale without extravagance. Mde. D'Albert anticipates all my wants and makes a spoiled child of me. I like these dear people better and better—everything is so in harmony with one's moral feeling that I really can almost say I never enjoyed a more complete bien-être in my life than during the last fortnight.

For M. D'Albert I love him already as if he were father and brother both. You must know he is not more than 4 feet high with a deformed spine—the result of an accident in his boyhood—but on this little body is placed a finely formed head, full in every direction. The face is plain with small features, and rather haggard looking, but all the lines and the wavy grey hair indicate the temperament of the artist. I have not heard a word or seen a gesture of his yet that was not perfectly in harmony with an exquisite moral refinement—indeed one feels a better person always when he is present. He was educated for theology and did not become an artist—did not even begin to draw till he was 21. He sings well and plays on the piano a little. It is delightful to hear

[1] *Letters*, I. 298.   [2] *Letters*, I. 301–2.

him talk of his friends—he admires them so genuinely—one sees so
clearly that there is no reflex egotism. His conversation is charming.
I learn something every dinner-time.

  Mde. D'Albert has less of genius and more of cleverness—a really
lady-like person, who says everything well. She brings up her children
admirably—two nice intelligent boys—the youngest particularly has
a sort of Lamartine expression with a fine head.[1]

  In this cheerful atmosphere Mary Ann passed five profitable
months. Her health improved steadily under the watchful eye of
Maman, as she was soon calling Mme D'Albert. She had a
pleasant room looking out into the street, where she could see the
Sisters of Charity coming out of their convent on the very site of
the house where John Calvin died. She had her own piano, hired
by the month, and a generous supply of candles. Theatres were
near. One night she went to hear Alboni, 'a very fat syren', at
the Opera. Every Monday evening a group of musical friends of
the D'Alberts gathered in the salon to play for each other and to
sing, often really difficult music. Sometimes they would read
poetry or recite their own verses or act little comedies and vaude-
villes. They were persons of some standing in Geneva—lawyers,
doctors—and compared very favourably with many of the celebrities at Rosehill. Mary Ann's social experience was widened
by her acquaintance with people wise enough to sense the rare
quality of the unprepossessing-looking English lodger. Incisive
vignettes still enlivened her letters, though the satirical tone was
milder, even about religion. The D'Alberts 'appear to be evangelical and conservative', she wrote, 'but one finds these views in
company with more breadth of culture here than one can ever
augur from them in England'.[2] Though she boasted that she could
say anything to them, she did not pour out much of her earlier
experience, hardly mentioning the strong hold Evangelicalism had
held on her for seven dark years. 'When I was at Geneva,' she
confessed to D'Albert in 1859, 'I had not yet lost the attitude of
antagonism which belongs to the renunciation of *any* belief—also
I was very unhappy, and in a state of discord and rebellion towards
my own lot.'[3] In the long walks they took she sometimes shocked
him with her pantheistic views on the state of the soul in a future
life; he could not be sure that it was not simply 'un jeu de votre
imagination'.[4]

[1] *Letters*, I. 316–17.   [2] *Letters*, I. 314–15.
[3] *Letters*, III. 230–1.
[4] F. D'Albert Durade to GE, 30 Nov. 1859 (Yale).

Little is known of her reading at this time, though it must have been extensive. Voltaire is one of the few authors mentioned. It seems unlikely that, living in his birthplace, she did not read more of Rousseau. One wonders about authors like Gibbon, too, or Proudhon or Pierre Leroux. But it is useless to speculate. We know that she studied a little mathematics and went twice a week to the Athénée to hear the lectures on experimental physics given that winter by the inventor of electroplating, Professor A. A. de la Rive, particularly for ladies. At D'Albert's request she sat to him for a little portrait sketch, of which he painted a copy for her to take back to England. 'The idea of making a study of my visage is droll enough',[1] she wrote to the Brays. Many lines had been added since Cara painted her in 1842. Even with the new coiffure and D'Albert's tact she is no beauty. Still, as Ladislaw insists, 'the true seeing is within; and painting stares at you with an insistent imperfection. I feel that especially about representations of women. As if a woman were a mere coloured superficies! You must wait for movement and tone . . . how would you paint her voice, pray? But her voice is much diviner than anything you have seen of her.'[2] Many people were to succumb to the charm of George Eliot's voice and through it first discern that inner beauty. François D'Albert, walking about with her in earnest conversation day after day, could hardly have missed it. Her affection may have gone out to him in the old expansive way.

As spring approached and she had to begin to think of returning home, she knew that she would feel real grief in parting from the D'Alberts.

I feel they are my *friends*—without entering into or even knowing the greater part of my views, they understand my character, and have a real interest in me. I have infinite tenderness from Mme. d'Albert. I call her always 'Maman'; and she is just the creature one loves to lean on and be petted by. In fact, I am too much indulged, and shall go back to England as undisciplined as ever.[3]

But she leaned even more on Maman's little husband. Something was said of his accompanying her as far as Paris—'but I am afraid he cannot afford the journey—and alas! I cannot afford to pay for him'.[4] In the event, however, he took her all the way to England, where he lingered for nearly two months. They left Geneva 18 March 1850, when the snow was still so deep in the passes of

---

[1] *Letters*, I. 330. [2] *Middlemarch*, ch. 19.
[3] *Letters*, I. 328. [4] *Letters*, I. 330.

the Jura that they had to go by sledge and suffered a good deal
from the cold winds. The crossing from Calais was also rough,
making Mary Ann too ill to leave the hotel in London for a day.
At last on the 25th she abandoned M. D'Albert to sightseeing and
fled to the sheltering arms at Rosehill.

Four days of reunion were scarcely enough to catch up the old
threads. In spite of staggering business losses she found Charles
Bray as jolly as ever, and dear Cara was her old, quiet, affectionate
self. What did Mary Ann mean in describing herself to Sara as
'idle and naughty—on ne peut plus—sinking into heathenish
ignorance and woman's frivolity'?[1] Her brothers and sisters had
all written, promising her the warmest welcome. When she set out
on her visits, she missed more than she expected the snug little
room high up in Geneva, with the charming housemaid Jeanie
asking her in the prettiest voice as she brought in her breakfast
whether Madame had slept well. She began her family visits with
Isaac at Griff, her old home, where she had not stayed since the
unhappy days of the Holy War. Before a week passed she is writing to Patty Jackson to say

I am not yet decided as to my future plans—whether I shall remain in
England or return to Geneva. If the former, I shall probably spend
many months of the year in London. In that case I shall see you sometimes, shall I not? Ah! dear Patty, I have seen much trial since we met,
and so have you. My return to England is anything but joyous to me, for
old associations are rather painful than otherwise to me.[2]

A week later she is asking Sara Hennell to learn Mr. Chapman's
prices for lodgers and anything she can of other boarding houses
in London.

I am really anxious to know. O the dismal weather and the dismal
country and the dismal people. It was some envious demon that drove
me across the Jura to come and see people who don't want me. However, I am determined to sell everything I possess except a portmanteau
and carpet-bag and the necessary contents and be a foreigner on the
earth for ever more.[3]

Griff was clearly not going to be a home for her. At Meriden,
where she went next, she found the Clarkes' house overcrowded
and noisy. She writes to Cara:

Dear Chrissey is much kinder than any one else in the family and I am
happiest with her. She is generous and sympathizing and really cares

[1] *Letters*, I. 332.   [2] Ibid. 334.   [3] Ibid. 335.

for my happiness. But I am delighted to feel that I am of no importance to any of them, and have no motive for living amongst them. I have often told you I thought Melchisedec the only happy man, and I think so more than ever.[1]

In the same letter she asks if she may come back to Rosehill and invite M. D'Albert to join her there for a few days. He came on 7 May, and she showed him Kenilworth Castle and Warwick and her favourite walks near Coventry before he departed on the 10th.

It was ten years before they met again, though they corresponded in friendly fashion to the end of her life. At first she wrote a good many letters in French, all of which he later burnt. As he explained to Cross, Mary Ann had asked and been granted Mme D'Albert's permission to *tutoyer* him and had used the locution for several years. Fearing that after his death persons finding the letters without knowing the reason for the familiar form might attach a malevolent significance to it, he thought it best to destroy them. He did it with regret, for the familiar form added to her style a *naïveté* not found in her English sentences. The only letters in French he kept were those to his wife—but none of these have been found.[2] His explanation is doubtless true. Still one wonders whether this was another case of Mary Ann's over-ready expansiveness betraying her into indiscretion. The Brays thought they saw traces of D'Albert in her portrait of Philip Wakem, a musician and a talented painter, who carried in his deformed body an ardent love for Maggie. George Eliot, however, knew that Maggie had for him only tender sisterly feelings.

She left Rosehill the day after D'Albert, perhaps to complete her family visits to Fanny Houghton and Robert Evans; but she was back 4 June, and for the next seven months made Rosehill her home. The Brays had other visitors during the summer; Cara's friend Edward Noel and his daughter came in June to stay a month, and Sara was there for a month in July and August. Charles and Rufa Hennell they did not see; he was suffering again from tuberculosis and died 2 September.

One permanent result of her Swiss sojourn was to change the spelling of her name from Mary Ann to Marian. Polly had long been her nickname. During their correspondence about Strauss Sara Hennell had transformed Mary Ann to Pollian in a pedantic pun on Apollyon, the Angel of Destruction in Revelation; most of her letters to the Brays and Sara were signed Pollian. While she

---

[1] *Letters*, I. 336.
[2] D'Albert Durade to Cross, 23 Feb. 1885 (Yale).

was in Geneva, where it was natural to use the French form, Marianne occurs a few times. From the spring of 1851 until the last year of her life (except with a few old correspondents) she signed herself Marian.

In October John Chapman arrived at Rosehill with Robert William Mackay, a bachelor at forty-seven, a man of some property, educated at Winchester and Oxford. Chapman had just published Mackay's *The Progress of the Intellect, as Exemplified in the Religious Development of the Greeks and Hebrews*, which contained much to interest Charles Bray. They both believed the moral and the physical were subject to the same 'inexorable law of consequences'; human duty was comprised in earnest study of that law and obedience to its teaching. Following Creuzer, Mackay traced the origin of all divinities to nature cults. If the book inevitably reminds one of Mr. Casaubon's Key to All Mythologies, there is little pedantry in it, and a great deal of sound learning and careful writing. Mackay was then almost alone among English theologians in accepting Strauss's view of the mythical character of the Bible. It was natural that Chapman should ask the Translator of Strauss to write an article on the book, which the editor of the *Westminster Review* had agreed to publish. Marian was only too glad of the opportunity.

Her review[1] began by pointing out that, though the Positivist science of Comte offers the only hope of extending man's knowledge and happiness, it was a serious mistake 'to suppose that the study of the past and the labours of criticism have no important practical bearing on the present'. Expulsion of error will be much quickened

if by a survey of the past it can be shown how each age and each race has had a faith and a symbolism suited to its need and its stage of development, and that for succeeding ages to dream of retaining the spirit along with the forms of the past, is as futile as the embalming of the dead body in the hope that it may one day be resumed by the living soul.

She does not hesitate to point out Mackay's weaknesses, like his occasional redundance, or to differ with his emphasis on the allegorical interpretation of Greek myths; she commends his independence in analysing the mythical character of the Old Testament. It is an impressive article, written with distinction, firm in its critical tone, revealing for the first time the extraordinary grasp of her massive intellect.

[1] 'The Progress of the Intellect', *WR*, 54 (Jan. 1851), 353–68.

When it was finished, Marian took it to London 18 November to deliver to Chapman and spent two weeks at his house, 142 Strand. Built originally as a hotel on the site of the old Turk's Head Coffee House, it was much larger than Chapman needed for his small family. He conducted his publishing and bookselling business on the ground floor, where two or three clerks were kept busy. On the floors above, Mrs. Chapman accommodated paying guests at a charge of 45 or 50 shillings a week for board and residence, depending on the room. Centrally located between the City and the West End, it looked from the back over Somerset House and towards the Thames. Many literary people who had connections with Chapman's publishing, especially Americans—Horace Greeley, Bryant, Emerson, for example—found 142 Strand convenient and recommended it to their friends.

John Chapman, then twenty-nine years old, was a strikingly handsome fellow, tall, vigorous, magnetic. He had been married for seven years to Susanna Brewitt, only daughter of a Nottingham lace manufacturer, who had left her a fortune ample enough to outweigh her lack of charm and the unhappy fact that she was fourteen years older than her husband. They had three children: Beatrice, aged six, and Ernest, now five, who lived with their parents, and Walter, aged three, a deaf mute, who lived with his uncle in Nottingham. The only other permanent resident of the house was Miss Elisabeth Tilley, a pretty woman of thirty, who served ostensibly as governess and helped with the housekeeping, but who also occupied the more intimate position of Chapman's mistress. If Susanna was aware of their relation, she chose to ignore it; she was a very circumspect lady, at the moment much exercised by the questionable tone of a novel by Eliza Lynn called *Realities*, which Chapman had agreed to publish, depicting the sordid life of the London theatre.

On Friday nights there were usually parties at 142 Strand of people with literary interests, many of them Chapman's authors. Here on the last Friday of her visit Marian met Eliza Lynn. 'She says she was "never so attracted to a woman before as to me" —I am "such a loveable person"', Marian reported to Cara. 'I have enjoyed my visit very much', she added, 'and am to come again in January.' Her mind was made up. If Eliza Lynn could write books, so could she. She would live in London and earn her living with her pen.

Marian went back to Rosehill, and, after spending Christmas with the Clarkes, returned to the Strand 8 January 1851, travelling

alone. Chapman, who met her at Euston Station, recorded in his
Diary[1] that 'her manner was friendly, but formal and studied'—
perhaps in consequence of two letters Miss Tilley had dispatched
to Coventry the week before. Her room, though rather dark and
high up at the end of a long passage, looked 'charmingly comfortable' to her, and she settled in to renew the freedom of her
life at Geneva. When Chapman went with her to choose a piano
for her room, they 'conversed much on *general topics*, and about
Miss Lynn and her social principles'. Marian, having read a proof
of a love scene in *Realities*, which was 'warmly and vividly
depicted', concurred in his disapproval of its tone and tendency.
The next morning, Sunday, 12 January, he

rose late, sat in Miss E[vans]'s room while she played one of Mosart's
Masses with much expression. Then went with her to call on Miss
Lynn in the hope of inducing her to cancel some objectionable passages,
and succeeded to the extent of a few lines only. I said that such passages
were addressed to and excited the sensual nature and were therefore
injurious;—and that as I am the publisher of works notable for their
intellectual freedom it behoves me to be exceedingly careful of the
moral tendency of all I issue.

Chapman's sudden enthusiasm for 'Mosart' probably explains
Susanna's acquiescence in the purchase a week later of a piano for
the drawing-room; thereafter Marian could perform less privately,
and Susanna herself sometimes played duets with Sara Hennell
or other visitors. Chapman next discovered a burning desire to
learn German and began to go regularly to her room to take
lessons from the Translator of Strauss. Now Elisabeth Tilley
evinced a sudden interest in the language, which barely concealed
a violent jealousy of Marian, in whose room her magnetic lover
was spending more and more time. To private lessons in German
Marian added readings of Latin and perhaps less abstruse subjects, sometimes at very curious hours.

She continued her own studies as she had done at Geneva,
enrolling in Francis Newman's course in geometry at the Ladies
(now Bedford) College, for which 'good-natured Mr. Chapman'
gave her a ticket—which, she told the Brays, she insisted on paying
for. She also heard Faraday's lecture at the Royal Society on the
magnetism of oxygen, for which 'good Mr. Mackay' gave her a
ticket. He invited her to come with the Chapmans to Sunday

---

[1] Chapman's Diary (Yale), the source of most of the information in this chapter,
is published in G. S. Haight, *George Eliot and John Chapman* (1940), pp. 122–220.

dinner at his house, calling in advance to tell her in his rather fussy bachelor way that his piano had been tuned. There she met Charles Leslie, the painter and biographer of Constable, with his wife and daughter; Dr. Neil Arnott, another 'delightful old bachelor', one of Queen Victoria's physicians; Mackay's young nephew, Vincent; and after dinner a new group of young people came in to tea, among whom were three of Constable's children.[1] There were also interesting people boarding at 142 Strand, some of whom Marian had met before. Dr. W. B. Hodgson, who had mesmerized her at Liverpool in 1844, now Principal of Chorlton High School, Manchester, and a member of the Council of University College, stayed for some weeks. Dr. Brabant was there, too, obviously impressed by the development of his Deutera, whom he took to the theatre. He kindly lent his telescope to Chapman, who, rising at 5.30, looked again at the crescent Venus, which he had seen for the first time on the day Marian arrived in the Strand.

Except for her teaching, which was gratuitous, Marian had not found the literary work she was hoping for. When Susanna grew annoyed at sarcastic letters from James Nesbitt about the proofs of his three-volume novel *The Siege of Damascus*, Chapman asked Marian 'to undertake the revision of the work henceforth, which she kindly consented to do'. There is no mention of any compensation. Her article on *The Progress of the Intellect* had appeared in the January number of the *Westminster*; in February she offered to write a review of W. R. Greg's *The Creed of Christendom*, which Chapman had just published, doing it 'not for money, but for love—of the subject as connected with the *Inquiry*'.[2] But the *Westminster* was in a precarious financial state; the subject did not suit; and the editor would not take it for money or love. Chapman, eager to advertise his publications, wrote to William Empson, editor of the *Edinburgh Review*, sending him a copy of Marian's article on *The Progress of the Intellect* and proposing that its author should write one for the *Edinburgh*, either on Mackay again, or on Harriet Martineau's new book, or on slavery, the subject on which Empson, knowing Chapman's American connections, had asked him to secure an article. None of these proposals was accepted. In sending the Brays the notes of rejection Marian remarked, 'You will be pleased to see that Mr. C. spoke of me to Empson as a man.'[2]

[1] *Letters*, I. 342–3.   [2] Ibid. 346.

Meanwhile, Chapman's relations with the three ladies at 142 Strand were growing more and more difficult. The first open hostilities occurred 22 January:

Invited Miss Evans to go out after breakfast; did not get a decisive answer. E. afterwards said if I did go, she should be glad to go. I then invited Miss Evans again telling her E. would go, whereupon she declined rather rudely. Susanna being willing to go out, and neither E. nor S. wishing to walk far, I proposed they should go a short distance without me, which E. considered an insult from me and reproached me in no measured terms accordingly, and heaped upon me suspicions and accusations I do not in any way deserve. I was very severe and harsh, said things I was sorry for afterwards, and we became reconciled in the Park.

Miss Evans apologized for her rudeness tonight, which roused all E.'s jealousy again, and consequent bitterness.

A few days later Chapman notes that 'Elisabeth has not spoken kindly to me since Thursday evening—on account of Miss Evans.' Two leaves containing the entries for the last week in January have been cut from the Diary, so we can only guess at how he soothed the ruffled feelings. The leaves for 4–7 and 11–17 February have also been removed. But on the 18th it is apparent that Susanna has joined forces with Elisabeth. After recording the unfortunate episode, Chapman carefully deleted the latter part of his entry:

I presume with the view of arriving at a more friendly understanding S. and E. had a long talk this morning which resulted in their comparing notes on the subject of my intimacy with Miss Evans, and their arrival at the conclusion ⟨ that we are completely in love with each other. —E. being intensely jealous herself said all she could to cause S. to look from the same point of view, which a little incident (her finding me with my hand in M.'s) had quite prepared her for. E. betrayed my trust and her own promise. S. said to me that if ever I went to M.'s room again she will write to Mr. Bray, and say that she dislikes her ⟩.—

The next day Chapman continues:

Sat in the dining room to write in the morning where M. joined me, we talked of course of the excited feelings of S. and E. I gave her an account of what had passed and urged her to talk with S. on the subject to give her an opportunity of dissipating her uncalled for hatred by expression.—E. made some bitter remarks on account of our being in the dining room (i.e. together), and I therefore passed the afternoon in S.'s room without a fire.—S. had a long talk with M. before dinner unsatisfactory to S. from the high tone M. took. Conversation renewed after dinner in my presence when M. confessed S. had reason to complain, and a reconciliation was effected.—

In the morning, 'Susanna made it a condition of our renewed treaties of amity that I should recommence my German lessons, which I grieve to think will pain Elisabeth;—I am sure I have no [other] feeling on the subject than to obtain peace at any cost.—' The following evening Chapman had to escort some visitors to a concert. Elisabeth, he wrote,

was kind to me before I went and kissed me several times. At parting she kissed me saying 'God bless thee thou frail bark!' But alas this morning she is all bitterness and icy coldness, the result I believe of conversation she had last night with M.—who was very severe and unjust to me yesterday.—

Two days later, when Marian came to his room for a dictionary and found Elisabeth there, the ladies had a further conversation, 'the result of which was increased bitterness in both their minds'. At this juncture Miss Kate Martineau carried Marian off to Highbury for the week-end. With her rival out of the way, Elisabeth became friendly again, and Chapman spent a good part of the next day working at arithmetic with her.

What happened when Marian returned we cannot tell, since the leaves with the entries for 25 February–3 March have been cut out. The antagonism among the ladies certainly reached some sort of climax. The fact that the long-suffering Susanna is henceforth as hard to placate as Elisabeth leads one to suspect another incident like that when she found Marian holding her husband's hand. It is clear that they joined forces against Marian and drove her back to Coventry. After nine days without comment the Diary notes a last round of theatres, exhibitions, concerts, and opera. Chapman took her to Tottenham to see Mr. Windus's famous collection of Turner water-colours, and to the Cyclorama in Albany Street for the 'Grand Moving Panorama of the Lisbon Earthquake': at Drury Lane they saw Boucicault's *A Morning Call* and *Azael, or the Prodigal*, a spectacle with scenes in Memphis. Susanna took her to Hullah's Concert, to hear the first English performance of the Credo from Bach's B-Minor Mass, and on Saturday night she went with Chapman to Her Majesty's Theatre to hear *Lucia di Lammermoor*. On Monday, 24 March he wrote—and deleted in part:

M. departed today, I accompanied her to the railway. She was very sad, and hence made me feel so.—She pressed me for some intimation of the state of my feelings,— ⟨ I told her that I felt great affection for her, but that I loved E. and S. also, though each in a different way. ⟩ At this avowal she burst into tears. I tried to comfort her, and reminded [her] of the dear friends and pleasant home she was returning to,—but the train whirled her away very very sad.—

Susanna was much excited today and perplexed with her packing, she reproached me, and spoke very bitterly about M.—

There can be little doubt that Marian was guilty of some indiscretion, probably more serious than holding hands. Her over-ready expansiveness, her incapability of practising the required conventionalisms, her unfortunately balanced moral and animal regions—all come again to mind. John Chapman was a notorious philanderer. In youth his friends called him 'Byron', surely not just for his noble profile or his literary bent. To his pervasive masculine attraction, which few women could resist, Marian's yearning for affection, the stronger for lying behind a plain exterior, made her doubly susceptible. When her father died she had had her vision of becoming earthly, sensual, devilish. Did John Chapman help her realize it? T. P. O'Connor told of walking along the Strand with Chapman in the 1890s and, as they passed 142, mentioning the rumour that Marian had once been in love with Herbert Spencer. He 'gave my arm an eloquent squeeze, and whispered, "You know, she was very fond of me!" He said no more; relapsed into that curious enigmatic silence which was part of his fascination.'[1]

Susanna departed the next day for Truro to join her children, who were visiting relatives there. Elisabeth was left in undisputed possession of the field. To Chapman the house seemed strangely empty, and he felt a sense of extreme loneliness. He took Elisabeth across to the Lyceum one evening to see Charles Mathews in *Cool as a Cucumber*, and, when he came home, sent Marian a 'packet of letters' that Susanna had written him since her departure. They touched with suspicion on a new project he was considering, an analytical catalogue of his more significant publications—concise critiques, prefaced perhaps by an outline sketch of philosophic writing in England that would appreciate his part in its development over the past decade. Obviously no one was better fitted to prepare such a book than the Translator of Strauss, who had shown gratifying enthusiasm for the plan. The bitter injustice of Susanna's remarks, impugning her motives, impelled Marian

[1] *M.A.P.*, 2 Dec. 1899, p. 519.

to write 4 April declining to do the catalogue; but after sealing her letter, she sent another with it:

Rosehill
April 4.

Dear Mr. Chapman

I send you in another envelope a note written under my first impression on reading your packet of letters. On further consideration I consent to continue the Catalogue, since I am ashamed of perpetual vacillations, on condition that you state or rather, I should hope, re-state to Mrs. C. the fact that I am doing it, not because I 'like', but in compliance with your request. You are aware that I never had the slightest wish to undertake the thing on my own account. If I continue it, it will be with the utmost repugnance, and only on the understanding that I shall accept no remuneration.

Yours etc.
Marian Evans.[1]

After sleeping with Elisabeth for the first time in a month, Chapman read some of *The Progress of the Intellect* aloud to her before breakfast and then wrote to Marian about Susanna's letters.

I begged her to be calm and not to let recent circumstances agitate and needlessly pain her. I told her that I feel even in the midst of the tumult of grief, and in the very moment of excitement the most intimate essence of my being, or some element of it, ⟨ remains ⟩ is still no sharer in the enacted scene, but continues a serene spectator, experiencing only shame and regret that any part of my nature with which it is allied should be so moved and agitated by events and affections or the selfish personalities of today and yesterday.[2]

Charles Bray came to London a few days later and took Chapman to the Crystal Palace, getting him admitted to the yet unopened Exhibition as his 'assistant'. It would be illuminating to have their comments on Marian. The correspondence continued for more than a month. Sometimes Marian wrote to Susanna directly, sending the letters to Chapman unsealed for him to read and forward, while he sent copies of his letters to them both. Before Susanna returned from Truro, he was hoping that they would 'become better friends'. But with Elisabeth it was not so easy. The mere sight of a letter from Marian, even if he offered to let her read it, threw her into a passion. A typical outburst is seen in a deleted entry in his Diary for 28 April:

⟨I had a short simple note from M. this morning, which E. read and then flew into a great passion, and begged me not to speak to her. We

---

[1] *Letters*, I. 348.   [2] Chapman's Diary, 5 Apr. 1851.

separated all morning, she came to me after lunch, expressed her regret, and observed that I was so cruelly calm. I wrote a short proper note to M. which she did not see, in answer to her question I said I had written, which caused another manifestation of excitement, from which however she soon recovered.⟩

Marian made her letters business-like, excluding all references to Elisabeth, who she probably knew would see them. But into these cool missives she sometimes slipped warmer *billets doux* to be disposed of secretly. After mentioning her calm letter of 20 June in his Diary, Chapman added and deleted: 'Miss Evans' little note is inexpressively charming, so quick, intelligent and over-flowing with love and sweetness! I feel her to be the living torment to my soul.' On Susanna's return from Truro, Marian wrote: 'I should think you are right glad to have Mrs. Chapman again to enliven you all.' When he took over Marian's old room for his study, moving his sofa into it, she wrote: 'I congratulate you on your migration but I hope the room has been duly exorcised since I left it.'[1]

One day in mid April 1851 Chapman received a letter from Edward Lombe, which changed his situation. Lombe was an eccentric gentleman of Melton Hall, Wymondham, who had not been in England for twenty-five years. He outraged his Norfolk neighbours by allowing his sixty-eight tenants to shoot game on their farms and to vote for Members of Parliament without con-sulting him on their merits, as other landlords required. With an income of £14,000 left him by a father he had not spoken to for years, he lived in Florence, bestowing by letter his bene-factions in support of free-thought and secular control of educa-tion. He now proposed to pay Chapman for reprinting Theodore Parker's *Discourse on Matters Pertaining to Religion*, or Hennell's *Inquiry*, or an abridgement of the translation of Strauss's *Leben Jesu*—in fact, to assist him generally in the publication of such works. He also offered to help in establishing a quarterly review that would be liberal enough for his views; he was then contribut-ing £200 a year to the *Westminster* for special articles. Nothing could have suited Chapman better. Some months before, he had discussed the possibility of taking over the *Westminster*; and when the proprietor W. E. Hickson called on him 1 May to ask whether he was still disposed to purchase it, they quickly agreed on a price

[1] *Letters*, I. 354.

of £300. In making the offer in form a week later Chapman got
Hickson to promise that he would insert Marian's article on *The
Creed of Christendom* in the July number, and wrote to tell her
so. The transfer was not made till 8 October. But Chapman did
not wait to begin planning. He set out at once to enlist support,
writing to Lombe, interviewing Joseph Parkes, getting promises
of help from Mackay, F. W. Newman, Dr. Brabant, Miss Susan
Hughes, and others. Though he was astute enough to recognize
that his education had not fitted him for the position, he was flattered when George Combe expressed his satisfaction 'that I
intended to be the chief editor of the review myself'. However,
he knew intimately a person with the intelligence and literary
ability needed to conduct a first-rate liberal quarterly of real
distinction, a person who, under his charm, would be content
to remain in the background and let him bask publicly in editorial
glory. But this was the ardent spinster in Coventry, who had been
banished forever from the Strand and was still smarting under a
mortification that she was sure she did not entirely deserve. There
was little hope that either Elisabeth or Susanna would tolerate her
return.

Charles Bray, calling on Chapman one day, suggested casually
that he come to Rosehill to discuss his plans. When Chapman told
Elisabeth of 'the urgent invitation of me to Coventry, which I
could not refuse without great difficulty, and that I had promised
almost to go',[1] she immediately became haughty and indignant
and left the room, remaining in a state of sullen anger for three
days. But as usual Chapman had his way, staying at Rosehill a
fortnight. He arrived 27 May. Mrs. Bray, Marian, and Mrs.
Thornton Hunt were there to greet him; Mr. Bray and Sara Hennell came in later from Leamington, where he had been lecturing
to young ladies! A deleted entry in Chapman's Diary says that
he 'Found Miss Evans shy calm and affectionate.' She was the
real object of his visit, not Bray, who is mentioned only two or
three times. Next day Chapman and Marian walked together
before breakfast. They came away from a concert when it was half
over to begin the prospectus for the *Westminster Review*. All his
magnetism was turned on her again. On the second day he

Walked with M. before breakfast, told her the exact condition of things
in regard to E. whom on every account I wish to stay at the Strand.
She was much grieved and expressed herself prepared to atone in any

[1] Chapman's Diary, 15 May 1851.

way she could for the pain she has caused, and put herself in my hands prepared to accept any arrangement I may make either for her return to the Strand or to any house in London I may think suitable in October. —She agreed to write the article on foreign literature for each number of the Westminster which I am very glad of. Wrote the greater part of the Prospectus today, and then gave it to M. to finish.

The next day he went with her to Leamington and, while she visited Fanny Houghton, called on Susanna's cousin on the South Parade. They went home by way of Kenilworth Castle. Chapman

was somewhat disappointed with the ruin, but the effect from the Leamington side is very striking. As we rested on the grass, I remarked on the wonderful and mysterious embodiment of all the elements characteristics and beauties of nature which man and woman jointly present. I dwelt also on the incomprehensible mystery and witchery of beauty. My words jarred upon her and put an end to her enjoyment. Was it from a consciousness of her own want of beauty? She wept bitterly.

'She was not fitted to stand alone'; but it was all too clear that John Chapman would never be the man she could lean upon. Still, to live in London, helping him unobtrusively with the *Review* would be better than never seeing him.

But how could it be contrived? In his Diary 31 May 1851 he wrote:

I find it a matter of great difficulty to determine what can be done in regard to M's return to Town. Both Susanna and Elisabeth oppose her return to the Strand, and I suspect they would be equally opposed to her residence elsewhere in London, and yet as an active cooperator with me in Editing the Westminster Review she must be in London much of her time. Oh how deeply I regret that any cause for distrust should ever have been given. I must and will recover the confidence I once possessed. I will act consistently with my own fairer thought and thus raise my own self respect and diffuse peace.—[Five lines deleted] For my own part I do not feel in raptures with any woman now, and my passionate moods are exceptional and transient and are rather *permitted* as a means of according the strongest evidence of *affection* than storms wh: I cannot controul. The beneficent affection, and pleasure of social intercourse, which I experience, seems to be equally distributed towards Susanna E and M, but in regard to *passionate enthusiasm*, my 'first love' will I believe also be my last. I wish I could make her happy!

Marian was calm now; though her heart cried out for 'passionate enthusiasm', she resigned herself to the 'beneficent' affection of Chapman, who had not yet reached his thirtieth birthday. In the evening she 'sang exquisitely' with Thornton Hunt and his wife, whose destinies were to mingle so strangely with hers. Alone in her room she read again the old pages of Thomas à Kempis; it flashed through her 'that all the miseries of her young life had come from fixing her heart on her own pleasure, as if that were the central necessity of the universe'.[1] She lent the book to Chapman, who copied a sentence on 'spiritual progress' into his Diary. During their walk three days later: 'we made a solemn and holy vow which henceforth will bind us to the right. She is a noble being. Wrote a chiding letter to Susanna.'[2] Marian worked steadily at the prospectus, going without dinner the last night to finish it and read it to him. As soon as the proofs came back from Mr. Bray's printer, they were dispatched to a dozen likely supporters with letters, which Chapman dated rather unwisely from Rosehill, for this implied that Bray was one of the chief backers of the *Review*, which was far from true. His business affairs were increasingly troubled, and he had been forced to retrench in many ways.

Marian was firmly opposed to Chapman's dream that he could succeed as the sole editor of the *Westminster*. He undoubtedly needed her, and she needed to be needed. Her eagerness to serve others anonymously had been shown long before in her offering to translate Vinet for Mr. Watts and Spinoza for Charles Bray, as well as in her enormous unsung labour over Strauss. She was quite willing to let Chapman pose as chief editor while she did the real work without public acknowledgement. The letters sent with the prospectus refer to 'the Editors', of whom Chapman alone was named. Those who knew him well doubted his ability to carry on in an editorial line that began with John Stuart Mill. 'In regard to the secret of the Editorship', she wrote 9 June, 'it will perhaps be the best plan for you to state, that for the present *you* are to be regarded as the responsible person, but that you employ an Editor in whose literary and general ability you confide.' The word *employ* was equivocal. Though Charles Bray, the night before Chapman left Rosehill, talked with him 'about the pecuniary arrangement with Marian', there is no evidence that she ever received any money for editorial work apart from the articles she wrote. Perhaps her board was given instead of salary. She worked, not for money, but for love—of the nominal chief editor. She had agreed to do the abridgement that Mr. Lombe wanted for a fee of £100; after two months she asked, 'Pray when

---

[1] *Mill on the Floss*, Bk. IV, ch. 3.
[2] Chapman's Diary, 5 June 1851.

are we to hear any more of the Strauss abridgement?'[1] But Chapman apparently let the hint drop in silence.

She was equally firm in opposing his itch to write for the *Westminster*. Soon after it was offered to him, he confided to his Diary, 'I should be glad to write an Article of Sociology for the first Number.'[2] Though Marian realized that he had neither the ideas nor the skill in expressing them required for the distinguished periodical she hoped to create, she was too astute to tell him outright. In September when he mentioned the possibility of writing the article on national representation that Lombe wanted for the first number, she put her objections on other grounds: 'Miss Evans thinks I should lose power and influence by becoming a writer in the Westminster Review, and could not then maintain that dignified relation with the various contributors that she thinks I may do otherwise.'[3] He accepted her advice. She meant to limit her own work to the editing and perhaps a few reviews in the sections headed Contemporary Literature. 'If I did only one of the Summaries, I should certainly prefer that of the English Literature', she wrote. 'I agree with you that Lewes would be likely to do an article on Modern Novelists very well. I advise you to ask him, as I should not like to engage myself to write anything not *ex officio* for the first number.'[4]

All summer long Chapman struggled to convince Susanna and Elisabeth that, if he was to succeed with the *Westminster*, Marian Evans must be in London, preferably at 142 Strand. She had gone to Bishop's Teignton, Devonshire, to chaperone Cara, who was visiting her friend Edward Noel. The Great Exhibition at the Crystal Palace was at its height; knowing that they would surely want to see it, Chapman wrote on 15 July, 'to invite Mr. and Mrs. Bray, and Miss Evans, and Miss Hennell to spend a week with us in August'. It was a safe gesture. On their way home, Charles Bray met Cara and Marian and took them to stay with Cara's old friend Mary Marshall in Wellington Terrace, St. John's Wood. There Chapman spent the evening with them, 13 August, in a long discussion of the much-amended prospectus. The next day, after going over the Royal Academy and Northumberland House with Charles and Marian, he took Susanna in the evening to call 'on the whole party, but especially to see Mrs. Bray'; and on the 15th, after showing them the Exhibition, brought Marian and Sara

[1] *Letters*, I. 354.   [2] Chapman's Diary, 21 May 1851.
[3] Ibid., 21 Sept. 1851.   [4] *Letters*, I. 357.

Hennell home with him so that 'Miss E. might "make a call" on Susanna, and afford the opportunity of a long Editorial Conference, in which after coffee we accomplished much. Susanna is very poorly with headache.' On the 16th Elisabeth was 'in tears again', and Marian back at Rosehill.

Twice more during the summer Chapman went to Coventry to consult her. She had suggested that for the first number he ask James Martineau to write the article Lombe wanted on 'Christian Ethics and Modern Civilization'. Martineau, left to determine the scope, asked in reply 'for some indications of the mode of treatment we wish to be adopted'. This was beyond Chapman's power. So he went to Rosehill 23 August to get help from his secret editor. She drafted a long tactful letter for him, assuring Martineau that the application to him was prompted, 'not only by a general sense of your ability to treat such a subject', but more especially by the perusal of his article in the July number of the *Westminster* on Greg's *Creed of Christendom*—(which, in spite of Hickson's promise, had kept hers from appearing there). 'The Future Editors of the Westminster desire that the article in question should contain'—and she went on to outline the argument in detail. It must be 'treated by a mind which to adequate critical knowledge unites thorough directness of purpose and deep sympathy with the onward movements of the age'.[1] Chapman copied her letter almost without change and sent it to Martineau. The rest of the week-end he spent discussing revisions in the prospectus, which was to head their first number, and the selection of other authors.

He returned to the Strand Monday night at 11, and, after reading the chapter on 'Christian Eclecticism' in Greg's book, went to bed with Elisabeth. The next day was Susanna's forty-third birthday. She was in 'an unhappy, excitable mood, and made Miss Evans the subject on which she gave vent to it, and hence I had a miserable morning, ⟨supplemental to Elisabeth's upbraidings before breakfast that every time last night I met her coldly the dear!⟩'[2] Sometime early in September, by what sort of persuasion one cannot say, both ladies were brought to consent to the co-editor's return to the Strand. Perhaps the George Combes, who had been charmed by her at Rosehill and spoke enthusiastically about her to the Chapmans, turned the balance in her favour. On 11 September Marian was writing to Chapman: 'I wish you would see if I can have the same piano again as I had when in town

[1] Draft in GE's hand, 23 Aug. 1851 (Yale).
[2] Chapman's Diary, 27 Aug. 1851.

before, and make the man let me have it for 16s. per month, which is quite enough.'

Chapman's second visit to Coventry took place on Saturday, 20 September. On the pretext of having to go to Birmingham on business, he planned to stop again at Rosehill for the weekend. Susanna reproached him so bitterly for not inviting her to accompany him that he was constrained to take her. They found Mrs. Bray very ill, the Noel family expected, and everyone painfully disturbed by their unexpected arrival. The visit was a failure from every side. But it served to ratify the truce under which Marian was allowed to return to the Strand. Elisabeth's jealousy still smouldered. She took offence at the phrase 'I count the days until Friday week' in a letter Chapman was writing to Marian.[1] But by now the co-editor knew better how to deal with her rival. On the 29th Marian was installed in her old room with her old piano. Elisabeth went off for a holiday in Berkshire. After 10 October the only entries in Chapman's Diary are reminders of family anniversaries, among which appears under 22 November, 'Miss Evans' Thirty-first birthday.' He had begun to write 'thirtieth'. It was actually her thirty-second. There may well have been further conflicts among the three ladies who shared so queerly in Chapman's heart, though we learn nothing about them, for the leaves covering 11–17 October and 15–21 November have also been cut out of the Diary.

Now that she understood the situation, Marian could afford to be magnanimous and treated Elisabeth with a sympathy that she never forgot. The star of Chapman's 'first love' was in its decline; by the time he moved from the Strand in May 1854 it had set. One shadowy glimpse of her came to Marian many years later, after the death of Lewes, in a letter from Germany:

Pension Anglaise
49 Anlage, Heidelberg
16 December 1878

My dear Mrs. Lewes

You will I am sure after the lapse of so many years be surprised at this signature. I have lately read the announcement of your bereavement, and knowing—remembering—how you will suffer, must be suffering now, I feel I must write and tell you how sincerely sorry I am for you and how much I sympathise with you in your distress and trouble and I do hope you will not think me impertinent—I don't think you will—not if you believe the feeling which impels me now.—

[1] Chapman's Diary, 17 Sept. 1851.

You are sure to have great choice of society, any friends you will, and much homage—I hope indeed there may be one or two to love and tend and sympathise with you as only true affection can do—

Since I saw you last I imagine your life has been a very happy one, and your domestic peace and comfort perfect. I have enquired a few times when I could do so quietly and of those who know you. It has not often been my fate to meet such. I must not now speak of your exalted position and the pleasure I have had in reading nearly all—not the latest yet—of your books, these things are as nothing to you now and possibly the gap in your affectionate nature can never be repaired. You have lost your trusting trusted loving friend and companion. May God help you to bear your loss as He only can. I wish you could return to the simple faith of your youth for consolation now in your time of distress.

Some acquaintance with grief and troubles of various kinds and a vivid recollection now of some kind words uttered makes me sympathise and grieve for you in the great trouble that has come upon you, but our afflictions are not for long. How time flies! 25 years ago seems to me but as yesterday and will you not look forward to a happy reunion!

I must only speak of myself to say I am here amongst strangers and that no one will know that I write to you. If you blame me, then pray forgive the mistake only believe that I am grieved for you from my heart and that I hope and trust you have some gentle loving friend with you to soothe and sustain you and that you may take comfort and trust in hope from Above in the future.

With earnest wishes for some continued happiness to you

I am dear Mrs. Lewes
Yours faithfully
Elisabeth Tilley

Marian now saw Chapman, too, more clearly. With a nature like his, how could she ever expect Mental Beauty to prevail over the more superficial charms of Elisabeth Tilley? The moral side of her character, if not spontaneously active, asserted its control over the animal. The 'solemn and holy vow' they made during that rainy walk in June would henceforth bind *her* at least, to the right. She would renounce the gratification of her own desires as Thomas à Kempis directed. She returned to the Strand, a loyal 'helpmate' in editing the *Westminster Review*, but nothing more.

CHAPTER IV

THE CONDITIONS ESSENTIAL TO
HUMAN HAPPINESS

※

A WEEK after Marian's return to the Strand Chapman completed his purchase of the *Westminster Review*. He and his self-effacing editor set out to collect articles for the initial number of the new series, January 1852. They were in close daily conference now and took long walks about town in the course of business. One of the first was to Chelsea, where Marian wandered alone up and down Cheyne Row while Chapman called on Carlyle and tried vainly to persuade him to write the article on the peerage that Lombe wanted to pay for. Carlyle, describing the visit to Browning, with a suggestion that *he* might contribute, reported that Chapman says he has capital for four years' trial, 'an able Editor (name can't be given), and such an array of "talent" as was seldom gathered before'. Herbert Spencer too refused to do the peerage, and they finally secured William Johnson Fox, who had written the very first article the *Westminster* ever published when Mill founded it in 1824; Fox thus initiated both series. Professor Edward Forbes of King's College, London, supplied a popular account of shell-fish; W. R. Greg discussed labour relations; Francis William Newman refuted proposed plans for direct legislation by popular vote; James Anthony Froude wrote on Mary Stuart; and George Henry Lewes on Julia von Krüdener, the Russian pietist who at the time of the Holy Alliance anticipated Rasputin in using religion to influence politics. James Martineau's 'The Ethics of Christendom', which had caused the editors so much anxious correspondence, failed to please either conservative readers or freethinkers like Lombe, who expected a slashing attack on orthodoxy.

The pattern set by this number is followed generally in all ten numbers edited by Marian Evans. There is always at least one article that may be classified under the heading Reform—reform in government, education, prisons, charity, industry, labour relations, and so on. Politics are usually represented—British foreign policy, the balance of power, Ireland, France, Italy, Turkey, Russia, the colonies, like Jamaica and India—all from the Radical point of view. Under History one finds the brilliant series of Froude's articles with their fresh interpretation of Tudor England, which formed the basis of his great book a few years later. Religion is covered, not only by articles on theology like Martineau's, but by accounts of religion in Germany and Italy and serious studies of sects like the Quakers and the Mormons. Under Philosophy the most important contributions are John Stuart Mill's article on Whewell and John Oxenford's pioneer essay on Schopenhauer, which, soon translated into German, formed the foundation of Schopenhauer's fame. In addition to articles on biology, geology, botany, the atomic theory in chemistry, fads like vegetarianism, homoeopathy, and water cures, the heading Science would include the four important articles by Herbert Spencer in which his theory of Evolution is first outlined. Under Literature there are occasional articles on classical subjects—Propertius and Martial—but most of them deal with recent or contemporary writers—Shelley (by Lewes), Moore, De Quincey, Balzac, Thackeray, Matthew Arnold, Mrs. Gaskell, and Charlotte Brontë.

Reviews of new books are collected into four groups entitled 'Contemporary Literature' of England, America, Germany, and France. The January 1852 number noticed 57 English, 13 American, 34 German, and 33 French books. On the average the *Westminster* reviewed about a hundred volumes in each of these ten numbers. From Lewes's account book[1] we learn that he was paid for doing the 'French Summary', as he calls it, for seven numbers, January 1852 through July 1853. Mrs. Edward Sinnett apparently wrote most of the German reviews. Many American books were noticed, because Chapman made much of his transatlantic market, and the *Westminster* was read even by the youthful William Dean Howells on the Ohio frontier. The long articles reviewing so many English books were necessarily of composite authorship. In the first number, for example, Spencer reviewed W. B. Carpenter's *Physiology* and probably the works of Garth Wilkinson, R. G. Latham, and E. P. Thompson that follow (pp. 274–81). The donnish account of R. W. Browne's *History of Classical Literature* is obviously by a different hand from the pages discussing historical books, while those on travel seem to show still

---

[1] 'Literary Receipts' (Berg Collection, NYPL) published in *Letters*, VII. 365–83.

another. There has been much loose attribution to Marian Evans of reviews in the *Westminster* during her editorship. Since it was her responsibility to link the contributions of various authors together, her touch is sometimes found in reviews she did not write. The collection of cuttings of her contributions to the *Westminster*, now in the Nuneaton Public Library, includes from the January 1852 number only the notices of Carlyle's *Life of Sterling* and Macready's *A Sketch of Suwarow* (pp. 247–52), and from April 1852, only *The Life and Letters of Joseph Story* (one of Chapman's publications) and Margaret Fuller's *Memoirs* (pp. 663–6). In July 1852 there are a few pages one is tempted to ascribe to her, knowing that some of the books would have interested her; but we learn from her letter given below that the author was Chapman's assistant Ebenezer Syme, a former Nonconformist minister from Nottingham. Beginning in January 1854 the 'Contemporary Literature' sections were re-classified into six groups, as Spencer suggested, by subject rather than geography: 'Theology, Philosophy, and Politics'; 'Science'; 'Classics and Philology'; 'History, Biography, Voyages and Travels'; 'Belles Lettres'; and 'Art'. We know that in 1854 James Martineau wrote the 'Theology', Froude the 'History', and Mrs. Sinnett the 'Belles Lettres'.[1] Marian's part in the *Westminster* 1852–4 was limited to advising on the choice of authors and subjects, editing the articles with cuts and rearrangements where necessary, careful proof-reading, and supervision of the letterpress. Occasionally she may have tucked into the 'Contemporary Literature' section a notice of some book she was especially interested in, but in the absence of strong evidence to confirm her authorship, attributions are hazardous. One thing certainly owed to her was the motto from Goethe on the title-page: 'Wahrheitsliebe zeigt sich darin, dass man überall das Gute zu finden und zu schätzen weiss.'[2]

Though the authors were all anonymous in the pages of the *Westminster*, many of them appeared in person at 142 Strand from time to time to discuss their articles with the editors or to attend the evening parties that the Chapmans gave almost every week. Here Marian talked with kind, but odd Robert Mackay. Scientists like Huxley and Richard Owen and Edward Forbes were there occasionally; the physicist Sir David Brewster came with his

[1] *Letters*, II. 159.
[2] Goethe, *Sprüche in Prosa: Maximen und Reflexionen*, I, no. 35: 'Love of truth shown in this: that one know how to find good everywhere and to treasure it.'

daughter Margaret, who long remembered the impression made on them by the quiet-voiced Miss Evans. Many of those who talked with her in the Strand remarked on their surprise at finding such intelligent, quick comprehension in the plain-looking editor. Shrewd old Crabb Robinson saw her there—'the translator of Strauss—no recommendation to me, certainly, but the contrary, and yet there was something about her which pleased me much both in look and voice.'[1] London was swarming with refugees from the 1848 revolutions, many of whom gravitated toward this centre of enlightened radicalism. Karl Marx was brought by Chapman's friend Andrew Johnson, a clerk in the Bullion Office at the Bank of England, where Marx instructed Engels to address letters to him when he had particularly '*wichtige* Sachen zu schreiben'. We have no record of Marian's meeting Marx. But she did see another friend of Johnson, Ferdinand Freiligrath, the revolutionary poet, who came to join Marx in London; he offered to write critical articles on German literature for the *Westminster*, which Johnson would put into good English. Marian, consulted about the proposal, remained non-committal. With Pierre Leroux she had long conversations in which he expounded his unique plan for a new society, a true *pont* uniting 'the love of self with the love of one's neighbour'.[2] Louis Blanc was another frequent visitor she enjoyed talking with. Mazzini was one of the few refugees Marian found acceptable as a contributor; she had long admired his efforts to unite Italy under a republican government. He came with his English sponsor Peter Alfred Taylor, a grandson of Samuel Courtauld, founder of the great silk firm, who was chairman of the Friends of Italy. Mrs. Taylor, once his sisters' governess, a charming person genuinely interested in literature, the arts, public education, and women's rights, became a lasting friend of Marian Evans, who used to visit her at Sydenham, and later at Aubrey House on Notting Hill.

Chapman's connections as publisher brought many American authors to 142 Strand, some of whom boarded there while in London. Horace Greeley, the rather eccentric editor of the New York *Tribune*, was there, expounding his favourite doctrines—temperance, socialism, high tariff, and the abolition of capital punishment. There the more moderate radical of the New York

---

[1] *Henry Crabb Robinson on Books and Their Writers*, ed. E. J. Morley (3 vols., 1938), II. 707. The MS. at Dr. Williams's Library reads 'Miss   , the translator'.
[2] *Letters*, II. 5.

Evening Post, William Cullen Bryant met 'a blue-stocking lady who writes for the Westminster Review named Ellans; and a Mr. Spencer, a bookseller'; but Bryant's son-in-law Parke Godwin, who was with him, soon discovered that Miss 'Ellans' was Marian Evans, the translator of Strauss, and Herbert Spencer, not a bookseller, but the author of *Social Statics*, published by Chapman in 1850.[1] Noah Porter, Professor of Moral Philosophy and Metaphysics, a Congregational minister, who was using Chapman's facilities in 1853 to buy books for the library of Yale College, also recorded his observation of Marian Evans; and thirty years later, when President of Yale, he stirred a violent controversy by objecting to the use of Spencer's *Sociology* as a textbook. The famous Swedish author Fredrika Bremer stayed at 142 Strand for a month on the way home from her American tour. As usual Marian's first impressions were frankly unfavourable: 'she is old —extremely ugly, and deformed—I should think she is nearly sixty. Her eyes are sore, her teeth horrid', adding a few days later, 'She is to me a repulsive person, equally unprepossessing to eye and ear.'[2] But soon her harsh opinion changed; she looked with delight at Miss Bremer's sketch-books filled with landscapes, flowers, portraits of Emerson, Jenny Lind, Oersted, and other famous people, all done by herself, listened with approval to her playing the piano at the Chapman's evening parties, and felt truly sorry when Miss Bremer left for Sweden.

Two notable visitors to the Strand—George Combe and Harriet Martineau—Marian had met before. Combe, whose books originally converted Charles Bray to phrenology, used to stop off at Rosehill on his way to and from Edinburgh. Like François D'Albert Durade, Combe was a very small man with a deformed spine, an abnormally large head, conspicuous for its phrenological development, and weak lungs, which took him to the Continent each year. In 1833 at the age of forty-five he had married the beautiful Cecilia Siddons, youngest child of the famous actress, and with her fortune of £15,000 retired from his family's brewery to make himself the foremost apostle of phrenology, writing constantly and lecturing on both sides of the Atlantic, advocating its use to reform education and the penal system. On first meeting Marian and the Brays at Rosehill, 29 August 1851, Combe recorded his impression that 'Miss Evans is the most extra-

---

[1] Parke Godwin, *Biography of W. C. Bryant* (2 vols., N.Y., 1883), II. 66.
[2] *Letters*, I. 365–6.

ordinary person of the party', her having translated the German, as well as the Hebrew, Greek, and Latin quotations in *Das Leben Jesu* 'without assistance' amazing him. 'She has a very large brain', he wrote in his Journal; 'the anterior lobe is remarkable for length, breadth, and height.' Perhaps her work on Strauss led Combe to see the 'organ' he calls Destructiveness prominently developed in her. The fallibility of phrenology as a guide to character appears in his finding Amativeness (sexual feeling) and Philoprogenitiveness (love of children) both rather small. She showed 'great analytic power and an instinctive soundness of judgment' in discussing phrenology; and her conversation on religion, economics, and political events persuaded Combe that 'with the exception perhaps of Lucretia Mott, she appeared to me the ablest woman whom I have seen, and in many respects she excells Lucretia. She is extremely feminine and gentle; and the great strength of her intellect combined with this quality renders her very interesting.'[1]

Harriet Martineau had met Marian once in 1845 at the house of Charles Holte Bracebridge of Atherstone. Miss Martineau was then recently recovered from a long and supposedly mortal illness, cured, she believed, by mesmerism. In 1852 she was still full of the marvels of the new 'science', which promised to expand man's knowledge beyond the limits of imagination. Her chief companion in this research was a queer young man, Henry George Atkinson, with whom she had written *Letters on the Laws of Man's Nature and Development*, published by Chapman in 1851. It was principally the work of Atkinson, who pretended to discover the phrenological centres of control by making mesmerized subjects describe their own brains. 'Now for the cerebrum!' exclaims Miss Martineau in one letter. 'Where do you begin?' Mesmeric revelation had freed her not only from her illness, but from 'the little enclosure' of theological dogma, leaving her mind at liberty to expatiate throughout the cosmos in a windy rodomontade not unlike that produced by hallucinatory drugs. Her faith in the new materialistic 'sciences', flaunted so blatantly, provoked Douglas Jerrold's quip, 'There is no God, and Harriet Martineau is his prophet.' One morning she brought Atkinson with her to 142 Strand, 'very kind and cordial', Marian wrote, 'but unhappily not able to stay long enough to dispel the repulsion excited by the *vulgarity* (I use the word in a moral sense) of her looks and gestures. . . . I honour Harriet Martineau for her powers and

[1] George Combe Journal, 29–30 Aug. 1851 (NLS).

industry and should be glad to think highly of her. I have no doubt that she is fascinating when there is time for talk.'[1] This usual negative beginning of Marian's acquaintance was quickly reversed on further meetings. Within a few weeks they were on intimate terms. By the end of March Miss Martineau added a codicil to her will making Marian joint trustee with Atkinson of a fund Mr. Lombe had set up for an abridgement of Comte and gave her a most cordial invitation to visit at Ambleside.

Marian often received invitations from friends she made during the parties at 142 Strand. William Ellis, a rich insurance underwriter, who had founded the Birkbeck schools, and his wife, a daughter of the historian Sharon Turner, asked her to their house several times. Sir James Clark, the Queen's physician, like the Ellises a friend of the Combes, who sometimes stayed with him, invited Marian quite often to dine with him in Brook Street, where she would meet Dr. Neil Arnott and other interesting people. Dr. Abraham Cox, Combe's nephew, also entertained her occasionally when the Combes' were staying with him at Kingston. Joseph Parkes, who had subsidized the publication of the Strauss, was naturally interested in its translator and had his wife and his daughter Bessie call on her soon after her return to the Strand. Bessie (Elizabeth Rayner Parkes) was educated at Leam, Warwickshire, in a boarding school kept by Cara Bray's friend, the wife of the Unitarian minister William Field. Bessie had met Marian Evans once at Rosehill, and came back often to talk with her in the Strand, sometimes attending the Chapmans' evening parties. 'Miss Parkes is a dear, ardent, honest creature', Marian told the Brays in February 1852, 'and I hope we shall be good friends.'[2] Bessie soon wrote to Barbara Leigh Smith: 'Miss Evans I see more of and she becomes a friend to me. She seems to love me, and, though I don't see exactly why, I am very glad at it. I suppose it is an "instinctive affection". As I know her better, the harsh heavy look of her face softens into a very beautiful tender expression.'[3] Bessie declared that the photograph taken in 1858 by Mayall gave

the only real indication left to us of the true shape of the head and of George Eliot's smile and general bearing. In daily life the brow, the blue eyes, and the upper part of the face had a great charm. The lower half was disproportionately long. Abundant brown hair framed a

[1] *Letters*, II. 4–5.   [2] *Letters*, II. 9.   [3] *Letters*, II. 16.

countenance which was certainly not in any sense unpleasing, noble in its general outline, and very sweet and kind in expression. Her height was good, her figure remarkably supple; at moments it had an almost serpentine grace. Her characteristic bearing suggested fatigue; perhaps, even as a girl, she would hardly have been animated; but when she was amused her eyes filled with laughter. She did not look young when I first saw her, and I have no recollection of her ever looking much older.

Bessie took her to concerts and to exhibitions at the Royal Academy, and Marian sometimes dined with the Parkeses. According to Bessie, whenever 'any special celebrity was invited to dinner, such as Thackeray, Grote the historian, or old Mr. Warburton', Mr. Parkes was never content 'unless he had also secured his young countrywoman Marian Evans'. The impression is perhaps correct, though Marian mentions none of these three guests. On such occasions, Bessie continues,

from 1851 to 1855, she used to wear black velvet, then seldom adopted by unmarried ladies. I can see her descending the great staircase of our house in Savile Row (afterwards the Stafford Club), on my father's arm, the only lady, except my mother, among the group of remarkable men, politicians, and authors of the first literary rank. She would talk and laugh softly, and look up into my father's face respectfully, while the light of the great hall-lamp shone on the waving masses of her hair, and the black velvet fell in folds about her feet.[1]

Marian also had invitations to two grand balls the Parkeses gave, which of course she declined, once explaining that her black velvet would not be appropriate and that she could not afford to buy a ball dress. 'It would be a crucifixion of my own taste as well as other people's to appear like a withered cabbage in a flower garden. At a dinner-party, when people think only of conversation, one doesn't mind being a dowdy, but it is the essence of a dance that every one should look fresh and elegant—at least as to their garments.'[2]

Bessie was coming to the Strand more often than her parents liked. There was undeniable impropriety in a young girl's going about alone, and Mr. Parkes knew quite well that the house at 142 Strand was no good place for his only daughter. But she had begun to write poems and wanted the advice of the lady editor of the *Westminster*, who was ten years her senior. The poems were

[1] Bessie R. Belloc, 'Dorothea Casaubon and George Eliot', *Contemporary Review*, 65 (Feb. 1894), 213.
[2] *Letters*, II. 138.

mostly topical pieces, revealing more determination than talent. They celebrate Bessie's enthusiasm for Goethe, Carlyle, Tennyson, Mrs. Browning, Emerson, freedom in Italy and Hungary, the beauties of Kenilworth, Stoneleigh Abbey, and Hastings, where the Parkeses lived for several years; there was even a sonnet beginning

> Dear smoky Birmingham, since long ago
> I left your native streets, . . .

The last poem in the group, 'To E[lizabeth] B[lackwell] at New York', shows the interest in feminist causes that occupied Bessie through most of her life. It is easy to imagine what advice Marian gave—and how it was ignored. The best she could say was, 'Publish the poems with all my heart, but don't stop there. Work on and on and do better things still.'[1] Issued by Chapman in November 1852, *Poems* by B. R. Parkes were reviewed by Lewes in the *Leader* beside Arnold's *Empedocles* ('graceful, thoughtful, but not individual. Her reading, not her heart, is here expressed.')[2] At the end of a short paragraph the *Westminster* said that 'she belongs to the contemplative school, and in some of her pieces reminds us of Emerson'.[3] As the daughter of a Radical reformer and great-grand-daughter of Joseph Priestley, Bessie may well have inherited a taste for rebellion. Her little gestures of defiance once brought a gentle caution from that earlier rebel Marian Evans:

Now, dear child, don't be playing pranks and shocking people, because I am told they lay it all to me and my bad influence over you. But I appeal to you whether I have not been the soberest properest of friends —whether the pink of conventionalism could have shewn a graver dis-approval of your *chaussure* than I? But thus it is that goodness is mis-apprehended and maligned in this ill-conditioned world—*human* world that is.[4]

But Marian was far too busy with problems of her own to worry much about Bessie, and their friendship developed slowly. Bessie wrote to Barbara Leigh Smith 12 February 1853:

Do you know, Marian Evans has changed to me lately, has seemed to have finally made up her mind to love me. It took her some time to consider those wretched poison drops of evil speaking, and I saw it, and shrunk from it just as you can fancy, but I have learnt my lesson

---

[1] *Letters*, II. 45. [2] *Leader*, 8 Jan. 1853, p. 43.
[3] *WR*, 59 (Jan. 1853), 287. It was probably by GE. [4] *Letters*, II. 44.

of patience somewhat bitterly, and held my tongue, and let her consider at leisure, and she has thrown them to the winds. She said the other day, having made me sit close to her, and looking full into my eyes: 'I thought when I first knew you, you had a great deal of self-esteem in the sense of putting forth your own opinions, but I have quite lost the impression. I suppose when we love people, we lose the sense of their faults.' I was inexpressibly touched. I nearly cried. The odd mixture of truth and fondness in Marian is so great. She never spares, but expresses every opinion, good and bad, with the most unflinching plainness, and yet she seems able to see faults without losing tenderness.[1]

Marian showed no hesitation, however, in liking Barbara Leigh Smith when Bessie introduced them in June 1852. Barbara was a grand-daughter of the great abolitionist William Smith, a Unitarian, who had defended Joseph Priestley in 1791 after his flight to London. His descendants were numerous and distinguished. The eldest son Benjamin Leigh Smith succeeded his father in Parliament, carrying on the family tradition by supporting repeal of the Corn Laws and most other Radical policies. About 1826, when he was a bachelor over forty, he saw in the street a ravishingly pretty girl of seventeen, followed her home, and discovered that she was a milliner's apprentice named Anne Longden, daughter of a Norfolk miller. Leigh Smith seduced her, 'took her under his protection', and though he never married, had five children by her before she died of tuberculosis in 1834. Barbara was the eldest. Despite his antipathy to marriage, Leigh Smith was devoted to his family, who lived with him very comfortably at 5 Blandford Square and at their country house near Hastings. Like his father he was an intelligent patron of the arts. When Barbara showed a talent for drawing, he had William Henry Hunt give her lessons, and she was allowed to visit the great Turner's studio; she became a painter of considerable ability. In 1848 when she came of age her father gave her an independent allowance of £300 a year, and after his death she inherited a large fortune. But because of their illegitimacy, the Leigh Smiths were 'the *tabooed* family',[2] and their numerous cousins, who included Florence Nightingale and the Bonham Carters, looked on them somewhat askance. So when her aunt Mrs. Samuel Smith brought Florence and Hilary Bonham Carter (Sara Hennell's friends) to the Strand to call on

[1] *Letters*, II. 87.
[2] Ibid. 45; Mrs. Belloc Lowndes to GSH, 19 Nov. 1942; *Letters of Mrs. Gaskell and Charles Eliot Norton*, ed. Jane Whitehill (1932), p. 52.

Marian, Barbara, of course, was not with them. Such a taboo would have been nothing to the emancipated Miss Evans. 'Tell your noble-looking Barbara—I cannot call her Miss Smith, at least to you—' she wrote to Bessie, 'that I only hope she will keep up her desire to make an "indelible impression" on me. It will be no hard task. The material she has to work on is very impressible and I am sure the mould is first-rate.'[1] Soon Marian was being invited to dine at Blandford Square to meet interesting friends of the Leigh Smiths, who included Mrs. Jameson and Robert Noel, a brother of Cara Bray's friend, Edward.[2]

The kind of problem Marian faced during her two years as editor of the *Westminster Review* may be seen in a typical letter to Chapman, written when the October number was being planned:

> Broadstairs
> Saturday Evening. [24 July 1852]

Dear Friend

I laid Mr. Gilpin's note with the accompanying pamphlet on my desk the morning I left London, meaning to commend them to your care. I dare say you will find them in my room. If not, I believe the purport of Mr. Gilpin's note was that the writer of said pamphlet wished to know if an article on 'Free Schools in Worcestershire' (the subject of the pamphlet) would be accepted for the Westminster. I am not sure whether it was requested that the pamphlet should be noticed by us.

I return Froude's letter and Martineau's. Of course you will let Froude have his 26 pages. As to Martineau, there is no doubt that he will write—'Self-interest well understood' will secure that. Pray, how came you to tell him that J. S. Mill was going to write? I have told you all along that he would flatly contradict Martineau and that there was nothing for it but to announce contradiction on our title-page. I think M. is right as to the 'idea' of a quarterly, but it is plain that the Westminster can't realize that 'idea.' However, if I were its proprietor and could afford to make it what I liked, it should certainly not represent the Martineau 'School of thought.' Not that I mean to decry him, or to speak superciliously of one so immeasurably superior to myself—I simply mean that I can't see things through spectacles of his colour.

What do you think of sending the note which I enclose to Miss

---

[1] *Letters*, II. 65.

[2] The Reverend Thomas Noel, an illegitimate son of Lady Byron's grandfather Viscount Wentworth, would have succeeded to the estate and title if his parents had married. Feeling it her duty to provide for her cousins, Lady Byron prepared one of them to succeed his father in the family living at Kirkby Mallory, made another agent of the estate there, purchased an estate for Edward on the island of Euboea, and settled Robert in Bohemia, where he married a German baroness.

Bronty? The thrice-announced parcel has just arrived. As to my disgraceful mistake about the stamps, I can only say—peccavi, peccavi. The only excuse I have to make is that I just glanced at the envelope in which you forwarded the same M.S. to me, and saw only two stamps on it. I need not say that I did not pause to use my reasoning faculty in the matter.

Don't suggest 'Fashion' as a subject to any one else—I should like to keep it.

Sunday—This morning came (with the Athenæum and Leader, for which thanks) a letter from Geo. Combe announcing Dr. S. Brown's refusal to write said article for October. I enclose the letters of both. Please return Geo. Combe's with *the one of his which I sent you some time ago*. (See last page of my letter.) I am sorry for Dr. B's defection as I am very favourably impressed with the character of his mind. I wish Mr. Bastard would wait until January and still get Dr. B. to write. I shall say so to Geo. Combe. If yes, what do you say to Lewes on Lamarck?

I have noticed the advertisement of the British Q[uarterl]y this morning. Its list of subjects is excellent. I wish you could contrive to let me see the number when it comes out. They have one subject of which I am jealous—"Pre-Raphaelism in Painting and Literature." We have no good writer on such subjects on our staff. Ought we not, too, to try and enlist David Masson, who is one of the Br[itish] Q[uarterly] set? He wrote that article in the Leader on the Patagonian Missionaries, which I thought very beautiful. Seeing 'Margaret Fuller' among their subjects makes me rather regret having missed the first moment for writing an article on her life myself, but I think she still may come in as one of a triad or quaternion.

I feel that I am a wretched helpmate to you, almost out of the world and incog. so far as I am in it. When you can afford to pay an Editor, if that time will ever come, you must get one. If you believe in Free Will, in the Theism that looks on manhood as a type of the godhead and on Jesus as the Ideal Man, get one belonging to the Martineau 'School of thought,' and he will drill you a regiment of writers who will produce a Prospective on a larger scale, and so the Westminster may come to have 'dignity' in the eyes of Liverpool.

If not—if you believe, as I do, that the thought which is to mould the Future has for its root a belief in necessity, that a nobler presentation of humanity has yet to be given in resignation to individual nothingness, than could ever be shewn of a being who believes in the phantasmagoria of hope unsustained by reason—why then get a man of another calibre and let him write a fresh Prospectus, and if Liverpool theology and ethics are to be admitted, let them be put in the 'dangerous ward,' *alias*, the Independent Section.

The only third course is the present one, that of Editorial compromise. Martineau writes much that we can agree with and admire. Newman ditto, J. S. Mill still more, Froude a little less and so on. These men can write more openly in the Westminster than anywhere else. They are amongst the world's vanguard, though not all in the foremost line; it is good for the world, therefore, that they should have every facility for speaking out. Ergo, since each can't have a periodical to himself, it is good that there should be one which is common to them—id est, the Westminster. The grand mistake with respect to this plan is the paragraph in the Prospectus which announces the Independent Section and which thus makes the Editors responsible for everything outside that railing—Ah me! how wise we all are après coup.

If we don't have Lewes's article on Lamarck, I think you had better sound him when he comes back and see what hope there is in him for October. Defective as his articles are, they are the best we can get *of the kind.*

An article on Chalmers would not be 'light.' It is important that this Hereditary Transmission business should be settled as soon as possible, and so I shall tell Combe, that we may know whether we want 1 article or 2. Apropos of Combe, I think you are too sore on the subject of the 'Copyright'—you did not tell him the terms when you agreed that he should write. Besides for your purposes his article is a bone picked quite clean—let him use it up in his Papin's digester if he will.

It is amusing to see J. Martineau so confidently setting down the Niebuhr article as Newman's and so deluding himself into praising it. It is to me the most entirely satisfactory article in the number. I thought Lewes's criticism in the Leader very poor and undiscriminating.

The publishing world seems utterly stagnant—nothing coming out which would do as a peg for an article. I am running on, scribbling to no purpose and you will hardly thank me. Miss Hennell writes the following opinion of the English article: 'I have just read Syme's Eng. article. Most of it is very good; whenever he is in earnest he is good. But in the theological it is mostly slash and scoff, without giving us any confidence that he has any opinions of his own, and in other parts his style is quite too coarse, especially Nell Gwyn. One feels that he does not write as a gentleman.' I congratulate you on your ability to be cheerful *malgrè tout.*

Yours etc.
Marian Evans.[1]

Even readers who disagreed strongly with the opinions of the *Westminster* conceded that its intellectual level was high. Since the new editors took over, said the *Leader*, 'it has recovered the former importance it acquired when under the editorship of John Stuart Mill'. But it could not live on praise alone. Mr. Lombe, who had subsidized several articles, died in Florence 1 March 1852, before the second number was ready for the printer. A few weeks

---

[1] *Letters*, II. 47–50.

later Dr. Brabant, who had lent Chapman £800, called with the unwelcome news that the money must be repaid within two years. Under the circumstances it would have been tempting to economize in payments to authors, which came to £250 a number, an enormous sum for a quarterly that printed only 650 copies and sold for 5s. The editors refused to yield. Chapman's friends did what they could for him. Combe was 'indefatigable in writing and thinking for us', Marian wrote, and got his friend T. H. Bastard to give £60 for articles. Bray, though his own business was in an alarming state, also concerned himself with the problem, and talked of supporting the *Westminster* for Marian's sake—a gesture she would not countenance. However, his friend Edward Flower, the Unitarian brewer, was persuaded to lend Chapman some money, though he would not increase the loan. At the end of 1852, when 'the affairs of Chapmandom' never looked more dismal, the philanthropic Samuel Courtauld *volunteered* to lend him £600, and the *Review* staggered on.

Its accounts were hopelessly entangled with those of Chapman's publishing and bookselling business. Since the beginning of the century the price of books had been fixed by a small group of London publishers who controlled the Booksellers' Association. To members they granted discounts of 30 to 45 per cent on condition that the books should not be retailed at a discount of more than 10 per cent. Each bookseller who signed the Regulations was given a ticket permitting him to purchase on these terms; but if he were found underselling—and the Association maintained spies to detect violations—his ticket was forfeited, and the publishers would furnish no books to fill his orders. Chapman had signed the Regulations under protest and adhered to them faithfully in his English trade. But he maintained that the London publishers had no jurisdiction over American books; in January 1852 he announced that henceforth he would sell imported books at cost plus a small commission. To his surprise his ticket was cancelled, and the majority of publishers refused to sell him their books.

Chapman was not the man to yield without a struggle. He set out to stir up rebellion. He wrote to Cabinet Ministers and Members of Parliament. He called on influential authors, who assured him of support. Most important of all, with Marian's help, he wrote for the April number of the *Westminster* an article entitled 'The Commerce of Literature', which exposed the shabby racket in effective but moderate terms and precipitated a public discussion. Soon the criticism of the monopoly had grown so strong that the Association was compelled to act. They agreed to submit their case to a committee, whose opinion was to be accepted without appeal.

In the meantime Chapman planned a meeting of the rebels to be held 4 May at his house in the Strand. Spencer went about with him to solicit help. When the meeting was called to order by Charles Dickens as chairman, the distinguished group present included Wilkie Collins, R. H. Horne, F. W. Newman, Lewes, Spencer, Charles Babbage, Dr. Roget of the *Thesaurus*, Tom Taylor of *Punch*, Henry Crabb Robinson, George Cruikshank, and Richard Owen. Many who could not attend sent letters, which Dickens read with enthusiasm. Chapman gave an able statement of the Free Traders' position, in the composition of which he had been aided by Spencer and Marian. She described the evening in a letter to the Brays:

> The meeting last night went off triumphantly, and I saluted Mr. Chapman with 'See the Conquering Hero Comes' on the piano at 12 o'clock, for not until then was the last magnate except Herbert Spencer out of the house. I sat *at* the door for a short time, but soon got a chair within it and heard and saw everything.
>
> Dickens in the chair—a position he fills remarkably well, preserving a courteous neutrality of eyebrow, and speaking with clearness and decision. His appearance is certainly disappointing—no benevolence in the face and I think little in the head—the anterior lobe not by any means remarkable. In fact he is not distinguished looking in any way —neither handsome nor ugly, neither fat nor thin, neither tall nor short.
>
> Mr. Chapman read his statement very well and looked distinguished and refined even in that assemblage of intellectuals. Letters were read from R. Chambers, Geo. Combe, MacCulloch, Cobden, James Wilson, De Morgan etc. Babbage moved the first resolution—an ugly man and a bad speaker but a great authority. Charles Knight is a beautiful elderly man with a modest but firm enunciation, and he made a wise and telling speech which silenced one or two vulgar, ignorant booksellers who had got into the meeting by mistake. One of these—Willis no—Sotheran—began by complimenting Dickens—'views held by such worthy and important gentlemen, *which is your worthy person in the chair.*' Dickens looked respectfully neutral. These four booksellers were a capital foil to all the other men in the room, and they happened to sit all in a row. Their faces contrasted with those of the authors were in every sense a primâ facie argument against them. The most telling speech of the evening was Prof. Tom Taylor's—as witty and brilliant as one of George Dawson's. Professor Owen's too was remarkably

good. . . . Owen has a tremendous head and looked, as he was, the greatest celebrity of the meeting. Geo. Cruikshank, too, made a capital speech, in an admirable moral spirit. He is the most homely, genuine looking man, not unlike the pictures of Captain Cuttle.

So now I hope poor Mr. Chap. will have a little time to attend to his business which is needing him awfully—in fact his private affairs are wearing a melancholy aspect. However he has worked well and in a good spirit at this great question and has shewn a degree of talent, and power of mastering a subject which have won him general admiration.[1]

The 'last magnate *except* Herbert Spencer' Marian had written in this account of the booksellers meeting. For some months now he had been her most intimate companion. Born in Derby, five months after Marian, Herbert Spencer was the only survivor of the nine children of a schoolmaster. All four of his grandparents were Wesleyans, and his birth was recorded in the Methodist Register Office in London instead of in his parish at Derby. His mother, daughter of a plumber and glazier, adhered strictly to their faith. His father, however, showed a more independent mind; he was secretary of the Derby Philosophical Society. He encouraged Herbert's taste for mathematics and practical science. At thirteen the lad was sent to live at Hinton Charterhouse, near Bath, with his uncle the Reverend Thomas Spencer, who under Simeon's influence at Cambridge had abandoned the Wesleyans. Thomas was a keen opponent of such evils as slavery, the Corn Laws, and drunkenness; in the cause of total abstinence he edited the *National Temperance Chronicle* and lectured widely. Marian heard him in 1845 at Coventry, where he stayed with the Brays and spoke so eloquently, Cara wrote, that 'We had to hold Mary Ann to prevent her going and taking the pledge.'[2] Under his uncle's tutelage Herbert showed no aptitude for the Classics, but developed unusual talent in mathematics and drawing. At seventeen he went to work as a civil engineer with the London and Birmingham Railway, laying out new lines and designing bridges. When this ended, he settled in London, dividing his time between engineering, mechanical inventions, and writing for periodicals on social and political subjects. In 1846 he met John Chapman the publisher of his uncle's temperance pamphlets; and when he took a place as subeditor of *The Economist* at a salary of 100 guineas a year with free rooms above its office in the Strand, he found himself just opposite the Chapman's house, where he sometimes spent the

[1] *Letters*, II. 23–4.
[2] Bray–Hennell Extracts, 6 Sept. 1845 (Yale).

evenings. His editorial duties he seems to have taken lightly, saving most of his energy for writing his first book, *Social Statics, or the Conditions Essential to Human Happiness Specified, and the First of Them Developed*, which Chapman published at the end of 1850.

Marian had been introduced to Spencer in August 1851, while she was in London with the Brays to see the Exhibition at the Crystal Palace, and after her return to the Strand in September she saw him there frequently. Part of his work for *The Economist* was reviewing the theatre and opera. One night she went with him to the Lyceum to see *The Chain of Events*, a play in eight acts, adapted by Lewes from the French.

It is a very long chain and drags rather heavily [she told Charles Bray]. No sparkle, but a sort of Dickens-like sentimentality all through—in short, I think it might please you. As a series of tableaux I never saw anything equal to it. But to my mind it is execrable moral taste to have a storm and shipwreck with all its horrors on the stage. I could only scream and cover my eyes. It was revolting to hear the cheers and clapping of the audience. But perhaps all that was pure philosophy, and they were so thoroughly imbued with your beloved optimism that they felt more than ever reconciled to the scheme of things.[1]

Spencer often had tickets for Covent Garden and sometimes asked her to go with him. 'I had two offers last night', she wrote to Cara, '—not of marriage, but of music—which I find it impossible to resist. Mr. Herbert Spencer proposed to take me on Thursday to hear William Tell, and Miss Parkes asked me to go with her to hear the Creation on Friday.'[2] Later she and Spencer heard *I Martiri* and *Norma* and *The Huguenots*. 'See what a fine thing it is to pick up people who are short-sighted enough to like one.'[3] As the spring days grew warmer she and Spencer would walk on the terrace of Somerset House, to which Chapman had a key; in those days before the Thames Embankment was built only a balustrate separated it from the river. There, with no noise but the gulls and the passing steamboats, they would pace backwards and forwards for hours, 'discussing many things'. To his friend Edward Lott, Spencer wrote 23 April 1852 about

Miss Evans, whom you have heard me mention as the translatress of Strauss and as the most admirable woman, mentally, I ever met. We have been for some time past on very intimate terms. I am frequently at Chapman's, and the greatness of her intellect conjoined with her

[1] *Letters*, II. 18.   [2] *Letters*, II. 16.   [3] *Letters*, II. 22–3.

womanly qualities and manner, generally keep me at her side most of the evening.[1]

But to Marian, Spencer seems very soon to have made it clear that his admiration was of her mental qualities only, for she wrote to the Brays 27 April: 'We have agreed that we are not in love with each other and that there is no reason why we should not have as much of each other's society as we like. He is a good, delightful creature and I always feel better for being with him.'[2] They sang together at the Chapmans' evening parties, and he helped her make copies of the resolutions to be offered at the booksellers meeting. 'My brightest spot next to my love of *old* friends', she wrote to Cara, 'is the deliciously calm *new* friendship that Herbert Spencer gives me. We see each other every day and have a delightful *camaraderie* in everything. But for him my life would be desolate enough now, with poor Mr. C. so occupied and so sad—but he runs away with a great deal of my time.'[3] On fine days they made longer excursions to the Chiswick Flower Show or to Kew Gardens, discussing possible articles for the *Westminster*. 'I went to Kew yesterday,' she wrote to Sara Hennell, 29 June, 'on a scientific expedition with Herbert Spencer, who has all sorts of theories about plants—I should have said a *proof*-hunting expedition. Of course, if the flowers didn't correspond to the theories, we said, "*tant pis pour les fleurs*." '[4] He brought his father to see her 22 June, 'a large-brained, highly informed man, with a certain quaintness and simplicity—altogether very pleasing'.[5]

Charles Bray, always eager to further Marian's happiness, had offered to invite Spencer to Rosehill while she was visiting there in July.

I told Herbert Spencer of your invitation, Mr. Bray, not mentioning that you asked him *with me*. He said he should like to accept it—but I think it would be better for him to go down when I am with you. We certainly could not go together, for all the world is setting us down as engaged —a most disagreeable thing if one chose to make oneself uncomfortable. 'Tell it not in Gath' however—that is to say, please to avoid mentioning our names together, and pray burn this note, that it may not lie on the chimney piece for general inspection.[6]

A week later she wrote to her 'Dear Trio' at Coventry: 'Your joint assurance of welcome strengthens the centripetal force that

[1] Herbert Spencer, *Autobiography* (2 vols., 1904), I. 394–5.
[2] *Letters*, II. 22. [3] *Letters*, II. 29. [4] *Letters*, II. 40.
[5] *Letters*, II. 37. [6] *Letters*, II. 35.

would carry me to you, but on the other hand sundry considerations are in favour of the centrifugal force which I suppose will
carry me to Broadstairs or Ramsgate. On the whole I prefer to
keep my visit to you as a *bonne bouche* when I am just in the
best physical and mental state for enjoying it.'[1] And two days
later, she added in a note to Mr. Bray:

> I have assured Herbert Spencer that you will think it a sufficiently
> formal answer to the invitation you sent him through Mr. Lewes if I
> tell you that he will prefer waiting for the pleasure of a visit to you
> until I am with you—if you will have him then. *Entre nous*, if Mr. Lewes
> should not accept your invitation now, pray don't ask him when I am
> with you—not that I don't like him—*au contraire*—but I want nothing
> so Londonish when I go to enjoy the fields and hedgerows and yet
> more, friends of ten years' growth.
>
> Mr. Chapman says I can't leave before today week, as he will be
> unable to escort me—that is to say, he and Mrs. C.—before then. I
> wish you could all go with me instead.[2]

As soon as the July number of the *Review* was out, Marian
—escorted by Mr. *and Mrs.* Chapman—went for her holiday to
Broadstairs on the Kentish coast, a 'pretty, quiet place, which
David Copperfield has made classic'.[3] Bray had apparently teased
her about her new friend. 'I am not going to the coast *with* any
one', she replied, '—but simply to do my health good.'[4] She took
two snug little rooms in a cottage, for which she paid a guinea
a week, with a motherly blue-eyed woman and a damsel of fourteen to wait on her, and liked the arrangement so well that she
stayed there two months. But she was not alone all the time. Of
this summer Spencer remarks with the careful vagueness in which
he veiled his *Autobiography*: 'Two of my weekly vacations were
spent at the sea-side: and, later on in the season, I had a few
pleasant days with Miss Evans's friends, the Brays, at Coventry.'[5]
In the context of their relations at this time there is little doubt of
where his seaside vacations found him. Perhaps it was on his
account that Marian said on 13 July, 'I am obliged to write very
hurriedly, as I am not alone.'[6] Mr. and Mrs. Bray came to spend
the first week-end in August with her at Broadstairs, Cara staying
on till the 12th. But in the middle of the month, Spencer, one
suspects, was back again to resume their walks along the shore,
picking up shells, gathering wild flowers, discussing Aristotle's

---

[1] *Letters*, II. 36.　　[2] *Letters*, II. 37.　　[3] *Letters*, II. 52.　　[4] *Letters*, II. 38.
[5] Spencer, *Autobiography*, I. 407.　　[6] *Letters*, II. 42.

view of the chief good and his own plan of the *Psychology*, for which he was reading the copy of Mill's *Logic* that Marian lent him. She wrote to Cara 19 August, 'Thanks for the sermon—it made us laugh well over our tea on Monday.'[1] Could *us* include any one but Spencer?

Though the beauties of sea and glorious evening skies were scarcely needed to stir Marian's expansive affection, the Specifier of the Conditions Essential to Human Happiness, who was to die a bachelor in his eighty-fourth year, was quite unripe for matrimony. With some lack of chivalry he later allowed it to be understood among friends that his intimacy with Marian had not led to marriage because of her lack of beauty. 'Physical beauty is a *sine quâ non* with me; as was once unhappily proved where the intellectual traits and the emotional traits were of the highest', he wrote late in life.[2] But the inadequacy of this reason is obvious from his objection to Miss Potter, 'a great beauty, alike in face and figure', because he did 'not quite like the shape of her head'. In Marian's case lack of beauty was a plausible reason, one she herself was all too prone to accept. We recall her bitter tears at Kenilworth the summer before, when Chapman dwelt on 'the incomprehensible mystery and witchery of beauty'. In her letters to the Brays there are never more references to her 'ugliness' than during the months of her involvement with Spencer. 'I am a hideous hag now', she will write, 'sad and wizened', 'haggard as an old witch', 'like one of those old hags we used to see by the wayside in Italy—only a little worse, for want of the dark eyes and dark hair in contrast with the parchment'.[3] Spencer in two essays on 'Personal Beauty', published in the *Leader* in 1854, singles out to illustrate ugliness some of the very features for which Marian's face was most conspicuous—the heavy under jaw, the large mouth, the long upper lip, the long, prominent nose—all so unlike the ideal Greek head. Quite illogically (and ignoring Socrates) he argues 'a *necessary* relationship' between ugly features and inferiority of intellect and character. 'The saying that beauty is but skin-deep is but a skin-deep saying', he concludes.[4]

Despite her lack of beauty, Spencer had a photograph of Marian in his bedroom until the day he died. The sisters who kept house for him in the 1890s used to tease him about it, trying to trap him

---

[1] *Letters*, II. 51.
[2] Spencer, *Autobiography*, II. 445.
[3] *Letters*, II. 11, 38, 25, 29.
[4] *Leader*, 15 Apr. 1854, pp. 356–7.

into admitting that he had once been in love with her. At last one of them, looking intently at the picture, exclaimed:

'What a long nose she had! She must have been very difficult to kiss, Mr. Spencer!'
'Yes, indeed!' he brightly acquiesced, to our intense delight at the apparent admission. He laughingly protested he was only speaking 'theoretically'; but would Herbert Spencer, the philosopher, have generalised from *à priori* reasoning?'[1]

Of those who knew her at this time Spencer was almost the only one to see in her physique 'perhaps, a trace of that masculinity characterizing her intellect; for though of but the ordinary feminine height she was strongly built'.[2] We must weigh this opinion against one of Kate Potter (Lady Courtney), who knew him for many years: 'In spite of his great intellect Mr. Spencer always seemed to me to have a strong element of the feminine in his character: an element which manifested itself in the weaknesses, as well as the attractive qualities of his personality.'[3] In 1842 at almost the same time the phrenologist was discovering that Marian Evans was 'of a most affectionate disposition, always requiring some one to lean upon', another phrenologist, aptly named J. Q. Rumball, was 'reading' Herbert Spencer's head. He found Firmness and Self-esteem both *very* large, with Amativeness only moderate—a just description, one would say, though his conclusion that Spencer should be either a poet, a painter, or a musician is another criticism of the value of phrenology as an index to aptitudes. In setting down the essentials of marriage for his friend Lott, Spencer wrote in 1845 that, first, lovers must serve as the type of each other's ideal; second, grant equality of rights ('no woman of truly noble mind will submit to be dictated to'); and third, forget as far as possible the 'legal bond', since passion alone is amply sufficient 'to ensure the permanence of the union'.[4] In 1852, confronted himself with passion, Spencer could rouse none to answer it.

His rejection of Marian's love caused no abrupt change in their association. He came to Rosehill for the long-postponed week-end in October, while she was there; they still took their long walks, discussing his *Psychology*, which probably owes a good deal more to her than the single happy phrase, 'Things which have a constant

---

[1] *Home Life with Herbert Spencer, by Two* (1906), p. 191.
[2] Spencer, *Autobiography*, I. 395.
[3] David Duncan, *Life and Letters of Herbert Spencer* (1908), p. 494.
[4] Spencer, *Autobiography*, I. 268.

PLATE V

HERBERT SPENCER 1855

MARIAN EVANS 1858
Etching by Paul Adolphe Rajon (1884) from a
photograph

relation to the same thing have a constant relation to each other', for which a footnote (p. 162) expressed his gratitude. He continued to call on her and took her occasionally to the opera. Even a year later we find: 'He made the pen with which I write. So you see he is a useful member of society.'[1] Like Sir James Chettam he had discovered 'the delight there is in frank kindness and companionship between a man and a woman who have no passion to hide or confess'.[2] But any dream she may have had of Spencer as the man she could lean upon had fled with the sunsets at Broadstairs. By 1853 her heart had turned in quite a different direction and found another heart to answer it. She could regard Spencer then with amused tolerance. In October 1853, when he stayed again with the Brays, arriving the day before she left, Marian wrote to Cara, 'I hope you are likely to survive the heavy dose of theories you have had.'[3] Spencer declared solemnly that Marian was not 'vivacious', and that 'the wit and humour which from time to time gave signs of their presence, were not frequently displayed'.[4] Could he have missed some of the signs? She saw his absurdities clearly enough now, and studied in him a human trait of which she was to be one of the greatest delineators—egoism. She had long since accepted the philosophy of necessity, that everything acts in accordance with its own nature; she did not expect more than was in him. Her suffering she kept to herself, possibly grumbling a little more about low spirits and the usual racking headaches, but facing the cause of them squarely. Her experience with John Chapman and even with the egregious Dr. Brabant had taught her renunciation.

But the Specifier of the Conditions Essential to Human Happiness had had little practice in renouncing. The death of his uncle in January 1853, though it brought him a welcome legacy of more than £500, cost him the stale excuse that lack of money prevented his marrying. He resigned his post on *The Economist* and set out 1 August 1853 for his first sight of the Continent. Change of scene failed to calm his agitated mind. Nothing he saw in Europe equalled his expectations: he was disappointed with the picturesque stretches of the Rhine; at Frankfurt he noted only two nights and a day of toothache (after an 'immunity of thirty-three years'); and he found Switzerland 'far inferior to Scotland' from the 'absence of fine colouring'.[5] With his friend Lott he spent two or three frantic

[1] *Letters*, II. 117.   [2] *Middlemarch*, ch. 8.   [3] *Letters*, II. 119.
[4] Spencer, *Autobiography*, I. 397.   [5] Ibid. 467.

weeks in the Alps, climbing in quick succession the Furkas-horn, the Faulhorn, the Wengernalp, the Riffelberg, and the Gornergrat. He felt no ill effects from the exertion, for he had always been a great walker since, at the age of thirteen, he ran away from school in Wiltshire and walked back to Derby, 120 miles in three days. But soon after his return to London in September 1853 he noticed 'signs of an enfeebled action of the heart', vague 'cardiac disturbances which never afterwards entirely ceased'.[1] He went home to father and mother. Marian commented on his condition to Sara Hennell: 'Herbert Spencer writes me word that he has had an attack of palpitation of the heart—but is quite recovered. I am going to quote to him a passage I found in Sainte-Beuve which just fits him: "Quand j'ai dit qu'il n'avait jamais eu de passion et d'excès, je me suis trop avancé; il a eu un excès de *raison*." '[2] After a few months at Derby, he went off to Wales to complete his *Psychology*. He had just finished the chapter on 'Feelings' and was in the midst of 'Reason', when his 'nervous system finally gave way'.[3] He felt a 'sensation in the head —not pain nor heat nor fulness nor tension, but simply a sensation, bearable enough but abnormal'.[4] At this price he bought safety from the perils of marriage.

Spencer lived another fifty years, holding his pulse in company, inserting ear-plugs if the conversation seemed likely to grow exciting, trying to sleep, sometimes, with his head wrapped in a towel soaked in salt water and encased in a rubber cap. Friends

---

[1] Spencer, *Autobiography*, I. 432–3.   [2] *Letters*, II. 128.
[3] In Spencer's *Psychology* (1855), pp. 601–2, the order of these two is reversed; it is difficult to see how 'Reason' could have been written after 'Feelings'. A few extracts from the latter are suggestive: [As a corollary] 'I may cite the passion which unites the sexes.... Added to the purely physical elements of it, are first to be noticed those highly complex impressions produced by personal beauty.... With this there is united the complex sentiment which we term affection, ... which assumes its highest activity between lovers. ... Next there must be added the feeling which phrenologists have named love of approbation. To be preferred above all the world, and that by one admired beyond all others, is to have the love of approbation gratified in a degree passing every previous experience: especially as, to this direct gratification of it there must be added that reflex gratification of it which results from the preference being witnessed by unconcerned persons. Further, there is the allied emotion of self-esteem, ... a practical proof of power, of superiority, which cannot fail agreeably to excite the *amour propre*. Yet again, the proprietary feeling has its share ... the pleasure of possession; the two belong to each other—claim each other as a species of property. Once more ... the love of unrestrained activity is gratified. Finally, there is an exaltation of the sympathies: purely personal pleasures are doubled by being shared with another.... All these, each excited in the highest degree, and severally tending to reflect their excitement on each other, form the composite psychical state which we call love.'
[4] Spencer, *Autobiography*, I. 467.

like Lott and Huxley and Potter, to whom he talked constantly
of his symptoms, even Comte, whom he called upon in Paris in
1853, recommended his taking a wife as the obvious cure. When
Mrs. Potter also prescribed it seriously, he told her:

I labour under the double difficulty that my choice is very limited and
that I am not easy to please. Moral and intellectual beauties do not by
themselves suffice to attract me; and owing to the stupidity of our
educational system it is rare to find them united to a good physique.
Moreover there is the pecuniary difficulty. . . . So, all things considered,
the chances are that I shall continue a melancholy Cœlebs to the end
of my days.

When she returned to the attack later, he admitted: 'No one is
more thoroughly convinced than I am that bachelorhood is an
unnatural and very injurious state. Ever since I was a boy (when
I was unfortunate in having no brothers or sisters) I have been
longing to have my affections called out.'[1] He knew all too well
that they had been called out and had not come when they were
called for.

Marian felt no rancour toward him; she never held grudges.
Spencer remarked how she was 'so tolerant of human weaknesses
as to be quickly forgiving; and, indeed, was prone to deprecate
harsh judgments. This last trait was I doubt not in part caused by
constant study of her own defects.'[2] Possibly some of his taught
her too. But she never turned on him the scorn Pope vented on
Lady Mary Wortley Montagu. The only hint of allusion to this
sad epoch in her life appears on the opening page of her last
book, where she makes her shadowy narrator Theophrastus Such
a bachelor whose friends are 'astonished at my never having told
them before of my accident in the Alps, causing me the nervous
shock which has since notably diminished my digestive powers', a
man whose acquaintances are 'as forgetful of my biography and
tenets as they would be if I were a dead philosopher'.[3] Writing to
Sara Hennell 10 July 1854, Marian described his *Westminster*
article on 'The Genesis of Science' as 'a grand one'.

You must read it. He will stand in the Biographical Dictionaries of
1954 as 'Spencer, Herbert, an original and profound philosophical
writer, especially known by his great work x x x which gave a new
impulse to psychology and has mainly contributed to the present
advanced position of that science, compared with that which it had

---

[1] Ibid. I. 478–9.   [2] Ibid. 396.
[3] *Impressions of Theophrastus Such* (1879), pp. 3–4.

attained in the middle of the last century. The life of this philosopher, like that of the great Kant, offers little material for the narrator. Born in the year 1820 etc.'[1]

The 'overstrained heart' served as a convenient explanation for a conspicuous alteration in Spencer's appearance and manner. Unable to sleep, he walked about London in a 'half-distracted' state. For many months he could do nothing. A photograph of him at this time has, he says, 'a worn anxious look, showing that waste was in excess of repair'.[2] But the true account of these months is hopelessly obscured in the *Autobiography*. No Victorian cultivated more sedulously what modern jargon would term his 'image'. He called in all his letters, extracting the portions that supported his view of himself; the manuscripts themselves have disappeared. Parts of the *Autobiography*, privately printed twenty years before his death and given to friends to read under the most solemn pledges of secrecy, were rewritten to answer in advance any criticisms that might arise when it was published. All his life Spencer engaged in acrimonious controversy to establish the priority of his ideas, refusing to admit that any one, even his own father, suggested or anticipated any of them. He believed in the evolution of everything except his own theories. Though there is no sign of it earlier, in the *Autobiography* he claims even the discovery of George Eliot's genius for fiction. It was her diffidence, he insists, that 'led her, in those days, to resist my suggestion that she should write novels. I thought I saw in her many, if not all, of the needful qualifications in high degrees—quick observation, great power of analysis, unusual and rapid intuition into others' states of mind, deep and broad sympathies, wit and humour [just denied her on the previous page], and wide culture. But she would not listen to my advice.'[3] He made quite a point of having first taken Lewes to see her in the Strand.

Spencer was even more concerned than she with how he might appear in 1954. Not content with tailoring his own 'image', he wanted to control Marian's view of him as well. A week after her death he wrote to the newspapers denying the statement in some obituaries that he had had anything to do with George Eliot's education. He was appalled to read in an interview he had given to an American visitor some months before: 'It is rumoured that

[1] *Letters*, II. 165.   [2] Spencer, *Autobiography*, I. 464.
[3] Ibid. 398.

he once loved George Eliot; but be that as it may, he has never married.' Discussing the report with close friends, he was shocked to learn that the rumour had been current for years that he and Marian 'were about to be married when Lewes came on the scene'. Potter dissuaded him from his impulse to 'publish the truth' at once, telling him, 'My dear Spencer, you will be eternally damned if you do it.'[1] So he wrote to Cross, asking him in the biography to 'contradict these statements in some general way', indicating 'the fact that high as was my admiration for her, and great as my feeling of friendship, yet my feeling did not grow into a warm one—or something to that effect'.[2] Three years later, hearing that the biography was nearly completed, he reminded Cross of the matter and suggested the wording of a note to be attached to her remark that 'we are not in love with each other': 'The intimacy naturally led to rumours. It was said that Mr. Spencer was in love with her. This however was not true. I have the best possible warrant for saying that his feeling did not pass the limits of friendship.'[3]

Naturally this cold disclaimer jarred upon Cross, who thought that the indirect evidence of the letter and the continued intimacy between Spencer and Marian were sufficient. Lord Bowen, whom Cross consulted, felt that the mention of 'rumours' was ambiguous and might give rise to gossip. Spencer next proposed another version: 'Of course the intimacy caused speculation. After some time it was concluded that Mr. Spencer was in love with her and that they were engaged. But I have the best possible warrant for saying that this was not true.'[4] That was equally repugnant to Cross, who suggested a note of his own, denying that she had jilted Spencer. This version Spencer would not accept. 'Much better no note at all than the one you propose', he wrote 23 October 1884. Accordingly, Cross took him at his word and omitted the note. But the problem continued to trouble him, and at the last moment he deleted from the text the words 'that we are not in love with each other', leaving the innocuous reading: 'We have agreed that there is no reason why we should not have as much of each other's society as we like.'[5]

On the day he received his copy of the *Life* Spencer wrote angrily to Cross about the omission:

[1] Beatrice Webb, *My Apprenticeship* (1926), p. 31.
[2] Spencer to Cross, 3 Apr. 1881 (Yale).
[3] 13 Jan. 1884 (Yale).   [4] 21 Oct. 1884 (Yale).
[5] Cross, I. 278. The American ed. (Harper, 1885), printed from earlier proofs, contains the whole sentence.

As the account now stands it is not only consistent with the report that I was jilted for Lewes, but tends to confirm it. Such a fact as that I was anxious to visit the Brays when she was there, and such a fact as that my name quietly drops out as a companion while Lewes' comes in, gives colour to the statement, and there is nothing that I can see to negative it. I cannot say that I have been fairly used.[1]

But after taking counsel with his friends, he wrote a week later in milder tone: 'It seems that you and your friend were right after all. From two to whom I have named the matter, I have had the opinion that the omitted words would have tended rather to cause misinterpretation than to prevent it. My friend Potter, too, thinks it quite as well that there was no note.'[2] Potter's daughter Beatrice Webb described her conversation with him:

Herbert Spencer deliciously conscious about the 'Miss Evans' episode —asked me seriously what was my impression of their relationship on reading those passages referring to him. Had wished John Cross to insert contradiction that there had ever been aught between them. Shows his small-mindedness in the extreme concern. But as George Eliot says, his friendship will always endure because of his truthfulness.

They recurred to the subject 9 June 1886:

'I was never in love,' he answered when I put the question straight. . . . Strange—a nature with so perfect an intellect and little else—save friendliness and the uprightness of a truth-loving mind. He has some-times told me sadly that he wondered at the weakness of his feelings even of friendship, and towards old friends and relations; that he thought it came from his mind being constantly busied with the perfection of this one idea—never once doubting the value of it.[1]

We shall never have the whole story, since none of Spencer's early letters to Marian survives. Some half-dozen of hers, carefully selected, no doubt, to confirm his account of their relations, are preserved, but sealed from all eyes till 1985. They can hardly alter the picture of an ardent, generous nature offering herself to an egoist who could love nothing but his 'image'. One of his trustees, who read them, exclaimed to a friend: 'What a pair it would have been, George Eliot and Hebert Spencer! He was just as capable of loving as of flying.' When the letters are finally published, they will, I predict, remind one of Sir Andrew Ague-cheek's pathetic remark, 'I was adored once, too.'

---

[1] 2 Feb. 1885 (Yale).   [2] 9 Feb. 1885 (Yale).
[3] *My Apprenticeship*, p. 30.

CHAPTER V

THE NEED TO BE LOVED

※

BACK from Broadstairs at the end of August 1852, Marian resigned herself to the unavoidable fact that 'my good friend Herbert Spencer', as Lewes called him, would never be more than a good friend to her either. Violent headache and sickness reflected the depression of spirit she felt on resuming her work in the Strand, labouring over great dreary articles that had to be pruned and shaped without excessively irritating their authors. Young William Hale White, who worked for Chapman at this time, remembered her sitting in that dark room at the back of No. 142, 'with her hair over her shoulders, the easy chair half sideways to the fire, her feet over the arm', reading endless proofs, though always willing to stop and talk with him. 'She never reserved herself, but always said what was best in her at the moment, even when no special demand was made upon her. Consequently, she found out what was best in everybody. I have never heard better talk than hers, even when there was nobody to listen but myself and the ordinary members of the Chapman household.'[1] September was cold and wet; after her sunny days on the coast the fog had never seemed more hideous. Though she wanted to escape into other lodgings, Chapman 'made a great point' of her staying till after Christmas. 'But ever since I came back', she wrote to Sara Hennell, 'I have felt something like the madness which imagines that the four walls are contracting and going to crush one.'[2] When the October number of the *Westminster* was safely out, she shook off the headaches, which were probably due to eye-strain and anxiety, and made a flight to the North to visit the Combes and Harriet Martineau.

She arrived in Edinburgh 5 October 1852, 'hardly recognizing myself for the same person as the damozel who left it by the coach with a heavy heart' to return to her father seven years before. The

---

[1] *Athenæum*, 28 Nov. 1885, p. 702; 8 Dec. 1894, p. 791.
[2] *Letters*, II. 54.

Combes had an elegant house in Melville Street with 'glorious
fires, and a comfortable carriage—in short just the circumstances
to nourish sleek optimism, convince one that this is "le meilleur
des mondes possibles", and make one shudder at the impiety of
all who doubt it'.[1] Mrs. Combe in her sixtieth year was still
beautiful, with 'a blooming complexion like a girl of fifteen and a
smile as bright and cheery as a flower-garden'.[2] With Mr. Combe
Marian enjoyed talking, especially about the men he had known
—or rather, listening to him, for 'all the interlocutors besides
Mr. Combe have little to do but shape elegant modes of negation
and affirmation like the people who are talked to by Socrates in
Plato's dialogues'. Not infrequently his wife would drop asleep
in the midst of his discourse, her lovely head inclined towards him
in reverent attention.[3] From her bedroom window Marian had a
pleasant view over the trees of Inverleith Park to the Firth of
Forth, sparkling in the sunshine three miles away. The Combes
drove her about, showing her Edinburgh at its finest and introducing her to many of their friends. 'She is thoroughly feminine,
refined, and lady-like', wrote Combe in his Journal, describing
her as 'pleasing but not pretty'.[4] Though they urged her to stay
longer than a fortnight, she adhered to her original plan and left
20 October for Ambleside.

Here she found Harriet Martineau 'charming in her own home
—quite handsome from her animation and intelligence. She came
behind me, put her hands round me, and kissed me in the prettiest
way this evening', Marian wrote, 'telling me she was so glad she
had got me here.'[5] Joined by Henry Atkinson next day, they
trudged about, looking at the model cottages Miss Martineau was
building and enjoying the fine scenery of Windermere and Der-
went Water. 'Miss Evans's visit was a vast pleasure,' she wrote to
Chapman. 'The only drawbacks were wet roads and that she would
not stay longer.'[6] She left 26 October for Coventry to crown her
holiday with a ten-day visit to the trio of 'affectionate and long-
tried friends' there, who always made her feel 'brave for anything
that is to come after'. From Rosehill she wrote to Bessie Parkes

[1] *Letters*, II. 59.   [2] Ibid. 31.
[3] Ibid. 59; Bray, *Autobiography*, p. 71. Bray wrote to Combe, 1 Nov. 1852: 'We are
pleased that your experience of our friend Miss Evans confirms our own . . . her
manners are much improved since she went into the world; they were tinged, I used
to think, with a slight degree of affectation. She speaks with much affection of
both you and Mrs. Combe, and she was pleased with all she heard from you and
did not, as far as I can ascertain, think your speeches at all too long.' (NLS).
[4] Combe Journal, 20 Oct. 1852 (NLS).   [5] *Letters*, II. 62.
[6] H. Martineau to J. Chapman, 29 Oct. [1852] (Yale).

that, being 'extremely comfortable, I am resigned. I have noticed that my resignation always flourishes best in that kind of soil.'[1]

Back once more in the fog of the Strand, her depression returned. 'My room here has the light one might expect midway up a chimney', she told Mr. Combe, 'with a little blaze of fire below, and a little glimmer of sky above.'[2] Her mind was dark, too. What was her life to be? Her thirty-third birthday was drawing near. She needed desperately some one friend to be all in all to her. Spencer, she knew, who came in the day she returned 'and spent the evening with me', could not be that friend. She had been planning to spend Christmas with the Clarkes at Meriden, and looked forward to sharing the warm family affection and the happy laughter of nephews and nieces. But it proved anything but merry. Word came on 20 December that Edward Clarke was dangerously ill; he died the same day. Marian dropped the unfinished proofs of the January *Westminster* to go to Chrissey, who was left with six children, the eldest not yet fifteen years old, the youngest not fifteen months, and with little to support them. Whatever expectations Edward Clarke had from his father's estate, like Chrissey's portion from Robert Evans, had all been anticipated by loans. The sale of the surgical practice and what small possessions were left would bring her an income of about £100 a year—quite inadequate for such a family. Isaac agreed to let her live rent free in the house at Attleborough, once her own, and tried to be kind to her, 'though not in a very large way'. For Isaac took his position as head of the family very seriously. He always had to have things done in his way, which was obviously the best. After a week Chrissey agreed that Marian could do her no substantial good by staying on at Meriden.

Isaac, however, was very indignant to find that I had arranged to leave without consulting him and thereupon flew into a violent passion with me, winding up by saying that he desired I would never 'apply to him for anything whatever'—which, seeing that I have never done so, was almost as superfluous as if I had said that I would never receive a kindness from him.[3]

Marian saw that her duty lay, not in helping with household work, but in earning more money by writing to add to Chrissey's meagre resources.

She returned to the Strand 30 December to shudder over the frightful mistakes in the latter pages of the January number of the

[1] *Letters*, II. 65.   [2] GE to Combe, 13 Nov. 1852 (NLS).   [3] *Letters*, II. 75.

Westminster, which her editorial eye would have caught, and to find herself in the middle of an angry dispute between Combe and Chapman over a book advertisement, accidently omitted. Her headaches recurred more persistently. At the end of January an acute rheumatic pain in the right shoulder sent her to bed for nearly a week; she was glad indeed when Charles Bray appeared 3 February to bear her off again to convalesce at Rosehill. When she felt stronger, she spent a few days with Chrissey, now settled in the overcrowded house at Attleborough, and took 'large doses of romping and doll-dressing' with the children, worrying about how she could help look after them. A well-meant offer by a friend to get some of the little ones admitted to the Infant Orphan Asylum naturally tore Chrissey's heart. 'I think she ought to be provided for without any such measures', Marian wrote.[1] But Isaac's help was far from generous. Was Marian thinking of him when she wrote that the Dodsons would never forsake their inconvenient kin, 'would not let them want bread, but only require them to eat it with bitter herbs'?[2] Another friend, a former patient of Mr. Clarke's, offered to send the eldest son to Australia. Marian recommended accepting; Australia might be a solution to the whole problem. 'What do you think of my going to Australia with Chrissey and all her family?', she asked the Brays in April, '—to settle them and then come back? I am just going to write to her and suggest the idea.' But her sister was not adventurous, and no more was heard of Australia.[3]

My chief trouble is poor Chrissey [Marian wrote to Cara]. Think of her in that ugly small house with six children who are inevitably made naughty by being thrown close together from morning till night. To live with her in that hideous neighbourhood amongst ignorant bigots is impossible to me. It would be moral asphyxia and I had better take the other kind—charcoal myself and leave my money, perhaps more acceptable than my labour and affection. Then I dare not incur the *material* responsibility of taking her away from Isaac's house and its attendant pecuniary advantages. My health might fail and other things might happen to make her, as well as me, regret the change.

Yet how odious it seems that I, who preach self-devotion, should make myself comfortable here while there is a whole family to whom, by renunciation of my egotism I could give almost everything they want. And the work I can do in other directions is so trivial![4]

[1] *Letters* II. 90.   [2] *Mill on the Floss,* Bk. IV, ch. I.
[3] The youngest son Christopher Charles Clarke (1845–1912) went out to Australia in 1864, married in 1867, worked on the railway for a time, and became partner in a tweed mill. His grandchildren still live in Sydney, N.S.W.
[4] *Letters,* II. 97.

In the same letter she spoke of Herbert Spencer's intention of quitting his position as subeditor of *The Economist* to trust to 'article-writing for bread', as his friend Lewes did. 'People are very good to me. Mr. Lewes especially is kind and attentive and has quite won my regard after having a good deal of my vituperation. Like a few other people in the world, he is much better than he seems—a man of heart and conscience wearing a mask of flippancy.'[1] When she first met Lewes, introduced by Chapman at Jeffs's bookshop in the Burlington Arcade 6 October 1851, Marian's impression—as usual—was negative. He was very unattractive looking, short and slightly built, 'a sort of miniature Mirabeau in appearance', she wrote. Perhaps she was recalling Carlyle's description of the 'born king of men . . . through whose shaggy beetle-brows and rough-hewn, seamed, carbuncled face there look natural ugliness, small-pox, incontinence, bankruptcy —and burning fire of genius'.[2] All of these could have been discerned in Lewes by one who knew him well enough. Or was it the Gallic note in his sprightly, vivacious manner? His hands, full of nervous expression, were in constant gesticulation. Born in London, he had lived as a child at Boulogne, gone to school in Jersey and Brittany from the age of eleven until he was sent at thirteen to Dr. Charles Parr Burney's famous seminary at Greenwich. There he acquired a good command of Latin and Greek as well as sound English. His school-days over, he worked (according to Francis Espinasse) 'successively in a notary's office and a Russia [leather] merchant's counting-house, before, having walked the London hospitals for a time [studying medicine], he threw himself into London Literature'.[3] None of his contemporaries was more versatile. By 1850 he had published a popular history of philosophy, two novels, a life of Robespierre, a tragedy in blank verse produced at Manchester, Liverpool, and London, besides scores of successful periodical articles on a wide variety of subjects, which he had been writing since he was seventeen.

Lewes's principal interest in 1852 was the *Leader*, a weekly newspaper, which he and his old friend Thornton Leigh Hunt had founded two years before. Hunt, a journalist all his life, covered the political and general news, while Lewes was responsible for the literary section, reviewing books, theatres, music, and the arts. The *Leader* office in Wellington Street was just round

---

[1] *Letters*, II. 98.
[2] T. Carlyle, *French Revolution*, Bk. IV, ch. 4.
[3] F. Espinasse, *Literary Recollections* (1893), p. 274.

the corner from 142 Strand, where Lewes and his friend Herbert Spencer often dropped in to chat with Marian Evans. On one of these visits, when Spencer rose to leave, Lewes signified that he was going to stay; this, said Spencer, was the beginning of their intimacy.[1] As references to Spencer in Marian's letters dwindle, those to Lewes grow increasingly sympathetic. On 22 November 1852 (her thirty-third birthday) she sat down to work on copy for the *Westminster*, 'thinking that I had two clear hours before dinner—rap at the door—Mr. Lewes—who of course sits talking till the second bell rings'.[2] He came more frequently to the Chapman's evening parties, too, where he was always welcome 'We had a pleasant evening last Wednesday', Marian wrote in March, '—Lewes, as always genial and amusing. He has quite won my liking, in spite of myself.'[3] As reviewer for the *Leader* he of course had the entrée of the theatres and soon began to take Marian with him. A grandson of the famous eighteenth-century comedian Charles Lee Lewes, he himself had acted occasionally and knew all the actors and managers. One evening he took Marian to see Rachel. 'When the drop-scene fell, we walked about and saw the green room and all the dingy, dusty paraphernalia that make up theatrical splendour.'[4] It was a glimpse of a new world. 'Lewes has been quite a pleasant friend to me lately', she told the Brays in April 1853—and then cancelled the sentence and ended her letter abruptly.[5]

Since Lewes had contributed regularly to the *Westminster Review* from 1840 to 1847, Chapman naturally turned to him for articles. Besides his summary of French books in the Contemporary Literature section, Lewes appeared in almost every number during Marian's editorship. She was not always pleased with his articles, which were sometimes less carefully planned and written than suited the high standard she set, but they were always interesting and covered a wide field: Julia von Krüdener, Goethe, Geoffrey St. Hilaire, George Sand, Jane Austen, Charlotte Brontë, Mrs. Gaskell and other 'Lady-novelists', Shelley, Alexander Smith—whatever the subject he could be counted on for intelligent, readable articles. Consultation about them necessarily threw him and Marian together. As she came to know him better, her aversion disappeared. He was certainly one of the ugliest men in London—with an 'immense ugliness', Mrs. Carlyle said in all kindness; she and other friends sometimes referred to him as 'Ape'

---

[1] Spencer to Cross, 13 Jan. 1884 (Yale).   [2] *Letters*, II. 68.
[3] *Letters*, II. 94.   [4] *Letters*, II. 104.   [5] *Letters*, II. 97.

because of his very narrow jaw and wide cheek bones and brow. His face was pale and deeply pock-marked, the nose straight with rather large nostrils, the lips full and red, partly hidden by straggling moustaches. His light-brown curly hair he wore quite long. His eyes, the best feature of his face, were large and dark and highly expressive, but with a sadness in repose oddly at variance with his gay banter. Despite this appearance there was something decidedly appealing about 'little Lewes', as Mrs. Carlyle called him: 'he is the most amusing little fellow in the whole world—if you only look over his unparalleled *impudence*, which is not impudence at all but man-of-genius *bonhomie*. . . . He is the best mimic in the world and full of famous stories, and no spleen or envy or *bad* thing in him.'[1] In any company he quickly attracted a fascinated circle about him and held them in animated discussion of philosophy or science or literature. Even his worst enemy, the spiteful Eliza Lynn Linton, admitted that 'Wherever he went there was always a patch of intellectual sunshine in the room.'[2]

After spending more than a year in Germany 1838–9, supporting himself by giving English lessons and sending articles to the magazines at home, Lewes had been introduced, probably as a tutor, into the family of Swynfen Jervis, M.P., of Darlaston Hall, Chatcull, Staffordshire.[3] He soon fell in love with the eldest daughter Agnes, whom he married at St. Margaret's, Westminster, 18 February 1841; she was nineteen and he, twenty-three. She was given away by her father, who signed the register as witness with Lewes's old friend Dr. Neil Arnott; an even older friend, Leigh Hunt, was among those present. The ceremony was performed by the Rector, the Reverend Henry Hart Milman. The contrast between bride and groom was striking, both in station and appearance. Agnes, a great-niece of the Earl of St. Vincent, was a dazzling beauty, very blonde and with lovely pink cheeks. She was as accomplished as she was beautiful. For several years she augmented their income by translating and adapting articles from the French and Spanish, which Lewes sold to the magazines. He was writing constantly—articles and novels and *A Biographical History of Philosophy* (4 vols., 1845–6), based on a series of lectures first given at W. J. Fox's Finsbury Chapel. They were very happy together. Carlyle recalled how 'They used to come down of an

[1] 5 Feb. 1849. *Jane Welsh Carlyle, Letters to Her Family 1839–1863*, ed. Leonard Huxley (N.Y., 1924), pp. 319–20.
[2] *Bookman*, 3 (1892–3), 522.
[3] Dante Gabriel Rossetti's father had taught Italian at Darlaston; his sister Christina visited the Jervises there in 1852.

evening to us through the lanes from Kensington, and were as merry as two birds.'[1]

The Leweses had four sons: Charles Lee (1842–91), Thornton Arnott (1844–69), Herbert Arthur (1846–75), and St. Vincent Arthy (1848–50). Charles was born at 3 Pembroke Square, Kensington, where they were living with Lewes's mother; Thornton at 2 Campden Hill Terrace, Kensington; and the others close by at 26 Bedford Place, where the Leweses lived 1846–55. I list these addresses because so much nonsense has been written about the 'Phalanstery' at Royal Hill House, Queen's Road, Bayswater, where the Leweses are incorrectly said to have lived in a co-operative household on Fourieresque principles with the Thornton Hunts, the Gliddons, and the Samuel Laurences. Actually, the house, a very large one, later a girls' school, was occupied by Anastasia Laurence's parents, the Arthur Gliddons. Thornton Hunt and his wife Katharine, niece of Mr. Gliddon, lived there with them 1845–9, when they went to live with her father John Gliddon at Broadway House, Hammersmith. So far as I can discover, the Hunts and the Leweses, though they undoubtedly spent much time together, never lived under the same roof.

Swynfen Jervis, a man of artistic interests and advanced views, had brought up his children in a liberal way. Agnes, like Lewes, held the freest ideas about social relations, including that of the sexes, for which his early devotion to Shelley and his bachelor days in Germany and France seem to have provided him practical models. Feelings could not be trammelled by legal bonds or religious sanctions; love would not be constrained; no one was to blame if his affections changed. For the first eight years of their marriage they were blissfully happy, working gaily together and enjoying their growing family. Lewes went several times alone to the Continent: for a month in 1842 (armed with John Stuart Mill's introductions to Comte, Victor Cousin, de Tocqueville, Michelet, and others) to Paris, where he collected material for articles on modern French philosophy and the last chapters of his *History*; in 1845 to Berlin, where he renewed his acquaintance with Varnhagen von Ense and met Boeckh, Schelling, Tieck, Fanny Lewald, Stahr, Bettina Brentano, and others; in 1847 he was again in France, trying (again in vain, it seems) to meet George Sand. In 1849 he was away from home for even longer periods. Between 7 and 24 February he gave a series of six lectures

[1] Note by Mrs. William Allingham (NLS: Acc. 1728.143 [1880]).

on the history of philosophy at the Liverpool Mechanics Institute; most of March and April he spent in Manchester, where in addition to repeating the series of lectures at the Athenæum, he appeared at the Theatre Royal as Shylock and as Don Gomez de la Vega in his own play *The Noble Heart*. The lectures and *The Merchant of Venice* were given again at Edinburgh in November. During these engagements, he made a good many visits to men like Salis Schwabe at Manchester, Rawlings and Holt at Liverpool, and Robert Chambers at Edinburgh, enlisting support for the *Leader*, which he and Thornton Hunt were then planning. On Christmas Day he wrote from Burton Rectory, near Lincoln, the home of the Reverend Edmund Larken, Lord Monson's radical brother-in-law, one of the most generous backers of the new paper. Whether these prolonged absences from home had anything to do with the collapse of his marriage it is impossible to say. Sharp-eyed Mrs. Carlyle had noticed a change between February and April 1849: 'I used to think these Leweses a perfect pair of love-birds', she wrote to her cousin Jeanie Welsh, 'always cuddling together on the same perch—to speak figuratively—but the female love-bird appears to have hopped off to some distance and to be now taking a somewhat critical view of her little shaggy mate!'[1]

The first number of the *Leader* was published 30 March 1850, just one week after the Lewes's youngest son, St. Vincent, died of whooping-cough. Two weeks later, 16 April, Agnes gave birth to a fifth son, whose father was Thornton Hunt. Perhaps acknowledging that he was partly to blame, certainly unwilling to stigmatize the child, Lewes registered him as Edmund Alfred Lewes and treated him exactly like his own boys. There were no recriminations on either side. Agnes had merely followed her feelings; it was a principle they all accepted. Thornton wrote that 'Human beings are born with passions; you will not discipline those passions by ignoring them, and nature always avenges herself by retorting upon the false moralist some depravity as the result of his handiwork.'[2] Lewes shared this view. His review of Mrs. Gaskell's *Ruth* attacked the intensity of grief afflicting little Leonard when he learns that his mother is unmarried:

This language is sheerly impossible. No child would at once realize any such shame, even were it a fact, that illegitimacy in actual life *did* bring

---

[1] *Jane Welsh Carlyle. Letters to Her Family* (1924), p. 329.
[2] 'The Discipline of Art', *Leader*, 3 July 1852, pp. 639–40.

with it disgrace . . .; the least reflection will tell Mrs. Gaskell that in our day no such brand affects the illegitimate child.[1]

In his column in the *Leader*, remarking on a pretended clair-voyante's absurd 'vision' of his family as 'two girls and a tall, pale, dark woman', Lewes declared that it really consists 'of four boys and a human Rose in the shape of their mother'.[2] He continued to live with them all at 26 Bedford Place. He was there on the night of 30 March 1851, when the Census records him as head of the house, married, aged thirty-three, 'author: general litera-ture', born in London; Agnes, his wife, married, aged twenty-eight, also born in London; the four sons, all born in Kensington, Charles and Thornton described as 'scholars'; Martha Baker, nurse, aged thirty-six, 'unmarried servant', born in Brighton; and Annie Bauce, servant, aged twenty-four, 'unmarried general ser-vant', born in Reading.[3]

With Thornton Hunt, Lewes continued to work harmoniously on the *Leader*. But the offence was repeated. Before Agnes bore Hunt a second child, Rose Agnes Lewes, 21 October 1851, Lewes had ceased to regard her as his wife. He still kept on friendly terms with her, however, coming to see her from time to time, writing to her when he was away, and contributing to support her and her illegitimate brood as long as he lived. Today a divorce would have set him free; but then divorce was out of the question. Even if he had had the hundreds of pounds it required for the cumbersome legal process, Lewes, having once condoned her adultery, was forever precluded from appealing for divorce. Eliza Lynn Linton, probably ignorant of the facts, tried to picture 'that faithful and loving man, that loyal and devoted friend, Thornton Hunt' as playing somehow the more honourable part in this curious triangle.[4] She could hardly have known that Hunt, the father of ten children by his own wife and four by Agnes Lewes, had twice had a child by his own wife and one by Agnes born within weeks of each other: Rose Agnes Lewes (21 October 1851) and Bryan Courthope Leigh Hunt (6 January 1852); Ethel Isa-bella Lewes (9 October 1853) and Beatrice Mary Leigh Hunt (16 November 1853). Thornton's connection with Agnes continued as late as 21 May 1857, when Mildred Jane Lewes was born.[5]

---

[1] '*Ruth* and *Villette*', *WR*, 59 (Apr. 1853), 485.
[2] *Leader*, 15 June 1850, p. 258.
[3] Public Record Office: H.O. 107/1468.
[4] Eliza Lynn Linton, *Autobiography of Christopher Kirkland* (3 vols. 1885), I. 278.　　　　　　　　　　　　　　　　　[5] Somerset House.

PLATE VI

AGNES JERVIS LEWES, GEORGE HENRY LEWES,
AND THORNTON LEIGH HUNT *c.* 1844

From a pencil sketch by W. M. Thackeray

By the time Marian Evans came to know Lewes, his home was hopelessly broken up. Though he did not blame Agnes and concealed his chagrin from the world behind a front of flippant banter, he was thoroughly disillusioned with free love. He always thought of this as 'a very dreary *wasted* period of my life. I had given up all ambition whatever, lived from hand to mouth, and thought the evil of each day sufficient.'[1]

Marian, too, for very different reasons, was in a despondent mood, growing increasingly restless at 142 Strand. Though she needed money to help her sister, Chapman's business affairs were in such a parlous state that he could pay her nothing for her work on the *Westminster* except perhaps her board. She longed to be free of the whole affair. George Combe said that he thought the *Review* 'under my management the most important means of enlightenment of a literary nature in existence—the Edinburgh, under Jeffrey, nothing to it etc. etc.!!!'[2] Yet she had to admit that the *Review* 'would be a great deal worse if I were not here'.[3] She told Chapman in March 1853 that she intended to leave after the next number was out; but she soon wrote to Mr. Bray: 'Instead of changing my street, I have changed my room only, and am now installed in Mr. Chapman's. It is very light and pleasant, and I suppose I must be content for a few months longer. Indeed I think I shall never have the energy to move—it seems to be of so little consequence where I am or what I do.'[4] Even the new room did not prevent her from catching cold and a severe cough, which persisted till the Brays again intervened and took her to Rosehill for three weeks in May.

When the July number of the *Review* was finished, Marian went with Sara Hennell and the Chapmans to spend a week-end with Bessie Parkes, Barbara Leigh Smith, and her aunt Miss Julia Smith at Ockley, Surrey. The Combes's invitation to go to Switzerland with them for the whole summer she refused without much deliberation. She was seeing more and more of Lewes. After two weeks at Tunbridge Wells, which she found expensive, she migrated to St. Leonard's, where she lodged first at Spa Cottage on a hill with 'a vast expanse of sea and sky for my only view. . . . The bright weather and genial air—so different from what I have had for a year before—make me feel as happy and stupid as a well-conditioned cow. I sit looking at the sea and the sleepy ships

---

[1] GHL Journal, 28 Jan. 1859.   [2] *Letters*, II. 33.
[3] *Letters*, II. 88.   [4] *Letters*, II. 93.

with a purely animal *bien-être*.[1] There are only slight hints of visits from Lewes during her six weeks at the coast. Her landlord was a German from Saxe-Weimar, who talked to her about *Mr.* Schiller and *Mr.* Goethe. '*Mr.* Goethe is one of my companions here', she told Sara.[2] One wonders whether she was reading Goethe's works or whether his chief English exponent George Henry Lewes may not have been there occasionally, walking on the beach with her in the evening, giving her 'the look and the hand of warm affection' she craved so much. 'This British Channel really looks as blue as the Mediterranean today. What weather!'[3] Some time during the summer Lewes poured out to her the miserable story of his marriage. One can easily imagine how Marian's ready expansiveness would respond with sympathy and affection, which in his cynical, lonely state he must have found more than welcome. Pity is a common step to love.

When Marian returned to London in mid September 1853, she set out at once to find lodgings. By the first week in October she had left the Strand and was established on the ground floor at 21 Cambridge Street, Hyde Park Square. In this house, kept by a Mrs. Pitt, who cooked her excellent little dinners, Marian could receive guests whenever she liked, free from the surveillance of the Chapman household. Oscar Browning believed that this change of address 'marked the commencement of the union with Mr. Lewes'.[4] Though his opinion could be formed only on inference or gossip (he was sixteen at the time), it is probably correct. Lewes was with her almost every day. Her depression lifted; her health improved. 'I am as well as possible', she wrote to Charles Bray, '—and certainly when I put my head into the house in the Strand I feel that I have gained, or rather escaped, a great deal physically by my change.'[5] Again, she wrote to Sara: 'Today is an exceptional day—that is, a fine one. I am hoping for a row (pron. *ro*) on the Serpentine.'[6] Of course, she could not go alone; do we hear in the casual pun the well-known voice of her companion? The same letter quotes a bit of Theodore Parker she had just read in Leigh Hunt's *Religion of the Heart*. On that same day Lewes, at the end of his notice of Hunt's book in the *Leader*, added a curious sentence: 'All we can say is, that a noble and accomplished woman was listening to her husband's reading of the book when we called one evening, and that her eyes were full of tears!'[7] The

---

[1] *Letters*, II. 112.   [2] *Letters*, II. 115.   [3] *Letters*, II. 113.
[4] Oscar Browning, *George Eliot* (1890), p. 37.   [5] *Letters*, II. 123.
[6] Ibid. 120.   [7] *Leader*, 22 Oct. 1853, p. 1024.

adjectives fit Marian well; he would hardly apply them to Agnes, just delivered of her third bastard. Was the caller beginning to think of himself as Marian's husband? Herbert Spencer, home from the Alps, called once or twice in September. It was immediately apparent that Marian's love, which he had rejected a year before, was now valued and fostered by his good friend Lewes. Spencer went again to Rosehill in October to visit the Brays, with whom Marian had been staying for a fortnight. The day after he arrived she returned to Cambridge Street. In the hurry of getting off she left behind 'a small gold brooch on the table in my room with my Father's hair in it'.[1] Freudians, recalling her vision of herself becoming earthly, sensual, and devilish for want of her father's 'purifying, restraining influence', might attach some significance to this slip. A month later she wrote to Sara in reply to her birthday greeting:

I begin this year more happily than I have done most years of my life. 'Notre vraie destinée,' says Comte, 'se compose de *resignation* et *d'activité*'—and I seem more disposed to both than I have ever been before. Let us hope that we shall both get stronger by the year's activity —calmer by its resignation. I know it may be just the contrary—don't suspect me of being a canting optimist. We *may* both find ourselves at the end of the year going faster to the hell of conscious moral and intellectual weakness. Still there is a possibility—even a probability—the other way.[2]

Perhaps the clearest evidence of her involvement with Lewes can be found in the way she helped him with his work. He was more pressed than usual in revising and reading proof of *Comte's Philosophy of the Sciences,* based on his articles in the *Leader* (April–August 1852). He was also working for the actor-manager Charles Mathews, who for nearly two years paid him £10 a week to write and adapt plays for the Lyceum under the pseudonym Slingsby Lawrence. And regularly each Saturday the *Leader* had to appear with his four or five pages headed Literature: reviews of the latest books and plays interspersed with lively comment over his pseudonym Vivian. Even during the summer of 1853, when Marian was at St. Leonard's, some of the articles on those pages seem more like hers than Lewes's. Her remark in a letter to Sara Hennell, 1 October, 'I have promised to do some work tonight and tomorrow for a person who is rather more idle than myself', is explained by Cross as 'Correcting "Leader" proofs for Mr. Lewes.'[3] But, since Marian wrote the letter on Saturday evening

---

[1] *Letters*, II. 120.   [2] *Letters*, II. 127.   [3] Cross, I. 314.

after the *Leader* was already out, her work was probably the review of Theodore Parker's *Theism, Atheism, and the Popular Religion*, with which Chapman had inaugurated his new Quarterly Series—a book more appealing to the Translator of Strauss than to Vivian; it fills nearly half his space for 8 October.

Yet we know that she did read the *Comte* proofs and was zealous in promoting the book on Lewes's account. Chapman had published Harriet Martineau's abridgement of Comte's *Positive Philosophy* a few weeks after Bohn brought out Lewes's book, *Comte's Philosophy of the Sciences*, and though they were very different in scope, reviewers naturally tended to draw comparisons. Marian had tried vainly to get someone to write an article on Comte for the *Westminster Review*; when Alexander Bain, the last hope, refused, the books were left for Huxley to treat in his Science summary, January 1854. As the last proof sheets were going through her hands, Marian wrote to ask Chapman not to send the Huxley article to the printer till he discussed it with her. In it Huxley, after warm praise of Miss Martineau's work, attacked Lewes as a mere 'book scientist' in a contemptuous notice that was not altogether fair. But in spite of Marian's loyal effort, it was too late to make changes, and Lewes's only recourse was a long signed letter in the *Leader* two weeks later, refuting Huxley's charges.

Of course, Lewes was not the only visitor at Marian's new lodgings. Harriet Martineau came to call several times (once bringing with her Mrs. Wills, a sister of Robert Chambers) and invited her to come to Lady Compton's, where she was staying while in London—'This, too, in spite of my having vexed her by introducing Mr. Lewes to her, which I did as a desirable bit of peace-making.'[1] Bessie Parkes, who was preparing another volume of poems, also came, perhaps oftener than Marian found convenient, a few times with Barbara Leigh Smith, who lent some of her water-colours for the new room. Mr. and Mrs. Chapman dropped by occasionally to see their former lodger. Kind Robert Mackay, no longer a bachelor, having married in his fiftieth year, called with his wife to invite Marian to a party, where she met Dr. Neil Arnott, Dr. John Elliotson, and other interesting people.[2] When she stepped across Bayswater to walk in the Park, she sometimes met acquaintances. 'Good Sir James Clark stopped me yesterday as I was sauntering along with eyes on the clouds and made very fatherly inquiries about me, urging me to spend a quiet

[1] *Letters*, II. 122.   [2] Ibid. 126.

evening with him and Lady Clark next week.'[1] At dinner at their house she first saw Arthur Helps: 'Very snug—only he and myself. He is a sleek man with close-snipped hair—has a quiet humourous way of talking, like his books.'[2] She knew that he was one of Lewes's closest friends. By November 1853 she had become an even closer friend; Lewes was the one person she saw constantly.

Besides her regular editorial work for the *Westminster Review* Marian was committed to another task, a translation of Ludwig Feuerbach's *Das Wesen des Christenthums*, which Chapman had advertised 18 June 1853 as 'in preparation' for his new Quarterly Series. The project had been in her mind since July 1851, when Robert Noel came to visit the Brays at Rosehill with Dr. Anton Springer, a Bohemian revolutionist, philosopher, and critic. Both men talked to her about Feuerbach, and Noel lent her a copy of *Das Wesen des Religions* (1845), a shorter book containing some of the fundamental ideas of *Das Wesen des Christenthums*, which he expressed great anxiety to see translated. Chapman, looking for titles to publish in his Quarterly Series, agreed to pay Marian two shillings a page for the translation—a little more than £30— surely not exorbitant wages for such skilled and arduous work. Though Lewes had little interest in religion or metaphysics, he knew about Feuerbach, who was mentioned in his *Biographical History of Philosophy*,[3] and he followed Marian's progress closely.

The powerful appeal the book had for her sprang, not from its bold humanism—'Homo homini deus est'—for she had long been familiar with that, but from Feuerbach's daring conception of love: 'Love is God himself, and apart from it there is no God . . ., not a visionary, imaginary love—no! a real love, a love which has flesh and blood, which vibrates as an almighty force through all living.'[4] She agreed whole-heartedly with Feuerbach's distinction between 'self-interested love' and 'the true human love', which 'impels the sacrifice of self to another'. Such love is, and must always be, particular and limited, finding its expression in the sexual relation, the frankest recognition of the divine in Nature.

But marriage—we mean, of course, marriage as the free bond of love —is sacred in itself, by the very nature of the union which is therein effected. That alone is a religious marriage which is a true marriage, which corresponds to the essence of marriage—of love. . . . Yes, only

---

[1] *Letters*, II. 120.   [2] *Letters*, II. 135–6.
[3] (4 vols., 1846), IV. 235.
[4] Ludwig Feuerbach, *The Essence of Christianity*, tr. Marian Evans (1854), p. 47.

as the free bond of love; for a marriage the bond of which is merely an external restriction, not the voluntary, contented self-restriction of love, in short, a marriage which is not spontaneously concluded, spontaneously willed, self-sufficing, is not a true marriage, and therefore not a truly moral marriage.[1]

How different this impassioned definition is from Herbert Spencer's cold analysis: a mixture of personal beauty, love of approbation gratified, self-esteem, proof of power, and the proprietary feeling with which lovers claim each other as a species of property![2]

When the *Leader* came to Rosehill 15 October 1853, during Marian's visit, there must have been some comment on its announcement of the birth, 9 October, at 26 Bedford Place of a daughter to 'the wife of G. H. Lewes, Esq.' The Brays had long known and liked the Hunts, and had been distressed to see Thornton living so blatantly in 'the category of the reckless'.[3] Knowing what she did of Lewes's generous conduct, Marian must surely have defended him; her sympathy made his troubles her own. As Feuerbach says, 'In feeling man is related to his fellow man as to himself; he is alive to the sorrows, the joys of another as his own . . .; the hand, the kiss, the glance, the voice, the tone, the word' —all impart the same emotion to them both.[4] She had long since penetrated the thin veneer of cynicism beneath which Lewes hid his despair. In reviewing Brough's farce *How to Make Home Happy* he wrote: 'As I have *no* home, and that home is not happy, I really stand in need of his secret.'[5] A week later of a play called *Whitebait at Greenwich* he asked:

What is the subtle link connecting gastronomy with matrimony (right and left-handed),—gulosity with what the French call 'overflowings of the heart'? There *is* such a link. . . . I, not feeling myself capable of gastronomic excellence, have never married. Shakspeare, who knew everything, calls Love, with sad irony,—

> 'A madness most discreet,
> A choking gall, and a *preserving sweet*,'

thereby profoundly, though obscurely, intimating the connexion between love and jam-pots, which our proverbial phrase 'cupboard love' has consecrated.[6]

On the opposite page, facing this (possibly indecent) remark appears the announcement of the birth 16 November 1853, at

---

[1] *Essence of Christianity*, p. 268.   [2] Spencer, *Psychology* (1855), p. 602.
[3] *Letters*, II. 12.   [4] *Essence of Christianity*, p. 277.
[5] *Leader*, 12 Nov. 1853, p. 1099.   [6] *Leader*, 19 Nov. 1853, p. 1124.

12 Bentinck Terrace of a daughter to 'the wife of Thornton Hunt, Esq.' The Hunts, who (says the *DNB*) were descended from one of the oldest settlers in the Barbadoes, had very dark complexions; and Carlyle once referred to Agnes's 'sooty skinned children' by Thornton Hunt.[1] Something of this dusky trait may be read between the lines of the blond Lewes's enigmatic review of Coyne's comedy, *The Hope of the Family*:

> When I was on the Gold Coast I met a boy so very unlike me in general appearance, that had not considerations of geography (and my own strict morals) rendered the belief absurd, I should have believed that there before me stood a son of mine—an indirect heir—an 'accident'—an 'Oat,' in short (that is, on the supposition of my having sown any wild oats!). . . .
> One is always the son of somebody; but, happily, one is not always the father of somebody. I congratulate myself in ranging under that category every time I see my friends revelling in the 'blessings of boys'. . . . But then, as I always say, if men will have sons, why their blood be on their own heads.[2]

'If you went to the Haymarket on Wednesday,' Marian wrote to Charles Bray, 'I hope you didn't carry away the impression that that stupid play—the "Hope of the Family"—was by Slingsby Lawrence.'[3]

While her new lodgings had many other advantages, they made Marian's editorial work for the *Westminster Review* more difficult. Proofs and manuscripts had to be taken to the Strand, there being then no telephone to settle questions that only conferences between the two editors could answer. With the publication of each number she tried to get out from under the burden. Her efforts to mediate between the complaisant Chapman and his authors were growing harder each day. About one problem she wrote to Mr. Combe, 'If I were sole editor I would take the responsibility on myself; but being a woman and something less than half an editor, I do not see how the step you propose could be taken with the naturalness and *bienséance* that could alone favour any good result.'[4] Combe had written a long, hopelessly diffuse article on 'Criminal Legislation and Prison Reform'—through the use of phrenology, of course—which Chapman had given her to edit. As one of the

---

[1] T. Carlyle to John Carlyle, 2 Nov. 1854 (NLS: 516.86).
[2] *Leader*, 10 Dec. 1853, p. 1195.
[3] *Letters*, II. 131.
[4] GE to Combe, 28 Nov. 1853 (NLS).

supporters of the *Review* Combe had to be handled carefully. The article was postponed from January to April 1854 to make room for a more timely one on strikes. Then Combe decided to print it privately as a pamphlet, and Marian had to prepare it for the printer, read the proofs, and send them out to several of his friends. Next, for its appearance in the *Westminster*, which the most tactful hints could not discourage, she had to reduce the ninety-six pages to thirty-six—no easy task with an author so firmly convinced of his literary prowess.

The January number reflected the intelligence Marian brought to it. Among the authors were both James and Harriet Martineau, Huxley, W. B. Donne, W. E. Forster, Froude, and Lewes—a strong list. The April number was almost as good; it had Harriet Martineau, Spencer, Froude, and Huxley, though (despite Marian's best efforts) it was not enhanced by Combe's still-too-long article. The 'Belles Lettres' section was worse than usual. 'How came you to imagine that I did the Belles Lettres in the Westminster?' Marian asked Sara Hennell, 3 June 1854. 'Mrs. Sinnett did them as usual—and she begs Mr. Chapman not to take this work from her at present, as the loss of it would make a serious deficit in her income.'[1] But it was one of the weakest parts of the *Review*, and Chapman had discussed the possibility of Marian's taking it over. 'It would be £16. 16 a quarter,' she told Cara, 'so I think it would be worth groaning over.'[2] This was somewhat more than Chapman paid Huxley, who got only £12. 12s. for articles of the same length on Science.[3]

Chapman's business affairs, inextricably mingled with those of the *Review*, were more desperate than ever. He owed £9,000, including £2,500 he had extracted from his wife's trustees; and as the loans fell due he tried to meet them by getting 'a G or an H to satisfy the claims of E and F'.[4] When he was actually faced with bankruptcy in June 1854, Harriet Martineau, partly to frustrate her brother James's desire to take over the *Westminster*, lent Chapman £500, and with further loans from Samuel Courtauld, Octavius Smith, and others, he paid seven or eight shillings on the pound and was allowed to stay afloat. Faced with these difficulties, Chapman suggested dropping the Quarterly Series.

---

[1] *Letters*, II. 159.   [2] Ibid. 149.
[3] Carlyle wrote to Chapman 18 July 1854, refusing to contribute to the *WR* because the prices paid were '(30 per cent below what I refused to work *under* and always was wont to be paid, 20 years ago, in the *Edinburgh* &c.)' (Yale). When GE began to write the 'Belles Lettres' in July 1855, she was paid £12. 12s.
[4] *Letters*, II. 162.

THE NEED TO BE LOVED 141

At its beginning he had announced *two* books by the Translator of Strauss: Feuerbach's *Essence of Christianity* and an original work, *The Idea of a Future Life*, which Marian had been considering ever since her Coventry days.[1] For this she would need to consult many books. In December 1853 she wrote to Chapman:

> You seem to be oblivious just now of the fact that you have pledged yourself as well as me to the publication of another work besides Feuerbach in your Series. For the completion of the historical part of that work, *books* are indispensable to me. If I could do as I pleased I would much rather become myself a subscriber to the London Library and save both myself and you the trouble of speaking to you on the subject. But as this said work will occupy nearly the whole of next year and as I am to have no money for it—since the 'half profits' are not likely to have any other than a conceptional existence, a 'gedacht-sein'—I don't see how I can possibly go to any expense in the matter.
>
> I bitterly regret that I allowed myself to be associated with your Series, but since I have done so, I am very anxious to fulfil my engagements both to you and the public. It is in this sense that I wish you to publish Feuerbach, and I beg you to understand that I would much rather that you should publish the work and *not* pay me than pay me and not publish it. I don't think you are sufficiently alive to the ignominy of advertising things, especially as part of a subscription series, which never appear. The two requests then which I have to make are first, that you will let me know whether you can, *as a matter of business*, undertake to supply me with the necessary books, and secondly, that you will consider the question of Feuerbach as one which concerns our *honour* first and our pockets after.[2]

It was costing her £9 a month to live in Cambridge Street, a good deal more than in the Strand; but, as she told Charles Bray, 'I have had frequent guests.'[3] 'Spent Christmas Day alone at Cambridge Street', she wrote in the only entry from her Journal that has survived from these years.[4] She was working hard at Feuerbach and pondering her future course with George Lewes. In the new year she went down to Meriden for five days with Chrissey, who was 'anxious about the placing of the boys, and Isaac's ideas on the subject seem to be rather at variance with her hopes. Alas!' Marian wrote to Fanny Houghton, 'I wish I had money enough to give her real help.'[5] Then she spent five days at Rosehill. During this visit she discussed her translation with Sara

---

[1] *Leader*, 18 June 1853, p. 600; *Letters*, III. 95.
[2] *Letters*, II. 130–1.   [3] Ibid. 122.
[4] Cross, I. 319, prints it as the beginning of a letter to Mrs. Bray.
[5] *Letters*, II. 134.

Hennell, who agreed to read the Feuerbach manuscript as she had done with the Strauss. Marian sent it in large batches. Though few of Sara's comments are recorded, she was more sympathetic with Feuerbach's radical views than Marian had feared. 'Your impression of the book exactly corresponds to its effect in Germany', Marian wrote. 'It is considered *the* book of the age there, but Germany and England are *two* countries'; it would not be easy to stir such enthusiasm in England.[1] 'I am too entirely without hope about the book to be sensitive', she wrote. 'The press will do nothing but abuse or ridicule it—which for those who know what " the press " means, as I do, is not of the slightest consequence to one's own view, but must affect a publisher's.'[2] When translating the long Appendix, in which some of Feuerbach's crudest statements occur, even Marian felt qualms about sending it to Sara and pleaded lack of time. She cut carefully from page 438 the concluding sentences of section 7 and dispatched it with her translation:

21 Cambridge St.
Saturday. [29 April 1854]

Dear Sara

I have yet another service to beg of you—a very great one. It is to read as quickly as you can the portion of the appendix which I send you by today's post, and to tell me how far it will be necessary to modify it for the Eng[lish] public. I have written it very rapidly and have translated it quite literally so you have the *raw* Feuerbach—not any of my cooking. I am so far removed from the popular feeling on the subject of which it treats that I cannot trust my own judgment. With the ideas of Feuerbach I everywhere agree, but of course I should, of myself, alter the phraseology considerably. Before I do this however, I want you to tell me what I *must* leave out. Mind, I want to keep in as much as possible. Send it me back as soon as possible, and don't think of the *style* but only of the matter and the crudity of expression. In great haste,

Your ever grateful
Pollian.[3]

Sara advised omitting the last six sentences, which contain such remarks as, 'You can rip the heart out of the body and still be a good Christian—but you must not meddle with the name; only in the name has the modern Christian any correspondence with the old.' Marian accepted her advice.[4] Printing was already under

[1] *Letters*, II. 137.   [2] Ibid. 152.
[3] Ibid. 153.   [4] *Essence of Christianity*, p. 288.

way. Proofs were finished by the first week in June. The advertisements 24 June announced as ready 'In a few days' *Das Wesen des Christenthums* by Ludwig Feuerbach, translated from the second German edition by the Translator of 'Strauss's Life of Jesus'. Perhaps at Lewes's suggestion, on the final proof of the title-page she inserted—for the first and only time—her own name, Marian Evans. The book appeared the second week in July as Number VI of Chapman's Quarterly Series, price 10*s*. 6*d*.

With Feuerbach finished, Marian's headaches and other discomforts lightened a little. But in mid April 'Poor Lewes' fell ill and was forbidden to put pen to paper for a month. His symptoms, which stemmed from a serious neurological disturbance, included intense, burning headaches, toothache, and a terrible singing in his ears that persisted for several years. His doctor sent him off to the country to stay with Arthur Helps at Vernon Hill, near Bishop's Waltham, Hampshire. 'No opera and no fun for me for the next month', Marian wrote to Cara.[1] His familiar pseudonym Vivian was absent from the *Leader*, 15 April to 20 May. Some of the reviews in his Literature columns during these weeks can be safely attributed to Marian Evans. The notice of the recent magazines, for example, dwelt at length on the *Westminster*, of which she had just finished reading proof; and in the review of three trashy novels one hears a note that she was often to sound: 'Although it is quite true that the lady-novelists are, if not the best, among the best, it is equally true that the female pen is capable of writing a very bad novel, when wilful women set their wits that way.'[2] Other friends of Lewes rallied, too. On this same page with Marian's review appeared the first of Spencer's two articles on 'Personal Beauty'! He had not quite recovered from his palpitations, she reported, but was better. When the month was over, Lewes came back and tried to work, but 'His poor head—his only fortune—is not well yet, and he has had the misery of being ennuyé with idleness without perceiving the compensating improvement. Still I hope the good he has been getting has been greater than he has been conscious of.' The doctor pronounced him 'better, but not yet fit for work. However he is obliged to do a little and must content himself with an *approximation* to his doctor's directions.'[3] Within a week he was ordered again to the country, and went off to try Dr. Balbirnie's water cure at Malvern. During the three

[1] *Letters*, II. 151.   [2] *Leader*, 15 Apr. 1854, p. 356.
[3] *Letters*, II. 157-8.

weeks he was there, Marian again loyally helped fill his columns in the *Leader*. The extremely long article 10 June on George Combe's pamphlet, *Criminal Legislation and Prison Discipline*, which she had rewritten and abridged at least twice, was easy material, and the review of Ruskin's Edinburgh lectures on architecture and painting recalled an old interest. The article on Sydney Smith 17 June may be from her pen as well as that on Wilkie Collins the following week. She was a practised hand at journalism now, and could tack together long quotations from books on Transcaucasia or New Zealand to make convincing reviews. We cannot say whether she was paid for these contributions; Lewes's Literary Receipts record his usual stipend of £20 for each month.[1]

Marian's own health was far from good. She felt 'regularly "done up" both in body and mind'. Though terribly out of spirits, she told Sara, 'the pleasantest thought I have is that whatever I may feel affects no one else—happens in a little "island cut off from other lands"'.[2] To Cara Bray, always her most sympathetic friend, she wrote:

My various aches determined themselves into an attack of rheumatism which sent me to bed yesterday; but I am better this morning and, as you see, able to sit up and write. My troubles are purely psychical— self-dissatisfaction and despair of achieving anything worth the doing. I can truly say, they vanish into nothing before any fear for the happiness of those I love. . . . When I spoke of myself as an island, I did not mean that I was so exceptionally. We are all islands—

> 'Each in his hidden sphere of joy or woe,
> Our hermit spirits dwell and roam apart'—

and this seclusion is sometimes the most intensely felt at the very moment your friend is caressing you or consoling you. But this gradually becomes a source of satisfaction instead of repining. When we are young we think our troubles a mighty business—that the world is spread out expressly as a stage for the particular drama of our lives and that we have a right to rant and foam at the mouth if we are crossed. I have done enough of that in my time. But we begin at last to understand that these things are important only to one's own consciousness, which is but as a globule of dew on a rose-leaf that at midday there will be no trace of. This is no high-flown sentimentality, but a simple reflection which I find useful to me every day.[1]

Transitory or not, Marian Evans's consciousness was important to her. She had always put her own integrity before what others might think of her.

---

[1] *Letters*, VII. 372.   [2] Ibid. II 154–5.   [3] Ibid. 155–6.

What should she do? The Chapmans, about to move from the Strand to a house at 43 Blandford Square, urged her to come live with them. Marian considered the plan. At the end of May she wrote:

I have finally decided not to live with the Chapmans. The consideration that determined me was, that I could not feel at liberty to leave them after causing them to make arrangements on my account, and it is quite possible that I may wish to go to the continent or twenty other things. At all events, I like to feel free. Apart from the comfort of being with people who call out some affection there would be no advantage in my living with the C's—at least none that *I* take into account.[1]

For the third time the Combes had invited her to go with them on their summer travels, and she had politely refused. But she was clearly thinking of going somewhere. She had already discussed her plan with John Chapman, and now she argued it at length with Charles Bray, who came by appointment and spent the whole day with her 11 June. They knew her thoroughly. While they could point out the troubles she would bring on herself by living openly with Lewes and the danger she would be exposed to if the connection did not last, they could not say that her course was wrong. At thirty-four her deeply passionate nature had at last found a wholly satisfying love that responded keenly to Lewes's more experienced sexuality. Though far different in intellectual temper, they had vigorous, philosophical minds, lively sense of humour, and romantic sentiments stirred by the same things. Both love and pity prompted their union. With his heavy responsibilities and precarious health, Lewes needed her help, and 'the need of being loved would always subdue her', as it did Maggie Tulliver.[2] No one else would be injured by their living together. Agnes had gone on steadily with Thornton Hunt since their third child was born and had no intention of giving him up. With a settled home Lewes would be able to work better and earn more to support her and her mingled brood. For Marian too it would be an economic advantage. No religious question was involved; all of them were freethinkers, indifferent to ecclesiastical frowns.

But the legal barrier was insurmountable. Though Agnes might be his wife in name only, flagrantly unfaithful, as long as she lived the archaic English law governing divorce would prevent Lewes from marrying anyone else. He paid dearly for his generosity in acknowledging Edmund. To Marian the law that upheld such a vicious relation seemed utterly immoral. In 1848 she had expressed her contempt for Jane Eyre's refusal to become Mr. Rochester's

---

[1] *Letters*, II. 158.   [2] *Mill on the Floss*, Bk. VI, ch. 4.

mistress, to accept his pledge of faith and live as his wife without marriage;[1] she doubtless approved of Jane's initiative in returning to offer herself to the widowed Rochester. In her Commonplace Book Marian noted: 'It is remarkable that Shakspeare's women almost always *make love*, in opposition to the conventional notion of what is fitting for woman. Yet his pictures of women are belauded. Is it so with contemporary dramatists?'[2] Perhaps it was with the contemporary dramatist she knew best, who made a profession of ridiculing conventional notions.

In their writings all the popular mid Victorian novelists, haunted by the canons of the circulating libraries, were sticklers for propriety. The most trifling violation of the sexual code by a Lady Dedlock or Little Em'ly inevitably brought death or banishment; yet in private life, if kept private enough, Dickens's Ellen Ternan might have a very different fate. Today one tends to accept the prudish literary picture for the reality of Victorian morals. Emerson was shocked in 1848 to hear Carlyle and Dickens agree that 'chastity in the male sex was as good as gone in our times, and in England was so rare that they could name all the exceptions'. When Emerson declared that young Americans of good standing and good education, 'go virgins to their nuptial bed, as truly as their brides', Dickens replied that 'incontinence is so much the rule in England that if his own son were particularly chaste, he should be alarmed on his account, as if he could not be in good health'. He added that Leigh Hunt too thought chastity 'indifferent'.[3] Not even Dickens would have yielded women the same liberty. Marian felt strongly about the injustice society displayed, winking at a man who associates with a 'light woman' but refusing to let him form 'a true union with a true and loyal wife'.[4] Her closest friends, Chapman and Charles Bray, keeping their pleasures private, lived as freely as the emancipated in any generation. Chapman's life she knew from her own experience, and she had probably heard gossip about Bray's. Rufa Hennell once confided to Chapman that 'Mrs. Bray is and has been for years decidedly in love with Mr. [Edward] Noel, and that Mr. Bray promotes her wish that Mr. Noel should visit Rosehill as much as possible, and that she in return tries to promote his happiness in any way that his wishes tend. That Miss Mary Hennell [Sara's eldest sister] used to live with the Brays, and that she was the especial object of

---

[1] *Letters*, I. 268.   [2] GE Commonplace Book, No. 25 (Yale).
[3] 25 Apr. 1848. *Journals of R. W. Emerson* (Boston and N.Y., 1912), VII. 441.
[4] Simcox Autobiography, 7 Nov. 1886, fol. 140.

his affections', and so on.[1] Some of it may have been true. Why should people like this think worse of those who chose to live openly and honestly together?

Marian made her last visit to the Brays at Rosehill 17–26 June; for the last time they had tea in the summer-house and lay on the bearskin under the old acacia, talking in the old free way. But she could not find the courage to tell Cara and Sara her decision. They did not like George—did not really know him. In any case, liberal as they were, they would never have approved of this drastic step. For her own good they would have thought her unwise to outlaw herself from society, especially (though they would not have dared say it) with a man as flighty and unprincipled as Lewes. Bray had probably warned her that people like Combe and Sir James Clark would probably cut her; she could not flaunt the code and maintain any social position. But as Marian looked at it, she had no social position to maintain. She lived remote from all her family; her life could have no effect on theirs.

Combe called the day after she returned to London, bringing her the news of his little circle before leaving on his summer journey. In the evening George took her to see *Sunshine through the Clouds*, which he had adapted for Mathews from Madame de Girardin's *La Joie fait peur*, 'a wonderfully original and beautiful piece', Marian wrote, 'which makes one cry rather too much for pleasure'.[2] She was in a flurry of preparation, her anticipation so high that she hardly had time to be annoyed with Sara for having reviewed Feuerbach in the Coventry *Herald* with personal praise of its translator.[3] She depended on Charles to explain to Sara and Cara that she was going abroad with George—as his wife. But while packing up Sara's Hebrew Grammar, Apocryphal Gospels, and a little Titian print to return to her, Marian thought it well to drop a hint: 'I shall soon send you a good bye', she wrote, 'for I am preparing to go to "Labassecour" '—Brussels, to readers of *Villette*.[4] Ten days later it came:

21 Cambridge Street
Wednesday Evening

Dear Friends—all three

I have only time to say good bye and God bless you. Poste Restante, Weimar for the next six weeks, and afterwards Berlin.

Ever your loving and grateful

Marian.[5]

[1] Chapman's Diary, 27 June 1851.   [2] *Letters*, II. 162.
[3] Coventry *Herald*, 7 July 1854, p. 2a.   [4] *Letters*, II. 165.   [5] Ibid. 166.

CHAPTER VI

'SOME ONE TO LEAN UPON'
WEIMAR AND BERLIN

※

Marian said her last good-bye to Cambridge Street on 20 July
1854 and took a hansom cab to St. Katharine's Wharf. Soon after
11 o'clock she found herself on the *Ravensbourne*, a fast new
steamer, 'about ½ an hour earlier than a sensible person would
have been aboard, and in consequence I had 20 minutes of terrible
fear lest something should have delayed G. But before long I saw
his welcome face looking for me over the porter's shoulder and all
was well.'[1] They were soon under way, gliding smoothly down the
Thames. Like Maggie and Stephen Guest aboard the Dutch vessel,
Marian paced up and down the deck, leaning on George's arm.
For months she had been tortured by scruples, fought fiercely
against an overmastering inclination, hesitated, refusing 'to begin
any future with a deliberate consent to what ought not to have
been'. Now she had taken the step. At last she had found some
one to lean upon.

They spent the whole night on deck.

The sunset was lovely but still lovelier the dawn as we were passing
up the Scheldt between 2 and 3 in the morning. The crescent moon,
the stars, the first faint blush of the dawn, reflected in the glassy river,
the dark mass of clouds on the horizon which sent forth flashes of
lightning, and the graceful forms of the boats and sailing vessels painted
in jet black on the reddish glow of the sky and water, made an unfor-
gettable picture. Then the sun rose and lighted up the sleepy shores of
Belgium with their fringe of long grass, their rows of poplars, their
church spires and farm buildings.

'The day was glorious and our passage perfect', she wrote.
'Mr. R. Noel happened to be a fellow passenger.'[2] Robert Ralph

---

[1] GE Journal, 20 July 1854.
[2] GE to John Chapman, 6 Aug. 1854 (Yale).

Noel, the eldest of Lady Byron's Noel cousins, lived on the estate
she had given him at Teschen, Bohemia, painting a little, translating a little, writing a little on history, on geology, on art, on
phrenology. Phrenology brought him sometimes to visit the Brays
at Coventry; indeed, he had just spent the week-end of 7–9 July
with them; though they had talked about Marian and her Feuerbach, they said nothing about her plan to go abroad. Noel, who
was married to a German baroness, held continental views on the
relation of the sexes. As Marian once remarked to Sara Hennell,
he was a man 'of large experience of life, especially among distinguished people and in remarkable places'[1]—which had included, it was said, an affair with Goethe's daughter-in-law
Ottilie.[2] From him, even if it were possible, Marian felt no need to
conceal their relations. Noel was able to give them helpful information about Weimar, where they were going to live for some
months while George collected material for the life of Goethe he
had worked at sporadically for ten years. At Antwerp Noel said
good-bye and, heading towards Bonn, left them with all good
wishes for a happy journey. They had found him 'a very pleasant
companion'. When writing to his English friends, however—the
Brays, the Leigh Smiths, Mrs. Jameson—he doubtless mentioned
the chance encounter. Rumour would soon be blowing the news
about.

After the 'usual ennui of having our boxes inspected', they
were safely lodged in the Hôtel du Rhein, a comfortable German
house close by on the Quai Van Dyck. They took a long rest,
walked out to find the Cathedral, duly admired the paintings by
Rubens, and passed through the Place Verte to look at his statue;
then, 'feeling we had our fill of beauty', went home to dine. In
the evening they took another walk by the royal palace 'under the
calm light of a lovely evening sky', and having arrived too late
to see the zoological gardens, 'went home to our pleasant room,
from which we could enjoy the evening red melting away over the
Scheldt and its shipping, the breaking out of the stars, and the
itinerant concerts which were delighting the groups of people
below us'.

There was no end to the hot dry weather. After a second day
of sightseeing at Antwerp they spent three more in Brussels in
much the same way. In the morning they took long rambles to
the Park or the Basse Ville, where the reminiscences of *Villette*

[1] *Letters*, II. 144.
[2] *Anna Jameson. Letters and Friendships*, ed. S. Erskine (1915), p. 109.

were most vivid, returning with 'aching legs and melting bodies' to lie on their beds through the middle of the day; again in the evening they wandered out to watch the sun set behind the spire of the Hôtel de Ville (which reminded Marian of the Scott monument at Edinburgh) and to hear a concert in the Park. On 27 July the rain came. They rose at five and went by railway through Namur to Liège, where they stayed at the Hôtel de l'Europe. Having 'had our tea in my bedroom', they spent the evening wandering about the town 'in a state of rapture' at the beauty of rich green foliage and picturesque houses set in the amphitheatre of wooded hills—'everything we saw was beautiful'. Liège was so charming that they decided to stay a second night. The unusually heightened tone in which Marian describes it implies a strong undercurrent of emotion. The church of St. Jacques was 'perhaps the finest thing we have seen on our journey, . . . all is harmony, and we sat for half an hour wrapt in delicious contemplation. . . . Next to this delight came the Palais de Justice', followed by a long drive through the town in an open carriage for a view from the Casino. In the evening, after going again to St. Jacques to hear the organ, 'we had another drive and then a farewell walk to our beloved Palais de Justice and to the Quay'.

The day's delay brought them a second chance encounter with an old friend. They set off on the nine o'clock train for Cologne, and at Vervier, who should appear on the platform but Dr. Brabant! He joined them in their carriage and talked incessantly all the way to Cologne. As they passed through town in the omnibus on the way to the Hôtel de Hollande, where she and George were to stay, Marian thought it looked very dismal. But there was a further surprise in store for her. 'After dinner Dr. Brabant called to tell us that Strauss was residing in Cologne and would receive us the next morning at 9.' Perhaps this unexpected prospect darkened still further her drab impression of Cologne, though later, when she and George rambled about alone, it 'looked more endurable by the soft evening light'. On returning to the hotel they found busy Dr. Brabant back again with the news that 'Strauss would *call on us* in the morning'. While they were breakfasting in the public room, he and Dr. Brabant joined them.[1] Though she knew German thoroughly, Marian had had little practice in speaking it; one imagines that Lewes and Dr. Brabant did most of the talking. Strauss looked 'worn and saddened', Marian told

[1] GE Journal, 29–30 July 1854.

Chapman, 'and gives one the impression of a man for whom life has lost all charm'.[1] To Charles Bray she confessed, 'It was rather melancholy. Strauss looks so strange and cast-down, and my deficient German prevented us from learning more of each other than our exterior, which in the case of both would have been better left to imagination.'[2] The interview was hardly a success. Marian had never whole-heartedly accepted Strauss's narrow intellectual approach—she had been 'Strauss-sick' while translating the account of the crucifixion. And Strauss's uneasiness with her may have come partly from his knowing that the fourth edition of *Das Leben Jesu*, which she had used, contained the most extreme statement of his position, incorporating the violent expression of feeling provoked by attacks of the orthodox, but few of the concessions with which he had mitigated it in the earlier editions. His views were now much altered. Both Strauss and Marian must have felt uncertain, uncomfortable, and relieved when the brief meeting was ended by their having to catch the steamboat up the Rhine to Coblenz. Even there she did not recover the romantic mood of Liège; though the view of Ehrenbreitstein from their windows at the Trois Suisses made a fine picture and their waiter's 'affectionate manners' were amusing, she was most impressed by the number of deformed people they saw in Coblenz. The voyage to Mainz next day was more satisfactory; the views from the steamer 'seemed to me really to deserve Byron's praise'. But as they landed it began to rain hard again, and they were soon driven back to the waiting-room at the railway station, where Marian spent her time admiring the 'prim architectural bouquets on the table and getting by heart the German faces about us', until the train left.

At Frankfurt they put up at the Weidenbusch near the house where Goethe was born. They went twice to the Goethe house, Lewes making notes for the biography, studied Schwanthaler's statue of him in the Goetheplatz and Marchesi's at the Library, and walked to the Judengasse, 'a striking scene', which impressed itself so strongly on her memory that she returned twenty years later to study it as the setting for Daniel Deronda's encounter with Joseph Kalonymos. Marian's *naïveté* in the arts comes out embarrassingly in her extravagant admiration of the Düsseldorf paintings at the Städel Museum: 'the one thing never to be forgotten was Hübner's picture of Job and his Friends. Lessing's pictures—Ezzelin in Prison and Huss before the Council of Constance are meritorious but not thrilling. We unfortunately missed

---

[1] GE to J. Chapman, 6 Aug. 1854 (Yale).   [2] *Letters*, II. 171.

Overbeck's picture of Christianity Triumphing over the Arts.'[1]
Such subjects she could recall humorously in *Middlemarch*, when
she had young Naumann paint Mr. Casaubon as Thomas Aquinas
—'a deep, subtle sort of thinker with his forefinger on the page',
Mr. Brooke says, 'while St. Bonaventure or somebody else, rather
fat and florid, is looking up at the Trinity. Everything is symbolical, you know,—the higher style of art.'[2] Next morning in a heavy
rain they went to the garden of the banker von Bethmann's house
to see Dannecker's Ariadne Seated on a Panther. 'I never saw
any sculpture equal to this—the feeling it excites is the essence of
true worship—a bowing of the soul before power creating beauty.'
At five o'clock the train left for Weimar. The second-class carriage
was so comfortable that the first half of the long journey was
delightful. They had a splendid view of Marburg in the setting sun.
But when dark came, the confinement grew 'tiring and leg-achy'.

Their arrival is described in her 'Recollections of Weimar':[3]

It was between 3 and 4 o'clock on a fine August morning (the 2d)
that after a ten-hours' journey from Frankfurt I woke up at the Bahn-
hof of Weimar. No tipsiness can be more dead to all appeals than that
which comes from fitful draughts of sleep on a railway journey by
night. To the disgust of your wakeful companion, who has been smiling
in envious pity upon you as you have stared wildly around at every
stoppage of the train and then instantly sunk into dreamland again,
you are totally insensible to the existence of your umbrella and to the
fact that your carpet bag is stowed under your seat or that you have
borrowed his books and have tucked them behind the cushion. 'What's
the odds so long as one can sleep?' is your '*formule de la vie*', and it is
not till you have begun to shiver on the platform in the cool morning
air that you are alive to propriety and [reality] and to the further necessity of keeping a firm grip upon it.

Such was my condition when I reached the station at Weimar. The
ride from thence to the town thoroughly aroused me and as usual by
the time I got into a bed room I had no longer any desire for bed.
The glimpse of the town which this ride gave me was in striking contrast with my pre-conceptions. The lines of houses looked rough and
straggling and were often interrupted by trees peeping out from bits of
garden. At last we stopped before the Erb-prinz, an inn of long standing in the heart of the town, and after some delay through the dreamy
doubts of the porter whether we could have rooms before the 'Herr-
schaft' had departed, we found ourselves following him along heavy-
looking corridors and at length were ushered into rooms which

---

[1] GE Journal, 1 Aug. 1854.   [2] *Middlemarch*, ch. 34.
[3] Written at the back of GE Journal.

overlooked a garden for all the world like one you may see in many an English village at the back of a farm house.

The beds were tolerable. By nine o'clock they had slept away their fatigue, and, after breakfasting, walked out in search of lodgings. Their idea of Weimar had come from reading about Goethe. They found it

more like a market town than the precinct of a court. And this is the 'Athens of the north,' we said. Materially speaking it is more like Sparta. The blending of rustic and civic life, the indications of a central government with those of drinking and smoking subjects has some analogy with the condition of old Lacedemon. . . . One's first feeling is: How could Goethe live here, in this dull, lifeless village?

It deserved the caricature in Thackeray's Pumpernickel.

They soon found lodgings at 62a Kaufgasse with Frau Münderloh, at the modest rent of nine thalers a month, and arranged to take their meals at the Erb-prinz table d'hôte. The Germans, Marian thought, excel the English in their cooking, being 'bolder and more imaginative in their combinations of sauces, fruits, and vegetables with animal food. But their meat bears almost the same relation to ours as cat and horseflesh do to theirs.' To the country girl from Warwickshire, a

melancholy sight is a flock of Weimarian sheep, followed or led by their shepherd. They are as dingy as London sheep and far more skinny. Some one who dined with us said the sight of the sheep had set him against mutton, and we resolutely refused it whenever it was brought to table, which however it very rarely was. But the variety of dishes they afford to give one at 10 groschen a head is something marvellous.

Their total expense, including wine and washing, was only £2. 6s. per week. Frau Münderloh, the widow of a confectioner, Marian described as 'a tall fat woman between 50 and 60, with a rudimentary nose and mouth looking like accidental inequalities on a large hemisphere of fat' and talk 'as monotonous as the sound of a Jew's harp'. Their sitting-room was long and narrow, 'like a room cut out of a wall', with four windows along the street, and two doors, one leading to the hall, the other to their bedroom. 'Our servant Lora (short for Leonora) was an inexhaustible joke to us. A little goitrous woman, capless of course, first cousin to Thackeray's "inhabitant of the Rhine country" in his *Kickleburys*.'

After a day or two George called on Gustav Schöll, Director of the Art Institute, to whom Strauss had given him a letter of introduction. Schöll, returning his call the same afternoon, took them both to the Schloss to show them the Dichter Zimmer in the west wing, decorated with scenes from the works of Goethe, Wieland, and Schiller. He proved a valuable friend in Weimar. An Austrian, hearty and cordial, with none of the Thuringian heaviness, Schöll had begun with teaching theology, till, under Strauss's influence, he gave up his professorship at Halle and turned to mythology and the history of art. He was well liked at Court, and had a wide circle of friends in the town; to know him and his excellent wife was to know the 'right people' of Weimar. Every visiting scholar and artist came sooner or later to their house in the Schiller-strasse. He had edited letters and essays of Goethe. Marian found him genial and unaffected—full of accurate knowledge on all literary and philosophical subjects. Through Schöll they met the family of Hermann Sauppe, Principal of the Gymnasium, who looked like a shoemaker but was a real Gelehrter, the editor of a series of classical texts. The Schölls and the Sauppes went with them at the end of August to Tiefurt, where they saw the 'queer little Schloss which used to be Amalia's residence' and was now crowded with the Duke Karl Friedrich's collections of engravings and rococo wares. Years later Marian recalled the excursion—'my own want of appreciation for the Sauer-milch, my bungling attempt to speak German, the thunderstorm, the tiny rooms, and the entertainment Professor Sauppe gave us by reading aloud "Das neueste von Plundersweilern".'[1]

There were a number of other residents of Weimar who proved agreeable acquaintances. Thomas Wilson, who had lost his faith when a curate at Norwich and resigned a professorship of geography at Bedford College after his orthodoxy was questioned, was now teaching at a girl's school in Weimar, married to a German lady and living near the town in a manor house given them by the Duke. There Wilson introduced Lewes to old Eckermann—'interesting to look at though shattered in mind and body', she wrote.[2] They were taken to call on Eckermann again by James Marshall, the Duchess's private secretary, a Scot, who often came by the Kaufgasse to walk with them.

But the most fascinating acquaintance they made at Weimar was Franz Liszt, Director of the Court Theatre and since 1848 the Duke's Kapellmeister—a position held in the eighteenth

---

[1] GE to Hedwig Sauppe, 22 Jan. 1864.
[2] GE Journal, 29 Sept., 8 Oct. 1854.

century by J. S. Bach. Liszt had been followed to Weimar by the Princess Caroline Sayn-Wittgenstein, whose husband, after many years of ignoring the liaison, was about to divorce her. They were now living openly together at the Altenburg in the Park across the Ilm. Lewes, who had known Liszt at Vienna in 1839, called on him on 9 August. The next day at half-past ten Liszt returned the call, and after chatting pleasantly for some time, invited George and Marian to breakfast.

On arriving at the Altenburg we were shewn into the garden, where in a saloon formed by overarching trees, the déjeûner was set out. We found Hoffmann von Fallersleben, the lyric poet, Dr. Schade, a Gelehr-ter who has distinguished himself by a critical work on the 11,000 virgins (!), and a Herr Cornelius, an agreeable looking artist. Presently came a Herr or Doctor Raff, a musician who has recently published a volume called Wagnerfrage. Soon after we were joined by Liszt and the Princess Marie, an elegant, gentle looking girl of 17, and last, by the Princess Wittgenstein with her nephew Prince Eugène and a young French (or Swiss?) artist, a pupil of Scheffer.

The appearance of the Princess rather startled me at first. I had expected to see a tall distinguished looking woman, if not a beautiful one. But she is short and unbecomingly endowed with embonpoint; at the first glance the face is not pleasing, and the profile especially is harsh and barbarian, but the dark, bright hair and eyes give the idea of vivacity and strength. Her teeth, unhappily, are blackish too. She was tastefully dressed in a morning robe of some semi-transparent white material lined with orange-colour, which formed the bordering, and ornamented the sleeves, a black lace jacket, and a piquant cap set on the summit of her comb, and trimmed with violet colour.

The breakfast was not sumptuous either as to the food or the appoint-ments. When the cigars came, Hoffmann was requested to read some of his poetry, and he gave us a bacchanalian poem with great spirit. I sat between Liszt and Miss Anderson, the Princess Marie's governess, an amiable but insignificant person. G. sat next the Princess and talked with her about Goethe, whom she pronounced to have been an egotist. My great delight was to watch Liszt and observe the sweetness of his expression. Genius, benevolence and tenderness beam from his whole countenance, and his manners are in perfect harmony with it. A little rain sent us into the house, and when we were seated in an elegant little drawing room, opening into a large music-salon, we had more reading from Hoffmann, and from the French artist who with a tremu-lous voice pitched in a minor key, read us some rather pretty senti-mentalities of his own.

Then came the thing I had longed for—Liszt's playing. I sat near him so that I could see both his hands and face. For the first time in my life I beheld real inspiration—for the first time I heard the true tones of the piano. He played one of his own compositions—one of a series of religious *fantaisies*. There was nothing strange or excessive about his manner. His manipulation of the instrument was quiet and easy, and his face was simply grand—the lips compressed and the head thrown a little backward. When the music expressed quiet rapture or devotion a sweet smile flitted over his features: when it was triumphant the nostrils dilated. There was nothing petty or egoistic to mar the picture. Why did not Scheffer paint him thus instead of representing him as one of the three Magi?[1]

They were soon on intimate terms with Liszt, meeting him every few days. He would drop in and chat for an hour, or, after dining with them at the Erb-prinz, come home to take coffee in the Kaufgasse, talking late into the evening. Once he introduced a young Russian composer named Anton Rubinstein,[2] whose opera *The Siberian Huntsmen* he was preparing to produce at the Theatre. There he also presented a number of Wagner's operas, some for the first time. Marian heard *Lohengrin, Der Fliegende Holländer*, and *Tannhäuser*. George, she wrote,

had not the patience to sit out more than two acts of Lohengrin, and indeed I too was weary. The declamation appeared to be monotonous, and situations in themselves trivial or disagreeable were dwelt on fatiguingly. . . . With the Fliegende Holländer I was delighted—the poem and the music were alike charming. The Tannhäuser too created in me a great desire to hear it again. Many of the situations and much of the music struck me as remarkably fine. And I appreciated these operas all the better retrospectively, when we saw Der Freischutz, which I had never before heard and seen on the stage. The effect of the delicious music with which one is so familiar was completely spoiled by the lack of recitative and the terrible *lapsus* from melody to ordinary speech. . . . The only other opera we heard was Flotow's Martha, or the Markt von Richmond, a collection of shreds and patches, the patch oftenest repeated being the Last Rose of Summer. . . . G. had the fidgets that evening and longed to turn out, so we went through the rain and paid four shillings to hear this trash. I told him to console himself by regarding the 4s. as an insurance against Flotow for the future.

The Princess too was very kind, inviting them to her evening parties, where they might hear Liszt play a new Prelude or demonstrate the instrument, half-organ and half-piano, he had constructed for himself. There they might watch Hermann the conjurer, or listen to Clara Schumann—'a melancholy, interesting creature', Marian noted in her journal. 'Her husband went mad a year ago, and she has to support eight children.'[1] The French Ambassador the Marquis de Ferrière was often there, 'a very favourable specimen of a Frenchman, but intensely French', whose genial face and perfect good humour 'gave one the same sort of bien-être as a well stuffed arm-chair and a warm hearthrug'. Though 'an awful old maid' Fräulein Becker was generally to be seen, one hears more of the gentlemen than the ladies at these parties; Liszt was somewhat out of favour with the Court since he had left the Erb-prinz to move into the Princess's house. Her property in Russia had been confiscated after she refused to return to the Prince. But Liszt was wealthy and indifferent to the snub.

Lewes was working hard on his *Goethe*. He rewrote the whole first half of the book, in which he had originally depended largely on the *Wahrheit und Dichtung*, now treating it as only one of the sources. The few biographical studies done by the Germans had used mostly printed materials, and the superiority of Lewes's book lay in his inclusion of so much primary information drawn from letters and from people who had known Goethe. Lewes interviewed everyone he could find who had seen the poet. His daughter-in-law Ottilie gave him permission to see Goethe's study and bedroom, which were not open to the public; Lewes described them carefully.[2] He got little out of his conversations with Eckermann, who was in the last few months of his life, his mind failing fast. Besides, like Kräuter, Goethe's last secretary, who was more helpful, Eckermann had known the poet only in old age. Frau Riemer gave him some interesting particulars about Minna Herzlieb, which threw light on the experience Goethe says he deposited 'as in a burial urn' in the *Wahlverwandtschaften*. And Lewes also talked with another old lady of the Court, who was only sixteen when Goethe came to Weimar, a lady so old that she was, as Liszt said, 'presque monumentale'.[3]

Lewes had other work to do as well. The *Goethe* could bring him nothing for another year; meanwhile, he had to find money to support Agnes and her six children in Bedford Place. Though the burning sensation in his head still troubled him, he somehow wrote enough to keep his columns for the *Leader* filled through August and September, the £20 earned each month being paid to Agnes. He got £50 for adapting a French farce for Wigan at the Olympic.

[1] GE Journal, 28 Oct. 1854.
[2] *Life and Works of Goethe* (2 vols., 1855), II. 178–9.
[3] *Letters*, II. 180.

Marian too had to count her pennies. She had been right in believing that the Feuerbach translation would bring her nothing beyond the £30 Chapman paid her before she left London. The reviewers, as she anticipated, were either violently hostile or, like the *Leader*, ignored the book entirely. She was living on £50 Charles Bray advanced against her half-yearly income, which Isaac would not pay her till December. She was more than glad therefore to have a letter from Chapman on 5 August—her first letter since leaving England—proposing that she or Lewes write an article for the *Westminster* on Victor Cousin's *Madame de Sablé*. The postmaster at first refused to give her the letter without seeing her passport, 'and when at last I did get it, I opened it with all sorts of grateful, affectionate feelings towards you for having written to me so soon'.

On reading your letter we determined to get Cousin's book and to unite it with several others as a subject for an article *by me* on 'French Writers on Women.' Do you approve of this? If so, I will endeavour to send you the MSS. early in September. I happen to have the material at hand to make such an article piquant and fresh, which are perhaps the qualities likely to be most welcome to you. (Tell me what space you want filled). . . . When we are at Berlin I shall be able to get Kingsley's works, without which an article on them might be like themselves, more imaginative than solid. You know, I have not been an industrious writer, otherwise I might by this time have been adept enough to criticise a man's works not only without having them at hand, but without having seen them.[1]

Her article entitled 'Woman in France: Madame de Sablé' was finished by the end of August; at Lewes's suggestion she revised the earlier portion, which needed to be expanded a bit, and sent it off to London on 8 September. It begins with a protest against believing that 'there is no sex in literature'. Woman under any social condition will necessarily have sensations and emotions— the maternal ones—that remain unknown to man. In the light of the future of George Eliot it is amusing to read that only in France have women had 'a vital influence on the development of literature'. One reason for this, she thought, was 'probably the laxity of opinion and practice with regard to the marriage tie'.

Heaven forbid that we should enter on a defence of French morals, most of all in relation to marriage! But it is undeniable, that unions formed in the maturity of thought and feeling, and grounded only on

[1] GE to J. Chapman, 6 Aug. 1854 (Yale).

inherent fitness and mutual attraction, tended to bring women into more intelligent sympathy with men, and to heighten and complicate their share in the political drama. The quiescence and security of the conjugal relation are doubtless favourable to the manifestation of the highest qualities . . ., but barely foster a passion sufficient to rouse all the faculties to aid in winning or retaining its beloved object—to convert indolence into activity, indifference into ardent partisanship, dulness into perspicuity. Gallantry and intrigue are sorry enough things in themselves, but they certainly serve better to arouse the dormant faculties of women than embroidery and domestic drudgery. . . . The dreamy and fantastic girl was awakened to reality by the experience of wifehood and maternity, and became capable of loving, not a mere phantom of her own imagination, but a living man, struggling with the hatreds and rivalries of the political arena. . . . Madame de Sablé was not a genius, not a heroine, but a woman whom men could more than love—whom they could make their friend, confidante, and counsellor; the sharer not of their joys and sorrows only, but of their ideas and aims.[1]

It is a bright, readable article, of which Lewes and Sara Hennell both thought highly. But Marian feared that Chapman 'did not approve it, as he has said no word of satisfaction about it, and though he had been urgent on me to write for the Review before, he has made no proposition to that effect since'.[2] Still, he paid her £15 for it, sending the bills, torn in half, by two separate posts. This made a welcome addition to their slender store, which was now so reduced that they had decided to forgo the visit to Dresden. Another scrap of work Marian found in translating and abridging a long article Liszt had recently published on Meyerbeer and Wagner, which Lewes sent with some dissenting preliminary comment to the *Leader*; it appeared as 'The Romantic School of Music'.[3]

She had never been so happy. 'I have had a month of exquisite enjoyment, and seem to have begun life afresh', she wrote to Charles Bray. 'I am really strong and well and have recovered the power of learning in spite of age and grey hairs.'[4] To John Chapman she was even more specific: 'I am happier every day and find my domesticity more and more delightful and beneficial to me. Affection, respect, and intellectual sympathy deepen, and for the first time in my life I can say to the moments, "Verweilen sie, sie sind so schön".'[5] When she wrote that 'Any London news will

---

[1] *WR*, 62 (Oct. 1854), 449, 451–2, 472.
[2] *Letters*, II. 188.
[3] *Leader*, 28 Oct. 1854, pp. 1027–8.
[4] *Letters*, II. 170–1.
[5] Ibid. 173.

be welcome',[1] she had no idea what ugly stories were going round town about her. A passage in the *Goethe*, which Lewes may have been writing about that time, speaks feelingly of how 'a rumour, originating perhaps in thoughtless ignorance, circulated by relentless malice, gains credence in the face of evidence, which no amount of evidence suffices to dissipate'.[2] An example is found in a letter from Thomas Woolner, the sculptor, to William Bell Scott, 4 October [1854]:

By the way—have you heard of a—of two blackguard literary fellows, Lewes and Thornton Hunt? They seem to have used wives on the ancient Briton practice of having them in common: now blackguard Lewes has bolted with a —— and is living in Germany with her. I believe it dangerous to write facts of anyone nowadays so I will not any further lift the mantle and display the filthy contaminations of these hideous satyrs and smirking moralists—these workers in the Agepemone—these Mormonites in another name—stink pots of humanity.[3]

Woolner could not have known that Scott was one of Lewes's old friends. To Weimar news of the rumours came from an even older friend, Thomas Carlyle. Lewes's Journal begins with 24 July 1856, the earlier volumes, of which there were nine, having been destroyed; so we have only Marian's brief note for 11 October: 'A painful letter from London caused us both a bad night.' Lewes replied on the 13th, 'explaining his position. The rain continued all day.' Though that letter too has disappeared, its envelope endorsed 'G. H. Lewes and "Strong minded Woman"' gives some hint of its impression on Carlyle. His reply, however, is noted in Marian's Journal on 19 October 1854 as 'a letter of noble sympathy from Carlyle', which George sat down at once to acknowledge:

Weimar Thursday night.
My dear Carlyle

Your letter has been with me half an hour and I have not yet recovered the *shock*—delightful shock—it gave me. One must have been, like me, long misjudged and harshly judged without power of explanation, to understand the feelings which such a letter creates. My heart yearned towards you as I read it. It has given me new courage. I sat at your feet when my mind was first awakening; I have honored and loved you ever since both as teacher and friend, and *now* to find that you judge me rightly, and are not estranged by what has estranged so many from me, gives me strength to bear what yet must be borne!

[1] GE to J. Chapman, 6 Aug. 1854 (Yale).
[2] *Goethe*, I. 410.
[3] *Letters*, II. 175–6.

So much in gratitude. Now for justice: On my *word of honor* there is no foundation for the scandal as it runs. My separation was in nowise caused by the lady named, nor by any other lady. It has always been imminent, always *threatened*, but never before carried out, because of those assailing pangs of anticipation which would not let me carry resolution into fact. At various epochs I have explicitly declared that unless a change took place I would not hold out. At last—and this more because some circumstances into which I do [not] wish to enter, happened to occur at a time when I was hypochondriacal and hopeless about myself, fearing lest a chronic disease would disable me from undertaking such responsibilities as those previously borne—at last, I say, the crisis came. But believe me the lady named had not only *nothing* whatever to do with it but was, I solemnly declare, ignorant of my own state of mind on the subject. She knew the previous state of things, as indeed others knew it, but that is all.

Then as to the 'letter to Miss Martineau'—not only is she totally incapable of anything she justly considers so foolish and unworthy; but in fact she has *not* written to Miss Martineau at all—has had no communication with her for twelve months—has sent no message to her, or any one else—in short this letter is a pure, or impure, fabrication —the letter, the purport, the language, all fiction. And I shall feel doubly bound to you if you will, on all occasions, clear the lady from such unworthy aspersions and not allow her to be placed in so totally false a position.

Thus far I give you a solemn denial of the scandal. Where gossip affects a point of honor or principle I feel bound to meet it with denial; on all private matters my only answer is *silence*. . . .

With kindest regards to your wife, Believe me, dear Carlyle,

Your very grateful

G. H. Lewes.[1]

The sage of Chelsea shook his head as he added at the bottom of Lewes's letter: 'Alas, alas!—I had (at his request) approved unequivocally of parting *such a marriage*; and advised to contradict, if he could, on his word of honour, the bad rumours circulating about a certain "strong minded woman" and him. He assures me, on his word of honour, the strong minded did not *write* etc.: as well assure me her stockings are both of one colour; that is a very insignificant point!—No answer to this second letter.'[2]

Marian, too, was hearing the rumours. When she wrote to Chapman about payment for her *Westminster* article she said:

I am sorry that you are annoyed with questions about me. Do whatever seems likely to free you from such importunities. About my own

[1] *Letters*, II. 176–8.   [2] Parrish Collection, Princeton.

justification I am entirely indifferent. But there is a report concerning Mr. Lewes which I must beg you to contradict whenever it is mentioned to you. It is, 'that he has run away from his wife and family.' This is so far from being true that he is in constant correspondence with his wife and is providing for her to the best of his power, while no man can be more nervously anxious than he about the future welfare of his children. The letters he has received from Mrs. Lewes since he has been away, as well as those which he has written to her, have confirmed everything he has told me about their past history and proved to me that his conduct as a husband has been in the highest degree noble and self-sacrificing. Since we have been here, circumstances (in which I am not concerned) have led to his determining on a separation, but he has never contemplated withdrawing the most watchful care over his wife and the utmost efforts for his children.

We have been told of a silly story about a 'message' sent by me 'in a letter to Miss Martineau' which letter has been shown at the Reform Club. It is hardly necessary to tell you that I have had no communication with Miss Martineau, and that if I had, she is one of the last persons to whom I should speak as to a confidante. The phrase 'run away' as applied to me is simply amusing—I wonder what I had to run away from. But as applied to Mr. Lewes it is more serious, and I have thought it right to explain to you how utterly false it is. You are in possession of the broad facts of the case, but there are very many particulars which you do *not* know and which are perhaps necessary to set his character and conduct in their true light. Such particulars cannot be given in a letter. He has written to Carlyle and to Robert Chambers, stating as much of the truth as he can without too severely inculpating others. Helps already knew, and his sympathy was a great comfort when he passed through Weimar.[1]

You ask me to tell you what reply you shall give to inquiries. I have nothing to deny or to conceal. I have done nothing with which any person has a right to interfere. I have surely full liberty to travel in Germany, and to travel with Mr. Lewes. No one here seems to find it at all scandalous that we should be together. Mr. Wilson and Mr. Marshall are as friendly and attentive as possible. But I do not wish to take the ground of ignoring what is unconventional in my position. I have counted the cost of the step that I have taken and am prepared to bear, without irritation or bitterness, renunciation by all my friends. I am not mistaken in the person to whom I have attached myself. He is worthy of the sacrifice I have incurred, and my only anxiety is that he should be rightly judged. . . .

Mr. Lewes was in doubt whether he should not return to London to refute the report of his having 'run away', but his health is so far from being established and he is so unequal to spending a winter of worry and

[1] GE Journal, 29–30 Aug. 1854.

PLATE VII

THORNTON LEIGH HUNT
From a drawing in chalks by Samuel Laurence

GEORGE HENRY LEWES *c.* 1858
Wood-engraving from a photograph

sadness there that he will not do so unless it should prove absolutely necessary. He has given up the Leader.

Do write to me when you can, and believe me always, sincerely

Your obliged friend

Marian Evans.

Has Miss Tilley sailed for Australia?[1]

We can only speculate about the 'circumstances (in which I am not concerned)' that led Lewes to determine on a separation. Perhaps Agnes had written that she was pregnant again. It was a full year since her third child by Hunt was born, and though another was not registered till 1857, she may have had a miscarriage. Carlyle, writing to his brother John about the affair on 2 November 1854, said: 'Lewes has cast away his wife—who indeed deserved it of him, having openly produced those dirty sooty skinned children which have Th[ornto]n Hunt for father, and being ready for a third; Lewes to pay the whole account, even the money part of it!'[2] That Carlyle did not know it was Agnes's fourth we may take as a sign of Lewes's moderation. In a letter to Charles Bray, 16 October—a 'dismal, rainy day', with the Michaelmas fair bringing 'an incessant buzz of voices under our windows, not soothing to the nerves'—Marian covered the same points, but added the detail that Agnes 'has had all the money due to him in London'.

I have been long enough with Mr. Lewes to judge of his character on adequate grounds, and there is therefore no absurdity in offering my opinion as evidence that he is worthy of high respect. . . .

Of course many silly myths are already afloat about me, in addition to the truth, which of itself would be thought matter for scandal. I am quite unconcerned about them except as they may cause pain to my real friends. If you hear of anything that I have said, done, or written in relation to Mr. Lewes beyond the simple fact that I am attached to him and that I am living with him, do me the justice to believe that it is false. You and Mr. Chapman are the only persons to whom I have ever spoken of his private position and of my relation to him, and the only influence I should ever dream of exerting over him as to his conduct towards his wife and children is that of stimulating his conscientious care for them, if it needed any stimulus.

Pray pardon this long letter on a painful subject. I felt it a duty to write it.

I am ignorant how far Cara and Sara may be acquainted with the state of things, and how they may feel towards me. I am quite prepared

[1] GE to J. Chapman, 15 Oct. 1854 (Yale).

[2] T. Carlyle to John Carlyle, 2 Nov. 1854 (NLS: 516.86).

to accept the consequences of a step which I have deliberately taken and to accept them without irritation or bitterness. The most painful consequence will, I know, be loss of friends. If I do not write, therefore, understand that it is because I desire not to obtrude myself.

Write to me soon and let me know how things are with you. I am full of affection towards you all, and whatever you may think of me, shall always be

Your true and grateful friend
Marian Evans.[1]

If Cara and Sara were still ignorant of the state of things, Marian could blame no one but herself. She dared not tell them her plans at Rosehill, trusting Charles to break the news. The allusion to her in this letter gave Sara an opportunity to let her long-smouldering feeling explode. Sara was a militant feminist. She saw no reason why a 'female friend' who for years had been Marian's 'Beloved Achates', could not be trusted with any facts that could be given to her admittedly 'leaky' brother-in-law or the notoriously lecherous John Chapman. Her letter must have sizzled with indignation. It brought an earnest protest from Marian:

62a Kaufgasse, Weimar
Tuesday October 31.

My dear Sara

The mode in which you and Cara have interpreted both my words and my silence makes me dread lest in writing more I should only give rise to fresh misconceptions. I am so deeply conscious of having had neither the feeling nor the want of feeling which you impute to me that I am quite unable to read into my words, quoted by you, the sense which you put upon them. When you say that I do not care about Cara's or your opinion and friendship it seems much the same to me as if you said that I didn't care to eat when I was hungry or to drink when I was thirsty. One of two things: either I am a creature without affection, on whom the memories of years have no hold, or, you, Cara and Mr. Bray are the most cherished friends I have in the world. It is simply self-contradictory to say that a person can be indifferent about her dearest friends; yet this is what you substantially say, when you accuse me of 'boasting with what serenity I can give you up,' of 'speaking proudly' etc. The only reply I can give to such an accusation is an absolute denial that I have been actuated by such a spirit as you describe with regard to any one thing which I have written, done, or left undone.

You say: 'You' shew that 'you wish to have communication with Charles only.' The reason why I wrote to Mr. Bray and not to you and Cara is simply this. Before I left England, I communicated, by Mr.

---

[1] *Letters*, II. 178–9, misdated [23 Oct. 1854].

Lewes's desire, certain facts in strict confidence to Mr. Bray and Mr. Chapman and I did so for special reasons which would not apply to any female friend. After your kind letters came to me, we heard much painful news from London as to reports which were partly a perversion of the truth, partly pure falsehood. I cannot, even now, see that I did anything deserving so severe a reproach as you send me, in writing to Mr. Bray who was already in possession of the main facts, and in intimating that my silence to you arose from no want of affection, but from what I, falsely perhaps, but still sincerely, regarded as the very reverse of *pride* and a spirit of *boasting*.

There is now no longer any secrecy to be preserved about Mr. Lewes's affairs or mine, and whatever I have written to Mr. Bray, I have written to you. I am under no foolish hallucinations about either the present or the future and am standing on no stilts of any kind. I wish to speak simply and to act simply but I think it can hardly be unintelligible to you that I shrink from writing elaborately about private feelings and circumstances. I have really felt it a privation that I have been unable to write to you about things not personal, in which I know you would feel a common interest, and it will brighten my thoughts very much to know that I may do so. Cara, you and my own sister are the three women who are tied to my heart by a cord which can never be broken and which really *pulls* me continually. My love for you rests on a past which no future can reverse, and offensive as the words seem to have been to you, I must repeat, that I can feel no bitterness towards you, however you may act towards me. If you remain to me what you have ever been, my life will be all the happier, and I will try not to be unworthy of your love so far as faithfulness to my own conscience can make me worthy of it.

I have written miserably ill, and I fear all the while I am writing that I may be giving rise to some mistake. But interpret my whole letter so as to make it accord with this plain statement—I love Cara and you with unchanged and unchangeable affection, and while I retain your friendship I retain the best that life has given me next to that which is the deepest and gravest joy in all human experience.

Marian Evans.[1]

Sara accepted this straightforward avowal by her former 'Gemahlin'[2] and resumed regular correspondence—'but I have a strange sort of feeling that I am writing to some one in a book, and not to the Marian that we have known and loved so many years. Do not mistake me, I mean nothing unkind.'[3] Cara, however, could not so easily overlook Marian's open defiance of convention, which offended her naturally refined instincts. After one letter of protest (which has not been found), she stopped writing. Cara had

[1] *Letters*, II. 181–2.   [2] See *Letters*, I. 186.   [3] *Letters*, II. 186.

brought Marian up from the awkward, troubled girl who turned to her during the conflict with Robert Evans; she had recognized her talent, yielded her the love and sympathy her family could not give, and made Rosehill her real home. Cara knew in her own private life the heart's need for love; she had borne her disappointments with dignity. Now, as always, her deepest disapproval was expressed in silence. None of the Coventry trio really liked Lewes. Cara deplored his lack of seriousness, Sara his contempt for metaphysics, Charles his persistent refusal to accept phrenology as a science.

Lewes's contempt for phrenology probably exacerbated George Combe's sense of outrage on learning that Miss Evans, whom they had entertained in their home, introduced to their friends, and urged three times to travel with them, was living with Lewes. England's foremost phrenologist, consultant to the royal family, had misread her character. Deeply mortified and distressed, he wrote to Bray:

I should like to know whether there is insanity in Miss Evans's family; for her conduct, with *her* brain, seems to me like morbid mental aberration . . . an educated woman who, in the face of the world, volunteers to live as a wife, with a man who already has a living wife and children, appears to me to pursue a course and to set an example calculated only to degrade herself and her sex, if she be sane. If you receive her into your family circle, while present appearances are unexplained, pray consider whether you will do justice to your own female domestic circle? and how other ladies may feel about going into a circle which makes no distinction between those who act thus, and those who preserve their honour unspotted?[1]

Even the radical Joseph Parkes, on hearing the news about Marian, came home 'in a white rage, as if on the verge of a paralytic stroke'.[2] The storm of horror that it produced matched the revulsion from the 'fallen woman' which Dickens was exploiting so profitably in Mrs. Dombey, Little Em'ly, and Lady Dedlock.

Most of Lewes's acquaintances were inclined to blame him as the seducer, though like Carlyle and Combe they believed him perfectly justified in leaving Agnes. But John Chapman, who knew Marian perhaps more intimately than anyone, hinted in

[1] G. Combe to C. Bray, 15 Nov. 1854 (NLS).
[2] So Bessie told Edith Simcox (Autobiography, 21 Feb. 1882, fol. 98). According to his granddaughter Mrs. Belloc Lowndes, Parkes himself 'did not remain faithful to his wife' ('*I, Too, Have Lived in Arcadia*', 1942, p. 31).

conversation with Robert Chambers that the responsibility was equally hers. In a letter Chapman added:

A word about Miss E.—I am very anxious that what I *said* to you about *her especially*, should be regarded as strictly confidential. I mention this because Mr. Bray connected your name with a rumour about her; and I should be sorry to be thought disposed to disparage her. I only dropped the word I did because I felt that Lewes was not as you imagined almost alone to blame. Still I think him much the most blameworthy in the matter. Now I can only pray, against hope, that he may prove constant to her; otherwise she is *utterly* lost. She has a noble nature, which in good circumstances and under good influences would have shone out.[1]

Harriet Martineau had never seen Lewes till Marian introduced them that day in Cambridge Street. Whether because of his severe criticism of her *Letters on the Laws of Man's Nature and Development* or because of the rivalry of their books on Comte,[2] she heartily disliked him and was more than willing to join the chorus of malicious gossip. Before waiting to learn the facts, she instantly extended her hatred of Lewes to cover Marian as well, spreading it among her numerous correspondents with a virulence that makes one consider pathological theories of sexual jealousy. Marian wrote to Chapman 30 October:

I hope you have contradicted the story of my writing to Miss Martineau. I cannot understand how it originated except in some communication of yours to Miss M. which you intended to be serviceable to me. You must have made this communication in a moment of hallucination as to Miss M's character. Amongst her good qualities we certainly cannot reckon zeal for other people's reputation. She is sure to caricature any information for the amusement of the next person to whom she turns her ear-trumpet.[3]

Until her death Harriet Martineau maintained this irrational antipathy. Marian was not greatly disturbed by it; she had expected that reaction from most people, though she may have hoped for a little more sympathetic understanding in a great liberal woman of letters. In 1856 after it was announced that she was dying of an incurable disease, Marian—though in need of the money—gave up to Miss Martineau the article on 'Missions and Missionaries', which Chapman had asked her write. 'I feel for her terrible bodily suffering', Marian wrote, 'and think of her with respect and

[1] J. Chapman to R. Chambers, 16 Oct. 1854 (W. & R. Chambers Ltd.).
[2] See *Letters*, II. 122–3.   [3] *Letters*, II. 180.

admiration.'[1] And she made an odd request of Chapman: 'When Harriet Martineau dies—if I outlive her—and her memoirs are published, I should like to write an article upon her. I need hardly say that mine would be an admiring appreciation of her.'[2] But Harriet Martineau did not die. She lived on for another twenty years—with never a word to Marian, even when the great novels compelled her increasing admiration. Her hatred of Lewes never faltered. When there was a rumour of his illness, she wrote hastily: 'Do you know that Lewes is likely to die? "All but hopelessly ill", Matt. Arnold told me the other day. What will she do? Take a successor, I should expect.'[3]

These painful matters cast a heavy shadow over the last weeks of the Leweses' stay in Weimar. Melancholy news came from Chrissey Clarke of the drowning at sea of her son Robert and from Chapman of the death by cholera of his cousin, another John Chapman,[4] a helpful supporter of the *Westminster,* over which James and Harriet Martineau were struggling for control. Marian was glad to be away from it all. At the end of her Recollections she wrote:

Dear Weimar! We were sorry to say good bye to it, with its pleasant group of friends—the grand, fascinating Liszt, the bright, kind Princess, the Marquis de Ferrière with his becoming embonpoint and agreeable chat, the hearty animated Schöll. . . . We breakfasted twice, by way of farewell, with Liszt and the Princess—the first time without any other visitors. The Princess Marie showed me a remarkable series of sketches from Dante, while Liszt went to rest and George talked with the Princess. After this, we all sat down together in the Princess Marie's room, Liszt, the Princess and her daughter on the sofa, G. and I opposite to them, and Miss Anderson a little in the rear. I like to recall this moment, and Liszt's face with its serious expression, as we talked about his coming to London and I asked the Princess if she should come too. The next time we breakfasted with them the Marquis de Ferrière and young Cornelius were there, and I had a long theological séance with the Princess on the sofa. She parted from us very prettily, with earnest wishes for my happiness in particular. G. was so grateful for this that he couldn't help saying 'God bless you' to her, and she repeated it, calling after me too, 'God bless you.' The evening before I left Liszt called while G. was away [at the Schloss, taking leave of the Duke] and brought me a paper of bon-bons which the Princess had sent us to refresh us on our journey.

[1] *Letters*, II. 229.   [2] *Letters*, II. 258.
[3] R. K. Webb, *Harriet Martineau* (1960), p. 14.
[4] GE Journal, 14 and 4 Oct. 1854.

While they were packing on the last morning, Schöll came, bringing Uhland's poems as a parting present for Marian and some letters of introduction for George at Berlin. After a stay of less than five minutes, he took a thoroughly German farewell, 'kissing G. again and again on the lips'. When they left for the train, their odd little maid Lora was out of the way,

so we could not give her the 10 groschen which I had laid by for her; but when we were walking quietly on the platform at the station lo! we heard a scream behind us and on looking round saw Lora running towards us with a bouquet in her hand, which she had been in quest of while we were leaving. It was touching to see her funny face wrinkled up into something meant for a smile as she said her goodbyes and held out her dirty hand that we might give it a parting shake. The morning had been sombre and bitterly cold from the beginning, and now it began to rain heavily. The train soon came up—we rushed under an umbrella into our carriage, and so on the 3d of November, after a stay of just three months, we turned our backs on Weimar to seek new streets and faces new.

Berlin was very different—an uninteresting modern city with broad, monotonous streets, little personality, and no flavour of the idyllic. The first night they spent at Kellner's Hôtel de l'Europe, in the Taubenstrasse, which they liked well enough to take most of their meals there for four months, though the service at the table d'hôte was so slow and the company so boring that they always carried books to read during dinner. They found comfortable lodgings with Frau Holzayer at 62 Dorotheenstrasse, for which they had to pay three times what their rooms at Weimar had cost. The next morning the sun was shining brightly, and they went to walk in the Linden, elbowing their way among the Sunday promeneurs, who looked remarkably smart and handsome after the Thuringians.

'We had not gone far when we met a nice-looking old gentleman with an order round his neck and a gold-headed cane in his hand, who exclaimed on seeing George "Ist's möglich?" and then bid him heartily welcome.' It was Varnhagen von Ense, whom Lewes had known well since his student days, introduced in 1839 by a letter from Carlyle. Varnhagen had been the husband of the celebrated Friederike Rahel, whose correspondence he published; he had written books on many subjects, including Goethe, and had been something of a literary arbiter in his younger days. He was now the most faithful habitué of Fräulein von Solmar's salon, where Lewes hastened to present himself again that same evening and was warmly welcomed. Fräulein von Solmar, an accomplished woman between fifty and sixty, was at home to her friends every night but Thursday. Marian, introduced to her at a party Varnhagen gave for them the first Thursday, was cordially invited to her salon; as Fräulein von Solmar was 'in the best society of Berlin', Marian told Bray, 'this is no slight advantage'.[1] She and George went to her house about once a week during the first two months of their stay in Berlin. There, besides Varnhagen and Fräulein Assing, his niece, they usually saw General Pfuhl, an old soldier with a good deal of learning and strong social sympathies. Baron Sternberg, the novelist, 'used frequently to glide in when we were there and cast strange cold glances around, talking quietly to Fräulein Assing or some other lady who sat in a distant parallel of latitude'.[2] Karl Vehse, the historian, was there once or twice, as noisy as Sternberg was quiet.

A more amusing acquaintance was another old friend of George's earlier visits to Berlin, Professor Otto Gruppe. The author of 'books on everything'—on the Greek drama, the cosmic systems of the Greeks, poetry, philosophy, and politics, he had also invented a superior marbled paper for binding books and was an enthusiastic boar hunter. He and his little wife, thirty years younger, with their two children formed a charming group in their flat up endless flights of stairs in the Leipzigerplatz, where George and Marian spent many pleasant evenings, chatting, playing whist or poker, and listening to readings from his epic poem *Firdausi*, about to be published.

A very different scholar was Adolf Stahr, who shared Lewes's interest in Goethe and Spinoza and wrote on the history of art and philosophy. Marian described him as 'pale, nervous, sickly looking, with scarcely any moral radiation, so to speak'; his literary egotism was ludicrously prominent. But she looked with peculiar fascination at his companion Fanny Lewald, the novelist, a crusader for the independence of women, who had been living openly with Stahr for nine years. Lewes, having known Fanny at Berlin in 1845, called on her soon after their arrival and probably explained about Marian. Fanny came to call the next day, and they saw her fairly often during their stay. Going to their house 6 February 1855, they discovered that Stahr and Fanny had 'gone to be married at last', and, as Marian later observed, they 'seemed the happier for it'. The Stahrs distressed both George and Marian by implying that the Princess Wittgenstein was 'an incubus' on

[1] *Letters*, II. 184.   [2] GE Journal, 'Recollections of Berlin'.

Liszt. 'We were both glad to be able to doubt the truth of this representation', wrote Marian, who was corresponding with the Princess from time to time.

Another pleasant friend at Berlin was Heinrich Magnus, the chemist, who invited them to a party at his house to introduce them to Johannes Müller, Du Bois Reymond, Christian Ehrenberg, and other distinguished scientists. His brother Eduard Magnus, the portrait painter, was equally kind; Marian considered him the only German she met 'who seemed conscious of his country's deficiencies—who would admit, for example, that they talked loudly, that they were given to "embarras," and that they were not polite'.

Ludwig Dessoir, the leading actor at Berlin's Court Theatre, she probably ranked in this category. He had played in London in July 1853. Lewes's review in the *Leader*,[1] though praising his intelligence and representative power, declared that he lacked the physique required for tragic heroes (a lack Lewes recognized plainly in himself). As soon as Dessoir heard that Lewes was in Berlin, he called and offered them free seats for the Theatre, which they used occasionally. He would frequently meet them on the street and walk with them, sometimes coming in to discuss Shakespeare: 'Shakespeare ist mein Gott,' he told them; 'Ich habe kein anderen Gott.' At his request they saw his Othello again, but still could not like it; and his Shylock Marian thought 'perfectly disgusting'.

Christian Rauch, the sculptor, she regarded as the most distinguished man they saw in Berlin, and—next to Liszt—in Germany. Schöll had given Lewes a letter to him; 'soon after it had been left at his house he called on us in the evening and at once won our hearts by his beautiful person and the benignant charm of his conversation. He is indeed the finest old man I ever saw—more than 76, I believe, but perfectly upright, even stately in his carriage.' Like most of the other men they saw at Berlin, Rauch told them interesting stories about Goethe, dwelling especially on his 'loveable nature. He described very graphically Goethe's way of introducing subjects, showing plates, etc., bringing in the cast of Schiller's skull and talking about it.' This conversation enabled Lewes in his *Goethe* to speak of Schiller's brow as 'narrow', in defiance of Dannecker's bust of the poet; 'the sculptor, as usual, had grossly departed from truth in his desire to idealize. Artists always believe they know better than Nature.'

[1] *Leader*, 30 July 1853, p. 741.

And the description of long-necked Schiller walking like a camel was told by 'Tieck, the sculptor, to Rauch, from whom I heard it'.[1]

Berlin afforded few of those charming walks they took almost daily at Weimar, and they had no time for excursions. They never went to Sanssouci. When the northern winter brought driving rains and heavy snow, they often had to make their way the half-mile to the Hôtel de l'Europe through icy streets for their meals. Marian as usual suffered excessively from the cold. She missed the strolls in the mild Weimar air through the alley of noble chestnut trees and under the tall limes and plane trees and birches about the Palace at the Belvedere or among the mountain ashes in full berry at Ettersburg, 'like bunches of coral standing out against the blue sky'. Those walks always relieved her tension and headache.

While Lewes was gathering valuable materials in Germany, Marian could find little profitable work. Writing on her thirty-fifth birthday to thank Sara for a letter on which she had stitched a tiny $A\chi$ (Achates) as a sign that her irritation was past, she wrote:

I should be very glad to have my pen employed in something that would yield immediate profit, and there are plenty of subjects suggested by new German books which would be fresh and instructive in an English Review. But I cannot bring myself to run the risk of a refusal from an editor. Indeed I cannot for several reasons make any proposition at present. So I am working at what will ultimately yield something which is secured by agreement with Bohn.[2]

This was the translation of Spinoza's *Ethics*, which occupied her during their whole stay in Berlin. Beginning 8 November 1854, she worked at it almost every day until they left for England, when Part III was nearly finished.

But another task of translation that occupied a good deal of her time in Germany has never been noticed—the many pages of quotation in Lewes's *Goethe*. Lewes remarks early in the book that, since 'to leave German untranslated is very unfair to those whose want of leisure or inclination has prevented their acquiring the language, I shall throughout translate every word cited'.[3] From Marian's Journal we know that she translated the genealogical tables (I. 10–11) and the long excerpts from Kestner's

---

[1] *Goethe*, II. 186.   [2] *Letters*, II. 189.   [3] *Goethe*, I. 7–8.

letters in the *Werther* chapter (I. 213-18). Though Lewes, who had published a good deal of verse in his early days, undoubtedly rendered the poetry, there is no question that most of the long prose passages were transcribed and translated by Marian. She also more than once, read the whole manuscript with scrupulous care. In some respects this important biography—a standard work on Goethe, which was immediately acclaimed in Germany and plagiarized in France—might be considered a composite production with George Eliot as silent collaborator.

Tantalizing references in the Journal to an apparently unsuccessful effort to get through Mrs. Robert Noel an introduction to Humboldt suggest that Marian may have had another article in mind. At last, in January 1855 she pocketed her pride and proposed as a subject for the *Westminster* Ideals of Womankind, perhaps inspired by close reading of Johannes Scherr's *Deutsche Cultur- und Sittengeschichte* and some of Fanny Lewald's books. But Chapman, ill, absorbed in desperate attempts to avoid bankruptcy, and in his own complicated relations with womankind, could not be interested in it nor in the more precise subject, Woman in Germany, which Marian proposed as a substitute. Instead, he agreed to accept an article on Eduard Vehse's *Geschichte des österreichischen Hofs und Adels*, of which eleven of the ultimate twenty-eight volumes had appeared. Marian borrowed the book from the author himself, who was pleased to have it noticed in England. She finished the article 3 March and sent it to London the next day. Though it consists largely of excerpts from Vehse, brilliantly selected and translated, and contains little criticism beyond the satirical undertone, 'Memoirs of the Court of Austria' well deserved the dignity of opening the April number of the *Westminster*. Chapman paid her a welcome £20.

For literary output Marian's eight months in Germany were not impressive. She produced two rather popular articles for the *Westminster Review*, a couple of short ones for the *Leader*; most of her work was translation—Liszt's article on Meyerbeer, the extended passages quoted in the *Goethe*, and half of Spinoza's *Ethics*. Sometimes when Lewes's head was painful she would write to his dictation—for example, the long article in the *Leader* on Sir Benjamin Brodie's *Psychological Inquiries*.[1] But it would be a great mistake to look on this as a wasted period of her life. During these months she read more intensively than at any time since her winter in Geneva; Cross fills nearly three pages with just the titles

[1] *Leader*, 31 Mar. 1855, pp. 306-7.

of books she read in Weimar and Berlin, drawn from her Journal, and by no means exhausts the list. German literature naturally predominates. She read probably every word of Goethe, a good deal of Schiller, Lessing, Schlegel, Heine, Uhland, and many more recent writers. There are few French authors on the list (though she and George had spoken French constantly with Liszt and his friends in Weimar) and few English. She wrote to Chapman: 'we have seen some very pleasant and varied society, partly made up of Mr. Lewes's old friends and partly of new ones. But we enjoy our evenings at home most of all—we read furiously and are trying to get very wise, in spite of Solomon's proverb about the unimprovability of bad materials.'[1] Her learning was deeply founded. Some of the easy allusiveness in George Eliot's novels can be traced to those long evenings of close reading at Berlin. 'How we used to rejoice in the idea of our warm room and coffee as we battled our way from dinner against the wind and snow! Then came the delightful long evening in which we read Shakespeare, Goethe, Heine, and Macaulay, with German pfefferkuchen and semmels at the end to complete the noctes cenæque deûm.'[2]

When her article on Vehse's *Court of Austria* was finished, they spent most of their last week in sightseeing, preparing to return to England. At the New Museum Kaulbach was still painting his frescoes on the staircase. With Professor von Olfers's help they got into the unfinished Hall of Northern Antiquities, and went from there to the Egyptian Gallery, in which, Marian thought, 'for the common eye there is nothing to compare with the stupendous relics of the British Museum'. At the Old Museum Marian saw 'three gems which remain in the imagination', a Titian and two Correggios; of the Dutch paintings she singled out the Jan Steen that Goethe describes in the *Wahlverwandtschaften*, which she was pleased to recognize. They went one evening to a concert, twice to the opera, and to the theatre. The day before they departed Eduard Magnus came, bringing Marian two lithographs of his paintings and 'took a farewell of hearty friendliness'.[3] On Sunday morning, 11 March, they set off in the snow, 'leaving behind us, alas! G's rug, which should have kept his feet warm on the journey'. They intended to go straight through to Calais, but the cold was so intense that they saw it would be folly to attempt

---

[1] GE to J. Chapman, 9 Dec. 1854 (Yale)
[2] GE Journal, 'Recollections of Berlin'.
[3] Ibid. 10 Mar. 1855.

it, and they got off at Cologne to spend another night at the Hôtel de Mayence. Next morning, after looking again at the cathedral ('Melancholy as ever in its impression upon me!') they resumed the journey. As far as Brussels they had some rather interesting companions,

two French artists who were on their way from Russia. Strange beings they looked to us at first in their dirty linen, Russian caps, and other queer equipment, but in this as in many other cases I found that a first impression was an extremely mistaken one, for instead of being, as I imagined, common, uncultivated men, they were highly intelligent. They told us a characteristic fact about the buildings in St. Petersburg —namely, that they are only solid and splendid where they are inevitably near the eye; everywhere else they are trumpery. They also told us of the trouble they had to see the Dresden Gallery, and the wretched way in which it is managed.[1]

The Hôtel de Saxe at Brussels was, 'a disagreeable place', though 'As we took our supper, we had the pleasure of looking at Berlioz' fine head and face, he being employed in the same way on the other side of the table.' The next afternoon at Calais after a cup of tea, they went aboard the Channel boat. 'We soon became ill, and so were even thankful to see the cliffs of Dover.' There at the Lord Warden they had a last night together before Lewes went up to London to arrange his affairs.

English mutton, an English fire, and an English bed were likely to be appreciated by creatures who had had eight months of Germany with its questionable meat, its stove-heated rooms, and beds warranted not to tuck up. The taste and quietude of a first-rate English Hotel were also in striking contrast with the heavy finery, the noise, and the indiscriminate smoking of German inns. But after all, Germany is no bad place to live in, and the Germans, to counterbalance their want of taste and politeness, are at least free from the bigotry and exclusiveness of their more refined cousins.[2]

The shadow of Mrs. Grundy was looming.

[1] GE Journal, 12 Mar. 1855.   [2] GE Journal, 'Recollections of Berlin'.

CHAPTER VII

A STRONG MINDED WOMAN

❋

THE next morning Lewes took lodgings for Miss Marian Evans
at 1 Sydney Place and went up to London. She did not see him
again for five weeks. Though her Journal provides only a fragmentary record, these weeks must have marked the most trying
period of her life. Chapman was praying 'against hope' that Lewes
would prove constant; the Brays thought that the connection
could not last; she dared not think that it could end. She began
bravely enough, working at Spinoza in the mornings, taking long
walks up Castle Hill or along the beach, and then coming home to
read and translate again. Every two or three days a letter came
from George. After so many months of constant companionship
she missed him terribly. She had comfortable lodgings and 'a
nice quiet woman' to wait on her, but made no acquaintances at
Dover. It was not so easy as she expected to give up old friends
and face the consequences of the step she had taken. She wrote to
Sara that she was 'well and calmly happy—feeling much stronger
and clearer in mind for the last eight months of new experience',
but added that news 'of you all at Rosehill' would be very
welcome.[1] She explained to Bessie, who (without telling Mr.
Parkes) had written to her at Berlin:

I have taken lodgings here for a short time while Mr. Lewes makes some
arrangements in town. . . . I am now rather enjoying the contrast of
perfect quiet and of a bright sun shining on cliff and softly rounded hill
and fringed sea after much paddling through the thawing snows of the
Berlin streets. . . . I can dilate on nothing now. I will only say that if you
knew everything, we should probably be much nearer agreement even
as to the details of conduct than you suppose. In the mean time, believe
no one's representations about me, for there is not a *single person* who
is in a position to make a true representation. My mind is deliciously
calm and untroubled so far as my own lot is concerned, my only anxieties
are sympathetic ones.

[1] *Letters*, II. 194.

She enclosed the note to Chapman, 'as I suppose you still wish me not to write to you directly'.[1] This was a subterfuge she had rejected in 1849, when she sent word to Mary Sibree (whose father objected to her writing to a freethinker) that 'I cannot carry on a correspondence with any one who will not avow it'.[2]

Marian's sympathy with Lewes in his numerous problems was perforce remote. His immediate need was for money. He had to make a bargain with some publisher for the *Goethe*, to which he had devoted most of a year's work. Charles Mathews paid him £39 for plays, and he got another £25 for a pot-boiling one-act farce called *Buckstone's Adventure with a Polish Princess*.[3] E. F. S. Pigott, who was now managing and financing the *Leader*, welcomed both his contributions and Marian's, though he could pay only at the low rate of £1. 1s. an article. Thornton Hunt had left the staff to become editor of a new morning paper, the *Daily Telegraph*. Lewes's most serious problem was to persuade Hunt to pay his share for the support of Agnes and her children, three of whom were his. Lewes's elder sons, Charles (now thirteen) and Thornie (eleven), were at Dr. Pearce's Bayswater Academy, where Bertie (nine) would soon follow them, and Lewes planned to find a school on the Continent where they could finish their education. Meanwhile, they lived cheerfully with Mamma and Nursie (and sometimes Uncle Thornton?), very fond of 'the children' and unaware of any irregularity in their relationship. For Agnes, who was probably still pregnant, Lewes felt no bitterness. We have no letters written by him during these weeks in March and April 1855, but if any are found they may well be dated from 26 Bedford Place, where most of his books and things remained until 1859. During his absence in Germany, Agnes had gone deeply into debt, and Thornton was slow to pay any part of her bills; Lewes, who was legally responsible, had to borrow money to settle her accounts.[4]

While these perplexing affairs were being argued in London, Marian walked alone on the cliffs at Dover. She tried to continue the readings of Shakespeare that had beguiled so many long evenings in their little room in the Dorotheenstrasse. She began

[1] *Letters*, II. 195–6.   [2] *Letters*, I. 306.
[3] Originally written for T. F. Robson as *Robson's Adventure with a Russian Princess*, it was revised for Buckstone, who produced it at the Haymarket 4 July 1855.
[4] *Letters*, VII. 383.

with *Venus and Adonis*, *The Passionate Pilgrim*, and some of the Sonnets. Of *Two Gentlemen of Verona* she wrote: 'That play disgusted me more than ever in the final scene where Valentine, on Proteus's mere begging pardon when he has no longer any hope of gaining his ends, says: "All that was mine in Silvia I give thee"! —Silvia standing by.'[1] Could men really bandy a noble woman's love about like that? Soon the fine weather changed. Walking along the beach one afternoon, she 'saw a sea fog come in with amazing rapidity—a thick cloud seemed to gather on the cliff in a moment'. Winter returned with icy winds; on 23 March snow fell. Marian caught cold and for several days had to stay indoors, translating Spinoza and reading *The Tempest* and *Macbeth*.

Once more in a dark moment a letter from Chapman brought her good news: he invited her to undertake the 'Belles Lettres' section of the 'Contemporary Literature' reviews in the *Westminster*, steady work that would add £50 a year to her income.[2] Marian celebrated with 'a delightful walk over the hills', and after working at Spinoza a little, read *Romeo and Juliet* and some of the *Nibelungenlied*, in which Liszt and Wagner had interested her. The next evening—the only time I can recall her mentioning it— she sewed. The last page of the manuscript of her 'Recollections of Berlin' is dated 'Dover, March 27. 1855'. On the 28th she suffered a bilious attack with terrible headache that kept her two days in bed. It was a genuine illness, followed by three weeks of monotonous working and waiting while Lewes's negotiations dragged on in London. Writing on 4 April 1855 to Charles Bray, whose letters, she complained, 'rival in curtness those of F.M. the Duke [of Wellington]', about the payment of her half-year's income into a London bank, Marian said: 'Mr. Lewes is gone to Arthur Helps's at Vernon Hill for a week or ten days, and on his return I shall join him in London, where—that is, in the environs—we shall establish ourselves till the big books are fairly through the press, when I hope our wings will be plumed for a new flight to the south of Germany and Italy, for which we both yearn.'[3]

Meanwhile, she slogged on through the *Ethics*, read more old German literature, following the *Nibelungenlied* with *Reineke Fuchs*, and put Shakespeare aside for Gibbon's *Decline and Fall* and Spencer's 'The Genesis of Science'. Her Journal for 9 April notes a 'Painful letter which upset me for work. Walked out and then translated 2 pages of Sp[inoza]. Read Henry V. In the evening

---

[1] GE Journal, 16 Mar. 1855.   [2] Ibid. 25 Mar. 1855.
[3] *Letters*, II. 197.

translated again.' The next day after translating she 'Walked, feeling much depression against which I struggled hard. Read Henry V and Henry VIII.' *Richard II* and all three parts of *Henry VI* followed. From 12 to 14 April she was 'Still feverish and unable to fix my mind steadily on reading or writing', though she did a little work on a Weimar article for *Fraser's*. We can only speculate about the crisis. Apparently Marian had stipulated that, before she would come to London as Lewes's wife, Agnes must declare her intention of never returning to him—making the separation definite, if not legal. Mrs. Bray told Edith Simcox that Marian 'insisted on the question being asked on both sides—Was there any possibility of bringing about a reunion?—and Mrs. Lewes—the *de facto* Mrs. Hunt—said, No, never, and she would be very glad if he could marry Miss Evans.'[1] It was probably Marian's insistence on getting this statement clearly formulated that prolonged her depressing stay at Dover. At length it was settled. The next entry in her Journal says simply: 'Wednesday 18 [April]. Came to town, to lodgings in Bayswater.' George had taken rooms for Mr. and Mrs. Lewes at 8 Victoria Grove Terrace, now called Ossington Street. It was the formal beginning of their marriage.

Little is known of the two weeks they lived in Bayswater. They spent the first few days wandering about the suburbs looking for lodgings; by 23 April they had fixed on 7 Clarence Row, East Sheen as a suitable residence. There are only two other entries in Marian's Journal during April: 'Wednesday 25. Went to the British Museum', and 'Saturday 28. Finished article on Weimar for Fraser.' She had three callers that we know of, though they are not mentioned in the Journal. Rufa Hennell came on the 28th, the first woman to risk her reputation by associating with the abandoned recreant. Chapman had come on the evening of the 26th, when George was out, and left him an invitation to write on 'Teetotalism' for the July *Westminster*. Marian, accepting for him, commented on the yet unwritten article Chapman had proposed to her at Weimar on the works of Charles Kingsley, to which the just-published *Westward Ho!* would now have to be added:

As to the Kingsley article, perhaps, since you cannot have it in July when 'Westward ho!' would belong to the publications of the quarter and thus present an obvious occasion for taking up the subject, it would be unwise to produce it in October when it would look like a belated article, and though the criticism might be of a different order from what would have appeared in newspapers and other periodicals, yet it would

[1] Simcox Autobiography, 12 June 1885, fol. 104.

come, at the very best, like a course of ham after several courses of
bacon. It is true that I should only treat 'Westward ho!' in the same
proportion as the other works, but on the whole perhaps it would be
well to defer the subject till the echoes of the Westward ho! criticisms
have died out, and substitute Dr. Cumming (if you like) for October.
I refer the matter to your reconsideration.

I was very sorry to hear from Mrs. Hennell that you were unable to
go to business after Thursday evening. I fear your kindness in coming
so far to return late may have done your body harm, though, like all
good nature, it must have done your soul good. For 'within narrow
limits'—but only narrow ones—the soul can prosper on the body's
harm.

I thought it was very good of Mrs. Hennell to call on me, and I
respect her for it.[1]

On the 30th Bessie Parkes called. It was a daring act. No record
of their conversation remains. When Marian wrote to her the
next day, she addressed the letter 'Miss Parkes | B. Smith Esq. | 5
Blandford Square'—another subterfuge.

I forgot to say yesterday that if you write to me at East Sheen, I must
beg you to enclose the letter to G. H. Lewes Esq. I will tell you the
reason of this when I see you. If you are ever able to come to me, let
me know the day before, that I may be at home and meet you at the
station.

I have not yet lost the glow of joy at the sight of you.[2]

Marian's great anxiety was lest friends who called or wrote
might address her as 'Miss Evans'. Bessie, whose feminist enthusiasm was aggressive, proved one of the most persistent offen-
ders. Marian cautioned Charles Bray similarly when she notified
him of her new address. She had never seen him together with
Lewes, and rather feared that Bray with his heavy jocularity might
embarrass her by quoting a remark she had made about Lewes
before she knew him well.

We go tomorrow to our new home at East Sheen, a charming village
close to Richmond Park. If you write to me, please to enclose the letter
to G. H. Lewes Esq. | 7 Clarence Row | East Sheen | Richmond |
Surrey. When you come to London again, I hope you will pay us a visit,
for I think, apart from any regard for me it will be a pleasure to you to
see that pretty place, and it is far less trouble to get there than to Bayswater. You have only to jump into the train at the Waterloo Bridge
Station and in ten minutes you will be at Mortlake where you must
get down. Mortlake, as I daresay you know, is a lovely village on the

[1] *Letters*, II. 198.   [2] *Letters*, II. 200.

bank of the Thames, and East Sheen is its twin sister lying close to it. Ask the way to East Sheen and in three minutes you will be at our door. Then you shall have a nice dinner and a nice snooze after it, and then a stroll, along the river or in the Park, such as you can't get at Coventry even by the help of a carriage.

And pray, when I see you again, don't *mis*quote something I said two or three years ago, which something you seem to have converted into a supercilious, impertinent expression of disapprobation on my part. If the discipline of years has taught me anything, it has taught me to be reverent to all good in others and perpetually mindful of my own need of tolerance, and surely few people can have had more opportunity than I have had for knowing the good in you, and still fewer can have put that goodness to an equally severe test.

We are panting to be in the country and resume our old habits of undisturbed companionship and work. Mr. Lewes has been much worse since he returned to town and the other evening he alarmed me terribly by fainting. Imagine that I had never seen any one faint before, and that I thought he was dead! You will be able then to understand my condition for three or four minutes until he returned to consciousness. However we hope that when we are far away from the roar of omni*bii* (as poor Joseph Hume is accused of calling them) we shall have no more of such attacks.

Mrs. Hennell called on me the other day, very kindly and nobly. I respect her for it. I was so stupified and heated by having sat in-doors writing all day, that she must have carried away anything but a charming image of me, but that was of slight consequence—it was enough that she did a good action.

Best love to Cara and Sara for whom, of course, I write as well as for you.[1]

On Wednesday, 2 May they settled into the new lodgings. East Sheen was a beautiful spot then, with many fine old villas in magnificent gardens. Lying just north of Richmond Park and a few minutes from Kew Gardens, it offered delightful walks starting right at their door. The idyllic régime of Weimar was resumed while they buckled down to finishing 'the big books' and to earning as much as they could to repay the money Lewes was forced to borrow to pay Agnes's debts. Marian had translated all Part III of the *Ethics* before leaving Dover. Before she could begin Part IV she had to write the 'Belles Lettres' section for the July *Westminster*.[2]

Though analysis of her 'Belles Lettres' articles, each covering

[1] *Letters*, II. 199–200.
[2] A complete list of GE's essays and periodical writings is given by Thomas Pinney, *Essays of George Eliot* (N.Y., 1963), pp. 453–5.

twenty or thirty books, would be out of place here, some comment on her treatment of the more famous works reviewed may be given as evidence of what Marian was reading. A third of her space in the July article was devoted to Kingsley's *Westward Ho!* Praising his stirring adventures and vividly painted scenes, she criticized the partisan spirit, which led him to eulogize the past and sneer at the present, to call his *own* opinion God, to ride down capitalists and Jesuits, and 'fight with that Protean personage he calls "the Devil"'. A second and worse fault was 'his perpetual hortatory tendency. . . . Until he shakes off this parsonic habit, he will not be able to create truly human characters, or to write a genuine historical romance.'[1] A second novel Marian discussed was Geraldine Jewsbury's *Constance Herbert*, a *Tendenz-roman*, which aims to show the value of sacrificing inclination to duty, in this case, abstinence from marriage where there is an inheritance of insanity. But the story seemed to show that nothing her characters gave up would prove to have been worth the keeping, all three lovers renounced by her heroines turning out to be good riddance.

In all this we can see neither the true doctrine of renunciation, nor a true representation of the realities of life. . . . It is the very perception that the thing we renounce is precious, is something never to be compensated to us, which constitutes the beauty and heroism of renunciation. The only motive that renders such a resolution as Constance Herbert's noble, is that keen sympathy with human misery which makes a woman prefer to suffer for the term of her own life, rather than run the risk of causing misery to an indefinite number of other human beings. . . . The notion that duty looks stern, but all the while has her hand full of sugar-plums, with which she will reward us by-and-by, is the favourite cant of optimists . . ., but it really undermines all true moral development.[2]

Interest in her own perplexities led Marian to give more space to this novel than it deserved. Matthew Arnold's *Poems. Second Series* she found not equal, though a worthy companion to the First Series (a judgement Arnold himself shared), selecting for special praise excerpts from 'Empedocles' and 'Resignation'; from the latter she quoted some forty lines describing the poet, who views human life with 'sad lucidity of soul'. Another book given careful criticism was Guillaume Guizot's *Ménandre*. Gautier's *Militona* she dismissed with a few sentences, complaining that it falls off terribly towards the end, 'like the baskets

<hr>

[1] *WR*, 64 (July 1855), 291.   [2] Ibid. 294–5.

of strawberries which tempt the thirsty pedestrian at Kew or elsewhere on a bright summer's day—all inviting, ripe, and fresh at
the beginning, and, as you near the end, poor, crude, and stale'.
Twenty-three books, English, French, and German, were treated
in the article. Chapman got good value for his £12. 12s.

In October 1855[1] Tennyson's *Maud* received nearly a third of
her space. The warmest admiration of the poet's earlier work is
followed by almost complete disapproval of *Maud* for its morbid,
melodramatic story and its 'faith in War as the unique social
regenerator'. In January 1856 Browning's *Men and Women* got
most attention. His so-called obscurity does not trouble Marian;
though a reader must exert himself, it is always worth the effort.
Browning's 'keen glance pierces into all the secrets of human
character, but . . . he reveals those secrets, not by a process of
dissection, but by dramatic painting'—as shown by the famous
passage she quoted from 'How It Strikes a Contemporary'. 'Fra
Lippo Lippi', from which she gave two pages, is better 'than an
essay on Realism in Art; we would rather have "The Statue and
the Bust" than a three-volumed novel with the same moral'.
Longfellow's *Hiawatha* she described sympathetically and justly:
mothers who love poetry were recommended to read it aloud to
their boys and girls. Another American book, though not new,
'interesting enough to make us break our rule by a retrospective
notice', was Thoreau's *Walden*. Marian praised Thoreau's keen
eye in the observation of nature, his deep poetic sensibility, and,
'throughout the book the presence of a refined as well as a hardy
mind'. She found plenty of sense mingled with his unworldliness,
and gave a page of well-chosen passages, italicizing several phrases
that particularly struck her—epigrammatic phrases like those we
find in her later novels. The new cheap edition of *Villette* was
noted, 'which we, at least, would rather read for the third time
than most new novels for the first'.[2]

In April 1856 when she covered both 'Art' and 'Belles
Lettres', Marian gave most space to Ruskin's *Modern Painters*
Volume III. She saw Ruskin's faults and absurdities well enough,
but recognized his importance as an influence on his age.

The truth of infinite value that he teaches is *realism*—the doctrine that
all truth and beauty are to be attained by a humble and faithful study
of nature, and not by substituting vague forms, bred by imagination on
the mists of feeling, in place of definite, substantial reality. The thorough

---

[1] *WR*, 64 (Oct. 1855), 596–615.   [2] *WR*, 65 (Jan. 1856), 290–312.

acceptance of this doctrine would remould our life; and he who teaches its application . . . is a prophet for his generation.[1]

Intelligent criticism of 'The Grand Style', 'Classical Landscape', 'The Pathetic Fallacy', and other chapters, showed how clearly she understood the significance of the book. Meredith's *The Shaving of Shagpat* she praised for originality, though she confessed to a rather languishing interest towards the end. The article concluded surprisingly with a comment on Walt Whitman's *Leaves of Grass*, from which she quoted some specimens.

The quarter for July 1856 offered Marian little besides Volume IV of *Modern Painters* and Victor Hugo's *Contemplations*. But she took a bad novel called *Perversion*, which had been praised by the weeklies, to demonstrate what a novel should *not* be. *The Vicar of Wakefield*, she declared, 'though we began to read it when we were eight years old, . . . is as inexhaustible as a really fine melody'. Not so *Perversion*. It should be called a tale for the season, which it is not likely to outlast. She then showed that the story is uninteresting, the character-sketching 'approximate, coarse, and often feeble', the satire without finesse; 'there is little appeal to the emotions; and the power of dramatic representation is entirely absent'. The life of the school and the home life of the brother and sister are 'merely described, not *presented*'. There is hardly any dialogue. The situations and characters are treated in a superficial, conventional style. And finally, the 'moral odour of the book is bad. There is the readiest imputation of the worst motives to all kinds of people; and it is clear that in the writer's view Christian charity has nothing to do with abstinence from abusing and slandering such men as Goethe and Carlyle.'[2] Though Marian had not yet begun 'Amos Barton', she was already thinking about what the writing of good fiction demands. Bessie Parkes's *Gabriel* was handled kindly with more than a page, while several other volumes of poetry were disposed of sarcastically. Mrs. Caroline Phillipson suffered worst with her *Lonely Hours*: 'This lady, having habitually solaced her "lonely hours" with writing sentimental doggrel, has liberally offered a thick volume of that literary commodity to the public, in the form of a new and enlarged edition, accompanied with a portrait conveying a very high idea of her personal charms—charms which we can only regard as a kind of compensation of Nature for the imbecility exhibited in her verses.'[3]

---

[1] *WR*, 65 (Apr. 1856), 626.   [2] *WR*, 66 (July 1856), 261.
[3] *WR*, 66 (July 1856), 264.

In the October number Marian discussed Mrs. Stowe's *Dred*, praising her for her *invention* of the Negro novel with its lofty religious fervour, reminiscent of the best parts of *Old Mortality*. But she indicated the weakness of its idealization of the Negro. 'If the negroes are really so very good, slavery has answered as moral discipline', and this one-sided view deprives Mrs. Stowe of 'the most terribly tragic element in the relation of the two races —the Nemesis lurking in the vices of the oppressed'.[1] Charles Reade's *It's Never Too Late to Mend* Marian found an exceptional novel with much that is talented and clever, but not a work of genius. Reade is always self-conscious, working his characters up after types, and not knowing where to stop, exaggerating contrasts, wearying emotion by taxing it too repeatedly, even bursting into capitals to impress a reader with the magnitude of an idea.

In January 1857 Marian wrote both the 'Belles Lettres' and the section called 'History, Biography, Voyages and Travels'. The latter, for which Chapman paid her an extra £10, was routine journalism, written crisply and well, but of no great interest to the biographer. The 'Belles Lettres' began with Mrs. Browning's *Aurora Leigh*. Marian like most of her contemporaries received the book with enthusiasm. It did not blind her, however, to the derivative quality of a story which borrowed its catastrophe from *Jane Eyre*. 'Life has sadness and bitterness enough for a disappointed philanthropist like Romney Leigh, short of maiming or blindness; . . . the lavish mutilation of heroes' bodies, which has become the habit of novelists, . . . weakens instead of strengthening tragic effect.'[2] To Mrs. Phillipson, who had retorted to the ridicule of her *Lonely Hours* with *A Song in Prose to the Westminster Owl*, Marian devoted another page that must have made the lady wish she had left reviewers alone. Believing that it was Lewes who had slashed the book, Mrs. Phillipson attacks the 'Westminster Reviewer!—Bard!—Dramatist!—Actor! (that is provincial actor), Biographer! Philosopher!', and so on, even stooping to nasty allusions to Bayswater and Kensington. 'Our talents are by no means so versatile as those of the gentleman whom she undertakes to punish for our sins', Marian remarked; 'we are bound in honesty to disclaim the honour of being either "bard", "dramatist", "actor", or "biographer" . . . . It is not fair that any one should endure even a squirt vicariously.'[3]

The 'Belles Lettres' articles during these seven quarters noticed

[1] *WR*, 66 (Oct. 1856), 572–3.   [2] *WR*, 67 (Jan. 1857), 307.
[3] *WR*, 67 (July, 1856), 314.

166 different books, and Marian doubtless looked at many more that were not worth mention. The work gave her a close practical acquaintance with the literary market-place. Some of the books she was able to review for the *Leader* also, which paid her £1. 1*s*. for each article. Between March 1855, when she returned to England, and August 1856 she notes in the account of her literary earnings[1] payment for thirty-one articles in the *Leader*. For the Weimar article in *Fraser's*, which was divided into two parts, she received £14, and for four in the *Saturday Review*, £7. 7*s*. But the major part of her income she derived from the five long articles Chapman commissioned for the *Westminster*. Soon after returning to London in 1855 she had proposed 'Evangelical Teaching: Dr. Cumming'. She began reading for it in June, and it was finished 24 August. John Cumming, D.D., a Scot whose evangelistic preaching had required rebuilding his church in Covent Garden to seat a thousand—bringing pew rents of £1,500 a year—had published numerous works like *Genesis and Geology*, *Rome the Babylon of the Apocalypse*, *The Church before the Flood*, and *Lectures on the Book of Revelation*, which offered Marian ample ammunition for an annihilating account of the beliefs she had held so earnestly in girlhood. She exposed the lack of scrupulous veracity, the absence of real charity, and the perverted moral judgement, not of Dr. Cumming alone, but of all Evangelicals. Published in October 1855, the article made a great impression. Lewes, of course, singled it out for comment in the Literature columns of the *Leader*, which since May he had again been writing regularly. Walking with Marian one day in Richmond Park, he told her that the article had convinced him of true genius in her writing.[2]

At East Sheen they saw few visitors. Professor Richard Owen, the naturalist, lived at Sheen Lodge, where Lewes often called on him, and Marian too met him at this time. John Chapman was always welcome. He came to dinner on Sunday, 24 June, bringing proof of a long article that he had written on 'The Position of Woman in Barbarism and among the Ancients'. Marian gave him the criticism he asked for in a long letter the next day:

In that part of your article which consists of digested narrative your style is on the whole clear, easy, and forcible; but whenever you pass from narrative to dissertation, certain old faults reappear—inexactness of expression, triads and duads of verbs and adjectives, mixed

---

[1] *Letters*, VII. 358–9.   [2] Cross, I. 384.

metaphors, and a sort of watery volume that requires to be reduced by evaporation. Passages with these characteristics chiefly occur in the manuscript sheets and I have marked most of them with a pencil line by the side; but by and bye I will specify one or two.

A whole page of specific objections follows.

So much for little points of style which I commend to your attention. 'Progressive improvement' (2d page of manuscript) is a questionable phrase. You mean *gradual* improvement. To 'emerge from a catalepsy' is also questionable. The sentence on the same page which I have marked with a pencil line and star is bad. Pray rewrite it. 'Stepping stones' cannot be 'forged into fetters.'

Your sentences would often be much improved by being broken up. That plan of linking propositions together into unvarying, long sentences gives your style a tough, gutta percha sort of consistence. It should be more brittle—as most clear and bright things are. The sentence on page *g* of manuscript is an example of this. . . .

The article is very interesting and able. The manuscript portion, with the exception of what relates to Rome, seems to me very inferior to the slips, and I think it is quite worth your while to revise it thoroughly, with a view to force, point, and clearness.

I have written as unceremoniously as I used to do in the old days, believing that you will like that best.[1]

Poor Chapman, understandably discouraged, wrote to ask whether he should not abandon the whole thing. Marian replied, 27 June:

Assuredly your article is worth publishing. I think it very valuable and interesting; indeed I thought I had said so in my letter. It is for that very reason that I dwelt on certain defects of style which you can remedy by giving a little more trouble. The opening of the article would be really beautiful if the sentences were pruned a little. . . .

There is no reason for you to be desponding about your writing. You have made immense progress during the last few years, and you have so much force of mind and sincerity of purpose that you may work your way to a style which is free from vices, though perhaps you will never attain felicity—indeed, that is a free gift of Nature rather than a reward of labour. . . .

I am sure you will not attribute these observations to any conceited assumptions on my part, but to their real motive—personal and intellectual sympathy. If in writing hastily I have said anything at all impertinent, it is the vice of my expression and not of my feeling.[2]

The rigorous standard Marian held up for Chapman she adhered to in her own work, even at its hastiest.

---

[1] *Letters*, II. 205–7.   [2] Ibid. 208–9.

She had been writing to Mr. Bray almost every week since her return to England, perhaps hoping to elicit news of Rosehill in return. When he announced his intention of coming to East Sheen early in July, Marian was delighted; she renewed eagerly her exact directions about trains. He 'must get down at the *Mortlake* station. I will meet you there and conduct you to our home—if possible. If not, you have only three minutes' walk to get here, and any one will tell you which way to take.'[1] But his visit, 10 July, was not an unqualified success. Lewes was in bed with a cold, pains in his head, and a large abscess in his face; Marian too had caught cold the day before. Bray soon got into acrimonious argument with Lewes about phrenology, and, when she took her husband's side, accused her of having abandoned her old belief in the 'science'. In writing to him a few days later, Marian mentioned 'the fact of my having been ill as some apology for the very imperfect companionship and entertainment I gave you'. But she defended George's view of phrenology:

I am not conscious of falling off from the 'physiological basis'. I never believed more profoundly than I do now that character is based on organization. I never had a higher appreciation than I have now of the services which phrenology has rendered towards the science of man. But I do not, and I think I never shall, consider every man shallow or unconscientious who is unable to embrace all Mr. Combe's views of organology and psychology—especially as some of the ablest men I have ever known are in that position of inability.

And at the end of her letter she added: 'I am glad to hear that you enjoyed the view from Richmond Hill and that you had thus some compensation for the trouble you so kindly took in coming to see us. Mr. Lewes sends his kind regards.'[2] During George's illness she had been reading him Scott's novels out of an edition borrowed from Bray in May, when she was planning an article for *Fraser's*. In returning them she said: 'Reasons occurred for my *not* writing the projected article, but the loan effected *one* beneficent object, for when Mr. Lewes was too ill to listen to anything else I read him Old Mortality and the Fair Maid of Perth.'[3]

About once a week Lewes would go to town to deliver their manuscripts, do errands, see Agnes and his sons in Bedford Place, and call on his mother Mrs. John Willim. The boys probably thought that his long absences were dictated by ill health. They were too young to be burdened with his domestic complications,

[1] *Letters*, II. 204.   [2] Ibid. 210.   [3] Ibid. 215.

and he said nothing to them yet about ·the new Mrs. Lewes at
East Sheen. In August, when he was a little recovered from a
second abscess in his face, he took his three boys to Ramsgate for
a week's holiday. While he was away Marian worked hard at her
article on Cumming and walked alone in Richmond Park. Her
correspondence with Sara was fairly steady; but it was more than
a year since they had seen each other, and the letters lack something of the old warmth. Marian would send autographs for Sara's
collection—of Liszt, Varnhagen, Bulwer, or Currer Bell—hoping
for news of Rosehill in return. 'I think of you *so* often', she wrote.[1]
One September day, without warning, perhaps on impulse, Sara
defied the taboo and called at 7 Clarence Row. We do not know
whether she asked for 'Miss Evans'. But Marian and George were
not at home. 'Our walk had beguiled us further than usual',
Marian wrote: '—indeed I think it was the day we had a boat on
the Thames and were obstinately resisted on our return by the
spring tides which, as the Boatman said, "tries a fellow, them
does"'. She ended her letter: 'The smallest detail about you
thankfully received by | Your affectionate friend | Marian.'[2]

Cara, after sending her one letter of remonstrance to Berlin,
had maintained a disapproving silence. Marian could hardly have
sat describing the absurdities of Cumming's Evangelicalism without often recalling Cara's kindness to her in those trying days of
her rebellion at Foleshill. Before the article was finished, she
received another letter from Cara, written ostensibly to ask what
she wanted done with the sheets and pillow-cases stored for her at
Rosehill since her father died. In it the remonstrance was repeated.
Marian answered with an extraordinary statement of her position:

7 Clarence Row
September 4

Dear Cara
No one has better reason than myself to know how difficult it is to
produce a true impression by letters, and how likely they are to be misinterpreted even where years of friendship might seem to furnish a
sufficient key. And it seems the more probable to me that I misinterpreted your letter to me at Berlin since I find that my answer to it
produced totally false conclusions in your mind. Assuredly if there be
any one subject on which I feel no levity it is that of marriage and the
relation of the sexes—if there is any one action or relation of my life
which is and always has been profoundly serious, it is my relation to
Mr. Lewes. If any expression or parallel in my letter bore an opposite

[1] *Letters*, II. 213.   [2] *Letters*, II. 217.

construction it must have been, because you interpreted as of general application what I intended simply in answer to what I considered Mr. Combe's petty and absurd views about the effect on his reputation of having introduced me to one or two of his friends. *Nothing* that I said in that letter was intended as a discussion of the principles of my conduct or as an answer to your opinions on the subject.

It is, however, natural enough that you should mistake me in many ways, for not only are you unacquainted with Mr. Lewes's real character and the course of his actions, but also, it is several years now since you and I were much together, and it is possible that the modifications my mind has undergone may be in quite the opposite direction to what you imagine. No one can be better aware than yourself that it is possible for two people to hold different opinions on momentous subjects with equal sincerity and an equally earnest conviction that their respective opinions are alone the truly moral ones. If we differ on the subject of the marriage laws, I at least can believe of you that you cleave to what you believe to be good, and I don't know of anything in the nature of your views that should prevent you from believing the same of me. *How far* we differ I think we neither of us know; for I am ignorant of your precise views and apparently you attribute to me both feelings and opinions which are not mine. We cannot set each other quite right on this matter in letters, but one thing I can tell you in few words. Light and easily broken ties are what I neither desire theoretically nor could live for practically. Women who are satisfied with such ties do *not* act as I have done—they obtain what they desire and are still invited to dinner.

That any unworldly, unsuperstitious person who is sufficiently acquainted with the realities of life can pronounce my relation to Mr. Lewes immoral I can only understand by remembering how subtle and complex are the influences that mould opinion. But I *do* remember this, and I indulge in no arrogant or uncharitable thoughts about those who condemn us, even though we might have expected a somewhat different verdict. From the majority of persons, of course, we never looked for anything but condemnation. We are leading no life of self-indulgence, except indeed, that being happy in each other, we find everything easy. We are working hard to provide for others better than we provide for ourselves, and to fulfil every responsibility that lies upon us. Levity and pride would not be a sufficient basis for that.

Pardon me, dear Cara, if in vindicating myself from some unjust conclusions, I seem too cold and self-asserting. I should not care to vindicate myself, if I did not love you and desire to relieve you of the pain which you say these conclusions have given you. Whatever I may have misinterpreted before, I do not misinterpret your letter this morning, but read in it nothing else than love and kindness towards me to which my heart fully answers yes. I should like never to write about myself again—it is not healthy to dwell on one's own feelings and conduct, but only to try and live more faithfully and lovingly every fresh day.

I think not one of the endless words and deeds of kindness and forbearance you have ever shewn me has vanished from my memory. I recall them often, and feel, as about everything else in the past, how deficient I have been in almost every relation of my life. But that deficiency is irrevocable and I can find no strength or comfort except in 'pressing forward towards the things that are before,' and trying to make the present better than the past. But if we should never be very near each other again, dear Cara, do bear this faith in your mind, that I was not insensible or ungrateful to all your goodness, and that I am one amongst the many for whom you have not lived in vain.

Those dreadful sheets and pillow cases! Pray give them away if you won't use them, for I don't want them, and can never set up housekeeping on that small stock.

I am very busy just now, and have been obliged to write hastily. Bear this in mind, and believe that no meaning is mine which contradicts my assurance that I am your affectionate and earnest friend

Marian.

My love to Sara. I can't write more today but will write to her another day.[1]

This letter proved more effective than the earlier efforts. Cara now resumed correspondence, though reservedly. It was four years before they met again face to face.

When the 'Belles Lettres' and several shorter articles for the *Leader* had been sent off, Marian and George left East Sheen finally on 19 September 1855 and went to Worthing for a fortnight's holiday, taking lodgings at 21 Steyne. They were both worn out, 'miserably bilious and headachy'. But the weather was bright and warm, and after a few days they were bathing in the sea and taking long walks on the beach looking for shells. Returning to Surrey 3 October, they settled in new lodgings at 8 Park Shot, Richmond, which was to be their home for three and a half years. Here they were just a few steps from the Richmond station, within sight of the Old Deer Park, not half a mile from the Thames nor much further from Kew Gardens. Their landlady Mrs. Croft kept everything in 'the pink of order and cleanliness'.[2] The lodger on the floor below them was a clergyman, whom they were sometimes afraid they might alarm with a sudden outburst of 'very dramatic singing of Figaro etc.'[3] But a still more disturbing fear was the old possibility that someone might arrive and ask to see 'Miss Evans'. After telling the Brays that a call from Edward Noel would be welcome, Marian added in a letter to Sara: 'Mr. Lewes wishes me to write again—though I think it hardly necessary—to say that if Mr. Noel comes to see us—and we shall be very happy if he will do so—we hope you will impress on his memory that he must ask for *Mrs. Lewes* and not for Miss Evans, as a misunderstanding on this matter would be very painful.'[1] Even the address of letters was a continuing anxiety. To Bessie Parkes Marian wrote 22 March 1856:

Your address to me as *Miss Evans* was unfortunate, as I am not known under that name here. We find it indispensable to our comfort that I should bear Mr. Lewes's name while we occupy lodgings, and we are now with so excellent a woman that any cause of removal would be a misfortune. If you have occasion to write to me again, please to bear this in mind.[2]

In the little sitting-room at 8 Park Shot they both worked away industriously, having few diversions beyond their daily walks. Though Marian did not complain of it at the time, many years later she confessed that the scratching of George's pen used to drive her nearly wild. His 'big book' was finished: *The Life and Works of Goethe: with Sketches of His Age and Contemporaries*, published by David Nutt in two volumes, 1 November 1855. Lewes dedicated it to Thomas Carlyle, 'who first taught England to appreciate Goethe', and 'as a memorial of gratitude for intellectual guidance, and of esteem for rare and noble qualities'. Carlyle could not help being enthusiastic about the book. In his letter of thanks to Lewes he called it 'an excellent Biography—altogether transcendently so as Biographies are done in this country'—no mean praise from England's foremost biographer, then deeply immersed in *Frederick the Great*.[3] Marian filled nearly three columns of the *Leader* with an account of the book, but, because of Lewes's known connection with the paper, delivered no judgement on it. There was no dearth of praise for it elsewhere. Nutt paid Lewes £350 for the first edition; the right to reprint it in America and on the Continent and to translate it immediately into German produced another £100. During his lifetime Lewes realized more than a thousand pounds from the *Goethe*—deservedly, for it is an excellent book, and was widely acclaimed everywhere. It established Lewes as a notable literary figure at home and abroad. It is still in print in the Everyman edition.

Marian's 'Evangelical Teaching' in the October *Westminster*

---

[1] *Letters*, II. 230–1.   [2] *Letters*, II. 232.
[3] T. Carlyle to GHL, 3 Nov. 1855 (Yale). Lockhart had died in 1854.

Review also attracted much favourable comment. At Coventry, Mary Sibree, now Mrs. John Cash, read it aloud to the trio at Rosehill; she and Mr. Bray were sure it was by Marian. When he wrote, asking her to tell, he added that he would like to come to Park Shot or *any*where to see her. Marian replied at once:

Since you have found out the 'Cumming', I write by to-day's post just to say, that it *is* mine, but also to beg that you will not mention it as such to any one likely to transmit the information to London, as we are keeping the authorship a secret. The article appears to have produced a strong impression, and that impression would be a little counteracted if the author were known to be a *woman*. I have had a letter addressed to 'the author of article No. 4.' begging me to print it separately for 'the good of mankind in general'. It is so kind of you to rejoice in anything I do at all well.[1]

More important than the praise of old friends was a letter from Chapman, asking her to write an article on Heine for the January 1856 number. She and George had often discussed Heine with Varnhagen, one of his early friends. During their winter evenings in Berlin they read aloud his *Geständniss*. 'The wit burns low after the first 50 pages', Marian wrote in her Journal, 'and the want of principle and purpose makes it wearisome.'[2] Though Heine had been reprinted in America and a few of his books translated there, he was little known in England. Arnold's famous essay on him did not appear till 1863, when Lewes published it in the *Cornhill*, which he was then editing. Marian's pioneer account 'probably did more than any other single work in introducing to English-speaking peoples the genius that was Heine's'.[3] She began with a careful distinction between humour and wit, in both of which she found the German mind deficient. But Heine 'to Teutonic imagination, sensibility, and humour, adds an amount of *esprit* that would make him brilliant among the most brilliant Frenchmen'.[4] He is 'one of the most remarkable men of this age: no echo, but a real voice, and therefore, like all genuine things in this world, worth studying, . . . a surpassing lyric poet, . . . a humorist, . . . a wit, who holds in his hand the most scorching lightnings of satire; . . . an artist in prose literature, who has shown even more completely than Goethe the possibilities of German prose; . . . a lover of freedom'. Throughout the article there are long quotations from Heine, which provided the earliest English version of some of his

[1] *Letters*, II. 218.　　　　　　　　[2] GE Journal, 21 Dec. 1854.
[3] S. L. Wormley, *Heine in England* (Chapel Hill, 1943), p. 113.
[4] 'German Wit: Heinrich Heine', *WR*, 65 (Jan. 1856), 1–33; 6–7.

writings. Here again Marian's achievement as a tactful translator from the German has not been adequately recognized. She declared in one of her *Leader* articles about this time that 'Though a good translator is infinitely below the man who produces *good* original works, he is infinitely above the man who produces *feeble* original works.' In addition to knowledge of the language, the task demands high moral qualities in a translator—patience, rigid fidelity, and 'the sense of responsibility in interpreting another man's mind',[1] 'German Wit: Heinrich Heine' was sent off 28 November; two weeks later the 'Belles Lettres' followed. Chapman's payment for the two—£32. 12s.—was the largest she had received at one time. Her earnings for 1855 totalled £119. 8s.

Marian set out for Attleborough to spend Christmas with Chrissey and her children more cheerful than she had been for several years. She was disappointed that Fanny Houghton could not come from Leamington to spend the day with them, but did not accept the invitation to stay a night with her there on the way back to London. We do not know whether or not she saw Isaac at this time: Griff is only three miles from Attleborough. However, it is clear that she told none of her family about her marriage. Chrissey, who wrote to her occasionally, continued to send letters in care of Mr. Chapman. One invitation during the holiday that we know she refused to accept came from Charles Bray. On New Year's Day when she was again at Richmond she sent

A happy New Year to you and yours! I have never answered your note in which you invited me to call at your house on my way to my sister's. I am sure that note was written with the kindest intentions, but if you had thought twice you would have seen that I was not likely to take a journey twice as long as necessary and walk all through Coventry in order to make a call where I had only the invitation of the master of the house. I went straight from London to Nuneaton by express in two hours and a half, and returned in the same way. In this season one likes to abridge railway journeying as much as possible.[2]

Lewes had gone to spend Christmas as usual with Arthur Helps at Vernon Hill, where he stayed till 5 January. 'I am trying to fill up the gap his absence makes by being as industrious as possible', Marian wrote. She was reading George Meredith's *The Shaving of Shagpat* and Kingsley's *Greek Heroes*, both of which she discussed in the 'Belles Lettres' section of the *Westminster* for April 1856. She gave the *Leader* another review of Meredith's book and

[1] *Leader*, 20 Oct. 1855, p. 1015.   [2] *Letters*, II. 224.

one of Peter Von Bohlen's *Introduction to Genesis*, a translation
of a long work on the Higher Criticism, which Chapman had
published. Apart from some dozen articles in the *Leader* her main
task in the early months of 1856 was to complete her 'big book',
the translation of Spinoza's *Ethics*.

One compensation for the isolation of her life at Richmond was
the unbroken time it gave her for serious reading. She had finished
reading the *Odyssey* before she wrote in her Journal 13 June 1855,
'I began the second book of the *Iliad* in Greek this morning.' In
December she was reading Sophocles in a new edition of the
Antigone, which she reviewed for the *Leader*.[1] By brief references
we can trace her course through Greek drama: the *Ajax* (22
September 1856), the *Oedipus* trilogy (14 February, 8 April, 22
April 1857), the *Electra* (12 August), the *Philoctetes* (25 October).
The Aeschylus trilogy followed: the *Agamemnon* (6 December
1857), the *Choephori* (17 January 1858), and the *Eumenides* (3
February). The practice of reading Greek she kept up throughout
the rest of her life. R. C. Jebb, meeting her at Cambridge in 1873,
recalled her saying that Sophocles had influenced her most by
his 'delineation of the great primitive emotions'.[2] Vernon Rendall,
the editor of *Notes and Queries*, in a series of interesting articles
on 'George Eliot and the Classics', remarked on her fondness for
Sophocles, 'I have never seen so many references to him in the
writings of any other author.' Her first published story, 'Amos
Barton', quoted a couplet from the *Philoctetes*, and in subsequent
works she went on, says Rendall, 'to a garland of Greek which I
have not seen equalled in the writings of any author, inside or
outside fiction'.[3] Her knowledge of Latin was even wider. Horace
she naturally quoted most frequently, but Virgil, Cicero, Persius,
Livy, Tacitus, Plautus, Quintilian, and Pliny are some of the others
who came easily to her mind. This genuine knowledge of the
classics—more solid than that Thackeray got at Charterhouse and
Cambridge, probably wider than that Trollope got at Harrow and
Winchester—was acquired during the long period of social ostra-
cism when, because of her honest avowal of the union with Lewes,
she was not invited to dinner.

Huxley's sneer that he was a mere 'book-scientist' stung Lewes
more sharply than he admitted. In the eighteenth century Goethe

[1] *Leader*, 29 Mar. 1856, p. 306
[2] C. L. Jebb, *Life and Letters of Sir Richard Claverhouse Jebb* (1907), p. 155.
[3] *Notes and Queries*, 13 Dec. 1947, p. 545; 27 Dec. 1947, p. 565.

had been called a 'facile amateur', and Lewes devoted a long chapter of his biography to defending 'The Poet as Man of Science'. Though conceding that Goethe was not one of 'those laborious and meritorious workers who with microscope and scalpel painfully collect the materials from which Science emerges',[1] Lewes showed the importance of some of his discoveries, citing the same modern authorities he had appealed to in defending himself against Huxley. The charge was not althogether true of Lewes, since he had been a medical student early in life, and his interest in comparative anatomy had revived in the 1850s, when Herbert Spencer was collecting evidence for his articles on the Development Hypothesis. Yet Lewes was not primarily a worker 'with microscope and scalpel'. One day by a pretty stream at Ilmenau they watched a caterpillar crawling on a leaf; when Lewes cut it in two, 'the fore part set to work to devour the other half', Marian wrote. 'I made a little paper box that we might carry it home and observe the phenomenon; but nothing came of it, for the head did not flourish on the tail, and soon became inanimate.'[2] At East Sheen in 1855 Lewes consulted his neighbour Richard Owen on some of the scientific problems concerning Goethe. He was willing now to confess himself 'an amateur, ignorant, but anxious to learn',[3] and when the *Goethe* was finished, he resolved to increase his knowledge of biology through careful research. Borrowing Arthur Helps's microscope, he began systematic study.

Marian described herself at this time as 'reading Homer and science and rearing tadpoles'.[4] Their holiday in September 1855 took them to Worthing in search of polyps as much as of health, and they were already planning as soon as the weather got warm 'to run away to mountains and molluscs and sea breezes'.[5] One day in April, Spencer took them to the Crystal Palace, re-erected in Sydenham as an enormous museum, and lectured them on his biological theories. He had gone to Tenby the previous autumn on the advice of Huxley, who spent his honeymoon there. Like every other place at that time, it disappointed Spencer, though his report of the marine life to be found on the coast was attractive. Lewes was far from well, still tormented by 'that terrible singing in his ears which has never left him since the commencement of his illness two years ago'.[6] But ill health was a minor pretext.

[1] *Goethe*, II. 135.
[2] GE Journal, 21 Sept. 1854; 'Recollections of Weimar'.
[3] *Sea-side Studies* (1858), p. 101.   [4] *Letters*, II. 202.
[5] Ibid. 235.   [6] Ibid. 253.

Lewes was determined by the observation and dissection of marine animals to try to discover some of the 'complex facts of life'. Marian could write for the *Westminster* and the *Leader* at the coast as well as at Richmond, and Lewes meant to draw from his work a series of articles on natural history that would be both popular and truly scientific.

They set out 8 May 1856, 'a cold, unfriendly day', Marian called it. They had to change first at Windsor with an interval between trains too short to let them walk around the Castle. Bristol, where they waited three hours, had little to show, and they sat—both headachy—in a dreary room at the dirty railway station. Reaching Exeter at ten, they 'were delighted to find a comfortable bedroom' at the station hotel. In the morning after breakfast they strolled into town to see the Cathedral.

As we passed the door it was ajar and we peeped in across the locked gate which shut out free entrance. The interior seemed very fine, but our glimpse was interrupted by the approach of the hard, dry-looking woman that alternates as key-keeper with the oily sexton in English cathedrals. 'Can we see the Cathedral?' I asked. 'Yes, I can *show* you the Cathedral.' We declined to be 'shown' and walked on, taking a few more glances at the pleasant streets.[1]

They had no sixpences to spare. At Barnstaple they said good-bye to the railway and 'took to the good old fashioned stage coach', which finally 'rattled and swung up the hilly street of Ilfracombe and stopped at the door of the Clarence Hotel'. Within an hour they had discovered a cheap and delightful lodging at Runnymede Villa, where they lived happily for the next seven weeks.

Marian's 'Recollections of Ilfracombe'[2] show her poised on the threshold of fiction. The lesson of realism that so impressed her in Ruskin's *Modern Painters* she was practising consciously in this account expanded from her Journal.

I never before longed so much to know the names of things as during this visit to Ilfracombe. The desire is part of the tendency that is now constantly growing in me to escape from all vagueness and inaccuracy into the daylight of distinct, vivid ideas. The mere fact of naming an object tends to give definiteness to our conception of it—we have then a sign that at once calls up in our minds the distinctive qualities which mark out for us that particular object from all others.[3]

---

[1] *Letters*, II. 239.
[2] *Letters*, II. 238–52, from GE's Journal.   [3] *Letters*, II. 251.

Another—perhaps less happy—influence of Ruskin is sometimes seen in the over-elaborate descriptions of scenery. They were not written for herself alone. Lewes, who declared half-seriously in *Sea-side Studies*, 'I have no descriptive power', put into the book a good deal of description, some of which (e.g. pages 30–1, 75–7) has been lifted bodily from Marian's 'Recollections'—another example of his helpmate's anonymous collaboration. Sometimes Lewes touches up the account with details Marian omitted: when they go out hunting specimens, she is wearing clothes that 'won't spoil' and carrying the landing net.[1] He puts in little sketches of their life at Ilfracombe:

> Wearied with hammering, clambering, and stooping in this blazing sunlight of a summer noon, we seat ourselves on a convenient boulder for half-an-hour's repose. My companion, whose legs are lolling in a shallow pool, brings out a pocket-pistol of sherry and a bag of biscuits. To this 'repast we do ample justice' (as detestable writers with unerring unanimity always say when they want to describe eating and drinking), and then the blue lazy curl of a mild havannah rises into the warm air, making contentment more content.[2]

Most of their mornings were spent 'naturalizing' along the shore, knocking anemones from the rock with hammer and chisel, and gathering polyps or annelids. In the afternoons after the specimens had been carefully sorted in the proper containers, they often took long inland walks, of which Marian gives detailed descriptions. Once, as they were coming home, 'we rested on a gate under the trees, and a blind man came up to rest also. He told us in his slow way what a fine "healthy spot" this was—yes a very healthy spot—a healthy spot. And then we went on our way and saw his face no more.'[3] Lewes's version, with an eye towards the magazine, tells how the blind man 'held down his head; alas! it was useless for him to hold it erect, fronting the lovely scene'.[4] He also describes their coming upon a little girl lying asleep on the rock, 'her rosy cheek resting on her little arm', the sun pouring down on her and on the milk in the can by her side. 'All I know is, that the picture was very touching, and I placed a penny in the child's half-closed hand that she might find it on awaking. She would think some fairy placed it there.' This episode is a little suspect both for its sentimental tone and because it is not mentioned by Marian.[5] She wrote to Charles Bray in March: 'You don't

[1] *Sea-side Studies*, p. 17.   [2] Ibid. p. 26.
[3] *Letters*, II. 249.   [4] *Sea-side Studies*, p. 77.
[5] Among Thornton Lewes's juvenilia at Yale is a 16-line poem 'The Milk Girl'.

know what a severely practical person I am become, and what
a sharp eye I have to the main chance. I keep the purse and
dole out sovereigns with all the pangs of a miser.'[1] So closely did
they figure expenses that in all their seven weeks at Ilfracombe
they ascended the Tors only twice; 'for a tax of 3d per head was
demanded on this luxury, and we could not afford a sixpenny
walk very frequently'.[2] A penny to a sleeping child is not likely
to have been overlooked.

Marian's translation of the *Ethics* was another example of silent
collaboration with Lewes. She had finished the whole manuscript
and revised it, ready for the printer, by 19 February; before leaving
for Ilfracombe Lewes delivered it with his brief introduction at
Bohn's office. Lewes had done much to make Spinoza more widely
known in England. He was the author of the unsigned articles on
Spinoza and Spinozism in the *Penny Cyclopaedia* (1843).[3] His long
article for the *Westminster Review* (May 1843) he reprinted as a
pamphlet (with the profit of which he paid some book bills) and
later incorporated in the Spinoza chapters of his *Biographical
History of Philosophy*. Bohn, who had published Lewes's book
on Comte, originally agreed with him to edit and annotate for
the Philosophical Library translations of the *Ethics* and the *Tractatus Theologico-politicus* to be done by a man named Kelly.
According to Bohn's account, Kelly was to have been paid £50
and Lewes, £25. But Kelly soon abandoned the difficult task.
Lewes, before he left for Weimar, discussed the project with Bohn's
son, who agreed that he might have the £75 if he supplied a translation of the *Ethics*, which had never been put into English, and
reprint such excerpts as he wished to quote from the seventeenth-
century version of the *Tractatus*.

But the elder Bohn, who suspected that Lewes had abandoned
his translation for the more lucrative *Goethe*, thought the price too
high, and wrote to him 3 June asking to see the agreement, of
which his son had kept no copy. 'It is so long since we entertained
the subject that I had lost sight of it, indeed, given it up till I
lately saw your M.S. and reminder. . . . I presume you mean the
printer to modernize the English of the printed volume, as it will

---

Founded on Fact', which tells the same story. GHL has endorsed it: 'June 1856.
Sent to Ilfracombe.' Perhaps Thornie invented it.

[1] *Letters*, II. 233.

[2] Ibid. 251.

[3] GHL's contributions to the *Penny Cyclopaedia*, collected by him, are in Dr.
Williams's Library (A. 12. 24).

want alteration.'[1] To tell the truth, Bohn was no longer eager to publish Spinoza. 'What two or three years ago might be a reasonable speculation may be a very doubtful one now', he wrote on 7 June. He thought that if half the volume was to be a mere reprint of the old translation, which he had never contemplated, £50 was a fair price. He had never dreamed of abridging, 'for I detest abridgements'. His uniform rule was to pay £3 or £3. 3s. per sheet of thirty-two pages for translations, and he saw no reason to vary it for the *Ethics*. But since his son had come to that understanding with Lewes, he would abide by their terms. 'Please bring it with you, and we will enter into a proper agreement.'[2]

On reading this Lewes flew into a violent rage. It is not quite clear what he hoped to accomplish by answering what he called Bohn's 'insulting letter' with one (if we may judge from his draft) even more insulting. 'I altogether decline to have transactions with a man who shows such wonderful facility in forgetting', he wrote. 'I beg you will send back my M.S. and consider the whole business at an end between us.' Perhaps he was hoping to find a publisher who would pay more for Marian's translation. In 1859 he offered it to A. & C. Black, who showed some interest, but when he again asked £75 for it, they declined. They in turn asked him to write a short article on Spinoza for their *Encyclopaedia Britannica*, which he in turn declined. So the manuscript of Marian's 'big book', the five parts still tied up in their blue wrappers, remains unpublished in the Beinecke Library at Yale University. Marian's Journal is silent on this unpleasant conclusion of her long labour.

The only real acquaintance they made at Ilfracombe was 'the charming little zoological curate' the Reverend George Tugwell. An Oriel man, not yet twenty-six years old, Tugwell had already published five small books—an essay on architecture, a tale, a devotional tract called *The Church in the Household*, and *The North Devon Handbook*. But it was his *Manual of Sea Anemones Commonly Found on the English Coast* that attracted Lewes, who called on him soon after they arrived. Tugwell, eager to help the well-known author, proved 'most good-natured in lending and giving apparatus and "critturs" of all sorts',[3] and invaluable practical instruction as well. They found him 'a delightful com-

---

[1] Henry George Bohn to GHL, 3 June 1856 (Yale).
[2] 13 June 1856 (Yale).
[3] *Letters*, II. 253.

panion on expeditions'. He was doubtless unaware that Mrs. Lewes was the Translator of Strauss and Feuerbach.

She was working on one of her finest articles for the *Westminster*, 'The Natural History of German Life', a review of W. H. Riehl's *Die bürgerliche Gesellschaft* and *Land und Leute*. Sharing in Lewes's biological researches had intensified her desire to 'escape from all vagueness'. Her mind absorbed a good deal of new scientific knowledge that was later to crop out in her novels. For example, in *The Mill on the Floss* when she asks how Mr. Stelling should 'be expected to know that education was a delicate and difficult business? any more than an animal endowed with a power of boring a hole through a rock should be expected to have wide views of excavation', she is recalling her acquaintance with the *teredo navalis*, whose habits Lewes describes in *Sea-side Studies*.[1] In his close examination of marine animals Lewes was pursuing 'the humble and faithful study of nature' advocated by Ruskin just as Riehl was in his analysis of German peasants. Marian was about to begin an equally truthful study of English provincial life. In her article she came out strongly on the side of realism. The painter, she wrote,

is still under the influence of idyllic literature, which has always expressed the imagination of the cultivated and town-bred, rather than the truth of rustic life. Idyllic ploughmen are jocund when they drive their team afield; idyllic shepherds make bashful love under hawthorn bushes; idyllic villagers dance in the chequered shade and refresh themselves, not immoderately, with spicy nut-brown ale. But no one who has seen much of actual ploughmen thinks them jocund; no one who is well acquainted with the English peasantry can pronounce them merry. The slow gaze, in which no sense of beauty beams, no humour twinkles, —the slow utterance, and the heavy slouching walk, remind one rather of that melancholy animal the camel, than of the sturdy countryman, with striped stockings, red waistcoat, and hat aside, who represents the traditional English peasant. Observe a company of haymakers. When you see them at a distance, tossing up the forkfuls of hay in the golden light, while the wagon creeps slowly with its increasing burthen over the meadow, and the bright green space which tells of work done gets larger and larger, you pronounce the scene 'smiling', and you think these companions in labour must be as bright and cheerful as the picture to which they give animation. Approach nearer, and you will certainly find that haymaking time is a time for joking, especially if there are women among the labourers; but the coarse laugh that bursts out every now and then, and expresses the triumphant taunt, is as far as

[1] *Mill on the Floss*, Bk. II, ch. 4; *Sea-side Studies*, pp. 81–4.

possible from your conception of idyllic merriment. That delicious effervescence of the mind which we call fun, has no equivalent for the northern peasant, except tipsy revelry; the only realm of fancy and imagination for the English clown exists at the bottom of the third quart pot.[1]

As Marian knew well from her youth in Warwickshire, the 'selfish instincts are not subdued by the sight of buttercups. . . . To make men moral something more is requisite than to turn them out to grass.' It is the function of painter or novelist to extend our sympathy with our fellow men by teaching us to feel, 'not for the heroic artisan or the sentimental peasant, but for the peasant in all his coarse apathy, and the artisan in all his suspicious selfishness'. Dickens (though the article does not name him) is our

one great novelist who is gifted with the utmost power of rendering the external traits of our town population; and if he could give us their psychological character—their conceptions of life, and their emotions —with the same truth as their idiom and manners, his books would be the greatest contribution Art has ever made to the awakening of social sympathies. But . . . he scarcely ever passes from the humorous and external to the emotional and tragic, without becoming as transcendent in his unreality as he was a moment before in his artistic truthfulness . . ., encouraging the miserable fallacy that high morality and refined sentiment can grow out of harsh social relations, ignorance, and want; or that the working-classes are in a condition to enter at once into a millennial state of *altruism*, wherein everyone is caring for everyone else, and no one for himself.[2]

If a man of sufficient moral and intellectual breadth, Marian continues, would devote himself to studying 'the natural history of our social classes' and give us the results in a book 'well nourished with specific facts', his work would be a valuable aid to the social and political reformer. The article is one of the richest she ever wrote. In it we see her mind turning back to the memories of her childhood among the common people of Warwickshire with the vivid sympathy that was soon to flower in her fiction. Any one who wishes to understand the origin of George Eliot's novels should read the essay on Riehl.

When it had gone off to Chapman in London together with the 'Belles Lettres', she and George left Ilfracombe, 26 June, for Tenby on the coast of South Wales. The flight across the Bristol Channel now takes only a few minutes. In 1856 it took all day—

[1] *WR*, 66 (July 1856), 51–79; 53.   [2] Ibid., 55.

by boat to Swansea, by railway to Narberth Road, then by coach to Tenby. During the journey Marian's quick eye found pictures everywhere, even at 'dismal, smelly Swansea', There it

was the sight of two 'cockle women,' who would make a fine subject for a painter. One of them was the grandest woman I ever saw—six feet high, carrying herself like a Greek warrior, and treading the earth with unconscious majesty. They wore large woollen shawls of a rich brown, doubled lengthwise, with the end thrown back again over the left shoulder so as to fall behind in graceful folds. The grander of the two carried a great pitcher in her hand, and wore a quaint little bonnet set upright on her head. Her face was weather-beaten and wizened, but her eyes were bright and piercing and the lines of her face, with its high cheek-bones, strong and characteristic. The other carried her pitcher on her head, and was also a fine old woman, but less majestic in her port than her companion. The guard at the railway told us that one of the porters had been insolent the other day to a cockle woman, and that she immediately pitched him off the platform into the road below![1]

At Tenby they stayed five weeks. Marian roamed the sands she had first walked with the Brays and the Hennells in 1843, collecting molluscs and medusae for George's microscope, and in the evenings reading zoology and Shakespeare aloud. At the end of July Edward F. S. Pigott, now the mainstay of the *Leader*, came to spend a few days with them while waiting for his brother to take him away on his yacht. Lewes showed him some 'microscopic marvels', and two delightful puppies, Sambo and Rose. After lunch they all went in an open pony carriage to Lydstep, but the tide was so high that they could not enter the caves. Back at Tenby they heard a Mormon preacher after dinner

holding forth to some sailors, their wives, and a tribe of children. The whole scene was very ludicrous. The preacher, not above twenty, was fluent but perfectly *un*influential, grinding the same barren chaff, and never hitting on any topic which could arrest the hearers. The two Elders who stood beside him—caryatides of imbecility—were memorable figures! There was a troublesome foreground of boys and girls, fighting, playing and making noises. But the men were silent and respectful.[2]

Then they rambled on the sands, where the tide was now low enough to let them enter the second cave of St. Catherine's. Here Lewes made the pools phosphorescent by stirring them with his stick; as they came out they admired the grand buttresses and pillars, 'which reminded us of the Egyptian Idols at Sydenham'.

[1] *Letters*, II. 251–2.   [2] GHL Journal, 28 July 1856.

At the end of a week Pigott's brother arrived in his yacht, had them all aboard for lunch, and sailed away the next day, leaving them 'once more quiet and alone'.[1]

Their other visitor at Tenby was Barbara Leigh Smith. Though Marian had met her several times as Bessie Parkes's friend, they were not at all intimate. But soon after Marian was settled at East Sheen in July 1855 Barbara wrote her a sympathetic letter, 'a manifestation of her strong noble nature', which Marian sent on to Sara Hennell, asking her to burn it.[2] In January 1856 Barbara, an active champion of women's rights, asked Marian to sign a petition to Parliament urging enactment of a law to permit married women to own property. Marian signed it. Possibly she was the one responsible for revising the clause about the husband's responsibility for debts contracted by his wife, which (as she knew full well) 'often produces much injustice'.[3] At Ilfracombe Marian had received another letter from Barbara suggesting that she might come down for a few days of sketching. 'I wish I could drink in the sight of you among other pleasant things', Marian replied; and

perhaps if the weather will have the goodness to clear up, you can make a little expedition to Ilfracombe before we leave. . . .

I am heartily pleased to hear of the success your pictures have, and especially of Ruskin's encouragement. What books his two last are! I think he is the finest writer living.

I shall say nothing of sorrows and renunciations, but I understand and feel what you must have to do and bear. Yes—I hope we shall know each other better, and that you will know Mr. Lewes too, for he is far better worth knowing than I.[4]

The 'sorrows and renunciations' probably allude to another experience Marian and Barbara shared in common: they had both been in love with John Chapman. His extraordinary affair with Barbara reached its climax in the summer of 1855, when he urged her to announce to her family that she intended to live with Chapman, even though he was married; she would then, in Chapman's words, 'be able, without fear and undue anxiety and without the knowledge of the world, to be really united with me and to look forward with joyous anticipation to becoming a Mother'.[5] Barbara hesitated, not sure that she loved him enough

[1] GE Journal, 3 Aug. 1856.　　　　　　　　　[2] *Letters*, II. 211.
[3] Ibid. 227.　　　　　　　　　　　　　　　　　[4] Ibid. 255.
[5] For an account of this affair see G. S. Haight, *George Eliot and John Chapman* (1940), pp. 87–92.

for this drastic step. One day when she spoke in a general way of her belief in free love, her father advised her to go to America to practise it. Chapman tried to compose a letter that would make the arrangement clear to Mr. Smith, but found it too difficult; 'I scarcely knew what to say.' Still, he was optimistic. 'Try to be hopeful and peaceful', he wrote to Barbara, on 17 September 1855; 'rely upon it we shall be happy yet. Lewes and M. E. seemed to be perfectly so.' Spurred on, perhaps, by their notorious example, Barbara finally found courage to tell her father that she intended to live with Chapman. Mr. Smith's strenuous objections must be inferred, but he quickly put an end to the affair. These were Barbara's sorrows and renunciations, and they could not fail to give her a deeper sympathy with Marian.

Barbara came to Tenby 12 July and stayed four days, walking the sands with them, painting landscapes, sketching a new genus of annelid for Lewes, and passing long hours in most intimate conversation with Marian. The warm friendship they formed here was never broken. Marian wrote in her Journal:

> We enjoyed her society very much, but were deeply touched to see that three years had made her so much older and sadder. Her activity for great objects is admirable, and contact with her is a fresh inspiration to work while it is day. On Tuesday evening she came to tell us about her interview with her 'Aunt Patty'—a scene beyond the conception of Molière. We parted from her at the door of the Coburg at about ½ past 11.[1]

During this visit Barbara came to know and like Lewes, too. Before leaving Tenby she wrote to Bessie: 'I do wish, my dear, that you would revise your view of Lewes. I have quite revised mine. Like you, I thought him an extremely sensual man. Marian tells me that in their intimate marital relationship he is unsensual, extremely considerate. His manner to her is delightful. It is plain to me that he makes her extremely happy.'[2] Without using the exact words, Barbara explained that the Leweses practised some form of birth control, and intended to have no children. She could see that Chapman's account of their happiness was not exaggerated.

Their health had improved with the daily exercise in the bright sunshine and sea air. The satisfying sexual life gave Marian a sense

[1] GE Journal, 20 July 1856.
[2] These words are not Barbara's, but are taken from a description of the letter given me by Bessie's daughter Mrs. Belloc Lowndes, 31 Aug. 1942, soon after she had destroyed it.

of well-being she had never known before. In her Journal 20 July she noted that 'The fortnight has slipped away without my being able to show much result from it'—beyond a review for the *Leader*, her 'Recollections of Ilfracombe', and an introduction to an article on Edward Young begun in April. 'Besides these trifles', she continued, 'I have done no *visible* work. But I have absorbed many ideas and much bodily strength; indeed I do not remember ever feeling so strong in mind and body as I feel at this moment.' Her creative life was about to begin.

From early childhood Marian had dreamed of writing stories. 'Edward Neville' is the earliest fragment we have. The description of the Staffordshire village mentioned in the autobiographical section of her Journal called 'How I Came to Write Fiction', may date from 1846, when Sara Hennell fancied she 'must be writing her novel'.

It had always been a vague dream of mine that some time or other I might write a novel, and my shadowy conception of what the novel was to be, varied, of course, from one epoch of my life to another. But I never went farther towards the actual writing of the novel than an introductory chapter describing a Staffordshire village and the life of the neighbouring farm houses, and as the years passed on I lost any hope that I should ever be able to write a novel, just as I desponded about everything else in my future life. I always thought I was deficient in dramatic power, both of construction and dialogue, but I felt I should be at my ease in the descriptive parts of a novel. My 'introductory chapter' was pure description though there were good materials in it for dramatic presentation. It happened to be among the papers I had with me in Germany, and one evening at Berlin, something led me to read it to George. He was struck with it as a bit of concrete description, and it suggested to him the possibility of my being able to write a novel, though he distrusted—indeed disbelieved in, my possession of any dramatic power. Still, he began to think that I might as well try, some time, what I could do in fiction, and by and bye when we came back to England and I had greater success than he had ever expected in other kinds of writing, his impression that it was worth while to see how far my mental power would go towards the production of a novel, was strengthened. He began to say very positively, 'You must try and write a story,' and when we were at Tenby he urged me to begin at once. I deferred it, however, after my usual fashion, with work that does not present itself as an absolute duty. But one morning as I was lying in bed, thinking what should be the subject of my first story, my thoughts merged themselves into a dreamy doze, and I imagined myself writing a story of which the title was—'The Sad Fortunes of the

Reverend Amos Barton'. I was soon wide awake again, and told G. He said, 'O what a capital title!' and from that time I had settled in my mind that this should be my first story.[1]

If that Tenby lodging-house is still standing, it might justly display a plaque saying: 'George Eliot was born here.'

By the end of July their work at Tenby was nearly done. Lewes, no longer a mere 'book-scientist', had made himself a practical zoologist, had described some unknown species of marine animals, and collected enough material for several articles in *Blackwood's*. They packed up the precious specimens and their books and papers and equipment, took the steamer to Bristol on 8 August, spent the night at Bath, and were at home in Richmond the next day. Marian was eager to get to her story. But first she had to write an article for the October *Westminster* and finish the 'Belles Lettres' and the 'History' sections of the reviews, which she had agreed to do as well—a total of twenty-seven books to be covered. Charles Bray sent her an appreciative letter about the article on Riehl. 'Such things', she replied, 'encourage me and help me to do better. I never think what I write is good for anything till other people tell me so, and even then it always seems to me as if I should never write anything *else* worth reading.'[2] It was the Brays' last summer at Rosehill, which his dwindling income had compelled them to give up for Ivy Cottage nearby. He did not tell her that Mrs. Thornton Hunt and two of her children were visiting them for a fortnight, lying on the bearskin under the old acacia, which Marian was never to see again.

Lewes began at once arranging to put Charlie and Thornie in boarding school. Marian inquired of Sara Hennell about the possibility of placing them with her old friend John Sibree, then a tutor near Stroud, who could not take them. Sara, however, sent Marian a circular describing Hofwyl, where the Noel brothers had been educated. It was an interesting school near Berne, founded in 1806 by von Fellenberg on Pestalozzian principles. It proved to be exactly right for the Lewes boys. On Monday, 25 August, Agnes and Baker (Nursie) brought the boys to George at London Bridge Station, and they started for Switzerland. In Paris the boys 'were in ecstasies with the shops, wanting to buy everything to send home to Mamma and the children', he wrote in his Journal.

[1] 'How I Came to Write Fiction', in GE's Journal. *Letters*, II. 406–10.
[2] *Letters*, II. 260.

They reached Hofwyl 28 August. The boys were enchanted with the school, and Lewes was pleased with the headmaster, Dr. Müller, and his wife. He stayed three days, roaming about the place, going with them to bathe, rowing on the lake, and in the evenings playing games with them. But 'Boys not sorry to be left', he noted.

Marian described how she spent the interval in a letter to Charles Bray, who was proposing to come and see them:

> I had counted on this space of solitary time to get an article written which I had promised to let Mr. Chapman have for his next number. But lo! on Tuesday came seven large devils of toothache in place of one little devil that had been teazing me now and then, and from Tuesday till Saturday I was nothing but a frightful energumen. The doctor came and said it was neuralgia, and dosed me with quinine. That didn't do so we sent for the dentist, who decided that it was simply my good-for-nothing wisdom tooth. So I was chloroformed *twice*, and at last —on Saturday evening—the tooth was got out.
>
> I had written to Mr. Chapman begging him to let me off and get a substitute, but he cruelly wrote back that he *must* have the article. So here am I on this blessed 1st of September, with this odious article to write in a hurry and with Mr. Lewes coming home to reduce my writing time to the minimum. *That* is why I am vexed you are coming on the 6th, for we MUST see you, if everything else goes wrong. Send me word exactly when you shall be here.[1]

The 'odious article' was 'Silly Novels by Lady Novelists'.[2] It had been suggested to Marian in July by *Compensation*, a novel of what she called the 'mind-and-millinery species', and she thought that a discussion of it and a few others might be made the 'vehicle of some wholesome truth as well as of some amusement'.[3] The heroine of *Compensation* is a phoenix, so learned that she reads the Bible in the original *tongues*, and 'can talk with perfect correctness in any language except English'. Its absurd plot is 'a wonderful *pot pourri* of Almack's, Scotch second-sight, Mr. Rogers's breakfasts, Italian brigands, death-bed conversions, superior authoresses, Italian mistresses, and attempts at poisoning old ladies, the whole served up with a garnish of talk about "faith and development", and "most original minds" '. The most objectionable feature of such books is the absurd diction, of which Marian exhibits some choice specimens. A second species of silly novel is the 'oracular', in which the writer's religious, philo-

---

[1] *Letters*, ii. 261.   [2] *WR*, 66 (Oct. 1856), 442–61.
[3] *Letters*, ii. 258.

sophical, or moral theories are expounded. As a general rule 'the ability of a lady novelist to describe actual life and her fellow-men is in inverse proportion to her confident eloquence about God and the other world'. Marian used the epithet 'silly' advisedly. 'If as the world has long agreed, a very great amount of instruction will not make a wise man, still less will a very mediocre amount of instruction make a wise woman. And the most mischievous form of feminine silliness is the literary form.' For all their display, these ladies are not well educated. They mistake 'vagueness for depth, bombast for eloquence, and affectation for originality'.

A really cultured woman, like a really cultured man, is all the simpler and the less obtrusive for her knowledge. . . . She neither spouts poetry nor quotes Cicero on slight provocation. . . . She does not write books to confound philosophers, perhaps because she is able to write books that delight them. In conversation she is the least formidable of women, because she understands you, without wanting to make you aware that you *can't* understand her. She does not give you information, which is the raw material of culture,—she gives you sympathy, which is its subtlest essence.[1]

Novels of the 'oracular' species are inspired by some form of High Church interest. But those of an even more numerous class, the 'white neck-cloth species', take their tone of thought and feeling from the Evangelical party. In one respect they are meritoriously realistic: 'their favourite hero, the Evangelical young curate is always rather an insipid personage'. And though it is less excusable for an Evangelical to 'seek her subjects among titles and carriages', the novels of the 'white neck-cloth' school are as snobbish as the rest. 'The real drama of Evangelicalism—and it has abundance of fine drama for any one who has genius enough to discern and reproduce it—lies among the middle and lower classes. . . . Why can we not have pictures of religious life among the industrial classes in England as interesting as Mrs. Stowe's pictures of religious life among the negroes?' Marian asked. The article ends with some remarks about the critics, who treat a silly lady's novel with 'the choicest phraseology of puffery', praising in inverse proportion to the degree of excellence, while 'Harriet Martineau, Currer Bell, and Mrs. Gaskell have been treated as cavalierly as if they had been men.' The old excuse that women write because they have few other spheres of occupation cannot serve if they write badly. 'A cluster of great names, both living and dead', prove that

[1] *WR*, 66 (Oct. 1856), 455.

women can produce novels not only fine, but among the very finest; —novels, too, that have a precious speciality, lying quite apart from masculine aptitudes and experience. No educational restrictions can shut women out from the materials of fiction, and there is no species of art which is so free from rigid requirements. Like crystalline masses, it may take any form, and yet be beautiful; we have only to pour in the right elements—genuine observation, humour, and passion. . . . But in novel-writing there are no barriers for incapacity to stumble against, no external criteria to prevent a writer from mistaking foolish facility for mastery.[1]

Marian's long employment as a reviewer gave her sound knowledge of the weaknesses of ephemeral fiction. When she began to write, she would run no danger of adding to the number of silly novels by lady novelists.

Her article was finished and dispatched to Chapman 12 September; the 'Belles Lettres' followed on the 19th. The next night she and George celebrated by going to the theatre for the first time since returning from Germany eighteen months before. On 23 September she recorded in her Journal: 'Began to write "The Sad Fortunes of the Reverend Amos Barton," which I hope to make one of a series called "Scenes of Clerical Life." '

[1] *WR*, 66 (Oct. 1856), 461.

CHAPTER VIII

THE REAL DRAMA OF EVANGELICALISM
SCENES OF CLERICAL LIFE

※

'THE real drama of Evangelicalism—and it has abundance of fine drama for any one who has genius enough to discern and reproduce it—lies among the middle and lower classes,' Marian had written. In 'Amos Barton' she reproduces a drama she had witnessed during those earnest Evangelical years of her adolescence. She took for her hero, not a curate of the 'white neck-cloth' school of fiction, but 'a man whose virtues were not heroic, and who had no undetected crime within his breast; who had not the slightest mystery hanging about him, but was palpably and unmistakably commonplace'. He was middle class, middle-aged. 'His very faults were middling—he was not *very* ungrammatical. It was not in his nature to be superlative in anything; unless, indeed, he was superlatively middling, the quintessential extract of mediocrity.'[1] This unheroic hero was drawn from keen observation of the Reverend John Gwyther, Curate of Chilvers Coton, 1831–41, whose sermons she had heard, who had officiated at her mother's funeral and her sister's wedding. Gwyther graduated B.A., 1828, St. John's College, Cambridge, where he had been under the powerful influence of Charles Simeon. Two or three years of experience at Birmingham had developed in him no more tact than Amos Barton has. When he came to Coton in 1831, he pressed his Evangelical reforms on the parish with more zeal than wisdom. He moved at once to replace the old Sternhold and Hopkins version of the Psalms, which (accompanied by a bassoon and two key-bugles) had been sung there lustily for generations, with new hymns set to unfamiliar tunes. The episode described in Chapter 1, where Amos interrupted the 'wedding psalm' by calling out 'Silence!' and then 'gave out a hymn himself to some meeting-house tune' actually occurred on 12 February 1832, when

---

[1] 'Amos Barton', ch. 5.

Robert Evans noted in his Journal: 'Mr. Gwyther preached and stopd the Singers.' The following November he is found opposing another ancient parish tradition, the Coton wakes, on the dubious ground that people coming from places around might bring the cholera with them. In August 1833 he had his beadle William Lenton held for 'eating his Bread and Cheese, receiving some felloniously from his Servant Girl', and when the man was discharged, had him taken into custody again and before the Magistrates, who again liberated him, 'the Reverend Gentleman failing to make out his charge'.[1] These petty episodes indicate well enough that George Eliot did not exaggerate Amos Barton's personal deficiencies. The story, of course, was imaginary. No one has ever produced convincing prototypes of the Countess Czerlaski or her brother, who cause Amos's downfall. Milly's six children, so appealingly depicted, remind us at once of Chrissey's six little ones at Attleborough, to whom their Aunt Polly was tenderly devoted. The whole parish was rendered with a clarity and vigour that distinguish the tale from most fiction of the time.

In retrospect, Lewes seems to have been rather slow to discover George Eliot's genius, which her excessive diffidence helped to conceal. His 'prevalent impression', she recalled, was that, 'though I could hardly write a *poor* novel, my effort would want the highest quality of fiction—dramatic presentation'. Still, he kept urging her to try. After she had read him the opening chapter of 'Amos Barton', he no longer had any doubt about her ability; it was clear that she could write good dialogue.

There still remained the question whether I could command any pathos, and that was to be decided by the mode in which I treated Milly's death. One night G. went to town on purpose to leave me a quiet evening for writing it. I wrote the chapter from the news brought by the shepherd to Mrs. Hackit, to the moment when Amos is dragged from the bedside, and I read it to G. when he came home. We both cried over it, and then he came up to me and kissed me, saying 'I think your pathos is better than your fun.'[2]

They had determined from the start that if the 'story turned out good enough, we would send it to Blackwood'.

Next to Lewes, John Blackwood did most to develop and sustain George Eliot's genius as a novelist. The sixth son of the Edinburgh

---

[1] 'Occurrences at Nuneaton', Aug. 1833 (Nuneaton).
[2] *Letters*, II. 407.

publisher and founder of *Blackwood's Magazine*, John was educated at the High School and then sent with a tutor to live for two years in France and Italy before being placed in London in 1838 to learn the book-selling trade. In 1840 at the age of twenty-three he was made a partner in the firm and given charge of their London office at 22 Pall Mall. John was a most attractive, energetic young Scot, gracious and enthusiastic as well as prudent. His sincerity and personal charm soon won him many life-long friends, among them Thackeray, Bulwer Lytton, and J. T. Delane, the editor of *The Times*. Part of his duty was to secure contributions for *Maga*, as *Blackwood's* was usually called. One manuscript that he accepted was 'Lesurques', a tale by Lewes, which was published in January 1843; and in 1848, after being recalled to Edinburgh to be editor of the magazine, he published another entitled 'The Great Tragedian'. At Richmond, Lewes, hardpressed for money, reworked one of his old plays into a long story, 'Metamorphosis', which he sent to Blackwood; it appeared in three instalments, May–July 1856. The next month *Maga* began the long series of 'Sea-side Studies', the fruit of his research at Ilfracombe, which was not completed till October 1857. It was quite natural, then, that Lewes should submit 'Amos Barton' to Blackwood on 6 November 1856 as the manuscript of 'a friend who desired my good offices with you'.

I confess that before reading the m.s. I had considerable doubts of my friend's power as a writer of fiction; but after reading it those doubts were changed into very high admiration. I don't know what you will think of the story, but according to my judgement such humour, pathos, vivid presentation and nice observation have not been exhibited (in this style) since the 'Vicar of Wakefield'—and in consequence of that opinion I feel quite pleased in negotiating the matter with you.

This is what I am commissioned to say to you about the proposed series. It will consist of tales and sketches illustrative of the actual life of our country clergy about a quarter of a century ago; but solely in its *human* and *not at all* in its *theological* aspect; the object being to do what has never yet been done in our Literature, for we have had abundant religious stories polemical and doctrinal, but since the 'Vicar' and Miss Austen, no stories representing the clergy like any other class with the humours, sorrows, and troubles of other men. He begged me particularly to add that—as the specimen sent will sufficiently prove—the tone throughout will be sympathetic and not at all antagonistic.

Some of these, if not all, you may think suitable for Maga. If any are sent of which you do not approve, or which you do not think sufficiently interesting, these he will reserve for the separate republication and for this purpose he wishes to retain the copyright. Should you only print one or two he will be well satisfied; and still better if you should think well enough of the series to undertake the separate republication.

He calculates the present story will make two parts for Maga.[1]

Blackwood's response was prompt:

I am happy to say that I think your friend's reminiscences of Clerical Life will do. If there is any more of the series written I should like to see it, as until I saw more I could not make any decided proposition for the publication of the Tales in whole or in part in the Magazine. This first specimen Amos Barton is unquestionably very pleasant reading.

Perhaps the author falls into the error of trying too much to explain the characters of his actors by descriptions instead of allowing them to evolve in the action of the story; but the descriptions are very humorous and good. The death of Milly is powerfully done and affected me much. I am not sure whether he does not spoil it a little by specifying so minutely the different children and their names.

The windup is perhaps the lamest part of the story, and there too I think the defect is caused by the specifications as to the fortunes of parties of whom the reader has no previous knowledge and cannot consequently feel much interest. At first I was afraid that in the amusing reminiscences of childhood in church there was a want of some softening touch as the remembrance of a father or mother lends in after years to what was at the time considerable penance.

I hate anything of a sneer at real religious feeling as cordially as I despise anything like cant, and I should think this author is of the same way of thinking although his clergymen with one exception are not very attractive specimens of the body. The revulsion of feeling towards poor Amos is capitally drawn, although the asinine stupidity of his conduct about the Countess had disposed one to kick him.

I daresay I shall have a more decided opinion as to the merits of the Story when I have looked at it again and thought over it, but in the meantime I am sure that there is a happy turn of expression throughout, also much humour and pathos. If the author is a new writer I beg to congratulate him on being worthy of the honours of print and pay. I shall be very glad to hear from you or him soon.[2]

Lewes replied on 15 November:

I have communicated your letter to my clerical friend, who, though somewhat discouraged by it, has taken my advice and will submit the second story to you when it is written. At present he has only written what he sent you. His avocations, he informs me, will prevent his setting to work for the next three weeks or so; but as soon as he is at liberty he will begin.

[1] *Letters*, II. 269–70.   [2] Ibid. 272.

I rate the story much higher than you appear to do from certain expressions in your note, though you too appreciate the humour and pathos and the happy turn of expression. It struck me as being fresher than any story I have read for a long while, and as exhibiting in a high degree that faculty which I find to be the rarest of all, viz. the dramatic ventriloquism. At the same time I told him that I perfectly understood your editorial caution in not accepting from an unknown hand a series on the strength of one specimen.[1]

Blackwood, protesting that he had not intended to convey 'anything like disappointment to your friend,' acknowledged that he always hesitated before accepting a manuscript, especially one of a series, from a stranger.

I am sorry that the author has no more written but if he cares much about a speedy appearance I have so high an opinion of this first Tale that I will waive my objections and publish it without seeing more; not, of course committing myself to go on with the other Tales of the series unless I approved of them. I am very sanguine that I will approve as in addition to the other merits of Amos I agree with you that there is great freshness of style. If you think also that it would stimulate the author to go on with the other Tales with more spirit I will publish Amos at once. He would divide into two parts. I am blocked up for December but I could start him in January.

I am glad to hear that your friend is as I supposed a Clergyman. Such a subject is best in clerical hands and some of the pleasantest and least prejudiced correspondents I have ever had are English Clergymen.[2]

Lewes's response to this contains his first warning to Blackwood about George Eliot's extreme diffidence:

Your letter has greatly restored the shaken confidence of my friend, who is unusually sensitive, and unlike most writers is more anxious about *excellence* than about appearing in print—as his waiting so long before taking the venture proved. He is consequently afraid of failure though not afraid of obscurity; and by failure he would understand that which I suspect most writers would be apt to consider as success—so high is his ambition.

I tell you this that you may understand the sort of shy, shrinking, ambitious nature you have to deal with. I tried to persuade him that you really *did* appreciate his story, but were only hesitating about committing yourself to a *series* and your last letter has proved me to have been right. Although, as he never contemplated binding you to the publication of any portion of the series to which you might object, he could not at first see your position in its true light. All is, however, clear now.

He will be gratified if you publish Amos Barton in January, as it will give him ample time to get the second story ready, so as to appear when Barton is finished, should you wish it. He is anxious, however, that you should publish the general title of 'Scenes of Clerical Life'—and I think you may do this with perfect safety, since it is quite clear that the writer of Amos Barton is capable of writing at least one more story suitable to Maga, and two would suffice to justify the general title.

In this letter Lewes also dropped the first word of caution about anonymity. He knew that only the prospect of appearing anonymously and successfully in *Maga* had induced Marian to begin the series, and that the revelation of her authorship would soon end it.

Let me not forget to add that when I referred to 'my clerical friend' I meant to designate the writer of the clerical stories, not that he was a clericus. I am not at liberty to remove the veil of anonymity—even as regards social position. Be pleased therefore to keep the whole secret —and not even mention *my* negotiation or in any way lead guessers— (should any one trouble himself with such a guess—*not* very likely) to jump from me to my friend.[1]

The avocation that prevented the author from writing the second of the Clerical Scenes was a great pile of work that she had promised Chapman for the January 1857 *Westminster*, which came to eighty pages in print, nearly one-fourth of the whole number. Besides the 'Belles Lettres' she wrote the section entitled 'History, Biography, Voyages, and Travels', reviewing altogether thirty-three books. But her principal contribution was the essay that led off the number: 'Worldliness and Otherworldliness: the Poet Young.'[2] She had begun it in April 1856; not thinking well of what she had written, she gave it up. When she read those first pages to Lewes at Ilfracombe, however, 'he said he thought it would be the best article I had written',[3] and so, after 'Amos Barton' was done, she finished and sent it off to Chapman on 4 December.

Young's *Night Thoughts* had been Marian's favourite reading in her teens, when—like Burke—she committed long passages of it to memory; she agreed heartily with Dr. Johnson's praise of the poem as 'original', 'variegated with deep reflections and striking allusions'.[4] But now, in maturity, she saw it as the shallow reflection of 'a mind in which the higher human sympathies were

[1] *Letters*, II. 276–7.
[2] 'Worldliness and Other-worldliness: The Poet Young', *WR*, 67 (Jan. 1857), 1–42.   [3] *Letters*, II. 258.
[4] Boswell, *Life of Johnson*, ed. Hill and Powell, IV. 60.

inactive', and thought its 'religious and moral spirit low and false'.[1] With cutting sarcasm she convicted Young of 'radical insincerity as a poetic artist' and 'want of genuine emotion', denying outright his contention that virtue springs only from the hope of immortality. Young was 'a sort of cross between a sycophant and a psalmist'; he 'fluctuates between rhapsodic applause of King George and rhapsodic applause of Jehovah'. Some merits she still grants him: occasional grandeur of thought, startling vigour of imagery. Of an example that may pass for sublime,

> His hand the good man fixes on the skies,
> And bids earth roll, nor feels her idle whirl,

she says: 'But pause a moment to realize the image, and the monstrous absurdity of a man's grasping the skies and hanging habitually suspended there, while he contemptuously bids the earth roll, warns you that no genuine feeling could have suggested so unnatural a conception.'[2] When this test of realism (the same harsh test that Dr. Johnson turned on *Paradise Lost*) is applied to *Night Thoughts*, all is 'remote, vague, and unknown', ready for Marian's final contrast with Cowper, who presents the commonest objects 'truthfully and lovingly', cherishing them in proportion to their nearness.

Young's worldliness, which (after a foolish youth spent in pursuit of preferment) led him to take orders, has a close parallel in 'Amos Barton'. Amos was Curate, not Vicar, of Shepperton. 'Those were the days when a man could hold three small livings, starve a curate a-piece on two of them, and live badly himself on the third.' So it was with the incumbent of Shepperton, Mr. Carpe, who lived in another county, pocketed £35. 10s. a year from Shepperton, and gave Amos £80 for doing all the work. Carpe's prototype, the Reverend George Hake, Vicar of Chilvers Coton, also held livings at Rocester and Ellastone in Staffordshire, where he resided—all three on the recommendation of Francis Newdigate. Like Edward Young, Mr. Hake entered the Church rather late in life, having originally been a soldier. He had no university degree, having kept only two terms at Cambridge. Intellectually he was as badly fitted for his profession as Amos Barton.[3] It was not for any scandal, but because he wanted to give the curacy to his brother Henry, whose qualifications were as slight as his own, that he forced John Gwyther to leave Coton.

[1] *WR*, 67 (Jan. 1857), 19.   [2] Ibid. 27.
[3] *Letters*, III. 171.

Chapman paid Marian £20 for the article on Young, and a few days later, apparently with no more prompting than the favourable comments on it, added £5 more, bringing her earnings from the January number to £44. 1s. He could ill afford to lose her pen. But Blackwood had sent her 50 guineas for 'Amos Barton', which she had written with far less pain, and Marian foresaw a future in fiction more remunerative than reviewing or translating. Money was still a problem. Sometimes at Richmond they had not even enough food. Once when for economy they were lunching on bread and butter only, 'their landlady, who had had a present of game, sent them up some partridges, and after eating it they felt so much better that they agreed they could not be having enough to eat'.[1] One day, walking with Marian, Lewes said, 'We ought to live better than we do; we'll begin to have beer for lunch.' He told Charles Eliot Norton that in those days 'we were very poor, living in one room, where I had my little table with my microscope making my observations, and my wife another close at hand where she wrote; we were trying to pay off debts'.[2]

Needless to say, the debts were not Marian's. Lewes noted in his Journal 6 December 1856: 'Have been agitated and distressed lately by finding Agnes £150 in debt, mainly owing to T's defalcations. Angry correspondence and much discussion. Jervis [her father] has, however, given some temporary aid, and more is hoped.' But Thornton continued recalcitrant. Ten days later Lewes wrote:

Tuesday 16th. *This evening Thornton sent me a challenge!*—through Redford[3]—as I would not withdraw the 'offensive expression' of my disbelief in his statements and promises. There is something ludicrous in the extravagance of this—A challenge from him to me, and on such grounds! Wrote to Redford declining to withdraw the expression, and declining to name a friend; but offering as an alternative that Thornton should name some gentlemen to act as a Court of Honor, before which my charges and his explanations could be heard.

Sunday 21st. Thornton, declining the appeal to a Court of Honor, proposed that Pigott should see Redford, on my behalf, and to this with some reservation I consented. To-day Pigott, Redford, and I met, and Pigott agreed with me that I could *not* withdraw the offensive expression; and Reford declined to go further on with the case.

[1] Simcox, *Autobiography*, 18 Jan. 1881, fol. 88.
[2] *Letters of Charles Eliot Norton*, ed. S. Norton and M.A. de W. Howe (2 vols., 1913), I. 307.
[3] George Redford (1816–95), a surgeon lately returned from the Crimean War, devoted himself to the arts, writing for the *Leader* and *The Times* and planning exhibitions. He played the 'cello well, and like Pigott, had an excellent voice.

In her Journal Marian wrote: 'Christmas Eve. Alone at Park Shot', and 'Christmas Day. Began "Mr. Gilfil's Love Story", the second of my series.' Lewes had gone off as usual 24 December to spend two weeks at Vernon Hill, where Arthur Helps this year had 'had a theatre erected in which we played Charades for the amusement of the county families'.[1] On New Year's Day *Blackwood's* came out with the first instalment of 'Amos Barton', which Lewes read aloud one evening. 'The women', he reported to Blackwood, 'were charmed. Helps said it was "pestilently clever", and John Major, a clergyman,[2] was very much pleased with it. They were all sure that the author was a clergyman—a Cambridge man.'[3] Other comments were heard after Lewes came home: Richard Owen 'does not remember when he has read a better story', and Mrs. Owen thought it 'very clever'.[4] 'Agnes', Marian wrote, 'thought I was the father of a family— was sure I was a man who had seen a great deal of society etc.'[4a] In Edinburgh Blackwood too was collecting opinions. Critics there were a good deal divided. His friend W. G. Hamley, with whom he could not recollect ever having differed in opinion before, startled him by 'declaring dead against Amos', complaining of the 'obscure and laboured' style and finding too much 'sniffing and dirty noses' to please him. 'He thought the Author very possibly a *man of Science* but not a practised writer', said Blackwood. 'The idea of a man of Science had occurred to me before from some of the illustrations.' He had shown Thackeray, who was visiting him, part of the manuscript of Chapter 2, but could not get much opinion except that 'he would have liked to have read more'.[5]

When Blackwood sent the February number of *Maga* with the last half of 'Amos Barton', he was still ignorant of the new contributor's name and began his letter, 'My Dear Amos'. In her reply Marian declared:

Whatever may be the success of my stories, I shall be resolute in preserving my incognito, having observed that a *nom de plume* secures all the advantages without the disagreeables of reputation. Perhaps, therefore, it will be well to give you my prospective name, as a tub to throw to the whale in case of curious inquiries, and accordingly I subscribe myself, best and most sympathizing of editors,

> Yours very truly,
> George Eliot.[6]

[1] GHL Journal, 7 Jan. 1857.
[2] Headmaster of the King's College School.
[3] *Letters*, II. 408.
[4] *Letters*, II. 294–5.   [4a] *Letters*, II. 408.
[5] *Letters*, II. 291.
[6] *Letters*, II. 292.

She chose this name, she told Cross, because 'George was Mr. Lewes's Christian name, and Eliot was a good mouth-filling, easily-pronounced word.'[1] She probably did not remember that a George Elliot was Parish Clerk at Baginton, where Fanny Houghton used to live,[2] or that the *Leader*, 15 October 1853, announcing the birth of a daughter to Agnes Lewes, listed in the same column the birth of a daughter to the wife of Captain George Elliot, R.N., of 108 Cambridge Street, Warwick Square—not Hyde Park.[3] Jane Eyre, befriended by the Rivers family, told them that her name was Jane Elliott. As a not uncommon name, it was well suited to the purpose. Blackwood was already speculating about the mystery. His London manager Joseph Langford, like Lewes a playwright and dramatic critic, asked Blackwood 27 January 1857, 'Who wrote Amos Barton? Can you tell me? I have heard a hint that I dare not entertain and from no bad judge.'[4] Blackwood could not tell. But he told George Eliot that Albert Smith, the popular lecturer and entertainer, had been moved more than he thought possible in reading it (it 'made me blubber like a boy'), adding that 'from his account the luminaries of the Garrick generally seem to have mingled their tears with their tumblers over the death bed of Milly. It will be great fun if you are a member of that society and hear yourself discussed. I sympathize with your desire for the incognito, although I hope to break through it erelong as far as regards myself.'[5] Blackwood got his clerk to turn up some letters written ten years before by Captain George Warburton because of a fancied similarity in the handwriting, though 'Amos does not seem to me anything like what that good artillery man would or could write'.[6] Soon Langford had another clue. He wrote to Blackwood 16 February: 'I heard a curious thing about Amos Barton, namely that it is the actual life of a clergyman named Gwythir who at the time the incidents occurred lived at a place called, I think, Coton in one of the midland counties and who is now vicar of a small parish in Yorkshire. Indeed his daughter wrote to a lady, a friend of mine, telling her to be sure to read the story as it was their family history.'[7] Concerning this strange development Blackwood prudently said nothing to his unknown George Eliot.

'Mr. Gilfil's Love-story', like 'Amos Barton', was drawn from Marian's childhood memories. Cheverel Manor is a faithful copy

[1] Cross, I. 431.   [2] F. White, *Warwickshire* (1850), p. 601.
[3] *Leader*, 15 Oct. 1853, p. 1005.   [4] *Letters*, II. 298.
[5] Ibid. 293.   [6] Ibid. 294.   [7] Ibid. 298.

of Arbury Hall, and, though Sir Roger Newdigate died long before her birth, Marian made convincing descriptions of him and his lady from her recollection of their full-length portraits by Romney (not Reynolds), which still hang in the saloon. Maynard Gilfil, the hero, however, she had known in the Reverend Bernard Gilpin Ebdell, Vicar of Chilvers Coton and of Astley until his death in 1828. He was in a sense her earliest acquaintance, since he christened her in 1819. While the background and characters are studied with the careful realism that marks all George Eliot's fiction, the plot is entirely imaginary. Caterina's prototype Sarah Shilton was not an Italian orphan found by Lady Cheverel in Milan, but a collier's daughter from a cottage on the estate, who was educated by Lady Newdigate and enjoyed some local reputation as a singer. But she had no love affair with Sir Roger's nephew, who had married her supposed rival before Sarah was nine years old. Caterina's marriage to Mr. Gilfil lasted only a few months, Sarah's to Mr. Ebdell for more than twenty-three years. The melodramatic episodes—finding the infant Caterina at her father's death-bed, and her infatuation with the impossible Captain Wybrow, who, just before she arrived, dagger in hand, to murder him, died conveniently of a heart attack—all this is the romancer's invention.

To Blackwood, who was about to begin Bulwer Lytton's new novel *What Will He Do with It?* in *Maga*, melodrama was less disturbing than the realism of 'sniffing and dirty noses'. His critical instinct told him, however, that some of the things worrying him in George Eliot's stories were evidence of freshness; their commonplace, middle-aged heroes and brilliant depiction of ordinary surroundings struck a new note. George Eliot defended herself against objections like Hamley's, which 'arise from a dislike to the *order* of art rather than from a critical estimate of the execution. Any one who detests the Dutch school in general will hardly appreciate fairly the merits of a particular Dutch painting. And against this sort of condemnation, one must steel oneself as one best can. But objections which point out to me any vice of manner or any failure in producing an intended effect will be really profitable.'[1] After reading the first chapters of 'Mr. Gilfil' Blackwood was 'puzzled as to how the love part is going to be managed',[2] and in sending George Eliot the proof, he gently hinted his doubt:

It is not a pleasant picture to see a good fellow loving on when the lady's heart is *openly* devoted to a Jackanapes, and I am a little puzzled

[1] *Letters*, II. 292.   [2] *Letters*, II. 296.

as to how you are to bring the excellent Gilfil out without making him too abjectly devoted a lover for a man of character. I think the objection would be readily met by making Caterina a little less openly devoted to Wybrow and giving a little more dignity to her character. Understand that I by no means object to her; on the contrary I think that she promises to be most interesting and I look with great anxiety for the picture of her half-broken heart turning to Gilfil. I hope she finally rejects the insufferable Wybrow—but I must not speculate upon your plot, and if I am wrong in my opinions about the demeanour of Caterina with Wybrow recollect that I write to some extent in the dark.[1]

Against this pressure to turn her hero and heroine into conventional figures of popular romance George Eliot stood firm. She accepted Blackwood's advice on minor details like the omission of French phrases, which, she agreed, were not in keeping with her story.

But I am unable to alter anything in relation to the delineation or development of character, as my stories always grow out of my psychological conception of the dramatis personæ. For example the behaviour of Caterina in the gallery is essential to my conception of her nature and to the development of that nature in the plot. My artistic bent is not at all to the presentation of eminently irreproachable characters, but to the presentation of mixed human beings in such a way as to call forth tolerant judgment, pity, and sympathy. And I cannot stir a step aside from what I *feel* to be *true* in character. If anything strikes you as untrue to human nature in my delineations, I shall be very glad if you will point it out to me, that I may reconsider the matter. But alas! inconsistencies and weaknesses are not untrue.[2]

Truth was her aim, psychological truth as well as truth of background to make her story plausible. Lewes, in returning the proof, gave her loyal support: 'the subtle truth in delineation of complex motives is better than anything he has yet done in that way'.[3] But Blackwood as editor of a family magazine still had grave doubts about Caterina and her dagger, 'beautifully as the impossibility of her using it is indicated. I daresay George Eliot will kick furiously at the base idea of altering a syllable at this point, but I am pretty sure that his dear little heroine would be more sure of universal sympathy if she only dreamed or felt as if she could stab the cur to the heart, and I think it would be more consistent with her character than the active step of getting hold of the lethal weapon.'[4] George Eliot was adamant: 'it would be

---

[1] *Letters*, II. 297.   [2] Ibid. 299.
[3] Ibid. 307.   [4] Ibid. 308.

the death of my story to substitute a dream for the real scene. Dreams usually play an important part in fiction, but rarely, I think, in actual life.'¹ In a postscript to Lewes, Blackwood had written: 'By all means let the incognito be kept. Shall I say to anxious inquirers that the Scenes are by one George Eliot of whom I know nothing?' To this Marian heartily agreed.

For several reasons I am very anxious to retain my incognito for some time to come, and to an author not already famous, anonymity is the highest *prestige*. Besides, if George Eliot turns out a dull dog and an ineffective writer—a mere flash in the pan—I, for one, am determined to cut him on the first intimation of that disagreeable fact.

The Fates have willed that this shall be a very melancholy story, and I am longing to be a little merrier again. Ever, my dear Sir,

Yours very truly (incognito apart)

George Eliot.²

At this point Marian and George set out for the Scilly Isles to continue his 'Sea-side Studies', the first series of which had proved successful in *Blackwood's*.They slept at the Great Western Hotel in London, 15 March, before taking the express to Plymouth; there they put up at the Globe, from which the coach started for Truro. George Eliot's Journal is full of carefully observed details, stored for possible use in fiction.

17 [March]. We set off by coach to Truro at 10½ under a cloudy sky. We had the back places outside, and, hard seats excepted, a very agreeable journey. Our travelling companions were a stout elderly gentleman who had travelled a great deal, bald and benevolent; an old Scotch sailor, who had come over in the vessel where the drunken captain had flogged a boy to death, and who was now travelling from Dundee to Penzance, to give his evidence in the captain's trial; a pretentious, vulgar young man with smart clothes, dirty nails, and original information in physiology; and, for part of the way, a Devonshire lass, who shook hands with us all round at parting, and a Devonshire lad with scarlet flowered plush waistcoat and yellow and flowered silk neckerchief, who ate buns industriously from the time we started till his large stock was exhausted. The old sailor was a fine specimen of a simple, brave, kind-hearted man—a natural gentleman. For part of our way, until after we reached Bodmin, the country was charming—clear, rushing, winding streams, great hills, their sides clothed with woods hoary with grey lichen, and deep valleys which the unfinished railway spanned with its viaducts. But by and bye we got into the dreariest scenery of Cornwall; treeless, rough wastes, the relics of former mines; works for

---

¹ *Letters*, II. 309.   ² *Letters*, II. 309–10.

the preparation of the white clay used in making porcelain, where the chief objects were hovels for packing the blocks of dried, purified clay, as white as chalk, and oblong tanks where the clay is put to be purified; and throughout all this region of mines and clay works, the streams are thick and coloured or else milky white. At St. Austell, where there is a fine church tower, we got inside, and found an intelligent companion, who told us something of the miners and their customs. At St. Probus, a little village through which we passed, there is another exquisite church tower, but the landscape all the way is bare and dreary. It was nearly dark when we reached Truro and exchanged our stage coach for the railway. We arrived terribly weary at Penzance about half past eight.

After a 'chop tea' they went to bed, expecting to cross to Scilly early the next morning. But 'the morning was so dismal—the rain pouring down and the wind reported to be "due west,"—that we gave up our voyage'.

Since the packet boat sailed only twice a week, they set out to find lodgings, unhappily choosing the worst. Lewes describes them humorously in his Journal, and adapts the entry for *Sea-side Studies*:

Were you ever in nautical lodgings? Do you remember their ornaments 'above all reach of art'[1]—the cases of stuffed birds and fish, the shells on the mantelpiece, and the engravings irradiating the walls: a 'Sailor's Departure,' with whimpering wife and sentimental offspring; a 'Sailor's Return,' with joyous wife and capering juveniles? All these adorned my rooms, which were further adorned by a correct misrepresentation of the brig Triton, as she appeared entering an impossible harbour of Marseilles, flanked by a portrait of the defunct husband, master of the aforesaid brig, painted in the well-known style: a resplendent shirt-front with a head attached, sternly inexpressive, on a mahogany background. The defunct mariner seemed blank with astonishment at my courage in coming to such a house—a ruin, not a lodging. Everything in it was afflicted with the rickets. The chairbacks creaked inharmonious threats, if you incautiously leaned against them. The fire-irons fell continually from their unstable rests. The bed-pole tumbled at my feet when I attempted to draw the curtain. The doors wouldn't shut. Even the teapot had a *wobbly* top, which resisted all closing.[2]

Here for eight days they were marooned, waiting for less tempestuous weather. When they finally embarked for Scilly 26 March, they were as seasick as if they had gone at once.

[1] Cf. Pope, 'Essay on Criticism', I. 155.
[2] *Sea-side Studies*, pp. 182–3.

But at St. Mary's they found clean, comfortable lodgings at the Post Office, large but low rooms at the reasonable cost of 14*s*. per week with 1*s*. 6*d*. for fire, and soon 'sat down to our desks in home fashion', Lewes working at his marine specimens, George Eliot going on with 'Mr Gilfil's Love-story'. As usual they spent the evenings reading aloud. The books Marian mentions in her Journal during these months are of unusual interest. They began with Mrs. Gaskell's *Cranford*, followed by her *Life of Charlotte Brontë*, to which Lewes had contributed his important correspondence with Charlotte; later they read *The Professor*. Marian reread Hawthorne's *Scarlet Letter* and Mrs. Browning's *Aurora Leigh*. But the most significant name in the list is that of Jane Austen. Between February and June 1857 the Journal shows them reading aloud every one of the novels except *Pride and Prejudice*, which may simply have missed mention. George Eliot had read many of them before, and Lewes was one of the earliest Janeites. His article on 'The Lady Novelists' in the *Westminster Review* calls Jane Austen 'the greatest artist that has ever written, using the term to signify the most perfect mastery over the means to her end. . . . To read one of her books is like an actual experience of life: you know the people as if you had lived with them, and you feel something of personal affection for them'.[1] In this atmosphere 'Mr. Gilfil' was finished, the Epilogue being written 'sitting on the Fortification Hill' at St. Mary's one sunshiny morning early in April.

Marian's life on this tiny isle was no more isolated than it had been at Richmond. Though she had re-established correspondence with her Coventry friends, the old *rapport* could never be quite restored. In the summer of 1856 Sara Hennell kept asking her advice about an essay on *Christianity and Infidelity*. Her interminable letters and Marian's evasive replies make it impossible to ignore the wide divergence between them. Sara was a theist, believing in an anthropomorphic 'Design of Creation', which Marian could not accept. Lewes, appealed to, did his best to avoid an answer that he knew must contradict Sara's view.[2] In the press of finishing her article on Young, Marian had forgotten their

---

[1] *WR*, 58 (July 1852), 134.
[2] Perhaps GHL alluded to Sara and Marian in *Sea-side Studies* (p. 290) when he mentioned 'a witty friend of mine, who, upon hearing that one of her own sex was fond of reading metaphysics, and was feared to be suffering from softened brain, drew her own conclusion as to this masculine course of study, exclaiming, " *Man is but woman with a softened brain.*" '

common birthdays 22–23 November, which Sara observed by sending a photograph of herself. 'The portrait is very *beautiful*, dear Sara', Marian wrote, 'and I think it a treasure. Yet greedy thing that I am, I long for one of Cara too.'[1] And looking back to the days they had passed together, she said: 'I feel what a poor, narrow cup I held out to receive all that, and how often I wounded when I might have helped you, if I had only had a larger and more reverent heart. . . . But now we are separated, and I shall never be able to make up for my past failures. There is so little we can make up for!'[2] Charles Bray had suggested a second time that Marian visit them—without Lewes. 'Thanks for your kind wish', she replied,'—but though I love my friends quite as much as I profess to do—which is saying a great deal, as human nature goes—I love home better.'[3]

Her family too had grown further away. In 1856 for the first time since her winter at Geneva the Christmas holiday passed without a visit to Warwickshire. Letters, even from her dear Chrissey, came more rarely. At the end of March, Chrissey and two of her children came down with typhus; she 'lost her pretty little Fanny, and I am still waiting anxiously for news of Katy and herself'.[4] Isaac sent a letter to say that Chrissey was better but not yet out of danger; ten days later Mrs. Isaac Evans reported that both she and Katy were still very ill.[5]

In this gloomy atmosphere, herself constantly ailing, the weather cold and dreary, Marian began her third story, later to be named 'Janet's Repentance'. In their seven weeks on Scilly, Lewes had done all he could with the marine specimens available there. On 11 May they departed for Jersey. The journey took nearly five days: by boat to Penzance, by coach to Falmouth, by steamer to Plymouth, and again by steamer to Jersey. The arrival was an exciting experience for Lewes, who had been at school at St. Helier in 1829. The Royal Square, no longer disgraced by the pillory, seemed to have shrunk to a third of its old dimensions, and the Theatre had lost the magical and imposing aspect of those days 'when it seemed the centre of perfect bliss'.[6] After lunch they set out from Jeune's Union Hotel to buy boots, get hair cut, get letters, and look for lodgings. The next day at Gorey they found what they wanted at Rosa Cottage with a family named Amys—

[1] *Letters*, II. 276.   [2] Ibid. 278.
[3] Ibid. 279.   [4] Fanny died 26 Mar. 1857.
[5] GE Journal, 18 Apr. 1857.   [5] *Sea-side Studies*, p. 270.

a sitting-room, a work room for Lewes adjoining it, and a bedroom —the three rooms and attendance costing only 13*s*. a week. So they returned to St. Helier, 'bought wine, brandy, groceries, paper, map etc., hired an easy chair and a bath', and, after dining at the Hotel, had a fly to carry them and their things to Gorey, where they unpacked and went tired to bed.[1]

During the first few days they took leisurely walks, wrote letters, sat in the sun on the Castle Hill while Marian read *Emma* aloud, and in the evening strolled on the sands, where Lewes spoke with the fishermen, trying to engage them to bring him refuse from their trawls. They found the people friendly. One day, passing through a garden belonging to a cottager, 'we were agreeably surprised by the woman's offering us a bunch of lilac; she then brought out a telescope for us to see the coast of France, and was altogether obliging, smiling, and good'.[2]

Marian, having written her 'Recollections of the Scilly Isles' in her Journal, went back to work on the first part of 'Janet's Repentance', which she finished 30 May. For this tale she returned again to memories of her childhood at Mrs. Wallington's School. Mr. Tryan, her hero, is an idealized portrait of Mr. Jones, the Evangelical curate at Nuneaton. Her version of his persecution at the hands of Janet's husband, the brutal Lawyer Dempster, was derived from Jones's staunchest disciples, Maria Lewis and Mrs. Buchanan, and heavily slanted towards the Evangelical side. But her description of the town of Milby (Chapter 2), a brilliant analysis of provincial English society in 1830, forms an essential background against which the drama of opposition to Evangelical reform is played. Through the perspective of twenty-five years Marian studied the inhabitants of Nuneaton with scientific objectivity.

The luxuriant beauty of Jersey, 'the grassy isle', so welcome after stormy, rocky Scilly, made Marian homesick for the familiar old lanes of Warwickshire. Her thoughts kept turning to Chrissey and her children in that fever-stricken house at Attleborough, and to the trio at Coventry, now crowded into the diminished compass of Ivy Cottage. 'I wonder if I should have had the happiness of seeing Cara, if I had been at Richmond now', she asked Sara 22 May. 'I would rather see her than any one else in the world—except poor Chrissey.'[3]

[1] GHL Journal, 15–16 May 1857.   [2] Ibid. 20 May 1857.
[3] *Letters*, II. 329.

When they were well settled at Gorey, Marian made a great decision. Possibly it was prompted by news of the birth of a third daughter to Agnes on 21 May, who was duly registered as Mildred Jane Lewes, though Thornton Hunt was her father. She wrote first to Isaac:

Rosa Cottage | Gorey | Jersey | May 26th 1857

My dear Brother

You will be surprized, I dare say, but I hope not sorry, to learn that I have changed my name, and have someone to take care of me in the world. The event is not at all a sudden one, though it may appear sudden in its announcement to you. My husband has been known to me for several years, and I am well acquainted with his mind and character. He is occupied entirely with scientific and learned pursuits, is several years older than myself, and has three boys, two of whom are at school in Switzerland, and one in England.

We shall remain at the coast here, or in Brittany for some months, on account of my health, which has for some time been very frail, and which is benefited by the sea air. The winter we shall probably spend in Germany. But any inconvenience about money payments to me may, I suppose, be avoided if you will be kind enough to pay my income to the account of Mr. G. H. Lewes, into the Union Bank of London, Charing Cross Branch, 4, Pall Mall East, Mr. Lewes having an account there.

I wrote to you many weeks ago from Scilly, enclosing a letter to Chrissey, which if you received it, you would of course put by for her, as it was written in ignorance of her extreme illness. But as I have not received any intimation that my letter reached you, I think it safest to repeat its chief purport, which was to request that you would pay £15 of my present half year's income to Chrissey.

I shall also be much obliged if you will inform me how Chrissey is, and whether she is strong enough to make it desirable for me to write to her.

Give my love to Sarah and tell her I am very grateful to her for letting me have news of Chrissey. I received two notes of hers through Fanny, and subsequently another, in answer to mine.

The enclosed letter to Fanny I shall be glad if you will address for me as I fear 'Leamington,' which was all I could put on a previous letter I wrote to her, may hardly suffice in a large town where there may be several Mrs. Houghtons.

We are not at all rich people, but we are both workers, and shall have enough for our wants.

I hope you are all well and that Sarah is recovered from her fatigues and anxieties. With love to her and all my tall nephews and nieces, I remain, dear Isaac,

Your affectionate Sister
Marian Lewes.[1]

[1] *Letters*, II. 331–2.

The letter to Fanny Houghton was much the same. Beginning with a hope that previous letters had reached her and that Henry was recovering from his accident, she wrote:

Next, let me ask you to open your eyes and look surprized, for I am going to tell you some very unexpected news. I am sure you retain enough friendship and sisterly affection for me to be glad that I should have a kind husband to love me and take care of me. Our paths in life lie far apart, but I, at least, shall always remember with gratitude how kind you were to me in old days, and how much pleasure it gave me to talk with you.

My husband has been well known to me for years, and marriage is a very sober and serious thing when people are as old as we are, so that the future is as little of a problem to me, as it can be to any of us. He is older than I am, not at all full of wealth or beauty, but very full indeed of literature and physiology and zoology and other invisible endowments, which happily have their market value. Still better, he is a man of high honour and integrity and the kindest heart, of which, of course, I think all the better because it is devoted to me.

We shall both be hard workers, for we have three little boys to keep as well as ourselves. Two of them are in Switzerland, at a delightful school there, and the youngest is at school in England. We shall live chiefly abroad for some time, for while the boys are at school, there is no necessity for our having a fixed residence near London.

My thoughts are very much with dear Chrissey. I have asked Isaac to send me word if she is well enough for me to write to her without a risk of agitating her too much.[1]

The next day she wrote to John Chapman, who for three years had served as 'Miss Evans's' post office for her family. After some months of study in London he had just secured an M.D. degree from St. Andrews University, which with only one professor and almost no resident students conferred more medical degrees than any other university in Scotland or England—a total of 605 in 1862.[2] Marian addressed him as 'My dear M.D.'

I dare say I am the slowest of all your friends in expressing my sympathy, but I have been waiting because I wanted to tell you at the same time that I had taken a step which I have long been meditating— that of telling my brother and sister that I am married. I wrote for that purpose on Monday, so now I shall not need to trouble you further with the transmission of letters, and you must henceforth remember that I am Mrs. Lewes to all my relatives. . . .

Such grassy vallies in this delicious island, with sleek cows turning mild faces on us as we pass them! Such shadowy lanes and glimpses of

---

[1] *Letters*, II. 333.　　[2] *George Eliot and John Chapman*, pp. 93–4.

the sea at unexpected openings! Everything that you must long for as you walk hot and dusty and deafened along the Strand. But no—I dare say you are too full of review articles and pathological wisdom to have space for dreamy longings. . . .

All happiness attend you as editor and physician! That is the warm wish of

Your sincere friend
Marian E.[1]

She also wrote to Sara Hennell, explaining that her family 'are now acquainted with what is *essential* in my position, and if any utterly false report reaches them in the first instance, their minds will be prepared not to accept it without reserve. I do not think Chrissey will give up correspondence with me in any case, and that is the point I most care about, as I shall still be able to help her as far as my means will allow.'[2]

Fanny was first to respond. Though her letter has not survived, she seems to have written cordially, probably not realizing the informal nature of the 'marriage'. Perhaps she suggested coming with her husband to join the Leweses at Jersey; they had long been wanting a milder climate. Marian replied on 2 June:

I wish I could help you with experienced advice as to a suitable place of residence for recruiting Henry's health. The only places I can think of as likely to answer your purpose, which I suppose includes easy transit, cheapness, and a sufficiently bracing air, are Tréport and St. Valery in Normandy, which are easily reached from Brighton. . . .

Jersey is very warm—which is just what I want. It is very pretty—a paradise of green vallies, but disappointingly English in habits and *prices*. The mild genial air has done me immense good already; but of course one can't tell whether July heat may not prove too much even for me.

Thanks—a thousand thanks, dear Fanny for your letter. I have just written to Chrissey, being unable to wait another post after hearing that I *might* write to her, and finding I have yet a few minutes I write to you also. I hope Chrissey *will* be able to have some change of air for I begged Isaac to pay her £15 from me for that purpose. I do trust the money will not be absolutely wanted for anything else. I wish I could do more, but my poverty, not my will restricts me. Pray do something, if you can to urge that the money should be so applied. I don't mean that you should do it *obviously* or directly, or that you should appear to know anything about that sum, but simply that you should insist on the importance of leaving that hotbed of fever for a time.

[1] GE to J. Chapman, 27 May 1857 (Yale).
[2] *Letters*, II. 342.

One item of local news Fanny had sent her concerned some stories in *Blackwood's*, all about Chilvers Coton and Arbury, written, she had been told, by Mr. Liggins of Attleborough. Marian commented on the report with some disingenuousness:

You are wrong about Mr. Liggins or rather your informants are wrong. We too have been struck with the 'Clerical Sketches', and I have recognized some figures and traditions connected with our old neighbourhood. But Blackwood informs Mr. Lewes that the author is a Mr. Eliot, a clergyman, I presume. *Au reste*, he may be a relation of Mr. Liggins's or some other 'Mr.' who knows Coton stories.

Have you read Currer Bell's Life by Mrs. Gaskell? Do—it will deeply interest you.

With kindest regards and best wishes for Henry's recovery, I am ever, dear Fanny

Your affectionate Sister
Marian Lewes *alias* Polly.[1]

Isaac remained ominously silent. Marian had miscalculated the rigorous demands of his Pearson respectability, forgotten how angry he had been when, after Edward Clarke's funeral, she left Meriden without consulting him. Commenting on Maggie Tulliver's childish quarrel with Tom, she wrote: 'We learn to restrain ourselves as we get older. We keep apart when we have quarrelled, express ourselves in well-bred phrases, and in this way preserve a dignified alienation, showing much firmness on one side, and swallowing much grief on the other.'[2] So it was with Isaac and Marian. He handed her letter to Mr. Holbeche, the family solicitor, to answer:

Sutton Coldfield
9th June 1857

Dear Mrs. Lewes

I have had an interview with your Brother in consequence of your letter to him announcing your marriage. He is so much hurt at your not having previously made some communication to him as to your intention and prospects that he cannot make up his mind to write, feeling that he could not do so in a Brotherly Spirit. I have at his request undertaken to address you in the belief that you will receive my letter as coming from an old Friend of your Family. Your Brother and Sister (who is gradually gaining a little strength) are naturally anxious to obtain some information respecting your altered state. Perhaps you will not object to make some communication to me which I may convey to them. Permit me to ask when and where you were married and what is the occupation of Mr. Lewes, who I think you refer to in your letter

---

[1] *Letters*, II. 336–7.   [2] *Mill on the Floss*, Bk. I, ch. 5.

as being actively employed, and where his residence is as you request a remittance to be made to his Bankers in London by the Trustees under your Father's Will. I shall be happy to hear from you and trust the result of your communication may be that of your Brother corresponding directly with you, and remain, Dear Mrs. Lewes,

Yours very faithfully
Vincent Holbeche.

Mrs. G. H. Lewes.[1]

Marian answered immediately:

Rosa Cottage | Gorey | Jersey | June 13, 1857

My dear Sir

I have just received your letter written to me by my brother's request, and I willingly reply to it at once by a statement of the facts concerning which you desire information; the more so, because I anticipated the probability of my having to correspond with you as joint Trustee under my Father's Will.

My brother has judged wisely in begging you to communicate with me. If his feelings towards me are unfriendly, there is no necessity for his paining himself by any direct intercourse with me; indeed, if he had written to me in a tone which I could not recognize (since I am not conscious of having done him any injury) I must myself have employed a third person as a correspondent.

Mr. Lewes is a well-known writer, author among other things, of the 'Life of Goethe' and the 'Biographical History of Philosophy'. Our marriage is not a legal one, though it is regarded by us both as a sacred bond. He is unable at present to contract a legal marriage, because, though long deprived of his first wife by her misconduct, he is not legally divorced.

I have been his wife and have borne his name for nearly three years; a fact which has been known to all my personal friends except the members of my own family, from whom I have withheld it because, knowing that their views of life differ in many respects from my own, I wished not to give them unnecessary pain. Other considerations, however, have at length determined me to inform them of my circumstances and of the responsibilities for life, which I have undertaken.

It may be desirable to mention to you that I am not dependent on any one, the larger part of my income for several years having been derived from my own constant labour as a writer. You will perceive, therefore, that in my conduct towards my own family I have not been guided by any motives of self-interest, since I have been neither in the reception nor the expectation of the slightest favour from them.

Mr. Lewes, as I have already stated, has an account at the Union Bank of London, Charing Cross Branch, 4 Pall Mall East. I have

[1] *Letters*, II. 346.

requested that any money due to me may be paid to his account there, because, as we are frequently out of England and away from town, the transmission of cheques is attended with much inconvenience. I presume that I have a legal right to appoint the payment of interest due to me to any person I may choose to name. But if there is any point necessary to be taken into consideration, which I have overlooked or of which I am ignorant, you will be good enough to set me right.

I have satisfaction in communicating with you in this case, rather than with anyone else, not only because you kindly undertook, from friendship to my Father, to become my trustee, but because I learned from him that it was owing to your considerate suggestion that some provision was made for me during the first year after my Father's death. I daresay you have forgotten the circumstance, but I have always remembered gratefully that instance of thoughtfulness on my behalf, and am glad to have an opportunity of acknowledging it. I remain, my dear Sir,

Yours very truly,
Marian Lewes.

Vincent Holbeche Esq.[1]

Forwarding it to Isaac, 17 June, Mr. Holbeche wrote: 'I send you a letter I have this morning received from *Mrs.* Lewes in reply to mine to her, of which you have a copy on the other side. Her letter needs no comment from me at present.' It received none that we know of from Isaac. Under his pressure Fanny and Chrissey on the same day sent letters breaking off all communication with their lost sister. From her family Dear Polly, in whom the domestic affections were so deeply ingrained, was now a complete outcast.

With her mind intensely agitated by this reception of her news, Marian was trying to get on with 'Janet's Repentance', which was also meeting strong objection. With the proof of Part I Blackwood wrote again that he was rather 'puzzled':

It is exceedingly clever and some of the hits and descriptions of character are first rate, but I should have liked a pleasanter picture. Surely the colours are rather harsh for a sketch of English County Town life only 25 years ago. The glimpse at the end of the part shows that a powerful and pathetic story is coming and I rather wish you had plunged sooner into it instead of expending so much humour in the delineation of characters who do not seem likely to assist materially in the movement of the Story and who are not in themselves interesting.

The first scene especially I think you should shorten. It is deuced

[1] *Letters*, II. 349–50.

good but rather a staggerer in an opening scene of a Story of Clerical Life. Dempster is rather too barefaced a brute and I am sorry that the poor wife's sufferings should have driven her to so unsentimental a resource as beer. Still it is true to nature. The case is but too common, and I have no right to pass any opinion on this part of the story until I see more of it. I shall be very glad if in returning the proof you can send me a further portion of M.S. as I feel very confident that what is coming will more than dissipate the slight doubts I feel about the popular qualities of this first part.

I greatly regret not being able to give applause altogether unqualified, but I may mention a capital sign that both my brother and I liked it better on the second reading than on the first. For the meantime I feel certain that I am right in advising you to *soften* your picture as much as you can. Your sketches this time are all written in the harsher Thackerayan view of human nature, and I should have liked to have seen some of the good which at page 10 you so neatly indicate as existing at Milby. When are you going to give us a really good active working clergyman, neither absurdly evangelical nor absurdly High Church?

The Scene at the Linnets is capital. Thackeray is I think rather disposed to claim you as a disciple of his, and I daresay the beautiful touch about the flutter in the female hearts at page 17 is something in his style. . . .

If my comments upon Janet disappoint you, consider that I am wrong and attribute my want of appreciation to a fortnight of hot weather and hotter dinners in London.[1]

Even the postscript saying that he had paid £22. 10s. into Lewes's account for Part IV of 'Gilfil' could not overcome George Eliot's disappointment at Blackwood's failure to understand her aim. He seems to have been hoping that she would write him another *Cranford*, which would 'puzzle' no one.

Marian's long letter to him 11 June earnestly defends the artistic integrity of her realism:

I am not much surprized, and not at all hurt by your letter received today with the proof. It is a great satisfaction—in fact my only satisfaction, that you should give me your judgment with perfect frankness. I am able, I think, to enter into an editor's doubts and difficulties, and to see my stories in some degree from your point of view as well as my own. My answer is written after considering the question as far as possible on all sides, and as I feel that I shall not be able to make any other than *superficial* alterations in the proof, I will, first of all, say what I can in explanation of the spirit and future course of the present story.

The collision in the drama is not at all between 'bigotted churchman-

[1] *Letters*, II. 344–5.

ship' and evangelicalism, but between *ir*religion and religion. Religion in this case happens to be represented by evangelicalism, and the story so far as regards the *persecution*, is a real bit in the religious history of England that happened about eight-and-twenty years ago. I thought I had made it apparent in my sketch of Milby feelings on the advent of Mr. Tryan that the conflict lay between immorality and morality—irreligion and religion. Mr. Tryan will carry the reader's sympathy. It is through him that Janet is brought to repentance. Dempster's vices have their natural evolution in deeper and deeper moral deterioration (though not without softening touches) and death from intemperance. Everything is softened from the fact, so far as art is permitted to soften and yet to remain essentially true. The real town was more vicious than my Milby; the real Dempster was far more disgusting than mine; the real Janet alas! had a far sadder end than mine, who will melt away from the reader's sight in purity, happiness and beauty.

My sketches both of churchmen and dissenters, with whom I am almost equally acquainted, are drawn from close observation of them in real life, and not at all from hearsay or from the descriptions of novelists. Dempster is no more like a dissenter than Jonathan Oldbuck is like Davie Deans. If I were to undertake to alter Dempster's language or character, I should be attempting to represent some vague conception of what may possibly exist in other people's minds, but has no existence in my own. Such of your marginal objections as relate to a mere detail I can meet without difficulty by alteration; but as an artist I should be utterly powerless if I departed from my own conceptions of life and character. There is nothing to be done with the story, but either to let Dempster and Janet and the rest be as I *see* them, or to renounce it as too painful.

I am keenly alive, at once to the scruples and alarms an editor may feel, and to my own utter inability to write under any cramping influence, and on this double ground I should like you to consider whether it will not be better to close the series for the Magazine *now*. I daresay you will feel no difficulty about publishing a volume containing the story of Janet's Repentance, though you may not like to hazard its insertion in the Magazine, and I shall accept that plan with no other feeling than that you have been to me the most liberal and agreeable of editors and are the man of all others I would choose for a publisher.

Blackwood's wish that she would exhibit 'some of the good which at page 10 you so neatly indicate as existing at Milby' must have disheartened George Eliot, for her remarks on the qualities that make it 'now a refined, moral, and enlightened town' were clearly ironic.

My irony, so far as I understand myself, is not directed against opinions—against any class of religious views—but against the vices and weaknesses that belong to human nature in every sort of clothing. But it is possible that I may not affect other minds as I intend and wish to affect them, and you are a better judge than I can be of the degree in which I may occasionally be offensive. I should like *not* to be offensive —I should like to touch every heart among my readers with nothing but loving humour, with tenderness, with belief in goodness. But I may have failed in this case of Janet, at least so far as to have made you feel its publication in the Magazine a disagreeable risk. If so, there will be no harm done by closing the series with No. 2, as I have suggested. If, however, I take your objections to be deeper than they really are—if you prefer inserting the story in spite of your partial dissatisfaction, I shall of course be happy to appear under Maga's wing still.

When I remember what have been the successes in fiction even as republications from Maga I can hardly believe that the public will regard my pictures as exceptionally coarse. But in any case there are too many prolific writers who devote themselves to the production of pleasing pictures, to the exclusion of all disagreeable truths for me to desire to add one to their number. In this respect, at least, I may have some resemblance to Thackeray, though I am not conscious of being in any way a disciple of his, unless it constitute discipleship to think him, as I suppose the majority of people with any intellect do, on the whole the most powerful of living novelists.

I will retain the proof until I receive an answer from you. In the meanwhile, I remain, my dear Sir,

Yours with sincere regard and obligation

George Eliot[1]

Lewes, sending the proof of another of the 'Sea-side Studies', added his opinion against Blackwood's impression:

I was in raptures with 'Janet's Repentance' when Eliot first read it to me and declared it would be the finest thing he had written. Your letter therefore considerably staggered me, as I have much confidence in your judgement; accordingly I reread the part with a critical eye to detect the objections you spoke of. In vain! Two readings have left me in the dark. Either you or I must be under a profound misconception of the effect likely to be produced. I agree with you in thinking the description of the town and its inhabitants the least successful part of what is printed—but I agree with Eliot that it was necessary to paint the locale for the truth of the story. Only in such an atmosphere could such a story move freely and naturally. Dempster seems to me a marvellous creation—Dr. Johnson turned rascal, or rather dissolute. Janet is a striking figure, too. And when I think of my ignorance of clerical life and squabbles, yet find myself so interested in this story, I feel that all persons better informed must be greatly moved.[2]

[1] *Letters*, II. 347–9.   [2] Ibid. 351.

The prospect of losing his new contributor was more than Blackwood could contemplate. Taking his cue from Lewes, he wrote to George Eliot at once, assuring her of his

great confidence that in spite of my objections to this first part of Janet's Repentance the Tale as it goes on will prove one of your best. Indeed the glimpse of what was coming in the last pages left this impression on my mind at first.

I do not fall in with George Eliots every day and the idea of stopping the Series as suggested in your letter gave me 'quite a turn' to use one of Thackeray's favourite phrases. There is nothing in the part that can make me 'afraid' to publish it. On the contrary no one can read it without being impressed by the ability and truth of the individual pictures, and I only wished to convey my fear that you are wasting power in sketching in so many figures who would not help on or add to the popularity of your story.

From the tone of this first part I do not think that it will be much liked, but you know what groundwork you require, and when I have not seen the whole of your M.S. you must always take my remarks as those of one writing to some extent in the dark. I wish much now that I had the rest of your M.S. as I feel sure that it would enable me to write and heartily congratulate you upon a new success.

I liked the religious feeling in Gilfil much, and I am very glad to see what you say on that head in your letter. I feel sure that we shall agree in disliking canters of all creeds and respecting real religious feeling whatever form it takes. Send the proof direct to Edinburgh where I hope to be on Thursday.

I leave this 'damned distracting Town' tomorrow morning and, many friends as I have in it, I am not sorry to get away. . . . Thackeray was here today to say good bye to Mrs. Blackwood and had there not been some other parties in the room I would have read what you said about him, as I do not think it would have been otherwise than gratifying to the old Trojan.

In continuing to write for the Magazine I beg of all things that you will not consider yourself hampered in any way. Of course I will say when I think you are failing to produce the effect you intend or otherwise missing the mark, but unless you write entirely from the bent of your own genius or knowledge or observation it would not be worth my while to make any comments at all.

The cordial tone of your letters gives me great pleasure, and after reading your last I should have liked very much to have shaken hands with you and expressed the hope which I now write that there are many years of happy friendly and literary intercourse before us.[1]

[1] *Letters*, II. 352–3.

George Eliot's reply 16 June closed this round of their discussion of realism:

Thanks for your kind letter. It shows that you have understood me, and will give me confidence for the future. I have attended, I think, to all your marginal observations except one, and have been able to make several omissions and introduce several touches which I hope you will find an agreeable modification of the second chapter, when you read it in revise. I wish I could send you more M.S., but unfortunately I have not enough in readiness for you, to make that worth while.

The descriptions of character are not so alien to the drama as they possibly appear to you at present, and several other things that seem to have puzzled you will I dare say, become clear as the story proceeds. I will forward the next part as soon as I can possibly get it in a state of completeness and now I have your cordial words to give me confidence it will go on more swimmingly.

I heartily respond to your wish that our literary intercourse may continue—for that wish includes many good things. It means that I shall go on writing what will stir men's hearts to sympathy as well as that I shall have all the pleasures and advantages involved in the possession of a generous editor. That that editor may one day become a personal friend is a prospect which I hope I may indulge without proving too sanguine.[1]

Some of the omissions she alludes to here are given by Thomas A. Noble in his *George Eliot's 'Scenes of Clerical Life'*.[2] Where she had written of Mr. Crewe in the pulpit: 'His brown wig was hardly ever put on quite right, and sometimes, when he spat, he made noises not in the rubric', the latter clause was deleted.[3] In discussing drunkenness at Milby she had written: 'It is true there were three or four substantial men who had a reputation for exceptional sobriety, and not more than half a dozen married ladies were frequently observed to become less sure of their equilibrium as the day advanced, so Milby habits were really not as bad as possible.' All printed texts omit the clause about the ladies.[4] A longer passage on Dempster's drinking disappeared entirely. After the account of Mr. Jerome's goodwill in giving 'sacks of potatoes to the poor', George Eliot had written:

That sort of virtue was not common at Milby, in spite of Mr. Dempster's alarm at the introduction of a doctrine which would invalidate the efficacy of good works. The virtue there, I imagine, was chiefly of that negative kind which consists in not pretending to be better than

[1] *Letters*, II. 353.   [2] (New Haven, 1965), pp. 155–7.
[3] MS: fol. 14 (Morgan Library); *Blackwood's Magazine*, 82 (July 1857), 60.
[4] MS: fols. 11–12.

one's neighbours, and in this it might safely challenge comparison with the most ingenuous of provincial towns. Drunkenness was indulged in with great candour; no one put on very charming manners to his wife when in company; neighbours on the best of terms imputed boastful lying and spiteful detraction to each other without any affectation of disgust; and other sins prayed against in the litany were the subject of very free allusion and were committed with considerable openness. Dempster's life, to be sure, was thought too flagrantly irregular; his drinking was out of all bounds, and he often abused his wife beyond what was reasonable. Still he was one of those valuable public characters in whom society has at all times tolerated an extra amount of aberration; he was very well received in most houses, and there were several ladies rather proud of 'knowing how to manage Dempster', or of jocosely twitting him with being a sad husband.[1]

None of these passages was restored to the text when the *Scenes* were reprinted.

Neither George Eliot nor Blackwood was converted by this correspondence. But through it she learned to respect his practical wisdom as the editor of a family magazine and a publisher of fiction that had to be kept acceptable to circulating libraries; and he learned to be chary of trying to mould her genius into the conventional pattern. Sending the proof of Part II, he protested mildly that the bishop conducting the confirmation in Chapter 6 'is doubtless a true sketch, but I wish he had been a better sample of the cloth', and complained that the mock play-bill in Chapter 9 'did not make me laugh'.[2] George Eliot answered both objections, 12 July:

I think you have rather mistaken the intention of the jokes in the play-bill. They are not meant by any means as Attic wit, but as *Milby* wit, and any really fine sarcasm would be out of place. I have altered the conclusion a little to prevent that mistake in the reader. It would not do, I think, to substitute vagueness for particularity in this instance, and omit the play-bill. In the real persecution, a play-bill of an equally insulting kind was printed and circulated and thought the finest joke imaginable.

My own impression on rereading very carefully the account of the confirmation is, that readers will perceive, what is the fact—that I am not in the least occupying myself with confirmation in general, or with Bishops in general, but with a particular confirmation, and a particular Bishop.

The letter ended with a summary of her position:

Art must be either real and concrete, or ideal and eclectic. Both are good and true in their way, but my stories are of the former kind. I

[1] MS: fols. 22–3.   [2] *Letters*, II. 360.

undertake to exhibit nothing as it should be; I only try to exhibit some
things as they have been or are, seen through such a medium as my
own nature gives me. The moral effect of the stories of course depends
on my power of seeing truly and feeling justly; and as I am not conscious
of looking at things through the medium of cynicism or irreverence,
I can't help hoping that there is no tendency in what I write to produce
those miserable mental states.[1]

Lewes, who had watched the disturbing effect of Blackwood's
criticism, reiterated his caution:

Entre nous let me hint that unless you have any *serious* objection to
make to Eliot's stories, *don't* make any. He is so easily discouraged, so
diffident of himself, that not being prompted by necessity to write, he
will close the series in the belief that his writing is not relished. I laugh
at him for his diffidence and tell him it's a proof he is *not* an author.
But he has passed the middle of life without writing at all, and will easily
be made to give it up. *Don't allude to this hint of mine.* He wouldn't like
my interfering.[2]

Blackwood quickly caught on. When there was matter to praise,
as there always was, he praised it generously. But he was careful
to avoid or pass lightly over unfavourable impressions. When he
sent the proof of Part III, at the end of which the brutal Dempster
thrusts his wife out of doors in her night-gown, he pronounced it
'admirable'.[3] Part V, in which Dempster, after falling out of the
gig and breaking his leg, has a wild attack of delirium tremens
and dies of the 'mortified' limb, was the severest test of his control.
And the concluding chapters, in which the heroine struggles against
the 'unpoetic' temptation of the brandy bottle and the hero dies
of consumption, must have bothered Blackwood more than he
admitted.

I was a little puzzled when I came to the climax about the bottle of
brandy but you have rearranged it beautifully and it contributes to the
air of truth. Should there be so much of Dempster's delirium? I daresay
the effect would be lessened if it was shortened. Tryan's death is finely
painted and I think few can fail to be affected by the closing scenes of
the good man's life.[4]

Blackwood probably agreed with the remark of his friend the
Reverend G. C. Swayne on the 'disagreeable' story with 'the
evangelical parson's contracting at the end a passion for the re-
formed gin-drinker, the explosion of which in scandal is happily

---

[1] *Letters*, II. 362.   [2] Ibid. 363–4.
[3] Ibid. 371.   [4] Ibid. 387.

prevented by his *timely* death'.[1] But he now concealed such sentiments from his sensitive author, who expressed herself as 'very
much gratified that my Janet has won your heart and kept up your
interest in her to the end'.[2] It was too late, however. His lack of
sympathy with the earlier instalments had annoyed her so much
that, 'although he came round to admiration at the third part',
she did not alter her determination to close the series with 'Janet'
and republish them in two volumes instead of the usual three.[3]

At Jersey they saw few people they knew. One day while out
walking they met Pierre Leroux, still in exile, who chatted with them
and promised to call one evening; but he is not mentioned again.
They were quite content with their own society, working hard,
Lewes on the physiology of the nervous system and Marian on
'Janet's Repentance'. Every day they took long walks, even if it
rained. When it was fine, they sometimes read in the mild air out
of doors. 'After lunch,' Lewes noted in his Journal 5 June, 'we
took *Sense and Sensibility* with us and, lying down in the shade
behind the Castle, read it aloud.' But these idyllic days could not
last indefinitely. His 'Sea-side Studies' were nearly finished, and
he had to be in London to arrange for their republication with
illustrations. Herbert, his youngest son, was to be taken to join
his brothers in Switzerland. Accordingly, they left Jersey on 24
July and, after a roughish crossing to Southampton, spent the
night at the Craven Hotel in London. Having done a little shopping,
they returned to Richmond, 'unpacked, and were settled in our
old home as usual by 6 o'clock'.[4] The next day, Sunday, Lewes
hurried over to Sheen Lodge to dine with Richard Owen (to whom
he dedicated *Sea-side Studies*), who was much impressed by his
discoveries. On Monday, his Journal notes: 'Went to see Agnes;
dined at 4. Went with Marian to the Opera: *Lucrezia Borgia*
with Grisi, . . . still lovely and impassioned. Afterwards we had
an act of *Macbeth* in Italian with Madame Ristori in the sleep-
walking scene.' A week later they saw Ristori again in her great
role of Medea, 'an immense treat to us both. . . . There is more
of the actress in her than in Rachel, but not so much intensity.'[5]
They had a few visitors at Richmond. Sara Hennell, put off
by Lewes on the pretext of Marian's headache when they went to
the opera, came on 31 July and stayed the night; no comment on

[1] G. C. Swayne to J. Blackwood, 8 Nov. [1857] (NLS).
[2] *Letters*, II. 387. [3] Ibid. 410.
[4] GE Journal, 26 July 1857. [5] GHL Journal, 3 Aug. 1857.

the visit survives from either side. Barbara came to dinner on 4 August, bringing her husband Dr. Eugène Bodichon, a Frenchman she had met in Algiers and married in London that June, despite the disapproval of her family. After dinner they took a boat up the river to Twickenham, and then walked home in the twilight. The Bodichons were about to leave for the United States to spend a full year in travel and painting. Lewes gave Barbara a copy of the new edition of his *Biographical History of Philosophy* inscribed 'Souvenir affecteux', and they said good-bye with regret.

While Marian continued 'Janet's Repentance', Lewes took Bertie on 24 August to join his brothers at Hofwyl. He was delighted to find them looking 'happy and ruddy, and picking up all sorts of practical knowledge as well as "school learning"'—more improved than he had dared hope in one year.[1] Having tea with the Headmaster Dr. Müller, he 'enjoyed a cigar in the open air while I heard all about the boys—report highly satisfactory as to morale and physique—and my inspection confirmed the report'.[2] The boys came to him at breakfast, Thornie gaily singing French songs; they rambled in the woods and by the lake, Thornie bringing his botanical box and butterfly net, with which they caught some locusts. One day Lewes took them all to Berne on a shopping expedition. In the evenings they sang and played, and 'Pater', as they called him, amused them with card tricks and sleight-of-hand. He returned to Richmond 3 September, much cheered by his visit.

Rufa Hennell, who had been the first woman to call on the Leweses, was now the first to invite them to dinner. Seven years a widow, she had just married Wathen Mark Wilks Call, a Cambridge man, who after a long inner struggle had given up orders and resigned his parish at Bideford. 'I was very much and agreeably struck with Mr. Call', Marian wrote to Chapman. 'He has a thoroughly cultured and refined mind—one of the few men one enjoys listening and talking to. That was my impression from a first interview.' She went on to suggest that 'in the dearth of superior writers, I can't help thinking he would be worth enlisting as a contributor',[3] Call became one of the most dependable writers in the *Westminster*.

Bessie Parkes, now editing the *Waverley Journal*, 'Conducted by Women', sent Marian some copies of it, hoping to enlist her in 'the Cause'. Marian gave her sound advice about the paper:

---

[1] *Letters*, II. 383.
[2] GHL Journal, 26 Aug. 1857.
[3] GE to J. Chapman, 27 Sept. [1857] (Yale).

For my own taste, I should say, the more business you can get into the journal—the more statements of philanthropic movements and social facts, and the *less literature*, the better. Not because I like philanthropy and hate literature, but because I want to *know* about philanthropy and don't care for second-rate literature. However, I am a wretchedly bad judge of what a newspaper should be—a person who dislikes wine can never be a good 'taster' and I only read newspapers as a hard duty. So my personal impressions are really of no value. . . .

I shall see you, I hope, some day before very long. We have a call to make in town and—topography being willing—I shall look in at 14A Princes Street.[1]

Marian came with Lewes to Princes Street, the office of the *Waverley*, 23 September before dining with the Calls. Here she was introduced as 'Miss Evans' to Bessie's partner Emily Faithfull, a decidedly queer young woman. The following day Marian wrote:

Dear Bessie

This letter comes by way of postscript to our interview yesterday.

First, it did me good to see you—the warm unmistakeable affection in your face was a sweet cordial to me.

Secondly, you must please not call me *Miss Evans* again. I have renounced that name, and do not mean to be known by it in any way. It is Mr. Lewes's wish that the few friends who care about me should recognize me as Mrs. Lewes, and my Father's Trustee sends me receipts to sign as Marian Lewes, so that my adoption of the name has been made a matter of business. There is not much probability of such a chance as that of your having to introduce me should occur again. But I think it better to write on the subject to you while it is in my memory, to prevent the possibility of a future mistake.

There is another thing I want to say, though perhaps it is super-fluous. Mr. Lewes was afraid you would misunderstand my words about 'Providence bringing you to Richmond' as an invitation, which it would be quite indelicate in me to give in the present state of our relative circumstances—i.e. of *your* circumstances and *mine*. I don't think you would misunderstand me so far—you know that I would not for the world have you do anything that should cause 'your good to be evil spoken of'. I meant that some unforeseen good luck might bring you to Richmond and that I might see you without causing offence to any one.

Ever your loving
Marian E. Lewes.[2]

Herbert Spencer came to see them, of course, his heart now quite healed, looking well again and 'brimful of clever talk as

---

[1] *Letters*, II. 379–80. [2] *Letters*, II. 384–5.

usual'.[1] In the course of their conversation after dinner Marian—somewhat injudiciously—entrusted him with the secret of her pseudonym. She was very close to revealing it again 10 December, when Major William Blackwood came to discuss a chemistry book that Lewes was editing for the firm. Writing to his brother John, he said: 'I have just returned from Richmond. G. E. did not show: he is such a timid fellow, Lewes said. He was very pleasant, and talked in a very handsome way of his connection with us, saying of all editors he had ever had to do with, and he had had to do with many, you and Lord Jeffrey were the most agreeable. I saw *a* Mrs. Lewes.'[2] In her Journal Marian described William as 'an unaffected agreeable man. It was evident to us when he had only been in the room a few minutes that he knew I was George Eliot.' She did not reveal herself, however. The incognito was clearly growing thin at the Blackwood office in Edinburgh. If George Eliot had reasons for maintaining it, the Blackwoods were now equally anxious to. The rumour that Langford dared not entertain in January had proved all too true. In Warwickshire 'keys' to the characters in the *Scenes* were being circulated, and everyone was speculating about who might be the 'chield amang them taking notes'. The leading contender was Joseph Liggins, son of a baker at Attleborough, who had been rusticated from Cambridge in 1824 after a short residence, and retired for a time to the Isle of Man. From thence came a note by a friend of his in the *Manx Sun*, 4 July 1857, which Blackwood forwarded to Lewes: 'We have simply to state our firm belief that the facts [of the *Scenes*] are in the main literally true. Moreover, unless we be thoroughly and grievously in error, the writer is a gentleman of our own acquaintance, an old Cantab, and well-known in this island some five-and-twenty years or more ago. The gentleman we mean is named Liggers, and doubtless will contradict our guess should we be in error.' The mis-spelling of the name was corrected in later comments in the *Sun*.

Lewes, thanking Blackwood for the note, treated 'Liggers's' claim to the authorship as a great joke:

We were both amused with the divination of the Manx Seer and his friend Liggers. Quel nom! How can you wonder at the anonymous being desired, when its removal would disclose a somewhat antique Liggers who had sown wild oats in Manx society, and was now subdued to the grave proprieties of Maga. Liggers would look well on a title

---

[1] *Letters*, II. 405.   [2] Ibid. 410.

page! Liggers's New Novel. | The Manx Cat. | By Joshua Liggers. |
3 vols. £1. 11. 6*d*.

'In the *Manx Cat* the brilliant Liggers has produced a work which
may vie with the finest productions of his pen.' *Sun*.

'In the *Manx Cat* Liggers shows a master hand.' *Observer*.

'We were the first to recognize the genius of Liggers. The *Manx Cat*
may go forth with our recommendation.' *Athenæum*.[1]

Nevertheless, in the proof for the reprint of the *Scenes* a significant change was made. The opening pages of 'Mr. Gilfil's Love
Story' mention a Mrs. Liggins, an elderly widow, 'well left', who
says that from the time she was married 'till Mr. Liggins died,
nine years ago come Candlemas, I niver was out of black two year
together!'[2] In all subsequent printings *Liggins* appears as *Higgins*.

In August word came from another direction. The Reverend
W. P. Jones of Preston wrote asking

Messrs. Blackwood to inform him if there will be any more Parts of
Scenes of Clerical Life, *Janet's Repentance*. Parts 1 and 2 of that allude
to his deceased Brother, who died 23 years ago last December, and he is
utterly at a loss to conceive who could have written the statements or
revived what should have been buried in oblivion. W. P. Jones with his
only surviving sister had his attention drawn to the Paper by a clerical
friend who knew all the Parties alluded to, *most* if not *all* of whom have
long been in Eternity. If Messrs. Blackwood will oblige Mr. Jones by
an answer they will confer a kindness on him.[3]

'I hope', said Blackwood in forwarding the note, 'the old gentleman is under a delusion and that our friend has not in his love of
reality said anything to identify his story with living characters. . . .
I shall be curious to hear from Eliot.'[4] George Eliot's answer came
at once:

Mr. Tryan is not a portrait of any clergyman, living or dead. He is
an ideal character, but I hope probable enough to resemble more than
one evangelical clergyman of his day.

If Mr. Jones's deceased brother was like Mr. Tryan, so much the
better, for in that case he was made of human nature's finer clay. I
think you will agree with me that there are few clergymen who would
be depreciated by an identification with Mr. Tryan. But I should rather
suppose that the old gentleman, misled by some similarity in outward
circumstances, is blind to the discrepancies which must exist where no
portrait was intended. As to the rest of my story, so far as its elements
were suggested by real persons, those persons have been, to use good
Mr. Jones's phrase 'long in eternity'.

---

[1] *Letters*, II. 366. [2] *Blackwood's*, 81 (Mar. 1857), 319.
[3] *Letters*, II. 375. [4] *Letters*, II. 374.

I think I told you that a persecution of the kind I have described did actually take place, and belongs as much to the common store of our religious history as the Gorham Controversy, or as Bishop Blomfield's decision about wax candles. But I only know the *outline* of the real persecution. The details have been filled in from my imagination.

I should consider it a fault which would cause me lasting regret, if I had used reality in any other than the legitimate way common to all artists who draw their materials from their observation and experience. It would be a melancholy result of my fictions if I gave *just* cause of annoyance to any good and sensible person. But I suppose there is no perfect safeguard against erroneous impressions or a mistaken susceptibility. We are all apt to forget how little there is about us that is unique, and how very strongly we resemble many other insignificant people who have lived before us. I shouldn't wonder if several nieces of pedantic maiden ladies saw a portrait of their aunt in Miss Pratt, but I hope they will not think it necessary, on that ground, to increase the already troublesome number of your correspondents.[1]

Plans for reprinting the *Scenes* were being discussed. In first introducing the new author Lewes had said that his friend wished to retain the copyright. Blackwood, in spite of his private distaste for 'Janet', paid George Eliot the unusual compliment of opening the November number of *Maga* with the conclusion of the story. George Eliot proposed a motto from Fielding for the title-page, but Blackwood thought it had been used before, and she gave it up; 'though I copied it into my note-book when I was re-reading "Amelia" a few months ago, it is one of those obvious quotations which never *appear* fresh, though they may actually be made for the first time'.[2] She enclosed the following list of persons to whom she wished copies of the *Scenes* sent: Froude, Dickens, Thackeray, Tennyson, Ruskin, Faraday, Albert Smith, Mrs. Carlyle, and 'The author of *Companions of my Solitude*'. This last was Arthur Helps, with whom George Lewes would be staying over the Christmas holidays; not wanting the presentation to be connected with him, she ordered the book sent through his publisher. Faraday, whom she once heard lecture at the British Society on the magnetism of oxygen, is the most difficult to account for. It is a curious list.

The Blackwoods had paid her generously for the *Scenes*. Each month the cheques for £20 or more arrived, made payable to Lewes's account in order to preserve the incognito, a total of £263 for the eleven instalments. Again on the advice of Lewes,

[1] *Letters*, II. 375–6.   [2] Ibid. 414.

the veteran journalist, George Eliot left the terms of the reprint to the Blackwoods, and gladly accepted their offer of £120 for an edition of 750 copies—a small number, even for serialized stories. But the type was left standing, and before publication Major Blackwood increased the number to 1,000, giving her an additional £60. With his finger on the pulse of popular taste John Blackwood knew that the realism that 'puzzled' him was not likely to appeal to 'lady readers', who would devour any amount of 'Silly Novels' from the circulating libraries. Mudie's, the largest of these, when the book was subscribed 4 January 1858, took 350 copies, thanks to an extra 10 per cent discount. The fate of the book would have to await the reviews. But Marian was no longer worried about money. With 'Amos Barton' included, she had earned £443 in 1857 and Lewes £433. 9s. 2d.

On Christmas Day Marian wrote in her Journal: 'George and I spent this lovely day together—lovely as a clear spring day. We could see Hampstead from the park so distinctly that it seemed to have suddenly come nearer to us. We ate our turkey together in a happy "solitude à deux".' The next day Lewes went off as usual to 'Helps's hospitable and delightful mansion' at Vernon Hill, where the holidays were very jolly. Alone again on New Year's Eve, Marian, poised on the brink of her career as a novelist, wrote in her Journal:

The last night of 1857. The dear old year is gone with all its *Weben* and *Streben*. Yet not gone, either; for what I have suffered and enjoyed in it remains to me an everlasting possession while my soul's life remains. This time last year I was alone, as I am now, and dear George was at Vernon Hill. I was writing the Introduction to Mr. Gilfil's Love Story. What a world of thoughts and feelings since then! My life has deepened unspeakably during the last year: I feel a greater capacity for moral and intellectual enjoyment, a more acute sense of my deficiencies in the past, a more solemn desire to be faithful to coming duties, than I remember at any former period of my life. And my happiness has deepened too: the blessedness of a perfect love and union grows daily. I have had some severe suffering this year from anxiety about my sister and what will probably be a final separation from her—there has been no other real trouble. Few women, I fear have had such reasons as I have to think the long sad years of youth were worth living for the sake of middle age. . . . So goodbye, dear 1857! May I be able to look back on 1858 with an equal consciousness of advancement in work and in heart.

George returned from Vernon Hill 2 January.

On coming upstairs he said, 'I have some very pretty news for you— something in my pocket!' I was at a loss to conjecture and thought confusedly of possible opinions from admiring readers, when he drew the 'Times' from his pocket,—today's number, containing a review of the 'Scenes of Clerical Life'. He had happened to ask a gentleman in the railway carriage coming up to London to allow him to look at the 'Times', and felt quite agitated and tremulous when his eyes alighted on the review. Finding he had time to go into town before the train started, he bought a copy there.[1]

Blackwood's old friend Delane, the Editor of *The Times*, had written on 27 December to ask for an early copy of the book, which he gave to Samuel Lucas to review. It was a long article, filling nearly two columns of the vast pages of *The Times*, and included many excerpts from the stories. 'It is a favourable notice, and as far as it goes, appreciatory', George Eliot wrote. No new novelist could ask for a more propitious start.

[1] GE Journal, 2 Jan. 1858.

CHAPTER IX

ADAM BEDE

✳

Adam Bede was conceived as another Clerical Scene. In discussing possible subjects for her series, George Eliot told Lewes a story that she had heard her Methodist aunt Mrs. Samuel Evans tell about visiting in prison a young girl condemned to death for child murder, bringing her to confess, and riding with her to the scaffold.[1] Lewes remarked that the scene in the prison would make a fine element in a story. Marian had other stories in mind that she also wanted to write, one in particular called 'The Clerical Tutor'. But Blackwood's lack of enthusiasm for the realism of 'Janet's Repentance' made her resolve to close the series. She decided to combine 'my aunt's story' with certain points in her father's life and character and make them into a long novel. 'I have a subject in mind which will not come under the limitations of the title 'Clerical Life', and I am inclined to take a large canvas for it and write a novel', she told Blackwood. 'It will be a country story—full of the breath of cows and the scent of hay.'[2] She set to work on 22 October 1857, soon after the last proof of 'Janet' had gone back to Edinburgh.

The story advanced very slowly. Though she was returning again to her childhood at Griff, there is less of personal experience in *Adam Bede* than in 'Amos' or 'Janet'. Critics who like to draw a sharp distinction between George Eliot's early novels, 'inspired by imagination working through memory', and the later ones, 'contrived laboriously by intellect', do not realize how carefully George Eliot studied the background for the most natural of them, *Adam Bede*. Her acquaintance with Methodists was limited to one or two visits of her aunt. Now she got out Southey's *Life of Wesley* and made careful notes on such matters as women's preaching, visions, the drawing of lots, divination of God's will

---

[1] *Letters*, II. 502. The account of the episode from the Nottingham *Journal*, 20 Mar. 1802, is reprinted in *Adam Bede*, ed. G. S. Haight (N.Y., 1948), p. vii.

[2] *Letters*, II. 381, 387.

by opening the Bible at hazard and reading the first text the eye falls upon, belief in present miracles, visits to prisons and mad-houses, and Wesley's description of his preaching in the open air, standing 'in the calm still evening, with the setting sun behind me', as Dinah Morris does in the second chapter of *Adam Bede*. The realistic effect of such details convinced many readers that Dinah must be a 'portrait' of an actual person. But physically the stately, dignified Dinah with her pale reddish hair and mild grey eyes was totally different from the supposed original. Mrs. Evans was a 'tiny little woman' with bright, small, dark eyes and black hair; in temperament she was 'a woman of strong natural excitability', who under the promptings of her zeal was sometimes led into indiscretions.[1]

For further historical background George Eliot went to the *Gentleman's Magazine* of 1799. In her Commonplace Book she copied out lists of the dates when flowers bloomed—foxglove July 3rd, elder, the 9th; ripe cherries were gathered the 10th; the hay harvest was begun the 13th, and oats the 29th. August that year was rainy, and the 'oldest person cannot remember', says the *Gentleman's Magazine*, when the beans were not all in by September 8th. She made careful notes on various trees—the ash, the lime, the elm, on the different kinds of clouds, and the signs of high winds approaching, on the wages paid, the rising prices of bread, on Jenner's vaccination, on lead mines in Derbyshire. Many of these proved useful. One interesting note describes the celebration at Belvoir Castle of the coming of age of the fifth Duke of Rutland in 1799 with the great feast and dancing and fireworks. There are several notes on the clergy, on plurality of livings, the evils of non-residence, and the poverty of curates. From such facts alone no novelist—not even George Eliot—could have created the world of *Adam Bede*; but her concern for details helps explain the sense of authenticity, the remarkable density of background her realism achieves. By Christmas time, after two months' work, she had written only through Chapter 3; Chapter 4 was finished 6 January 1858, the day *Scenes of Clerical Life* was published in two volumes.

The reception of her stories had heartened Marian. While 'Mr. Gilfil' was still appearing in *Maga*, George had come upstairs to her with a letter in his hands, 'his face bright with gladness, saying, "her fame's beginning already"'.[2] The letter, from the Reverend Archer Gurney, a 'brother author and old reviewer'

[1] *Letters*, III. 175.   [2] *Letters*, II. 409. Gurney's letter, 14 May 1857 (Yale).

whom they had never heard of, praised George Eliot's 'great and characteristic charm', Nature. He wondered about her work to come. 'Will you always remain equally natural? That is the doubt. Will the fear of the critic, or the public, or the literary world, which spoils almost every one, never master you?' George Eliot was determined that they should not.

The presentation copies of the *Scenes* all brought appreciative responses. Froude, declaring that he had been attracted to 'Janet' when it first appeared in *Maga*, told of the delight the book gave him and his wife, and expressed the hope that 'the acquaintance which we seem to have made with you through your writings may improve into something more tangible. I do not know whether I am addressing a young man or an old—a clergyman or a layman.'[1] Dickens was one of the few to discern a feminine hand in the author of the *Scenes*, whom, he said, he would have been strongly disposed to address as a woman. 'If they originated with no woman, I believe that no man ever before had the art of making himself mentally so like a woman since the world began.'[2] In a separate letter to Blackwood, Dickens cited 'such marvels of description' as Mrs. Barton sitting up in bed, mending the children's clothes, and the portraits of both Wybrow and Janet as 'taken from a woman's point of view'.[3] But sharp-eyed Jane Carlyle did not sense a woman's touch. She thought the book was written by 'a man of middle age, with a wife from whom he has got those beautiful *feminine* touches in his book, a good many children, and a dog that he has as much fondness for as I have for my little Nero! for the rest, not just a clergyman, but Brother or first cousin to a clergyman!' She praised the *Scenes* as a human book—written out of the heart of a live man, not merely out of the brain of an author—'full of tenderness and pathos without a scrap of sentimentality, of sense without dogmatism, of earnestness without twaddle'. And like most of the rest she looked forward 'to shaking hands with you some day'.[4] Faraday, the scientist, had probably not read his copy when he thanked the author for the two volumes. 'They have been, and will be again, a very pleasant relief from mental occupation among my own pursuits. Such rest I find at times not merely agreeable, but essential.' The comment illuminates Faraday more than the *Scenes*; perhaps Lewes was exaggerating in writing to Blackwood that George Eliot treasured Faraday's letter beside that of Dickens,[5] of which she said: 'There can hardly

[1] Cross, II. 5–6.   [2] *Letters*, II. 423–4.
[3] *Letters*, II. 427–8.   [4] Ibid. 425–6.   [5] Ibid. 429.

be any climax of approbation for me after this, and I am so deeply moved by the finely felt and finely expressed sympathy of the letter, that the iron mask of my incognito seems quite painful in forbidding me to tell Dickens how thoroughly his generous impulse has been appreciated.'[1]

Adam Bede was originally planned as a serial novel for *Blackwood's*. By the end of January, when Chapter 8 was finished, the editor was already pressing George Eliot to show him some of it. But she was not ready and wanted to avoid his piecemeal comments, which she had found so disturbing while writing the *Scenes*. Even when he called at 8 Park Shot at the end of February she did not give him the manuscript.

On Sunday the 28th Mr. John Blackwood called on us, having come to London for a few days only. He talked a good deal about the 'Clerical Scenes' and George Eliot, and at last asked, 'Well, am I to see George Eliot this time?' G. said, 'Do you wish to see him?' 'As he likes—I wish it to be quite spontaneous.' I left the room, and G. following me a moment, I told him he might reveal me. Blackwood was kind, came back when he found he was too late for the train, and said he would come to Richmond again.[2]

Writing to his wife the next morning he said:

I drove to Richmond to see Lewes, and was introduced to George Eliot—a woman (the Mrs. Lewes whom we suspected). This is to be kept a profound secret, and on all accounts it is desirable, as you will readily imagine. She is a most intelligent pleasant woman, with a face like a man, but a good expression. I am not to tell Langford the secret even. . . . Lewes says he [i.e. George Eliot] would do ten times the work for me that he would do for any other man, and he does not think any other editor in the world would have been able to induce George Eliot to go on. It was very flattering, as his experience of editors is very great and he is a monstrous clever fellow.[3]

On the following Friday, 5 March, Blackwood went again to Richmond. He

chatted very pleasantly—told us that Thackeray spoke highly of the 'Scenes' and said *they were not written by a woman*. Mrs. Blackwood is *sure* they are not written by a woman. Mrs. Oliphant, the novelist, too is confident on the same side. I gave Blackwood the M.S. of my new novel to the end of the second scene in the wood. He opened it, read the first page, and smiling said, 'This will do.' We walked with him to Kew,

---

[1] *Letters*, ii. 424.   [2] Ibid. 435.   [3] Ibid. 436.

PLATE VIII

JOHN BLACKWOOD 1857

From a portrait by Sir John Watson Gordon

and had a good deal of talk. Found, among other things, that he had lived two years in Italy when he was a youth, and that he admires Miss Austen.[1]

'I picked up a Cab about Hammersmith and got to town in good time after a very pleasant afternoon at Richmond', Blackwood wrote to Lewes on 11 March. 'Best regards to George Eliot when you see him.' In spite of all injunctions he began reading *Adam Bede* on the train on his way home to Edinburgh, 'and felt very savage when the waning light stopped me as we neared the Scottish Border'. Though he assured her 'that I think Adam Bede all right, most lifelike and real', Blackwood wished to read the manuscript quietly over again before writing in detail about it. 'I write this note to allay all anxiety on the part of George Eliot as to my appreciation of the merits of this most promising opening of a picture of life. Is there much more written or is it merely blocked out?' To this Lewes returned word that 'no more is yet *written*, although all is laid out; but before he goes away he will send m.s.s for another *part*'.[2]

They were planning to go to Munich early in April; 'before I go,' George Eliot wrote, 'I shall send you a small packet of M.S. forming the fourth part of "Adam Bede", if he is destined to appear in parts, which your last pleasant letter has made me regard as probable. In that case, I leave entirely to you the decision when he shall make his début. I feel ready to begin now at any time.'[3] Meanwhile, she received Blackwood's comments on the story, written on 31 March. He praised the lifelike quality of the scene in the carpenter shop and the rustics waiting for Dinah's sermon, which he thought beautiful: 'I did not think you could possibly have managed such an outré proceeding . . . with such delicacy and skill—freedom from cant or offence of any kind.' But, scattered among the compliments, the anxieties of the editor of a family magazine often appear:

The meaning of the proverb about Chad's Bess should be made clear or it may be taken to imply something more than I suppose it does. . . . It strikes me that the passage page 53 about the identity of Love, religious feeling, and Love of Art would be better modified a little. . . . The Vicar is a capital fellow and the visit to the sick room is very touching, but I wish for the sake of my Church of England friends he had more of 'the root of the matter in him.' However I hope he is to sublime as the story goes on.

[1] *Letters*, II. 435–6.   [2] *Letters*, II. 439.   [3] *Letters*, II. 442.

The description of Mrs. Poyser is first rate. The Captain's inquiries as to Hetty walking in the Chase are direct enough. Dinah and the clergyman are good together and Hetty is certainly very attractive. . . . The Captain's unfortunate attachment to Hetty will I suppose form a main element in the Tragic part of the story. I am not quite sure how far I like the scenes in the wood and I hope things will not come to the usual sad catastrophe! . . .

The story is altogether very novel and I cannot recollect anything at all like it. I find myself constantly thinking of the characters as real personages, which is a capital sign. It will be very different from anything that has ever appeared in the Magazine and as far as I can at present judge will do well there, but if you will allow me I shall not decide on the form of publication until I have seen more.

When you send down the two other parts you mention will you give me a sketch of the rest of the story?[1]

George Eliot replied at once, refusing to tell him the rest of the story. Perhaps fear of the restraint magazine publication inevitably imposed made her incline towards publishing the novel separately. Blackwood, writing to Lewes 30 April, said: 'Give my best regards to George Eliot and tell him that he will find me quite ready to meet his wishes by the publication of Adam Bede as a separate work at once. In whatever form the Tale first sees the light I am sure it will be an excellent thing both for the pocket and for the reputation of the author.'[2]

Before leaving for Germany Marian sent her Coventry friends a copy of the photograph taken of her by Mayall a month before. In announcing the gift she wrote on 27 March [1858]:

The feeling that you and Sara have been and always will be the women I have loved best in the world—the women I have had most reason to love and admire—strengthens instead of fading with time and absence. It is impossible ever to revive the past, and if we could recover the friend from whom we have parted we should perhaps find that we could not recover precisely the old relation. But that doesn't hinder the past from being sacred and belonging to our religion. I have some faith, too, that we should never lose our old fitness for each other, and that our talks together, and looks at each other must always be fuller of mutual understanding than we could find elsewhere.

In this faith I shall venture to recommend to you and Sara, a lady of my acquaintance in whom I have a peculiar interest. She will present herself to you shortly, with a note from my hand, and I believe that for my sake you will receive her with indulgence. I can't say much that is good of her, but I am confident that she will not misconduct herself in your society. She will sit in modest silence, looking ready to enjoy any joke that is passing.[1]

The letter brought an immediate invitation from Mrs. Bray to come visit them. 'Impossible, my dear Cara, though I give you twenty spiritual kisses for wishing it. We set out next Monday, and there are all sorts of insuperable reasons why I couldn't leave home in the interim. But the aforesaid lady will not fail to make her appearance at Ivy Cottage and *she* will not turn Nelly out of her bed.'[2]

Another preparation that Marian made was to write her will, probably at Lewes's suggestion; and one day when they went to town to do errands, she signed it in the presence of Dr. Chapman and his assistant Mr. Birt.[3] Lewes had been having 'Another very painful proof that my kindness to Agnes has not been appreciated. In spite of the last year's affair she is 184£ beyond her increased income this year. Resolved to change my line of conduct altogether, until I see a different character in her. I fear she is quite *hardened*.'[4] But her debts had to be paid before he could go away. He had decided on Munich as a place where they could live cheaply, and, while Marian worked quietly at *Adam Bede*, he could carry on his studies for *The Physiology of Common Life*.[5]

They left London in the evening 7 April and after a rough crossing stopped for breakfast at Lille, where—unfortunately— Marian left her ring behind. The journey was broken with nights spent at Cologne, Frankfurt, and Nürnberg. At Bamberg they were joined in their carriage by 'a pleasant looking elderly couple who spoke to each other and looked so affectionately, that we said directly "Shall we be so when we are old?" It was very pretty to see them hold each other's gloved hands for a minute, like lovers.' Nürnberg was the highlight of the trip. Marian filled pages of her Journal with vivid descriptions of the quaint streets, the old houses with their painted fronts and wonderful tiled roofs. On Sunday morning they stopped to look into St. Sebald's Church, where a Protestant minister was reading a prayer in a cold, formal voice, and, 'as the air and floor were yet colder, we

---

[1] Coventry *Herald*, Supplement, 7–8 Nov. 1919, p. 8. [2] *Letters*, II. 443.
[3] GE Journal, 7 Mar. 1858. [4] GHL Journal, Mar. 1858.
[5] *The Physiology of Common Life* had a wide influence. Pavlov, for example, got his first interest in physiology, he said, from reading it. His copy in the German translation is at Yale. In *Crime and Punishment* (ch. 2) Marmeladov tells Raskolnikov that Sonia has read Lewes's *Physiology* and 'even recounted extracts from it to us'.

hurried out again in less than a minute'. But at the Frauenkirche, where mass was being said, the atmosphere was different. The 'delicious sound of the organ and voices drew us farther and farther in among the standing people, and we staid there I don't know how long—till the music ceased'. Her old feeling of hostility towards organized religion had evaporated since she began to write the *Scenes of Clerical Life*, and though her agnosticism remained, she never again spoke contemptuously of any sincerely held faith.

How the music warmed one's heart! I loved the good people about me, even to the soldier who stood with his back to us, giving us a full view of his close cropped head, with its pale yellowish hair standing up in bristles on the crown, as if his hat had acted like a forcing-pot. There was a little baby, in a close-fitting cap on its little round head, looking round with bright black eyes as it sucked its bit of bread. Such a funny little complete face—rich brown complexion and miniature Roman nose. And then its mother lifted it up, that it might see the rose-decked altar, where the priests were standing. How the music that stirs all one's devout emotions blends everything into harmony,—makes one feel part of one whole, which one loves all alike, losing the sense of a separate self. Nothing could be more wretched as art than the painted Saint Veronica opposite me, holding out the sad face on her miraculous hand-kerchief. Yet it touched me deeply, and the thought of the Man of Sorrows seemed a very close thing—not a faint hearsay. The music ceased, and the hard prosaic voices began. So we turned out again in search of the Gänse männchen.

In the afternoon they went on to Munich, and by ten o'clock were sitting at the Bayerische Hof, 'quietly eating our supper in our own room—a great frescoed comfortless place, with beds shut off by glass doors'. For the first time on the journey they 'had a carpetless room and mattresses instead of spring beds. It was Germany *pur et simple*.'[1] The next day they found lodgings at 15 Luitpoldstrasse—

'zwei elegant möblirte Zimmer,' where there has been an immense expenditure on wax and china ornaments and the least possible outlay in basins. We have two time-pieces under glass shades, several crucifixes also under glass shades, several bouquets of artificial flowers under glass shades, a Schranke with glass doors crammed full of the most brittle and tiny articles to be found in the German shops, selected apparently for the brittle-minuteness, and seventeen bad pictures. These

[1] GE Journal, 14 Apr. 1858.

are the chief advantages of our lodgings. As secondary ones, we have a very clean old maid as our landlady, and a good-natured ruddy *dummes mädchen* for servant; we have a clean Abtritt (!) and two very large gilt framed mirrors hung in dark corners.[1]

For all this they paid the modest price of 10*s*. per week, and their meals at the table-d'hôte at the Bayerische Hof cost 1*s*. 3*d*. each for an 'admirable dinner'.[2]

Lewes had brought a few letters of introduction. They were scarcely needed, for his *Goethe* was very much under discussion, and his portrait had appeared in the German magazines. At the University of Munich the new King Maximilian II had gathered a brilliant group of men. The scientists included the famous chemist Liebig, the physiologist Bischoff, the zoologist and anatomist von Siebold, the palaeontologist Andreas Wagner, and the botanist Martius—all men of distinction. The historians included Löher and von Sybel, the great authority on the Crusades. Among the literary, who held honorary professorships, were the novelist Paul Heyse, and the poets Bodenstedt and Geibel. The most renowned of the painters was Kaulbach, who for the King's admiration was turning out huge Weltgeschichtliche Bilder like *The Battle of the Huns*. The Leweses were soon on familiar terms with all this intellectual circle. 'I dare say we shall have quite as much society as we shall care for', Marian wrote.[1]

They began their work early in the mornings, 'just as if we were at Richmond'. After dining at one o'clock they would often stroll in the Englischer Garten, where (Lewes wrote) they occasionally saw the Queen 'walking quietly with another lady and a servant behind. We had met her once before, but not knowing who she was, took no notice. Today we stopped and I raised my hat as she passed and bowed pleasantly.'[3] There seems to have been no closer meeting. One day as they sat there listening to the military band and watching the crowds smoking, drinking beer, eating, and enjoying themselves, they saw ex-King Ludwig 'walking among them, bowing with his hat off to everybody'.[4] Sometimes they went to the breezy Theresien Wiese, where Schwanthaler's colossal bronze *Bavaria* had been erected, watching the effect of the light on the snow-crowned Alps beyond. Marian always had an eye out for human interest. Caught one day in a shower near the

---

[1] *Letters*, II. 450.   [2] GHL Journal, 14 Apr. 1858.
[3] Ibid. 23 Apr. 1858.   [4] Ibid. 15 May 1858.

Ruhmeshalle, they took shelter in the Keeper's cottage, where, she noted, they saw

a mother with her three children; the eldest a boy with his book, the second a three-year old maiden, the third a sweet baby girl of a year and a half; two dogs, one a mixture of the setter and pointer, the other a turnspit; and a relation or servant ironing. The baby cried at the sight of George in beard and spectacles, but kept turning her eyes towards him from her mother's lap, every now and then seeming to have overcome her fears and then bursting out crying anew. At last she got down and lifted the table-cloth to peep at his legs, as if to see the monster's nether parts.[1]

In the evenings they tried to keep up their habit of reading aloud, taking *Mary Barton* and *Wuthering Heights* in the first weeks with a little Wordsworth and Tennyson. But they were soon drawn so busily into the cheerful social life that there were few evenings left for reading. At least once a week they went to the theatre or opera. Much oftener there were evening parties— sometimes impromptu—that began about seven o'clock with tea in the home of a friend and went on till midnight or after. The Journals record such evenings at the houses of von Sybel, Martius, Liebig, von Siebold, Bodenstedt, Löher, and their earliest friend Oldenbourg, the publisher. There were fascinating and informative day-time engagements, too, that cut into the working hours. Marian found the men more interesting than their wives. In a letter to Sara she wrote: 'It is quite an exception to meet with a woman who seems to expect any sort of companionship from the men, and I shudder at the sight of a woman in society, for I know I shall have to sit on the sofa with her all the evening, listening to her stupidities, while the men on the other side of the table are discussing all the subjects I care to hear about'.[2] She was exaggerating, of course. She would certainly have made exceptions of Frau Martius, Frau Bodenstedt, and Frau von Siebold, who was kindness itself when Marian was ill in bed for a week with what the doctor called cholerine.[3]

Liebig was exceedingly genial and invited them to come and see him. Having done the requisite small talk with his wife ('a typical Frau', according to Lewes), they descended into the laboratory and stayed there with Liebig an hour and a half. 'He explained to Marian the whole process of silver mirror manufacture, and gave her one as a remembrance.'[4] A few days later they dined with

[1] GE Journal, 16 Apr. 1858.　　　[2] *Letters*, II. 454.
[3] GE Journal, 30 June 1858.　　　[4] GHL Journal, 5 May 1858.

him. Marian wrote, 'His manners are charming—easy, graceful, benignant, and all the more conspicuous because he is so quiet and low-spoken among the loud talkers here. It is touching to look at his hands, the skin begrimed and the nails black to the roots. He looks best in his laboratory with his velvet cap on, holding little phials in his hand and talking of Kreatine and Kreatinine in the same easy way that well bred ladies talk scandal.' And when they left at 4 o'clock he 'begged that he might see us very often, "for you interest yourself in the same ideas and like the same works of art that I like" '.[1]

Marian's taste in art had ripened since her Weimar days. At Munich Rubens gave her more pleasure than any other painter.

Rubens more than any one else makes me feel that painting is a great art and that he was a great artist. His are such real, breathing men and women—men and women moved by passions, not mincing and grimacing and posing in mere apery of passion! What a grand, glowing, forceful thing life looks in his pictures—the men such grand bearded grappling beings fit to do the work of the world, the women such real mothers.[2]

She saw nothing to admire in the 'elaborate lifelessness' of the modern German painters like Kaulbach.

It is an unspeakable relief, after staring at one of his huge pictures, the Destruction of Jerusalem, for example, which is a regular child's puzzle of symbolism, to sweep it all out of one's mind—which is very easily done, for nothing grasps you in it—and call up in your imagination a little Gerard Dou that you have seen hanging in a corner of one of the cabinets.[3]

This little cabinet with the Dutch paintings—Gerard Dou, Teniers, van Ostade, Breughel, Metsu—appealed most strongly to her. She was writing Chapter 17 of *Adam Bede*, 'In Which the Story Pauses a Little', with its famous plea for the beauty of the commonplace: 'content to tell my simple story, without trying to make things seem better than they were; dreading nothing, indeed, but falsity. . . . Falsehood is so easy, truth so difficult.'

It is for this rare, precious quality of truthfulness that I delight in many Dutch paintings. . . . I turn without shrinking, from cloud-borne angels, from prophets, sibyls, and heroic warriors, to an old woman bending over her flower-pot, or eating her solitary dinner, while the

[1] *Letters*, II. 453; GHL Journal, 9 May 1858.
[2] *Letters*, II. 451.   [3] Ibid. 455.

noonday light, softened perhaps by a screen of leaves, falls on her mob-cap, and just touches the rim of her spinning-wheel, and her stone jug, and all those cheap common things which are the precious necessaries of life to her. . . .

'Foh!' says my idealistic friend, 'what vulgar details! What good is there in taking all these pains to give an exact likeness of old ugly women and clowns? What a low phase of life!—what clumsy, ugly people!'

But bless us, things may be lovable that are not altogether hand-some, I hope? . . . human feeling is like the mighty rivers that bless the earth: it does not wait for beauty—it flows with resistless force and brings beauty with it.

All honour and reverence to the divine beauty of form! Let us culti-vate it to the utmost in men, women, and children in our gardens and in our houses. But let us love that other beauty too, which lies in no secret of proportion, but in the secret of deep human sympathy. Paint us an angel, if you can . . .; paint us yet oftener a Madonna . . .; but do not impose on us any aesthetic rules which shall banish from the region of Art those old women scraping carrots with their work-worn hands, those heavy clowns taking holiday in a dingy pot-house, those rounded backs and stupid weather-beaten faces that have bent over the spade and done the rough work of the world—those homes with their tin pans, their brown pitchers, their rough curs, and their clusters of onions. In this world there are so many of these common coarse people, who have no picturesque sentimental wretchedness! It is so needful we should remember their existence, else we may happen to leave them quite out of our religion and philosophy, and frame lofty theories which only fit a world of extremes. Therefore let Art always remind us of them; therefore let us always have men ready to give the loving pains of a life to the faithful representing of commonplace things.

In mid June, as she was beginning Book III with the description of Arthur's birthday feast, Lewes went for a week to Hofwyl to see his boys. Again he found them looking remarkably well. They rambled together in the wood, Thornie collecting plants, Bertie picking strawberries; they took long walks to the Reichenbach and up the Gürten; and he watched them bathe every day in the great circular swimming pool with its pavilion and diving boards. Among the presents he brought were some from 'Miss Evans', who sent Charlie a volume of Scott's poems. But again Lewes told them nothing about his relation with her. On the way back to Munich he stayed overnight at Zurich, where, after buying a brooch for Polly, he called on the physiologist Moleschott. His wife, answering the door, said that he was not at home. But when Lewes gave her his card, she recognized him from his portrait in the magazine as the biographer of Goethe, and insisted on his coming in. Moleschott, a Dutchman who spoke English with evident satisfaction, was delighted to make Lewes's acquaintance, and they 'had a glorious evening of it till 1 o'clock' discussing physiology.

During his absence Marian had been working at Chapters 23 and 24, 'Dinner-Time' and 'The Health-drinking'. The sympathetic von Siebolds bore her off one day to Nymphenburg to call on Liebig's sister Frau Knapp. Four days later she wrote in her Journal: 'Tired of loneliness, I went to the Frau von Siebold, chatted with her over tea, and then heard some music.' The next day her 'kind little friend' brought her a lovely bouquet of roses and an invitation to go with them to the theatre and see the new comedy, which she did to her regret: 'A miserably poor affair.' At last, the next day, 'in the evening at ten o'clock—after I had suffered a great deal in thinking of the possibilities that might have prevented him from coming', George returned.[1] 'Much to hear and tell!' he wrote in his Journal. In the morning she read him all that she had written of *Adam Bede* during his absence, 'and he approves of it more than I expected'.

They were to leave Munich 7 July. For Lewes it had been a most fruitful stay; the physiologists had given him expert advice and put 'extensive apparatus and no end of frogs' at his disposal. The day before their departure Bischoff invited him to the Institute to meet Jacubowitsch. While he was gone, Strauss, who had come to Munich for a week, called on Marian: 'I had a quarter of an hour's chat with him alone, and was very agreeably impressed', she wrote to Sara Hennell. 'He looked much more serene, and his face had a far sweeter expression than when I saw him in that dumb way at Cologne. He speaks with very choice words, like a man strictly truthful in the use of language.'[2] Then she and George 'dined cozily with the von Siebolds and took coffee with them in their pleasant garden. . . . A very affecting parting' from these kind friends ended the delightful day. But the next morning, in spite of heavy rain, they found von Siebold at the railway station, where he 'came to see the last of us'.

There was a good deal of rain during the brief holiday they took in the Tyrol. At six o'clock their first evening at Salzburg, where they stayed at the Goldenes Schiff opposite the Cathedral, they were pleasantly startled 'by the striking up of the chimes, playing

[1] GE Journal, 17–24 June 1858. [2] *Letters*, II. 472.

a tune of Mozart's. We clung to each other and listened.' As they were mounting the steps of the Mönchberg, the rain began again more heavily. 'Never mind; we must go on', Marian wrote in her Journal. 'Precious time, paid for at hotels, must be used to some purpose. So we went under our umbrellas, and got a very grand view of the mountains for our pains.'[1] The weather continuing rainy, they gave up the Königsee and went on to Ischl, a magnificent drive in the Stellwagen, crossing the Gmundensee the next day, to go by rail to the Falls of the Traun. There again as they waited for the train 'it began to rain, and the good-natured-looking woman asked us to take shelter in her little station-house —a single room, not more than eight feet square, where she lived with her husband and two little girls, all the year round. The good couple looked more contented than half the well-lodged people in the world'. Marian added in her Journal: 'He used to be a droschky driver, and after that life of uncertain gain, which had many days quite penniless and therefore dinnerless, he found his present position quite a pleasant lot.' Spending the night at Linz, they went by steamboat up the Danube to Vienna, with rain incessant till they had passed all the finest views.

Vienna was familiar ground to Lewes, who lived there for six months as a gay bachelor in 1839. They put up at the Drei Rosen, all the other hotels being full, and took three days for strenuous sightseeing that included a view of his old lodgings in the Kärntner Tor, soon to be demolished in the interest of progress. After three hours over the pictures at the Belvedere they had dinner and went a second time into St. Stephen's (according to Lewes 'while mass was going on'),[2] and then to the theatre. At the Liechtenstein Gallery, Rubens and the other Dutch painters delighted them. One of their greatest pleasures, however, was a visit to the anatomist Hyrtl, who showed them some of his preparations of the vascular and nervous systems in animals. Marian in her usual way got from him a story of his loss of fortune in the 1848 revolution:

He was compelled by the revolutionists to attend on the wounded for three days running. When at last he came to his home to change his clothes, he found nothing but four bare walls! His fortune, in Government bonds, was burnt along with the house, as well as all his precious collection of anatomical preparations. He told us that since that great

[1] GE Journal [8 July 1858]; 'Recollections of Our Journey from Munich to Dresden'.
[2] GHL Journal, 13 July 1858.

shock his nerves have been so susceptible that he sheds tears at the most
trifling events, and has a depression of spirits which often keeps him
silent for days. He only received a slight sum from government in
compensation for his loss.[1]

On the overnight journey to Prague a family of Wallachians
shared the railway carriage with them, 'one of whom, an elderly
man, could speak no German and began to address George in
Wallachian as if that were the common language of all the earth'.
After breakfast they rambled about the wonderful old town. 'The
most interesting things we saw were the Jewish burial-ground
(the Alter Friedhof) and the old Synagogue', Marian wrote. 'We
saw a lovely dark-eyed Jewish child here, which we were glad to
kiss in all its dirt. Then came the sombre old synagogue with its
smoky groins, and lamp forever burning. An intelligent Jew was
our cicerone and read us some Hebrew out of the precious old
book of the Law.'[2] They were both much impressed. George Eliot
never forgot it. The synagogue, described in these very words from
her Journal, appears in her tale 'The Lifted Veil'. Prague is also
made the scene of Mirah's escape from her father in *Daniel
Deronda*. Vienna, too, figures briefly in both stories.

The journey to Dresden on 17 July was made easily enough,
and by four o'clock they were dining comfortably at the Hôtel
de Pologne. Early the next morning—Sunday—they found lodgings on the second storey at 5B Waisenhausstrasse—'a whole
apartment of six rooms all to ourselves for 18s/. per week'.
Munich had been delightful. At no time in her whole life did
Marian go about among people so freely as there; the irregularity
of her marriage was unknown, and she ran no danger of being
saluted as 'Miss Evans'. But the constant social distraction had
prevented her from getting on as fast as she had hoped with
Adam Bede. Now, at Dresden they determined to live like hermits.
'In Munich', Lewes admitted to Blackwood, 'we had too much
society; it was pleasant but prevented work; and as it is not easy
for me to know one family in these small places without being
forced to know a great many more, I have resolved on complete
seclusion. It is amazing how well one can do without "society"!'[3]
'And so we did', Marian declared in her Journal. 'We were as
happy as princes—are not; George writing at the far corner of

[1] GHL Journal, 14 July 1858.   [2] GHL Journal, 16 July 1858.
[3] *Letters*, II. 474.

the great salon, I at my Schranke in my own private room with closed doors. Here I wrote the latter half of the second volume of Adam Bede in the long mornings that our early hours—rising at six o'clock—secured us.'

On Tuesdays, Thursdays, and Fridays they went at noon to the Gallery to study the paintings. Dresden offered even better examples of the Dutch School than Munich, many by Gerard Dou and Terborch, to say nothing of two of the finest Vermeers. The Holbeins and the great Titians—especially *The Tribute Money* —fascinated her. But the climax of her delight was Raphael's *Sistine Madonna*; 'all other art seems only a preparation for feeling the superiority of the Madonna di San Sisto the more'.[1] They saw it first within an hour of securing their lodgings. The *Madonna* cabinet was crowded. Marian 'sat down on the sofa opposite the picture for an instant, but a sort of awe, as if I were suddenly in the presence of some glorious being, made my heart swell too much for me to remain comfortably, and we hurried out of the room'.[2] Lewes merely noted that their rapid glance at the Gallery 'set us both in a perfect flutter, but as we were tired and the rooms were crowded, we contented ourselves with the "whet" to our appetite'—and went to dinner. Yet when they returned two days later, even he looked at the *Madonna* 'till I felt quite hysterical'.[3] Each day after studying other paintings they would return last to 'this sublimest picture', which they found harder and harder to leave.

'It was a charming life—our six weeks at Dresden', Marian wrote, with the long mornings of undisturbed work, the 'quiet afternoons in our pleasant salon'; their occasional walks in the open 'with the grand stretch of sky all round us', the concerts in the Grosser Garten or the Brühl'sche Terrace—all helped 'to make an agreeable fringe to the quiet working time'. But the days were now growing shorter, and they had to think of returning to England. They were anxious to have both *Adam Bede* and *The Physiology of Common Life* published before Christmas. They set off for Leipzig 30 August. After calling on Tauchnitz, the publisher of continental reprints of many British books, they dined at the house of Heinrich Brockhaus, head of the great publishing firm. Here they were introduced to Victor Carus, the Professor of Comparative Anatomy, who was to translate *The Physiology of Common Life* for Brockhaus and many of Darwin's works. The

[1] *Letters,* II. 471.   [2] GE Journal.
[3] GHL Journal, 20 July 1858.

following day Carus showed them his museum and took them to an open-air concert. The next morning at seven they set off again, and travelling day and night for more than forty hours, arrived at Richmond just before midnight, 2 September 1858.

George Eliot had finished all but the last chapter of Volume II of *Adam Bede* before she left Dresden; that—Chapter 35, 'The Hidden Dread'—was soon written 'in the old room at Richmond', and the manuscript sent off to Blackwood on 7 September. It was nearly a month before she received his comments. 'The story is a very striking one and I cannot recollect anything at all of the same kind', he wrote on 4 October. 'I long to see how it will work out.' He praised a number of the characters. 'Hetty is a wonderful piece of painting. One seems to *see* the little villain.' But the point that troubled him most was the fight between Adam and Arthur in Chapter 27.[1] Lewes in discussing the plan with her during the first weeks at Munich had

expressed his fear that Adam's part was too passive throughout the drama, and that it was important for him to be brought into more direct collision with Arthur. This doubt haunted me, and out of it grew the scene in the Wood between Arthur and Adam: the fight came to me as a *necessity* one night at the Munich opera when I was listening to *William Tell*.[2]

This was one of the first chapters she composed in the long, quiet mornings at Dresden. Blackwood wrote to her:

I have thought a great deal over the encounter between Adam and Arthur, indeed I daresay it is pondering over that scene which has prevented me from sooner sitting down to write to you. The picture of Adam's feelings before he gets the fatal glimpse of the scene in the wood is perfection. The point is worked up to with wonderful skill. It is very difficult to imagine what would happen between any two men brought so suddenly into such a total revulsion of feelings and change of relative positions as happens to Adam and Arthur, but on the whole I think you have hit the mark and sustained in a very trying climax the characters of the two men you are drawing. I am ashamed of myself for not feeling more sorry for Adam, but I have no doubt the sympathies will gather round him keenly when the full force of his affliction comes upon him and the tender and stern fibres in his heart of oak fairly begin to struggle.[3]

---

[1] *Letters*, II. 483–4.
[2] 'History of *Adam Bede*', GE Journal; *Letters*, II. 504.
[3] *Letters*, II. 484.

At another time George Eliot would have been more disturbed over the failure of her hero to win his entire sympathy. But now she was completely absorbed in her work.

The opening of the third volume—Hetty's journeys—was, I think written more rapidly than the rest of the book, and was left without the slightest alteration of the first draught. Throughout the book, I have altered little, and the only cases, I think, in which George suggested more than a verbal alteration, when I read the M.S. aloud to him, were the first scene at the Farm [Ch. 6] and the scene in the Wood between Arthur and Adam [Ch. 48], both of which he recommended me to 'space out' a little, which I did. When, on October 29, I had written to the end of the love scene at the Farm, between Adam and Dinah, I sent the M.S. to Blackwood, since the remainder of the third volume could not affect the judgment passed on what had gone before.[1]

Blackwood 'wrote back in warm admiration':

I fastened upon the 3d volume of Adam Bede and read the whole of the M.S. that afternoon. I am happy to tell you that I think it capital. I never saw such wonderful effects worked out by such a succession of simple and yet delicate and minute touches. Hetty's night in the fields is marvellous. . . . Adam going to support her at the Trial is a noble touch. . . . Mr. Irwine is always good. So are the Poysers, life-like as possible.

Dinah is a very striking and original character, always perfectly supported and never obtrusive in her piety. Very early in the book I took it into my head that it could be 'borne in upon her' to fall in love with Adam. Arthur is the least satisfactory character but it is true too. The picture of his complacent happy feelings before the bomb shell bursts upon him is very good.

We have been trying pages so as to start with the printing immediately. The extent is not so great as I imagined and I cannot help thinking that our people have rather underestimated the quantity.

Inclosed I send our formal offer for the book which will I hope come up to your expectations and, congratulating you upon having worked out the climax of your story so splendidly, I am always,

yours very truly
John Blackwood.

George Eliot Esq.[2]

His offer was £800 for the copyright for four years—£400 at six months, the remainder at nine. George Eliot accepted at once with the modification that the first payment should be at the time of publication, the second at nine months, to which Blackwood

---

[1] *Letters*, II. 504.   [2] *Letters*, II. 492–3.

agreed. The specimen pages were disappointing in appearance, for the printers had greatly underestimated the quantity, and Blackwood, writing 15 November, promised a new specimen 'in a day or two'. The first sheets of proof (pages 1–32) reached her 23 November. In ordinary circumstances the novel would have been printed and bound within a month. But the printing office was struggling with the four volumes of Bulwer Lytton's *What Will He Do with It?*, which, after its run in *Maga*, was being rushed through to catch the Christmas trade. Lytton was slow in returning his proof; about a ton and a half of the same type being used for *Adam Bede* was locked up.

The delay troubled George Eliot. She wrote to Blackwood:

I am very nervous about the preservation of the incognito, for I have reason to believe that some rumour of the authorship of C.S. has escaped from a member of my own family, who, however, could only speak on *suspicion*. This makes me anxious that the publication of 'Adam' should not be delayed longer than is necessary after the Christmas Holidays, for I wish the book to be judged quite apart from its authorship.[1]

We cannot be sure who the member of her family was. Fanny Houghton, who in June 1857 first told her that Liggins was the author of the *Scenes*, or Chrissey, who lived near that eccentric fellow, may have wondered at Marian's certainty that he was not. Perhaps her tight-lipped brother Isaac at Griff had been struck by the close knowledge of Arbury shown in 'Mr. Gilfil' and, recalling their roaming about the place together in childhood, surmised that it might be from her pen. The Brays had long wondered what she was doing. Since her article on Young in January 1857 they could find nothing they could identify as hers. 'Do not guess at authorship—it is a bad speculation', she advised Sara in October 1858. 'I have *not written a word* in the Westminster.'[2] But what was she writing, then? Charles thought it might be fiction. In March he had jokingly asked her in a letter when her *novel* was coming out. Marian tried to pass it off with a jest in the same vein by asking when his *poem* was going to appear; 'I don't see why I shouldn't suppose you are writing a poem, as well as you suppose that I am writing a novel', she said. But she ended the letter: 'Seriously, I wish you would not set false rumours, or any other rumours afloat about me. They are injurious. Several people, who

---

[1] *Letters*, II. 505.　　[2] *Letters*, II. 486.

seem to derive their notions from Ivy Cottage [Spencer, for example?], have spoken to me of a supposed novel I was going to bring out. Such things are damaging to me.'[1]

In December, with the publication of *Adam Bede* delayed, Lewes decided that they should meet any inquiry about its authorship with direct contradiction. They were reading Lockhart's *Life of Sir Walter Scott*, who had more than once declared, 'On my honour, I am *not* the Author of Waverley', defending the lie on the ground of his right to avoid self-incrimination. 'An incognito can be maintained on no other condition', Marian said.[2] And Lewes reported to Blackwood that

G.E. is very uncomfortable about the delay in printing. He thinks—and I agree with him—that *mystery* as to authorship will have a great effect in determining critical opinion, and although when once a success has been made, the knowledge of the authorship cannot affect it, it might have a prejudicial influence if the rumour to which he alluded in his letter to you should spread—as spread of course it will. The evil consequences of the mystery being disclosed before the book appears seem to him, and to me, far greater than any disadvantages of contemporaneous appearance with 'What will he do with it'—the more so as that book having already been for 18 months in the mouths of men, will necessarily be less of a novelty, less *talked* about, than if it were now first appearing. Under these circumstances don't you think it very desirable to crowd all sail? Your own experience must have shown you the immense advantage there is in a mystery about authorship. . . . When Jane Eyre was finally known to be a woman's book the tone noticeably changed. Not that I believe in the possibility of anything adventitious permanently hurting a *good* book, but there is always something temporary in the success of a novel, and one may as well secure all adventitious aids.[3]

Harriet Martineau tried deliberately to make her articles 'look like a man's writing' in the *Edinburgh Review*. 'As we earnestly wish the authorship not to become known', she wrote to Henry Reeve, 'I have used the mannish way of talking about needlework.'[4] Lewes knew the Press Gang well and realized that if *Adam Bede* were known to be by Marian Evans, the strong-minded woman who was living with him, 'every newspaper critic would have written against it'.[5] That was the worst of the 'evil consequences'. Though he did not speak of it, Blackwood knew it too. 'Keep your secret all you can', he wrote.[6] Bulwer Lytton's book was at

[1] *Letters*, II. 442–3.   [2] Ibid. 505.
[3] Ibid. 506.   [4] 31 Jan. and 6 Feb. 1859 (John Martineau).
[5] *Letters*, III. 103.   [6] Ibid. II. 508.

last out of the way, and he expected *Adam Bede* to be all in type
by the end of the year.

But the rumour was spreading in London too. Herbert Spencer,
coming to dine with the Leweses on 5 November, 'brought the
unpleasant news that Dr. Chapman had asked him point-blank
if I wrote the Clerical Scenes'. Marian sent off a letter to Chapman
at once to check further gossip:

I have just learned that you have allowed yourself to speak carelessly
of rumours concerning a supposed authorship of mine. A little reflection
in my behalf would have suggested to you that were any such rumours
true, my own abstinence from any communication concerning my own
writing, except to my most intimate friends, was evidence that I regarded
secrecy on such subjects as a matter of importance. Instead of exercising
this friendly consideration, you carelessly, certainly, for no one's
pleasure or interest, and to my serious injury, contribute to the circulation of idle rumours and gossip, entirely unwarranted by any
evidence. . . . Should you like to have unfounded reports of that kind
circulated concerning yourself, still more should you like an old friend
to speak idly of the merest hearsay on matters which you yourself had
exhibited extreme aversion to disclose?[1]

Three weeks passed without word. In her Journal, 30 November
1858, Marian noted 'by way of dating the conclusion of an acquaintance extending over eight years, that I have received no answer from
Dr. Chapman to my letter of the 5th and have learned from Mr.
Spencer that the circumstances attending this silence are not more
excusable than I had imagined them to be. I shall not correspond
with him or willingly see him again.' A month later his answer
came, explaining his failure to reply sooner, and Marian started
the new year by breaking her resolution with an acknowledgement.

If that letter of mine implied any misconception or contained any word
not strictly just, I beg so far, to apologize for it. Several of your observations and statements I have read with much surprize, but I forbear
commenting on them, since it does not seem likely that further letter-
writing would advance our mutual understanding.

This frosty note brought an immediate appeal to let him come and
explain his explanation in person. But his old magnetism had lost
its attraction for Marian. She declined:

We are in the midst of that exciting anxious business—taking a house.
We have not yet decided what house it shall be, and are having constant

journeyings with that object. For the next month or more, I imagine, our leisure time will be taken up with the details of furnishing and settling, and I think we must deny ourselves the pleasure of seeing any visitors until we are fairly at ease in our new home.[1]

The new door was not quite shut against him. In February he was writing to her again, hinting at his knowledge of the incognito. Though she was very reluctant to have him do it, Lewes, taking example from Sir Walter Scott, replied for her:

My dear Chapman,

Not to notice your transparent allusion in your last, would be improperly to admit its truth. After the previous correspondence, your continuing to impute those works to Mrs. Lewes may be *meant* as a compliment, but *is* an offence against delicacy and friendship. As you seem so very slow in appreciating her feelings on this point, she authorizes me to state, as distinctly as language can do so, that she is not the author of 'Adam Bede'.

Yours faithfully,

G. H. Lewes.[2]

He noted in his Journal that 'the very existence and possibility of anonymity would be at an end if every impertinent fellow could force you by confession or implication to admit the truth of his questions . . . ; and if the thing is to be denied at all I am for distinct, effective denial rather than equivocation'.[3]

The house they had chosen was Holly Lodge at Southfields, Wandsworth. In the little sitting-room in Park Shot, where they had to write at tables close to each other, the scratch of pen and rustle of paper had always distracted her; the long mornings in the spacious rooms at Dresden had shown the value of quiet and isolation for her best work. They were also planning to make a home for Lewes's sons when they should be finished at Hofwyl. For several weeks they had been looking over houses at Putney and Mortlake and Wandsworth before they made the offer for Holly Lodge. Marian described it in a letter to Sara:

Our house is very comfortable—with far more of vulgar indulgences in it than I ever expected to have again; but you must not imagine it a snug place, just peeping above the holly bushes. Imagine it, rather, as a tall cake, with a low garnish of holly and laurel. There was a house after my own heart at Mortlake, which we were kept in suspense about

---

[1] *Letters*, III. 3. [2] Ibid. 13.
[3] GHL Journal, 12 Feb. 1859.

for some weeks—a place where I should have liked to think of living
and dying; but it turned out at last to have a premium affixed to the
lease, which made it too expensive for prudence. As it is we are very
well off, with glorious breezy walks and wide horizons, well-ventilated
rooms and abundant water. If I allowed myself to have any longings
beyond what is given, they would be for a nook quite in the country,
far away from Palaces crystal or otherwise, with an orchard behind me
full of old trees and rough grass, and hedgerow paths among the endless
fields where you meet nobody. We talk of such things sometimes along
with old age and dim faculties and a small independence to save us
from writing drivel for dishonest money. In the meantime the business
of life shuts us up within the environs of London and within sight of
human advancement, which I should be so very glad to believe in
without seeing.[1]

The rainy Christmas Day of 1858 they spent 'alone together'
at Park Shot, reading proofs of *Adam Bede* and, in the evening,
Lockhart's *Scott* aloud. This book, said Lewes in his Journal, was
a great *stimulus* to them both,

extremely valuable to all literary men as an exemplar of work. Even I
who have not much to reproach myself with in the way of deficient
regularity or industry, feel the book act like a spur. And it has also
given me many valuable hints for our remotely contemplated establishment of a Publishing House, when Charles is qualified to begin. . . .
The book has given me a personal love for Scott.[2]

When George left her 27 December to visit Helps, Marian
devoted her evenings to 'reading through Horace in this pause'.
The weather continued cold and wet; at Vernon Hill George was
laid up with a sore throat and was glad to get home again on
New Year's Day. It was the last time he left her alone during the
holidays. 'Our double life is more and more blessed, more and
more complete', Marian wrote in her Journal at the end of the
year, while Lewes, whose *Physiology of Common Life*, No. 1, was
published that day, noted 'a deepening of domestic happiness, an
extension of reputation, and a great advance in culture'. They
walked along the Thames towards Kew 28 January, Lewes wrote
in his Journal,

to meet Herbert Spencer, who was to spend the day with us; and we
chatted with him on matters personal and philosophical. I owe him
a debt of gratitude. My acquaintance with him was the brightest ray
in a very dreary *wasted* period of my life. I had given up all ambition

---

[1] *Letters*, III. 14–15. [2] GHL Journal, 25 Jan. 1859.

whatever, lived from hand to mouth, and thought the evil of each day sufficient. The stimulus of his intellect, especially during our long walks, roused my energy once more, and revived my dormant love of science. His intense theorizing tendency was contagious, and it was only the stimulus of a *theory* which could then have induced me to work.—I owe Spencer another, and a deeper debt. It was through him that I learned to know Marian—to know her was to love her—and since then my life has been a new birth. To her I owe all my prosperity and all my happiness. God bless her!

The last proofs of *Adam Bede* had been read 15 January. With high hopes they awaited its publication.

Much had to be done before they could move into Holly Lodge. The most difficult problem was to find a good servant. There were endless things to buy—furniture and curtains, bedding and linen, crockery and hardware, china and glass, and plate. On one shopping trip they visited St. Paul's, which Lewes had not entered since he was eight or nine, then went to a wholesale warehouse in Watling Street to buy carpet and rugs, walked up Fleet Street and the Strand to the banker's, bought 'a watch, which is to be Polly's present to Charlie', and an 'elegant tea caddy, and came home thoroughly tired'.[1] Finally, on 5 February 1859, they 'went to take possession of Holly Lodge, which is to be our dwelling, we expect for years to come. It was a deliciously fresh, bright day: I will accept the omen', George Eliot wrote in her Journal. They moved on the 11th. After the bookcases came, Lewes went to 26 Bedford Place and packed up his books and pictures for removal, reaching home again in time to superintend their unloading and stowing away. After years spent in lodgings, a house of their own presented many problems.

Adam Bede was published 1 February 1859. With his cheque for £400 Blackwood sent a charming letter congratulating the author:

Whatever the subscription may be I am confident of success, great success. The book is so novel and so true. The whole story remains in my mind like a succession of incidents in the lives of people whom I know. Adam Bede can certainly never come under the class of popular agreeable stories, but those who love forever real humour and true natural description will stand by the sturdy Carpenter and the living groups you have painted in and about Hayslope.

My brother joins me in congratulations and good wishes for a triumph in this case and many more which we think your pen will yet achieve.[2]

[1] GHL Journal, 28 Jan. 1859.   [2] *Letters*, III. 6.

The subscription was distinctly disappointing—only 730 copies. Of the circulating libraries, Mudie—the largest—offered only fifty at first, and hesitated to take even 500 copies with an extra 10 per cent. discount. Blackwood was confident, however, that when the reviews appeared and people began to talk about the book, the movement of sales would begin. Lewes was less sanguine. Though he breathed no word of doubt to Marian, he wrote in his Journal:

I continue to have firm faith in the *ultimate* triumph of the book; but I confess to be a little shaken as to the immediate success. Literature is such a strange thing. In Fiction readers love to see a reflection of their own egoism. They like to fancy themselves doing and feeling what the heroes and heroines do and feel. Now in Adam Bede there can be but slender gratification of this desire. No one would care to be a merely upright carpenter who does not rise to be more than a master builder at the end. Few women would care to be Dinah—they would like to have her beauty and goodness, but not her Methodism and mob cap. Nous verrons.[1]

Blackwood sent copies to his friends and to the press 'in all directions'. On the list of press copies George Eliot substituted the name of Émile Montégut of the *Revue des deux Mondes* for that of Émile Forgues, who had reviewed the *Scenes* as an example of the evils of a married clergy! Copies inscribed by the London manager Joseph Langford 'From the Author' went to Dr. John Brown, Mrs. Carlyle, Dickens, Thackeray, Froude, Charles Kingsley, and Richard Owen.

The first comment to be relayed to her came from Richard Simpson, a brother of Blackwood's clerk, a cabinet-maker in Edinburgh, who maintained that the author 'must have been bred to the business or at all events passed a great deal of time in the workshop listening to the men'.[2] This tribute disposes of Carlyle's sneer: 'I found out in the first two pages that it was a woman's writing—she supposed that in making a door, you last of all put in the *panels*!'[3] Carlyle read no further. George Eliot had wanted him to read it because his childhood 'lay among the furrowed fields and pious peasantry. If he *could* be urged to read

---

[1] GHL Journal, 9 Feb. 1859.   [2] *Letters*, III. 9.
[3] According to Mrs. Allingham, who reported the comment, this was the only reference he made to GE or her works. He recalled vaguely calling during one of his daily rides and making her acquaintance soon after they 'took up with each other, when they were living somewhere in the Sydenham direction' (NLS: Acc. 1728/143 [1880]).

a novel! I should like to give him the same sort of pleasure he has given me in the early chapters of *Sartor*', she told John Blackwood.[1] But Mrs. Carlyle wrote ecstatically to George Eliot:

5 Cheyne Row Chelsea
20th February /59

Dear Sir

I must again offer you my heartiest thanks. Since I received your *Scenes of Clerical Life* nothing has fallen from the skies to me so welcome as *Adam Bede, all to myself*, 'from the author.'

My husband had just read an advertisement of it aloud to me, adding: '*Scenes of Clerical Life? That* was *your* Book wasn't it?' {The '*your*' being in the sense not of possession but of prediliction} 'Yes,' I had said, 'and I am so glad that he has written another! *Will* he send me this one, I wonder?'—thereby bringing on myself an utterly disregarded admonition about 'the tendency of the Female Mind to run into unreasonable expectations'; when up rattled the Parcel Delivery cart, and, a startling double-rap having transacted itself, a Book-parcel was brought me. 'There it is!' I said, with a little air of injured innocence triumphant!—'There is *what*, my Dear?'—'Why, *Adam Bede* to be sure!'—'How do you know?' {I had not yet opened the parcel} 'By *divination.*'—'Oh!—Well!—I hope you also *divine* that *Adam Bede* will justify your enthusiasm now you have got it!'—'As to *that*' {snappishly} 'I needn't have recourse to divination, only to natural logic!'—Now; if it had turned out *not Adam Bede* after all; where *was* my 'diminished head' going to have hidden itself?—But Fortune favours the Brave! I had foretold aright, on both points! The Book was actually *Adam Bede*, and *Adam Bede* 'justified my enthusiasm'; to say the least!

Oh yes! It was as good as *going into the country for one's health*, the reading of that Book was!—Like a visit to Scotland *minus* the fatigues of the long journey, and the grief of seeing friends grown old, and Places that knew me knowing me no more! I could fancy in reading it, to be seeing and hearing once again a crystal-clear, musical, Scotch stream, such as I long to lie down beside and—*cry* at (!) for gladness and sadness; after long stifling sojourn in the South; where there [is] no *water* but what is stagnant or muddy!

In truth, it is a beautiful most *human* Book! Every *Dog* in it, not to say every man woman and child in it, is brought home to one's 'business and bosom,' an individual fellow-creature! I found myself in charity with the whole human race when I laid it down—the *canine* race I had *always* appreciated—'not wisely but too well!'—the *human*, however, —Ach!—*that* has troubled me—as badly at times as 'twenty gallons of milk on one's mind'![2] For the rest; why you are so good to *me* is still a *mystery*, with every appearance of remaining so! . . . I give it up; just

---

[1] *Letters*, III. 23.   [2] Mrs. Poyser's worry in ch. 32.

'taking,' gratefully and gladly, 'the good the gods {under the name of George Elliot} have provided me.'

Now, Heaven knows if such a long letter to read be not illustrating for *you* also 'the tendency of the female mind to run into unreasonable expectations'! But just consider! Is it possible that, with my opportunities, I should not know perfectly well, what a 'distinguish-author' *does* with letters of compliment *that bore him*; either by their length or their stupidity? He lights his pipe with them or he makes them into spills; or he crushes them into a ball, and pitches them in the fire or waste-paper basket; does anything with them *except read them!* So I needn't take fright about having *bored* you; since, long before it came to that, I should have, or shall have been slit up into spills, or done good service in lighting your pipe! It is lawful for *Clergymen* to smoke, I hope,—for their own sakes? The newspaper critics have decided you are a Clergyman, but I don't believe it the least in the world. You understand the duties and uses of a Clergyman too well, for *being* one! An old Lord, who did not know my Husband, came up to him once at a Public meeting where he had been summoned to give his 'views' {not *having* any} on the 'Distressed Needle Women,' and asked; 'pray Sir, may I inquire, are *you* a Stock-Broker?'—'A Stock-Broker! certainly not!'—'Humph! Well I thought you *must* be a Stock-Broker; because, Sir, you go to the root of the matter.' —If that be the signal of a Stock-Broker I should say you must certainly be a *Stock-Broker*, and must certainly *not* be a *Clergyman!*

Respectfully and affectionately yours, whatever you be,

Jane W. Carlyle.[1]

Mrs. Carlyle was soon recommending *Adam Bede* to everyone she knew: Miss Catherine Macready promised her to get it at once; for 'it must be worth reading to win such praises'.[2] Annie Thackeray, whom she regaled with the story of the book's arrival, had already devoured the copy sent to her father. From Thackeray himself no word could be elicited. Overworked in his effort to bring *The Virginians* to a close, he had no time for reading. Two years later he confessed to a friend, 'I admire but can't read *Adam Bede* and the books of that Author.'[3] From Dickens there was no comment until July. Owen thought it the finest work since Scott.[4] Froude wrote admiringly that *Adam Bede* 'gave no pleasure. It gave a palpitation of the heart. That was not pleasure; but it was a passionate interest.'[5] The day his letter came she was reading in Horace, 'Non omnis moriar.' *Her* work was just beginning.

[1] *Letters*, III. 17–19.
[2] Catherine Macready to Jane Welsh Carlyle, [20 Feb. 1859] (NLS: 1774, fol. 150ᵛ).   [3] *Thackeray Letters*, ed. G. N. Ray, IV. 238.
[4] GHL Journal, 22 Apr. 1859.
[5] J. A. Froude to GE, 13 Mar. 1859 (Yale).

In Edinburgh the response was equally gratifying. John Caird, a celebrated preacher from Glasgow, coming to call on Mrs. Blackwood more than an hour late, said that he had been so fascinated by the book that he had forgotten time altogether. Dr. John Brown wrote to Blackwood, raving about it, and sent the author a copy of his little story *Rab and His Friends*, which George Eliot read twice, once aloud, and once to herself very slowly. The Reverend William Lucas Collins, of Great Houghton, Northamptonshire, wrote in a letter to Blackwood that he thought the plot the weakest part of the book, but the philosophy and the humour struck him as excellent. 'Altogether it is far beyond the ordinary run of novels, and will, I should think, make the writer (whose name I think you told me was *not* Eliot) a lasting reputation.'[1] Collins, who had criticized Mrs. Gaskell's novels in *Maga* in 1858 (rather severely, she felt), gladly agreed to review *Adam Bede* for the April number.

All the reviews were laudatory. The weekly newspapers spoke first. The *Athenæum*, in an article by Geraldine Jewsbury (who may have caught some of her friend Jane Carlyle's enthusiasm) called it 'a work of true genius, . . . a novel of the highest class, . . . a book to be accepted, not criticized'.[2] The *Leader* declared that 'The novel has not a weak point about it, nor a commonplace character.'[3] The *Literary Gazette*, the *Critic*, and *Bell's Weekly Messenger* all praised it, though *Bell's* ranked it after Bulwer Lytton's novel. Lewes, irritable and weary of 'the moil and turmoil of moving', was annoyed by such praise. The *Statesman*, for example, said that *Adam Bede* was ' "One of the best novels we have read for a long time." The nincompoop couldn't see the distinction between Adam and the mass of novels he had been reading.'[4] Langford told him of three young ladies who were 'delighted' with it. But to Lewes 'delighted' was no more than young ladies said of fifty books during the season. 'If people are only "delighted" with *Adam Bede* there will be no adequate success for that work.'[5] The *Saturday Review*, though generally laudatory, suggested that George Eliot had evidently 'sat at the feet of Mr. Kingsley', and (like the *Examiner*), took exception to the details of Hetty's pregnancy, which 'read like the rough notes of a man-midwife's conversation with a bride'.[6] On seeing this the watchful Blackwood sent the book to James Simpson, the Professor of

[1] W. L. Collins to J. Blackwood, 16 Feb. 1859 (NLS).
[2] *Athenæum*, 26 Feb. 1859, p. 284. [3] *Leader*, 26 Feb. 1859, p. 270.
[4] GHL Journal, 12 Feb. 1859. [5] Ibid. 9 Feb. 1859.
[6] *Saturday Review*, 26 Feb. 1859, pp. 281–3.

Midwifery at Edinburgh University. Simpson could find no in-delicacy in the episode, which twentieth-century readers object to as excessively reticent; but he pointed out that Hetty's baby, being premature at six or seven months, wouldn't have been a noisy, squalling child. For his part, he said, George Eliot was 'a Teniers and Titian of a novel writer, . . . a grand and glorious fellow'.[1]

In the midst of this gratifying reception of her novel, Marian received a letter from her sister Chrissey—'ill in bed—consumptive —regretting that she ever ceased to write to me. It has ploughed up my heart.'[2] To Sara Hennell, who had heard the news and offered to go see Chrissey, she wrote:

I think not, dear Sara, thank you. I have written to Chrissey and shall hear from her again. She has the materials for knowing and inferring all that is necessary.

I think her writing was the result of long quiet thought—the slow return of a naturally just and affectionate mind to the position from which it had been thrust by external influence. She says, 'My object in writing to you . . . was to tell you how very sorry I have been that I ceased to write and neglected one who under all circumstances was kind to me and mine. *Pray believe* me when I say it will be the greatest comfort I can possibly receive to know you are *well* and *happy*. Will you write once more etc. etc.' I wrote immediately, and I desire to avoid any word of reference to anything with which she associates the idea of alienation. The past is abolished from my mind—I only want her to feel that I love her and care for her.[3]

The Brays at once offered Marian their hospitality. If Chrissey expressed a wish to see her, she would go; but 'much as I should like to sit with you all by your own fire' the necessity of hurrying back to George 'will forbid me that pleasant renewal of the past. People who have been inseparable and found *all* their happiness in each other for five years are in a sort of Siamese-twin condition that other people are not likely to regard with tolerance or even with belief.'[4] In a few days Chrissey wrote 'by her daughter Emily, saying that she would love to see me, but fears the excitement. She writes herself a few words in pencil this time as if she were weaker—alas—.' On 14 March Emily wrote that her mother had been taken worse and could not live many days. The following morning she was dead.

[1] James Young Simpson to J. Blackwood, 4 Mar. 1859 (NLS).
[2] *Letters*, III. 23.   [3] Ibid. 26.   [4] Ibid. 27.

The succeeding days are a blank in Marian's Journal. She carried on as usual, went to town with George to look for a servant, walked in Richmond Park, saw the Head Keeper's dogs, and in the evenings read Balzac's *Un grand Homme de Province.* The day after Chrissey's funeral the manuscript of *Adam Bede,* which Lewes had requested, came from Blackwood, beautifully bound in red russia. Marian inscribed on the fly-leaf: 'To my dear husband, George Henry Lewes, I give this M.S. of a work which would never have been written but for the happiness which his love has conferred on my life. Marian Lewes March 23. 1859.' Some interesting facts about its composition she also noted there:

The first volume was written at Richmond, the second at Munich and Dresden, the third at Richmond again. The work was begun on the 22d October 1857, and finished on the 16th November 1858. A large portion of it was written twice, though often scarcely at all altered in the copying; but other parts only once, and among these the description of Dinah and a good deal of her sermon, the love-scene between her and Seth, 'Hetty's World', most of the scene in the Two Bedchambers, the talk between Arthur and Adam, various parts in the second volume which I can recal less easily, and in the third, Hetty's journeys, her confession and the cottage scenes.[1]

Collins's review in the April *Blackwood's* had been carefully tailored by the editor with respect to George Eliot's sensibilities. Though Collins had been afraid of praising the book too much, John Blackwood encouraged him to strengthen his remarks, which he gladly did, and to delete his objections to the conventional nature of the plot. 'I think I was *good*', Collins said in a letter to Blackwood, 'not to mention Donnithorne galloping up with the reprieve.'[2] In April the quarterlies began to join the chorus of praise. The *Westminster* carried, not a review, but an article of twenty-seven pages, space rarely given to a single work of fiction. But a paragraph at the end, inserted by Chapman, annoyed Lewes. Having forced Spencer to admit that George Eliot was Marian Evans, Chapman then pretended to an unwarranted astuteness.

We speak of the author as of the masculine gender, but the deliberate appreciation of feminine feelings conveyed in this question—'What woman was ever satisfied with apparent neglect, even when she knows it is the mask of love?'—would alone suffice to make us skeptical as to whether *George Eliot* ever wrote it.

[1] Except for *Scenes of Clerical Life* (Morgan), and 'Brother Jacob' (Yale) the MSS. of GE's works are in the British Museum, Add. 34020–43.
[2] W. L. Collins to J. Blackwood, 24 Mar. 1859 (NLS).

And he cited Hetty as a character that could have been drawn only by an author with 'the intense feelings and sympathies of woman'.[1] It was not fairly done.

In those days a three-volume novel was sold for 31*s.* 6*d.*, a price only the rich could afford. Most people borrowed novels from the circulating libraries like Mudie's, which gave them as many as they could read for £2. 2*s.* a year. As the fame of *Adam Bede* grew, Mudie had to increase his supply to 1,000 copies. The book was making its way not only with the ordinary novel readers, but— according to Langford—'people who are scholars and most fastidious are greatly pleased with it'.[2] By mid March of the 2,100 copies of the first edition 1,800 had been sold. Novels rarely needed more than one edition in three volumes. The type had been distributed.[3] But it was reset, and a second edition of 750 copies run off. Even this failed to satisfy the increasing demand; a second impression of 500 was required. Then, early in June, *Adam Bede* was reprinted in two volumes selling at 12*s.* In this form more than 10,000 copies were sold in 1859, and it was reprinted on the Continent and in America before the so-called Cheap edition in one volume at 6*s.* appeared. There were translations into German, Dutch, Hungarian, French, and Russian. The Russian translation went through three editions in 1859. One of them was read by Tolstoy, who placed it among the examples of the 'highest art'.[4] *Adam Bede* became a sensational success, taking precedence over *A Tale of Two Cities* and *The Virginians.* No book had made such an impression since *Uncle Tom's Cabin* swept the world. As *The Times* declared 12 April in a long review filling three full columns, 'It is a first-rate novel, and its author takes rank at once among the masters of the art.' The Thunderer had pronounced. No caviller could ever reverse that judgement.

While the 'whole town was ringing with applause', the effect of success on George Eliot was 'almost sad instead of joyful— but the sadness lies near joy—and you will understand the effect on such a nature', Lewes told Blackwood.[5] He had cautioned him long since to handle George Eliot tenderly. 'Some people's Pegasus seems to have the mouth (as well as the *pace*) of a cart horse; but

[1] *WR*, 71 (Apr. 1859), 510–11.
[2] J. Langford to J. Blackwood, 4 Apr. 1859 (NLS).
[3] *Letters*, III. 33.
[4] Tolstoy read it 11 Oct. 1859 (Jubilee ed., LX, p. 300). *What is Art?* (World's Classics ed.), p. 242. See W. Gareth Jones, 'George Eliot's *Adam Bede* and Tolstoy's Conception of *Anna Karenina*', *Modern Language Review*, 60 (July 1966), 473–81.   [5] *Letters*, III. 36.

your thoroughbred—all bone and nerve—requires other treatment.'[1] Blackwood had managed her skilfully. On 7 March he
wrote that 'we may now consider the Bedesman fairly round the
corner and coming in a winner at a slapping pace'.

Early in May a letter arrived from Barbara Bodichon, who in
Algiers had read excerpts from *Adam Bede* in some obscure newspaper which 'instantly made me internally exclaim, that is written
by Marian Evans, there is her great big head and heart and her
wise wide views. . . . It is an opinion which fire cannot melt out of
me, I would die in it at the stake.'[2] Marian answered at once:

> Holly Lodge, May 5. 59
> God bless you, dearest Barbara, for your love and sympathy. You
> are the first friend who has given any symptom of knowing me—the first
> heart that has recognized me in a book which has come from my heart
> of hearts. But keep the secret solemnly till I give you leave to tell it,
> and give way to no impulses of triumphant affection. You have sense
> enough to know how important the *incognito* has been, and we are
> anxious to keep it up a few months longer.
> Curiously enough, my old Coventry friends who have certainly read
> the 'Westminster' and the 'Times' and have probably by this time read
> the book itself, have given no sign of recognition. But a certain Mr.
> Liggins, whom rumour has fixed on as the author of my books and whom
> they have believed in, has probably screened me from their vision.—I
> am a very blessed woman, am I not? to have all this reason for being
> glad that I have lived, in spite of my sins and sorrows—or rather, by
> reason of my sins and sorrows. I have had no time of exultation; on the
> contrary these last months have been sadder than usual to me, and I
> have thought more of the future and the much work that remains to be
> done in life than of anything that has been achieved. But I think your
> letter today gave me more joy—more heart-glow, than all the letters or
> reviews or the other testimonies of success that have come to me since
> the evenings when I read aloud my manuscript—to my dear dear
> husband, and he laughed and cried alternately and then rushed to kiss
> me. He is the prime blessing that has made all the rest possible to me—
> giving me a response to everything I have written, a response that I
> could confide in as a proof that I had not mistaken my work.

To this letter Lewes added a postscript that Marian did not see:

> You're a darling, and I have always said so! I don't know that I
> ever said it to you—my modesty may have held me back, as usual; but
> I say it now. You are *the* person on whose sympathy we both counted,
> and only just escaped having the secret confided to you before you went;

---

[1] *Letters*, II. 448.   [2] *Letters*, III. 56–7.

but we are glad you found it out for yourself. The success of the book is *inoui*.

And he closed with a word of caution: 'But, dear Barbara, you must not call her Marian Evans again: that individual is extinct, rolled up, mashed, absorbed in the Lewesian magnificence!'[1]

When the secret was out, Barbara wrote that she had known Marian for seven years and had 'a kind of delight in her presence which could only be explained by a sonnet. I never knew she had written fiction only philosophy and criticism and yet I knew Adam Bede was by her—for in it I saw her peculiar and surpassing tenderness and wisdom. I know no one so learned, and so delicate and tender. I read what I have written to Dr. Bodichon—he knows her too and says I can't exaggerate.'[2]

The failure of her Coventry friends to recognize Marian was partly due to her own careful indirection. Sara had given her an account of Joseph Liggins, which Marian copied and sent to Blackwood on 10 April 'for your amusement':

'I want to ask you if you have read "Adam Bede" or the "Scenes of Clerical Life", and whether you know that the author is Mr. Liggins. . . . A deputation of dissenting parsons went over *to ask him to write for the Eclectic*, and they found him washing his slop-basin at a pump. He has no servant and does everything for himself, but Mr. Rosevear' (one of said parsons) 'said that he inspired them with a reverence that would have made any impertinent question impossible. The son of a baker, of no mark at all in his town, so that it is possible you may not have heard of him. You know he calls himself "George Eliot". It sounds strange to hear the Westminster doubting whether he is a woman, *when here he is so well known*. But I am glad it has mentioned him. *They say he gets no profit out of "Adam Bede", and gives it freely to Blackwood, which is a shame.* We have not read him yet, but the extracts are irresistible.'

Conceive the real George Eliot's feelings, conscious of being a base worldling—not washing his own slop-basin, and *not* giving away his M.S.! Nor even intending to do so, in spite of the reverence such a course might inspire. I hope you and Major Blackwood will enjoy the myth.[3]

In her reply to Sara, Marian alluded to the matter disingenuously: 'Mr. Lewes has read *Adam Bede*, and is as dithyrambic about it as others appear to be so *I* must refresh my soul with it now, as well

[1] *Letters*, III. 63–5.
[2] Barbara Bodichon to Patty Smith, 29 Nov. [1859] (W. E. Stockhausen).
[3] *Letters*, III. 44.

as with the Springtide. Mr. Liggins I remember as a vision of my childhood—a tall black coated genteel young clergyman-in-embryo.'[1]

The Times remarked at the end of its review that nobody seemed to know who the author is;

it was even surmised that he must be a lady, since none but a woman's hand could have painted those touching scenes of clerical life. Now, the question will be raised, can this be a young author? Is all this mature thought, finished portraiture, and crowd of characters the product of a 'prentice hand and of callow genius? If it is, the hand must have an extraordinary cunning, and the genius must be of the highest order.

A few days later an unknown clergyman named Anders wrote to the editor from a remote village in Lincolnshire announcing that *Adam Bede* was written by Joseph Liggins of Nuneaton. 'You may easily satisfy yourself of my correctness by inquiring of any one in that neighbourhood. Mr. Liggins himself and the characters he paints in the *Scenes of Clerical Life* are as familiar there as the twin spires of Coventry.'[2] Blackwood had heard the same story nearly a year before, in May 1858 at Epsom Downs. He had described it to Lewes:

I was smoking my cigar and watching the betters in the enclosure in front of the Stand on the Derby day when I was accosted by Newdegate, the member for Warwickshire, who after some talk on politics etc. said, 'Do you know that you have been publishing a capital series of stories in the Magazine, the Clerical Scenes, all about my place and County.' My disbelief availed nothing. He knew the author, a Mr. Liggers. This is, I think, the same unfortunate patronymic that the *Manx Cat* selected as the author's.

Liggers has not acknowledged the authorship, but Newdegate said he had written to him accusing him of it but saying that the stories were told with so much delicacy, good taste, and good feeling that no offence could possibly be taken. Oldinport he said was old Sir Roger Newdigate, and he could send me a key to the whole characters. The date he considered about the beginning of the present century although more recent characters were introduced. The perfect conviction of Newdegate in the truth of his surmises was very curious, and G.E. must write me a line with a message to him. Newdegate is a capital specimen of an honest high minded English gentleman and Squire, and his opinion is excellent evidence as to the existence of the qualities he attributed to the Tales.[3]

His request for a line from George Eliot brought this reply:

[1] *Letters*, III. 46. [2] *The Times*, 15 Apr. 1859, p. 10 f.
[3] *Letters* II. 457–8.

You were right in believing that I should like to hear Mr. Newdegate's opinion of the Stories. His testimony to the spirit in which they are written is really valuable, for I know he deserves the character you give him.

As to details, he seems, from what you say, as likely to be mistaken about them as he is about the authorship; but it is invariably the case that when people discover certain points of coincidence in a fiction with facts that happen to have come to their knowledge, they believe themselves able to furnish a key to the whole. That is amusing enough to the author, who knows from what widely sundered portions of experience —from what a combination of subtle shadowy suggestions with certain actual objects and events, his story has been formed. Certain vague traditions about Sir Roger Newdigate (him of 'Newdigate-Prize' celebrity) which I heard when I was a child are woven into the character of Sir Christopher Cheverel, and the house he improved into a charming Gothic place with beautiful ceilings, I know from actual vision—but the rest of 'Mr. Gilfil's Love Story' is spun out of the subtlest web of minute observation and inward experience, from my first childish recollections up to recent years. So it is with all the other stories. It would be a very difficult thing for me to furnish a key to them myself. But where there is no exact memory of the past any story with a few remembered points of character or of incident may pass for a history.[1]

Blackwood wisely let the matter drop, though he did not forget it. But a year later Mr. Anders's letter in *The Times* could not be ignored. Lewes wrote at once in George Eliot's name denying the statement about Liggins. 'I declare on my honour that that gentleman never saw a line of those works until they were printed, nor had he any knowledge of them whatever.'[2] There Lewes should have stopped. He went on to say that the attempt to pry into what was obviously meant to be concealed is 'indefensible'. The newspapers, always ready for argument, stirred a long controversy about the public's 'right to information'.

Anders had derived his information from the real 'inventor' of Liggins, the Reverend James Quirk, Curate of Attleborough, where that neglected genius lived. After the *Scenes* began to appear in *Maga*, Liggins let him see a 'manuscript' of them in his own hand. The gullible Quirk spread the news about, discussing it at the monthly clerical meeting, from which it was disseminated to parsonages all over the Kingdom. When *Adam Bede* was published, Liggins explained that he had written it ten or twelve years before and sent it to the Blackwoods, who, he said quite truthfully, had never paid him a penny for it. This new development

Quirk, who was born at Peel, reported in the *Manx Sun*, 21 May 1859. When the Blackwoods protested, he declared: 'I *know* that Mr. Liggins wrote Clerical Scenes as at first printed.' Why should they keep him from helping a literary man in distress? Staggered by their repeated denials, Quirk asked to see a copy of George Eliot's letter to *The Times*. Marian wrote it out for him and sent it through Blackwood with a note reading: 'Herewith the copy of the letter. I hope that Mr. Quirk feels a little gravel in his boots this morning. I am fond of Liggins, compared with Quirk.'[1] Poor Quirk had to confess that it was not Liggins's hand. But, he added, Liggins was going to publish another work soon; then the whole mystery would be solved. In September, Quirk was still writing to the real George Eliot, who would have ignored his letters but that she knew he had been kind to Chrissey in her last days.[2]

The most troublesome champion of Liggins was Charles Holte Bracebridge, a muddle-headed magistrate of Atherstone. Like Mr. Brooke in *Middlemarch*, he had gone into a good many things at one time—archaeology, politics, philanthropy. His wife was a dear friend of Florence Nightingale, whom the Bracebridges had rescued from her family in 1847 to take her to Italy; later they travelled with her in Egypt, Greece, and Germany; and in 1854 they accompanied her on her famous campaign in the Crimea. There Bracebridge's irrelevant bumbling soon proved too much for the authorities, and on the excuse of health he was shipped home in July 1855. Though Miss Nightingale had implored him to say nothing, in a lecture at Coventry a few weeks after his return he made a 'furious and inaccurate attack' on the Army authorities and doctors, which was printed in *The Times*. Of course, it was believed that Miss Nightingale had inspired the attack; all her work for a year was undone by his hour of stupid twaddle.[3] Ready for a new 'cause', Bracebridge, on learning the 'facts' from Quirk, quickly gave Liggins his support, gave it 'spontaseiously', Bracebridge wrote (his spelling being as vague as his thought), for Liggins 'has wanted bread, run up a score at the grocery, lives in a house of 1/6 or 2/0 a week value, and often forgoes the ministrations of the charwoman. His conversation is wonderful and his long days passed at home till evening with his

---

[1] *Letters*, III. 78.
[2] Ibid. 147.
[3] Cecil Woodham-Smith, *Florence Nightingale* (1951), pp. 159–60.

Cats.[1] (His detractors suggested less innocent occupation for the evenings.) Bracebridge imparted this intelligence to his numerous correspondents—Harriet Martineau, Mrs. Gaskell, Catherine Winkworth, the Brays, and many more. Another volunteer named Nicholas, a 'Student in Medicine and undergraduate of the University of London', wrote to the *Athenæum* as Liggins's 'only male relative in England' to vouch for his veracity,[2] and on the same day someone reported in the *Literary Gazette* that a barmaid at Aylesbury, who was reading the *Scenes*, declared that she knew both Janet and the author, a man named Higgins—later explained as a printer's error for Liggins.[3]

Blackwood came again to Wandsworth and together they concocted a second letter to *The Times* to state that George Eliot's books were not written by Liggins, and that 'if any person is receiving charitable contributions on the ground of being the author', he is doing so under false pretences. George Eliot 'was full of fun', John reported to his brother, 'and gave me more the idea of the creator of her humorous characters than I have ever seen'.[4] This second letter, reprinted in *Bell's Weekly Messenger*, soon reached in the little village of Fewston, Yorkshire, the Reverend John Gwyther, who was prompted to write to the Editor of *Blackwood's* on 13 June 1859:

I have been a subscriber to your Magazine for about 12 years, and was much perplexed when I read the 1st number of 'Amos Barton'— on shewing it to my Eldest Daughter she said 'Who in the world could have written this—have you Papa?' So strongly were we certain it was an episode in my own life—the succeeding numbers confirmed the opinion:—and the Two succeeding Stories of Mr. Gilfil and Janette's Repentance, ⟨were⟩ are Historical reminisences of the Former Vicar —where I was Curate and of a Clergyman and the persecutions to which he was subject, all in the immediate Neighbourhood where I resided, during the events recorded in the Story of Amos Barton. All confirmed that I was the party delineated, and that it must have been written by some one intimate with me. My own suspicions fixed upon the Revd W. H. King who was Curate of Nuneaton, adjoining me, at that time —who afterwards went to Manchester and since then I learn is resident in Scotland. The Countess too and her (professed Father) the Rev. Sir John Waldron went in 1836–7 to Holyrood, since which time I have heard nothing of them.

---

[1] To C. Bray, 3 July [1859]; *Letters*, III. 110.
[2] *Athenæum*, 18 June 1859, p. 811.
[3] *Literary Gazette*, 18 June 1859, pp. 711–12.
[4] *Letters*, III. 75.

Time passed away and my pained feelings at the making public my private history abated, when our attention was called to it by a correspondent and we were asked if we knew who wrote it, but we said No —And were in reply assured it was 'Mr. Liggins'! Now we had known a little of Mr. L. whilst resident at Chilvers Coton, where the scene is laid, but never thought him equal to writing such a tale—but we were assured it was ⟨him⟩ he. In consequence of this, we gave the information to a friend in London who had interested herself in the subject; and I presume it is through that Medium that Mr. Liggin's name has been bruited. But of what is meant by 'Charitable Contributions' I know nothing, as all that I have done is giving the name of our gratuitous Historian, as I was assured of it. If it were not Mr. L— I am thrown back upon my first suspicion Mr. King, who alone of all my acquaintances of the time, was competent or had sufficient information to write it. If it was ⟨him⟩ he, and you have any communication with him, you may make my kind remembrances to him, and say that now the pain I felt at the first publication is past off—although I thought it unkind and taking a great liberty with a living Character—yet I fully forgive for old acquaintance sake. For we are as assured that I am intended by Amos Barton as I am of the Truth of any Fact soever.[1]

Mr. Gwyther's uncertainty about his pronouns recalls a similar failing of Amos Barton, who was 'not *very* ungrammatical'. The letter was sent to George Eliot, who drafted this reply for Blackwood on 15 June 1859:

The author of the 'Scenes of Clerical Life' and 'Adam Bede' begs me to inform you that he is not the Rev. W. H. King, but a much younger person, who wrote 'Amos Barton' under the impression that the clergyman whose long past trial suggested the groundwork of the story was no longer living, and that the incidents, not only through the license and necessities of artistic writing, but in consequence of the writer's imperfect knowledge, must have been so varied from the actual facts, that any one who discerned the core of truth must also recognize the large amount of arbitrary, imaginative addition.

But for any annoyance, even though it may have been brief and not well-founded, which the appearance of the story may have caused Mr. Gwyther, the writer is sincerely sorry.[2]

The correspondence produced by the Liggins affair was not all unpleasant. Mrs. Gaskell sent a letter addressed

Dear Mr. 'Gilbert Elliott',
Since I came from Manchester to London I have had the greatest compliment paid me I ever had in my life. I have been suspected of

---

[1] *Letters*, III. 83–4.   [2] *Letters*, III. 85–6.

having written 'Adam Bede'. I have hitherto denied it; but I really think, that as you want to keep your real name a secret, it would be very pleasant for me to blush acquiescence. Will you give me leave?

Well! if I had written Amos Barton, Janet's Repentance and Adam Bede I should neither be to have nor to hold with pride and delight in myself—so I think it is very well I have not. And please to take notice I knew what was coming up above the horizon from the dawn of the first number of Amos Barton in Blackwood.—After all it is a pity so much hearty admiration should go unappropriated through the world. So, although to my friends I am known under the name of Mrs. Gaskell, to you I will confess that I *am* the author of Adam Bede, and remain very respectfully and gratefully yours,

Gilbert Elliot.[1]

It was not these diversions that broke the incognito. The truth, ferreted out by Chapman, was spreading generally in literary circles. Delane, the editor of *The Times*, sent Blackwood 'a very strange story' to ask whether he wanted it published, probably the same story that Langford had heard from someone in the City: 'that these books were written by a lady who lives with Mr. Lewes, "a very clever woman". I should be sorry for such a notion to get about', added Langford.[2] Pigott was reported to have guessed it from hearing Spencer say that he knew the 'authoress', and from seeing how the Leweses' style of living had changed. Mrs. Owen Jones noticed how Lewes's eyes kindled at any praise of *Adam Bede* or the *Scenes*. It would be impossible to maintain the secret much longer.

From Warwickshire, where attention was still fixed on Liggins, there also came some indications that the real author was no longer unknown. Isaac Evans was reported to have said that no one but his sister could have written *Adam Bede*; there were things in it about his father that she must have written.[3] Before the word should reach her Coventry friends, Marian resolved to tell them herself. They were coming to London for the Handel Festival at the Crystal Palace on 20 June; she and Lewes arranged to meet them afterwards. The *Messiah* ended at half past five. As it was raining in torrents, they had some difficulty getting a cab, but at length arrived at the Brays' lodgings, where they were to dine. Marian and her dear trio were together again after five years of

---

[1] *Letters*, III. 74. Perhaps Mrs. Gaskell thought that Gilbert Elliot, Dean of Bristol, was GE. To C. E. Norton she wrote: 'I think I have a feeling that it is not worthwhile trying to write, while there are such books as Adam Bede and Scenes from Clerical Life.' *Letters of Mrs. Gaskell and C. E. Norton* (1932), p. 39.
[2] 13 June 1859. *Letters*, III. 77. [3] *Letters*, III. 98.

alienation. Soon, in tears, she revealed the great secret: she was the author of *Adam Bede*. 'It was inevitable to me to have that outburst when I saw you for a little while after the long silence, and felt that I must tell you then or be forestalled, and leave you to gather the truth amidst an inextricable mixture of falsehood.'[1] When she told them, Marian noted in her Journal, 'they seemed overwhelmed with surprize. This experience has enlightened me a good deal as to the ignorance in which we all live of each other.'

Sara had brought with her the manuscript of her new book, eventually entitled *Thoughts in Aid of Faith*, anticipating a long discussion of it with her old Pollian. But the great and unexpected news swept her poor work aside. The next day she came with the Brays to dine at Holly Lodge. 'After dinner', Lewes said, 'I had the disagreeable office of conveying to Sara our decided disapprobation of her m.s.—which made her very unhappy.'[2] As Sara explained to Marian,

I have been fancying you, as ten years ago, still interested in what we then conversed together upon—I was not sure that the writing that now occupied you was not the 'Idea of a Future Life' that was then in nubilas—that perhaps your thoughts had not been flowing in a parallel track to my own—I see now that I have lost the only reader in whom I felt confident in having secure sympathy with the *subject* (not with *me*) whom I most gratefully believe—believed in—that she has floated beyond me in another sphere, and I remain gazing at the glory into which she has departed, wistfully and very lonely.[3]

Sara went home and composed a sonnet beginning,

> Dear Friend, when all thy greatness suddenly
> Burst out, and thou wert other than I thought,
> At first I wept—for Marian, whom I sought,
> Now passed beyond herself, seemed lost to me.[4]

And Marian wrote a letter of apology for having 'from too much egoism and too little sympathy' blundered in discussing Sara's manuscript, a letter Sara found 'full of the tenderness of heart and conscience that comes with happiness! . . . How for ever remote we should have felt if you had made a pretence of being quite unchanged from your former self, and tried to converse as of former times!'[5] To Charles Bray Marian confessed her uneasiness at having

---

[1] *Letters*, III. 99.   [2] GHL Journal, 23 June 1859.
[3] *Letters*, III. 95–6.
[4] Dated 21 June 1859; found in the pocket of GE's Diary for 1880.
[5] *Letters*, III. 96–7.

listened with apparent acquiescence to statements about poor Agnes, which a little quiet reflection has convinced me are mingled with falsehood—I fear of a base sort. And I am also angry with myself for having spoken of her faults—quite uselessly to you and Cara. All such talk is futile. And I always hate myself after such attempts to vindicate one person at the expense of another.[1]

Bray like Sara, was delighted to find Marian famous 'and my convictions confirmed'. Lewes sent him a word of caution: '*Don't* say you know the authorship. Let fools and dupes continue their folly and pay for it.'[1]

As the incognito wore thinner, George Eliot, no longer amused by the farce, wanted some positive acknowledgement from Liggins to undeceive his supporters. She sent another longer letter to the editor of *The Times*, repeating that if Liggins implied he had contributed a single detail to George Eliot's books, '*he is an imposter*. And if he received money knowing at the time the money was intended for the author of these works—*he is a swindler*.'[2] It was strong language, more like Lewes's than hers. When the letter was in type, Delane sent the proof to Blackwood with the comment that, since Liggins was so entirely in the wrong, he thought George Eliot could afford to treat him more leniently. Together they prevailed on her to soften the language. But, she remarked to Blackwood, now that a manuscript of the *Scenes* by Liggins was being handed about, 'we can no longer consider the matter a joke or believe that only fools will be taken in. The thing will soon come to a pitch that would oblige me publicly to declare myself the author.'[3]

Though the Blackwoods could not tell her so, this possibility struck terror into their hearts. What form could such an announcement take? That *Adam Bede* was written by 'Mrs. Lewes'? Mrs. Lewes, alas, lived at 26 Bedford Place with four young children—not his, but all bearing Lewes's name. By 'Miss Marian Evans'? Except on legal documents Miss Evans had ceased to exist. 'My *name* is Marian Evans *Lewes*', she reminded Charles Bray after he had referred to her as Miss Evans in a letter to Bracebridge.[4] In the fastness of 45 George Street, Edinburgh, the Blackwood partners ruminated darkly on the result such a declaration might have, certain that it must affect the circulation in families of any future work by George Eliot.[5] She and Lewes were well aware of

[1] *Letters*, III. 91.   [2] 25 June 1859. *Letters*, III. 93.
[3] *Letters*, III. 102.   [4] *Letters*, III. 111.   [5] *Letters*, III. 221.

the danger too. Since Isaac had recognized her in it, they couldn't help other people's saying that the books were hers; but they were as anxious as Blackwood to 'make no categorical statement which can be taken as absolute authority'.[1] Blackwood's calm arguments and persuasive charm prevailed: 'I *wish* to suppress the letter', Marian wrote 29 June. There was no hope of suppressing the fact.

To a letter that Marian wrote to Barbara 30 June, Lewes added this postscript:

> Since the above was written we have come to the resolution of no longer concealing the authorship. It makes me angry to think that people should say that the secret has been kept because there was any *fear* of the effect of the author's name. You may tell it openly to all who care to hear it that the object of anonymity was to get the book judged on its own merits, and not prejudged as the work of a woman, or of a particular woman. It is quite clear that people would have sniffed at it if they had known the writer to be a woman but they can't now unsay their admiration. . . .
>
> P.P.S. *Entre nous.* Please don't write or tell Marian anything *unpleasant* that you hear unless it is important for her to hear it. She is so very sensitive, and has such a tendency to dwell on and believe in unpleasant ideas that I always keep them from her. What other people would disregard or despise sinks into her mind. She knows nothing of this second postscript, of course.[2]

Two days later the *Athenæum* published a savage paragraph in its Weekly Gossip column which he could not keep from her:

> It is time to end this pother about the authorship of 'Adam Bede'. The writer is in no sense a 'great unknown'; the tale, if bright in parts, and such as a clever woman with an observant eye and unschooled moral nature might have written, has no great quality of any kind. Long ago we hinted our impression that Mr. Liggins, with his poverty and his pretensions, was a mystification, got up by George Eliot. . . .
>
> Mr. Nicholas, it is true, answers for Mr. Liggins; but who answers for Mr. Nicholas? Liggins, Eliot, and Nicholas are like Sairy Gamp, Betsy Prig, and Mrs. Harris. Roll all three into one and you turn up a rather strong-minded lady, blessed with abundance of showy sentiment and a profusion of pious words, but kept for sale rather than for use. Vanish Eliot, Nicholas, Liggins,—enter, (let us say, at a guess,) Miss Biggins! . . . The elaborate attempt to mystify the reading public, pursued in many articles and letters at the same time, but with the same Roman hand observable in all, is itself decisive of the writer's power.

[1] *Letters*, III. 99.   [2] Ibid. 106.

No woman of genius ever condescended to such a *ruse*,—no book was ever permanently helped by such a trick.[1]

This vicious personal attack, written by William Hepworth Dixon, hurt Marian cruelly.

Her sensitiveness was further exacerbated by the meddlesome activities of Mr. Bracebridge, which her Coventry friends reported in painful detail. Having been forced to acknowledge that Liggins was not George Eliot, Bracebridge propounded the theory that he had probably supplied the material for the books. While visiting the Nightingales at Leahurst, Bracebridge heard them speak of the family apothecary, 'old Poyser', and learned that Poyser was a common name in Derbyshire. So he instituted a Pickwickian investigation into the 'origins' of *Adam Bede*. He interviewed the Evans relatives at Wirksworth and discovered that the wife of Mr. Nightingale's tailor was actually a daughter of the 'original' of Dinah. Under his leading questions she gratified him with the information that 'Cousin Marian' had frequently visited her mother at Wirksworth (she actually spent only one night there, 18 June 1840), and had copied Dinah's sermon out of Mrs. Evans's papers. The defence of Liggins soon turned into an exposure of what Bracebridge called 'the phenomenal farmer's daughter'. He wrote to Mr. Bray:

their is intirnal evidence as to Clerical Scenes and the author of that claims the honor of Adam. The sermon etc. is riverse from what may be supposed the views of the translator of Strauss. I am sorry that our opinions of the non-advantage of that work to English literature restrained us from any attempt to improve our acquaintance with Miss Evans.[2]

It required the concerted efforts of all his correspondents, including Florence Nightingale, who greatly admired *Adam Bede*, to make Bracebridge desist. 'I doubt whether I ever met with so obtuse a man before', Harriet Martineau wrote to Henry Reeve, editor of the *Edinburgh Review*. 'He goes about like a chuckling detective on the track of a swindler.'[3]

Marian's most painful suffering at this time however, came from the marked change in Herbert Spencer's conduct. He had spent the day with them in March.

[1] *Athenæum*, 2 July 1859, p. 20.
[2] C. H. Bracebridge to C. Bray, 3 July [1859] (Yale). The Brays had taken GE with them to Atherstone in 1845 to meet Harriet Martineau.
[3] H. Martineau to Henry Reeve, 25 Dec. 1859 (John Martineau).

But [Lewes wrote in his Journal] his coming was only pain and disappointment to Polly, on account of his coolness. He used to be one of
our friends on whom we most relied; but jealousy, too patent and too
unequivocal, of our success, acting on his own bitterness at nonsuccess,
has of late cooled him visibly. He always tells us the disagreeable
things he hears or reads of us and never the agreeable things. His
jealousy of me has been growing these last two years; and it is more
excusable than his jealousy of her.—His visit was one we were glad to
see the end of.[1]

When the Brays and Sara came to Holly Lodge in June, they had
been told of Spencer's betrayal of the secret. They spoke so
frankly that Marian, always uneasy in criticizing others, took the
precaution of warning Mr. Bray

not to regard the last thing Mr. Lewes told you about Herbert Spencer,
as a thing incapable of being so explained as to make it more consistent
with our previous conviction concerning his character. Mr. Lewes and
I both hope in the possibility of such an explanation. And I need hardly
say that anything we have told you about him, has been told in full
confidence that you would allow no symptom of such knowledge to
escape you either to him or others. *We* shall be doubly careful to speak
only of what we admire in him to the world generally.[2]

There can be no doubt that the coldness of their 'good friend
Herbert Spencer' was painfully felt.

Under these assaults, which might well have shaken a more
seasoned campaigner, Marian was naturally miserable. Even the
news that Blackwood intended to pay her an extra £400 in consideration of the success of *Adam Bede*, which had sold more than
5,000 copies in a fortnight, could not console her for the undeserved
malice of the *Athenæum*—or 'even for the inflictions of friendship, which are certainly the hardest of all'.[3] Lewes had been
planning to make his annual visit to his sons in Switzerland. He
had just had a letter from Charlie, now nearly seventeen, ending,
'Give my love to Mamma and Nursie, Grandmamma, Miss Evans,
the children, Mr. and Mrs. O. Jones, when you see them, and take
the same yourself.'[4] He could not now leave Marian alone for
ten days. He told her peremptorily that she must go with him, and
she was glad to go. They set out 9 July under a lovely sky, crossed
the Channel, smooth as it had been five years before, and reached
Paris at 11 p.m., staying the night at the Hôtel du Danube. After

---

[1] GHL Journal, 24 Mar. 1859.   [2] *Letters*, III. 111.
[3] *Letters*, III. 118.   [4] CLL to GHL, 3 July 1859 (Yale).

breakfast, they strolled through the Tuileries Gardens, where they met an old acquaintance of Lewes's early days, Father Prout (Francis Mahoney), now Paris correspondent for the *Globe*—a conjunction of pseudonymous luminaries that never recurred. They spent a quiet hour with the paintings at the Louvre, took a drive in the Bois, rambled in the Palais Royal, looked at the shops, bought some books, dined at Véfour, drove again about the Boulevards and the Champs-Élysées—and so passed the day till their train left for Strasbourg. The next night they were at Basel, and on the 12th reached Lucerne.

Their days in cheap lodgings were over. Lewes took a charming room on the first floor at the Schweizerhof, with a superb view of the Lake. Here Polly would stay while he went to Hofwyl. The Richard Congreves, their new friends and neighbours at Wandsworth, were spending a month in Lucerne. Mrs. Congreve, who came to pass the afternoon with them, was soon told the secret of *Adam Bede*. After tea they rowed about the Lake as the sun set behind the mountains.

Lewes's Journal describes his next momentous day:

Wednesday 13th. Up at 4. Started at 5 for Zollikofen, which was reached at 10. Found the boys awaiting me, and looking in splendid condition. After a hot walk through the wood and along the dusty road a little lemonade and quiet chat in the shade with Dr. and Mrs. Müller and the boys was grateful enough. We then went to the Inn where I unpacked and distributed the presents I had brought.

For Charlie there was the new watch, a present from Miss Evans. She had sent Bertie a fine pocket knife—with a corkscrew attached.[1] When Lewes said he had brought Thornie a novel, all three boys shouted 'Is it *Adam Bede*?'—for at Hofwyl as at Paris everyone was talking excitedly about the book.

Dined at the school. Coffee and fruit in the drawingroom, followed by cigar in the shade. The boys then accompanied me to the wood, and there lying on the moss I unburthened myself about Agnes to them. They were less distressed than I had anticipated and were delighted to hear about Marian. This of course furnished the main topic for the whole day.—Came back and heard Charles play—surprised and delighted with his progress. Took tea at the school. Cigar and chat as we watched the sunset over the Bernese Alps. Bed at 9.

Lewes stayed two more days at Hofwyl, rambling about with the boys, going with them to bathe, and getting a half holiday for

[1] Cf. Jacob Cohen's knife in *Daniel Deronda*, ch. 33.

the whole school, which made him popular. His talk with his sons was 'mainly about the domestic changes, and future arrangements'. On the 16th they got up at four to accompany him to the station, where they 'said a painful good-bye'. Reaching Lucerne at ten, he found Polly waiting eagerly to hear how the news had been received, and they had a long chat about the boys. After two more pleasant days with the Congreves, they started home.

At Holly Lodge they found nothing but good news. 'The Bedesman never tires', Blackwood had written, 'and we are reprinting as fast as possible.'[1] Though the next payment on the book was not due till November, he offered to send it now if she desired. Once when they had been talking about dogs, he had heard her say: 'I wish some nobleman would admire *Adam Bede* enough to send me a pug!' Canny John Blackwood with an eye towards George Eliot's next novel took her at the word. He sent his sporting cousin Colonel Steuart to comb 'the Fancy' looking for a suitable puppy. With great difficulty he secured one. It cost 30 guineas, Blackwood told Langford ruefully; 'but *Adam Bede* flourishes, so I grins and bears it'.[2] A week after her return, Langford brought the dog to Wandsworth and stayed to dinner. 'Pug is come!' she wrote gratefully to Blackwood, '—come to fill up the void left by false and narrow-hearted friends. I see already that he is without envy, hatred, or malice—that he will betray no secrets, and feel neither pain at my success nor pleasure in my chagrin.'[3]

[1] *Letters*, III. 113.   [2] Ibid. 125.   [3] Ibid. 124.

CHAPTER X

THE MILL ON THE FLOSS AND *SILAS MARNER*

⁂

AFTER the quick dash to Lucerne, George Eliot felt more discontented than ever with Holly Lodge. Since her father's death ten years before she had always lived in lodgings, economically and with varying degrees of comfort. A house of her own, though providing more independence, also brought back the old responsibilities of housekeeping—buying furniture of all kinds, finding and managing a servant, ordering meals—a task which Lewes sometimes undertook to leave her free for work. Holly Lodge in Wimbledon Park Road was inconveniently far from the railway station and altogether too near her neighbours. She had not occupied it six months before she was writing that she wanted to transfer the house, 'into which we were driven by haste and economy, to some one who likes houses full of eyes all round him. I long for a house with some shade and grass close round it—I don't care how rough—and the sight of Swiss houses has heightened my longing'.[1]

The sense of 'eyes all round', intensified by the Liggins affair and the unsuccessful efforts to preserve her incognito, may be reflected in the title of a short story called 'The Lifted[2] Veil', which she 'began one morning at Richmond as a resource when my head was too stupid for more important work'. *Adam Bede* was hardly finished before Blackwood was pressing her for another 'tale' for *Maga*. She had been busy since January 1859 with *The Mill on the Floss*, which, she explained, 'will be a novel as long as Adam Bede, and a sort of companion picture of provincial life, . . . a work which will require time and labour. But', her letter continues,

I have a slight story of an outré kind—not a *jeu d'esprit*, but a *jeu de mélancolie*, which I could send you in a few days for your acceptance

---

[1] *Letters*, III. 118.
[2] In her Journal, 26 Apr. 1859, GE originally wrote 'Hidden'.

or rejection as a brief magazine story—of one number only. I think nothing of it, but my private critic says it is very striking and original, and on the strength of that opinion, I mention it.

Do write me good news as often as you can.

Ever yours hungrily
George Eliot.[1]

'The Lifted Veil' proved a *jeu de mélancolie* indeed. It is the account of a young man named Latimer, who is *cursed* with exceptional intelligence, *afflicted* with clairvoyance, *suffering* from 'the miseries of true prevision', which extends even to a precise view of his own death. The 'stream of thought' in people near him rushes upon him 'like a preternaturally heightened sense of hearing, making audible to one a roar of sound where others find perfect stillness'.[2] This experimental study of the stream of consciousness, with time sequence shifting to both past and future in a mode that Virginia Woolf was to develop, gives 'The Lifted Veil' a curiously modern quality. Except for *Theophrastus Such* it is the only one of George Eliot's narratives in the first person. The method emphasizes the hero's weakness in not trying to avoid any of the evils he foresees. The one person whose mind is closed to him is his wife Bertha, a beautiful but evil blonde, the earliest version of the sylph-like, water-nixie female, whose serpentine traits George Eliot traced more subtly in Rosamond Vincy and Gwendolen Harleth. Bertha's inadequtely motivated plan to poison Latimer is exposed through the revival of a dying maid by means of blood transfusion, a melodramatic expedient worthy of Poe, whose tales 'The Lifted Veil' occasionally reminds one of with the abnormally heightened consciousness of its hero, its foreign setting—Geneva, the Tyrol, Vienna, Prague—and its pseudo-scientific climax. Little wonder that John Blackwood found it difficult to write to George Eliot about it. In sending her the proof he said:

I wish the theme had been a happier one, and I think you must have been worrying and disturbing yourself about something when you wrote. Still, others are not so fond of sweets as I am, and no judge can read the Lifted Veil without deep admiration and the feeling that it is the work of a great writer.

I very much dislike the revivifying experiment at the end and would

---

[1] *Letters*, III. 41.
[2] 'The Lifted Veil', in *Works of George Eliot*, Cabinet ed., reprinted with *Silas Marner* (1878), pp. 275–341; p. 301.

strongly advise its deletion. I cannot help thinking that some of our excellent scientific friend's experiments on some confounded animalcule must have suggested it.[1]

Of course, she did not accept his advice. The story was not altered. In sending her cheque after its publication in the July *Maga* (£37. 10*s.* and £50 from Tauchnitz for reprinting *Adam Bede* on the Continent), Blackwood said:

The Veil is making very much the impression I expected. All admire the excellence and power of the writing, lovers of the painful are thrilled and delighted, others like me are thrilled but wish the author in a happier frame of mind and not thinking of unsympathising untrustworthy keepers of secrets.[2]

He was touching a very tender spot. The extraordinary success of *Adam Bede* had lifted the veil of anonymity, exposing Marian to a public gaze from which her ambiguous position as Lewes's wife, quite understandably, made her shrink. In June, before they resolved to abandon secrecy, Lewes wrote to Blackwood: 'It has occurred to us that if the name were affixed to "Lifted Veil" it might effectively put a stop to any rumours. It not being likely the Liggins would write on such a subject; or that he would continue to write when not paid. Qu'en dites vous?'[3] *Blackwood's* hardly ever published names of authors, though an exception had recently been made with Bulwer Lytton's pseudonym. John replied tactfully that he 'thought it better not to fritter away the prestige', which should be kept fresh for the new novel. 'In this', he added in writing to William, 'I am sure you will agree with me, although I daresay I am the only Editor who would have objected to the name in the present furor.'[4] William readily concurred: 'Though I don't like the story and don't think it fulfills the promise which the finely written opening holds out, yet I have no doubt it is one which will catch much attention. The conclusion is very disagreeable and it is strange that George Eliot should have written it.'[5] He was still hoping that the secret could be kept, but had great misgivings. To the sensitive author at this delicate moment the Blackwoods' reluctance to use her pseudonym with 'The Lifted Veil' implied a degree of mistrust. It was easy for her to fancy herself at Holly Lodge 'with houses full of eyes' all round her.

[1] *Letters*, III. 67.   [2] *Letters*, III. 112.   [3] *Letters*, III. 83.
[4] J. Blackwood to W. Blackwood, 15 June 1859 (NLS).
[5] W. Blackwood to J. Blackwood, 16 June 1859 (NLS).

The one charm of the place was her new friendship with Mrs. Richard Congreve, who lived very near them. She was the daughter of John Bury, the Coventry surgeon who had cared for Robert Evans in his last years; he had retired to live with the Congreves at Wandsworth, where he had died just a month before the Leweses moved into Holly Lodge. Charles Bray, having called on Mr. Bury there in 1858, wrote to Marian about the Congreves. Marian replied that Mr. Congreve had been

mentioned to us by our landlord as a gentleman who visited with no one in the neighbourhood—which eccentric course we had declared our intention of following. Amusingly enough, said landlord, Captain Rivers, and his wife, had begun to recommend the place by saying, '*We* visit with every one about here, and there are very pleasant soirées.' Oh! we exclaimed, in horror, 'Pray tell "every one" that we don't visit and don't desire to be called on.' Whereupon Mr. Richard Congreve was cited as an encouraging proof that we might be as isolated as we desired. He takes pupils, however, and I should imagine is not in the interesting state of destitution that Mr. Bray's enthusiastic sympathy gave us the idea of. We have met a pleasant-faced, bright-glancing man whom we set down to be worthy of the name Richard Congreve. I am curious to see if our *ahnung* will be verified.[1]

It soon was.

Maria Congreve was seventeen years younger than George Eliot. As a girl of fourteen she had once seen her at Foleshill, coming there when her father was making a professional call on Mr. Evans, and the passionate interest that Marian always excited in younger minds never faded. She remembered every detail of the visit: how she heard the piano as she was approaching the house; her surprise at the contrast between Mr. Evans's homely appearance and the culture evident in the music and books everywhere. She recalled how Miss Evans took her to walk in the garden, and having set her at ease, drew her out to say how she wanted to learn German, and so on.[2] When gossip came from Coventry and people were speaking unkindly about Marian and Lewes, old Mr. Bury declared that he was certain from what he had seen of her during her father's long illness that 'she could not have done anything she did not in her conscience feel to be right'.

Richard Congreve, a Warwickshire man, was born in 1818 at Leamington. He spent four years at a school kept by his uncle at Boulogne before entering Rugby in 1832, where he was contem-

---

[1] *Letters*, III. 16.
[2] Simcox Autobiography, 18 Jan. 1881, fol. 88.

porary with Clough and Matthew Arnold, going up to Oxford with them. He graduated B.A. with a first in 1840. After three years as a master at Rugby he returned to Wadham College as Tutor in 1848. Having survived the pressure from Newman's conversion to Rome, Congreve met Auguste Comte in Paris and gradually accepted Positivism, of which he was to become the chief English exponent. In 1854 he resigned his fellowship and married Maria Bury, earning his living by taking private pupils.

Mrs. Congreve herself has recorded the beginning of their acquaintance with the Leweses:

We decided to call not only because we were both strongly interested in her, knowing some of her most intimate Coventry friends, and knowing the high opinion entertained for her as a nurse as well as of her intellectual powers by my Father, who attended hers for some years, I believe, certainly for the last years of his life. She had also some years before declined to meet Dr. Congreve as being a clergyman. This objection was now removed but we thought it quite doubtful whether they would care to know us and were, I remember, glad that they were out when we called, so that they might take no notice if they chose. But the inducement to call was the scorn we both had of the unfairness with which a connection like theirs was visited by society—the man cut off from scarcely anything, the woman from all she most values. . . . The call however was very quickly and cordially returned and we were friends with her at once. Those who knew her will know how impossible it was that one could have any friendship with her exclusive of Mr. Lewes. How deeply she cherished all the pieties of her early life, even towards those who had ceased all intercourse was perhaps the more evident to me that I had just lost my Father and that she must have felt me the better able to feel with her in the illness and death of her sister, which followed so soon on our becoming acquainted.[1]

The friendship between the two households who 'visited no one' was instantaneous. Marian had said in a moment of bitterness that she would never have any *friends* again, only *acquaintances*.[2] But Mrs. Congreve made her change her mind. The Leweses returned the call on 27 February and were soon spending two or three evenings a week together in pleasant talk at their house or at Holly Lodge. 'We are so happy in the neighbourhood of Mr. and Mrs. Richard Congreve', she wrote in a letter to Sara. 'She is a sweet, intelligent, gentle creature. I already love her; and his fine beaming face does me good, like a glimpse of an Olympian.'[3] When they left at the end of April to take her young sister Emily

---

[1] Bodleian: MS Eng. let. e.   [2] *Letters*, III. 69.   [3] Ibid. 53.

Bury for five months on the Continent, Mrs. Congreve began to write immediately. Her first letter, sent from Dieppe the next day, shows what a powerful attraction George Eliot possessed:

I slept about a dozen times I should think, and woke once with a full persuasion that I was coming to call upon you in the afternoon. You must have a very strong influence over me. I usually wake so entirely mistress of the situation, but you do make such a difference to me in my rising up and lying down and in all my ways—now I actually know you, and that you will let me love you and even give me some love too. Since that one time I saw you years ago very frequently and more frequently as I grew older I have thought of you and often said to myself that if you were living still near Coventry I would have gone to you and told you my troubles and difficulties, and I never felt that towards any one else except of course Richard. Sometime I should like to talk over my difficulties, past though they are, with you. I should never be afraid of your misunderstanding them or me. I have such a perfect confidence in you. I do not think I should venture to write this though but for what you said to me once about your requiring to be told that people love you. . . .[1]

The feeling between the two husbands was less fervid. Congreve had known Lewes through the chapters on Comte in his *Biographical History of Philosophy* and his *Comte's Philosophy of the Sciences*; though they were both members of the company that founded the *Leader*, they had never met. Perhaps the former Tutor of Wadham, a notable example of Dr. Arnold's Christian Gentleman, could not help feeling some slight Olympian disdain for Marian's vivacious little companion, talking so brilliantly at her side, but so obviously not a University man. 'I like what I see of her', Congreve wrote to his wife soon after the acquaintance began. 'It is rather unfortunate that they are so inseparable.'[2] And Lewes observed in his Journal that Congreve had caught some of Comte's extreme contempt for 'men of specialities'—like physiology?—and had accepted his expansion of Positivism into a new religion. Lewes had broken with Comte after the publication of the *Catéchisme positive* in 1852, which Congreve had just translated (1858).

Yet the Leweses, isolated as they were from other society, found the sympathy of the Congreves delightful. To George Eliot the new friendship was of the highest importance. When the

---

[1] Maria Congreve to GE, 1 May 1859 (Yale).
[2] Bodleian: MS Eng. let. e. 51, fol. 307ᵛ.

Congreves went abroad, she missed them greatly. She picked flowers in their garden, and took their dog Rough on walks with the terrier bitch Vic, which had settled unbidden in the stable at Holly Lodge. She welcomed the letters from her new friend describing their travels, urging Marian to use their servant or put up any guests she liked in their house, and begging her to join them in Switzerland when Lewes went to visit his boys. 'I want to get rid of this house', she wrote to Mrs. Congreve, '—cut cables and drift about. I dislike Wandsworth, and should think with unmitigated regret of our coming here if it were not for you. But you are worth paying a price for.'[1] And in July, when it was time for Lewes to go to Hofwyl, she was glad to accompany him.

Her intimacy with the Congreves deepened in the six days Marian spent at Lucerne. After revealing the secret of her authorship, she presented a copy of *Scenes of Clerical Life* inscribed: 'Mrs. Congreve. In remembrance of February 1859, when her friendship first enriched the life of George Eliot.'[2] Much of their conversation dealt with Positivism. Marian had, of course, long been familiar with Comte and knew Lewes's books and Harriet Martineau's abridgement of the *Positive Philosophy*. But since the *Westminster Review* days she had lost her old 'delight in expressing intellectual difference', and she now delighted rather 'in feeling an emotional agreement'.[3] Though the basic rationalism of her thought was unchanged, she was seeking a new object for reverence in sympathy with the feelings of 'our struggling fellow men'. On the idea of a future life, which she had pondered so long, her views were similarly tempered, perhaps through her grief at the death of Chrissey; the subjective immortality of the Religion of Humanity as expounded by her new friends she found very appealing.

The extent of George Eliot's concern with Positivism has been greatly exaggerated. Most of her references to it occur in her letters to Mrs. Congreve, which must be read in the light of the strong emotional involvement between them. To her feelings the Religion of Humanity appealed strongly; but she could never bring her reason to unqualified acceptance of it: 'I cannot submit my intellect or my soul to the guidance of Comte.'[4] She told Benjamin Jowett that she 'was never a Comtist, but as they were a poor

---

[1] *Letters*, III. 79. Maria Congreve witnessed the wills that GE and GHL signed 21 Nov. 1859.
[2] Now in the collection of Gordon N. Ray.
[3] *Letters*, III. 231.   [4] Mathilde Blind, *George Eliot* (1883), p. 212.

unfortunate sect, she would never renounce them'.[1] Her contribution was never more than £5 a year. Congreve himself wrote in 1880 that 'she is not nor ever has been more than by her acceptance of the general idea of Humanity a Positivist'.[2] W. M. Simon, who has made the most thorough study of the subject, finds in all her works only a handful of brief passages that will bear any sort of Positivist interpretation, the principal one being the poem 'O May I Join the Choir Invisible'.[3] There is certainly little sign of Positivism in *The Mill on the Floss*, which she was writing during the first months of her friendship with the Congreves.

George Eliot's earliest allusion to *The Mill on the Floss* is found in a brief entry in her Journal, 12 January 1859: 'We went into town today and looked in the Annual Register for cases of *inundation*.' She copied into her Commonplace Book several passages, mostly of 1771, describing ships driven on to flooded fields, bridges washed away, and a family rescued from the upper storey of their house—all of which appear in the final pages of the novel. But Dorlcote Mill she drew from vivid memory of Arbury Mill, close by her birth-place, with its great heaps of corn for little girls to slide upon and its family of 'fat, flour-dusted spiders'. From the tiny stream that turned its wheel, however, there was no possibility of a catastrophic flood; she had written all the childhood scenes that fill the first volume before she could find a suitable river to flow beside Dorlcote Mill. The story grew very slowly, while she struggled against many interruptions. February was largely taken up with the move to Holly Lodge and repeated disappointments in finding a satisfactory servant. Then came the pleasant, but equally distracting, excitement of the first reviews of *Adam Bede* and the gratifying letters about it; in March, the news of Chrissey's illness and death, and the pain caused by Spencer's changed attitude. In April both she and George felt too feeble to work and went off to the Isle of Wight for three days of rest, reading J. L. Stephens's *Incidents of Travel in Central America* aloud. A fortnight after their return George Eliot, having finished 'The Lifted Veil', wrote in her Journal: 'Resumed my new novel, of which I am going to rewrite the first two chapters. I shall call it,

[1] E. Abbott and L. Campbell, *Benjamin Jowett* (3rd ed., 2 vols., N.Y., 1897) I. 182.

[2] To Sophie Edger, 10 May 1880 (Bodleian: Eng. let. e. 67, fol. 119).

[3] W. M. Simon, *European Positivism in the Nineteenth Century* (Ithaca, 1963, pp. 207–17. See also Thomas Pinney, 'More Leaves from George Eliot's Notebook', *Huntington Library Quarterly*, 29 (Aug. 1966), 360–2.

provisionally, "The Tullivers", for the sake of a title *quelconque*—or perhaps, "St. Ogg's on the Floss".[1] By 1 June she had reached page 85, and when Blackwood came to lunch two weeks later, she gave him the first six and a half chapters—110 pages—to read. 'I am perfectly delighted with the opening of the new story', he wrote. 'You may go ahead with perfect confidence that St. Ogg's on the Floss or Maggie will be a grand success.'[2]

Despite his assurance and the never-failing encouragement of Lewes, to whom every few days she would read what she had written, the book advanced slowly. She could not seem to work at Wandsworth. Even the pleasure of walking on the Common with her new puppy Pug, watching his astonishment at the sight of cows, could not reconcile her to Holly Lodge. Pug was not yet old enough to bark, but sneezed 'powerfully', George Eliot wrote to Blackwood: 'He sneezes at the world in general, and he looks affectionately at *me*.'[3] She made a great pet of him. One day Lewes took him to Kensington to show him to Agnes, 'who was delighted with him, as were the children'.[4] A week later Lewes returned there to arrange with Nursie (Martha Baker, now Mrs. Bell) to stay at Holly Lodge and look after Pug while they went off to Wales for a fortnight. Sara Hennell had recommended Penmaenmawr enthusiastically, and Marian was eager to see the northern coast.

For people in 'feeble' health the Leweses were rugged travellers. They left Euston Station at seven in the evening of 26 August by mail train to Conway, arriving about half past three after a 'very wearisome, sleepless night', to find not a bed to be had in the whole town. They rambled about in the dawn, went down to the beach, looked at the fine Castle, and came back to the station, where they 'had a nap on a truck'. After breakfast at a temperance hotel, just opening its shutters, they had another nap on a sofa before taking the train to Llandudno. There, though the scenery was tempting, the newness and 'fashionable watering place style both of houses and people' seemed hideous. So they took the next train to Penmaenmawr, where they found everything they could wish as to scenery and quiet, but unhappily no lodgings to be had. By the next train they returned to Conway and settled into a room over the shop of a grocer named Jones in Castle Street. The next day was spent in equally fruitless search for lodgings at Abergele.

[1] GE Journal, 27 Apr. 1859. [2] *Letters*, III. 88.
[3] Ibid. 133. [4] GHL Journal, 13 Aug. 1859.

For two or three days they tried to follow their usual régime, rising at seven, Marian writing while George zoologized, and in the afternoons taking long walks on the sands towards Penmaenmawr. But then the weather turned cold and rainy, and on 31 August they abandoned Wales for Weymouth on the Dorset coast.[1]

They broke the long journey at Lichfield to see Chrissey's daughters Emily and Katie Clarke, who through the kindness of their father's brother Henry Clarke had been put at Miss Eborall's School. They stayed at the Swan, where Marian had been with her father in 1826 and again in 1840. She was much comforted by the sight of the children, 'looking happy and apparently under excellent care'.[2] She brought them back to the Swan to meet their new uncle, and they all went out together to see the Cathedral and call on Miss Eborall, who promised Marian that she would attend to getting clothes for the girls. The next morning at eight Emily and Katie were at the station to take leave and wave good-bye. Aunt Polly soon had a letter from Emily telling her that Miss Eborall had bought her a dress and boots for dancing, which she liked very much and wore when Queen Victoria passed through Lichfield.[3]

At Weymouth in lodgings at 39 East Street, 'with some good Wesleyans, honest and kind', Lewes set up his microscope and little marine tank, while Marian at the top of the house, out of the way of disturbers, worked every morning at her novel.[4] The weather was so tempting, 5 September, that they resolved to give up the morning to a walk along the river.

Having made our way, in rather a roundabout manner and some trespassing to Radipole, we there went all over a Mill which was kindly shown us by the Miller. This was the very thing for Polly, who has a Mill in her new novel and wanted some details. We were so delighted with the spot that we enquired about lodgings, thinking a day or two might pleasantly and profitably be spent near the mills (there are five within three miles) and the stream. A laborer seemed willing to let his cottage, which we found very clean, and quite comfortable enough. We left him to ask his wife, and then rambled about.[5]

But when they returned the next day, they were put out to find that the labourer's wife was decidedly opposed to letting her cottage;

---

[1] Details from GHL's Journal.
[2] GE Journal, 25 Aug. 1859.
[3] Emily Clarke to GE, 20 Oct. [1859] (Yale).
[4] GE Journal, 25 Aug. 1859; *Letters*, III. 152.
[5] GHL Journal, 5 Sept. 1859.

after talking with a little old woman who might have had a lodging to let, they looked over another mill up the river and came home very tired to spend the evening reading Layard's *Nineveh* and *The Excursion* aloud. A few days later they went to Dorchester to see if the river Frome 'would suit Polly's purposes'. Lunching at an inn, they learned from the landlord that the stream was 'insignificant'. Nevertheless, they rambled through the meadows beside it and found it deliciously clear—'clear as the pure River of Life shown to the Evangelist', Thomas Hardy would say of it in *Tess of the d'Urbervilles*.[1] At this time Hardy was a nineteen-year-old apprentice in a Dorchester architect's office (which the Leweses probably walked past), spending his spare hours studying Greek tragedies and arguing vehemently with his fellows in defence of infant baptism. What a splendid imaginary conversation a Landor might write between George Eliot and young Thomas Hardy, meeting by chance on the banks of the Frome!

They returned to Wandsworth 16 September, finding the faithful Nursie there to meet them and 'Pug, somewhat sceptical at first, but finally acknowledging us.' Ten days later they were on the road again, this time bound for Newark and Gainsborough, 'Polly wanting to lay the scene of her novel on the Trent. . . . We took a boat from Gainsborough and rowed down to the Idle, which we ascended on foot some way, and walked back to Gainsborough.'[2] At last she had found a river that could provide a plausible flood for the catastrophe in her novel.

The form of publication had not yet been decided. With his eye on Dickens's great success Lewes dreamed of George Eliot's novel appearing in monthly parts. One day in June he got from Frederic Chapman 'an estimate of cost and profit of a serial novel, such as Dickens's'. He then called on Samuel Lucas, editor of *Once a Week*, who had thrice written to ask George Eliot for her next novel; finding him out, Lewes 'Dined with Mother and Agnes and came home early.'[3] John Blackwood was very eager to have the novel for *Maga*. He spent a long day with George Eliot and Lewes at Holly Lodge 25 June. Blackwood wrote to his brother William:

It is impossible not to like her excessively. She gives irresistibly the impression of a real good woman. It is impossible not to like him too. It is most melancholy that their relations cannot be put straight. . . .

[1] Ch. 16. [2] GHL Journal, Nov. 1859.
[3] GHL Journal, 8 June 1859.

She honestly confesses to a most deep seated anxiety to get a large price for the new Tale and I think we will be well able to afford to give it. It should be a little fortune to her. You would have been pleased with the way she spoke about it.[1]

But the dropping of the incognito a few days later somewhat cooled Blackwood's enthusiasm to have the story in *Maga*, and beyond general inquiries about its progress and the assurance that 'Every bit of what I read is distinctly before me now',[2] he said little about it during the summer. Writing to them at Weymouth he asked Lewes, 'How does the new Novel get on? Do you think we can start before the end of the year?'[3] But he made no clear offer for it. Nearly 15,000 copies of *Adam Bede* had been sold. Before they left Weymouth, George Eliot wrote to him frankly:

> The very large sale of 'Adam Bede' has necessarily modified my prospects as to the publication of my next book, and before troubling you with further manuscript, I want to tell you my thoughts on the subject.
>
> I have now so large and eager a public, that if we were to publish the work without a preliminary appearance in the Magazine, the first sale would infallibly be large, and a considerable profit would be gained even though the work might not ultimately impress the public so strongly as 'Adam' has done.
>
> Now surely publication in Maga, in the case of a new writer concerning whose works there is some expectation and curiosity, would inevitably reduce what would otherwise be the certain demand for three-volumed copies. The Magazine edition would be devoured, and would sweep away perhaps 20,000—nay, 40,000—readers who would otherwise demand copies of the complete work from the libraries. To say the least, there is enormous risk that the sale of the completed novel would be diminished. Again, the book might be in some respects superior to Adam, and yet not continue in the course of periodical reading to excite the same interest in the mass of readers, and an impression of its inferiority might be spread before republication:—another source of risk.
>
> The large circulation of 'Adam' renders the continual advertisement afforded by publication in a first-rate periodical—an advertisement otherwise so valuable—comparatively unimportant.

In this careful calculation Lewes's long experience with publishing is plainly visible.

> I don't at all know what are your views as to the amount you could afford to pay me for publishing in the Magazine—I have no doubt you

[1] *Letters*, III. 94.　　[2] Ibid. 131.　　[3] Ibid. 143.

would do the utmost for me consistently with publishing rules—but in my ignorance I am unable to believe that you would find it worth while to compensate to me for the inevitable subtraction from subsequent proceeds. I shall be much obliged to you if you will let me know precisely what arrangement you contemplate.

You see, I speak to you without circumlocution, and I am sure you will like that best. You know how important this money question is to me. I don't want the world to give me anything for my books except money enough to save me from the temptation to write *only* for money.[1]

This business-like inquiry caused some searching consultation in Edinburgh. Major William Blackwood, always less susceptible to George Eliot's charm, feared the effect of her name on the circulation of *Maga*, and his warning voice kept John uncertain. Privately John assured the Major that he 'would rather give £4000 than lose the book for the Mag. if it keeps up to sample'.[2] But, yielding to his brother's caution, he offered £3,000 for the copyright for four years after its publication in *Maga*.

We hope that this sum will meet your views. The prospects of the book are great but there is no certainty under the sun. Who would have supposed that Clerical Scenes, admirable as they are, would not have been carried off in thousands by the flood tide of Adam's popularity.

In the Magazine we would not put any author's name, and it would be great fun to watch the speculations as to the author's life. The style would be to me easily recognisable but no one, especially of the puffing writing and publishing order, would suppose that we would throw away such an advantage as putting the magic words by George Eliot at the head of a series of papers. In the long run however ours is the wisest course, as nothing equals the excitement of uncertainty.[3]

Speculations as to the author's life promised anything but fun for George Eliot. In John Blackwood's long relation with his sensitive author this extraordinary lapse of tact was never repeated. His jocular tone in announcing the abandonment of the most valuable name in the literary market hurt her more than he could have realized, and his reminder that the *Scenes of Clerical Life* had not sold well seemed less than kind. She replied at once.

When I wrote to you, I felt no disposition to publish in the Magazine beyond the inclination to meet your wishes—if they still pointed in that direction, and if I could do so without sacrifice.

[1] *Letters*, III. 151–2.
[2] J. Blackwood to W. Blackwood, 18 Sept. 1859 (NLS).
[3] *Letters*, III. 161.

Your letter confirms my presupposition that you would not find it worth your while to compensate me for the renunciation of the unquestionable advantages my book would derive from being presented to the public in three volumes with all its freshness upon it.

It was an oversight of mine not to inform you that I do not intend to part with the copyright, but only with an edition. As, from the nature of your offer, I infer that you think my next book will be a speculation attended with risk, I prefer incurring that risk myself.

I don't know whether you have had any glimpse of the annoyances I am still suffering from Mr. Bracebridge and the other friends of Liggins.[1]

She gave a detailed account of them.

Since the Blackwoods had told her that they intended to pay £400 more than their agreement required, *Adam Bede* had sold increasingly. They were about to print 2,000 more, and were contemplating another *douceur* in recognition of its success. Despite the risk of losing George Eliot to some other publisher, William wanted to say nothing about the additional sum till the negotiations for the new novel were completed; her quick rejection of their offer confirmed his view. It was three weeks before John acknowledged her letter. He wrote pleasantly to her 14 October, telling of the new printing of *Adam Bede*, and expressing regret that the Liggins affair was annoying her. 'No whisper of your persecution has reached me', he declared. 'Newdegate was with us for a day not long ago, and, like a gentleman as he is, said not a word on the subject beyond an incidental praise of your books.' At the end of the letter he wrote casually: 'The Major and I are very sorry indeed that you cannot entertain our proposal for the new Tale. I hope Maggie gets on as gloriously as she promised.'[2]

Answering the next day, George Eliot began by pointing out a few misprints that had crept into the two-volume edition of *Adam Bede*—like *vale* for *veil*—and with commendable care for the integrity of her text, urged Blackwood to see that it was taken from the *first* edition, which she had corrected carefully. After giving some further details of her 'persecution' by Mr. Bracebridge, she adverted to the new novel:

If you were living in London instead of at Edinburgh, I should ask you to read the first volume of 'Sister Maggie' at once, for the sake of having your impressions; but it is inconvenient to me to part with the M.S. The great success of 'Adam' makes my writing a matter of more anxiety than ever: I suppose there is a little sense of responsibility mixed up with a great deal of pride. And I think I should worry myself still more if I began to print before the thing is essentially complete. So on all grounds it is better to wait.[1]

Her letter closed with a report of Pug's development 'in three months of our intellectual society'. For the first time she signed, not 'George Eliot', but 'Marian Evans Lewes'. The Major, forwarding the letter to John in the country, said,

I am rather sorry to see the change of signature. On the whole I think you may be as well without the new tale for Maga. It is evident there is going to be no secret about the authorship now, which is one reason for its not appearing there to which considerable weight may be due: and another is the author's strong feeling about the advantage to be gained by having it brought out at once with the éclat of its being known to be by the author of A.B. Feeling sure that we are right as to the mode of publication we recommended I would not, were the author's position different, mind about pressing our ideas on him. But considering how that position may possibly affect the new book I think we might be placed in disagreeable circumstances by doing so.[2]

But John Blackwood, though he now addressed her as 'My Dear Madam', kept his relations with George Eliot cordial. Sending her the final payment of £400 for *Adam Bede* 27 October 1859, he spoke again of their intention to give her 'a further pecuniary share in the triumph of Adam. Since I so wrote the success has gone on, and instead of £400 we now intend to send you £800 at the beginning of the year.' He added a word about his delight in hearing of 'the progress of Maggie, in whom I shall always feel a very keen interest'.[3] But he was not destined to secure the new book solely by generous payment for the old. Marian replied:

I beg that you and Major Blackwood will accept my thanks for your proposal to give me a further share in the success of 'Adam Bede', beyond the terms of our agreement, which are fulfilled by the second cheque for £400, received this morning.

Neither you nor I ever calculated on half such a success, thinking that the book was too quiet and too unflattering to dominant fashions ever to be very popular. I hope that opinion of ours is a guarantee that there is nothing hollow or transient in the reception 'Adam' has met with.[4]

'The enclosed *cool* note from George Eliot has given me a fit of disgust', John wrote, in sending it to William, 'and I think I shall

[1] *Letters*, III. 185.   [2] *Letters*, III. 188.
[3] *Letters*, III. 190.   [4] *Letters*, III. 191.

notice it distinctly when I get home.'[1] His natural prudence prevailed, however, and he held his peace. To Langford in the London
office he confessed his chagrin at the tone in which his proposal for
the new book had been replied to:

I think my offer was a very fair one and I certainly shall make no
other. I do not much care about the matter and am more vexed at
being disappointed in G.E. If some very large sum has been offered
she should have told me, and she has sense enough to know that I am
the last person in the world to stand between any one making the best
they can of their work. Our kindness too in doubling the original price
of Adam Bede has been acknowledged in the most painfully unhand-
some way with hardly thanks.

There may be some crotchet at the bottom of it, as her letters have
been in such marked contrast to her warm written and spoken thanks.
Possibly my saying that I would publish the book anonymously may
have caused some suspicion but I did not care to use her name.[2]

Langford was being kept secretly informed by Blackwoods'
devoted manager at Edinburgh, George Simpson, who was convinced that 'George Eliot has sold herself to the highest bidder.
I said very early that he was an avaricious soul, but even with this
failing, if he had known what dealing with Gentlemen was, I
think he would have explained the matter to the Messrs. B. before
accepting the offer of another party. I have no doubt the tempter
is that fallen angel C.D.'[3]

His suspicion had some basis in fact. Charles Dickens had
broken with Bradbury and Evans over their refusal to publish in
Punch a personal statement about his separation from his wife.
He had replaced *Household Words* with a new weekly called *All
the Year Round*, and in April 1859 ordered his manager to invite
the then unknown George Eliot to write for it. She did not reply
until the incognito was abandoned. In July, just before going to
Lucerne, she wrote to Dickens, expressing interest in his proposal.
His answer 10 July 1859 explained that he had not acknowledged
her gift of *Adam Bede* because he could have done it only through
Blackwood; and knowing what changes he was about to make in
his publishing arrangements, 'had a great delicacy in suggesting
to the Scotch-Publishing-Mind through any after-splicing of this
and that together, that I had been waylaying you!' So he waited
until he could write to her in person. After some discriminating
comments on *Adam Bede*, Dickens added,

(Blackwood not now being the medium of communication), if you should ever have the freedom and inclination to be a fellow labourer with me, it would yield me a pleasure that I have never known yet and can never know otherwise; and no channel that even you could command, should be so profitable as to yourself. Secondly, I hope you will let me come to see you when we are all in or near London again, and tell you —as a curiosity—my reasons for the faith that was in me that you were a woman, and for the absolute and never-doubting confidence with which I have waved all men away from Adam Bede, and nailed my colors to the Mast with 'Eve' upon them.[1]

Dickens came to dine with them at Holly Lodge on 10 November; four days later he wrote to Lewes about George Eliot's doing a new novel for *All the Year Round*

on any terms perfectly satisfactory to Mrs. Lewes and you. Of course the copyright would remain her own, and the perfect liberty to select her own publisher for the completed story, and to publish it immediately on its completion, would remain her own likewise. An immense new public would probably be opened to her, and I am quite sure that our association would be full of interest and pleasure to me.[2]

There was never any prospect of her giving Dickens *The Mill on the Floss*. He wanted her *next* story, to begin in July 1860, when *The Woman in White* was concluded. After due consideration, she wrote in her Journal, 'We have written to Dickens saying that *Time* is an insurmountable obstacle to his proposition as he puts it', and dismissed the proposal from her mind.[3]

On 15 November Lewes went by appointment to see Samuel Lucas, the editor of *Once a Week*, which Bradbury and Evans had set up in competition with Dickens's new magazine. It is an index of their difficulty in securing contributions that they invited Lewes, who had published two mediocre novels in the 1840s, to write a novel for *Once a Week* on his own terms;

but [he wrote in his Journal] having agreed with Polly that it was desirable I should not swerve from Science any more, at least just now, I declined. They then asked me to contribute articles on my own terms. After this they approached the subject of a story from Polly, and wanted to know whether her new novel was in the market. I told them I thought it unlikely that she would publish in 'Once a Week' and that she felt bound to give Blackwood the refusal; but they assured me that *whatever* Blackwood offered they would give more. We parted on the understanding that they were to make an offer.[4]

[1] *Letters*, III. 115.   [2] *Letters*, III. 203.
[3] GE Journal, 18 Nov. 1859.   [3] GHL Journal, 15 Nov. 1859.

A number of other feelers were out. An American offered £1,200 for a story in twelve parts for the *Century Magazine*. George Smith, who was founding the new *Cornhill Magazine* with Thackeray as editor, engaged Lewes to do a series of papers on natural history, which would afterwards form a volume. He 'evidently wishes to *nouer des relations*', Lewes noted in his Journal.[1] But Smith's plans were far-ranging; he had Trollope's *Framley Parsonage* and Thackeray's *Adventures of Philip* scheduled, and made no such obvious move as to approach George Eliot at present.

During this uncertainty there were some cheering notes for George Eliot. Her old friend and schoolfellow Martha Jackson wrote to ask if the author of *Adam Bede* was *her* Marian Evans.[2] Mrs. Gaskell, who had been a dupe of the Liggins myth, when the truth became known refused at first to believe that the 'noble grand book' could have been written by one whose life did 'so jar against' it. She first begged George Smith to deny it, and then complained that he was too 'curt about Madam Adam', and pleaded with him for details of the author:

send us *please* a long account of what she is like &c &c &c &c,—eyes nose mouth, *dress* &c for *facts*, and then—if you would—your impression of her—which we won't tell anybody. *How came she to like Mr. Lewes so much?* I know he has his good points but somehow he is so soiled for a woman like her to fancy.[3]

Assured that Marian Evans was indeed the author, she reread both *Adam Bede* and the *Scenes* and then wrote George Eliot a generous letter, telling her once more

how earnestly fully, and humbly I admire them. I never read anything so complete, and beautiful in fiction, in my whole life before. . . . Perhaps you may have heard that I upheld Mr. Liggins as the author for long,—I did it on evidence, quite independent of, and unknown to the Bracebridges. He is a regular rascal. But I never was such a goose as to believe that such books as yours could be a mosaic of real and ideal. I should not be quite true in my ending, if I did not say before I concluded that I wish you *were* Mrs. Lewes. However that can't be helped, as far as I can see, and one must not judge others.[4]

In spite of this personal allusion, George Eliot responded warmly to the assurance of fellow-feeling from one who also knew an artist's pains:

[1] GHL Journal, 27 Oct. 1859.   [2] GE Journal, 25 Aug. 1859.
[3] *The Letters of Mrs. Gaskell*, ed. J. A. Chapple and A. Pollard (Manchester, 1966), pp. 586–7.   [4] *Letters*, III. 197.

You know, without my telling you, how much the help is heightened by its coming to me afresh, now that I have ceased to be a mystery and am known as a mere daylight fact. I shall always love to think that one woman wrote to another such sweet encouraging words—still more to think that you were the writer and I the receiver.

I had indulged the idea that if my books turned out to be worth much, you would be among my willing readers; for I was conscious, while the question of my power was still undecided for me, that my feeling towards Life and Art had some affinity with the feeling which had inspired 'Cranford' and the earlier chapters of 'Mary Barton'. That idea was brought the nearer to me, because I had the pleasure of reading Cranford for the first time in 1857, when I was writing the 'Scenes of Clerical Life', and going up the Rhine one dim wet day in the spring of the next year, when I was writing 'Adam Bede', I satisfied myself for the lack of a prospect by reading over again those earlier chapters of 'Mary Barton'. I like to tell you these slight details because they will prove to you that your letter must have a peculiar value for me, and that I am not expressing vague gratitude towards a writer whom I only remember vaguely as one who charmed me in the past. And I cannot believe such details are indifferent to you, even after we have been so long used to hear them: I fancy, as long as we live, we all need to know as much as we can of the good our life has been to others.[1]

Even more welcome to Marian was a reconciliation with Herbert Spencer. Lewes had written to him in September, probably mentioning the inhibiting effect his critical comments were having on Marian's writing. Some explanatory correspondence ensued. Before long she received a letter from him about *Adam Bede*: 'What am I to say?' Spencer wrote. 'That I have read it with laughter and tears and without criticism. Knowing as you do how constitutionally I am given to fault-finding, you will know what this means.' He then praised the book as a work of art and as a moral force: 'I feel greatly better for having read it.' He came to dine at Holly Lodge on 23 October, looking 'spry' and cheerful, and apparently unconscious of 'the negations which wounded me'.[2]

To her irritation over the Bracebridge correspondence a new annoyance was added in October, when the publisher T. C. Newby advertised as 'Just ready' a book called *Adam Bede, Junior. A Sequel*. Lewes wrote at once to John Blackwood in 'hot indignation' that 'surely Newby might be stopped by a letter threatening legal proceedings'.[3] Blackwood's lawyers advised him that the advertisement was not actionable, but Lewes kept urging him to

[1] *Letters*, III. 198–9.   [2] *Letters*, III. 170, 199, 192.   [3] *Letters*, III. 189.

move. John was at St. Andrews playing golf. In forwarding one note to him the Major said: 'Lewes of course exaggerates the importance of the matter, and I have endeavoured to tone him down by recalling Pickwick Abroad and the many similar felonies on popular authors.'[1] This nonchalance of the Blackwoods contributed to the coolness of George Eliot's acknowledgement of their doubled payment for *Adam Bede*. 'A propos of Pickwick', she remarked, 'and quite *entre nous*, think a little kindly of Dickens on this ground: he has both written and spoken with the warmest, most generous admiration of "Adam"'[2]—a fact received suspiciously in Edinburgh.

Both sides waited. Lewes dropped a word occasionally about the progress of the novel, and hinted at competition, but did not enter openly into the negotiations. 'What days these are for furious speculation in the periodical world!' he wrote in a letter to Blackwood, 18 November. 'My precious time is occupied with declining offers on all sides—every one imagining that he can seduce George Eliot, simply because he (the every one, not G.E.) *wants* that result!' (a remark that made Simpson exclaim, 'I say no wonder when Mr. Lewes has shown them the way!')[3] Dickens, seeing his advantage, told Lewes about Newby's unscrupulous methods of selling *Adam Bede, Junior* and asked him to write an account of 'that most shameful and abominable proceeding' for *All the Year Round*. In her Journal 22 November—her fortieth birthday—Marian complained that the Blackwoods 'are slow to act in the matter—hitherto, have not acted at all: not being strongly moved, apparently by what is likely to injure me more than them'. Lewes suggested that the Blackwoods write a letter to *The Times*. The only result was a single anonymous sentence in the *Athenæum* and the *Daily News* denying George Eliot's authorship of the book. Thereupon Lewes himself wrote to *The Times* in her name.[4] This marked the culmination of her discontent with the most excellent of publishers.

She could bear the uncertainty no longer. Nearly half of her novel was written when she sent Blackwood this letter, 26 November 1859:

As the time for the publication of my next work is not very far removed, and as thorough frankness is the condition of satisfactoriness in all relations, I am induced to ask you whether you still wish to remain

---

[1] W. Blackwood to J. Blackwood, 28 Oct. 1859 (NLS).
[2] *Letters*, III. 192. [3] Ibid. 208–9. [4] *The Times*, 2 Dec. 1859, p. 10 d.

my publishers, or whether the removal of my incognito has caused a
change in your views on that point.

I have never myself thought of putting an end to a connection which
has hitherto not appeared inauspicious to either of us, and I have looked
forward to your being my publishers as long as I produced books to
be published; but various indications, which I may possibly have misinterpreted, have made me desire a clear understanding in the matter.[1]

Blackwood protested that his only expectation of not continuing
to be her publisher had arisen from her previous letter.

I was very much annoyed or rather, I should say, hurt at the tone
in which my offer for the new novel was replied to and also at the very
dry way in which our conduct in doubling the purchase money of Adam
Bede was acknowledged.

In regard to the new Novel other people may take a more sanguine
view than I do of what it will produce and to secure a great popular
author may offer a sum such as I would neither think it right nor prudent to give. If such an offer has been made, I would be the very last
man who would wish for a moment to stand in the way of your doing
what you thought best for yourself, but I think I should have been told
so frankly instead of having my offer treated as if it were not worth
consideration at all.

As to the withdrawal of the incognito, you know how much I have
been opposed to it all along. It may prove a disadvantage and in the
eyes of many it will, but my opinion of your genius and confidence in
the truly good, honest, religious, and moral tone of all you have written
or will write is such that I think you will overcome any possible detri-
ment from the withdrawal of the mystery which has so far taken place.[2]

'It is clear that there has been a misunderstanding between us',
George Eliot replied, 'and I will try to explain my part of it.' When
they first discussed the publication of the new book, he declared that
he would pay as much for its appearance in *Maga* as it would bring
in any other way. But when the success of *Adam Bede* had been some
months 'in a perpetual crescendo', she had begun to doubt whether
publication in a periodical would be the most advantageous, and had
written frankly to him from Weymouth, expressing all her doubts.

In your reply, you took no notice whatever of the specific contents of
my letter, but stated that you would give me 'at least as much' for
publication in Maga as in any other way. I think you will perceive,
on reconsideration, that this reply was a stultification of my letter.
Your proposition at the same time to publish the story without the
name of George Eliot seemed to me (rendered doubly sensitive by the
recent withdrawal of my incognito) part of a depreciatory view that

[1] *Letters*, III. 215.   [1] Ibid. 216-17.

ran through your whole letter, in contrast with the usual delicacy and generosity of your tone.

She had no thought of any breach with the firm and had received at that time no offers from publishers except those he was aware of, so that his words about standing in her way could not properly apply. She had never dreamt of any doubt about his publishing the book till something Langford said to Lewes seemed to presuppose that he would not.

After this, came what appeared to us, a manifestation of indifference to my wishes, if not to my interests, in the matter of Newby, which was hardly what was due from publisher to author or from friend to friend. On all hands we have heard surprize expressed at your silence. And, in declining to write to the Times, to write to the Athenæum, a paper which has grossly insulted me, to ask them to insert a paragraph without the mention of your name, indicated, I thought, a forgetfulness which implied a very considerable alteration of feeling towards me.

This is the chapter of my unpleasant impressions, which at length became so strong, that I determined to write and ask you a simple question, that our mutual feeling might be ascertained. But up to this moment, I have said to every one that the Messrs. Blackwood are my publishers, and that I see no reason to leave them; but the contrary. It was important to me on every ground to know that I was not speaking on a false basis; for if you did *not* wish to publish for me, I should necessarily be in a different attitude towards proposals which I have hitherto waived.

I prefer, in every sense, permanent relations to shifting ones, and have the strongest distaste for the odour of mere money speculation about my writing. Moreover, I should be sorry to entertain any exorbitant notions, inconsistent with a rational, just regard to other people's motives and interests. But I may say without cant—since I am in a position of anxiety for others as well as myself—that it is my duty to seek not less than the highest reasonable advantage from my work. It did appear to Mr. Lewes and myself that, for the sum you mentioned, it would be unwise to give up my book for *five* years, losing time also by a slow form of publication.

She closed her long letter with an expression of sincere regret that her acknowledgement of the Blackwoods' intention to give her another £400 for *Adam Bede* 'appeared to you curt and unresponsive'. Having expressed herself strongly on previous occasions, she felt that the simple 'thank you' seemed the most natural.[1]

John Blackwood, just setting out for a week-end with Charles Newdegate at Arbury when the letter came, took it along to

[1] *Letters*, III. 217–19.

answer. 'I need not describe this fine quaint place to you, of all people in the world', he wrote. Each point that her letter had made he this time treated carefully.

As to proposing that the Tale should be anonymous in the Magazine, it is our usual custom and is I think the wisest plan. We departed from it in the case of My Novel and What Will [He Do with It?] as they were a sort of series and Sir Edward wished Pisistratus to be prefixed to them. I now see how with your susceptibilities painfully excited by your persecution the proposition might fall disagreeably upon you and I wish I had said more than I did in explanation.

I regretted the partial removal of the incognito but I never thought of ceasing to be your publisher on that account nor did I dream that such an idea would ever occur to you. As to the effect of the spread of the secret on the new book there must be, and I know there are, different opinions. My opinion is that George Eliot has only to write her book quietly without disturbing herself about what people are saying and she can command success.

In the Newby affair he had twice said that he thought it better to let the rubbish die a natural death. He would be in London on Monday, hoping to see them on Wednesday or Thursday. 'If we cannot agree in our opinions as to a fair sum for Maggie, possibly we may arrange some plan for a certain payment in the first instance and further instalments according to the sale of the book.'[1] George Eliot answered at once: 'I hope you will be able to be with us at luncheon on Wednesday. . . . I congratulate you on having seen that fine old place, Arbury. You must have passed by my brother's house, too—my old, old home.'[2]

Their discussion at Holly Lodge was long, but on the whole satisfactory. Lewes pressed again for publication in one-shilling numbers, which, from the estimates he had got, promised a profit of £5,000 on a sale of 10,000 copies. Since her letter to Blackwood, an offer had come from Bradbury and Evans: £4,500 for publication in *Once a Week* and in two subsequent editions.

I told her the offer was a very large one [John wrote to the Major] and that I would not offer any wild sum such as I was sure people trying to start a periodical and help off other things would give. She said she did not wish any such offer from me and that this one was entirely dismissed and that I was not to consider what others would give for the purpose of assisting them in their speculations but simply what was likely to produce a fair profit to myself with a good sum to her. She means what she says too I think. Lewes is much the keener of the two.

[1] *Letters*, III. 222-3.   [2] *Letters*, III. 224.

I was glad to see how she was looking, and she said herself that she had got over her worry and annoyance very much. She looked better than I have seen her and had not the vexed anxious look which was generally painfully visible.[1]

Blackwood carried away a volume and a half of the manuscript. To William he reported: 'It is wonderfully clever and shows an almost incredible wealth of fun and illustrations and power of painting character.' He found it impossible to read quickly, partly because it lacked 'the hurrying on interest of a taking narrative': by the middle of the second volume the hero and heroine are not above sixteen.

At William's suggestion John Blackwood offered George Eliot £2,000 for an edition of 4,000 copies (3 volumes, 31*s*. 6*d*.), a royalty of more than 30 per cent, and payment at the same rate for every copy beyond that number. For a two-volume edition at 12*s*. the royalty was to be 25 per cent; and for the cheap one-volume edition at 6*s*. she was to have 20 per cent.[2] Lewes still wanted to try the shilling numbers, but, Blackwood told William, 'she is dead against it and I think will have her way. She fears the nervous excitement of the trial and thinks her story will tell better in a mass. Her canvass is very wide and she could extend the story to anything. She is a fine character—all my former good opinion of her is restored. I am sure I cannot be mistaken both in her language and the expression of her face.'[3] On 20 December Marian wrote: 'I think we have fairly dissipated the nightmare of the Serial by dint of much talking. So we may consider the publication of Maggie settled'—with the understanding that payment was to be made at the date of publication. This was rather hard for the firm, which was accustomed to pay at intervals of six, nine, and twelve months, but they agreed to two sums of £1,000 each at six and nine months. Lewes, an old hand at such bargaining, got Harpers to give £300 for the American rights, promising early proof-sheets. Baron Tauchnitz, who had called on a 'visit of homage' 9 December—'a tall, fresh-complexioned, small-featured, smiling man in a wig', George Eliot noted—offered through his London agents £80 for the reprint in Germany; but when Lewes held out for £100 they finally agreed.[4] For the German translation he got £25 and for the Dutch, £10.

---

[1] *Letters*, III. 233.   [2] *Letters*, III. 235.   [3] *Letters*, III. 235–6.
[4] Ibid. 268. This was higher than any English novelist was getting, except perhaps Dickens. See Simon Nowell-Smith, 'Firma Tauchnitz 1837–1900', *Book Collector*, 15 (1966), 433.

Blackwood, sending her the cheque for £800, the extra acknowledgement for *Adam Bede*, made another handsome gesture: he proposed to place the book, when the present edition should be exhausted, on the same terms as the new novel, and returned the copyright to her, giving up the firm's remaining years. 'I never before had so pleasant a New Year's greeting', Marian wrote 4 January 1860.[1] George's gift to her had been a set of the Waverley Novels in forty-eight volumes; on the fly-leaf of Volume I he wrote: 'To Marian Evans Lewes, The best of Novelists, and Wives, These works of her longest-venerated and best-loved Romancist are given by her grateful Husband 1 January 1860.'[1] In his summary for 1859 Lewes noted that he had 'written comparatively little', most of his work having gone into experiments in physiology. But it would be difficult to over-estimate his contribution to George Eliot's triumphant achievement as a novelist. Without his affectionate encouragement she would probably never have written or published any fiction. It had brought them prosperity; George Eliot's income in 1859 was over £2,000; Lewes had earned only £353. Their union had been good for him, in other ways, too. Those who had known him in his flippant, reckless years marked the happy change in both his character and his work. He was sincere when he inscribed a copy of Chappell's *Popular Music of the Olden Time* 'To Her who makes the music of my life. From G. H. Lewes Feby 1860.'[2]

The title of the new novel was still undecided. They had called it in their letters *Maggie*, *Sister Maggie*, and *St. Ogg's on the Floss*, while *The Tulliver Family* and *The House of Tulliver, or Life on the Floss* were other possibilities considered. Blackwood suddenly thought one day of *The Mill on the Floss*, which George Eliot accepted gladly. 'The only objections are, that the Mill is not *strictly* on the Floss, being on its small tributary, and that the title is of rather laborious utterance', she wrote 6 January.[3] As the story drew towards its climax, the writing went on faster. Volume II was finished 16 January 1860; the whole of Volume III was written in eight weeks. George Eliot was anxious to have the book out before Easter (8 April), when she wanted to be in Italy on her last holiday 'before the boys are about us, making it difficult for us to leave home'.[4] Printing began in Edinburgh at the end of January. Blackwood, rereading the story in proof, wrote

---

[1] *Letters*, III. 240. [2] *Letters*, III. 247.
[3] *Letters*, III. 245. [4] *Letters*, III. 249.

enthusiastic comments to the author. There were also occasional words of caution. For example, he disliked 'the word lymphatic applied to Mrs. Tulliver. It interferes with the pleasure one has in *looking* at her.'[1] The description of Mrs. Moss as 'a patient, loosely-hung, child producing woman' troubled him, and Marian altered the phrase to 'patient, prolific, loving-hearted woman'.[2] Mrs. Pullet's graphic picture of old Mrs. Sutton's dropsy—'her legs was as thick as my body. .... They'd tapped her no end o' times, and the water—they say you might ha' swum in it, if you'd liked'[3]—survived in the text only because Blackwood did not see the proof before it went to the author. His old predilection for the conventional and romantic reappeared in his wish that 'noble Maggie had a more goodly lover' than the hunchback Philip Wakem—though he saw (as some critics have failed to see) that 'she does not seem really in love'.[4] He would also have liked Mrs. Tulliver to show 'some trait of feeling for her husband to enable one to sympathise with her woes', and thought Mr. Deane shabby in not helping Mr. Tulliver out of his difficulties, as he could have done 'without any great expenditure of breath or coin, but this would have played the deuce with the story'.[5] Lewes read all the proofs, too, and helped by taking over most of Marian's correspondence. One problem that worried her was Mr. Tulliver's lawsuit and the consequent bankruptcy. She consulted Henry Sheard, an attorney in the City, to make certain that she had allowed enough time for a Chancery order to be issued directing the sale of the Mill and the furniture. Proof of that portion (Book III, ch. 7) was sent to Sheard, 'he having promised to see that her *law* is all right. She is as fidgety about minute accuracy as if she were on oath', Lewes wrote.[6]

Blackwood was 'wearying for Volume III'.[7] Two-thirds of it came the first week in March; he read it at once and wrote to George Eliot, expressing his delight. He felt 'the misfortunes impending on Maggie like a personal grief'.[8] And a few days later, when fifty pages more arrived (brought by the Major's young son Willie), he devoured them excitedly. 'I do not envy the man who can read the scene where Lucy appears and falls on Maggie's neck without being affected to tears', he wrote.

Several times in reading these last chapters I have found myself start from my seat and walk to the Major's adjoining room exclaiming 'By

[1] *Letters*, III. 256.   [2] *Letters*, III. 259.   [3] Bk. I, ch. 7.
[4] *Letters*, III. 264.   [5] *Letters*, III. 265.
[6] *Letters*, III. 263. Sheard drew wills for both GHL and GE, which they signed 21 Nov. 1859.   [7] *Letters*, III. 265.   [8] *Letters*, III. 272.

God she is a *wonderful* woman.' The exclamation was irreverent, quite superfluous, and has a rude sound but I felt impelled to speak and the emphasis conveyed volumes of heartfelt admiration, so I hope to be excused. I await with trembling impatience the Catastrophe.[1]

Marian too was moved. She 'is getting her eyes redder and *swollener* every morning as she lives through her tragic story', Lewes wrote to Blackwood. 'But there is such a strain of poetry to relieve the tragedy that the more she cries, and the readers cry, the better say I. She is anxious to hear your opinion of the part you have got; although she knows you don't like disagreeable and uncomfortable situations.'[2] And in a letter to Barbara Bodichon he described Marian as 'reddening her eyes, and blackening her paper, over the foolish sorrows of two foolish young persons of her imaginary acquaintance'.[3] The sorrows were not all imaginary. A letter had come to her 3 March from Emily Clarke at Lichfield 'saying that dear little Katie is dead'.

By 16 March only two chapters remained to be written; on the 20th, having missed two days from headache, Marian was within seventeen pages of the end. The final paragraphs from the moment when Maggie is carried out upon the water in her boat were written on 21 March and dispatched at once to Edinburgh. 'Lying awake in the night and living through the scene again', Marian thought of three slight verbal changes, which she sent off in the morning —Thursday. Since they were leaving on Saturday to reach Rome for Holy Week, Lewes asked Blackwood to forward the final proof to Paris. But on Friday it arrived at Holly Lodge; and after finishing their packing, they corrected it and returned it to Edinburgh. Do we marvel more at the speed of the post or the speed of the Edinburgh printers in putting this proof in the hands of the author forty-eight hours after it was written?

After a farewell dinner with the Congreves, they left Holly Lodge again in the care of Mrs. Bell and set off early 24 March 1860 for Paris. On the train they met Dr. Richard Deakin, a resident physician at Rome, who made himself agreeable and gave them plenty of useful advice, which eventually brought him one of the few inscribed copies of *The Mill on the Floss*. With him they went to the Hôtel du Louvre—'a magnificent hotel where there is everything at hand'. In the morning, after Lewes had 'bought a pretty bonnet for Polly', they began their sightseeing with Notre Dame, the interior of which 'did not detain us many

[1] *Letters*, III. 276–7.   [2] *Letters*, III. 269.   [3] *Letters*, III. 269–70.

minutes'. The Sainte Chapelle, however, charmed and satisfied them. They went to the Louvre, rambled in the Palais Royal, and in the evening heard Tamberlik in *Otello*. The following day passed mostly in leisurely shopping before they took the evening train for Italy.

In 1860 the railway ended at St. Jean de Maurienne, which they reached at four the next afternoon. After dining they were tightly packed into a diligence with Marian's knees jammed against the bag of a soldier opposite containing the pay for his regiment, which cramped her legs sadly. At Lanslebourg about 11 o'clock they took to a sledge to go over the Mont Cenis pass. Gulping a cup of coffee in the waiting-room with the crowd round the hot iron stove, they went out into the starlight night to watch the men put the mules to the sledges and change the luggage. 'The air was cold and thin, but the change from the room was delightful. The scene was picturesque and confused. A number of mules, sledges, diligences, and drivers with lanterns were darkening the quiet snow-fields, while above and around were the sky and grand snowy mountains.' Packed even more tightly in the closed sledge, they felt surprisingly comfortable and napped often during the slow climb. Near the summit they saw by starlight the vast sloping snow-fields and the sharp lines of the mountains. On the descent they caught occasional glimpses of the sledges winding down ahead of them and heard the bells and the 'yup, yup!' of the muleteers. Morning dawned bright under a blue Italian sky, though the wind was so violent as they changed again into a diligence that it nearly blew Marian off her feet on the slippery ground. At Susa they had breakfast before taking the railway to Turin, where they rested a few hours. At the Turin station they saw Count Cavour, waiting to receive the new Viceroy of Tuscany, the Prince de Carignan, 'a large, stout "moustache"', squeezed in at the waist with a gold belt, looking like one of those dressed-up personages among the chessmen that the Cavours of the world play their games with'.[1] Five hours more by rail brought them to Genoa, where for the first time in seventy-two hours they 'slept the sleep of—travellers'.[2]

In the sunshine of Genoa they were out early in the morning for a brisk round of sightseeing. They walked about the Palladian streets, climbed the tower of Santa Maria di Carignano to view the city, and went in the evening to hear *Rigoletto* with a 'fat, robust tenor' and an 'incompetent and ugly soprano', who was first hissed and then warmly applauded. The following day was

[1] *Letters*, III. 287.   [2] GHL Journal, 26–8 Mar. 1860.

also spent in sightseeing, until at 7 o'clock they boarded the steam packet. The Mediterranean, calm as a lake, reflected the evening star—with great brilliance. They both slept soundly till the boat approached the harbour at Leghorn, where it tarried most of the day. The Leweses drove about the town and at their driver's suggestion stopped to see the Synagogue. It was the Jews' Sabbath, and the congregation was just separating, though a few men were 'still occupied in a final muttering of prayer', wrapped in their white scarves. The interior reminded Marian of a dissenting chapel at home. After lunch they made a brief excursion by rail to Pisa, returning at 5 o'clock to board the packet. Though they landed at Civitavecchia early the next morning—Palm Sunday, a four hours' delay in the custom house prevented their reaching Rome till noon.

Approaching the Eternal City, they both felt disappointed that 'there was nothing imposing to be seen'; after a 'weary length of dirty uninteresting streets', their first sight of St. Peter's dome was 'unimpressive'; the Castle of St. Angelo seemed 'but a shabby likeness of the engravings'.[1] The city was overflowing with visitors during Holy Week, and all the good hotels were full. After one night in a little room 'at an extravagant height of stairs and price', they found comfortable lodgings at 117 San Carlo al Corso with a Frenchman named Peureux and his little dark wife, who, speaking nothing but Italian, served as *parlatrice* to revive Marian's memory of the language. The vast crowds made it difficult to get about. On Maundy Thursday, when they spent the whole morning in St. Peter's, Lewes 'lost Polly, who went out by mistake before the appointed time'. While they were separated, the Pope came past, and she knelt down with the rest to receive his blessing. 'But altogether', she wrote to Mrs. Congreve, 'these ceremonies are a melancholy, hollow business, and we regret bitterly that the Holy Week has taken up our time from better things. I have a cold and headache this morning, and in other ways am not conscious of improvement from the Pope's blessing. I may comfort myself with thinking that the King of Sardinia is none the worse for the Pope's curse.'[2] On Good Friday they returned to St. Peter's to hear the Miserere. On Saturday, Lewes noted in his Journal,

our landlord and his wife came to ask if we would allow the priest to bless the house. We of course assented, and a young priest with some

---

[1] GE 'Recollections of Italy, 1860', in her Journal.   [2] *Letters*, III. 288.

attendant hurried into the room, sprinkled holy water and gabbled out some phrases with indifference and haste that were shocking. He then went into the bedroom and blessed the conjugal bed in the same style.[1]

After that, Lewes took Polly out shopping. They looked at cameos and bought Liddell's *History of Rome* and some Italian stories to practise their Italian. These books, to which Coindet's *Histoire de la peinture en Italie* was soon added, constituted most of their reading at Rome. In the evening they went to the Vatican Museum to see the statues by torchlight. Easter Sunday it rained all day. They had had enough of Holy Week and what Lewes called its 'hateful shams'. They did not even try to go to St. Peter's. Having found the Borghese Palace closed, they drove to the Cloaca Maxima, which, he noted, 'after 24 centuries still performs its duties'.[2] But it was too cold and wet for further exploration, and they soon returned home to read and write letters.

They took their sightseeing very seriously, studying Liddell and the guide-books. Except for Dr. Deakin, who called on them during Holy Week and took Lewes to some artists' studios, they saw no one they knew at Rome. They were not unobserved, however. Mrs. Browning, writing to her sister-in-law about *The Mill on the Floss*, added: 'The author is here, they say, with her elective, and is seen on the Corso walking, or in the Vatican musing. Always together. They are said to visit nobody, and to be beheld only at unawares.'[3] As they grew better acquainted with Rome, their initial disappointment gave way to enthusiasm, and Marian filled many pages of her Journal with the things that delighted her. Her first view of the interior of St. Peter's 'was perhaps at a higher pitch than any subsequent impression either of its beauty or vastness; but then on later visits the lovely marble, which has a tone at once subdued and warm, was half-covered with hideous red drapery'. This unhappy effect she recalled in *Middlemarch*:

in certain states of dull forlornness Dorothea all her life continued to see the vastness of St. Peter's, the huge bronze canopy, the excited intention in the attitudes and garments of the prophets and evangelists in the mosaics above, and the red drapery which was being hung for Christmas spreading itself everywhere like a disease of the retina.[4]

The illumination of St. Peter's the first Sunday after Easter struck Marian as 'magically beautiful', and Lewes's account of it was

[1] GHL Journal, 7 Apr. 1860.   [2] GHL Journal, 8 Apr. 1860.
[3] *The Letters of E. B. Browning*, ed. F. G. Kenyon (2 vols., 1897), II. 388.
[4] Ch. 20. The Casaubons's Roman honeymoon occurred in December. GE did not realize that the liturgical colour for Christmas is white.

even more rapturous. Their longest excursions took them to Frascati, Tusculum, and Tivoli, where the rain destroyed all possibility of seeing Hadrian's Villa. Under obtrusive umbrellas they spent two hours in the valley of the waterfalls, and then 'draggled' to the hotel, lunched, and drove home with the carriage covered.

At Naples, where they arrived on 30 April after a hot and uncomfortable night on the steamer, the weather improved. They took rooms on the first floor at the Hôtel des Étrangers, commanding a fine view of the Bay and Posilipo. They visited all the principal sights, enjoying the brilliant blue of sky and water. One day they went to Pompeii with a Russian couple with whom George had struck up an acquaintance at the table-d'hôte. Later, in the Museo Borbonico they studied with keener interest the objects excavated from the ashes. A coachman (nicknamed 'Baboon' by Marian) drove them everywhere about Naples and on a week's excursion to Salerno, Paestum, Amalfi, Sorrento, and other delightful spots, returning them to Naples on 13 May. Two days later they were on the steamer again bound for Leghorn on the way to Florence. During the stop at Civitavecchia they remained on board, reading and chatting with the other passengers. Among these was a very agreeable Genevese named Faesch-Michele, whom they agreed to accompany to the Pension Suisse, 'the quietest hotel in Florence', where they could be clear of the stream of English and Americans who make the main tracks of travel seem like 'a perpetual noisy picnic'.[1] On the railway journey from Leghorn they paused to see Pisa again. While they were admiring the reliefs on the pulpit, 'a baby came in to be christened, and we assisted at the ceremony with interest'.[2]

Their two weeks at Florence were pleasant. The weather was good. They had a comfortable salon and a large bedroom for only 10 pauls (about 5 shillings) a day. They passed the mornings in diligent sightseeing with impressions carefully noted in their Journals, and every afternoon drove out to the Cascine or the Boboli, to San Miniato or Fiesole. They made an excursion to Siena 29 May. They continued reading Coindet, to which they added Kugler's *Handbook of Italian Painters* as well as the autobiographies of Benvenuto Cellini and Alfieri. Lewes called on Thomas Adolphus Trollope, who was in England. But Mrs. Trollope chatted with him for half an hour, and called at their

---

[1] *Letters*, III. 294.   [2] GHL Journal, 17 May 1860.

hotel the next day. The Leweses were unfortunately out, and when they returned the call two days later, she was not at home. But they got together at last on 27 May, when, Lewes's Journal says, 'Mrs. Trollope called bringing with her an awful visitor, a Miss Blagden, who beset Polly.' This was Isabella Blagden, Browning's 'Dearest Isa'. The Leweses were invited to spend the evening at the Villino Trollope on 30 May, after Tom returned. Lewes found Tom 'a frank, serious, interesting man. They showed us over their house and we descended into the garden, where the fire flies (the first I have seen) were abundant. Two American women and some Italians came in. Home at 11.' One of the Americans was Kate Field, who described the meeting in a letter.[1] Fred Chapman and Charles Lever were also there.

A few days after she came to Florence George Eliot made a momentous decision. Lewes had been reading in a guide-book about Savonarola; 'it occurred to me that his life and times afford fine material for an historical romance. Polly at once caught at the idea with enthusiasm. It is a subject which will fall in with much of her studies and sympathies; and it will give fresh interest to our stay in Florence.'[2] The next day they went to San Marco. While Marian remained in the outer cloister contemplating Fra Angelico's *Crucifixion*, George went over the monastery where ladies were not admitted and took notes for her. On the way home they stopped to buy Savonarola's poems and Perrens's *Jérôme Savonarole, sa vie, ses prédications, ses écrits*.[3] In the Magliabecchian Library they examined a manuscript volume by Savonarola, 'written in a minute, shortsighted hand, but very clear'. They visited the Great Hall in the Palazzo Vecchio 'built under Savonarola's direction', and two days later went to the Palazzo Corsini to see a painting by Pollaiuolo called *The Death of Savonarola*—a curious and to us interesting bit of history'. Before they left Florence, Lewes commissioned a painter named Buonarotti to copy a fresco in San Marco by Fra Angelico, 'one of whose works Polly wishes to hang before her as she writes'.[4]

When they hurried out of England George Eliot had been anxious to get *The Mill on the Floss* out of her mind. But they were

[1] Lilian Whiting, *Kate Field* (1899), p. 101. Compare (pp. 395–401) the fancifully embroidered account of this meeting written for the N.Y. *Tribune*, 22 Dec. 1880, purporting to quote intimate confidences about her writing.

[2] GHL Journal, 21 May 1860.

[3] (2 vols., Paris, 1859), now in Dr. Williams's Library.

[4] GHL Journal, 31 May 1860.

hardly settled in Rome before she was inquiring about it and sending Blackwood their address. 'I tremble rather, to hear of its reception, lest high hopes should be speedily checked. But then, I am always in a state of fear, more or less rational; and if any good news comes, it will be the more welcome.'[1] Word soon came that 4,600 copies had been sold four days after publication—which spurred them to celebrate by the extravagance of buying some expensive prints, among them, one of Guido's *Aurora*. In Naples three weeks later they learned that about 5,600 copies had been sold; Mudie was nibbling at his third thousand. It was an immense sale for a three-volume novel, not equalled, Major Blackwood wrote, since the Waverley novels.[2] Still, a hint that comment on it had been less favourable than it was on *Adam Bede*[3] made Lewes describe it as rather 'chequered news'. In his Journal, 5 May he wrote:

The disclosure of the authorship would have much influence in that direction, which would be increased by the fact of its being a 'second book'. Moreover I doubt whether it is intrinsically so interesting as 'Adam'. Neither the story nor the characters take so profound a hold of the sympathies. Mais nous verrons. It is early days yet.

Polly, of course, was anxious, believing as usual in failure. For three weeks they awaited further reports. Lewes dreamt one night that 'John Blackwood told me "We can do nothing with the Mill".' But the next morning came a letter from Major Blackwood (writing for John, who was bound for the Derby) containing the welcome news that Mudie had taken his third thousand and that all 6,000 copies of *The Mill* were sold and 500 more were being printed.[4] This assured George Eliot of £3,250. There could be no doubt of the book's success.

On 19 May *The Times* published a long review beginning 'George Eliot is as great as ever'. Though very favourable in regard to the author, it objected strongly to the 'odious Dodson family, . . . stingy, selfish wretches'. George Eliot commented on it in a letter to Major Blackwood 27 May:

It is written in a generous spirit, and with so high a degree of intelligence, that I am rather alarmed lest the misapprehensions it exhibits should

---

[1] *Letters*, III. 285.   [2] W. Blackwood to GHL, 19 July 1860 (NLS).
[3] Langford heard such comments at the Garrick Club. The *Punch* circle spoke of the work as 'dreary and immoral', and thought Bradbury and Evans were lucky not to have secured it. Henry Silver's Diary, 11 Apr. 1860. (*Punch*).
[4] *Letters*, III. 296; GHL Journal, 26 May 1860. Before the end of 1860 the book had secured GE £3,985.

be due to my defective presentation, rather than to any failure on the part of the critic. I have certainly fulfilled my intention very badly if I have made the Dodson honesty appear 'mean and uninteresting', or made the payment of one's debts appear a contemptible virtue in comparison with any sort of 'Bohemian' qualities. So far as my own feeling and intention are concerned, no one class of persons or form of character is held up to reprobation or to exclusive admiration. Tom is painted with as much love and pity as Maggie, and I am so far from hating the Dodsons myself, that I am rather aghast to find them ticketed with such very ugly adjectives.[1]

At the end of her letter she dropped a tantalizing hint: 'There has been a crescendo of enjoyment in our travels, for Florence, from its relation to the history of modern art, has roused a keener interest in us even than Rome, and has stimulated me to entertain rather an ambitious project, which I mean to be a secret from every one but you and Mr. John Blackwood.' John complained that her hint was 'so vague that I cannot guess the style' of the new work, but she refused to tell what 'my great project is by letter, for I am anxious to keep it a secret. It will require a great deal of study and labour, and I am athirst to begin.'[2]

The Leweses left for Bologna by diligence about 7 p.m., 1 June, having taken the whole coupé. In the passage of the Apennines Marian noted

certain grand and startling effects that came to me in my occasional wakings. Wonderful heights and depths I saw on each side of us by the fading light of the evening. Then in the middle of the night while the lightning was flashing and the sky was heavy with threatening storm-clouds, I waked to find the six horses resolutely refusing, or unable, to move the diligence; till, at last, two meek oxen were tied to the axle, and their added strength dragged us up the hill.[3]

Though they had slept little, they were ready soon after reaching Bologna to begin studying the paintings, and in the evening took a carriage for two hours to drive about the town. The next day they left for Ferrara—Savonarola's birthplace—a long, dusty journey that ended about 8 p.m. They started at dawn for Padua, which they reached in clouds of dust about 2 o'clock. After a brief rest and a quick look at the frescoes they took the train into Venice. At 10 o'clock 4 June they were in a gondola, 'gliding mysteriously along', between moonlit buildings reflected in the water. 'What

[1] *Letters*, III. 299. [2] *Letters*, III. 305–7.
[3] 'Recollections of Italy', GE Journal.

stillness! What beauty!' Marian exclaimed. 'Looking out from
the high window of our hotel on the Grand Canal, I felt that it was
a pity to go to bed. Venice was more beautiful than romances had
feigned. And that was the impression that remained and even
deepened during our stay of eight days.'

Between Rovigo and Ferrara they had picked up a returned
courier named Domenico and engaged him as *valet de place* during
their stay in Venice. He suggested the Hôtel de la Ville, an excellent inn in the former Palazzo Grassi, and made life very pleasant
for them, seeing to their gondola, guiding them tactfully about the
city, advising them in the purchase of lace or glass or jewellery,
singing Venetian songs as they floated about the Lagoon. He took
them one day to Chioggia with four gondoliers, and they sailed
home in the sunset. After tea, while Lewes was writing to Agnes,
he was interrupted by the sound of music; looking out of the
window he saw a large gondola with coloured lanterns followed by
a crowd of smaller craft with ladies in summer dresses. Under the
Rialto Bridge they paused and sang for some time. 'It was more
like a scene from a novel than anything I have yet seen.'[1] These
enchanting moments soon ended. They left Venice on 12 June for
Verona, and went on to Desenzano, where they had a perfect view
of Lake Garda, but dined 'greasily' and 'passed a horrible night
of heat, headache, and fleas'. At Milan they lodged at the Albergo
Reale, where Marian had stayed with the Brays in 1849, and retraced her route to Lake Como, crossed quickly over the Splügen
Pass to Chur where they got a train to Zurich. Here they had a
good day with the Moleschotts before going to Berne on 23 June.

From their balcony at the Bernerhof they had a splendid view
of the Bernese Alps. After dinner Lewes rushed to Hofwyl to see
the boys, who were all well and much grown since his last visit.
The next day—Sunday—they came to the hotel to meet their new
'Mutter' and spend the whole day with her. On Monday she and
Lewes both went to the School. This visit had been the subject
of some concern for the boys, who were probably more troubled
than their father realized by his revelation of Agnes's relations with
Thornton Hunt. When they first learned that Marian was coming to
Hofwyl with their father on the return from Italy, Thornie wrote to
him in perplexity as to what they should tell their friend Empson;

as he has seen Mamma, and knows her, he will of course see that Mother
is not she, so that we have agreed, viz. Charles and I, that we had better

[1] GHL Journal, 10 June 1860.

tell him, enjoining at the same time secresy, as at any rate he would know it 3 or four months later, when he goes home. Mother will have therefore when we present him to say 'How d'ye do!' etc. etc. And we only wait for your permission to tell him. . . . You have told Mamma, that you had told us, didn't you? In ⟨your⟩ her last letter there were one or two sentences from which Charles and I concluded you had.

Thornie signed his note, 'Dear father, Your rascally pup.'[1] Empson's presentation seems to have been managed without embarrassment. Marian was shown everything at the School, dined there, had tea with the Müllers, and did not reach Berne till 10 o'clock.

The next morning Charles came to the hotel, 'having bid adieu to School forever'. He accompanied them to Geneva, where Marian wanted to visit her old friends the D'Albert Durades. She had not seen them since 1850. There had been occasional letters between them; she had told them of her marriage, and asked for suggestions about the boys' schooling, but for more than two years the correspondence had lapsed. After the success of *Adam Bede*, she wrote again, 18 October 1859:

Does it ever happen to you now to think of a certain Englishwoman, née Marian Evans? . . . In these last three years a great change has come over my life—a change in which I cannot help believing that both you and Madame D'Albert will rejoice. Under the influence of the intense happiness I have enjoyed in my married life from thorough moral and intellectual sympathy, I have at last found out my true vocation, after which my nature had always been feeling and striving uneasily without finding it. What do you think that vocation is? I pause for you to guess.

I have turned out to be an artist—not, as you are, with the pencil and the pallet, but with words. I have written a novel which people say has stirred them very deeply—and *not* a *few* people, but almost all reading England. It was published in February last, and already 14,000 copies have been sold. The title is 'Adam Bede'; and 'George Eliot', the name on the title page, is my *nom de plume*. . . . I write you word of it, because I believe that both your kind heart and Madame D'Albert's too, will be touched with real joy, that one whom you knew when she was not very happy and when her life seemed to serve no purpose of much worth, has been at last blessed with the sense that she has done something worth living and suffering for. And I write also because I want to give both you and her a proof that I still think of you with grateful affectionate recollection. . . .

I am very much changed from the Minie of old days: the years have altered me as much inwardly as outwardly. In some things, however,

---

[1] TAL to GHL, 20 Mar. 1860 (Yale).

I am just the same—in some of my failings, I fear:—but it is not a failing to retain a vivid remembrance of past scenes, and to feel warmly towards friends whose kindness lies far back in the distance, and in these things I am the same as when I used to walk on La Treille with you or Madame D'Albert.[1]

In his reply D'Albert said that while reading *Scenes of Clerical Life* he had thought 'c'est ainsi que Minie devrait écrire', and felt that he would like to translate it into French. He was glad to know that her marriage was happy: 'Telle que je vous connaîssais, le mariage devait être pour vous l'enfer ou le paradis.'[2] Reading *Adam Bede* he saw her in many pages, though there were others where he could not have recognized her, so greatly had a few years changed her thought since she used to shock him with her almost pantheistic views on the idea of a future life. Her response provides one of the most illuminating statements of her religious belief:

I can understand that there are many pages in 'Adam Bede' in which you do not recognize the 'Marian' or 'Minie' of old Geneva days. We knew each other too short a time, and I was under too partial and transient a phase of my mental history, for me to pour out to you much of my earlier experience. I think I hardly ever spoke to you of the strong hold Evangelical Christianity had on me from the age of fifteen to two and twenty and of the abundant intercourse I had had with earnest people of various religious sects. When I was at Geneva, I had not yet lost the attitude of antagonism which belongs to the renunciation of *any* belief—also, I was very unhappy, and in a state of discord and rebellion towards my own lot. Ten years of experience have wrought great changes in that inward self: I have no longer any antagonism towards any faith in which human sorrow and human longing for purity have expressed themselves; on the contrary, I have a sympathy with it that predominates over all argumentative tendencies.

I have not returned to dogmatic Christianity—to the acceptance of any set of doctrines as a creed, and a superhuman revelation of the Unseen—but I see in it the highest expression of the religious sentiment that has yet found its place in the history of mankind, and I have the profoundest interest in the inward life of sincere Christians in all ages. Many things that I should have argued against ten years ago, I now feel myself too ignorant and too limited in moral sensibility to speak of with confident disapprobation: on many points where I used to delight in expressing intellectual difference, I now delight in feeling an emotional agreement. On that question of our future existence, to which you

---

[1] *Letters*, III. 186–7.
[2] D'Albert to GE, 23 Oct. 1859 (Yale).

allude, I have undergone the sort of change I have just indicated, although my most rooted conviction is, that the immediate objects and the proper sphere of all our highest emotions are our struggling fellow-men and this earthly existence.[1]

In this letter she asked D'Albert about possible translators of *Adam Bede*; when he declared that he would like to undertake it himself, she sent him her authorization.[2]

She was naturally eager to go to Geneva again and to introduce George, whom she described as 'a person of the readiest, most facile intercourse, . . . a very airy, bright, versatile creature—not at all a formidable personage'. The meeting occurred on 26 June. The Leweses had refused Mme D'Albert's kind invitation to stay with them and took rooms at the Hôtel des Bergues. After tea they called at the D'Alberts' new apartment, Boulevard des Tranchées, 520. 'It was a great delight to me', Lewes wrote, 'to see how truly they loved and prized Polly, and we spent an exciting evening with them.'[3] After breakfast the D'Alberts called for them with a carriage and took them to the Athénée Museum, of which he was Director, and to call at Calame's studio. D'Albert read Marian some of his translation of *Adam Bede* and was given permission to translate *The Mill on the Floss*, too. The following day the D'Alberts put them on the train for Paris. 'Mamam', Marian said as she was leaving, 'écrivez-moi; cela me fera du bien.'[4] Though she never saw her friends again, Marian kept up the correspondence all her life.

They reached Holly Lodge after midnight on 1 July, and Charles for the first time slept in his own room, which Marian had urged Nursie to make as comfortable as possible.[5] Charles, a thoroughly good, intelligent, loving fellow with a strong sense of duty, was soon warmly devoted to his new little Mutter, as he called her, and richly repaid the affection she gave him. Passionately fond of music, he played Beethoven duets with her almost every evening. The three of them went quite regularly to the Pop concerts; they heard the *Messiah* at Exeter Hall, *Don Giovanni* at Her Majesty's, and *Le Prophète* at the opening of the Opera, for which Langford brought them a box.[6] Charles's other interests were not neglected. They took him to a course of Professor Hofmann's lectures on

[1] *Letters*, III. 230–1.
[2] GE to D'Albert Durade, 7 Feb. 1860 (copy at Yale).
[3] GHL Journal, 26 June 1860.
[4] Mme D'Albert Durade to GE, 16 July 1860.
[5] *Letters*, III. 304.
[6] 19 Oct., 7 Dec. 1860, 2 Apr. 1861.

chemistry at the Museum of Economic Geology and made occa-sional visits to the Crystal Palace to see the sculpture and other exhibitions.

Soon after their return to England, Lewes spoke to several people about a place for Charles in the Civil Service. Though asked only for information, Anthony Trollope (perhaps with some remembrance of his own uncertain beginning at St. Martin's-le-Grand) kindly wrote to the Duke of Argyll, then Postmaster General, for a nomination to compete for a vacancy in the Post Office. Both Marian and Lewes coached Charles for the examina-tion, which he passed easily ahead of all his competitors. He entered the service as a supplementary clerk, second class, in the Secretary's Office 15 August 1860 at a salary of £80 a year.

Thornie was a lad of very different temperament—imaginative, witty, vivacious, charming, but without the keen sense of self-discipline that guided his elder brother. He sang delightfully and wrote amusing tales and verses. His absorbing hobby at sixteen was natural history. He collected moths and butterflies; he stuffed birds and animals to present to Mutter. One wonders why his father did not head him towards a career in medicine or set him to work under one of his scientific friends like Richard Owen or Huxley. In those days the greatest opportunities for a young man to make his way were found in the Colonies. Lewes decided to remove Thornie from Hofwyl to give him a year of concentrated preparation for the East Indian service. D'Albert Durade had asked 3,000 francs to take charge of him for a year, which was more than Lewes could afford. He resolved to put the lad in the High School at Edinburgh under Dr. Schmitz to make him more familiar with British ways and to prepare him for the examinations. Thornie came to London on 27 September 1860; three days later his father took him to Edinburgh and established him in the family of a schoolmaster suggested by Blackwood.

If Holly Lodge was inconvenient for his elders, it was entirely too far from the City for Charles, who had to be at his office from ten to four. Soon after he was appointed, the Leweses set out to find a house in town. They offered £1,600 for one in Park Village West near Gloucester Gate, but failing to get it, were not alto-gether dismayed, for Marian did not want to be fixed in such an expensive house until she knew how their life in London would go. So they took most of a furnished house at 10 Harewood Square (now covered by the Marylebone Station), sent their furniture to the Pantechnicon, and moved 24 September. Though near enough to the Post Office for Charles, and convenient for concerts, it was in most respects an unattractive house with 'staring yellow curtains' and other disagreeables.[1] They abandoned it without regret three months later, when they moved into a house of their own near by at 16 Blandford Square, 'which we have taken for three years, hoping by the end of that time to have so far done our duty by the boys as to be free to live where we list'.[2] Marian begrudged more than ever the time-frittering details of shopping and housekeeping. In the latest move, 'to crown my sorrows, I have lost my pen—my old favourite pen with which I have written for eight years;—at least it is not forthcoming'.[3] The manuscript of *The Mill on the Floss*, the last to be written with it, came handsomely bound from Blackwood. Marian inscribed it: 'To my beloved Husband, George Henry Lewes, I give this MS. of my third book, written in the sixth year of our life together, at Holly Lodge, South Fields, Wandsworth, and finished March 21st, 1860.'

One advantage of 16 Blandford Square was its close proximity to Barbara Bodichon, who had kept her father's house at number 5 and spent only the winters at Algiers. But Marian now saw Mrs. Congreve less often. Occasionally she came from Wandsworth to call and was sometimes invited to stay the night, but there were no more daily walks on the heath. Visits from Sara Hennell were not encouraged. Two copies of her *Thoughts in Aid of Faith* awaited the Leweses on their return from Italy. Marian's copy, now in Dr. Williams's Library, is inscribed: 'Marian Evans Lewes. To the dearly-beloved Translator of Feuerbach's "Essence of Christianity"—in grateful remembrance of how much I owed to her during the season of happy intercourse which formed the "German" period of our lives. S. S. H. May 22d 1860.' Marian read it quickly; and while she found something to praise in the 'largeness and insight', confessed that she saw no logical consistency between the parts of the book and felt the meaning at times obscured in folds of abstract phraseology.[4] Lewes's comments were more brutally frank. He wrote a long letter to Sara, specifying passages where the meaning was in 'utter darkness!' or so wordy, involved, and vague that it was 'lost as in a mist',— an opinion in which Marian concurred.[5]

If it upset her to discuss Sara's writings, she was even more disturbed by Sara's insistence on discussing her novels with equal

---

[1] *Letters*, III. 358.   [2] GE Journal, 17 Dec. 1860.
[3] *Letters*, III. 364.   [4] Ibid. 316.   [5] Ibid. 318–21.

candour. Sara volunteered a suspicion that *The Mill on the Floss* seemed 'unfinished' because of Marian's intense sympathy with Maggie Tulliver, which, Sara thought, must have made her 'rush upstairs as you used to do, to give ease to the flood of passionate tears in your own room'. In every word of the book, said Sara, she could hear Marian's voice of ten years before. 'Go on!' she advised, '—write once more, and give us something as much better than this, as this, if finished, would be better (in moral tone) than *Consuelo*. For *Consuelo* is the only thing to compare with it.'[1] Such comments the sensitive George Eliot found less than helpful.

In Blandford Square the Leweses could see their London friends more easily. On Saturday evenings they were usually at home. George Redford, leaving his 'cello with them, would come then to play trios with Charles and Marian. Spencer and Pigott too became fairly regular visitors. One evening when Anthony Trollope dined with them, having come to inquire about a German school for his boys, Arthur Helps, recently named Clerk of the Privy Council, called unexpectedly, bringing Marian news that she found

extremely agreeable. He told me the Queen had been speaking to him in great admiration of my books, especially the Mill on the Floss. It is interesting to know that Royalty can be touched by that sort of writing —and I was grateful to Mr. Helps for his wish to tell me of the sympathy given to me in that quarter.[2]

Queen Victoria had also read *Adam Bede*, beginning it at Balmoral in September 1859 and finishing it at Windsor in October, according to the note in her copy; she read much of it aloud to the Prince Consort. 'It has made a deep impression upon me', she wrote in her journal, adding that 'Albert likes and is much interested' in it.[3] To her uncle, Leopold I, King of the Belgians, she wrote: 'If you have not read *Adam Bede*, a novel published a few months ago, I strongly recommend it, as one of the finest written for a long time.'[4] To the Princess Royal she wrote the next day:

Dear Papa is much amused and interested by Adam Bede, which I am delighted to read a second time. There is such knowledge of human

[1] S. S. Hennell to GE, 28 June 1860 (Yale).
[2] GE Journal, 28 Nov. 1860.
[3] Queen Victoria, Journal, 29–30 Oct. 1859. In her Journal 15 Jan. 1861 the Queen also mentions her reading of the *Scenes of Clerical Life*; she was 'much interested and touched by the Love Story of Mr. Gilfil'. The books are at Windsor Castle.
[4] 1 Nov. 1859 (Royal Archives: Y 104/38).

nature, and such truth in the characters, I like to trace a likeness to the dear Highlanders in Adam—and also in Lisbeth and Mrs Poyser. I am sure it is only a true picture of what constantly (and very naturally) happens.[1]

She commanded two water-colours of scenes from the story by Corbould (now at Buckingham Palace), one of Dinah preaching, the other—after a design by the Princess Alice—of Hetty making butter.

Possibly Marian felt the more grateful for the Queen's sympathy because her guests at Blandford Square included so few ladies. Mrs. Peter Taylor, who had written so generously to her in 1856, wrote again in 1861. Marian, replying 1 April, said bravely:

It was never a trial to me to have been cut off from what is called the world, and I think I love none of my fellow-creatures the less for it; still I must always retain a peculiar regard for those who showed me any kindness in word or deed at that time, when there was the least evidence in my favour. The list of those who did so is a short one, so that I can often and easily recall it.

Mrs. Taylor, a leader in the feminist cause, had addressed her as Miss Evans.

For the last six years I have ceased to be 'Miss Evans' for any one who has personal relations with me—having held myself under all the responsibilities of a married woman. I wish this to be distinctly understood; and when I tell you that we have a great boy of eighteen at home who calls me 'mother', as well as two other boys, almost as tall, who write to me under the same name, you will understand that the point is not one of mere egoism or personal dignity, when I request that any one who has a regard for me will cease to speak of me by my maiden name.[2]

Calling a few days later, Mrs. Taylor expressed a wish to have the Leweses at her house. But Marian explained that she found it a necessity of her London life

to make the rule of *never* paying visits. Without a carriage, and with my easily perturbed health, London distances would make any other rule quite irreconcilable for me with any efficient use of my days; and I am obliged to give up the *few* visits which would be really attractive and fruitful in order to avoid the *many* visits which would be the reverse. It is only by saying, 'I never pay visits', that I can escape being

---

[1] Archives of Schloss Friedrichshof. [2] *Letters*, III. 396.

ungracious or unkind—only by renouncing all social intercourse but such as comes to our own fireside, that I can escape sacrificing the chief objects of life.[1]

There was some self-deception in this renunciation of society by George Eliot, whose feminine visitors could be numbered on one hand. Mrs. Taylor accepted the arrangement, however, and came to call frequently.

The move to Blandford Square marked a more significant recognition—Marian's introduction to Lewes's mother, Mrs. John Willim, who lived with the irascible, gouty, eighty-six-year-old Captain Willim not far away in Clifton Road. Agnes used to visit her, sometimes when George was there too. During the first years of his union with Marian Mrs. Willim did not meet her; but in 1860, after George Eliot had become famous, Mrs. Willim accepted the situation, and, when they moved to Blandford Square, she wrote to her son, 'I am so pleased to think I shall be able to call and know your *aimable Wife*. I long to do so.'[2] Thereafter she lunched with them quite often. One day she sent word that she was coming to consult Lewes about the Captain's treatment of her. He 'won't let any one come to the house, and is so irritable that she can't sit in the room with him', Lewes wrote in his Journal. 'I told her to tell him that unless he could treat her better she should come and live with us. She stayed all day and seemed to pick up wonderfully.'[3] She was obviously proud of her son's new and distinguished wife.

In Warwickshire Marian's own family, though they read her novels avidly, maintained their icy silence. What did they think of the page on family likeness in *Adam Bede*? 'We hear a voice with the very cadence of our own uttering the thoughts we despise; we see eyes—ah! so like our mother's—averted from us in cold alienation; and our last darling child startles us with the air and gestures of the sister we parted from in bitterness long years ago.'[4]

Marian seldom felt well during the three years in Blandford Square. She complained of 'physical weakness', 'feeble body', 'heavy eyes and hands', and other vague symptoms; worst of all was a state of mental depression which Lewes's utmost efforts could not always alleviate. Marian blamed it on the 'London air'. She had never liked life in London, had never ceased to miss the country.

---

[1] *Letters*, III. 398.
[2] Mrs. J. Willim to GHL, Thursday [Dec. 1860] (Yale).
[3] GHL Journal, 16 Apr. 1861.   [4] *Adam Bede*, ch. 4.

When she grew especially despondent, Lewes would carry her off for a few days to some inn at Dorking or Tunbridge or Englefield Green, where her spirits rallied overnight and she would feel strong enough to tramp for hours about the lanes and fields. 'I felt a new creature as soon as I was in the country', she wrote to Mrs. Congreve. . . . 'I suppose we must keep soul and body together by occasional flights of this sort.'[1] The malaise and languor that oppressed her in London would also vanish as soon as she reached the Continent, where she took strenuous all-night journeys by rail or diligence and endured long days of relentless sightseeing. One looks inevitably for some psychological explanation to reconcile these contradictions. The most tempting one is to be found in her equivocal marital state, which since she had become famous, was painfully conspicuous. 'I never can think of her position without positive pain', Blackwood told Langford.[2] Barbara Bodichon's friend Mrs. Benjamin Brodie suggested that Lewes might obtain a divorce abroad tnat would enable him to regularize their union. A barrister, 'very accomplished in foreign and English law', whom he consulted, Marian wrote,

pronounces it *impossible*. I am not sorry. I think the boys will not suffer, and for myself I prefer excommunication. I have no earthly thing that I care for, to gain by being brought within the pale of people's personal attention, and I have many things to care for that I should lose—my freedom from petty worldly torments, commonly called pleasures, and that isolation which really keeps my charity warm instead of chilling it, as much contact with frivolous women would do.[3]

None the less, she smarted under the injustice of a society that ostracized her as a violator of the marriage tie while regarding the impenitent Agnes as a blameless abandoned wife.

Marian's intense sadness at this period appears most clearly in the portrait that Samuel Laurence drew of her in 1860. He was an old friend of Lewes. His wife, Anastasia Gliddon, was a cousin of Mrs. Thornton Hunt, and in the 1840s the Hunts and Laurences had shared the big house in the Queen's Road, Bayswater, with her parents the Arthur Gliddons. On 4 March 1860 Laurence came to lunch with the Leweses at Wandsworth and asked if he could take George Eliot's portrait—'because he felt he *could*', Lewes wrote

[1] *Letters*, III. 376.
[2] J. Blackwood to J. Langford, 6 Feb. 1861 (NLS).
[3] *Letters*, III. 366-7.

to Blackwood.[1] She was in the midst of the final book of *The Mill on the Floss* and preparing to leave soon for Italy, so there was no time for the six sittings he required. But in August he set to work. 'He is a very interesting man', George Eliot told Sara Hennell, '—with plenty of sadness in his life, like the rest of us.'[2] In her Journal she noted that she was feeling 'much depressed just now with self-dissatisfaction and fear that I may not be able to do anything more that is well worth doing'.[3] Laurence caught that mood in this finest portrait of George Eliot. Her oval face is framed in loosely waving hair, parted in the middle, the cameo at her throat repeating the form unobtrusively. The nose is very long and narrow, the chin strongly cleft; the eyelids are heavy, the eyes, observant, pensive, sad. The full, well-formed lips reveal the powerful sensual element noted by those who knew her intimately, and something of the 'cold, subtle, and unconscious cruelty of expression which might occasionally be detected there'.[4] The pervading melancholy is lightened by no hint of the quick animation and rich humour that she usually showed. Lewes had promised Blackwood that, if the portrait turned out well, he might have a copy of it. But when it was finished Lewes was dissatisfied (perhaps because it was too revealing?) and refused to accept it or to let Laurence exhibit it anywhere outside his own studio. Blackwood, who had noticed that pensive, sad look in George Eliot the first time he met her, thought it a good portrait. When he asked Laurence for a copy, he was told that he might have the original. It hung in the back parlour of Blackwood's office at 45 George Street until 1914.[5] It is reproduced in the frontispiece.

The sadness that Laurence saw in George Eliot is also reflected in her writing at this time. If money can be considered an index of success, she had no reason to doubt her achievement. *The Mill on the Floss*, as Blackwood predicted, had proved 'a little fortune to her'. In her Journal, 28 November 1860, Marian wrote: 'I have invested £2000 in East Indies Stock, and expect shortly to invest another £2000, so that with my other money, we have enough in any case to keep us from beggary.' Lewes had it put into shares in the Great Indian Peninsular Railway, which paid 5 per cent interest.

---

[1] *Letters*, III. 328.   [2] *Letters*, III. 329.   [3] GE Journal, 28 Aug. 1860.
[4] Mathilde Blind, *George Eliot* (1883), p. 208.
[5] Its present whereabouts is unknown. GE gave Laurence nine sittings in Aug. 1860. A preliminary sketch, signed by Laurence and dated 1857 (three years before he met GE), was given to Girton College by M. Llewelyn Davies in 1923. See Plate IX.

Money plays an important part in a story she wrote at Holly Lodge in the summer of 1860, which was first called 'Mr. David Faux, Confectioner', later 'The Idiot Brother', and was finally published in the *Cornhill Magazine* in 1864 as 'Brother Jacob'.[1] It is unique among George Eliot's works in its complete lack of sympathy for any of the characters, even the idiot. It is told in a bantering, cynical style as 'an admirable instance of the unexpected forms in which the great Nemesis hides herself'. The frivolous names she uses suggest the allegorical nature of the tale. The scene of it is the town of Grimworth, the actors are David Faux (alias Edward Freely), Penny Palfrey, and John Towers, while minor figures are called Sally Lunn, Zephaniah Crypt, Mr. Prettyman, Mr. Fullilove, and so on. David's theft of his mother's little hoard of golden guineas and his ultimate exposure as a social hypocrite are the two significant elements of the plot. Both theft and exposure recur in *Silas Marner*, which George Eliot began to write immediately after 'Brother Jacob'. Her often-quoted statement that the idea of that book 'thrust itself between me and the other book I was meditating', has allowed her earlier treatment of these themes to pass unnoticed.

Silas Marner has no trace of the cold sarcasm of 'Brother Jacob'; its characters are vivid, living people, not puppets constructed to act out the workings of Nemesis. In telling Blackwood of her plan for a story about Savonarola, George Eliot said that first she wanted to write another English story to be published when the Italian one was advanced far enough to begin publication in *Maga* without her name, so that it might escape some of the criticism that greets a writer 'when he does something other than what was expected of him'.[2] The move to Harewood Square delayed *Silas Marner*; only sixty-two pages were written by the end of November. But in Blandford Square it advanced steadily. On 15 February the first thirteen chapters were sent to Blackwood, who read it with admiration. Grieving over his brother William, who was suffering from an incurable illness, Blackwood found the first hundred pages of the story

very sad, almost oppressive, but relieved by the most exquisite touches of nature and natural feelings hit off in the fewest and most happily chosen words. I wish the picture had been a more cheery one and embraced higher specimens of humanity, but you paint so naturally that

[1] MS: Yale.   [2] *Letters*, III. 339.

PLATE IX

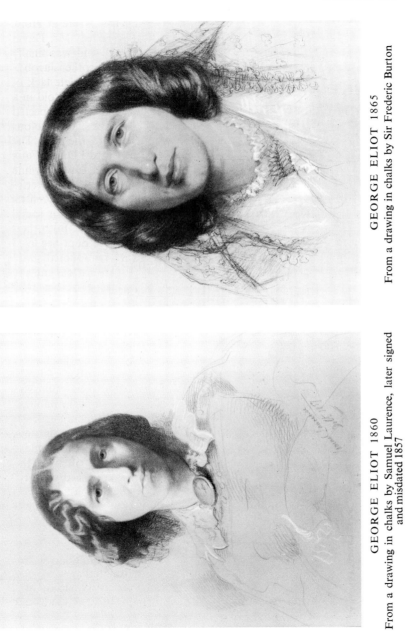

GEORGE ELIOT 1865

From a drawing in chalks by Sir Frederic Burton

GEORGE ELIOT 1860

From a drawing in chalks by Samuel Laurence, later signed and misdated 1857

in your hands the veriest earthworms become the most interesting perfect studies in fact.

After his usual praise of characters and scenes, Blackwood returned to his first objection, 'the want of brighter lights and some characters of whom one can think with pleasure as fellow creatures', but he ended by congratulating her upon her 'unfailing powers, which seem as inexhaustible as ever'.[1] In her reply, 24 February 1861, George Eliot wrote:

I don't wonder at your finding my story, as far as you have read it, rather sombre: indeed, I should not have believed that any one would have been interested in it but myself (since William Wordsworth is dead) if Mr. Lewes had not been strongly arrested by it. But I hope you will not find it at all a sad story, as a whole, since it sets—or is intended to set—in a strong light the remedial influences of pure, natural human relations. The Nemesis is a very mild one. I have felt all through as if the story would have lent itself best to metrical rather than prose fiction, especially in all that relates to the psychology of Silas; except that, under that treatment, there could not be an equal play of humour. It came to me first of all, quite suddenly, as a sort of legendary tale, suggested by my recollection of having once, in early childhood, seen a linen-weaver with a bag on his back; but, as my mind dwelt on the subject, I became inclined to a more realistic treatment.[2]

It was agreed that the story would go easily into one volume selling at 12s.; for an edition of 4,000 copies Blackwood offered her £800—a royalty of 33 per cent—with the same rate for any further copies sold. 'It is a relief to try to think upon your book or anything', he added, 'as sorrow is pressing hard upon us here. My dear brother's state leaves little or no hope.'[3] On 4 March she sent the manuscript of the next five chapters—through p. 308 —'the end of the fourth act', and the motto from Wordsworth's 'Michael'. The final pages went off on 10 March. The printers worked with marvellous speed. They had assured Blackwood, 'Oh, we'll blaw it out like a bottle',[4] and were as good as their word. On the 18th all the proof had been read and Lewes took Marian off to Hastings, where exactly a week later she received the bound volume. The only presentation copy she ordered was for Mrs. Willim. The subscription totalled 5,500 copies before the book was published on 2 April 1861. The sale of the 12s. edition reached 8,000 copies, and with reprint rights and translations, *Silas Marner* brought her £1,760 in 1861.

[1] *Letters*, III. 379–80. [2] *Letters*, III. 382.
[3] *Letters*, III. 384. [4] *Letters*, III. 383.

The Leweses stayed a week at Hastings. 'I feel already a new creature with a day's draught of sea-air', Marian wrote to Blackwood. They strolled along the beach looking for zoological specimens without much success and took long walks over the cliffs and through the meadows, 'talking of the Italian Romance Polly is contemplating'.[1] In the evenings they read aloud Volume V of Macaulay's *History of England*, just published, and sometimes strolled about in the moonlight after tea. One day they walked to St. Leonard's, where after listening to the band they

> went up to Polly's old lodgings and saw the old German, a Weimaraner who remembered Goethe and Schiller, both of whom were kind to him as a boy. He told us how frightened he once was on going into Schiller's room and finding him (as he thought) dead upon the floor. Schiller used to take opium—and sometimes took too much![2]

They returned to Blandford Square on 26 March.

Soon the reviews of *Silas Marner* began to come in. Lewes showed few of them to Marian, though almost all were favourable. One Scottish Freekirk newspaper discovered from the story 'that George Eliot has much of the Roundhead in her—the union of religious fervor with clear, calm insight and good sense. A queer notion, not without a sort of plausibility', Lewes remarked in his Journal.[3] *The Times* gave it a long discriminating review. The *Saturday Review* praised its portrayal of humble life, placing George Eliot above Scott, Bulwer Lytton, and Dickens. Of the company at the Rainbow the reviewer said: 'We know that these poor are like real poor people, just as we know that the characters in Shakspeare are like real men and women. The humour of the author, of course, pervades the representation, just as it does in the comic parts of Shakspeare.'[4] Huxley spoke to Lewes in the highest terms of *Silas* as 'a book to do great *good* to people',[5] and Henry Crabb Robinson, now converted to admiration, called it in his Diary 'an admirable novel, perhaps George Eliot's best'.[6]

The death of Major William Blackwood on 8 April prevented John from sharing fully the satisfaction in the success of *Silas Marner*. But he was soon writing to George Eliot again, reporting that Mudie had brought his purchases of the story to 3,000 and hoping that she would send him news of the progress of *Romola* during her second visit to Italy.

---

[1] GHL Journal, 24 Mar. 1861.   [2] GHL Journal, 22 Mar. 1861.
[3] GHL Journal, 4 Apr. 1861.   [4] *Saturday Review*, 13 Apr. 1861, 369–70.
[5] GHL Journal, 18 Apr. 1861.
[6] Henry Crabb Robinson, Diary, 19 Apr. 1861 (Dr. Williams's Library).

CHAPTER XI

ROMOLA

❊

GEORGE ELIOT undertook her second Italian journey with 'grave purposes', she told Blackwood.[1] To write convincingly about fifteenth-century Florence she needed more detailed knowledge than she had gathered during her two weeks there in 1860. She intended to return and immerse herself in the history and atmosphere of Florence, hoping that a story would grow around the events of Savonarola's life. She set out with George on 19 April 1861—the day after his forty-fourth birthday—leaving the dependable young Charles Lewes in Blandford Square with Mrs. Bell to look after him. At Paris they paused for a day, glancing at the pictures in the Luxembourg, visiting the tomb of Abelard and Héloïse in Père Lachaise, and buying Charles de Brosses's *Lettres sur l'Italie* to read on the way. After a good dinner at the Café Anglais they boarded the night train for Avignon, paying an extra 20 francs for the coupé.

Besides the Cathedral at Avignon, Marian wanted especially to see the handsome tomb that John Stuart Mill had erected to his wife, who died there in 1858, 'the whole surface of which is too small for the overflowing of his tender praises'.[2] The railway line then ended at Toulon. There Lewes persuaded Polly to let him hire a private carriage to take them to Nice. They had never travelled in such luxury. The weather was delicious. They could get down whenever they liked to walk a little among the orange trees and enjoy the views. The contrast in their comments is interesting. Lewes was struck by the orange trees 'bearing their golden fruit', the palms, and the grand clouds, 'which gave a fine sombre effect to the scene, the mountains in the drear distance looking very phantasmal'. Marian saw 'Everywhere a delicious plain covered with bright green corn, sprouting vines, mulberry trees, olives, and here and there meadows sprinkled with buttercups',[3] a comment

---

[1] *Letters*, III. 393.   [2] GHL Journal, 21 Apr. 1861.
[3] GHL Journal, 24 Apr. 1861; *Letters*, III. 408.

to remind one of the little wench standing between Robert Evans's knees as they drove through the Midlands. At Nice, where they stayed two nights, they saw a play called *Le Père Prodigue*, which Lewes in his Journal pronounced 'prodige-ux! Certainly any amount of prudery is better than the licence of French literature. We left after the end of the third act, disgusted with the audience for not rising to protest against such desecration of honest feelings.'[1] He arranged with a vetturino to take them in his 'new and elegant' carriage from Nice to Genoa and, if they were content, on to Pisa for 22 napoleons. They took four days along the Grande Corniche to Genoa. There they rested for two days, rambled about the town, read in the Doria gardens, or just sat in the sunshine watching the lizards darting about or the ships lying in the bay. Before leaving Genoa Lewes bought Varchi's *Storia Fiorentina*[2] and an unnamed Italian novel about Savonarola, of which no more is heard. Travelling again by easy stages, they reached Pisa on 4 May. For several days Polly had been ailing with a slight cold, and she was sick twice during their last morning's drive. But the sight of Pisa 'roused her a little, and after some bouillon she was well enough to set forth and enjoy for the third time this marvellous Cathedral, Campo Santo, Baptistry, and Campanile'. They boarded a train once more and were in Florence before 7 o'clock, settled at the Hôtel de l'Europe.

Marian's cold soon developed into an unpleasant case of *grippe* with headache and fever that continued through her first week in Florence. Even wood fires could not dispel the chill, and Lewes, one morning, after ineffectually walking her up and down the salon, 'danced with Polly to warm her feet'.[3] But soon he too was down with sore throat, fever, and sickness, and Polly was applying wet towels to relieve his raging headache. Nevertheless, the next day they both strolled out to study the cloister of Santa Maria Novella, and then went to 'feast our eyes on Giotto's tower and the Cathedral'. At the bookstalls in the Piazza Gran Duce, Lewes bought Charlotte M. Yonge's *The Daisy Chain*, which Anthony Trollope had warmly recommended, for Marian to read aloud in the evenings. Unfortunately, no comment about it has been recorded.

They spent five days in the Maglibecchian Library looking through old books and manuscripts. 'It is a delightful library to

[1] GHL Journal, 25 Apr. 1861.
[2] 1 May 1861. This copy (3 vols., 1852) is now in Dr. Williams's Library.
[3] GHL Journal, 5 May 1861.

study in', Lewes wrote, 'and the books are brought rapidly and without trouble.'[1] Here Marian copied into her Notebook[2] information about the Florence of Savonarola's day—costume, language, etymologies of names, descriptions of fairs and ceremonies, jesters, barbers, matchmakers, street lighting, bonfires, games, the making and marketing of woollen cloth. Twice after leaving the Library they went out near the Porto San Niccolo to see a silk weaver, who showed them her loom in operation and told a sad tale of the pitifully meagre income it brought her. 'Gave her a day's earnings and departed rather sorrowful', Lewes noted in his Journal.[3] He too copied out details for Marian; his Travel Notebook contains several pencil sketches of costumes with notes about them. He rendered a more vital service in visiting again the parts of the San Marco monastery to which women were not then admitted: 'From refectory a spiral staircase leads to ⟨room⟩ cells —a few paces from the top to the right is the other staircase opposite which the Annunciation.' After carefully locating several of the Fra Angelico frescoes, he added: 'The corridor leads to another on the right at the end of which a chapel *not* then existing. This leads to two cells, one salle d'audience; next Savonarola's cell 5 paces long 4 broad.'[4]

During their month at Florence the Leweses saw few acquaintances. Mrs. Benham Hay, an English painter who had lived there for some years, called on them. They had met her first at the Tom Trollopes' in 1860. Tom was out of town when the Leweses arrived in Florence, but they saw his wife and his daughter Bice a number of times. There was always an interesting company at the Villino Trollope—four or five English and Italians—sitting about in the cool loggia, smoking, drinking lemonade, and talking about the latest fad, spirit rapping, which Lewes discussed with his usual scepticism. One of the company was Colonel J. W. Peard, 'Garibaldi's Englishman', who commanded the English legion in the advance on Naples, a gigantic athlete with a 'fine massive energetic head' and a 'huge iron-grey beard'. He had been pointed out to Lewes at the hotel in Genoa. He stood towering over them as they talked on the balcony during the celebration of Italian liberation, 2 June. Another friend of the Trollopes, Signor Tibaldi,

[1] GHL Journal, 15 May 1861. Slips for books they consulted are reproduced in *Romola*, ed. Guido Biagi (2 vols., 1906), I, facing pp. xxxii–xxxiii.
[2] British Museum: Add. 40768.   [3] GHL Journal, 21 May 1861.
[4] GHL Travel Journal, pp. 38–9 (Yale). GE did not see the interior till 24 Apr. 1869.

gave them tickets to a great ceremony in memory of the Tuscan heroes of 1848 held in Santa Croce, 29 May. The church was hung with draperies, and all the altars were ablaze with lights. In the centre stood a grand catafalque with a figure of a crowned angel before it. The aisles were lined with troops, and when the military band struck up the dead march, the effect was profoundly moving. After the mass, Padre Angelico, a little blind priest, mounted the pulpit and gave an impassioned sermon on the theme of a free and united Italy. George Eliot recalled his tense emotion when describing Savonarola's sermon.[1]

Tom Trollope, who had been in England, returned later that day, called at once, and persuaded them to stay a little longer to go and see the monasteries at Camaldoli and La Vernia. Lewes's Journal, 3–6 June 1861, contains the fullest account of the expedition:

Monday 3 June. At 7 this morning Trollope came, as agreed on, with the carriage and we started for Prato Vecchio which we reached at 2. On the way one of the horses fell and cut his head severely. At first we thought him dead; it was with some difficulty he was got up again.—At Prato we ordered some coffee, and with the cold food we brought with us, had a tolerable luncheon. At 3 we started for *Camaldoli.* Polly mounted on a well trained poney which also carried the portmanteau. I occasionally took her place, and thus alternately walking and riding, we got to Camaldoli about ½ 6. The views were lovely; and when after crossing a space of arid hills—like a vast mud sea hardened into rock —we came upon the delicious valley of Camaldoli which was seen in the tender evening light we felt it worth any amount of fatigue.

We were received by a very handsome, graceful young friar (Cistercian order) who attended on us till the Padre Foresteraio came. He brought us wine and cold water, and said we should dine at sunset. As my throat was still bad and cough troublesome, they sent for their Padre Speziale, a thin, active, lively old man of nearly seventy—quite like a comedy apothecary—who with great volubility and benevolence first gave us a Lecture on the Cause of Cough and its Cure (sounding as if fresh from Hippocrates) and then departed to prepare me a calming potion. Which turned out very agreeable and very efficient. At supper (an excellent one) the Padre Foresteraio, a stout genial man over fifty sat by us and chatted. His delight when Trollope gave him a prime cigar was worth witnessing! T. slept in the monastery; and it was arranged that I might sleep with Polly in the cowhouse where the ladies are sent to sleep. This was about a mile higher up the hill, and we went there accompanied by a boy and his lantern. Capital beds; perfect cleanliness.

Tuesday 4th. Up at 6. From our windows the prospect was enchanting —made one long to live in the peaceful valley. Walked to the Foresteria

[1] *Romola*, ch. 24.

and breakfasted. We there saw the Padre Superiore—an elegant and intellectual man, also very handsome and full of the most suave courtesy. They took us with pride to see their saw mill, and we then started for the *Sacro Eremo*: an ascent of about 1½ hours, through delicious wood of firs, and beeches. Polly had to remain outside looking down the valley while T. and I went over the monastery, and saw the separate houses, each with its four rooms and little garden. The monks only dine together 13 times a year, and are allowed to speak 3 days in the week. We looked over their good Library. The Padre, hearing that a Signora was outside, instantly got his straw hat and came out to see her and conduct her to an elevated point from which she might *see* the monastery. He was very gallant. He seemed perfectly healthy and very happy. He said there was 'no remorse there as is in the world'. We then walked (I rode) along the hilltops to the *Casotto* having exquisite views all the way, through woods of pine, beech, and chesnut,—one whole mountain side covered with asphodels—and descended once more to the Foresteria where we dined well. The Padre who followed us about like a dog again enjoyed his cigar with us, and then took T. and me over the monastery. Looked over the strangers book, Wordsworth,[1] and Sismondi among the names inscribed. The usual amount of folly and egotism from unknown noodles. At ½ past 3 we started for *Bibbiena* which we reached at 7. En route Polly's horse fell on the edge of a precipice, but she was neither hurt nor shaken. I who saw her fall felt very sick and faint from the shock.

Wednesday 5 June. Up at ½ 6 and after breakfasted walked (as before) to La Vernia. Quite different landscape. The heat was intense and the fatigue at last overpowering. While waiting to be admitted we cautiously drank and washed our mouths out at the well. At last the padre (Franciscan order) appeared. Very civil and prevenant, but the Franciscans are quite another guess kind of friars, much lower in type, taken from the poorest classes. After a good dinner we went over the monastery and saw the marvels. Then reposed awhile and chatted (N.B. all the journey we have had fine talk with Trollope, who is a most loveable creature) till we thought ourselves able to ramble among the rocks and pines of this lovely place. This fairly knocked me up. My pulses fluttered so with fatigue I could scarcely get along. After coffee Polly rode down to her sleeping place and T. and I talked enthusiastically about her over our cigars. We slept in the monastery. Beds very rough—but weariness will snore upon a flint—and we were weary.

Thursday 6 June. Up at 6. Dismayed to find a pelting rain, with no prospect of cessation, and a three hours walk before us, with no 'change'! After breakfast and adieu to the monks we descended the

---

[1] Wordsworth wrote: 'Inglese—grateful for the hospitable attention of these benevolent monks and pleased with that courtesy which from the severity of their order might not have been expected. 1837 May 29th.' GHL Travel Journal.

steeps of La Vernia, and called for Polly who was still in bed, thinking we should not start such weather. While she dressed and breakfasted we stayed warming and drying ourselves by kitchen fire. Then began our descent to Bibbiena through mud and clouds—rain fine but steady. About halfway down the rain abated; and we reached Bibbiena without much damage. After a second breakfast we started in the carriage for Pontassieve, through rain and mist, and then through the most furious winds. Dined there and home to Florence by the evening lights. Bed at once.

The next morning they packed up and prepared to leave Florence. Calling on the Trollopes to say goodbye, they heard the sad news of Cavour's death—a great blow to Italian hopes, in which they all shared. Little Bice sang to them for the last time, and they parted from her parents with sincere regret. Trollope, who had lived in Italy since 1843, had just finished his first novel, *La Beata. A Tuscan Romeo and Juliet* (2 vols., 1861), a copy of which he presented to Marian, and was deep in his *History of Florence* (4 vols., 1865). He was an excellent authority for her to appeal to on questions about her novel.

They left for Genoa on their way to Hofwyl to see Bertie. The route lay by rail and boat and carriage, along Lake Maggiore, over the St. Gotthard pass amid rain and snow, the whole length of Lake Lucerne, and on to Berne, which they reached at mid-morning on 11 June. Lewes went off to Hofwyl and brought Bertie back in the afternoon. 'The dear boy is improved', Marian noted.[1] They took him about the town, had ices on the Platform as usual, and tea at the Bernerhof, where he spent the night with them. He was rather shy with his 'parents', but in the evening they had a long talk in which he 'came out'.[2] Next morning after breakfast they all walked by the river and then at 9.30 took leave of him and started for Paris. They were back in Blandford Square on 14 June. In her Journal of the stay in Florence, Marian counted 'thirty-four days of precious time spent there. Will it be all in vain? . . . I am in excellent health, and long to work steadily and effectively. If it were possible that I should produce *better* work than I have yet done! At least there is a possibility that I may make greater efforts against indolence and the despondency that comes from too egoistic a dread of failure.'[1]

Blackwood, who had been waiting in London for her return,

---

[1] GE Journal, 19 June 1861.   [2] GHL Journal, 11 June 1861.

came to lunch the next day and talked about her book. He wrote to Mrs. Blackwood:

Her great difficulty seems to be that she, as she describes it, hears her characters talking, and there is a weight upon her mind as if Savonarola and friends ought to be speaking Italian instead of English. Her description of how she realised her characters was very marvellous. I never heard anything so good as her distinction between what is called the real and the imaginative. It amounted to this, That you could not have the former without the latter and greater quality. Any real observation of life and character must be limited, and the imagination must fill in and give life to the picture. 'Silas Marner' sprang from her childish recollection of a man with a stoop and expression of face that led her to think that he was an alien from his fellows. The dialect of Lisbeth in 'Adam Bede' arose from her occasionally hearing her father when with his brothers revert to the dialect of his native district, Derbyshire. She could not tell how the feeling and knowledge came to her, but when Lisbeth was speaking she felt it was a real language which she heard. Lewes and she are going to dine with me one day at Greenwich.[1]

Blackwood's dinner party at Greenwich, 17 June 1861, was an attempt to counteract the paralysing diffidence of his firm's most valuable author. Returning from Florence, Marian had resolved to go nowhere for the rest of the year, but she made an exception for him. No other ladies were present.

He drove us there with Colonel Stewart, and we had a pleasant evening —the sight of a game of Golf in the Park, and a hazy view of the distant shipping with the Hospital finely broken by trees in the foreground. At dinner Colonel Hamley and Mr. [Moncrieff] Skene joined us: Delane who had been invited, was unable to come. The chat was agreeable enough, but the sight of the gliding ships darkening against the dying sunlight made me feel chat rather importunate. I think, when I give a white bait dinner I will invite no one but my second self, and we will agree not to talk audibly.[2]

The gentlemen have left no comment on the evening; it was probably rather heavy going on both sides.

George Eliot settled at once into the prolonged study for the background of her novel. Her Journal is peppered with the names of old authors, her notebooks filled with carefully copied extracts. She read Gibbon and Hallam and Michelet for accounts of the Middle Ages and the Revival of Learning; Montalembert, and Mrs. Jameson, and Helyot for the history of the monastic orders.

---

[1] *Letters*, III. 427. [2] *Letters*, III. 427–8.

She pored over books on the topography and history of Florence
—Nardi, Varchi, Sismondi, Nerli, Litta, Ammirato, Villani, and
especially, Lastri's *L'Osservatore Fiorentino*, which she indexed
in her Notebook.[1] The biographies of Savonarola by Burla-
macchi and Villari she used of course, and those of the Medici
by Roscoe, and the lives of the painters by Vasari. Not content
with histories of Italian literature like Tiraboschi's and Manni's,
she read widely in the original works—Sacchetti, Boccaccio, Fil-
elfo, Politian, Machiavelli, Petrarch, Marullo, Pulci, and many
others. Langford brought her *Le moyen âge illustré*, in which she
studied details of costume. Lewes described her to Blackwood as
'buried in old quartos and vellum bound literature which I would
rather *not* read; but she extracts nutriment, I have no doubt'.[2]
She herself sometimes hunted in the second-hand book shops for
scarce works. Her Journal for 8 December 1861 says: 'In the
Afternoon walked to Molini's and brought back Savonarola's
Dialogue de Veritate Prophetica and Compendium Revelationum,
for £4!' From Cambridge Lewes's friend W. G. Clark sent her
scarce books on the condition of Greece in the Middle Ages, and
she consulted others in the London Library. She went to the British
Museum to verify particulars about Lorenzo de' Medici's death,
the possible retardation of Easter, the celebration of Corpus
Christi, and Savonarola's preaching in the Quaresima of 1492.
On another visit she 'picked some details from Manni's life of
Bartolommeo Scala—also from Borghini's Discorsi, about the
simplicity of Florentine table equipage'.[3] She looked at prints in
the Print Room.[4] One day her Journal notes: 'Busied myself with
a plan of rational mnemonics in history.'[5]

From her immersion in all these primary materials George Eliot
hoped that a story would somehow emerge. She dwelt constantly
'with much depression on the probability or improbability of my
achieving the work I wish to do', and her thoughts kept turning
to an English novel instead. One day she 'Got into a state of so
much wretchedness in attempting to concentrate my thoughts on
the construction of my story that I became desperate, and suddenly
burst my bonds, saying, I will not think of writing'![6] Her headaches were acute and frequent. George did his best to hearten her.
Every day as they walked in Regent's Park, often to the Zoological

---

[1] GE's copy of Lastri (16 vols. in 5, Firenze, 1831) is at Yale.
[2] *Letters*, III. 430.   [3] GE Journal, 26 Jan., 19 Feb., 1862.
[4] GHL Journal, 17 May 1862.   [5] GE Journal, 7 July 1861.
[6] GE Journal, 30 July, 12 Aug. 1861.

Gardens, they would talk about her book. In the course of one of
these conversations she wrote, 'I struck out an idea with which
he was thoroughly satisfied as a "backbone" for the work', and
a few days later she felt that she 'conceived the plot of my novel
with new distinctness'.[1] Lewes reported 20 August 1861 that it was
'slowly crystallizing into what will be a magnificent programme.
Until quite lately I thought she would relinquish altogether in
despair, her singular diffidence being exaggerated in this case.
But now I think it will really be written. If only I could see the
first chapter!'[2] Despite all his efforts it was not begun. By the end
of the month she was 'Utterly despondent about my book', 'trying
to write, trying to construct, and unable', 'brooding, producing
little', 'Dreadfully depressed about myself and my work', 'So
utterly dejected that in walking with G. in the Park, I almost
resolved to give up my Italian novel.' Ideas for the English novel
kept intruding. Then, while walking again with George in the
Park, 'the Italian scenes returned upon me with fresh attraction'.
On 8 December she 'told him my conception of my story, and he
expressed great delight. Shall I ever be able to carry out my ideas?
Flashes of hope are succeeded by long intervals of dim mistrust.'
A few days later she wrote out a scheme of the plot, 'of which
I must make several other draughts before I begin to write my
book'.[3]

Since none of these sketches has been found, we can only speculate about the plan that tormented her for so long. We do not
even know what she intended to call the book. In her Journal and
letters it is referred to only as 'my novel' or 'my Italian story'.
The heroine's name is not mentioned until 1 January 1862, when
George Eliot noted, 'I began my Novel of Romola.' No one seems
to have commented on the origin of the name. Romola is not a
Christian but a place name. South-west of Florence towards
Certosa there is a little hamlet on a hill called Romola, which
appears in a list of nine mountains that Lewes scribbled down for
her in his Travel Notebook.[4] That she was to be of the Bardi
family was probably determined before the Leweses left Florence.
Twice at the Magliabecchian Library they consulted *Marietta de'*
Ricci (6 vols., Florence, 1845), a long historical novel by Agostino
Ademollo, to the second edition of which Luigi Passerini had

[1] GE Journal, 15–20 Aug. 1861.   [2] *Letters*, III. 446.
[3] GE Journal, 28 Oct., 6, 10 Nov., 11–12 Dec. 1861.
[4] Travel Notebook, p. 121.

appended elaborate learned notes. In Lastri's *Osservatore Fiorentino* there is found a good deal about the power and wealth
of the Bardi and their interest in international trade, to which
George Eliot alludes in Chapter 5 of *Romola*. Lastri tells the story
of a Florentine Romeo and Juliet based on the Bardi's feud with
the Buondelmonte family,[1] which George Eliot may have considered using. At the feast of John the Baptist, Ippolito Buondelmonte saw Dianora de' Bardi going into church and fell madly
in love with her. Their meetings in her room were achieved with
a rope ladder, which eventually caused the discovery and arrest
of poor Ippolito; he was led to his execution past the house of the
Bardi, from the window of which his disconsolate Dianora was
watching. From Lastri, George Eliot also took some information
about the shop of Burchiello, the barber-poet,[2] for her Nello, and
the unusual spelling of Baldassarre, which she found in Lastri's
account of the quondam Pope John XXIII, Baldassarre Coscia,
who died at Florence in 1419 and was buried in the Baptistry
beneath a splendid monument by Donatello.[3]

For her Baldassarre's relations with his ungrateful adopted son
Tito, however, George Eliot had a quite different source. One
evening in the winter of 1855 at Fräulein Solmar's in Berlin old
General Pfuhl told her a story of 'noble vengeance', which impressed her so much that she wrote it down in her Journal and
later (with slight variation) in her Commonplace Book.[4]

Edle Rache. A man of wealth in Rome adopted a poor boy he had
found in the street. This boy turned out a great villain and having previously entered the church managed by a series of arts to possess himself
of a legal title to his benefactor's property, and finally ordered him to
quit his own house, telling him he was no longer master. The outraged
man killed the villain on the spot. He was imprisoned, tried, and condemned for the murder. When in prison he refused to have a confessor.
He said, 'I wish to go to Hell, for *he* is there, and I want to follow out
my revenge.'

This may well have been the element of plot that Lewes pronounced adequate as a 'backbone' for Marian's novel. She told
Sara Hennell that Romola's 'Drifting Away' and the village with
the plague 'belonged to my earliest vision of the story and were by
deliberate forecast adopted as romantic and symbolical elements'.[5]

¹ Lastri, *Osservatore Fiorentino*, XIV. 81–5.
² *Osservatore Fiorentino*, VII. 8–17.   ³ *Osservatore Fiorentino*, VI, 10–15.
⁴ The story is found in the Journal at the end of the 'Recollections of Weimar';
in the Commonplace Book, No. 48. This is the latter.
⁵ Chs. 61, 68. *Letters*, IV. 104.

In the summer of 1861 while labouring to devise her plot, George Eliot 'ran through' Bulwer Lytton's *Rienzi*, 'wishing to examine his treatment of an historical subject', and reread one of her earliest favourites, Scott's *The Pirate*.[1] Years before, in the *Westminster Review* Lewes had glibly declared that in order to write a romance one 'needs only to study Scott and the historical novelists; to "cram" for the necessary information about costumes, antiquated forms of speech, and the leading political events of the epoch chosen'.[2] He may have regretted this easy formula as he watched Marian grubbing through collections of Tuscan proverbs to cull archaic colloquial phrases and to discover precisely what kind of cloth 'the *sajo*, or tunic' was made of, how 'the purse, or *scarcella*' was worn, and where 'the *deschi*, or stalls' were placed in the old Market. He reported to Blackwood that she was 'buried in musty old antiquities, which she will have to vivify. I am a sort of Italian Jackal, hunting up rare books and vellum bound unreadabilities in all the second hand book stalls of London.'[3] Bulwer Lytton had warned against dangers that he himself had not avoided; in his Preface to *The Last Days of Pompeii* (1834) he wrote: 'To impart anything like fidelity to the dialogues of classic actors, we must beware (to use a university phrase) how we "cram" for the occasion! Nothing can give a writer a more stiff and uneasy gait than the sudden and hasty adoption of the toga.' He blamed the biographer of Rienzi for appearing 'more like the historian of Rienzi's clothes, so minute is he on all details of their colour and quality,—so silent is he upon everything that could throw light upon the motives of the wearer.'[4] This was the very root of Marian's despondency. To Blackwood, who was coming to London before Christmas, Lewes wrote:

Polly is still deep in her researches. Your presence will I hope act like a stimulus to her to make her begin. At present she remains immovable in the conviction that she *can't* write the romance because she has not knowledge enough. Now as a matter of fact I know that she has immensely more knowledge of the particular period than any other writer who has touched it; but her distressing diffidence paralyses her.

This between ourselves. When you see her, mind your care is to discountenance the idea of a Romance being the product of an Encyclopædia.[5]

[1] GE Journal, 4, 21 Aug., 17 Nov. 1861.
[2] *WR*, 45 (Jan. 1846), 34.   [3] *Letters*, III. 457.
[4] *Rienzi* (1848), Appendix I.   [5] *Letters*, III. 473–4.

Charming as ever, John Blackwood came to lunch in Blandford Square on 22 December, and returned the next day bringing Mrs. Blackwood, who was introduced to George Eliot for the first time. This little attention must have meant more to her than her bare record of the visit admits. On New Year's Day 1862 Blackwood sent her a letter from Montalembert, author of *The Monks of the West*, filled with enthusiastic praise of *Silas Marner*, and a delightful pug in Dresden china as a memorial of the flesh-and-blood Pug, who had died about a year before. In thanking him George Eliot wrote:

> The year opens with good auguries. I have begun my novel this morning, and now a second Pug is come to be a faithful companion through my life—reminding me always of two things that I care for a good deal —the memory of my poor black-nosed pet, and the kindness of the Friend who gratified my too extravagant desires.
>
> Montalembert's words are very precious to me coming after I have learned to admire his book as I do.
>
> All happiness to you and Mrs. Blackwood in this coming year. I wish I could believe that I shall contribute to it by writing a book you will like to read.[1]

To reassure her of his interest this most assiduous of publishers called again on 2 January and again on the 12th.

Though she had made another start, her progress with *Romola* was painfully slow. On the last day of January she read George some entries from her Journal 'in which I recorded my *malaise* and despair. But it is impossible to me to believe that I have ever been in so unpromising and despairing a state as I now feel.— After writing these words, I read to G. the Proem and opening scene of my novel and he expressed great delight in them.' By 17 February only the first two chapters were finished, for she had been rewriting and adding to them with 'an oppressive sense of the far-stretching task before me, health being feeble just now'.

On 23 January 1862 George Smith had called. He had known Lewes since the 1840s and had enlisted him among the first contributors to the *Cornhill Magazine* in 1860. Lewes's interesting 'Studies in Animal Life' naturally related zoological observations to Darwin's new evolutionary theory, of which he was a strong proponent. Though Smith's firm published all Darwin's books before the *Origin of Species*, he may have been timid about

---

[1] *Letters*, IV. 3.

parading such controversial matter in a popular magazine. Whatever the reason, the 'Studies' were discontinued after six numbers. Now Smith wanted to start a new series, which Lewes, 'disgusted with his behaviour', declined to do. But he could not refuse to reprint in a small volume the papers that had appeared, since his agreement called for it.[1] Marian did not see Smith. But he asked George 'if I were open to "a magnificent offer". This made me think about money—but it is better for me not to be rich.'[2] A month later Smith returned to Blandford Square, bringing the proofs of Lewes's whole book. He had larger game in sight, however. Thackeray's *The Adventures of Philip*, which had started in the January number of the *Cornhill*, was clearly not going to be popular, and Trollope's *Framley Parsonage*, which had been, would conclude in April. Smith needed a new novel by a celebrated novelist to buoy up the declining sale. In the course of their chat, wrote Lewes,

he made a proposal to purchase Polly's new work for £10,000. This of course includes the entire copyright. It is the most magnificent offer ever yet made for a novel; and Polly, as usual was disinclined to accept it, on the ground that her work would not be worth the sum! Moreover she felt it impossible to begin publication in April or May—the period when Smith wishes it to begin to appear in the 'Cornhill Mag.' Unless she sees her book nearly completed and such as she considers worthy of publication she objects to begin printing it. I went down to Smith to tell him of her difficulties. He was much put out, April or May being the months when the Magazine will stand in need of some reinforcement, as Thackeray's story is quite insufficient to keep up the sale. Smith then proposed to print her story of *Brother Jacob*, written in 1860, if it can be split up into three numbers, and thus tide over the three months; and then to commence in August or September with the new work. She has consented to let him see the story to see if this arrangement will do. If not some other proposal will be made by him.[3]

As the first editor of the *Cornhill* Thackeray had never found his duties very congenial; and they absorbed a good deal of time that he should have put into work on his novel. In 1861 Smith bought the serial rights of Harriet Beecher Stowe's *Agnes of Sorrento*, a sentimental historical novel of fifteenth-century Italy and began to run it along with *The Adventures of Philip*. Though it had nothing to do with slavery or the American Civil War, it provided Thackeray, whose sympathies lay strongly with the South, one more reason

[1] GHL Journal, 23 Jan. 1862.   [2] GE Journal, 23 Jan. 1862.
[3] GHL Journal, 27 Feb. 1862.

to consider resigning. Finally, in March 1862, after publishing a
Roundabout Paper entitled 'Half a Loaf', a vigorous attack on the
Yankees, he stepped down from the 'thorn-cushioned chair'.[1]
Soon Smith was knocking again at the door of 16 Blandford
Square, looking for a new editor as well as a new novel for the
Cornhill. Though Lewes refused the post, he agreed that, if Smith
would get a subeditor of whom Lewes approved, he would act
as consulting editor, selecting the articles and suggesting subjects,
but taking no other responsibility. His salary was £600 a year.[2]
Frederick Greenwood was engaged as subeditor.

Smith immediately returned to his efforts to capture *Romola*. First
he had to dispel Lewes's old dream of publishing George Eliot's
novels in parts. Smith drew up for him a plan of weekly sixpenny
numbers with one plate. He called by appointment on 12 May
1862, and Marian read him several chapters 'in order that before
making any proposals he should know the kind of work it was
to be'. Part of her anxiety may have sprung from her knowledge
that the setting of her story would parallel that of *Agnes of Sorrento*, which had just concluded in the May number with the lurid
melodrama of Savonarola's execution. After hearing her, Smith
easily dissuaded them from the notion of parts by saying that he
believed *Romola* 'would not *tell* in small portions. He wishes to
publish it in the "Cornhill Magazine", but in considerable instalments—of 45 or 40 pages each number, with two illustrations.
He is to send a proposal on that basis.'[3] In two days the terms were
settled: £7,000 for publication in twelve monthly parts to begin
in July, the copyright reverting to George Eliot after six years.[4]

Frederic Leighton, who had lived in Florence in boyhood and
knew Italy well, was chosen to draw the illustrations at £20 each.
After calling with Smith to discuss the first plates, he described
George Eliot in a letter to his father:

Miss Evans (or Mrs. Lewes) has a very striking countenance. Her face
is large, her eyes deep set, her nose aquiline, her mouth large, the under
jaw projecting, rather like Charles Quint; her voice and manner are
grave, simple, and gentle. There is a curious mixture in her look; she

[1] See G. N. Ray, *Thackeray. The Age of Wisdom* (1958), pp. 320–1.
[2] GHL Journal, 8 Apr. and 8 May 1862.
[3] GHL Journal, 17 May 1862.
[4] A note by Sir John Murray, 19 Mar. 1902, after George Smith's death gives
the terms: £7,000 for twelve parts to fill 384 pages of the *Cornhill*. Smith, Elder were
to have the copyright including foreign rights for six years, and after that could sell
the stock and reprint the book until 1905 in any one form they determined. They
chose a volume at 2*s*. 6*d*. The £10,000 offer was for the entire copyright.

either is or seems very short-sighted. Lewes is clever. Both were
extremely polite to me; her I shall like much.[1]

George Eliot was now faced with the unpleasant task of inform-
ing her good friend John Blackwood of her desertion. With the
£1,600 from *Silas Marner* his payments to her since their relations
began amounted to £8,330. In the autumn of 1861 he proposed
to purchase the remaining copyright on her four books for £3,000
—a generous offer, which she would have done well to accept.
But after much perturbation Marian decided ('in consequence of
a letter from Bradbury and Evans') to decline.[2] Instead she agreed
to take £60 per thousand for a uniform edition of the novels selling
at 6s., with *Silas Marner* and the *Scenes* in the same volume—the
so-called Cheap Edition. It would be hard to imagine a more considerate publisher than John Blackwood. He saw to it that his
London manager brought books for her researches and sometimes
a box at the Opera. When she voiced the perennial complaint of
authors that her books were not being advertised, he had Simpson,
his clerk at Edinburgh, send her the list, which she confessed was
'a sufficient vindication of his advertising energy, and I am sorry
to have worried him on the subject'.[3] When Simpson came to
London in March 1862, he was sent to call, and 'brought us a
pleasing account of Thornie'. Blackwood himself always called
when he was in town. 'Of course you will be up in May, as usual',
Lewes wrote, 'and we shall then see you.'[4]

But before Blackwood arrived, the thunderbolt fell:

16 Blandford Square
May 19. 1862

My dear Sir

I fear this letter will seem rather abrupt to you but the abruptness is
unavoidable.

Some time ago I received an offer for my next novel which I suppose
was handsomer than almost any terms ever offered to a writer of Fiction.
As long as I hesitated on the subject I contemplated writing to you
to ascertain your views as to the arrangement you would be inclined
to make for the publication of the same work; since I was not willing to
exchange my relations with you for any new ones without overpowering reasons. Ultimately I declined the offer (on various grounds) and
there was therefore no need to write.

[1] Mrs. Russel Barrington, *Life, Letters and Work of Frederic Leighton* (2 vols.,
1906), II. 95. The original drawings were purchased by Philip Hofer, who kindly
gave me a number of them.
[2] GE Journal, 17 Oct. 1861.   [3] *Letters*, IV. 18.   [4] Ibid. 28.

But another offer, removing former objections, has been made, and after further reflection, I felt that, as I was not at liberty to mention the terms to you, and as they were hopelessly beyond your usual estimate of the value of my books to you, there would be an indelicacy in my making an appeal to you before decision. I have consequently accepted the offer, retaining however a power over my copyright at the end of six years so that my new work may then be included in any general edition.

I know quite well from the feeling you have invariably shewn, that if the matter were of more importance to you than it is likely to be, you would enter fully into the views of the case as it concerned my interests as well as your own.

I remain, my dear Sir

Always yours very truly
M. E. Lewes.

John Blackwood Esq.[1]

Blackwood's instant reply shows at its finest the sterling quality of the man:

Edinburgh
May 20/62

My Dear Madam

I am of course sorry that your new Novel is not to come out under the old colours but I am glad to hear that you have made so satisfactory an arrangement.

Hearing of the wild sums that were being offered to writers of much inferior mark to you, I thought it highly probably that offers would be made to you, and I can readily imagine that you are to receive such a a price as I could not make remunerative by any machinery that I could resort to.

Rest assured that I feel fully satisfied of the extreme reluctance with which you would decide upon leaving your old friend for any other publisher, however great the pecuniary consideration might be, and it would destroy my pleasure in business if I knew any friend was publishing with me when he thought he could do better for himself by going elsewhere. We have had several most successful enterprises together and much pleasant correspondence and I hope we shall have much more.

In a few days we go to Derbyshire where we leave the children with their aunts and intend to move on London about the end of next week. I hope therefore to see you soon and trust I shall find you in good health and spirits with your work progressing.

always yours truly
John Blackwood.

Mrs. Lewes.[2]

[1] *Letters*, IV. 34-5.   [2] Ibid. 35-6.

Two days later Langford was startled to receive from Smith, Elder & Co. copy for an advertisement in *Blackwood's*: 'A New Novel by the Author of "Adam Bede" Will Be Commenced in the Next Number of the Cornhill Magazine.' Sending it on to Mr. Blackwood, Langford wrote that 'in the first flirt of temper I thought you should refuse insertion, but it will certainly be more dignified to insert it. I shall have an opportunity of talking over with you this disgusting transaction, which certainly does not surprise me on her part, but does rather on the part of Mr. Smith.'[1] Blackwood replied from Derbyshire:

The conduct of our friends in Blandford Square is certainly not pleasing nor in the long run will they find it wise however great the bribe may have been. It is too bad after all the kindness she has experienced but I am sure she would do it against her inclination. The going over to the enemy without giving me any warning and with a story on which from what they both said I was fully intitled to calculate upon, sticks in my throat but I shall not quarrel—quarrels especially literary ones are vulgar.

In reality I do not care about the defection and it has not disturbed me a bit. From the voracity of Lewes I saw that there would be great difficulty in making the arrangement with them and marchanding or bidding against any one else is a thing I could not stand, so 'let them go'. Besides if the story is the one I suppose, I have no doubt it will be a fine thing but it was doubtful in my mind how far it would bear being given in fragments in the Magazine and certainly it would not suit the readers of the Cornhill. I intended to have decided on the form of publication when I had read the M.S.[1]

Forwarding the advertisement to his nephew William for insertion in *Maga*, Blackwood wrote: 'I am sorry for and disappointed in her but with their extortionate views we could not have made an arrangement so all is for the best. She does not know how strongly her desertion and going over to the enemy will tell upon the public estimate of her character and most justly. Literary quarrels are vulgar and I shall not quarrel but I shall make myself much more effectively understood and felt by not doing so.'

Though neither Lewes nor George Eliot mentions his visit on 17 June, there can be no doubt that Blackwood made himself felt. His interview is described in a letter to William:

Lewes was taken unwell while I was with them yesterday and she accompanied me down stairs to speak. She said that 'under all the circumstances she had felt that she must accept the enormous offer

[1] *Letters*, IV. 38.

that had been made—that she could never feel to another publisher as she felt towards me—that pleasure to her was gone in the matter and she did not feel sure now whether she had acted right'—whether she meant this last as towards me or as wisely regarding herself I could not tell. She also said that she 'hoped another time would arise', apparently meaning that she would then show how strong her feeling was. I did not wish any *confidences* nor in her peculiar circumstances to hit her, so merely looked her full in the face and shaking hands said, 'I'm fully satisfied that it must have been a very sharp pang to you' and came away.[1]

When George Eliot agreed to let the *Cornhill* have *Romola*, she had written only ten chapters of it, enough for the first two parts; only three parts were finished when publication began in July 1862. But by then the story was carefully planned. The writing now proceeded steadily, keeping about two months ahead of its appearance in the magazine. This left ample time for reading proof and consulting about the illustrations. Leighton proved very affable. She was delighted with his designs, which the wood engravings inevitably coarsened and exaggerated. 'He is an invaluable man to have', George Eliot wrote, 'because he knows Florence by heart.'[2] His knowledge was shown in the details of architecture and landscape he put into the plates and the vignette initials that opened each part. As he read proof, looking for subjects, Leighton occasionally queried some word like *ciompi* or some detail of costume that she had studied so scrupulously—the green serge *gamurra* or gown on Monna Ghita, the *berretta* for Tito, or the white hood on Tessa's head. George Eliot would refer him to Varchi or to the engravings of the Ghirlandajo frescoes in support of her choice. When Sara Hennell wrote appreciatively about the opening of the story, Marian warned her not to

make up your mind about anything that is to come, else whatever it is will disappoint you. Of necessity, the book is addressed to fewer readers than my previous works, and I myself have never expected—I might rather say *intended*—that the book should be as 'popular' in the same sense as the others. If one is to have freedom to write out one's own varying unfolding self, and not be a machine always grinding out the same material or spinning the same sort of web, one cannot always write for the same public. I forewarned the proprietor of the Cornhill on that point, read a large portion to him, and made him fully aware what the book was to be—but he is confident and happy—so I am acquitted of all scruple or anxiety except the grand anxiety of doing my

---

[1] *Letters*, IV. 44.   [2] *Letters*, IV. 49.

work worthily. Alas, I want to do something very much better than I ever *can* do it—if fasting and scourging oneself would make one a fit organ, there would be more positive comfort.[1]

She used the same image after the book was finished. When Sara described Romola as 'pure idealism . . . you have painted a goddess, and not a woman', Marian replied: 'You are right in saying that Romola is ideal—I feel it acutely in the reproof my own soul is constantly getting from the image it has made. My own books scourge me.'[2]

Marian's difficulty in the writing of *Romola* was aggravated by her ill health and her dislike for the city. She wrote to Barbara Bodichon, 'The wide sky, the *not*-London, makes a new creature of me in half an hour. I wonder then why I am ever depressed— why I am so shaken by agitations. I come back to London, and again the air is full of demons.'[3] In her own room in Blandford Square the scratch of George's pen no longer distracted her. But for complete concentration she needed the quiet seclusion of the country. From time to time Lewes would carry her away to little villages in Surrey or Sussex. At Englefield Green they found a pleasant lodging at the Barley Mow Inn—where Barbara Bodichon had spent her honeymoon—in beautiful country with delicious walks to Runnymede, Virginia Water, and Windsor Park. One day their landlord Mr. Bone drove them in his pony chaise to see the Queen's staghounds throw off. Another day they saw the foxhounds start: 'a lovely sight it was, the dogs on the hill, the horsemen under the trees grouped about—the bright sun and general joyousness'.[4] Much of Part VI (Chapters 27–32) was written at Littlehampton, where they stayed for three weeks in September. The Beach Hotel was 'luxurious and quiet. The sands are delightful and *with no one on them*', Lewes wrote to Charles. 'There is no variety; but all is so peaceful that the Mutter drinks in enjoyment, and scribbles away in perpetual thanksgiving.' In the evenings Lewes would read Beaumont and Fletcher to her.[5]

Her favourite refuge from London was Dorking, where they went repeatedly to the White Horse Inn or to lodgings in the Parsonage House on Station Road. Lewes left her there in April 1862 to see Charles off for his holiday in Switzerland, and again for nearly a fortnight in April 1863, when he went to Hofwyl

[1] *Letters*, IV. 49.   [2] *Letters*, IV. 103–4.   [3] *Letters*, IV. 102.
[4] GHL Journal, 12 Mar. 1862.   [5] *Letters*, IV. 54.

to see Bertie.[1] Many chapters of *Romola* were written at Dorking.
Cross remembered Marian's telling him how cruelly she had suffered there 'from working under a leaden weight at this time. The
writing of "Romola" ploughed into her more than any of her
other books. She told me she could put her finger on it as marking
a well-defined transition in her life. "I began it a young woman,—
I finished it an old woman."'[2] She told Blackwood in 1877 that
'there is no book of mine about which I more thoroughly feel
that I could swear by every sentence as having been written with
my best blood, such as it is, and with the most ardent care for
veracity of which my nature is capable'.[3]

Marian felt so much better away from London that she would
have liked to live always in the country; yet they had to be in
town to make a home for Charles. 'But he is a dear, precious boy,'
she wrote to Frau von Siebold, 'worth a great deal of sacrifice for
the sake of preserving the purity and beauty of his mind. He is very
tender to us old people and pets us very much.'[4] Though he made
their evenings lively with Beethoven duets on the new Broadwood
grand piano, she looked forward to his Swiss holidays when they
could again enjoy their 'dual solitude'.[5] 'I shall not regret his
absence just now', she admitted to Sara in February 1863, 'because
it will make our quiet more absolute.'[6] At the end of his first year
in the Post Office Charles was passed over in the usual promotions.
Anthony Trollope, inquiring into the cause, wrote Lewes 'a kind,
candid, but painful letter telling me that the boy was not doing
well, was careless, slow, and inefficient', which completely upset
his father and brought on a bilious attack.[7] Charles himself was
unconscious of any slackness, which was probably attributable to
the difference in his education. He was very generally liked by both
his comrades and his superiors, and, once his shortcomings were
explained, there was no further anxiety about him. He was pro-
moted in 1863, became a Second Class Clerk in 1868, and Principal Clerk in 1880.

Thornie was a more difficult problem. He was a bright young-
ster, leading his class during much of his first year at the High
School in Edinburgh. He lived at 1 Duncan Street in the house of
George Robertson, a classics master at the Grange House School,
who had been highly recommended by Dr. Schmitz. The Blackwoods kept a kindly eye on him. Mr. Simpson took him out to the

---

[1] *Letters*, IV. 82.   [2] Cross, II. 352.   [3] *Letters*, VI. 335–6.
[4] *Letters*, III. 449.   [5] *Letters*, III. 460.   [6] *Letters*, IV. 75.
[7] *Letters*, IV. 34.

Pentland Hills for a Sunday, Mrs. Blackwood had him to dinner, and Willie, eight years his senior, helped give him the 'rounding' he needed. In writing to Willie on business George Eliot said: 'Apropos of boys, we are sincerely obliged to you for thinking of Thornie at all, and only hope he will not bore you. Young gentlemen of seventeen have often immense resources for boring their elders.'[1] An exploit which won Willie's hearty admiration is described in Thornie's letter to his father, 22 December 1861:

On Friday night I went to the theatre, having won a shilling from Mrs. R. by a bet. I came out at a quarter to 11, and was home by 10 minutes past. I found the gate and door locked, and nobody opened though I rang four times. I know that Mr. R. was still up as his light was burning.

Thornie jumped over the wall of the garden, climbed into his room through the window, and went to bed. The next day Mr. Robertson said that he had been locked out because he was beyond the hour, and that he would report the matter to his father. Thornie answered:

'So you can!' This put him in an awful rage, so, calling me an insolent dog, he made his shoeleather acquainted with my posterity. You need not ask me what I did; I did what you would have done in my place—knocked him down. (This is what his face is like today [a sketch is inserted], a dark red mark under the eye, 2 spots above the mark, and two bruises on the forehead.)

I of course left the house, as he told me to, and proceeded to Dr. Schmitz's to ask his advice, because I did not think it possible that R. would take me back after flooring him. So I spent the night at the Dr's. In the evening R. came, not knowing that I was there, and Dr. Schmitz showed him so ably how wrong he had been, that he wrote me a full apology, which of course I willingly accepted, and came back here this morning. When he saw me he shook hands and said that he was very sorry for it, but that he hoped it would be buried in oblivion and forgotten, and that we should go on as formerly. And so we are all right again. You will of course not speak about it to him, as it is forgiven and forgotten. . . .

P.S. Charles will no doubt be desirous of knowing whether I got any blows, so you can inform him that I got one on the cheek, which cut it slightly internally. That is all, as Sayers said to Heenan when he split the latter's eye open. Dr. Schmitz said to me after having seen Mr. R., 'Lewes, you have given him a terrible pummelling, he has got a black eye.'

[1] *Letters*, III. 463.

Blackwood recounted Willie's version of 'Caliban's exploit' when he took Mrs. Blackwood to call on George Eliot, 23 December 1861, adding that his brother Archie is in an ecstasy with it and will certainly ask Thornie to his club on the first opportunity.[1]

When this lively, high-spirited Caliban was at home with Charles during his summer holidays, the house resounded with laughter which penetrated even to the room where the Mutter was wrestling with *Romola*. As she had done with Charles, she helped Thornie prepare for the first of his three examinations for the Civil Service. He passed it early in June 1861, and was dispatched to Hofwyl for a month, during which the house resumed its usual state of quiet. In June 1862 he took the examination for the Indian Service. Ranked 38th on a long list, he was summoned home from Hofwyl after only a fortnight to begin grinding at Sanskrit and Indian law. But his final year at Edinburgh he spent less diligently. The passion for taxidermy had given way to the collecting of postage stamps, which he begged the Leweses to send him when they were travelling. With another youth, who was destined to become a noted philatelist,[2] he published *Forged Stamps: How to Detect Them . . . Containing Accurate Descriptions of All Forged Stamps*, 36 pages, Edinburgh, 1863. 'Unknown to us', Marian told D'Albert Durade, 'he had during his last year in Edinburgh contracted a dislike to the thought of going to India and did not work heartily and thoroughly in preparation for the final examination. He failed, and we found that he had expected to fail; and this for a time was a great grief and disappointment to us.'[3] His father wanted Thornie to try once more, but he 'refused to go through the two years' ordeal again. Indeed he refused for a long while to choose any other career, having set his mind on going out to Poland to fight the Russians'.[4] Lewes sent him to Hofwyl to cool down, while he went to Knebworth to consult Bulwer Lytton, a former Secretary of State for the Colonies, about prospects for the lad in Vancouver Island or some other spot.

When Lewes brought Bertie home from Hofwyl in July 1863 to join his brothers, Marian felt 'up to the ears in Boydom and imperious parental duties'.[5] What was to be done with Bertie? Less intelligent than his brothers, he could never have succeeded in the Civil Service or in an English business. Lewes considered openings in Australia or New Zealand, and, after a plan for farm-

---

[1] *Letters*, III. 474. [2] Edward L. Pemberton.
[3] *Letters*, IV. 117. [4] GHL Journal, 22 Aug. 1863. [5] *Letters*, IV. 84.

PLATE X

GEORGE HENRY LEWES 1859

THORNTON ARNOTT LEWES
1863

CHARLES LEE LEWES 1865

ing in Algiers fell through, Bertie was sent to a farmer in Lanark-
shire recommended by Robert Chambers, Jr.[1] At Christmas time
he came home for a week, 'his wits a little sharpened', and improved in many ways, 'his face bright with a new interest in things
and his body getting stalwart as well as graceful'.[2] In lieu of more
intellectual entertainment they played whist with him in the evenings. After two years in Scotland Bertie got further experience on
a farm at Snitterfield, Warwickshire. 'He is a fine fellow physically', Marian wrote, 'and has pleasant social qualities, but he is
not suited to any other life than that of a farmer, and in England
farming has become a business that requires not only great capital
but great skill to render it otherwise than hazardous.'[3]

By January 1863, when she was finishing Part IX of *Romola* it
had become apparent that she could not complete the novel in
twelve instalments. She extended the plan to fourteen, and might
easily have made it into the sixteen instalments for which George
Smith had offered £10,000. In May she made 'a large excision of
matter for the sake of rapidity' in Part XIII,[4] at the end of which,
her Journal records, she 'Killed Tito in great excitement!'[5] The
final chapters were soon written. On 9 June she 'Put the last stroke
to Romola. Ebenezer!' and was borne off to the opera to celebrate.

As the work progressed she had lost a little of her self mistrust.
But she could not rely enough on her imagination to fill in the
picture and give life to it as she did in her English stories; to the
end she persisted in painstaking research to authenticate every
detail of costume, manners, speech, and history. Thomas Trollope,
arriving from Florence in May 1862, read the proof of Part I
and gave her some useful advice on antiquarian problems—her
assumption that the Bardi were originally *popolani*, what *netto di
specchi* really signified, and the use of *in piazzi*, an elliptical colloquial expression, admittedly current in the fifteenth century, but
'barbarous' to modern Italian ears.[6] Of *boto* for *voto* he later
recalled that, while it was historically correct, 'the vast majority
of strangers would never hear it, or understand it if they did.
George Eliot no doubt met with it in some of those old chroniclers
who wrote exactly as not only the lower orders, but the generality

---

[1] GHL to Robert Chambers, Jr., 21 Aug. 1863 (W. & R. Chambers Ltd.).
[2] *Letters*, IV. 124. [3] *Letters*, IV. 212.
[4] In ch. 62, 'The Benediction' (ch. 61 in MS), about thirteen pages were deleted
and the rest of the part renumbered.
[5] GE Journal, 16 May 1863.
[6] In the Cabinet ed. I. 28 GE changed it to 'into the piazza'.

of their fellow citizens, were speaking around them. And her use
of it testifies to the minuteness of her care to reproduce the form
and pressure of the time of which she was writing.'[1] His brother
Anthony Trollope, amazed at the toil George Eliot had endured
in getting up the background, cautioned her not to 'fire too much
over the heads of your readers. You have to write to tens of
thousands, and not to single thousands'. The 'descriptions of
Florence,—little bits of Florence down to a door nail, and great
facts of Florence up to the very fury of life among those full living
nobles,—are wonderful in their energy and in their accuracy. The
character of Romola is artistically beautiful,—a picture exceeded
by none that I know of any girl in any novel.'[2] Within two months
Trollope's own Lily Dale would be standing beside Romola during
the rest of her run in the *Cornhill*.

Serial publication gave novelists an opportunity to study the
public's response to their work while it was being created. Trollope, overhearing two members of the Athenæum declare their
weariness of Mrs. Proudie, went home and killed her before the
week was out.[3] Month after month Dickens played skilfully on
the mood of his vast audience much as a TV performer does. But
with George Eliot morbid diffidence deprived her of what might
often have been helpful criticism. Knowing their disastrous effect,
Lewes rarely let her see unfavourable comments. While writing
Part IX, which 'I think will be the dullest that has yet come',
Marian noted in her Journal: 'Yesterday a pleasant message
from Mr. Hannay about Romola.'[4] A few days later there were
more 'Pleasant words from Anthony Trollope.'[5] Lewes, after
dining at Theodore Martin's, brought her 'the encouraging word
that Arthur Helps highly enjoys Romola, and thinks it the finest
thing I have done'.[6] George Smith passed along this comment—
gratefully noted in her Journal: 'Millais reported that at a party
at Lady de Grey's she said it was the finest book she had ever read:
the expression of opinion passed round the company and it was
unanimous in the same sense. Ebenezer!'[7] Browning, who had

---

[1] T. A. Trollope, *What I Remember* (2nd ed., 2 vols., 1887), II. 301–3. GE kept
boto.
[2] A. Trollope to GE, 28 June 1862. *Letters of Anthony Trollope*, ed. B. A. Booth
(1951), p. 115 reads 'close nail'.
[3] Michael Sadleir, *Anthony Trollope. A Commentary* (Boston and N.Y. 1927).
p. 267.
[4] GE Journal, 31 Dec. 1862.   [5] GE Journal, 4 Jan. 1863.
[6] GE Journal, 8 Jan. 1863.   [7] GE Journal, 2 Feb. 1863.

found Tennyson reading *Romola* in bed, could not get the book
'—spite of my repeated applications at Mudie's—and shall give
up subscribing to him in consequence'. After reading the first
two volumes he wrote to George Eliot:

> 19. Warwick Crescent, | Upper Westbourne Terrace,
> August 2. '63. *5 a.m.*
>
> My dear Mrs. Lewes,
> I had hoped that the last thing I should do before going away would
> be, on shutting 'Romola's' last volume, to use pen and paper in at least
> an attempt to express my gratitude for the noblest and most heroic
> prose-poem that I have ever read: but I go miserably away at the end
> of the chapter, 'on San Miniato'.—Well, if I had just read *all*—going
> up to the height I expect—I probably could not have said even this
> poor word—which you must take for what it is worth: thank you once
> more heartily.
> All regard to your Husband from his and yours affectionately
> Robert Browning.

But when Browning finished the last volume he was disappointed
at too much dwelling on the delinquencies of Tito, while the great
interests—Savonarola and the Republic—'dwindled strangely'.
He told Isa Blagden: 'My impression of the great style and high
tone remain, of course,—but as a work of art, I want much. Other
people like it—I heard Gladstone loud in its praise the other day
at a dinner', Browning added.[1] This revised judgement was naturally never revealed to George Eliot.

One of the few published criticisms she noticed was Richard
Holt Hutton's in the *Spectator*,[2] which Lewes read aloud to her.
She wrote two letters to Hutton about it. Commending his grasp
of the relation she intended in Bardo and Baldassarre, and the
relation of Florentine political life and the development of Tito's
nature, she said:

there is scarcely a phrase, an incident, an allusion, that did not gather
its value to me from its supposed subservience to my main artistic
objects. . . . It is the habit of my imagination to strive after as full a
vision of the medium in which a character moves as of the character
itself. The psychological causes which prompted me to give such details
of Florentine life and history as I have given, are precisely the same as
those which determined me in giving the details of English village life
in 'Silas Marner', or the 'Dodson' life, out of which were developed
the destinies of poor Tom and Maggie. But you have correctly pointed

---

[1] E. C. McAleer, *Dearest Isa* (Austin, 1951), p. 178.
[2] *Spectator*, 18 July 1863, pp. 2265–7.

out the reason why my tendency to excess in this effort after artistic vision makes the impression of a fault in 'Romola' much more perceptibly than in my previous books. And I am not surprised at your dissatisfaction with Romola herself. I can well believe that the many difficulties belonging to the treatment of such a character have not been overcome, and that I have failed to bring out my conception with adequate fulness. I am sorry she has attracted you so little; for the great problem of her life, which essentially coincides with a chief problem in Savonarola's, is one that readers need helping to understand.[1]

Lewes's watchful eye also hovered over Marian's letters to intercept anything that might upset her work. When Sara Hennell wrote appreciatively of the opening of *Romola*, Marian was 'really glad to know' that it interested her.[2] But three months later when Sara quoted with disapproval some unfavourable comments that others had levelled at the story, Lewes, reading the letter to Marian at the breakfast table, suppressed the criticism and then conveniently 'lost' the letter. Though Marian 'asked him for it very shortly after, he could not find it. Such magical disappearances are effected now and then by the sleight of hand of some spirit that doesn't rap',[3] she said. Lewes, in town on business, wrote to Sara, explaining

why I 'mislaid' and suppressed that portion of your letter. . . . After the publication of 'Adam Bede' Marian felt deeply the evil influences of talking and allowing others to talk to her about her writing. We resolved therefore to exclude everything as far as we could. No one speaks about her books to her, but me; she sees no criticisms. The sum total of success is always ascertainable, and she is not asked to dwell on the details.

Besides this general conviction, there is a special reason in her case— it is that excessive diffidence which prevented her writing at all for so many years, and would prevent her now, if I were not beside her to encourage her. A thousand eulogies would not give her the slightest confidence, but one objection would increase her doubts. With regard to 'Romola' she has all along resisted writing it on the ground that no one would be interested in it; but a general sense of its not being possibly popular would not be half so dispiriting to her as the knowledge that any particular reader did not like it; and as it is very desirable she should suffer no more pain in this life than can possibly be avoided, I suppressed your mention of those whose bad judgement you reproved because I knew it would occupy her thoughts and worry her during my absence. If you only knew the wonderful eulogies which have reached her from learned Florentines, and Englishmen of high culture (F. Maurice

---

[1] *Letters*, IV. 97.   [2] *Letters*, IV. 48–9.   [3] *Letters*, IV. 60.

Bulwer, Anthony Trollope etc.) you would be surprised that she should be made miserable by doubts as to whether the book will be a success; and would understand why I contrived she should not see your letter.

Of course you will take no notice of this letter. I only wanted to explain a general principle àpropos of a particular case. The principle is this: *never tell her anything that other people say about her books, for good or evil*; unless of course it should be something exceptionally gratifying to her—something you know would please her apart from its being praise.[1]

This 'principle' had obvious disadvantages. Lewes's isolation of George Eliot used to be blamed for the alleged abstruseness of her later novels, which, it was assumed, would have been more 'popular' if he had let her take the brunt of public opinion. But he knew very well the conditions under which she could write. Though some harm may have come from his zealous over-protection, without it she would probably have written nothing. Edith Simcox puts it hardly too strongly in saying that 'we owe to Mr. Lewes the complete works of George Eliot, not one of which would have been written or even planned without the inspiriting influence of his constant encouragement'.[2] George Eliot's prolific contemporary Mrs. Oliphant regarded literature as 'a commodity —a product sold in the market place', and the only diffidence she showed over turning out more than 200 volumes of fiction was in having to acknowledge them.[3] Comparing her own career with George Eliot's, she asked wistfully, 'Should I have done better if I had been kept, like her, in a mental greenhouse and taken care of?'[4]

George Eliot no longer needed to write for money. During seven years as a novelist she had acquired 'an abundant independence',[5] earned nearly £16,000—more than enough to support her comfortably for the rest of her days. Her supposed mercenary trait, which the back office at 45 George Street discussed so harshly, was really a concern for Lewes and his boys. His health was wretched—more precarious than her own. What would happen if he were no longer able to work? Charles's salary at the Post

[1] *Letters*, IV. 58–9.
[2] Edith Simcox, 'George Eliot', *Nineteenth Century*, 9 (May 1881), 773.
[3] V. and R. Colby, *The Equivocal Virtue. Mrs. Oliphant and the Victorian Market Place* (New Haven, 1966), p. 3.
[4] Margaret Oliphant, *Autobiography* (1899), p. 5.
[5] GE Journal, 31 Dec. 1862.

Office was scarcely enough for him to live on; Thornton and Herbert would require capital to set them up somewhere in the colonies. And always in the background lay an awareness that Lewes was legally responsible for supporting Agnes and her four illegitimate children. Since they separated, Lewes had paid her an average of £250 a year, and he never ceased considering her welfare. In November 1862 he took her some clothes for Edmund, which his boys had outgrown. 'Found her in bed, having fallen down in the street yesterday and hurt her back. Chatted with her for a couple of hours', he wrote in his Journal.[1] To faithful Nursie Lewes was also paying £50 a year, and there were pressing demands on him by his brother's widow and her son Vivian. Marian had joined her life to George's for better for worse, for richer for poorer, in sickness and in health. Everything they earned went into one bank account. While she could not afford to take less than the best price for her writings, she never compromised artistic integrity for the sake of money. None of her works can be described as a pot-boiler. Because she believed that *Romola* would be better understood in longer instalments she took £7,000 instead of £10,000 for it. What other novelist ever made such a sacrifice? She can hardly be blamed because *Romola* did not bolster the circulation of the *Cornhill* as much as Smith had hoped, or that, when it was issued in three volumes in July 1863, the sale was not large. Sir Sidney Lee's authorized 'Memoir of George Smith', saying plainly that 'The whole transaction was not to Smith's pecuniary advantage',[2] almost implies that it was somehow George Eliot's fault rather than Smith's lapse of judgement. She sent him as a gift the story 'Brother Jacob', for which he had once offered her £250, and it appeared in the *Cornhill* in July 1864. This was not the gesture of a mercenary author.

The irregularity of her marriage to Lewes undoubtedly contributed to George Eliot's morbid diffidence. Outwardly she wore a brave unconcern that so few ladies came to 16 Blandford Square. Barbara Bodichon was in and out daily when she was in London, but spent half the year in Algiers and many weeks at her house near Hastings. Bessie Parkes came in occasionally, rather worried about meeting others in the house. 'If you would like to come, and have no reason to the contrary, do', Marian once wrote. 'If not, there has been no harm done by an invitation *entre nous*.'[3]

---

[1] GHL Journal, 8 Nov. 1862.
[2] *DNB, Supplement* (1909), p. xxx.   [3] *Letters*, IV. 114.

Mrs. Congreve was loyal, of course, but inconveniently distant in Wandsworth. Rufa and Mr. Call had left London. Cara Bray and Sara were rarely in town, though their cousin Mary Marshall, whose mother lived near by, came in to chat, and sometimes Mrs. Marshall would come and play the piano for them.

But their circle of masculine visitors was widening. Frederic Burton, the artist, whom they had met in Munich in 1858, became one of their close friends. When they invited him with Arthur Helps, George Scharf, Secretary of the National Portrait Gallery, and Anthony Trollope to a dinner on 27 May 1862 to welcome Tom Trollope, just arrived from Florence, Polly went out with George to buy claret glasses and other things to befit the occasion. Lewes's old friend Owen Jones, the architect, who had super-intended the decoration of the Crystal Palace, was a regular visitor, though Marian seems never to have met his wife. Robert Browning, now a widower, first came to call on 12 December 1862 and returned quite often. One day he brought Marian a photograph of an early portrait of Elizabeth Barrett.[1] On Saturday evenings the Leweses were ordinarily at home. Friends might then drop in without ceremony for an evening of music, Redford playing his 'cello, with Marian or Charles at the piano, while Pigott and Spencer joined Lewes in singing. Wilkie Collins was sometimes with them.

The lease of 16 Blandford Square expired in November 1863, and the Leweses had to find another house. In May they first looked at one called the Priory at 21 North Bank, a pretty, secluded house, set far back from the street in a garden full of roses along the Regent's Canal, now covered by the Electric Power Station. Though it was very tempting, Marian could not decide—'hardly liking to lock up any money in land and bricks, and yet frightened lest we should not get a quiet place just when we want it'.[2] They weighed a less expensive one in the Circus Road. But in August they bought the Priory, paying £2,000 for a forty-nine year lease. There Marian was to stay till the last year of her life. The rooms were spacious and well proportioned with large windows reaching almost to the ceiling. When the few altera-tions had been made, they put the decorating and furnishing entirely in the hands of Owen Jones. He designed a beautiful wallpaper for the drawing-room, chose elegant carpets and draper-ies and sconces, ruthlessly discarded all their drawing-room fur-niture and bought new. He made 'a very exquisite thing of it', wrote Lewes, though the expense was staggering.

[1] GE Journal, 28 July 1863.   [2] *Letters*, IV. 87.

These problems and uncertainty about the younger boys kept them in anxious turmoil all summer. After Thornie failed his examination, Marian felt so ill that George took her off to Worthing for a week. In September she went again to Richmond for a fortnight, leaving the Lewes men alone to battle over Thornie's future, to dispel, if they could, his 'fixed idea of going to fight for the Poles against the hated Russians. His father felt that it would be a sin to allow a boy of nineteen to incur the demoralization of joining coarse men engaged in guerrilla warfare, to say nothing of Thornie's utter unfitness for military subordination and other inevitable hardships.'[1] For a long time there was no moving him. At length, warm-hearted, practical Barbara Bodichon talked with the young rebel and fired his imagination with the prospect of shooting big game in Natal. She had good friends there, to whom she wrote letters for him. On 16 October 1863, in excellent spirits, already with a smattering of Dutch and Zulu picked up from his grammars and dictionaries, 'with a large packet of recommendatory letters to all sorts of people, and with what he cares much more for—a first-rate rifle and revolver', Thornie '*at last*' sailed for Durban.[2]

Three weeks later the Leweses moved into the Priory. George wrote:

It took us the whole week to get the things in and the books on their shelves, though even now they are not arranged, only put up, and the drawing room is still uninhabitable. Besides the trouble and vexation incident to moving we have had extra annoyances. The [piano] tuner was sick over our elegant drawing room paper, which Owen Jones had decorated, and over the carpet! This obliges us to have fresh paper made, as there are no remnants of the old, and it was originally made for us. —Polly having imprudently left her purse in the drawer of her dressing table, one of the workmen stole it. Still, in spite of annoyances, we are highly delighted with the house now we are in it, and hope to continue so. The idea of removal is too formidable.[3]

The house was charming and comfortable. 'Mr. Owen Jones has been unwearied in taking trouble that everything about us may be pretty', Marian wrote. 'He stayed two nights till after twelve o'clock, that he might see every engraving hung in the right place.'[4] He had determined every detail, 'so that we can have the pleasure

---

[1] *Letters*, IV. 117.   [2] *Letters*, IV. 109.
[3] GHL Journal, 13 Nov. 1863.   [4] *Letters*, IV. 116.

of admiring what is our own without vanity'.[1] In his concern for harmony Owen Jones took even Marian's wardrobe into account, and in consequence of a severe lecture on 'her general neglect of personal adornment', she appeared 'splendid in a grey moiré antique'[1] at the housewarming on 24 November, when they celebrated Charles Lewes's twenty-first birthday. Charles had H. Buxton Forman, his colleague at the Post Office, to dinner, and invited another colleague to come in for the evening party. All the loyal old friends were there—Spencer, Pigott, Redford, Burton, E. S. Dallas, Mr. and Mrs. Robert Noel, Owen Jones, Mrs. Peter Taylor, Mrs. F. R. Malleson with her sister Emily Whitehead, and Mary Marshall. Leopold Jansa, the violinist of the old Beethoven Quartette, played, to everyone's delight. Marian was so pleased with him that she arranged to take some lessons from him in accompanying the violin. When the party was over and she was stretched out in a wonderful reclining chair given her by a munificent friend (George Smith?), she thought herself 'in danger of being envied by the Gods, especially as my health is thoroughly good withal'.[2]

On New Year's Day 1864 Lewes summed up 1863 in his Journal: 'In a domestic sense it has been a chequered year. Much trouble about the two boys; much bother about the new house; continued happiness with the best of women.' On the first page of the bound manuscript of *Romola* the best of women wrote: 'To the Husband whose perfect Love has been the best source of her insight and strength this manuscript is given by his devoted Wife, the writer.'

[1] *Letters*, IV. 124.   [2] *Letters*, IV. 116.

CHAPTER XII

FELIX HOLT AND *THE SPANISH GYPSY*

※

On 30 December 1863 Lewes walked over to Kensal Green Cemetery to attend Thackeray's funeral. 'There was a very large gathering—between 1000 and 1500 people,' he wrote in his Journal, 'among them most of the literary and artistic celebrities. Theodore Martin drove me home, and came in to be introduced to Polly.'[1] Martin had known Lewes since the 1840s, when they both wrote for *Fraser's*. In 1851 he married Helen Faucit, whom Lewes once called 'the finest tragic actress on our stage';[2] she still appeared occasionally. Martin, an admirer of *Adam Bede*, was happy to make George Eliot's acquaintance. On 4 February 1864 he and Trollope dined at the Priory and had very pleasant talk, somewhat broken by a visit from Ben, the 'lovely bull terrier, . . . who is fast becoming the pet and tyrant of our household'. On 7 February Martin called, bringing his wife 'to see Polly', Lewes noted, 'and I hope the two will get on together'. The next day Lewes took Polly to see Kate Bateman in *Leah the Forsaken*.

While wondering at the badness of the piece and the success it has with the playgoing public, I thought of writing one for Helen Faucit and amused myself with sketching a plot. The idea laid hold of me, and during a sleepness night, I made out the skeleton of the whole five acts. In the morning I suggested to Polly that *she* should do the piece. She rather liked the suggestion, and when I had written out the barest possible outline of my plot, I read it to her. She thought the subject a good one, and one that she could work out. So I wrote to Helen Faucit to arrange a meeting next Sunday that I might learn from her, before Polly begins, whether she is prepared to return to the stage if a good play were ready for her.[3]

The Martins, 'extremely delighted at the idea', soon called again, bringing copies of Burton's portrait of Helen. It was agreed

---

[1] GHL Journal, 1 Jan. 1864.   [2] *Leader*, 31 Jan. 1852, p. 580.
[3] GHL Journal, 8 Feb. 1864.

that the Leweses would go to Glasgow at the end of March to see her act some of her favourite Shakespearean roles.[1] They stayed five days at the same hotel and saw each other constantly. Marian was charmed with Helen—'a flash of real acting in the evening twilight of the stage', she wrote.[2] On the way home they stopped to see Bertie on the farm near Thankerton, watched him weave at the loom of one of the cottagers, and had dinner with the farmer, after which Bertie drove them over the hills to the station in a blinding snow-storm.

Nothing is known for certain about the plot Lewes outlined. A sketch of a play called *Savello*, in three acts, written hastily in pencil by Lewes and inked over by George Eliot survives.[3] Savello, a cynical Don Giovanni, seeing the lovely Cassandra in church, is smitten and follows her home. When he makes 'discreet love' to her, she

takes the occasion to paint a picture of what his life might be and what it is—the misery he recklessly causes—the waste of his own life—he who is so noble, young, with great capacities. He is moved and in a transport kisses her hand, says she has saved his soul as well as given a meaning to his life, and departs resolved to act up to what she says.

But soon he sends a passionate letter, asking to see her alone 'to have his resolution of reform strengthened'; he has planned to have her jealous husband lured away to Pisa for the night. Cassandra replies that she would place a lamp in the window if it was safe to come. She then tells her husband all, but insists that by murdering Savello he will not shield her honour. Her husband 'quickly places lamp and the curtain falls'.

Act III

Savello's corpse. C. sobbing over body brings lamp and lights up the noble face. Her grief and pity rouse his jealousy. She covers the body and awaits the friends who burst in and take her off to prison.

Though this may not be the plot sketched for Helen Faucit, it is perhaps like it in character, closer to Lewes's manner than Marian's.

[1] GHL Journal, 6 Mar. 1864. Martin says: 'The plan of the drama was discussed between them, with the result, that the idea was dropped by George Eliot in accordance with my wife's opinion. The subject, I believe, was made use of afterwards in *The Spanish Gypsy*. But of this, as what passed between the two ladies was confidential, I cannot speak with certainty.' *Helena Faucit* (2nd ed. 1900), p. 265.   [2] *Letters*, IV. 143.

[3] Ibid. 132–3. Charles Lewes showed Edith Simcox a 'skeleton for a three-act tragedy, to be written some day if they went to Sicily'. Simcox Autobiography, 6 Apr. 1884.

The very different idea for her play, which developed into *The Spanish Gypsy*, came to her in Venice in May 1864. Frederic Burton, the painter, whom they had known in Munich, was one of their most faithful visitors at the Priory. He had never been in Italy, and when they proposed his joining them on their holiday there, he accepted gladly. They set out 4 May, going from Paris and Chambéry over the Mt. Cenis Pass. At Turin they paused a day or two before going on to Milan and Venice. From Burton, later the Director of the National Galley, the Leweses received valuable practice in looking at pictures. His trained eye gave them a more discriminating view of Venice, where they stayed three weeks. On going into St. Mark's Lewes wrote: 'Cannot understand how it was that we were not greatly struck with the interior on our former visit. To-day it seemed to us awful and beautiful —barbaric splendour.'[1] At the Scuola di San Rocco he discovered 'glorious, and even poetical merits' in Tintoretto's *Annunciation*, 'though the ugliness and vulgarity of Mary depoetizes the whole'.[2] Marian's Journal, while commenting on other paintings in the same room, is silent about this one. Yet in her Notes on *The Spanish Gypsy*, written in 1868, she declares that the poem was suggested to her by another *Annunciation* over the door;

this small picture of Titian's, pointed out to me for the first time, brought a new train of thought. It occurred to me that here was a great dramatic motive of the same class as those used by the Greek dramatists, yet specifically differing from them. A young maiden, believing herself to be on the eve of the chief event of her life—marriage—about to share in the ordinary lot of womanhood, full of young hope, has suddenly announced to her that she is chosen to fulfil a great destiny, entailing a terribly different experience from that of ordinary womanhood. She is chosen, not by any arbitrariness, but as a result of foregoing hereditary conditions: she obeys. 'Behold the handmaid of the Lord.' Here, I thought, is a subject grander than that of Iphigenia, and it has never been used.

In reflecting on it George Eliot concluded, rather strangely, that

nothing would serve me except that moment in Spanish history when the struggle with the Moors was attaining its climax, and when there was the gypsy race present under such conditions as would enable me to get my heroine and the hereditary claim on her among the gypsies. I required the opposition of race to give the need for renouncing the expectation of marriage.[3]

---

[1] GHL Journal, 13 May 1864. [2] Ibid. 16 May 1864.
[3] Cross, III. 42–3. It is curious that GE does not mention Bulwer Lytton's *Leila, or The Siege of Granada* (1838), in which the heroine, a Jewish maiden, faces a similar conflict of loyalties.

Leaving Venice, they took another three weeks of leisurely travel through Padua, Verona, Milan, and the Lakes, over the St. Gotthard Pass to Lucerne, and enjoyed a few days in Paris before returning to London 20 June.

Charles Lewes met them with the news that he was engaged to Gertrude Hill, a granddaughter of Dr. Southwood Smith. 'It startled us at first,' Lewes wrote, 'made Polly happy, and me rather melancholy—the thought of marriage is always a solemn and melancholy thought to me.'[1] They had observed Charles's fondness for Gertrude, who was four years older than he, a 'remarkably handsome' young lady, with a fine contralto voice. In assuming that she 'would hardly fall in love with our amiable bit of crudity' both the physiologist and the keen analyst of psychological motive proved to be mistaken. 'One never knows what to wish about marriage', Marian remarked; 'the evils of an early choice may be easily counterbalanced by the vitiation that often comes from long bachelorhood.'[2]

Before they left for Italy, Burton had asked George Eliot to let him take her portrait; having seen his pleasant one of Helen Faucit, she was quite willing to let him try. Her photographs were so unflattering that she was anxious to suppress them, and commonly denied that any existed. The Laurence drawing had not satisfied. She would try again with Burton. She gave the first sitting on 29 June 1864. There must have been several studies before one was achieved that satisfied the artist, the subject, and her friends. In August Marian wrote to Barbara that 'George saw it for the first time the other day, and was in raptures with it whereupon Mr. Burton told him it was *his* (George's). I don't know myself whether it is good or not.'[3] Barbara was sent to the studio to see it in October and Mrs. Congreve in January 1865.[4] On 22 July 1865, more than a year after the work began, Marian wrote in her Journal, 'Sat for my portrait, I suppose for the last time.' This was clearly a fresh study, for when it was given to the National Portrait Gallery after her death, Burton wrote: 'The portrait was drawn in 1865, in July, as I find by a diary of the time.'[5] It is in chalks on paper. Though it sympathetically softens

[1] GHL Journal, 23 June 1864. [2] *Letters*, IV. 155.
[3] GE to Barbara Bodichon, 12 Aug. 1864 (Berg Collection, NYPL).
[4] *Letters*, IV. 167, 174. It is reproduced in Plate IX, facing p. 340.
[5] F. Burton to George Scharf, 10 Feb. 1883 (National Portrait Gallery).

the harsh features one would expect from her photographs, it is probably a good likeness—certainly the best record available of George Eliot's fair complexion, light brown hair, and grey eyes. Mrs. Burne-Jones thought there was 'more keenness of expression than Burton caught, the eyes especially being more piercing'.[1] Mrs. Bray, who drew the earliest portrait and knew Marian well, objected to the 'fleshiness' of the face; and Grace the cook complimented her mistress on her healthy appearance by saying that she looked 'just like my portrait'. It was hung over the mantel in Lewes's study, next to the dining-room. A plan to reproduce it in colour proved impractical.[2] It was not copied till 1882, when Rajon made the unfortunate etching from it, which served as frontispiece for Volume I of *George Eliot's Life*, where it is dated 1864.

In trying to plan her drama of renunciation during the summer of 1864 George Eliot suffered more than her usual pangs. She re-read Gibbon's *Decline and Fall* in connection with the ecclesiastical histories of J. L. von Mosheim and J. L. K. Gieseler, and studied the rites of Dionysia as the origin of tragedy. Her Journal confesses to 'Horrible scepticism about all things—paralyzing my mind. Shall I ever be good for anything again?—ever do anything again?'[3] In the midst of Prescott's *Ferdinand and Isabella* in September she noted that she was 'reading about Spain and trying a drama on a subject that has fascinated me—have written the prologue, and am beginning the First Act. But I have little hope of anything satisfactory.'[4] Anxiety about George, who was growing thinner and thinner, increased her depression. The circulation of the *Cornhill* had continued to decline, and with the October number Lewes's work as consulting editor ceased. Though he regretted the loss of income, it was a relief.

On Smith's advice Lewes had tried riding for his health, but the exercise seemed 'to stir up my liver into unpleasant activity', and he soon abandoned it. Instead, they turned to the old therapy, change of scene. In September they went to Harrogate, where they drank the waters for ten days, and then on to Scarborough. Even at Tenby, Marian declared, 'the sands are not so fine as these'.[5] The weather was perfect, the North Sea blue as sapphire. They were never idle. Marian was studying Spanish grammar; Lewes

---

[1] *Memorials of Edward Burne-Jones*, II. 4.   [2] *Letters*, IV. 212.
[3] GE Journal, 17 July 1864.   [4] GE Journal, 6 Sept. 1864.
[5] *Letters*, IV. 164.

read *Don Quixote* aloud and heard her translate it 'like a good child'. Soon after their return to the Priory she had the first draft of Act I of her play ready to read to him, and rewrote it, incorporating his suggestions. Act II was completed in October while George was alone at Malvern for another water cure. When he returned 3 November, 'much benefited', she read it to him: 'It is written in verse—my first serious attempt at blank verse. G. praises and encourages me.'[1] But in the construction of the remaining three acts she was 'sticking in the mud continually', floundering in 'a swamp of miseries'. She suffered from dyspepsia and bilious headache. It was a month before she had fifteen pages of Act III ready for George, who, of course, 'approved it highly';[2] it was not finished till Christmas Day. Bertie's holiday and the unusual festivities entailed by Charles's engagement hindered her work. 'We acted charades and sang both before and at supper and were very merry', Lewes wrote.[3] In mid January he took Marian to Paris for ten days. She could not get on with the play. Much depressed, 'feeling my work worth nothing', she talked over Act IV with George and 'recovered some hope'. A note in her Journal, that 'I have only just written in verse the opening of my 4th act', indicates that she composed it in prose before versifying it.[4] Though George did all he could to give her assurance, praising her verse as 'triumphantly successful',[5] her headaches and feebleness of mind and body defeated his best efforts. He had always mistrusted her dramatic powers, and he had to confess that the play was flat and monotonous. On 21 February 1865 Marian wrote: 'George has taken my drama away from me.'

The termination of Lewes's editorial connection with the *Cornhill* did not end his relations with George Smith. Smith was already planning a new evening newspaper, the *Pall Mall Gazette*, for which he engaged Lewes as adviser, a purely consultative post, at a salary of £300 a year.[3] The brief trip to Paris in January 1865 was made primarily to arrange with Eugène Fourcade, editor of the *Revue des deux Mondes*, to contribute articles. The first number appeared 7 February 1865. Throughout the year Lewes wrote extensively for the *Pall Mall* on all sorts of subjects with a spriteliness reminiscent of his early *Leader* days. A long discriminating review of *As You Like It* at Drury Lane, signed 'L' praised Helen

---

[1] GE Journal, 4 Nov. 1864.
[3] GHL Journal, 25 Dec. 1864.
[5] GE Journal, 1 Jan. 1865.

[2] GE Journal, 5 Dec. 1864.
[4] GE Journal, 6 Feb. 1865.

Faucit's Rosalind with some reservations, but objected to the supporting cast: 'the subordinate characters were not so much filled as stuffed', Lewes wrote. 'A great writer, who sat near me during the performance, asked, with something of triumph, whether this did not satisfy me that it was a great mistake ever to see one of Shakspeare's plays acted!'[1] George Eliot helped Smith's new venture by contributing four brief articles, some of them, like 'The Logic of Servants', infused with an ironic humour that belies the despondency oppressing her.

Before agreeing to serve as adviser for the *Pall Mall Gazette*, Lewes withdrew from another position he had accepted. This was the editorship of the *Fortnightly Review*, which Anthony Trollope, Fred Chapman, Henry Danby Seymour, Laurence Oliphant, and others were projecting on the pattern of the *Revue des Deux Mondes*. Lewes gave as his reason for withdrawing his 'fears lest it should be too much for my health and disturb our domestic habits'.[2] Trollope forgave the defection, which he regretted most because they needed 'some one who would know what he was about in arranging the work of such a venture as we propose'; some one with whom he 'could hold close friendly intercourse'.[3] But he kept urging Lewes to reconsider. And, finally, after lunching at the Priory 21 March, Trollope bore him off to the meeting of the stockholders, who agreed to give him 'absolute power' over the conduct of the *Fortnightly*, a salary of £600 a year, a subeditor John Dennis, and a clerk to do all the routine work. Lewes was soon writing twenty letters in a day soliciting articles, and Polly, who dreaded the worry and anxiety, regretted that he had not persisted in his refusal. 'Dear George is all activity, yet is in very frail health. How I worship his good humour, his good sense, his affectionate care for every one who has claims on him! That worship is my best life.'[4] Loyal as ever, she wrote for the first number of the *Fortnightly* a long article on Lecky's *History of the Rise and Influence of the Spirit of Rationalism in Europe*, severely castigating its too-easy assumption that rationalism was the cause of progress. She also contributed a brief notice of the new edition of Owen Jones's *Grammar of Ornament*. Both were signed 'George Eliot', for Lewes had made the rule—a momentous one in the history of English journalism—that there were to be no anonymous articles in the *Fortnightly*.

---

[1] *Pall Mall Gazette*, 10 Mar. 1865, p. 10.   [2] GHL Journal, 25 Dec. 1864.
[3] A. Trollope to GHL, 24 Dec. 1864. *Letters of A. Trollope*, p. 160.
[4] GE Journal, 25 Mar. 1865.

On 20 March 1865 Charles Lewes and Gertrude Hill were married by Dr. Thomas Sadler in the Rosslyn Hill Unitarian Chapel.

The day was remarkably brilliant, but piercingly cold from a bitter and fierce east wind. No one was invited to the wedding except Polly and I, the Aunts, Gertrude's mother and sisters; yet there were many people in the Church. We went back to Church Row and had a quiet and pleasant talk with them all. The young couple started at ½ past 1 for Folkestone on their way to Italy. Happier prospects never smiled upon a marriage. Polly and I then called on Mother. Drove home and were quiet and cozy together all day.[1]

Polly could now think again about her play. She was reading Aeschylus, Klein's *History of the Drama*, and *The Theatre of the Greeks*, hoping vainly for inspiration to carry on Act IV. But, as she once observed to the hapless Sara Hennell, 'Inspiration is a rare incalculable thing—it will flash out sometimes in a mere bit of sky and water and weed, and leave you only to wonder at its absence in a picture where all sorts of rare and beautiful things have been brought together and studied with immeasurable pains.'[2] There could hardly be a better statement of her own plight. While she pondered melodramatic Spanish heroics, her English story kept intruding itself in front of the uncongenial task, as *Silas Marner* did with *Romola*. At last she yielded to it. On 29 March she wrote in her Journal: 'I have begun a Novel.'

This was *Felix Holt, the Radical*. Here—as the epigraph facing the title-page announced—she had returned to the Midlands, her 'native country', where in imagination she constantly saw the bushy hedgerows of catkined hazels, the golden corn-ricks clustered near the long roofs of the homestead, and the full-uddered cows coming in from the pastures to the early milking.[3] Her habit of scrupulous accuracy still demanded research. She read through *The Times* and the *Annual Register* for 1832–3, studied Neale's *History of the Puritans*, Macaulay's *History* and Hallam's, Mill's *Political Economy*, Fawcett's *Economic Position of the British Labourer*, and Samuel Bamford's *Passages in the Life of a Radical*, copying long extracts into her Notebook. But the vivid touches that illuminate the novel were drawn from her childhood memories

---

[1] GHL Journal, 20 Mar. 1865. GHL signed the Register with Gertrude's mother, her sister Florence, and 'Aunt' Margaret Gillies.

[2] Apropos of Holman Hunt's *Afterglow in Egypt. Letters*, IV. 159.

[3] *Felix Holt*, 'Introduction'.

of Nuneaton at the time of the Reform Bill, when she was a school-girl at Mrs. Wallington's. She had clear recollection of the soup kitchens for unemployed weavers and miners and of the excitement during the election riots in December 1832. The sentiment of the majority of the townspeople was strongly Radical. Dempster Heming, lately returned from successful practice of the law in India, had decided—like Harold Transome—to stand for the Radicals. In a fair election he would have won easily. But the Tories, seeing the tide going against them, suspended the poll, and called in a detachment of Scots Greys, which had been kept in readiness at Meriden; the Riot Act was read, and when the mob did not disperse, horse soldiers with drawn swords rode through the town, charging the people, cutting and trampling them down. One man died of his injuries.[1] These were events not to be forgotten. Though one seldom feels she is sketching characters from originals, as in the earlier novels, these memories gave a convincing density of background.

As she grew absorbed in the new work, Marian's malaise lightened. 'My health has been better of late', she noted in her Journal, 'and I am anxious to use the precious hours well.'[2] She sat in the garden at the Priory 'for two hours' discussing her novel and its 'psychological problems' with George,[3] who was always ready with sympathy. Before going to dine with the Congreves on 20 June, they 'walked together on Wimbledon Common in outer and inner sunshine, as of old', talking about the opening of the story, which she had read to him that morning. Her days were spent in planning, sketching characters and plot, but writing little.

With two numbers of the *Fortnightly* ready in advance, Lewes took her away on 10 August for a month in Normandy and Brittany, which they penetrated as far as Carnac and Nantes, returning through Tours and Chartres. On their return *Felix Holt* began to go forward faster. By the end of October she had written to page 107; on 22 November (her forty-sixth birthday) Chapter 7 was finished. When she read Chapter 9 to George on 4 December, he 'was much pleased and found no fault'. But at Christmas time, with Bertie home for his holiday, she was again 'sticking in the mud, from doubt about my construction: I have just consulted G. and he confirms my choice of incidents'.[4] Lewes told Tom

---

[1] Details drawn from 'Occurrences at Nuneaton', 21 Dec. 1832. The election cost Mr. Dugdale, the successful Tory candidate, nearly £12,000, £1,200 in Nuneaton alone, where his bill at the Newdigate Arms was £400 (Jan. 1835).

[2] GE Journal, 7 June 1865.   [3] GHL Journal, 13 June 1865.

[4] GE Journal, 24 Dec. 1865.

Trollope that 'Polly is miserable over a new novel.' A little later he described her as 'gestating, and gestation with her is always perturbing. I wish the book were done with all my heart.'[1] She was struggling to work out the intricacies of the Transome inheritance by studying Blackstone's *Commentaries*.

One evening in January 1866 when Spencer, Huxley, and Burton dined at the Priory, Frederic Harrison, who had written on trades unions for the *Fortnightly*, called by invitation. George Eliot had met him five years before at the Congreves'. Since his undergraduate days at Wadham College he had been a disciple of Congreve, and in London, where he was called to the Bar by Lincoln's Inn in 1858, he was closely associated with him in the Positivist movement. His interest in the Working Men's College and in problems of industrial co-operation made his advice peculiarly useful to George Eliot at this moment. Her request for books on the law of entail and the statutes of limitations initiated a long correspondence and many conferences on the legal aspects of *Felix Holt*, the first volume of which she gave him to read in manuscript.

Hitherto [she wrote] I have read my M.S. (I mean of my previous books) to Mr. Lewes, by 40 or 50 pages at a time, and he has told me if he felt an objection to anything. No one else has had any knowledge of my writing before their publication (I except, of course, the publishers). But now that you are good enough to incur the trouble of reading my M.S. I am anxious to get the full benefit of your participation.[2]

With Harrison's expert knowledge and sympathetic support, she advanced more confidently. In April near the end of Volume II she wrote to Barbara Bodichon: 'I am finishing a book, which has been growing slowly, like a sickly child, because of my own ailments; but now I am in the later acts of it. I can't move till it is done.' Her word 'acts' is interesting, for she had been reading Aristotle's *Poetics* and Aeschylus and Sophocles, and as Professor F. C. Thomson has shown, the original conception of *Felix Holt* was probably the tragedy of Mrs. Transome rather than the political plot.[3]

Soon after the second volume was finished, Lewes gave the manuscript to George Smith with the warning that George Eliot

---

[1] T. A. Trollope. *What I Remember* (1887), II. 314.
[2] *Letters*, IV. 221–2.
[3] 'The Genesis of Felix Holt', *PMLA*, 74 (Dec. 1959), 576–84, and 'Felix Holt and Classical Tragedy', *Nineteenth-Century Fiction*, 16 (June 1961), 47–58.

would expect at least £5,000 for the copyright. Having read it to his wife, Smith 'came to the conclusion that it would not be a profitable venture', and declined it.[1] Without mentioning the rejection, Lewes wrote immediately to John Blackwood, who replied:

> I am delighted to hear that Mrs. Lewes has so nearly finished her Novel and also much pleased that she should think in the first instance of her old friend as the publisher.
> That such a Novel as you describe by her will be first rate I have no manner of doubt but it would be against the principle upon which I really enter into and take a pleasure in my own business were I to decide finally on such a matter without having some opportunity of forming an opinion of the book by seeing a volume or so. I think she knows me well enough not to object to this and I would give an answer within a couple of days after receiving the M.S.
> As to what my opinion will be I feel nearly certain and the more serious matter is the terms. I contemplate giving from four to five thousand Pounds for the copyright for five years from date of publication and if this does not come up to your ideas I cannot see my way to anything like a fair chance of making the transaction remunerative by giving more. Of course I understand that it is a novel of the ordinary length in three volumes. I should like of all things to publish another great success by George Eliot and I do hope we may be able to agree about terms.
> Will you give her my regards and tell her that I have been thinking so much of her Novel since receiving your note that I have found it very difficult to attend to my ordinary work, of which I have more than enough at this period of the month.[2]

The fear and trembling with which George Eliot waited to hear of the safe arrival of her manuscript were augmented by anxiety to know her old friend's opinion of it. Blackwood 'broke the Sabbath' to begin reading, and after only eighty pages wrote to Lewes:

> I am lost in wonder and admiration of Mrs. Lewes' powers. It is not like a Novel and there may be a complaint of want of the ordinary Novel interest, but it is like looking on at a series of panoramas where human beings speak and act before us. There is hardly a page where there is not some turn of expression, witty or wise or both which one loves to dwell upon, but there is no time to write more.[3]

The next day he sent his formal offer of £5,000 for the copyright for five years. In accepting it, George Eliot said:

---

[1] *The House of Smith, Elder*, ed. Leonard Huxley (privately printed 1923), p. 103.
[2] *Letters*, IV. 240–1.   [3] Ibid. 243.

It is a great pleasure to me to be writing to you again, as in the old days. After your kind letters, I am chiefly anxious that the publication of 'Felix Holt' may be a satisfaction to you from beginning to end.

Mr. Lewes writes about other business matters, so I will only say that I am desirous to have the proofs as soon and as rapidly as will be practicable. They will require correcting with great care, and there are large spaces in the day, when I am unable to write, in which I could be attending to my proofs.[1]

She wanted the proofs, of course, for Harrison's scrutiny, lest any legal error should creep in.

As usual, Blackwood's warm appreciation of the book heartened George Eliot. He wrote of it with unfeigned enthusiasm to Langford:

The book is a perfect marvel. The time is 1832 just after the passing of the Reform Bill and surely such a picture or rather series of pictures of English Life, manners, and conversation never was drawn. You seem to hear and see the people speaking. Every individual character stands out a distinct figure. . . .

It is a great publishing triumph her returning to us, and she expresses the warmest feeling of gratification in resuming her old relations with me. Lewes too says it has quite cheered her up. Keep the sum paid strictly a secret.[2]

Any doubts that the staunch Tory Blackwood may have had about her politics were quickly dissipated: 'I suspect I am a radical of the Felix Holt breed', he told George Eliot, 'and so was my father before me.'[3] George Eliot now wrote with increasing speed, finishing Volume III within six weeks. The book was announced on 1 May, and proofs began to come within the week. George Eliot was still worrying about historical details, asking Blackwood to inquire of authorities in Edinburgh: Was imprisonment of civilians exceptional during the Napoleonic wars? Did transportation to the colonies involve hard labour? Who were the famous conveyancers of 1833? Harrison was helpful to the end. After reading the manuscript of the trial scene, he made many useful suggestions. The opinion of the Attorney-General, which he drafted simply as an example of the language of Lincoln's Inn, she inserted unchanged in Chapter 35.[4]

On 1 June 1866 Lewes wrote in his Journal:

Yesterday Polly finished *Felix Holt*. The sense of relief was very great and all day long suffused itself over our thoughts. The continual ill

---

[1] *Letters*, IV. 243–4.   [2] *Letters*, IV. 247.   [3] *Letters*, IV. 246.
[4] F. Harrison, *Memories and Thoughts* (1906), pp. 149–50.

health of the last months, and her dreadful nervousness and depression, made the writing a serious matter. Blackwood . . . thinks the book superior to *Adam Bede*. I cannot share that opinion; but the book is a noble book and will I think be more popular than the *Mill*.

In a letter to Mrs. Bray Marian said: 'As soon as I had done and read the last page to George, I felt better, and have been a new creature ever since, though a little overdone with visits from friends and attention (miserabile dictu!) to petticoats etc.'[1] The final proof was returned on 2 June, when Blackwood and his nephew called to express their delight in the wind-up of the story. Ten days later *Felix Holt* was on sale.

The Leweses were already across the Channel, headed for rest in the German watering places. Part of the route retraced their first journey together in 1854. They rambled again about Brussels 'to see our favorite spots (13 years ago! You may imagine the memories!)' Lewes wrote to his mother. It was actually only twelve years. At Antwerp they went to high mass at the Cathedral and in the evening to the theatre to see the Oberammergau company perform the *Passion Play*. At Coblenz the town was crowded with troops, for Bismarck had just opened his war on Austria and was preparing for the crushing battle of Sadowa. But in those happy days even Prussian wars did not interfere much with civilians. Marian and George lolled on the bridge 'over which we had looked on the Moselle 13 years ago talking of Goethe', and came back to sup on trout and venison, with a good bottle of wine.[2] At Schwalbach, despite the alarms, they stayed a fortnight, drinking the water, taking long walks in the woods, and reading under the beech trees. They always dined in their room, and at the end of the afternoon, strolled on the promenade, listening to the music of the bands and watching the gay company until tea time. 'As we do not speak to a soul here, we have all possible advantages without any of the drawbacks attendant on being thrown with a miscellaneous set of uninteresting people in a small place',[3] Lewes said. And Marian wrote to Mrs. Congreve:

It would have marred the *Kur* for me if I had had every day to undergo a *table d'hôte* where almost all the guests are English, presided over by the British chaplain. Please don't suspect me of being scornful towards my fellow country men or women; the fault is all mine that I am miserably *gênée* by the glances of strange eyes.[4]

[1] *Letters*, IV. 267–8.   [2] GHL Journal, 20 June 1866.
[3] GHL Journal, 28 June 1866.   [4] *Letters*, IV. 279.

At Schlangenbad, whither they migrated for another fortnight, they led the same 'indolent, dreamy, languorous' life, rambling and reading in the woods, taking 'the most luxurious and soothing of baths, like warm milk', and following the course of the war in the papers.[1] With Polly's now considerable investments Lewes studied the shares list in *The Times* closely; because of the war the daily figures were far from satisfactory.

Reports of the reception of *Felix Holt*, however, were entirely so. 'I do not know that I ever saw a Novel received with a more universal acclaim', Blackwood wrote.[2] The *Saturday Review* led off with a highly favourable article (it was by John Morley), and the *Spectator* was equally enthusiastic. *The Times* devoted three whole columns to a review (by E. S. Dallas), highly laudatory throughout, though the suggestion that Esther's rising to testify at the trial was taken from a story by Charles Reade, which neither of the Leweses had read, struck everyone as odd. The article in *Blackwood's* (by W. L. Collins) was naturally appreciative; but the disagreeable Transome plot troubled him as well as the reviewer in the *Edinburgh* (G. S. Venables), who found it 'purposeless and painful'. Bulwer Lytton shared this objection, 'but what does it signify', he said to Blackwood; 'the writing is wonderful and what is an author unless he is a Great Writer'.[3] Harrison, who had worked so hard over the book, reread the copy that George Eliot sent him four or five times, more like poetry than a novel. He wrote that he knew 'whole families where the three volumes have been read chapter by chapter and line by line and reread and recited as are the stanzas of In Memoriam'[4]—a hyperbole that attests his admiration, though it makes one marvel at his friends. Sales of the book lagged behind the critical opinions. Of the 5,250 printed in the three-volume edition at 31*s*. 6*d*. more than 300 were still unsold when the second edition in two volumes was published in December 1866. George Eliot had nothing more to gain, for the copyright was Blackwood's.

Cheered by these reports, the Leweses started homeward, pausing for a few days at Bonn and Aix and Liège, where again their delight was 'immense—greatly from old recollections'.[5] At the suggestion of a pleasant Englishman on the train they spent several

---

[1] *Letters*, IV. 283–4.   [2] *Letters*, IV. 289.   [3] *Letters*, IV. 280.
[4] Ibid. 285. From America a man named Holt sent GE word 24 June 1879 (Yale) that he had named his first child Felix in honour of her hero, and invited her to come visit them. Felix Holt grew up to be a novelist and wrote a popular novel about his native Kentucky, *The Gabriel Horn* (1951).
[5] GHL Journal, 24 July 1866.

days in Chaudfontaine. Taking their leisurely way through the Belgian cities to Ostend, they reached London on 2 August 1866.

Soon came a letter from Thornie with the news that he had got a grant of land from the government of Natal, some 3,000 acres on the Orange River; he urged them to send Bertie out to join him. Bertie came at once from Warwickshire, and they spent the next month outfitting him and arranging the transfer of funds to stock an African farm. On 8 September they gave him a farewell family party; old Nursie (Mrs. Bell) came in after dinner to say good-bye; and the next day Bertie took his final look at England as the ship headed for Durban.

As George Eliot's fame increased, the little circle of staunch friends—Spencer, Barbara Bodichon, the Calls, the Coventry trio, Bessie Parkes, Mary Marshall, Pigott, Redford, Mrs. Peter Taylor, the Congreves, Burton—widened steadily. Robert Browning, at first a rather reluctant admirer, became one of the heartiest, and called frequently at the Priory. One Sunday afternoon the Leweses walked home with him to Warwick Crescent. Marian wrote that they 'saw the objects Mrs. Browning used to have about her, her chair, tables, books etc. An epoch to be remembered. Browning showed us her Hebrew Bible with notes in her handwriting, and several of her copies of the Greek dramatists with her annotations.'[1] Sometimes he inscribed copies of his poems for her. The most conspicuous lion-hunter of his day, Richard Monckton Milnes, who was about to be raised to the peerage as Baron Houghton, had known Lewes for at least twenty years; he now began to invite him to his extraordinary parties in Upper Brook Street. Matthew Arnold described one on 14 June 1863 where he

met all the advanced liberals in religion and politics, and a Cingalese in full costume; so that, having lunched with the Rothschilds, I seemed to be passing my day among Jews, Turks, infidels, and heretics. But the philosophers were fearful! G. Lewes, Herbert Spencer, a sort of pseudo-Shelley called Swinburne, and so on. Froude, however, was there, and Browning, and Ruskin.[2]

At breakfast there one day Lewes met Robert Lytton, Huxley, Lord Wentworth, Grant-Duff, Twisleton, and Story the American sculptor. A week later he met Holman Hunt, Browning, Spedding, Spencer, the two Lushingtons, Congreve, Arthur Russell,

---

[1] GE Journal, 15 Oct. 1865.
[2] *Matthew Arnold Letters 1848–1888* (2 vols., 1895), I. 227–8.

and an Indian—a 'very pleasant' party. At the Priory on 25 June 1864, just after the Congreves arrived, Lord Houghton came in unexpectedly, 'bringing Polly a copy of his poems. He sat with us at lunch.'[1] It was her first meeting with him. Lord Houghton asked whether Mrs. Lewes had any fixed day for visitors and was soon appearing fairly often at the Sunday afternoons for which the Priory was becoming noted.

One of George Eliot's pleasantest new friendships, that with Mr. and Mrs. Frederick Lehmann, began by chance when she sat next to them at Covent Garden on 25 April 1864. Nina Lehmann was a daughter of Lewes's old friend Robert Chambers, at whose house in Edinburgh he had seen her in 1849, when she was nineteen. Frederick, born near Hamburg, was a partner in Naylor, Benzon & Co., the iron and steel firm later combined with Vickers Ltd. He had a fine collection of paintings and played the violin well. The Lehmanns invited the Leweses to dinner on the following Sunday, offering to send their carriage to take them to their house at Highgate. Nina's sister Amelia Chambers was married to Frederick's brother Rudolf Lehmann, a portrait painter, who settled in England in 1866. Their sister Elizabeth Lehmann was the wife of Ernst Leopold Schlesinger Benzon, senior partner in the Naylor firm, 'round as a ball all over, quite fat and enormous —or abnormous', as his great-nephew recalled, and with a strong German accent, but a conspicuous patron of the arts, though less discriminating than the Lehmanns.[2] At the houses of this closely linked group of wealthy people George Eliot met many distinguished musicians, painters, scientists, scholars—some of whom were invited to the Priory. Marian did not often go to their elaborate dinners and musicales, especially when she was working hard on a book; but the gregarious George Lewes dined out everywhere, talking enthusiastically about the absent George Eliot.

By the spring of 1865, when the *Fortnightly* was launched, George Eliot's Sunday afternoons had largely supplanted the open Saturday evenings, and some of the old names began to drop out of the lists of guests. Lewes's editorial connections inevitably attracted a new lot of men, writers for the *Cornhill*, the *Pall Mall Gazette*, or the *Fortnightly*. Trollope usually spent his week-ends in the country; but Huxley, Tyndall, John Morley, Frederick Greenwood, Alexander Bain, Viscount Amberley, and Walter Bagehot were seen at the Priory. Another group, somewhat overlapping

---

[1] GHL Journal, 25 June 1864.
[2] J. Lehmann, *Ancestors and Friends* (1962), p. 195.

those of the *Fortnightly*, have been loosely referred to as the Positivists. The Congreves with Frederic Harrison, E. S. Beesly, J. H. Bridges, and Albert and Henry Crompton were the chief of these. Lord Amberley, who was just the age of Charles Lewes, might stand in either group. Flaunting the conventions of both State and Church, he wrote in the *Fortnightly* a strong argument for disestablishment.[1] Like many earnest Victorians, he and his charming young wife, a daughter of Baron Stanley of Alderley, were looking hopefully towards the Religion of Humanity as a possible substitute for lost faith in Christianity.

They were among those who gathered on 5 May 1867 at the Sussex Hotel in Bouverie Street to hear the first of Richard Congreve's Sunday morning lectures. It was 'a considerable audience —about 75, chiefly men—' Marian told Sara Hennell, 'of various ranks, from lords and M.P.'s downwards, or upwards, for what is called social distinction seems to be in a shifting condition just now'.[2] Others Lewes noted were Lord Houghton, G. O. Trevelyan, Butler Johnstone, Mrs. Peter Taylor, Beesly, and Harrison. 'Introduced Lady Amberley to Polly; she wanted us to go back and lunch with her; but this was against rules, so she is to come to us next Sunday.'[3] Justin McCarthy confessed that he knew 'one, at least, who attended the lectures, less for the sake of what he heard than because such listeners as the authoress of *Romola* were among the audience'.[4] The second lecture attracted a smaller audience; the third, George Eliot described (possibly from the weather) as 'chilling. New faces in great part'; the fourth was 'rather better'; but there is no mention of the remaining five in the series. Lewes, though accepting the philosophy of Comte, refused to follow him when he 'assumed the part of pontiff'. In the *Fortnightly* he avowed his open and direct dissent from the doctrine of the *Politique Positive*, in which Comte stated his apostolic mission: 'All the true positivists regard me as a heretic', Lewes wrote. However, he added: 'My attitude has changed now that I have learned (from the remark of one very dear to me) to regard it as an utopia, presenting hypotheses rather than doctrines.'[5] He would not stand among the disciples, however, and Marian could not go without him.

The Amberleys called duly at the Priory. Polly, habitually slow in liking people, was 'not so favorably impressed with Lady

[1] 'Liberals, Conservatives, and the Church', *Fortnightly*, 1 (Sept. 1864), 16 ff.
[2] *Letters*, IV. 363.   [3] GHL Journal, 5 May 1867.
[4] 'The English Positivists', *Galaxy*, 7 (Mar. 1869), 373.
[5] 'Auguste Comte', *Fortnightly*, 3 (1 Jan. 1866), 404.

Amberley's nature as others are', Lewes observed.[1] And the daring young noblewoman (there in spite of her mother's frowns) took a critical look at the famous novelist: 'Mrs. Lewes sat on the sofa by me and talking to me only in a low sweet voice; her face is repulsively ugly from the immense size of the chin, but when she smiles it lights up amazingly and she looks both good and loving and gentle.' They talked about a book on the Social and Political Dependence of Women; Lady Amberley, having read only a quotation from it in the *Pall Mall*—'that a man ought to be able to be punished for a rape on his wife'—was surprised when George Eliot would not allow that the book was coarse. They talked about Browning's poems and agreed that Mrs. Browning's love poems were 'the finest expressions of love in the language'.[2] On later meetings her impression of George Eliot warmed. The Amberleys became fairly regular visitors at the Priory. One day they took little Frank (soon to succeed his grandfather as the second Earl Russell) in a cab to see Mrs. Lewes. 'Frank played in the garden while we were there,' Lady Amberley wrote, 'coming in to the maid of the house when there were snow-storms. I liked my visit. Mr. Otter, Mrs. Bodichon, and Browning were there, but I talked entirely to Mrs. Lewes and liked her very much.'[3] Earlier that day jolly Mrs. Benzon had called with her son Henry, who grew up to distinguish himself as the 'Jubilee Plunger' by gambling away his huge fortune in two years.

Without Marian, Lewes dined at the Amberleys on 7 May 1867. Lord John Russell and Lady Russell, Lord Amberley's parents, were there, with the Countess of Airlie, Sir John Bowring, W. E. Forster, Alexander Fraser (the Edinburgh philosopher), William Hanna (the radical theologian of the Scottish Church), Henry Crompton (the Positivist), and several others. Lewes found 'Lady Amberley more charming than ever, but her sister Lady Airlie even pleased me more—perhaps because her talk was mainly about Polly, whom she seems thoroughly to appreciate. Lord Russell talked to me about Spain. Home at 12.' The following week Lady Airlie invited Lewes to her first 'drum', or garden party, at Airlie Lodge, Campden Hill. Again he went without Marian.[4]

---

[1] GHL Journal, 26 May 1867.

[2] *Amberley Papers* (2 vols., 1937), II. 58. Lady Amberley's mother had forbidden her in 1860 to read the last volume of *The Mill on the Floss*; but, as Mr. Brooke says of Dorothea's reading Smollett's novels, 'She may read anything now that she's married, you know' (ch. 30).

[3] 28 Feb. 1869. *Amberley Papers*, II. 260. Frank's younger brother Bertrand, third Earl Russell, was born in 1872.   [4] GHL Journal, 18 May 1867.

It was a charming sight. The grounds are lovely and the groups of lovely well-dressed women variously scattered over the lawn and under the trees presented quite a Watteau. Nothing could exceed the attention with which I was treated. As the servant announced my name I heard a woman's voice in the conservatory say 'Here he is', so that they had been talking about me. Lady Amberley and Lady Airlie seemed anxious to introduce me to every one, first to their whole family and then to all the more distinguished guests, so that I had to bow to more Lords and Ladies than I ever met before. Lady Stanley [Lady Airlie's mother] expressed great pleasure in seeing me, having as she said, read all my works, subscribed to the *Fortnightly* as soon as it appeared, and gave it up directly I gave it up. Lord Airlie produced a very pleasant impression on me. We strolled about the grounds and sat under the trees till past six, when I had to hurry home to dinner.

Marian, who had been rewriting the opening scenes of *The Spanish Gypsy*, doubtless heard a good deal about the party; but no comment of hers has been preserved. The next day George took her to South Kensington to see the exhibition of historical portraits. 'It is really worth a little fatigue to see the English of past generations in their habit as they lived', she wrote to Sara Hennell, '—especially when Gainsborough and Sir Joshua are the painters. . . . We have been to nothing else yet, and have been keeping ourselves as quiet as possible.'[1]

Rosalind Howard, another sister of Lady Airlie and Lady Amberley, was an ardent champion of feminist causes all her days. Her husband, George Howard, a painter of considerable ability, was a friend of Burne-Jones and Morris. At Trinity College, Cambridge, in 1861 he had been one of the few undergraduates chosen to attend private lectures with the Prince of Wales. In 1889 he succeeded his uncle as ninth Earl of Carlisle. The Howards began to come to the Priory in 1869, when he was only twenty-six years old. They were among the most constant callers.

Lewes's social activity was more than vanity. Deep in Marian's nature he sensed that crying need to be recognized, respected, admired, which is reflected in several anecdotes of her childhood. Their marriage, though not legal, was essentially moral. Why should it not be acknowledged? Now that her genius was bringing the great of the world to her door, Lewes intended to use them in every possible way to enhance her image. The 'mercurial little showman', as George Meredith sneeringly called him, was playing no selfish part. He devoted the last decade of his life almost

---

[1] *Letters*, IV. 363–4.

entirely to fostering her genius. Lord Acton, preparing to review Cross's *Life of George Eliot* for the *Nineteenth Century* in 1885, wrote in an unpublished note:

Mr. Cross, loyal to the memory of Lewes, does not hint that there was any project of making straight a position which had become hard to bear, or that she ever awoke to the fact that she had sacrificed herself to an illusion. Tolerable at first. But as she grew famous, the strain grew heavy upon her—the contrast between the position she had and that which was due. About 1867 when the hard barrier yielded to her prodigious fame, she received its advance with excessive joy.

Yet, Lord Acton added, 'Hypotheses non fingo. I will not supply conjectures.'[1] Malicious stories about their relations were already circulating in 1867, spread by envious gossips, most of whom had never been inside the Priory. There is no evidence whatever that Marian repented of her decision to live with George or that he was ever unfaithful in his love for her. In accepting him she had felt—like Esther Lyon—that it was

the best thing that life could give her. But—if it was to be had at all—it was not to be had without paying a heavy price for it, such as we must pay for all that is greatly good. A supreme love, a motive that gives a sublime rhythm to a woman's life, and exalts habit into partnership with the soul's highest needs, is not to be had where and how she wills: to know that high initiation, she must often tread where it is hard to tread, and feel the chill air, and watch through darkness. It is not true that love makes all things easy: it makes us choose what is difficult.[2]

Rejection by her brothers and sister hurt Marian most keenly. Her half-brother Robert, informed by some clergyman that Marian's name was appended to a book 'bordering on infidelity', told Isaac that he wished 'her talents were turned to a different account'.[3] For nine years Isaac and Fanny had maintained their disapproving silence, though they followed her swelling fame with astonishment. At a bookseller's Fanny saw a photograph of Lewes among those of other literary celebrities and purchased it in order to gratify her curiosity about what sort of looking man Marian had chosen for a husband. She wrote to Isaac: 'Never in my life have I beheld a presentment of the human face with so

---

[1] Lord Acton's note (Cambridge University Library, MS. 5109, item 1035). Cf. *Nineteenth Century*, 17 (Mar. 1885), 476.

[2] *Felix Holt*, ch. 49.

[3] Robert Evans II to Isaac Evans, 23 Mar. 1857. (This letter and the two of Mrs. Houghton following belong to Mrs. Michael Womersley.)

very little of *human* beauty in it.' On asking the bookseller for George Eliot's picture, she was disappointed to find there was none; but he volunteered the information that she was 'the wife of the editor of the *Fortnightly*!'[1] When *Felix Holt* was announced, Fanny wrote:

I am on the tip-toe of expectation to see the forthcoming novel by Mary Ann. It is too much to hope that no member of her own family will figure in it. [Maggie and Tom *had* touched them, after all!] The subject is one of general interest and will be much more to the taste of the ordinary novel reader than Romola was. She has never written a line in the Fortnightly since she wrote those articles in the first number. It is too bad. They were only a decoy.[2]

After reading the novel Fanny wrote: 'I cannot expect you to join in my admiration of her last work. "Felix" is a Radical, and I know radicals find no favour in your sight. But all the same the Book is marvellously clever; that you *must* confess.'[3] What would Marian have given for that word from Fanny! But—like the news referred to on the last page of *Felix Holt*—it was among the things she had 'not heard, not having correspondence in those parts'.

The younger Evanses were more charitably disposed towards their famous aunt. When Robert died in February 1864, his son wrote the news to Marian, who thanked him sincerely, and sent her best love and sympathy to his mother. 'If she were ever to come to London, I hope that she would let me have the great pleasure of taking her by the hand again.'[4] Two days later Marian wrote directly to her sister-in-law to express her sympathy.

I will not believe [she added] that you will think there is no good in my saying these things to you, for good is always felt from the simple utterance of feelings that bind us poor struggling men and women to one another—And you must be very changed from what I remember you if you do not give a very gentle and loving welcome to any word or look of affection. But I cannot imagine you much changed—even your face I fancy would look familiar to me and bear few traces of the years that have passed since we last saw each other. To see you again or to hear from you, if ever you had the prompting or opportunity, would be a very sweet renewal of the past.[5]

Two years later young Robert, now the head of the family, wrote to Marian again, inviting her to come with Mr. Lewes to Notting-

[1] Mrs. Houghton to Isaac Evans, 11 Dec. 1866.
[2] Idem. 13 June 1866.
[3] Idem. 11 Dec. 1866
[4] *Letters*, IV. 131.   [5] *Letters*, IV. 134.

ham and make the acquaintance of his wife. In declining, she thanked them for their 'willingness to receive Mr. Lewes and myself', and asked him for news, which he gladly supplied, of his Aunt Houghton, 'my affectionately remembered sister',[1] who was living with his mother in Nottingham. 'I cling strongly to kith and kin,' Marian told Barbara, 'even though they reject *me*.'[2]

Her family would have been surprised to know how thoroughly conservative Marian had become. The revolutionary sentiments of those years in the Strand were gone forever. When Mrs. Peter Taylor asked her to contribute to the Mazzini fund, she firmly refused, explaining that, though she would gladly give for Mazzini's personal use, she feared this fund would ultimately be used to promote conspiracy, perhaps to acts 'more unsocial in their character than the very wrong they are directed to extinguish'.[3] Garibaldi, of course, was a respectable revolutionist, approved by the British government. When 'the working classes' presented their deputation to him at the Crystal Palace on 18 April 1864, Owen Jones got the Leweses places, and they 'had a carriage and pair and all three drove to Sydenham' to see him in his red shirt. While they were waiting, 'the Reverend F. D. Maurice came up and was introduced to Polly, sitting by her some time and chatting—also Bunsen and Saffi'. But the author of *Felix Holt* obviously did not consider the ballot a panacea for political ills—'as if Bribery in all its Protean forms could ever disappear by means of a single external arrangement!'[4]

At Blackwood's suggestion, after the passage of the Second Reform Bill in 1867, she wrote an 'Address to Working Men, by Felix Holt', putting into the mouth of her hero, that most conservative radical, an eloquent appeal to 'us artisans, and factory hands, and miners, and labourers of all sorts' to use their new power of the ballot with restraint, so that the 'common estate of society, . . . that treasure of knowledge, science, poetry, refinement of thought, feeling, and manners' shall not be lost, as it was in the French and Spanish revolutions. Blackwood found this kind of radicalism quite to his taste and was sure that it would do great good. As the opening article in *Maga* for January 1868 it was probably read more by conservatives than by 'us working men'. The day after the manuscript went off to Edinburgh, George Eliot sat for eight hours in the gallery of the House of Commons,

[1] *Letters*, IV. 140.   [2] *Letters*, V. 74.
[3] *Letters*, IV. 200.   [4] *Letters*, IV. 496.

listening to the debate on Abyssinia, where Napier had been sent to take control, one of the first steps towards British imperialism in Africa.[1] Even her disapproval of Queen Victoria was tempered. When Arthur Helps gave her the *Leaves from the Journal of Our Life in the Highlands*, which he had edited, she wrote in thanking him that she had read it 'with more sympathy because I am a woman of about the same age, and also have my personal happiness bound up in a dear husband whose loss would render my life simply a series of social duties and private memories'.[2]

Misled by George Eliot's open defiance of the marriage convention, reformers of all kinds tried to enlist her help. When John Stuart Mill introduced his amendment to extend the franchise to women, Mrs. Peter Taylor urged Marian to lend her influence in support of the cause. It was impossible to move her. To John Morley, who had discussed the issue with her, she wrote: 'If I were called on to act in the matter, I would certainly not oppose any plan which held out any reasonable promise of tending to establish as far as possible an equivalence of advantages for the two sexes, as to education and the possibilities of free development.' But the very fact that 'woman seems to me to have the worse share in existence', she thought, should be the 'basis for a sublimer resignation in woman and a more regenerating tenderness in man'. However, she added, 'The peculiarities of my own lot may have caused me to have idiosyncrasies rather than an average judgment.'[3] They always prevented her from appearing in the campaigns her feminist friends were promoting. Though Harrison saw in this reluctance evidence of her acceptance of the Positivist conception of 'woman's sphere', her view can be traced back long before her acquaintance with Comte, and shows no sympathy for his cult of the Vierge Mère.

On the education of women the reformers found her more receptive. Having heard from Barbara Bodichon that Emily Davies was working to establish a women's college, Marian invited her to come and discuss it.[4] Miss Davies, who was pleased to find her warmly in favour of the plan 'and on good grounds', was much envied by her fellow workers for having this excuse to call on the great George Eliot; one of them said 'it would be like a gin palace to have the temptation so close at hand'. Though Marian sub-

[1] *Letters*, IV. 404.   [2] Ibid. 417.
[3] GE to J. Morley, 14 May 1867 (L. W. Smith Collection. Morristown, New Jersey). A similar remark to Jowett is given in Abbott and Campbell, *Benjamin Jowett*, II. 274.
[4] *Letters*, IV. 399.

scribed £50 'From the Author of *Romola*' and followed with
interest the development of what became Girton College, her
attitude was always conservative. She wrote to Mme Bodichon:

What I should like to be sure of as a result of higher education for
women—a result that will come to pass over my grave—is, their recognition of the great amount of social unproductive labour which needs
to be done by women, and which is now either not done at all or done
wretchedly. No good can come to women, more than to any class of
male mortals, while each aims at doing the highest kind of work,
which ought rather to be held in sanctity as what only the few can do
well. I believe—and I want it to be well shown—that a more thorough
education will tend to do away with the odious vulgarity of our notions
about functions and employment, and to propagate the true gospel
that the deepest disgrace is to insist on doing work for which we are
unfit—to do work of any sort badly. There are many points of this
kind that want being urged, but they do not come well from me, and
I never like to be quoted in any way on this subject. But I will talk to
you some day, and ask you to prevail on Miss Davies to write a little
book which is much wanted.[1]

To Miss Davies she insisted on the special moral influence of
women that springs from physical and psychological differences.

And there lies just that kernel of truth in the vulgar alarm of men lest
women should be 'unsexed'. We can no more afford to part with that
exquisite type of gentleness, tenderness, possible maternity suffusing a
woman's being with affectionateness, which makes what we mean by
the feminine character, than we can afford to part with the human love,
the mutual subjection of soul between a man and a woman—which is
also a growth and revelation beginning before all history.
    The answer to those alarms of men about education is, to admit
fully that the mutual delight of the sexes in each other must enter into
the perfection of life, but to point out that complete union and sympathy can only come by women having opened to them the same store
of acquired truth or beliefs as men have, so that their grounds of judgment may be as far as possible the same.[2]

The *Fortnightly Review* under Lewes's editorship was at least
a *succès d'estime*. But the responsibility of planning an issue of
128 pages twice a month and writing extensively for it himself
was more than his frail physique could stand. At the end of the
first year Lewes told the Council that he wanted to resign. Trollope
prevailed on him to continue, undertaking to do part of his work

    [1] *Letters*, IV. 425.   [2] *Letters*, IV. 468.

while Lewes and Marian went off to Germany in the summer of
1866. The holiday revived him for a time. Then, within weeks of
his return, his health was again precarious. He called on Robert
Browning in October, 'very kind and pleasant and *useful*, but
looking so ill!', Browning wrote to Isa Blagden. 'The Fortnightly
turns into a Monthly next year, and Lewes in all likelihood leaves
the Editorship.'[1] A week at Tunbridge Wells in December failed
to restore him. He got 'worse and worse, thinner and thinner',
until in desperation he determined to go to the south of France,
leaving unfinished his *History of Philosophy*, which he was rewriting for the third edition. Polly packed her fine new travelling
bag, a Christmas present from George Smith, with initials on all
the fittings, the sort of bag she had always longed for, she said in
thanking him, and always denied herself as 'too great an indulgence. For I am a luxurious person with an uneasy conscience.'[2]
On 27 December they set out for Paris. There at Mme Mohl's they
dined with the Schérers and some French scholars; they returned
two days later for breakfast when Ernest Renan and two sculptors
—the Duchesse Colonna di Castiglione and Thomas Woolner—
were the only other guests. Woolner's opinion had changed since
he wrote to W. B. Scott in 1854 about 'the blackguard Lewes'
and the unmentionable creature he had 'bolted with'. When he
saw them in the Louvre, he went about with them, commenting
on the sculpture; they agreed to dine with him, but were too tired
to do it. Woolner became a caller at the Priory, on excellent terms
with them both to the end.

Leaving Paris on New Year's Day 1867 and breaking their
journey at Orléans, Bordeaux, and Bayonne, they arrived on
6 January at Biarritz, whose beauties Browning and other friends
had told them of. 'The stormy grandeur of the Bay of Biscay' with
waves dashing spray twenty or thirty feet into the air, the snow-
covered Pyrénées, the miraculous sunsets, the change of air
promptly exerted the usual healing effect. The 'Mutter burst out
laughing yesterday at my *fat face*', Lewes wrote to Charles when
they had been there just a week.[3] They were planning after a time
to take the new railway to Barcelona, the ultimate goal of their
travel. Before they left London Mrs. Nassau Senior had told them
about a house in the south of Spain. But the length of the journey

---

[1] E. C. McAleer, *Dearest Isa* (1951), p. 249.
[2] *Letters*, IV. 324. Other gifts from Smith include an oyster dish, and boxes of
bonbons.
[3] *Letters*, IV. 332.

and the nature of Spanish cooking ('a suggestion of oil and garlick in his food would cause him endless gastric miseries') made them decline it regretfully.[1] One morning as they were walking on the sands at Biarritz, Polly 'opened to me her secret desire of going from Barcelona to Granada. The idea quite fired me and it was *almost* resolved on. To prepare ourselves bought a Spanish conversation book and grammar; and taking the former in my pocket, as we walked I asked her words and phrases over and over again to impress them on our minds.'[2]

Before setting out, however, they made a three-days' excursion to Pau to see Mrs. Frederick Lehmann, who had been sent there for the winter on account of an alarming cough. She asked the Leweses to tea, 'and a very sweet evening we had', she wrote to her husband, 'There is such a gentle graciousness about Mrs. Lewes, one must love her, and she seems to adore him. He is worn out and thin and languid, has lost his old spirits, but they'll come back with change and rest.'[3] The next day the Leweses came at noon to breakfast with her. In the afternoon Nina sent George off to call on another invalid, the journalist Marmion Savage, while Marian talked with her. 'She made me tell her the whole story of our courtship and marriage, which seemed to interest her intensely. In fact, she was like a dear, loving elder sister to me the whole time.' Marian endeared herself further by being attentive to the German governess —'such a contrast to the way that upstart Miss Plumley treats her'. They came back again for dinner.

When she went away last night I said something of hoping she would like me, and we should be friends. She said, 'I do; I love you better every hour.' She said it so sweetly with her soft penetrating voice, it did not sound as such a compliment would from any other lips.

On the last morning, when the Leweses called to say good-bye, Mrs. Lehmann gave her a boxwood rosary and a knitted woollen shawl, and walked with them to the station. 'The weather has been glorious these two days, and the old white fellows so grand; in fact, the little visit has been a complete success', Nina wrote.

I have got to know her as I never should have done in years in London, and I think she loves me—we are sworn friends. What a sweet, mild, womanly presence hers is—so soothing too, and *elevating* above all. It is impossible to be with that noble creature without feeling *better*.

[1] *Letters*, IV. 317.   [2] GHL Journal, 10 Jan. 1867.
[3] *Letters*, IV. 335.

I have never known any one like her—and then her modesty, her humility. A modesty, too, that never makes her or you awkward, as many modesties do. I am full of her. She makes a great impression on me, and I long to see more of her and be with her. She said, without my asking it, she would write me from Barcelona to tell me how it went with 'George', and if they were going on as they now intend.[1]

Their journey through Spain was the most strenuous the Leweses ever attempted, entailing stretches of seventeen or eighteen hours by diligence, and as long as twenty-eight hours by railway in cold weather. Paradoxically, it did them both great good. Lewes returned after ten weeks looking 'like a healthy brother of his thin and pale self such as it was two months ago', 'plumper and ruddier', declaring that he had never enjoyed a journey so much.[2] They divided the long trip from San Sebastián to Barcelona by overnight stops at Zaragossa and Lérida. After a week at Barcelona filled with sightseeing, theatre or opera nearly every evening, and reading *Gil Blas* while they rested, they embarked on the steamer to Alicante. Since there were no other ladies aboard, Lewes was allowed to join Polly in the ladies' cabin. The voyage took two nights and a day. Though the weather was perfect, Lewes was sick as usual, and they were glad of a full day and night ashore to recover before taking another steamer to Malaga. On 15 February in a diligence hauled by ten mules they started on the long climb up the winding road to Granada, which they reached at 10 the next morning, horribly tired and hungry.[3]

At Granada they stayed a week at the Fonda Ortiz. Two Frenchmen, 'a pleasant American' named Taylor, and his sister were the only other guests. The Leweses made their first visit to the Alhambra with the Taylors, who departed the next day. Ramon the guide took them to a potter he knew in the Albaicin where they watched the men making and painting vases. After selecting two or three small ones, they were taken into the kitchen with the family, who entertained them with songs accompanied by the guitar and danced fandangoes. The 'natural grace and refinement of these people was very striking', Lewes wrote,

especially the two girls, who were shy and modest but wholly without affectation, and the old mother sitting by the hearth in the corner, smiling and putting in a word now and then, also singing her copla while the dance was going on, and the large mild dog who came in and curled himself by the hearth after saluting us all. We sat there a long

---

[1] *Letters*, IV. 336–7.   [2] Ibid. 347, 349.
[3] Details from GHL's Journal, Feb.–Mar. 1867.

while perfectly delighted with this poetical scene. It was simple life seen at its best.[1]

Their sympathetic view was in strong contrast to that of two Englishwomen '—girls almost, who had ridden from Córdova on horseback—excited our curiosity by speaking in the strongest terms against the Spainards, especially the lower orders, whom they pronounced little better than savages'. Another day, after dinner, they were entertained at the Fonda by a gypsy troop, the Captain, three or four men, and six girls in full costume, who danced fandangoes and gypsy dances, accompanying themselves with castanets, tambourines, and 'wild howling meant for singing'. Antonio, the Captain, was superbly handsome, and they gazed on him 'much as we should have gazed on a fine Greek statue' as he played the guitar and sang with a fine, resonant, baritone voice, and danced with rare grace and agility. At parting he shook hands with Lewes and with Polly too. On their last day at Granada they sought out the dwelling of the Captain, who was a blacksmith. He was delighted to see them again, called his wife to invite them upstairs, treating them like friends and showing them his photograph album; without any hint from the visitors, he took his guitar and played and sang for them. They knew better than to offer him money; but when Lewes suggested giving his workmen something to drink their health, Antonio patted him on the shoulder and said 'Bueno, bueno'.[2]

Lewes usually scribbled his name with deliberate illegibility in the hotel registers; at Granada, seeing only the two Frenchmen, he had written it legibly. Before they left, the hotel filled up with English and Americans, one of whom recognized the name. It was whispered around who they were. Before they started for Córdova one of the Americans, a Mrs. Stone, 'came to the window of the coupé and told Polly how delighted she was to have met the author of *Romola* and begging for her autograph'.

Two days were too much for Lewes in Córdova, 'this deadest of dead cities', though Marian was fascinated by the mosque, which her imagination peopled with the Moorish characters she was creating for her drama. At Seville, the Cathedral and the Murillos were worth the nuisance of the mosquitoes, which annoyed them constantly during their four days there. 'Altogether we feel very glad to be going away from Andalusia', Lewes wrote. From Seville to Madrid took over twenty-eight hours on a train

[1] GHL Journal, 19 Feb. 1867.   [2] GHL Journal, 22 Feb. 1867.

jammed with three or four hundred soldiers, noisy, smoking incessantly, yet 'not brutal'. At Madrid the pictures in the Prado, which they visited each day, made a fitting climax. 'They and the Cathedral at Seville are enough to justify western civilization, with all its faults', Marian wrote to Barbara Bodichon.[1] They started on 6 March on another long railway journey of nearly twenty-three hours back to France. On this last lap Marian caught cold and was kept in her room by cough and cold most of a week at Biarritz before they took another seventeen-hour journey to Paris and home. When they reached the Priory on 16 March 1867, a cold east wind was blowing the snow across Regent's Park.

Marian plunged at once into work on *The Spanish Gypsy* while her impressions of Spain were fresh. Her town of Bedmar was imaginary but recollected details gave some actuality to the settings, though with a strong theatrical quality. To John Blackwood's inquiry about what she was writing, Marian replied that it

is not a Romance. It is—prepare your fortitude—it is—a poem. I conceived the plot, and wrote nearly the whole as a drama in 1864. Mr. Lewes advised me to put it by for a time and take it up again, with a view to recasting it. He thinks hopefully of it. I need not tell you that I am *not* hopeful—but I am quite sure the subject is fine. It is not historic, but has merely historic connections. The plot was wrought out entirely as an incorporation of my own ideas. Of course, if it is ever finished to my satisfaction, it is not a work for us to get money by, but Mr. Lewes urges and insists that it shall be done. I have also my private projects about an English novel, but I am afraid of speaking as if I could depend on myself. At present I am rather dizzy, and not settled down to home habits of regular occupation.[2]

Her progress was painfully slow. To the usual problems of deciding on characters and motives she had added the difficulty of blank verse, imposed on the prose version of the story. Echoes of Milton and Tennyson and Wordsworth abound. Marian's old symptoms of headache and diffidence returned, requiring all Lewes's efforts to sustain her. He himself was suffering again

---

[1] *Letters*, IV. 351. GE's Notebook for *The Spanish Gypsy*, 120 pages, sold at Sotheby's, 27 June 1923, was broken up and bound with some MS. letters into volumes of *The Works of George Eliot*, large paper ed. (25 vols., Houghton Mifflin, Boston and N.Y., 1924), to form a limited ed. The set bought by W. M. Matthews contained sixteen pages of the Journal (fols. 37–40, 51–4) and a letter to Mrs. Bell, 8 June 1860. GE's Journal of her Spanish travel, 26 Jan.–7 Mar. 1867, sold at the same time, may have suffered the same mutilation. Owners of this set should examine the volumes for other fragments of the Journal.

[2] GE to J. Blackwood, 21 Mar. 1867; *Letters*, IV. 354–5.

from dyspepsia. When two weeks at Niton failed to restore them, he proposed a return to Germany to see if they could recapture the creative mood in which she had written *Adam Bede* in 1858. They left 29 July 1867 by the familiar route—Brussels, Liège (where their old room was already occupied), Cologne (where they supped with Helen Faucit and Theodore Martin), and on to Wetzlar to visit the scenes of Goethe's *Werther*. In Lotte's room 'Polly played the air from "Richard Coeur de Lion" on the old harpsichord with its black keys and plaintive jingling sounds, [which, Lewes wrote,] like the quavering of an old woman's voice, affected me.'¹ At Ilmenau they spent a fortnight, writing in the morning, wandering in the afternoon over the walks they had first taken in 1854. They passed through Weimar on the train with a tug at the heart at sight of the familiar spots, and went on to Dresden. Here in their old lodgings at 5B Waisenhausstrasse they resumed something of the old pattern of life. They visited the Gallery only a few times, and there is no mention of the Raphael, which stirred them so in 1858. When they did not go to the theatre or opera in the evenings, they would read aloud to each other. The poems of Tennyson are particularly significant at this point: Marian read 'Enoch Arden' aloud one day, and on another Lewes read 'Sea Dreams', 'The Northern Farmer', and 'Tithonus' to her. In the mornings Marian wrote and rewrote scenes of her drama, striving to make industry and determination answer for inspiration. Back in London 1 October, she plodded on, till at the end of the month Part I was finished.

Blackwood, shown a sample of the drama in June, had been 'puzzled what to say' about it. Now, wishing to be useful, he suggested putting Part I into type so that she could revise it more conveniently.² With the variant readings set one above another, it filled 122 pages. The sight of it gave Marian fresh hope, while Lewes, she told Blackwood, was 'in an unprecedented state of delight' with the poem, pleased by the sense of variety it gives.

At Christmas time Lewes went to see his mother and Gertrude, and then to the Benzons' to see their children enjoy the Christmas tree. He had begun *Problems of Life and Mind*, a pioneer study of psychology, to which he was applying all his knowledge of the nervous system. On 27 December he went off to Bonn and Heidelberg for ten days to consult the physiologists about his theories, leaving Polly at home, unwilling to put down her poem. When Mrs. Congreve urged her to attend one of the Positivist meetings

¹ GHL Journal, 2 Aug. 1867.   ² *Letters*, IV. 398.

in his absence, Marian told her that Mr. Lewes objected, 'on grounds which I think just, to my going to any public manifestation without him'.[1] She laboured away at Part II, writing each scene in prose before versifying it. In mid March Lewes took her to Torquay for a month, where she could work without interruption while he zoologized for his important series of articles on Darwin in the *Fortnightly*. As she read the scenes to him, he advised omitting 'some motives which prolonged the action'.[2] To Blackwood's relief this made the poem less tragic than she had threatened, leaving Silva alive to seek pardon at Rome for having killed Fedalma's[3] father, while she takes over the leadership of the Gypsy people. *The Spanish Gypsy* was chosen as the title, George Eliot said, 'because it is a little in the fashion of the elder dramatists, with whom I have perhaps more cousinship than with recent poets'.[4] The last lines were written on 29 April 1868, and the book was published early in June.

The Leweses were already in Germany on the way to Baden. At Bonn there were visits with the men Lewes had met in January —Wilhelm Preyer and Eduard Pflüger, the physiologists, and von Sybel, the historian they had known at Munich. After a week of fashionable Baden they were bored and went off to the little spa at Petersthal in the Black Forest, where they stayed a fortnight, taking the waters, wandering about the mountain paths, and reading Morris's *Earthly Paradise* aloud. From there they went to Freiburg, where they met other distinguished scientists—Funcke, Weismann, Kussmaul, Ecker, Manz, and others. Polly came in for her share of lionizing, too, before they drove off some fifteen miles to St. Märgen, a tiny watering-place. Here, though it was cold, they stayed four days. They made a memorable visit to a peasant's cottage in company with the Gräfin von Baudissin and her daughter, which provided material for the poem 'Agatha'. After a week at Interlaken, they started for home. They were back in London 23 July.

The reviews of *The Spanish Gypsy* were surprisingly laudatory— not only those in *The Times* (by Dallas) or *Blackwood's* (Colonel E. B. Hamley), where friendship coloured criticism. The *Spectator* called it 'undoubtedly much the greatest poem of any wide scope

---

[1] *Letters*, IV. 413.   [2] Ibid. 431.
[3] The heroine's name is spelt *Fidalma* in the first 322 folios of the MS.
[4] *Letters*, IV. 428.

and on a plan of any magnitude, which has ever proceeded from a woman'; even the hostile *Athenæum* found much to praise. More considered judgements soon appeared. The *Pall Mall Gazette* described the story as melodramatic and unnatural, and blamed George Eliot for 'casting the most modern of all philo-sophies . . . back into the mouths of people who hadn't the faintest glimmer of it'.[1] Henry James wrote perhaps the fairest estimate: '*The Spanish Gypsy* is not a genuine poem', he declared. 'It lacks the hurrying quickness, the palpitating warmth, the bursting melody of such a creation. . . . We see the landscape, the people, the manners of Spain as through a glass smoked by the flame of meditative vigils.'[2] Fedalma's rejection of marriage with Duke Silva for her 'grand submission' to the call of Gypsy blood struck even Positivists as wildly improbable. Harrison, one of the few to whom George Eliot gave copies of the book, was frankly dis-appointed. He had been hoping that she would use her art to promote the ideal of 'healthy moral control over societies', and the conduct of Fedalma and Zarca seemed 'treason to human life'.[3] Congreve's precise opinion of the poem is not known. His much-quoted allusion to it as a 'mass of Positivism' occurs only in George Eliot's quotation of the phrase after she had spent the night at Wandsworth, 3 November 1868; without the context one cannot be certain of his opinion. W. M. Simon, who has studied the question most closely, finds only a few brief passages in *The Spanish Gypsy* that bear any sort of Positivist interpretation; he suggests that this phrase of Congreve's may have started the whole erroneous view of George Eliot as a Positivist.[4]

Sales of *The Spanish Gypsy* attest George Eliot's reputation as a novelist more than her achievement as a poet. Of the first edition 2,000 copies were printed, selling at 10s. 6d., and a cautious second edition of 250 copies, incorporating a few corrections, was issued in August. Lewes pointed out to Blackwood that even Mrs. Browning's *Aurora Leigh* sold less than 3,000 copies in the first year. Reset with further revisions in November 1868 to sell at 7s. 6d. (of which George Eliot received 1s. 6d. for each copy sold), a third edition of 1,000 was printed; and a second 1,000 from stereotype plates answered the demand for the poem for the next

[1] *Pall Mall Gazette*, 3 July 1868, pp. 43-4.
[2] *North American Review*, 107 (Oct. 1868), 620-35.
[3] *Letters*, IV. 289, 485.
[4] *European Positivism* [1963], p. 211.

five years. In the United States, however, Ticknor and Fields sold over 8,000 copies of it, paying the author 1*s*. for each. 'I am happy in having fallen into honourable hands across the Atlantic, where dishonourable hands are abundant', she wrote.[1] In a letter to Lewes Robert Lytton mentioned the fact that Zincalo was properly accented on the first syllable, not the second, as she has it.[2] This was the sort of error most disturbing to Marian. But the stereotype plates had been cast, and to correct it would have required resetting more than 100 pages. The change was not made until the poem was included in the Cabinet edition in 1878.

By then *The Spanish Gypsy* had earned over £1,000 for its author. Writing to Mrs. Bray, she said:

Don't you imagine how the people who consider writing simply as a money-getting profession will despise me for choosing a work by which I could only get hundreds where for a novel I get thousands? I cannot help asking you to admire what my husband is, compared with many possible husbands—I mean, in urging me to produce a poem rather than anything in a worldly sense more profitable.[3]

They were now prosperous enough to indulge such lofty sentiment, far from the days when every sixpence had to be counted. She told Lucy Clifford that in those days they used to buy things and call them after the books that provided the money. 'We still have some table cloths that Maggie Tulliver gave us', she said.[4]

Social acceptance was harder to achieve than financial independence. During the first years at the Priory, George Eliot's genius gradually overcame society's refusal to countenance her relation to Lewes. Lord Acton, noting the change, believed that 'her conduct was explained by the current of her life'.[5] The fact was not forgotten but it was regarded as an exception. The attraction of her name and personality made the Priory the centre of the most interesting society in London. Some of the visitors were old friends whom Lewes invited deliberately. In 1868 he called on William Bell Scott, for example, whom he had known intimately in the 1840s, and 'asked me to dine and get acquainted with his new wife, whom I found the most bland and amiable of plain women, and most excellent in conversation'.[6] Another early friend, the Reverend W. H. Brookfield and his wife Jane, whom Lewes

---

[1] *Letters*, IV. 481.   [2] *Letters*, V. 32.   [3] *Letters*, IV. 438.
[4] 'A Remembrance of George Eliot', *Nineteenth Century*, 74 (July 1913), 115.
[5] Cambridge University Library: MS. 5109, item 139.
[6] *Autobiographical Notes of the Life of William Bell Scott*, ed. W. Minto (2 vols., N.Y., 1892), II. 71.

was meeting again at the Benzons', were happy to come and see George Eliot. Others like Mrs. Orr and Eliza Lynn Linton—never really a friend of Lewes or of Marian, whose success she could not forgive—came without being strongly urged.

Their most interesting guests were younger people, intellectuals, many of them bachelors, untroubled about the social shibboleth. Emanuel Deutsch, whom they first met at the Lehmanns', had come over from Germany in 1855 to be an assistant in the British Museum. Learned in Sanskrit and the Indo-European languages as well as in the Semitic—Chaldaic, Aramaic, Amharic, and Phoenician—he won wide acclaim by his article on the Talmud in the *Quarterly Review* in 1867. W. R. Shedden-Ralston, whose department was the Russian and Slavic, was another bachelor assistant at the British Museum, like Deutsch a prolific writer in the magazines. A somewhat younger man John Burnell Payne, who wrote for the *Pall Mall Gazette*, had begun life headed towards the Church, but, with many of his generation, lost his faith and settled for a career in teaching and journalism. He and his brother Joseph Frank Payne, who became a distinguished physician, were welcomed even more warmly when George Eliot discovered that they were cousins of her old teacher Miss Franklin. After John's untimely death in 1869 Dr. Payne laid his doubts about a future life before George Eliot. Another young physician at the beginning of a great career was T. Clifford Allbutt, inventor of the clinical thermometer. He too discussed his religious perplexity with her, and after his removal to Leeds, consulted her about the problem of his long engagement.[1] George Eliot, always avid in studying such human relations, followed his career with interest. After his marriage she and Lewes spent two days at Leeds, inspecting his new Infirmary.[2] Another young bachelor who had studied medicine for a time was Thomas Sanderson, later known as Cobden-Sanderson, the bookbinder and printer; he became one of the regular callers. So did Charles Kegan Paul, an Oxford graduate, who after some years as a chaplain at Eton and a co-worker with F. D. Maurice in London, left the Church altogether to become a publisher. From Cambridge came an older friend of Lewes, the Public Orator William George Clark, a Fellow of Trinity College, who called in October 1869 to tell them of his intention to give up his oratorship and renounce all connection with the Church—a course in which another friend, Henry Sidgwick, also of Trinity, followed him.

[1] *Letters*, IV. 499.   [2] *Letters*, IV. 473–4.

It was Clark who introduced Oscar Browning at the Priory, suggesting him as the reviewer of Tom Trollope's *History of Florence* in the *Fortnightly*.[1] The Leweses found him an entertaining guest. In 1867 Browning asked them to visit Eton, where they watched a cricket match, rowed on the river, and dined with the boys in his house. When George Eliot happened to remark on how comfortable a certain chair was, he sent her one like it. In February 1868 Browning and Clark together invited the Leweses to see Cambridge. Browning, who as a Fellow had rooms at King's College, went down in the train with them and saw them established at the Bull.

> We dined in the evening [he wrote], a small party, in Mr. Clark's rooms. I sat next to her, and she talked to me solemnly about the duties of life, about the shallow immorality of believing that all things would turn out for the best, and the danger of fixing our attention too much on the life to come, as likely to distract us from doing our duty in this world. The next day she breakfasted with me in my rooms in college. I shall not readily forget her exquisite courtesy and tenderness to the ladies whom I had invited to meet her.[2]

Among them was Augusta Webster, the poetess, who with her husband, a Fellow of Trinity, soon called at the Priory. Henry Sidgwick, another Fellow, who was of the party, became a trusted friend of the Leweses.

One Sunday afternoon in February 1868 Mr. and Mrs. Edward Burne-Jones came to the Priory, brought probably by Frederic Burton. They were at the centre of the Pre-Raphaelite circle—the Rossettis and the William Morrises—interested in literature and art, and quite indifferent to conventional prejudices. Twenty years younger than the Leweses, they became warm friends at once. Edward never ceased to be astonished at George Eliot's intellectual power. 'There is no one living better to talk to', he wrote of her years later. 'Her knowledge is really deep, and her heart one of the most sympathetic to me I ever knew.'[3] They came often to lunch or dinner at the Priory and were frequent visitors on Sunday afternoons before the number of guests grew so large that conversation with the hosts was difficult. They had moved in 1867 into the Grange, the great house in North End Lane, Fulham, where Samuel Richardson wrote all his novels. The Leweses used to drive out there to call on them, sometimes taking books or toys for their

[1] *Letters*, IV. 186. The review was in the *Fortnightly*, 4 (15 Feb. 1866), 70–86.
[2] Oscar Browning, *Life of George Eliot* (1890), p. 99.
[3] *Memorials of Edward Burne-Jones* (2 vols., 1904), II. 4.

two children. They soon introduced to George Eliot their friend William Morris, who gave her the first volume of his *The Earthly Paradise*; but he was much preoccupied and never became intimate. Rossetti, too, they brought to the Priory.[1]

In August 1868 Lewes was invited by Dr. H. W. Acland, Regius Professor of Medicine, to attend the meeting of the British Medical Association at Oxford. There at breakfast with the Aclands he met Charles Eliot Norton, who had just arrived from America with his wife and children, his mother, and two unmarried sisters to live abroad for nearly five years. In January, when Lewes learned that the Nortons had taken a house at 16 Queen's Gate Terrace, he called and

asked us to come and see his wife, saying that she never made calls herself, but was always at home on Sunday afternoons. She is an object of great interest and great curiosity to society here. She is not received in general society, and the women who visit her are either so émancipée as not to mind what the world says about them, or have no social position to maintain. Lewes dines out a good deal, and some of the men with whom he dines go without their wives to his house on Sundays. No one whom I have heard speak, speaks in other than terms of respect of Mrs. Lewes, but the common feeling is that it will not do for society to condone so flagrant a breach as hers of a convention and a sentiment (to use no stronger terms) on which morality greatly relies for support. I suspect society is right in this;—at least since I have been here I have heard of one sad case in which a poor weak woman defended her own wretched course, which had destroyed her own happiness and that of other persons also, by the example of Mrs. Lewes. I do not believe that many people think that Mrs. Lewes violated her own moral sense, or is other than a good woman in her present life, but they think her example pernicious, and that she cut herself off by her own act from the society of the women who feel themselves responsible for the tone of social morals in England.

After a while, as Susan did not call, an invitation came for her and me to lunch, and this we very readily accepted.

This account, written by Norton in a letter to G. W. Curtis,[2] is slightly misleading. Though Mrs. Norton did not call, her sister-in-law Grace Norton did call the first Sunday after Lewes's invitation, and the following Sunday Mr. and Mrs. Norton came to the Priory for lunch.

---

[1] GHL Diary, 7 Feb. 1869.
[2] C. E. Norton to G. W. Curtis, 29 Jan. 1869 (Harvard).

Their house, called 'The Priory' is a little, square, two-story dwelling standing in a half yard, half garden, surrounded with one of those high brick walls of which one grows so impatient in England.

Lewes received us at the door with characteristic animation; he looks and moves like an old-fashioned French barber or dancing-master, very ugly, very vivacious, very entertaining. You expect to see him take up his fiddle and begin to play. His talk is much more French than English in its liveliness and in the grimace and gesture with which it is accompanied,—all the action of his mind is rapid, and it is so full that it seems to be running over. 'Oh, if you like to hear stories', he said one day, 'I can tell you stories for twelve hours on end.'—it is just the same if you like to hear science, or philosophy. His acquirements are very wide, wider, perhaps, than deep; but the men who know most on special subjects speak with respect of his attainments. I have heard both Darwin and Sir Charles Lyell speak very highly of the thoroughness of his knowledge in their departments. In fact his talents seem equal to anything. But he is not a man who wins more than a moderate liking from you. He has the vanity of a Frenchman; his moral perceptions are not acute and he consequently often fails in social tact and taste. He has what it is hard to call a vulgar air, but at least there is something in his air which reminds you of vulgarity.

He took us into the pleasant cheerful drawing rooms which occupy one side of the lower floor of the house, where Mrs. Lewes received us very pleasantly,—and we soon had lunch, the only other person present being his eldest, and married son. Lunch was set in the study, a cheerful room like the others, lined with well-filled bookshelves, save over the fire-place where hung a staring likeness an odious, vulgarizing portrait of Mrs. Lewes. Indeed all the works of art in the house bore witness to the want of delicate artistic feeling, or good culture on the part of the occupants, with the single exception, so far as I observed, of the common lithograph of Titian's Christ of the Tribute Money. The walls of the drawing room in which we sat after lunch were adorned with proof impressions (possibly the original drawings, I am not sure) of the illustrations to 'Romola'.

The portrait of Mrs. Lewes reminded me, not by its own merit, of Couture's drawing of George Sand,—and there is a strong likeness to this drawing in her own face. The head and face are hardly as noble as George Sand's, but the lines are almost as strong and masculine; the cheeks are almost as heavy, and the hair is dressed in a similar style, but the eyes are not so deep, and there is less suggestion of possible beauty and possible sensuality in the general contour and in the expression. Indeed one rarely sees a plainer woman; dull complexion, dull eyes, heavy features.

For the greater part of two or three hours she and I talked together with little intermission. Her talk was by no means brilliant. She said not one memorable thing, but it was the talk of a person of strong mind

PLATE XI

GEORGE HENRY LEWES 1867

From a drawing by Rudolf Lehmann

who had thought much and who felt deeply, and consequently it was more than commonly interesting. Her manner was too intense, she leans over to you till her face is close to yours, and speaks in very low and eager tones; nor is her manner perfectly simple. It is a little that, or it suggests that, of a woman who feels herself to be of mark and is accustomed, as she is, to the adoring flattery of a coterie of not undistinguished admirers. In the course of the afternoon three or four men came in,—the only one whom I knew was Professor Beesly.

The others were not undistinguished, however: Dr. Joseph Payne and his brother, Cobden-Sanderson, Edward Lyulph Stanley (later Baron Stanley of Alderley), Colonel Edward Bruce Hamley, and Frederic Burton, happily unrecognized as the painter of the 'odious, vulgarizing portrait'.

We came away just before sunset. As the gate shut behind us I said, 'Well, Sue, do you want to go there again?' 'No', said she, 'I don't care much about it.'

But the facts belie this Brahminical indifference. Two weeks later Mrs. Norton and her sister-in-law called again, when the company included Mrs. Mark Pattison, Mrs. Lynn Linton, Cobden-Sanderson, Burton, Mountstuart Grant-Duff, F. T. Palgrave, and Sir Henry Holland.[1] The following Wednesday the Leweses lunched at Queen's Gate Terrace, and the next Monday Mrs. Norton brought her two children with her to lunch at the Priory.[2]

Other American ladies were equally happy to be admitted to the Priory. James T. Fields, the Boston publisher who had done so well with *The Spanish Gypsy*, called on 13 May 1869 to propose a uniform American edition of the works of George Eliot and offered £300 to publish her poem 'Agatha' in the *Atlantic Monthly*. The following Sunday he returned to the Priory with Mrs. Fields and Miss Mabel Lowell, who had come abroad with them. She was the daughter of James Russell Lowell, whose *Under the Willows* Mrs. Norton had presented to George Eliot on her first visit. Lowell himself became a correspondent of Lewes; writing to him, 7 July 1871, Lowell described how in 1847 he had accidentally opened Lewes's novel *Ranthorpe* at a bookseller's and, astonished to find an Englishman who knew about Goethe, he bought the book and had it still.[3] Then he read Lewes's *Goethe*,

---

[1] GHL Diary, 31 Jan. 1869.   [2] GHL Diary, 3, 18 Feb. 1869.
[3] Both GE's copy of *Under the Willows* and Lowell's of *Ranthorpe* are now in my collection.

which he thought 'admirably done'. The Nortons kept telling him about George Eliot, but he *would* not read her novels till one day, on a fishing trip, he picked up *Adam Bede*, which a friend had with him, and was converted.[1] When Lowell came to England in 1873, he became acquainted with the Leweses.

Another American correspondent, one of the most famous, was Harriet Beecher Stowe. Out of the blue in May 1869 she sent 'a really noble letter', full of admiration of *Silas Marner*, and *The Mill on the Floss*, and *Adam Bede*, describing her winter home in an orange grove in Florida, and wondering about George Eliot's religious views. She wrote 'in a most loveable, womanly tone'. George Eliot responded gratefully:

> I value very highly the warrant to call you friend which your letter has given me. It . . . made me almost wish that you could have a momentary vision of the discouragement, nay, paralyzing despondency in which many days of my writing life have been past, in order that you might fully understand the good I find in such sympathy as yours—in such an assurance as you give me that my work has been worth doing. But I will not dwell on any mental sickness of mine. The best joy your words give me is the sense of that sweet, generous feeling in you which dictated them, and I shall always be the richer because you have in this way made me know you better.

Marian goes on to tell how her first glimpse of Mrs. Stowe as a woman came through a letter read to her by Mrs. Follen in 1853, the details of which she still recalled easily. As to her religion, George Eliot wrote,

> I believe that religion too has to be modified—'developed', according to the dominant phrase—and that a religion more perfect than any yet prevalent, must express less care for personal consolation, and a more deeply-awing sense of responsibility to man, springing from sympathy with that which of all things is most certainly known to us, the difficulty of the human lot. I do not find my temple in Pantheism, which, whatever might be its value speculatively, could not yield a practical religion, since it is an attempt to look at the universe from the outside of our relations to it (that universe) as human beings. As healthy, sane human beings we must love and hate—love what is good for mankind, hate what is evil for mankind. For years of my youth I dwelt in dreams of a pantheistic sort, falsely supposing that I was enlarging my sympathy. But I have travelled far away from that time.

Letters are necessarily narrow and fragmentary, and when one writes

---

[1] James Russell Lowell to GHL, 7 July 1871 (L. W. Smith Collection, Morristown, N.J.).

on wide subjects are liable to create more misunderstanding than illumination. But I have little anxiety of that kind in writing to you, dear friend and fellow-labourer—for you have had longer experience than I as a writer, and fuller experience as a woman, since you have borne children and known the mother's history from the beginning. I trust your quick and long-taught mind as an interpreter little liable to mistake me.[1]

Though they never met, the correspondence thus begun continued till George Eliot's death.

At the end of 1868 George Eliot noted in her Journal: 'We have made some new friendships that cheer us with the sense of new admiration of actual living beings whom we know in the flesh, and who are kindly disposed to us. And we have no real trouble. I wish we were not in a minority of our fellow-men.' She had set herself many tasks for 1869—a novel called *Middlemarch*, a long poem on Timoleon, the Corinthian enemy of tyrants, and a number of shorter poems. A list of themes in her Notebook includes The Congress of Rivers; *(Tubalcain) Vision of Jubal; The Death of Pan, v. Plutarch; *Agatha; a passage from Marcus Aurelius: 'But Gods there are undoubtedly, and they regard human affairs'; Libanius; *Stradivarius; 'Ex oriente lux'; Der arme Heinrich; Homeric Hymn to Ceres; The burning of the Crucifix; Daphnis; Theocritean Idyl, killing of the bull; Death of d'Aubigné; and *Arion, vide Herodotus I.[2] For Timoleon, which was to show the influence of personal character on destiny,[3] she read much Sicilian history, copying into her Notebook extracts from Grote and a detailed chronology extending from the foundation of Carthage in 878 B.C. to the death of Timoleon in 336.[4] Happily no more is heard of what might have been painful work for everyone. The four she marked with asterisks were published. 'Agatha', describing her visit to the old woman's cottage at St. Märgen, was finished on 23 January 1869, and 'How Lisa Loved the King', a rhymed story from Boccaccio[5] (not included in the list) on 14 February.

For two years after Bertie joined Thornie in Natal, they went on 'gloriously', thoroughly happy in their partnership of the farm. Before Christmas 1867 Bertie wrote optimistically about it.[6] Youthful vigour survived a monetary crisis in the colony and a

---

[1] *Letters*, V. 29–31.   [2] Notebook (Folger Library: M. a. 13, fol. 71).
[3] Notebook, fol. 7.   [4] Ibid. fol. 9.   [5] *Decameron*, X. 7.
[6] *Letters*, IV. 397, and GHL Journal, 25 Dec. 1867.

war with the natives. But in January 1869 a letter came that made Lewes very sad. Thornie was having severe and persistent pains in his back, which he once thought were caused by an injury in wrestling some months before, but were now attributed to kidney stone. He was losing weight alarmingly. His father wrote to him immediately sending £250 and urging him to come home at once to have the best advice and perhaps go through an operation. It would be many weeks before the letter could reach Natal, and many more before Thornie would be able to get home. 'The vision of him haunts me incessantly', his father wrote.[1]

On 15 February, the day after George Eliot finished 'How Lisa Loved the King', she sent it off to Blackwood to see if he wanted it for *Maga*. He had it set immediately,[2] and offered £50 for it, agreeing to depart from his 'wise rule of anonymity' and use her name, though he did not think 'that an article from one of the Apostles' would much affect the sale of *Maga*. She accepted the offer, 'liking the old ingle nook better than the new hearths', but protested that she had no idea of its appearing in the March number, because it was '*absolutely* unrevised'.[3] Lewes's plan of selling it to Ticknor and Fields for simultaneous publication in the May number of the *Atlantic* was prevented by Blackwood's contract with the American reprinters of *Maga*.[4] George Eliot took the proof with her to revise at leisure in Italy.

On 3 March 1869 they set out, taking the way down the Rhône and along the Riviera. The mistral was blowing, and they shivered in rain and hail. At Florence, where they stayed five days with the Tom Trollopes, Marian was in bed most of the time with a sore throat and other ailments. Lewes, in spite of sciatica, went to a party at Isa Blagden's, and on the last day Polly was strong enough to go with him to see Professor Schiff demonstrate a machine for measuring the speed of thought.[5] In hope of warmer weather, they went by train directly to Naples. It rained most of the ten days they were there. Though their stay in Rome was timed to avoid the crowds of Holy Week, they found the city celebrating the jubilee of Pope Pius IX, almost as bustling as in 1860. The banker at MacBean's, a friend of John Blackwood, recognized Lewes, but promised not to mention their presence. They had been dodging

---

[1] *Letters*, v. 4.
[2] A galley-proof with a few corrections is in the Parrish Collection at Princeton.
[3] *Letters*, v. 15–16.
[4] Fields, Osgood & Co. published the poem separately, Boston, 1869.
[5] GHL Journal, 20 Mar. 1869.

English travellers everywhere, dining in their room to avoid conversation at table.

Walking in the Pamfili Gardens one day, they encountered Mrs. William Henry Bullock, the eldest daughter of Mrs. William Cross, to whom Spencer had introduced Lewes at Weybridge during a walking tour in October 1867. Mrs. Cross, who was also in Rome, came to call on the Leweses on 18 April with her son John Walter Cross, a tall, handsome fellow, twenty-nine years old. Since leaving Rugby, John had been working in New York as a broker in the family's business, and was now about to enter the London office. It was Lewes's fifty-second birthday. 'Both Polly and I had forgotten it', he wrote in his Journal, 18 April 1869.

Even Rome could not hold them for long. Lewes was anxious about his mother, now eighty-two years old and in feeble health. Charles and Gertrude, who had been looking after her in his absence, were about to set out for their holiday on the Continent. Lewes left Rome with no regret. 'I have had enough of it and want to be at home and at work again', he wrote.[1] His usual high spirits were failing. Instead of being amused, he was irritated by the unscrupulous cabbies, the inefficient Italian railways, and the annoying travellers. At Florence they stopped again for a few days with the Trollopes, able this time to enjoy a little sightseeing, including the interior of the monastery of San Marco, now a museum. They dined with the American Ambassador George Perkins Marsh and his wife, who promised to ask no one but Isa Blagden—a stipulation that cost them a chance to meet Longfellow, who, when he learned that George Eliot was coming, begged in vain to be included. They went quickly through Ravenna and Verona and over the Brenner Pass to Munich. On 2 May at 5 a.m. they took the train for Strasbourg. By 'miserable accident' at Ulm they got into the same carriage with the old friend of John Chapman and of Karl Marx, Andrew Johnson of the Bullion Office, 'an acquaintance from whom George has been at great pains to guard me in London'. Since Johnson, who was returning from a wedding trip with his second wife, evidently planned to stay at the same hotel in Strasbourg, George whispered to Polly: 'Are you prepared to go on to Paris tonight? You know the alternative.' Polly was. So they stayed on the train, arriving in Paris after a twenty-four-hour journey, and drove to five hotels in the dawn before they could find a room.[2] They reached the

---

[1] GHL Journal, 20 Apr. 1869.   [2] *Letters*, V. 27.

Priory on 5 May, exhausted, but glad to be back among their books and the 'comforts o' the Saut Market'.[1]

Lewes went at once to see his mother and two days later took Marian to call on her. On returning home they were astonished to find that Thornie had arrived, six weeks before it was thought possible. The fine muscular lad was pitifully wasted, having lost 4 stone (56 pounds) in a few months. He was suffering excruciating pain, but bearing it manfully. He came downstairs the next morning. Unable to sit up, he lay on the floor of the dining-room, writhing in agony. Lewes set out to find a chemist and get some opiate. He was gone a long time, for the shops were closed. It was Sunday, the day for visitors at the Priory. Few friends knew that they had returned. But soon after 3 o'clock the bell rang. Amelia ushered into the drawing-room Miss Grace Norton and Miss Sara Sedgwick, introducing a stammering American youth named Henry James, who was about to experience his 'unsurpassably prized admission to the presence of the great George Eliot', on whose work he had written three long articles.

She came out of the dining-room 'in no small flutter', and James was 'infinitely moved . . . to see so great a celebrity quite humanly and familiarly agitated'. She explained the reason for it simply, apologized for Mr. Lewes's absence, and then talked a little of their Italian holiday—of the mistral that scourged them, and of the 'evil faces: oh the evil faces' that had poisoned the whole scene. Henry James, who was just a year older than Thornie and knew something of backaches, went with her into the dining-room to see if he could beguile the sufferer until his father returned. Thornie 'lay stretched on his back on the floor', James wrote, 'the posture apparently least painful to him—though painful enough at best I easily saw on kneeling beside him, after my first dismay, to ask if I could in any way ease him. I see his face again, fair and young and flushed, with its vague little smile and its moist brow.' After a few moments Lewes returned with some morphia, and James volunteered to save him a second errand by going himself to ask Paget, the surgeon, to come to Thornie. Shaking off the 'kind door-opening' Miss Norton, James flew away in a cab to leave the message at Paget's house.[2]

---

[1] *Letters*, v. 29.
[2] Henry James, *The Middle Years* (1917), pp. 60–72. James's tendency to fictionalize appears in his recollection that Thornie 'had been suddenly taken with a violent attack of pain, the heritage of a bad accident not long before in the West Indies,

In a letter to his father the next day James described George Eliot's appearance:

To begin with she is magnificently ugly—deliciously hideous. She has a low forehead, a dull grey eye, a vast pendulous nose, a huge mouth, full of uneven teeth, and a chin and jaw-bone *qui n'en finissent pas*. . . . Now in this vast ugliness resides a most powerful beauty which, in a very few minutes steals forth and charms the mind, so that you end as I ended, in falling in love with her. Yes, behold me literally in love with this great horse-faced blue-stocking. I don't know in what the charm lies, but it is thoroughly potent. An admirable physiognomy—a delightful expression, a voice soft and rich as that of a counselling angel—a mingled sagacity and sweetness—a broad hint of a great underlying world of reserve, knowledge, pride and power—a great feminine dignity and character in these massively plain features—a hundred conflicting shades of consciousness and simpleness—shyness and frankness—graciousness and remote indifference.—these are some of the more definite elements of her personality. Her manner is extremely good though rather too intense and her speech, in the way of accent and syntax peculiarly agreeable. Altogether, she has a larger circumference than any woman I have ever seen.[1]

James Paget, Serjeant-surgeon-extraordinary to Queen Victoria, was one of the foremost medical men of the time. Lewes, meeting him at Oxford the previous August, had been gratified to hear him speak of George Eliot as 'the greatest genius—male or female—that we could boast of'.[2] Paget was out when James's message came, but he went to the Priory in the evening, examined Thornie, and prescribed morphia, which Lewes administered four times during the night to dull the agony. Paget took a grave view of the case, but seems not to have recognized it as tuberculosis of the spine, though in his *Descriptive Catalogue of the Anatomical Museum at St. Bartholomew's Hospital* he had described the very specimen used by Percivall Pott, his great eighteenth-century predecessor, in the pioneer account of the disease.[3] Beyond observing the curvature of the spine and Thornie's difficulty in moving his ribs to breathe, Paget seemed unable to diagnose it. After five weeks he called into consultation Dr. J. R. Reynolds, an authority on disease of the nervous system, who suspected tuberculosis in some of the glands. There was little they

---

a suffered onset from an angry bull, I seem to recall, who had tossed or otherwise mauled him, and, though beaten off, left him considerably compromised'.
[1] Henry James to his father, 10 May [1869] (Harvard).
[2] GHL Journal, 13 Aug. 1868.
[3] (3 vols., 1846–62), I. 172.

could do but increase the doses of morphia. For six months the disease ran its course, periods of dreadful pain alternating with others of comparative ease.

Thornie's disposition, always cheerful, seemed to grow sweeter in his suffering. His father and the Mutter sat by him much of the time. When not in pain, he would talk about his African adventures or sing them Zulu songs. Charles was not told about his brother till he came home from his holiday, 1 June. Dreadfully shocked, he fainted on first seeing Thornie. But he and Gertrude soon took over as much as they could of the burden of amusing and caring for him. On warm days he was carried out on the lawn to lie in the sun, and in the evenings he sometimes lay on the sofa in the drawing-room while Marian played Beethoven and Schubert to him. His father would go to Covent Garden to get him strawberries and other fruit. Barbara Bodichon, 'wonderfully clever in talking to young people', would come at least twice a week, bringing chickens and fresh cream from the country, spending the afternoon with Thornie while George and Marian went out to walk or rested a little after a sleepless night. Mrs. Nassau Senior would come up from Worthing bringing flowers or grapes. Pigott would come in the evenings to play cards with him.

One day, while the Mutter was out, Agnes, his real mother, came and sat with him for two and a half hours.[1] Though no more such visits are recorded, she probably came on other occasions when Lewes had taken Marian off to the country for a brief change—to Chiselhurst, or Hatfield, or Sevenoaks, or Watford, or to Weybridge to lunch with the Crosses. They were also grieving; Mrs. Cross's eldest daughter Mrs. Bullock died on 22 September, a few days after the birth of her first child.

Thornie's suffering varied sharply. Some days he would have many hours without pain. On 7 August Lewes took Marian to walk in Hyde Park; they returned at 3 o'clock to find him 'writhing and shouting loud enough to be heard in the garden'. A few days later he was paralysed below the waist. Though he never entirely regained use of his legs, the pain was less acute. Till the end he kept his sense of humour; in the most distressing moments he would look up with his odd, quick smile and make a joke. But his face, Marian wrote, had 'more than ever of the wizened look that has come instead of its old beauty, and that pains me to see; I cannot shake off the impression it creates in me of slow withering'.[2] Though his father tried to be more hopeful, Paget confirmed

---

[1] GHL Diary, 18 May 1869.   [2] *Letters*, v. 57.

their suspicion that Thornie was 'drifting away'. For three or four days he was only fitfully conscious. On 19 October he died, very gently, with the Mutter at his side. 'Nurse and I raised him and his last breathings were quite peaceful', she told Cara.[1] In her Journal she wrote: 'Through the six months of his illness, his frank impulsive mind disclosed no trace of evil feeling. He was a sweet-natured boy—still a boy though he had lived for 25 years and a half. . . . This death seems to me the beginning of our own.'[2] After the burial at Highgate she wrote to Barbara Bodichon:

Thanks for your tender words. It has cut deeper than I expected—that he is gone and I can never make him feel my love any more. Just now all else seems trivial compared with the powers of delighting and soothing a heart that is in need.

We go tomorrow morning to Limpsfield, in Surrey, to nice people in an old-fashioned farm house, that we knew of beforehand. It is an unspeakable comfort to have an immediate retreat. Later on, we shall perhaps go to the Isle of Wight, but just now we are unequal to journeying and arrangements with new people.[3]

---

[1] *Letters*, v. 60.   [2] GE Journal, 19 Oct. 1869.
[3] *Letters*, v. 60–1.

CHAPTER XIII

MIDDLEMARCH

※

THOUGH *Middlemarch* is not mentioned before 1 January 1869, George Eliot had been brooding over her 'English novel' ever since *Felix Holt* was finished. She wrote to Blackwood in February 1869: 'I mean to begin my novel at once, having already sketched the plan. But between the beginning and the middle of a book I am like the lazy Scheldt; between the middle and the end I am like the arrowy Rhone.[1] . . . The various elements of the story have been soliciting my mind for years—asking for a complete embodiment.'[2] Its beginning was postponed by her trip to Italy, and its progress shattered by Thornie's return. During the months of his illness she worked at it fitfully. Professor Jerome Beaty's masterly study of the manuscript suggests that the Introduction George Eliot wrote in July 1869 probably gave Lydgate's early history. On 2 August her Journal noted: 'Began *Middlemarch* (the Vincy and Featherstone parts).' These first episodes, Beaty shows, probably included a breakfast scene somewhat like that in Chapter 11, Mrs. Waule's remark to Featherstone about Fred's gambling, Fred's arrival with Rosamond at Stone Court, his conversation with Mary Garth (originally called Mary Dove), the meeting of Rosamond and Lydgate, and Fred's presentation of the note to Featherstone.[3] The Brookes and Casaubon had then no part in the story. On 1 September Marian wrote: 'I meditated characters and conditions for Middlemarch, which stands still in the beginning of Chapter III.' She spent the week reading J. R. Russell's *Heroes of Medicine* and the *Encyclopaedia* on medical colleges. On 11 September she wrote: 'I do not feel very confident that I can make anything satisfactory of Middlemarch. I have need to remember that other things which have been accomplished by me

---

[1] Cf. Byron, *Childe Harold*, III. 71.
[2] *Letters*, v. 16.
[3] Jerome Beaty, Middlemarch *from Notebook to Novel* (Urbana, 1960), p. 39.

were begun under the same cloud. G. has been reading Romola again, and expresses profound admiration. This is encouraging. At p. 50—end of Chap. III.' But her next reference 21 September reported the work 'im Stiche gerathen'. Mrs. Congreve, coming to tea that day, was asked to get her 'some information about provincial Hospitals, which is necessary to my imagining the conditions of my hero'. Progress on the novel lapsed.

Marian turned again to poetry. Intensive meditation on the Warwickshire of 1830 revived poignant memories of her childhood with Isaac, which in July she cast into eleven sonnets under the title 'Brother and Sister'. As Thornie's end drew near, she could not concentrate on *Middlemarch*. Her mind dwelt increasingly on the idea of a future life, a subject that had occupied her for years. In 1865, when the Brays' adopted daughter Nellie died, Marian wrote to Cara:

I don't know whether you strongly share, as I do, the old belief that made men say the gods loved those who died young. It seems to me truer than ever, now life has become more complex and more and more difficult problems have to be worked out. Life, though a good to men on the whole, is a doubtful good to many, and to some not a good at all. To my thought, it is a source of constant mental distortion to make the denial of this a part of religion, to go on pretending things are better than they are. . . . So to me, early death takes the aspect of salvation— though I feel too that those who live and suffer may sometimes have the greater blessedness of *being* a salvation.[4]

Now, sitting at Thornie's bedside, she began to compose a poem called 'The Legend of Jubal'. The children of Cain had settled in a region far to the East of 'Jehovah's land'. Though death followed them even there, it was not entirely bad, for it brought them new awareness of the value of life:

> No form, no shadow, but new dearness took
> From the one thought that life must have an end.

Through realization of its brevity, the arts were born to enrich life and to live on after their creator's death. Marian wrote about 100 lines before Thornie died, and continued work on the poem at Limpsfield, where she and Lewes went the day after the funeral to stay at Park Farm. There in the quietest and most beautiful part of Surrey, four and a half miles from any railway station,

---

¹ *Letters*, IV. 183.

with 'three good young sisters' as their hostesses they withdrew
to recover from the strain of the harrowing experience. The deep
calm of fields and woods soon exerted their beneficent effect.
'But I have a deep sense of change within', Marian wrote, soon
after her fiftieth birthday, 'and of a permanently closer companionship with death'.[1] They returned to the Priory on 13 November.
Two months after Thornie's death a letter came for him from
Bertie in Natal, full of news and good wishes.

On Sunday afternoons the old friends were soon calling again
—Spencer, Mrs. Congreve, Trollope, the Burne-Joneses, the
Howards. During the holidays the Leweses lunched at the Grange
and took the Burne-Jones children some toys. Good-hearted
Mrs. Benzon persuaded them to dine quietly with her at 10 Palace
Gardens, and George went again on Christmas Eve to see the
Benzon children lighting their magnificent tree. On Christmas Day
he and Marian walked to Hampstead to attend the Unitarian
service at Rosslyn Chapel with Charles, then went with him to
Highgate Cemetery to see Thornie's grave, and dined in Church
Row with Gertrude, who was expecting a child. On New Year's
Eve, just on the stroke of 12, Lewes read to Polly the stanzas from
In Memoriam, 'Ring out the old, ring in the new.'

She could do little writing in those bleak winter months. 'Jubal',
finished on 13 January 1870, was sold for £200 to *Macmillan's* and
for £50 to the *Atlantic Monthly*, where it appeared simultaneously
in May. *Middlemarch* languished. After 28 November 1869, when
Marian read some of it to Lewes, there is no mention of it until
7 March 1870. Visitors occupied more and more of her time.
Among them were the Arnolds, Mrs. Arthur Clough, Wyville
Thomson, the biologist, just back from his deep-sea dredging with
the *Porcupine*, and Lady Colville, the wife of a retired judge from
Bengal. Rossetti came one Sunday to lunch and invited them to see
his paintings in Chelsea. Another day they went to Watts's studio,
which was 'crowded with fine things'. Dickens at lunch on 6 March
enthralled them with a dramatic story: Lincoln on the day he was
shot told the Cabinet that something remarkable would happen
because he had dreamt for a third time a dream which twice
before had preceded events momentous to the nation; he was in
a boat on a great river all alone—and he ended with the words,
'I drift—I drift—I drift.' Dickens told it very finely. On his
doctor's advice he had given up his public readings. Marian
thought he looked 'dreadfully shattered'. Three months later he

[1] *Letters*, v. 70.

was dead. In January 1870 the Leweses resumed their old places at the Saturday afternoon concerts at St. James's Hall, where they had long been familiar figures. On 5 February, when the famous violinist Mme Norman Neruda was playing with Charles Hallé, she asked to be introduced to George Eliot, and came the next day to call on her at the Priory.

It took longer for Lewes to recover from Thornie's death. He could not get on with his *Problems of Life and Mind*, in which he was trying to apply his physiological knowledge to psychology. In January he thought of a quick dash to Utrecht to consult some Dutch physiologists; but finding Polly made melancholy at the idea of being left alone, he gave it up.[1] The headaches and ringing in the ears that had troubled him for years recurred with new force during the long strain and would not go away. One night in February he fainted in bed before going to sleep, and woke the next morning feeling queer and numb in the extremities.[2] Spencer, who was also out of sorts, took Lewes off to the Isle of Wight for the first week in March. But the nervous symptoms continued. At last in desperation he and Polly packed up and set out again for Germany.[3]

On the assumption that 'there are more comforts for cold weather in northern countries than in southern', they headed for Berlin. They found a number of old acquaintances from their stay there in 1855—Gruppe, Magnus, Stahr, Dubois-Reymond—who were delighted to welcome their now-famous friends. Dubois-Reymond, the Professor of Physiology at the Charité, introduced Lewes to Reichert, Westphal, and others engaged in the latest neurological research, and brought them tickets for the great University Festival in honour of the King's birthday. There Lewes found himself 'seated apart from the public among the Princes, Professors, Ambassadors, and persons covered with stars and decorations. The American Ambassador [George Bancroft] and myself were the only *un*decorated persons there.'[4] Bancroft called at their hotel the same afternoon to make George Eliot's acquaintance, and returned two days later with an invitation to dinner at his house, where they met Mommsen the historian, Bunsen the chemist, and a dozen other distinguished men and their wives. Franz Duncker, publisher of continental reprints, was assiduous in attention; he and Frau Duncker took them into the diplomatic

[1] GHL Diary, 19 Jan. 1870.   [2] GHL Diary, 17–18 Feb. 1870.
[3] GHL Diary, 14 Mar. 1870.   [4] *Letters*, v. 83.

box at the Reichstag, where they heard Bismarck and others speak. Albert Cohn, director of Asher & Co., which was rivalling Tauchnitz, was also attentive. Prince Frederick VIII, the Duke of Schleswig-Holstein, hearing that Lewes was in Asher's bookshop,

begged to be introduced. I liked him amazingly, and the same day he called to see Polly, who also liked him. He is almost forty, speaks English like an Englishman; is highly cultivated, deep in Oriental history and languages and so Polly had plenty to talk about. He invited us to go and stay with him—which of course we shall not do—and begged he might come and see us in London. Altogether his Highness was as agreeable an acquaintance as if he had been Mr. Smith with a first rate education.[1]

When not at parties in Berlin, the Leweses went to concerts and four times to the opera. After hearing *Tannhäuser* Lewes wrote to Charles: 'The Mutter and I have come to the conclusion that the Music of the future is not for us—Schubert, Beethoven, Mozart, Gluck or even Verdi—but not Wagner—is what we are made to respond to.' In his Journal he added: 'Two performances of each of his operas have failed to give us a moment of rapture; and succeeded in giving hours of noise and weariness.'[2] This was a common reaction. Lady Radnor, who patronized annual public concerts in London 1881–96, came out of the concert Wagner conducted at the Albert Hall in 1877 'with the registered resolve that if this was the new music, the old was better'.[3] Lewes spent a good deal of time at the hospitals, seeing every variety of madness and talking psychiatry with Dr. Westphal, 'a quiet unpretending little man', who was delighted with his interest in what Marian called this 'hideous branch of practice'.[4]

The weather in Berlin was cheerless, frequently snowy. Soon after they arrived Marian caught a cold and a sore throat, which the constant round of entertainments gave her no chance to shake off. Almost every evening found her sitting on a sofa in some drawing-room while one person after another was brought up to bow and pay her the same compliments. 'I felt my heart go out to some good women who seemed really to have an affectionate feeling towards me for the sake of my books', she wrote to Mrs. Congreve. 'But the sick animal longs for quiet and darkness'[4]—which hardly consort with lionizing and strenuous travel.

[1] *Letters*, v. 84.
[2] *Letters*, v. 85; GHL Journal, 25 Mar. 1870.
[3] E. F. Benson, *As We Were. A Victorian Peep Show* (N.Y., 1931), p. 261.
[4] *Letters*, v. 86.

After a night on the train they had two days in Prague, where they revisited the synagogue they had seen in 1858. Another night's journey brought them to Vienna. Robert Lytton, whom Lewes had seen at Knebworth, now Attaché at the British Embassy, met them at the station with a servant to take care of their luggage and saw them installed in a spacious apartment at the Römischen Kaiser. Almost every evening they dined with the Lyttons. Robert did everything to make their visit pleasant, and Mrs. Lytton was very charming. Theodor Gompertz, the Professor of Classical Philology, who came in with his wife the first evening, introduced Lewes the next morning to Professor Meynert, Director of the Psychiatric Clinic, and Stricker, the pathologist, who exhibited interesting types of insanity. Polly's cold had been growing steadily worse since they left Berlin; her sore throat and hoarseness were so severe that Lewes wrote to Lytton saying that they could not go that night to the private theatricals at the palace of Count von Beust, the Austrian Chancellor—a disappointment, as 'all the Court and all the fashion of Vienna will be there'. After dining with the Lyttons and Mrs. Lytton's sister Mrs. Earle, they then went back to the hotel, 'changed our dress, and rambled in the starlit streets'.[1] The next day Lewes's old friend Dr. Fürstenberg declared that Polly's throat was badly ulcerated, and she was put to bed for three days. Mrs. Lytton came every day to see her, bringing barley water and soothing concoctions. Her illness forced the Leweses to miss the Maundy Thursday ceremonies on 14 April. On Good Friday she was able to dine again with the Lyttons, who called on Saturday to say good-bye. Early Easter morning, when the Leweses went to the station, they found Fürstenberg, who had come to see them off and get them a coupé to themselves. They were glad enough to say good-bye to Vienna, which, Lewes felt, had completely lost its old charm and character.[2] The grandeur of the diplomatic circle had been something of a strain.

At Salzburg, where they stayed a week at the Melböck, they were cheered to find themselves 'in a comfortable hotel, with friendly landlord and waiters, after the splendid discomfort of Vienna and Berlin'. It was a marked contrast to their few days at the Goldenes Schiff in July 1858, when they did their sightseeing under an umbrella because 'precious time paid for at hotels must be used to some purpose'. Marian's throat soon healed. They rambled about in glorious weather, dining on trout, venison, snipe, and champagne. It was Lewes's fifty-third birthday. This time their

[1] GHL Journal, 9 Apr. 1870.   [2] Ibid. 17 Apr. 1870.

expedition to Berchtesgaden and the Königsee was realized. After pausing two days in Munich to see the good von Siebolds, they started for home, breaking the journey at Nürnberg, Würzburg (to see von Rechlinghausen and Kölliker), Heidelberg, and Paris, arriving at the Priory on 6 May. They were glad to be at home again, having begun to feel that they had had enough of wandering to and fro upon the earth.[1]

A week after their return the Sunday afternoons commenced again. Spencer, Lord and Lady Amberley, Sir Henry Holland, and Sanderson came on 15 May; in the evening the Leweses dined at Lord Houghton's, where they met Annie Thackeray, Mrs. Procter, Mrs. St. Ives, Rossetti, Butler Johnstone, Gaskell, Locker, Arthur Russell, Kinglake, and Lecky. The next Sunday they had Dr. Payne, Crompton, Julian Goldsmid, Frederick Locker and his daughter (Lady Charlotte Locker sent an excuse), and Colonel Hamley. In spite of their resolution they were soon wandering again, this time to visit the Mark Pattisons at Lincoln College, 25–28 May 1870. It was Marian's first visit to Oxford. The meadows were beautiful with buttercups. At supper they met Mary Augusta Arnold, a charming girl of eighteen, soon to become Mrs. Humphry Ward, who left a vivid account of the evening:

George Eliot sat at the Rector's right hand. I was opposite her; on my left was George Henry Lewes, to whom I took a prompt and active dislike. He and Mrs. Pattison kept up a lively conversation in which Mr. [Ingram] Bywater, on the other side of the table, played full part. George Eliot talked very little, and I not at all. The Rector was shy or tired, and George Eliot was in truth entirely occupied in watching or listening to Mr. Lewes. I was disappointed that she was so silent, and perhaps her quick eye may have divined it, for after supper, as we were going up the interesting old staircase, made in the thickness of the wall, which led direct from the dining-room to the drawing-room above, she said to me: 'The Rector tells me that you have been reading a good deal about Spain. Would you care to hear something of our Spanish journey?'—the journey which had preceded the appearance of *The Spanish Gypsy*, then newly published. My reply is easily imagined. The rest of the party passed through the dimly lit drawing-room to talk and smoke in the gallery beyond. George Eliot sat down in the darkness and I beside her. Then she talked for about twenty minutes, with perfect ease and finish, without misplacing a word or dropping a sentence, and I realised at last that I was in the presence of a great writer. Not a great

[1] *Letters*, v. 93.

talker. It is clear that George Eliot never was that. Impossible for her to 'talk' her books, or evolve her books from conversation, like Madame de Staël. She was too self-conscious, too desperately reflective, too rich in second-thoughts for that. But in tête-à-tête, and with time to choose her words, she could—in monologue, with just enough stimulus from a companion to keep it going—produce on a listener exactly the impression of some of her best work. As the low clear voice flowed on, in Mrs. Pattison's drawing room, I *saw* Saragossa, Granada, the Escorial, and that survival of the old Europe in the new, which one must go to Spain to find. Not that the description was particularly vivid—in talking of famous places John Richard Green could make words tell and paint with far greater success; but it was singularly complete and accomplished. When it was done the effect was there—the effect she had meant to produce. I shut my eyes, and it all comes back:—the darkened room, the long, pallid face, set in black lace, the evident wish to be kind to a young girl.

Two more impressions of her let me record. The following day, the Pattisons took their guests to see the 'eights' races from Christ Church meadow. A young Fellow of Merton, Mandell Creighton, afterwards the beloved and famous Bishop of London, was among those entertaining her on the barge, and on the way home he took her and Mr. Lewes through Merton garden. I was of the party, and I remember what a carnival of early summer it was in that enchanting place. The chesnuts were all out, one splendour from top to toe; the laburnums, the lilacs, the hawthorns red and white, the new-mown grass spreading its smooth and silky carpet round the college walls, a May sky overhead, and through the trees glimpses of towers and spires, silver grey, in the sparkling summer air:—the picture was one of those that Oxford throws before the spectator, at every turn, like the careless beauty that knows she has only to show herself, to move, to breathe, to give delight. George Eliot stood on the grass, in the bright sun, looking at the flower-laden chesnuts, at the distant glimpses on all sides, of the surrounding city, saying little—that she left to Mr. Lewes!—but drinking it in, storing it in that rich, absorbent mind of hers.

And afterwards when Mr. Lewes, Mr. Creighton, she and I walked back to Lincoln, I remember another little incident throwing light on the ever-ready instinct of the novelist. As we turned into the quadrangle of Lincoln—suddenly, at one of the upper windows of the Rector's lodgings, which occupied the far right-hand corner of the quad, there appeared the head and shoulders of Mrs. Pattison, as she looked out and beckoned smiling to Mrs. Lewes. It was a brilliant apparition, as though a French portrait by Greuze or Perronneau had suddenly slipped into a vacant space in the old college wall. The pale, pretty head, *blond-cendrée*; the delicate smiling features and white throat; a touch of black, a touch of blue; a white dress; a general eighteenth-century impression as though of powder and patches:—Mrs. Lewes perceived it in a flash, and I saw her run eagerly to Mr. Lewes and draw his attention to the window and its occupant. She took his arm, while she looked and waved. If she had lived longer, some day, and somewhere in her books, that vision at the window, and that flower-laden garden would have reappeared. I seemed to see her consciously and deliberately committing them both to memory.[1]

Other events, even more absorbing than boat-races, filled Marian's days at Oxford. For this keen prober of human motives Dr. George Rolleston one morning dissected a brain. Sir Benjamin Brodie, the Professor of Chemistry, demonstrated in his laboratory the new techniques of measuring infinitesimal quantities. Mrs. Pattison drove Marian in a pony carriage round by her country refuge at Headington and past Newman's conventual retreat at Littlemore before taking her to Lady Brodie's for supper. One afternoon at the Sheldonian Theatre they heard reports on the explorations in Palestine, and Emanuel Deutsch read his paper on the Moabite Stone. Among the guests at supper on their last evening were Benjamin Jowett, soon to be Master of Balliol, and Walter Pater, a Fellow of Brasenose and 'writer of articles on Leonardo da Vinci, Morris etc.'[2] Jowett was to become a staunch friend; Pater a strong aversion.

Lewes's neurological symptoms had been little helped by their German holiday. Quite unable to work on his *Problems*, he consulted Dr. Reynolds, who first prescribed phosphates and cod liver oil; and when these failed, ordered rest and sea air. Accordingly, they set out again, 15 June 1870, for Cromer on the Norfolk coast. There for a fortnight they sat on the sands reading aloud Trollope's *Vicar of Bullhampton*, Balzac's *Illusions perdues*, Mendelssohn's *Letters*, Rossetti's *Poems*, and the latest volume of Morris's *Earthly Paradise*. When the weather turned cold and rainy, they migrated to Harrogate, where the springs had seemed to help Lewes in 1864. They proved efficacious again; he gained strength every day. But the waters were 'so strongly tonic', Marian wrote, 'that it will not be prudent to continue taking them longer than a fortnight'.

So they decided to go on to Whitby, which Dr. Reynolds had suggested at first. There, she hoped, the Burne-Jones family might join them for their holiday. Edward was unable to come, but

[1] Mrs. Humphry Ward, *A Writer's Recollections* (1918), pp. 107–10.
[2] GE Journal, 27 May 1870.

Georgiana and the two children arrived the same day as the Leweses and took lodgings very near them. For a fortnight they walked together, and, while the children played on the sands, had long talks, sometimes late into the evening. One of the subjects discussed was Goethe's *Faust,* which Marian promised to help interpret for her. Georgie described her clear, grey eyes as 'piercing; I used to think they looked as if they had been washed by many waters. Her voice was a beautiful one, sometimes full and strong and at others as tender as a dove's.'[1] During the long days at Whitby their friendship deepened. A letter that Georgie wrote the day after Marian left to return to London reflects the curious fascination she exerted:

Dearest Mrs. Lewes,

Don't laugh if I say that my impulse is to address you as 'Honoured Madame'—I wish you wouldn't think it ludicrous and would allow me to do so—it so exactly says what I mean. I miss your kind selves very much—and am only reconciled to your having gone by the hope that you will be the better for it. . . .

I think much of you, and of your kindness to me during this past fortnight, and my heart smites me that I have somewhat resembled those friends who talk only of themselves to you. . . . Forgive me if it has been so, and reflect upon what a trap for egotism your unselfishness and tender thought for others is. The only atonement I can make is a resolve that what you have said to me in advice and warning shall not be lost. Give me also, please, a little credit for bashfulness before you, and a fear of appearing inquisitive, and then I think I need spend no more time in this looking back—the balance of everything is that you have won my grateful affection, and I hope you will accept it.[2]

After a week in 'our comfortable house', while Lewes visited his mother each day and attended to some business, they flitted off for three weeks more at Park Farm, Limpsfield. There Marian wrote most of 'Armgart', a poem that had occurred to her at Harrogate. Entirely in dramatic form and without any commentary, this story of a great opera singer who loses her voice reflects something of George Eliot's depression and 'almost total despair of future work'.[3] From her old master Leo, whose early ambitions had come to little, Armgart learns to live like him for the good she can do for others. Abandonment by her former suitor Graf Dornberg teaches her that a woman's domestic affections cannot

---

[1] *Memorials of Edward Burne-Jones,* II. 4.
[2] Mrs. Burne-Jones to GE, 2 Aug. [1870] (Yale).
[3] GE Journal, 27 Oct. 1870.

be sacrificed to her artistic life—a theme George Eliot would return to with the Alcharisi in *Daniel Deronda*. Lewes sold 'Armgart' to *Macmillan's* for £200 and to the *Atlantic Monthly* for £100— 'a pretty little sum for the small poem'.[1] It appeared simultaneously in July 1871.

The only drawback at Limpsfield was difficulty in getting the newspapers. The Franco-Prussian War had broken out on 19 July 1870; the Germans rapidly entered Alsace and started towards Paris. Marian spent several hours a day over *The Times* and the *Daily News*—for which Mrs. Cross's son-in-law Henry Bullock was the correspondent—'an excess in journal-reading that I was never drawn into before'.[2] At first her sympathies lay with the Germans. She felt that the French people had been misled by Napoleon's iniquitous policies, and even after his capture at Sedan on 1 September she condemned the government. But as the Prussian machine rolled on, her feeling changed, and when the siege of Paris began, she could only bewail the 'sorrows of poor France!' When Colonel Hamley wrote to *The Times* protesting against the ruthlessness of the conquerors, she blessed him for the 'good sensible words' of one 'who is at once a soldier, a writer, and a clear-headed man of principle'.[3] To George Eliot, modern weapons, capable of 'making eight wounds at once in one body', seemed worse than devilish. 'This war', she wrote, 'has been a personal sorrow to every human creature with any sympathy who has been within reach of hearing about it; still more to those who have gone out to see and help the sufferers.'[3] Among these were Willie and Mary Cross, who helped Henry Bullock set up a soup kitchen at Sedan for the relief of the peasant victims.

Besides the war news George Eliot's reading in 1870 included Lockhart's *Life of Scott*, Carlyle's *French Revolution*, Wolf's *Prolegomena to Homer*, Goethe's *Wilhelm Meister*, Comte's *Lettres à M. Valat* (just published), essays by Hume and Macaulay, Froude's *History of England*, and *Tom Jones*. Most of these were read aloud to Lewes. In August came 'a letter from Bertie telling us, to our joy, that he was engaged to a "well-educated young lady, Eliza Stevenson Harrison", and we agreed to write to the young lady's father on the subject to see if any provision could be made for their early marriage'.[4] Mr. Harrison, 'a long-established colonist' in Natal, objected to the match. Nevertheless, Eliza was

[1] GHL Diary, 19 Apr. 1871.   [2] *Letters*, v. 117.
[3] *Letters*, v. 134.
[4] GE Journal, 27 Oct. 1870.

bravely determined to marry Bertie.[1] With the very practical help of his father and the Mutter, they overbore the opposition, and they were married in August 1871. Their first child, born in December 1872, they named Marian Lewes.

Before the news of that event arrived, Lewes's mother Mrs. Willim died quite peacefully on 10 December 1871, as she sat in her chair chatting with her servant. She was eighty-three years old. Lewes was now free to devote his whole attention to Polly. They spent Christmas week on the Isle of Wight with Barbara Bodichon, who had taken Swanmore Parsonage at Ryde, working a little in the mornings, and rambling about in the pleasant air. St. Michael's Church, to which the Parsonage was attached, was extremely 'High'; the Vicar even had a scourge hanging in his study, which Lewes one day got the maid to bring to table in a covered dish as 'a delicacy seen only at recherché tables'. Marian, with her eager eclecticism in religions, went with Barbara on Christmas Day to hear mass intoned by the 'delicate-faced, tenor-voiced clergyman' Mr. Hooker Wix, 'sweet singing from boys' throats, and all sorts of Catholic ceremonial in a miniature way'.[2] She had taken Lewes in November to the Metropolitan Tabernacle in London to hear the famous preacher C. H. Spurgeon, but disliked everything about his performance.

In George Eliot's Journal and letters there is less about the writing of *Middlemarch* than almost any of her books. She had written accounts of other important epochs in her career: 'How I Came to Write Fiction', 'The History of *Adam Bede*', and 'Notes on *The Spanish Gypsy*', On her fifty-first birthday Lewes bought her 'a lockup book for her Autobiography'.[3] Whether she continued to record her progress there under lock and key we cannot say, since the book has not been found. We have no consecutive account of the writing of *Middlemarch*. 'My novel, I suppose, will be finished some day', she wrote to John Blackwood, 7 March 1870; 'it creeps on'. When he came to see her in May, he reported to his nephew that she was working away at it, 'but is not so far on as she intended to be. She gave me a long account of their views, her hopes and fears about it. It promises to be something wonderful—English provincial life.'[4] In August she let Lewes read the early chapters of it, probably some of the material ultimately published in Chapters 11 and 12. Then, 'about the opening of

[1] CLL to GHL and GE, 16 July 1871.   [2] *Letters*, v. 131.
[3] GHL Diary, 22 Nov. 1870.   [4] *Letters*, v. 99.

November', she began a story called 'Miss Brooke', which she refers to in her Journal on 2 December 1870: 'I am experimenting in a story, which I began without any very serious intention of carrying it out lengthily. It is a subject which has been recorded among my possible themes ever since I began to write fiction, but will probably take new shapes in the development. I am today at p. 44.' Two days later, Lewes noted that 'Polly read what she has written of "Miss Brooke" aloud',[1] and John Blackwood, having lunched 'with Lewes and Madam' that day, reported that 'She is working but has nothing ready, having changed her plans.'[2] The change was her decision to combine 'Miss Brooke' with her 'Middlemarch' story. By the end of December about 100 pages were written.

The war on the Continent was now seriously hindering travel in France or Germany. The Leweses were looking about for a country refuge where they could work quietly. They were planning some extensive alterations on the Priory, including a new bathroom, which would banish them for at least four months. Lady Brodie suggested a house near her at Reigate, which they went down to see.[3] Mrs. Pattison offered them the cottage at Headington which she had shown George Eliot in May.

But Mr. Lewes, not having seen the place, shook his head without hesitation [Marian wrote]. We are in a vacillating state of mind as to the arrangements we should make for our short lives, and cannot yet decide whether we should keep a home in London and have a modest little refuge in the not-too-distant country, or give up London entirely. In the latter case our requirements would be rather *im*modest in the way of space for books and snugness suitable for rickety old people.[4]

They considered two houses near Weybridge, which Mrs. Cross told them about, and another at Edenbridge before they found 'a queer little cottage' at Shottermill, near Haslemere, that suited them exactly. Brookbank, as it was called, belonged to Mrs. Alexander Gilchrist, widow of the biographer of Blake. The country about had varied and delightful walks with views that gave Marian the 'sense of standing on a round world'. They took possession on 2 May 1870 and lived there till 1 August, when they had to surrender the house to George Smith, the water-

[1] GHL Diary, 4 Dec. 1870.
[2] J. Blackwood to W. Blackwood, 5 Dec. 1870 (NLS).
[3] GHL Diary, 12 Nov. 1870.   [4] *Letters*, V. 120.

colourist, and move into Cherrimans just across the road where they stayed till they could return to the Priory on 1 September.

During this long summer at Shottermill Marian wrote with less torment from diffidence and self-mistrust than she had felt in many years. Her decision to add the county families—the Brookes, Chettams, Cadwalladers, and Casaubons—to her 'Middlemarch' story gave the novel a panoramic view of provincial life more complete than any she had attempted. On 19 March 1871, when she had written about 236 pages, she began to fear that she had 'too much matter, too many "momenti"'.[1] It was clear that so many complex strands could not be woven into the compass of an ordinary three-volume novel. Lewes was giving much thought to forms of publication. From the beginning of her career he had dreamed of a fortune to be made by issuing her novels in numbers like Dickens's and Thackeray's. He nearly persuaded her to try it with *The Mill on the Floss*. As an artist she knew that in short sections her work could not tell as she wanted it to. Even the long instalments of *Romola* in the *Cornhill* had not entirely satisfied her. It was clear that the circulating libraries were in their decline. They alone maintained the three-volume format, floating many inferior novels and discriminating against the best.[2] Blackwood had noticed their injurious effect on the sales of *Felix Holt*. 'The next time we take the field together', he wrote to George Eliot, 'I think we must experiment in a new form, but we can keep our own counsel about this.'[3] His venture in 1867 of reissuing George Eliot's works in a cheap illustrated edition in sixpenny weekly parts had been a failure. Trollope, who had passed the peak of his popularity, was incurring losses in the original publication in weekly parts of *He Knew He Was Right* and of *The Vicar of Bull-hampton* and *Ralph the Heir* in monthly parts.

At Brookbank one day Lewes was reading aloud to Polly, Victor Hugo's *Les Misérables*. These volumes, published at irregular intervals in 1862, suggested to him a similar plan, which he laid before Blackwood on 7 May 1871:

Mrs. Lewes finds that she will require 4 volumes for her story, not 3. I winced at the idea at first, but the story must not be spoiled for want of space, and as you have more than once spoken of the desirability of inventing some mode of circumventing the Libraries and making the public *buy* instead of borrowing I have devised the following scheme,

[1] GE Journal, 19 Mar. 1871.
[2] See G. L. Griest, 'A Victorian Leviathan: Mudie's Select Library', *Nineteenth Century Fiction*, 20 (Sept. 1965), 103–26.   [3] *Letters*, IV. 307.

suggested by the plan Victor Hugo followed with his long *Misérables*—namely to publish it in *half-volume parts* either at intervals of one, or as I think better, two months. The eight parts at 5/- could yield the 2£ for the four volumes, and at two month intervals would not be dearer than Maga. Each part would have a certain unity and completeness in itself with separate title. Thus the work is called *Middlemarch*. Part I will be *Miss Brooke*.

If in a stiff paper cover—attractive but not bookstallish—(I have one in my eye) this part ought to seduce purchasers, especially if Mudie were scant in supplies. It would be enough to furnish the town with talk for some time, and each part thus keep up and swell the general interest. *Tristram Shandy* you may remember was published at irregular intervals; and great was the desire for the continuation. Considering how slowly the public mind is brought into motion, this spreading of the publication over 16 months would be a decided advantage to the sale—especially as each part would contain as much as one ought to read at a time.

Ponder this; or suggest a better plan![1]

Blackwood pondered it well. When he was invited to come to Shottermill on 31 May, he took Willie with him. They came away with the manuscript of Book I, 'Miss Brooke'. He began to read it on the train and spent the whole next day over it. Though Lewes had arranged to call for the manuscript in town on 3 June, Blackwood could not wait to express his intense delight with the story, praising everything. 'There may not be in this first part what are considered popular incidents', he said, 'but there is overpowering interest in such a picture of human nature and I am much deceived if you are not about to repeat if not excell all your previous triumphs.'[2] His clerk George Simpson, to whom he had confided his impressions, wrote: 'I most anxiously hope we may secure it, and would willingly be content with a moderate gain to ourselves rather than let it go past us.'[3]

Marian had been unwell since Blackwood's visit, suffering from what she called neuralgia (Lewes called it *tic douloureux*), probably caused by infected teeth, which had been tormenting her for months. On 6 June Lewes took her to London to see the eminent surgeon Erasmus Wilson. Finding that he was out of town, they went to old Sir Henry Holland, who prescribed quinine, and she returned to work, bearing the pain as she could. Lewes himself, she wrote, was

[1] *Letters*, v. 145–6. [2] Ibid. 149.
[3] G. Simpson to J. Blackwood, 4 June 1871 (NLS).

in an altogether flourishing condition, enjoying all things from his breakfast to the highest problems in statics and dynamics. I think I have never seen him in such undisturbed health for many years—though of course he feels the tether that Time gradually shortens. He has to leave off study early, to avoid exhaustion.[1]

He wrote a little on his *Problems* in the mornings, strolled to Haslemere to post letters and do other errands, trying out new walks to take Polly on in the long afternoons. She usually wrote steadily until their dinner at 2.

On 27 June she read Lewes as much as she had ready of Book II, not finishing till 11 o'clock. From the manuscript Professor Beaty has reconstructed with great ingenuity the changes and additions she was making in her original draft of *Middlemarch* to join it with 'Miss Brooke'.[2] Some of them were doubtless suggested by Lewes's comments. The manuscript was dispatched to Edinburgh on 14 July. Blackwood read it

with the greatest admiration. It is a most wonderful study of human life and nature. You are like a great giant walking about among us and fixing every one you meet upon your canvas. In all this life like gallery that you put before us every trait in every character finds an echo or recollection in the reader's mind that tells him how true it is to Nature.[3]

After his usual detailed praise of the characters, Blackwood added:

I think our plan of publication is the right one as the two parts are almost distinct, each complete in itself. Indeed there will be complaints of the want of the continuous interest of a story, but this does not matter where all is so fresh and true to life. Each group that you introduce is a complete little book or study in itself.[4]

He had noticed that Book II was longer than I, almost equivalent to a volume of an ordinary novel. Lewes suggested the obvious solution of transferring some of Book II to the end of Book I. But, George Eliot wrote to Blackwood,

it is too early for such definite arrangements. I don't see how I can leave anything out, because I hope there is nothing that will be seen to be irrelevant to my design, which is to show the gradual action of ordinary causes rather than exceptional, and to show this in some directions which have not been from time immemorial the beaten path—the Cremorne walks and shows of fiction. But the best intentions are good

[1] *Letters*, v. 157.   [2] Middlemarch *from Notebook to Novel*, pp. 41–2.
[3] *Letters*, v. 167.   [4] *Letters*, v. 168.

for nothing until execution has justified them. And you know I am always compassed about with fears. I am in danger in all my designs of parodying dear Goldsmith's satire on Burke, and think of refining when novel readers only think of skipping.[1]

On 21 August Lewes brought up the question of terms:

Last night Mrs. Lewes read to me what she has written of part III —'Dorothea Married'[2]—and my delight in it not only confirms the expectation of a great success, but also confirms my belief in the desirability of bi-monthly publication. This being decided, and since we ought to publish the first part at Christmas—to be out before the Americans with whom our arrangement has been made—it is now time to settle about the terms of publication.

Since the plan is novel and may not realize all that one hopes from its novelty the choice is open to you to speculate or not as you think fit. Assuming that the work will consist of 4 volumes to sell at 40/- if you propose to take the risk we should be willing to part with the *English* right only, for 4 years (which would bring it into your other term of copyrights) for the sum of £6,000—payable in the course of 1872–3 in any instalments you may think fit.

Or if we take the risk we should require a royalty of 2/- per copy sold, on each 5/- part, in the original form, and an equivalent royalty on copies in cheaper editions. Half yearly accounts.

We ought to sell 10,000 at this cheap rate, because soon the Libraries will find it more profitable than ordinary novels since they will have 8 volumes to distribute in lieu of 4. But no one can tell.[3]

Blackwood prudently accepted the royalty.

After various trials, a format was devised to suit both George Eliot and Lewes. For the wrapper of the separate books Mr. Simpson secured a design, crawling with vines and foliage and meaningless scrolls, which (unhappily) the author liked. At her suggestion a circular vignette was added. Owen Jones, consulted too late, advised slight changes in the spacing and objected to the paper they had selected as too yellow a green.[4] Other colours they had considered were a lilac or mauve, a buff, and (perhaps in memory of Thackeray) a yellow. They would have done better to consult Barbara Bodichon, who had a fine eye for colour. When Book I appeared, she wrote:

I do not like the cover at all, it is not artistic enough—much better have nothing on the cover than that riggle and landscape, which are not

---

[1] *Letters*, v. 168–9.   [2] The title was changed to 'Waiting for Death'.
[3] *Letters*, v. 179–80.   [4] *Letters*, v. 191, 196.

worthy of your work at all. The green is not a bad colour, much better than the blue of the Spanish Gypsy, which was a very hard wicked blue and made me unhappy, and a plain Roman letter on that green would have been very nice. Do not let them do what they like in dressing your children it does make a difference and I like to see your things in becoming clothes.[1]

The inclusion of advertising pages in the separate books was Lewes's idea, and proved a profitable addition. He also corrected all the proofs. The printing of Book I was completed on 6 November and it was published on 1 December 1871. In the daily and weekly papers the chorus of praise began at once. Langford, Blackwood's London manager, though he conceded the necessity of getting out of Mudie's clutches, had been sceptical about the new experiment;[2] but after reading 'Miss Brooke' he was converted, and his admiration grew with each number.

Lewes had not waited for Blackwood's offer before disposing of the American rights to *Middlemarch*. In April 1871 he had asked Osgood, Ticknor & Co. of Boston what arrangement they could suggest to anticipate the English publication without risk to the copyright. They wished to publish the novel in weekly instalments in *Every Saturday*, and offered £1,200 for it. When Trübner advised him that the paper was not seen in England, Lewes—in spite of Marian's dislike of being read in short instalments—accepted the offer.[3] Blackwood, ignorant of how much had been paid for the rights, was uneasy about 'their Yankee arrangement. It has a confounded trading look', he wrote to Willie, 'and bits will be published right and left in this country in spite of our teeth.'[4] His anxiety was needless. On 10 November Osgood cabled Lewes that they had transferred the copyright to *Harper's Weekly* in New York; there *Middlemarch* appeared in weekly instalments from 16 December 1871 to 15 February 1873.

The Continental reprint caused greater trouble. Tauchnitz had paid George Eliot only £100 for *The Mill on the Floss* and less for *Romola*. He had a stranglehold on English reprints on the Continent, many of which found their way into England. So Lewes began negotiating with Albert Cohn of Asher & Co. in Berlin. After much correspondence and telegraphing, Cohn agreed to a

[1] Barbara Bodichon to GE, [Dec. 1871] (Yale).
[2] *Letters*, v. 207.
[3] GHL Diary, 15 July 1871.
[4] J. Blackwood to W. Blackwood, 4 Sept. 1871 (NLS).

plan of royalty, and *Middlemarch* became the first of Asher's
Collection of English and American Authors, Copyright Editions.
It brought George Eliot £327. The competition forced Tauchnitz
to raise his offers for subsequent books.[1] Simpson in Edinburgh
by a great coup got £200 for serial rights in the *Australasian* of
Melbourne, winning from Lewes the sobriquet 'von Moltke' for
his strategy. For the Dutch translation George Eliot was paid £25,
and for a rather bad one in German by Lehmann's brother Emil,
£30.

During the summer at Shottermill the Leweses saw few visitors.
The Calls came to tea one day, and Barbara Bodichon stayed for
two days, sleeping at the hotel opposite the railway station.
W. G. Clark, who had been visiting the Tennysons at Aldworth
two or three miles from Shottermill, came to see them on 29 June;
packing up a lunch with biscuits and sherry and cigars, they went
off to Waggoner's Wells to spend the whole day in pleasant chat.
On the train coming down from London, 14 July, Lewes met
Tennyson, who drove him in his carriage to Brookbank and came
in to be introduced to Polly. He told his wife that George Eliot
looked 'like the picture of Savonarola'.[2] A week later Tennyson
brought his son Hallam to call on her. On their return Mrs.
Tennyson, again obviously curious, gleaned from them that
George Eliot 'is delightful in a *tête-à-tête*, and speaks in a soft
soprano voice, which almost sounds like a fine falsetto, with her
strong, masculine face'. The Leweses, too, were a little curious
about the Laureate. One day they took their walk round Blackdown, looking at Aldworth, and on 9 August they went in to return
Tennyson's call. He and Hallam had gone off for a brief holiday
in Wales, but they met Mrs. Tennyson and her younger son
Lionel. When Alfred returned, he and Mrs. Tennyson came to call
on George Eliot on 26 August. 'After a while', Lewes's Diary
noted, 'she left him with us and he read "Maud" and "Northern
Farmer" aloud. We then walked part of the way home with him.'
The day before they departed from Shottermill, Tennyson 'came
to say goodbye and brought his poems to read—Boadicea, Tears
Idle Tears, Modern Northern Farmer, Guinevere. We walked part
of the way home with him.'[3] Mrs. Tennyson, again eager for

---

[1] See Simon Nowell-Smith, 'Firma Tauchnitz 1837–1900', *Book Collector*,
15 (1966), 434.
[2] *Alfred, Lord Tennyson. A Memoir* (1897), II. 107.
[3] GHL Diary, 31 Aug. 1871.

details, noted in her journal that Alfred 'read to them, and last of all at G. H. Lewes' request "Guinevere", which made George weep'. Changes in the text when these passages were published in *Alfred, Lord Tennyson. A Memoir* (1897) indicate the delicacy that ladies felt about calling on George Eliot. Some few copies of the first edition contain (II. 109) the entry for 26 August: 'We called on Lewes and George Eliot. A. stayed to read "Maud".' But in most copies the page has been cancelled and reset to remove the incriminating entry.[1]

It was quite by chance that Marian was at Shottermill to meet the Tennysons. She had been planning a brief holiday in Scotland. The centenary of Sir Walter Scott's birth was being celebrated at Edinburgh on 15 August 1871, and George Eliot was among the notable guests who had been invited to sit at the head table. Averse as she was to public appearance, her intense veneration for Scott impelled her to accept the invitation. Within a few weeks, however, the prospect frightened her, and she asked Lewes to write to the Committee, withdrawing. Blackwood, who was a member of it, was probably a little relieved. Though he would be sorry not to see her, he confessed that 'at those sort of gatherings there are always forward vulgar monsters to jar upon one's feelings, so perhaps you escape something'.[2] She celebrated Scott's birthday by working quietly on *Middlemarch* and reading an article on the atomic theory of Lucretius.

Early in August 1871 George Eliot received a letter from a young Scot named Alexander Main, lauding *Romola* and inquiring whether it was not correctly accented on the first syllable. Marian assured him that it was. Her warm response to his appreciation of the novel was rewarded with another rhapsody, this time eleven pages long, declaring that no other writer but Shakespeare came near George Eliot. This letter too she answered gratefully, dwelling chiefly on her 'worship for Scott', whom she had begun to read at the age of seven. 'I have not much strength and time for correspondence,' she concluded, 'but I shall always be glad to hear from you when you have anything in your mind which it will be a solace to you to say to me.'[3] Upon this hint Main sent her within a few days two letters of eight pages each on *The Spanish Gypsy*, which made her cry because, unlike the reviewers, he had

---

[1] See note in *Letters*, V. 180–1.
[2] Ibid. 168.   [3] Ibid. 175.

understood so perfectly what she intended.[1] On 25 September Main wrote again, sending sample pages of selections from George Eliot's works and asking permission to publish a volume of brief selections or 'sayings'. Polly was ill when this arrived, and Lewes took over the correspondence. Well aware of the benefit such appreciation had on her, Lewes promised to write to Blackwood about Main's proposal. Blackwood, who owned the copyrights, was naturally less enthusiastic, but agreed to see him. Soon he reported to George Eliot that Main was about thirty years old, had abandoned study for the ministry, and lived with his mother at Arbroath, spending whole days reading aloud by the sea-shore the works of George Eliot, whom he pronounced to be 'concrete'. However, his proposal was accepted, and the book under the title *Wise, Witty, and Tender Sayings in Prose and Verse*— with a painfully eulogistic preface (which the Leweses had not seen)—was published in December 1871. 'I think the Gusher will boil over if we do not publish before Christmas', Blackwood wrote to Willie.[2]

Returning on 1 September to the Priory which still reeked with fresh paint, the Leweses faced the problem of rearranging the furniture and books, and the more serious one of replacing their servants the sisters Grace and Amelia, who after ten years of service gave their month's warning on 5 September. It was a great shock to Marian. 'We should never have dismissed them, and we looked forward to taking care of them when they were too old to work', she told Cara. 'But their oddities were a yoke which we were certain would get heavier with the years, and since they could think of going we are contented now that they should go.'[3] She was very lucky in securing two excellent servants from the Calls, who were going to Italy for a year; with the addition of a third (long needed, but Grace and Amelia would never tolerate any 'stranger') they soon had the household running smoothly.[4]

---

[1] *Letters*, v. 184.

[2] J. Blackwood to W. Blackwood, 6 Nov. 1871 (NLS).

[3] *Letters*, v. 197.

[4] A list in GE's hand details the housemaid's work at the Priory: 'Lay and light all fires and keep all stoves clean. Shake Mats, clean Entrance. Empty all slops, clean Baths and Washing stands and open Beds. Make beds and dust bedroom furniture. Wash up after Lunch. Prepare tray for dinner. Close dining and drawing room shutters and bring up lamps. Light the Hall gas. Wash up after dinner. Turn down beds etc. Bolt the outer doors and put out the gas.' A weekly calendar follows: when each carpet is to be swept, when the plate is to be cleaned, and the doorsteps and bell handle (Yale).

While Marian was working hard on *Middlemarch*, George helped supervise the household. She fell seriously ill with a gastric fever on 16 September 1871, which she attributed at first to the smell of the paint. Three weeks later she wrote to Cara: 'I am as thin as a mediæval Christ, and Mr. Lewes is exerting his ingenuity to feed me up. He has been housekeeper, secretary, and Nurse all in one—as good a nurse as if he had been trained in a hospital.'[1]

On 30 November 1871 they gave a small party to celebrate the publication of *Middlemarch*, Book I. Presentation copies had been ordered and sent to Charles and Herbert Lewes, Mrs. Edward Lewes, Sara Hennell, Mrs. Congreve, Owen Jones, and Alexander Main, with three copies for Mrs. G. H. Lewes.[2] Main was an afterthought added by Lewes, not 'one of the three exceptional people' to whom, Marian told Sara, the book was to go.[3] 'But do not write to me about it', she warned Sara, 'because until a book has quite gone away from me and become entirely of the non-ego—gone thoroughly from the wine-press into the casks— I would rather not hear or see anything that is said about it.'[3]

Books II and III were put into type early in December. The chapters describing Dorothea at Rome (19–22), which conclude Book II, were originally the opening chapters of Book III; they were transposed with the chapters dealing with Fred Vincy's problems that now open Book III to keep both sets of characters present in each book.[4] Marian was working steadily now. She 'proposed further developments' to Lewes on 16 December, and before Christmas she was at page 227 of Book IV.

Their Christmas Marian described as 'rather doleful'.[5] She read *David Copperfield* aloud to Lewes, who was writing his article on Dickens for the *Fortnightly*. They went to see Irving in *The Bells*—the first time in years that they had gone to an English theatre. Christmas Eve they called on Gertrude, who was pregnant and ordered to stay very quiet, having had two miscarriages. On New Year's Day, however, when they went to Weybridge to stay with the Cross family—'delightful Scotch people', George Eliot calls them in a letter to Blackwood[6]—the weather was delicious. They walked in the mornings, drove about the country in the afternoons, and filled the rest of the day with interesting talk and 'riotous fun', playing games and acting a charade. The other guests—Jowett, T. C. Sandars, and C. S. C. Bowen were, like

[1] *Letters*, v. 197. [2] *Letters*, v. 217.
[3] *Letters*, v. 214. [4] Middlemarch *from Notebook to Novel*, pp. 52–5.
[5] *Letters*, v. 231. [6] *Letters*, v. 208.

Bullock, Balliol men, who all became regular visitors to the Priory. Bowen, who was junior counsel to the Attorney-General John Duke Coleridge, got the Leweses seats for the Tichborne trial, and they heard Coleridge speak for three hours, until Lewes, feeling ill from the bad air, had to come away.[1] Mr. and Mrs. Bowen came to a dinner party at the Priory on 27 January with Spencer, Harrison, Dr. Liebreich, and Francis Otter, another barrister friend of the Crosses. In the evening Mr. and Mrs. Lehmann, Mr. and Mrs. Du Maurier, Mrs. Pattison, Burton, Richard Doyle, Dr. Payne, Charles Lewes, and Margaret Gillies came, and there was music and 'capital singing' till nearly 1 o'clock.[2]

Book V of *Middlemarch* was written amid such diversions. The Sunday afternoons were more crowded than ever. On 18 February, when the Bowens came to lunch, the list included Mrs. Alfred Morrison, Owen Jones, F. W. H. Myers, George Howard, Mrs. Pattison, Browning, Barbara Bodichon, William Allingham, Mrs. John Jay, whom the Leweses had met in Vienna, Benzon, C. T. Newton, the archaeologist, C. E. C. B. Appleton, the youthful editor of the *Academy*, and Theodore Martin. Two days later Mrs. Nassau Senior came to lunch, sang to them, and accompanied them into town while Polly bought a silk dress at Heilbronner's. The next day Lewes found her 'deep in consultation' with Owen Jones—recalling his advice on her antique grey *moiré* in 1863.

Every Saturday the Leweses went to the Pop concerts. But before the series ended on 22 March, they had begun to search for a country retreat where they could escape again from the pressure of company. They looked at houses in Guildford, Barnet, Watford, and Godalming before taking Elversley, in Park Road, Redhill, Surrey, for three months from 24 May. Polly was far from well, having serious trouble with her teeth and gums. She went often to the dentist; Paget came several times to see her and give what relief he could. One day he sat more than an hour chatting with her about 'things medical à propos of Middle-march'.[3] Book V was dispatched to Edinburgh early in May. She had begun to write Book VI before they went down to Redhill. There in the quiet mornings she finished it and sent it off on 2 July. It was written in five weeks, more easily than any of the earlier books. With only two more to come, Lewes proposed to Blackwood that VII and VIII should be published in November

[1] *Letters*, v. 237. [2] GHL Diary, 27 Jan. 1872.
[3] GHL Diary, 20 Apr. 1872.

and December instead of at two-month intervals. Blackwood accepted the plan. They were written rapidly. Book VII was finished on 7 August; by 11 September 1872 most of VIII was done.

The house at Redhill proved very comfortable, 'shut out from the world amid fields—not a sound except hens cackling and dogs barking reaches us—not a soul knows where we are', Lewes wrote, 'so we haven't even many letters to disturb us'.[1] But Marian was exhausted by her long effort. She told Mrs. Cross that her life for the last year had been 'a sort of nightmare in which I have been scrambling on the slippery bank of a pool, just keeping my head above water'.[2] Before leaving to rest at Homburg, they went to Six Mile Bottom for a week-end with Henry Bullock, who had inherited an estate there and taken the added surname of Hall. His mother-in-law Mrs. Cross was there with Emily, Florence, and Johnny Cross, and Albert Druce, the husband of Anna Cross. Polly arrived tired and ailing on 13 September 1872. They spent the days quietly, inspecting the farms, dogs, fowls, horses, cattle, and talking to the farmers. On the last night, accompanying Polly into her bedroom, Mrs. Cross 'caught fire with her widow's streamers at the candle. Fortunately, it was soon put out, and no great damage done, but Polly had a slight hysterical fit from the shock.'[3] She awoke next morning with dreadful headache and sickness, which postponed their departure till the midday train. After a day or two at the Priory reading proofs of Book VIII and packing, they set out on 18 September for Homburg.

The sale of *Middlemarch* in parts selling at 5s. was just under 5,000 copies. Though Lewes had hoped that 7,000 or 8,000 would go in this form, it was still a profitable venture all round. Mudie, who had threatened to burke the novel, found the demand for it too strong to resist. He soon took 1,500 copies of Book I, and about the same of each of the rest. W. H. Smith & Son increased their subscription of the parts from 600 to 1,000. In 1873, bound four volumes at 21s., *Middlemarch* had a surprising sale of nearly 3,000 more copies; and in 1874, when it was reprinted in one volume at 7s. 6d., more than 13,000 were sold in the first six months. By 1879, including foreign editions, nearly 30,000 copies of the book had been sold, bringing George Eliot about £9,000.

[1] *Letters*, v. 278. [2] *Letters*, v. 301.
[3] GHL Diary, 15 Sept. 1872.

Its commercial success was dwarfed by its triumph with the critics. From the start *Middlemarch* was acclaimed a masterpiece. In a long article of nearly three columns the *Telegraph* declared it 'almost profane to speak of ordinary novels in the same breath with George Eliot's'.[1] *Blackwood's* naturally praised the book. There was a surprising agreement of opinion in the *Edinburgh Review* (by Lord Houghton), the *Quarterly* (by Robert Laing), the *Fortnightly* (by Sidney Colvin), the *Spectator* (by Hutton), and even the often inimical *Athenœum* (by Williams). Seldom can there have been such deserved unanimity of praise. Edith Simcox wrote in the *Academy*: 'to say that *Middlemarch* is George Eliot's greatest work is to say that it has scarcely a superior and very few equals in the whole wide range of English fiction'. With singular perception she pointed out that it marks an epoch in the history of fiction in so far as its incidents are taken from the inner life, as the action is developed by the direct influence of mind on mind and character on character, and as the material background gives 'perfect realistic truth to a profoundly imaginative psychological study'.[2] Though Henry James, who had his own standards for novels, found *Middlemarch* 'a treasure-house of details' but 'an indifferent whole', he admitted that [Jamesian] concentration on one or two characters would have deprived us of many of the best things in the book. 'George Eliot seems to us among English romancers to stand alone. Fielding approaches her, but to our mind she surpasses Fielding. Fielding was didactic—the author of *Middlemarch* is really philosophic.' Though James found a dozen passages he marked 'obscure', the book 'remains a very splendid performance. It sets a limit, we think to the development of the old-fashioned English novel.'[3] *The Times*, almost the last to pronounce, held its fire till 7 March 1873. The blast was worth waiting for. The highly favourable review (by Frederick Broome) filling nearly four columns, began: 'There are few novels in the language which will repay reading over again so well as *Middlemarch*.' This official word probably had a part in the unexpectedly large sale of the four-volume edition.

The impact of *Middlemarch*, which was even stronger than the sales indicate, came more from word of mouth than from reviews. 'I do not believe any of her books since *Adam Bede* has been

---

[1] *Daily Telegraph*, 18 June 1872.

[2] *Academy*, 1 Jan. 1873, p. 1. Freud said that *Middlemarch* 'appealed to him very much, and he found it illuminated important aspects of his relations with Martha [his wife]'. Ernest Jones, *Life and Work of Sigmund Freud* (1953), I. 174.

[3] *Galaxy*, 15 (Mar. 1873), 428.

so much talked about', Joseph Langford wrote to William Black-wood. He had been prejudiced against the novel at the start, sceptical of the new plan of publication, disliking the 'Prelude', the diffusion of interest, and the way George Eliot stands back from her characters and comments on them. But Book IV he found 'marvellous—such a picture of English country life has never been drawn', and he thought Book VI with its analysis of Bulstrode's hypocrisy 'first-first rate. . . . I have never been so charmed with anything she has written.'[1] Before the final number appeared, this hardened veteran of Paternoster Row was com-plaining of being kept in 'cruel ignorance' of the winding up of the wonderful story. Taine, whom Morley tried in vain to persuade to review the book in the *Fortnightly*, pronounced George Eliot 'the greatest of English romancers'. When Bulstrode was being de-scribed in Book VII, a West End clergyman in a sermon on Hosea, said: 'Many of you no doubt have read the work which that great teacher George Eliot is now publishing and have shuddered as I shuddered at the awful dissection of a guilty conscience. Well, *that* is what I mean by the prophetic spirit.'[2] Judge Fitzgerald reported that

at the opening of the Dublin Exhibition he was struck with the atten-tion of the Archbishop [Trench] to the interior of his hat, which at first he took for devout listening to the speeches, but on close examina-tion saw he was reading something, and as this was so intent he was prompted to look also into the hat, and found the Archbishop had *Middlemarch* there laid open—what a much better way of listening to 'opening speeches'![3]

Harriet Martineau, reading it for a second time, found the experi-ence almost too poignant to be borne. 'The Casaubons set me dreaming all night', she wrote to a friend. 'Do you ever hear *anything* of Lewes and Miss Evans?'[4] Dr. Hodgson, who had mesmerized Marian in 1844 and known her at 142 Strand, began the book in the morning and read till his lamp waned at 2 a.m.[5] Emily Dickinson wrote from Amherst to a cousin in Boston: 'What do I think of Middlemarch? What do I think of glory? . . . The mysteries of human nature surpass the "mysteries of redemp-tion".'[6] She charged Colonel T. W. Higginson, who was taking

[1] J. Langford to W. Blackwood, 28 Nov., 29 May, 25 Sept. 1872 (NLS).
[2] *Letters*, v. 333.   [3] *Letters*, v. 291.
[4] Theodora Bosanquet, *Harriet Martineau* (1927), p. 214.
[5] J. M. D. Meiklejohn, *Life and Letters of W. D. Hodgson* (Edinburgh, 1883), p. 383.
[6] *Letters of Emily Dickinson*, ed. T. H. Johnson (3 vols., Cambridge, Mass., 1958), II. 506.

some autumn leaves to England for George Eliot, to report every detail about her if he succeeded in meeting her.[1] Everywhere the book was being talked about.

George Eliot's friends had been carefully schooled by Lewes not to discuss her books with her. But Herbert Spencer, never expansive in feeling for others, wrote to Lewes on finishing Book VII: 'It is altogether admirable. I cannot conceive anything more perfectly done . . . this last portion seems to me to fulfil the requirements of the highest art in every respect.'[2] Barbara Bodichon, of course, was always a law unto herself. After reading Book I she wrote to Marian:

> I think it *is* your best work—no that I won't say but being the last I have read it does seem to me today to be by far your best. I am sure it is the most interesting only I dread the unfolding and feel quite certain it is a horrible tragedy coming [to Dorothea].
>
> I hear people say it is so witty amusing and lively; so it is but all is shadowed by the coming misery to me. I can't help feeling it desperately. I am very sorry for the poor thing just as if she were alive, and I want to stop her. She is like a child dancing into a quick sand on a sunny morning and I feel a sort of horror at your story as if it were all real and going on at this moment. I do not know if you meant to produce this sort of terrible foreshadowing of inevitable misery and I see some of 'em have read it and only see wit, character, and liveliness, and call it light reading, now I find it heavy reading to my heart though I think it a most noble book and thank you for it.[3]

Though many reviews commented on the supposed melancholy of *Middlemarch*, few were so struck as Barbara by the impending tragedy. George Eliot reassured Blackwood, who was always hoping for happy endings, that 'there is no unredeemed tragedy in the solution of the story'.[4]

There were the usual pedants pointing out little errors. A barrister in the Temple wrote anonymously to George Eliot to say that by destroying his second will, as he tried to do in Chapter 33, Featherstone could not have revived the earlier one.[5] In the next book (Chapter 52) George Eliot let Mr. Farebrother explain that fact to Mary Garth. Paget had expressed his great delight in

---

[1] George Whicher, *This Was a Poet* (1939), pp. 216–17.

[2] H. Spencer to GHL, 11 Nov. 1872 (Sterling Library, London University Library).

[3] Barbara Bodichon to GE, [Dec. 1871] (Yale).

[4] *Letters*, v. 296. T. S. Eliot wrote that Rosamond Vincy frightened him 'far more than Goneril or Regan'. *Three Voices of Poetry* (N.Y., 1954), p. 18.

[5] Anonymous to GE, 4 June 1872 (Yale).

George Eliot's 'wonderful accuracy in medical matters'. A few days later she was distressed to receive a letter from a London surgeon declaring it wrong in Chapters 63 and 66 to describe Lydgate 'with bright, dilated eyes' from taking opium, which contracts the pupils. When she asked Paget whether she should change the passages, he replied that it was accurate enough: the eyelids can be wide with excitement even though the pupils are contracted. Nevertheless, in revising the text for the one-volume edition, she changed the passages to read 'with a strange light in his eyes' and 'the peculiar light in the eyes'.[1]

Leisurely publication, protracted over a full year, developed a remarkable *rapport* between George Eliot and her readers. Enthralled by her accurate perception of human nature, many felt that she was writing especially for them. Letters came to her from all over the world. One that found her, posted in France, was addressed simply: 'George Eliot | the world-known authoress | Londres.' Another, from a young man in San Mateo, California, began:

> Oh you dear lady, I who have been a Fred Vincy ever so long, only not so little ugly and not so little unintelligent, thank you very very much for Middlemarch, most of all for the last chapter. I almost know that even I who have played vagabond and ninny every since I knew the meaning of such terms, *may* reform to find my Mary too—perhaps. You, who are a great lady yet know so well how all the little fishes struggle, may smile a moment at my folly which dares to love you for your goodness and inspiring handiwork. I shall not read this over, as my courage, fast oozing now, would fail—
>
> With many thanks and best wishes to your great husband I am
> Your humble admirer,
Ralph Q. Quirk.

Mrs. Dana Estes, a respectable lady in Boston, wrote to George Eliot:

> I feel the most intense desire to know you. I care for you as the embodyment of my highest principles, and after reading your books with me, my husband shares my enthusiasm. If we may never see you, we have much true married happiness to thank you for.[2]

Many of George Eliot's acquaintances were confident that they recognized the 'originals' of her characters. Dr. Clifford Allbutt,

---

[1] George D. Brown to GE, 4 Dec. 1872; James Paget to GE, 7 Dec. 1872 (Yale). D. H. Lawrence made the same mistake in *Sons and Lovers*: Mrs. Morel, dying, is given morphia. 'Darker and darker grew her eyes, all pupil with torture' (ch. 14).

[2] Mrs. Dana Estes to GE, 3 May 1874 (Yale).

who had taken her over his new Infirmary at Leeds, was convinced, that she drew Lydgate from him; and his biographers, who seldom read the novel with care, repeat the error as if it were some high distinction to have posed for the story's most conspicuous failure.[1] A far likelier prototype can be seen in George Eliot's brother-in-law Edward Clarke, who like Lydgate was better born than the other country surgeons, went bankrupt with a debt of £1,000, and died young. It is difficult to explain the vanity of Oscar Browning, neither a doctor nor a husband, in confiding to Arthur Rickett the 'open secret' that he was the original of Lydgate.[2] Perhaps he was confusing him with Ladislaw.

With most candidates for the dubious distinction of being the original of Mr. Casaubon the resemblance can be reduced to their having married much younger wives. When George Eliot began to write 'Miss Brooke', she said that it had 'been recorded among my possible themes ever since I began to write fiction'.[3] It appears in the young Romola, who longed to become as learned as Cassandra Fedele 'and then perhaps some great scholar will want to marry me'.[4] The theme has been treated, usually comically, in English literature since Chaucer's time, and there are examples in most other literatures. George Eliot knew from her earliest days the old pedant Christopher Clutterbuck in Bulwer Lytton's *Pelham*, whose young wife is actually named Dorothea. She was reading Jean Paul Richter's *Quintus Fixlein* while writing 'Miss Brooke'.

Of living originals Robert William Mackay, her acquaintance of the *Westminster Review* days, who married (not very happily) at Casaubon's age of forty-eight, was sometimes said to have suggested him.[5] But the most commonly accepted original was the Rector of Lincoln College, Mark Pattison, who published his *Life of Isaac Casaubon* in 1875, three years after *Middlemarch*. George Eliot had been interested in the great French scholar since her winter in Geneva, where Casaubon was born, and knew his fine edition of Theophrastus' *Charactères*. Pattison himself never showed any sign that he thought a cruel caricature was directed at him. Like his wife he corresponded warmly with George Eliot before and after *Middlemarch* appeared and called often at the Priory till the end of her life. Both of them consulted her about

---

[1] H. D. Rolleston, *Sir Thomas Clifford Allbutt* (1927), pp. 59–61.
[2] *Bookman*, 17 (Jan. 1900), 113.
[3] GE Journal, 2 Dec. 1870.   [4] *Romola*, ch. 5.
[5] *Life of Frances Power Cobbe*, by Herself (2 vols., Boston, 1894), II. 430–1.

the last chapter of the *Life of Isaac Casaubon*;[1] the copy the author presented to her is now in Dr. Williams's Library. After her death the name of the book and gossip about strained relations between the Pattisons led some people to fancy that George Eliot had them in mind when writing *Middlemarch*. Mrs. Pattison's second husband Sir Charles Dilke declared: 'The grotesqueness of any attempt to find a likeness between a mere pedant like George Eliot's Casaubon and a great scholar like Mark Pattison, or between the somewhat child-like Dorothea and the tremendous personality of the real heroine, was never made by any but a simpleton.'[2] Others who knew them shared this opinion. Mrs. Humphry Ward wrote: 'I do not believe that she ever meant to describe the Rector . . . in the dreary and foolish pedant who overshadows " Middlemarch ".'[3] John Morley dismissed the identification as an 'impertinent blunder'.[4]

Yet the canard persists. In 1957 a writer made the quaint suggestion that George Eliot's insight into the Pattisons' marital relations may have been 'prophetic rather than historical'.[5] The Warden of All Souls College in his recent Clark Lectures accepts this kind of prophetic history and sees Sir Charles Dilke—three years after the novel was published—beginning to play in Mrs. Pattison's life 'a *rôle* exactly corresponding with the part played in *Middlemarch* by Will Ladislaw', an example, he says, of life imitating art.[6] The exactness of the parallel is a little blurred by the fact that in Dorothea's case the attachment did not begin till *after* her husband died. The Warden adds an interesting new hypothesis that the warm friendship the Rector showed for George Eliot was a pretence assumed to cover his chagrin at the 'portrait', which Mrs. Pattison 'may have sanctioned or actually encouraged' her to write.[7] A full discussion of this fanciful theory is found in Appendix II.

In George Eliot's own life the closest prototype to Casaubon is found in the egregious Dr. Brabant, with whom Marian Evans had that embarrassing experience at Devizes in 1843.[8] Mrs. Lynn

---

[1] *Letters*, VI. 108.
[2] MS. 'Memoir of E. F. S. Dilke' (British Museum, Add. 43946, fol. 25) later prefixed with slight changes to *The Book of the Spiritual Life* (1905).
[3] Mrs. Humphry Ward, *A Writer's Recollections* (1918), p. 110.
[4] 'On Pattison's Memoirs', *Critical Miscellanies. Works* (1921), VI. 240–1.
[5] V. H. H. Green, *Oxford Common Room* (1957), pp. 213–14.
[6] John Sparrow, *Mark Pattison and the Idea of a University* (Cambridge, 1967), p. 17.
[7] Ibid. p. 16.
[8] See pp. 49–51.

Linton, who had known Brabant under somewhat similar circumstances, had no doubt that he was the original of Casaubon.
When Harriet Beecher Stowe inquired whether Dorothea's marriage was like her own, George Eliot replied: 'Impossible to conceive of any creature less like Mr. Casaubon than my warm,
enthusiastic husband. . . . I fear that the Casaubon-tints are not
quite foreign to my own mental complexion. At any rate, I am
very sorry for him.'[1] When a young friend put the question direct:
'But from whom, then, did you draw Casaubon?' George Eliot,
with a humorous solemnity, which was quite in earnest, nevertheless, pointed to her own heart.'[2] Perhaps she had in mind the
morbid fear of criticism that she shared with him. Or was she
recalling her youthful expulsion from that 'little heaven' at
Devizes? In the pain and humiliation of that episode lay the venom
that gave Casaubon his horrible vividness.

We do not know what Marian's sister Fanny Houghton thought
of *Middlemarch*, though her admiration of the achievement may
be safely assumed. Did she see an allusion to Isaac Evans's son
Frederick in Fred Vincy's mistaken ambition to rise in society
by entering the Church? Fred Evans, after taking a third at
Exeter College, Oxford, where he distinguished himself as an
athlete, had taken orders; when *Middlemarch* appeared he was
Vicar of Kidderminster, and soon to be Rector of Bedworth. One
wonders whether Isaac and Fanny could have read about Fred
Vincy's beloved Mary Garth without seeing some allusion to
'the family'. Mary is not pretty, but no one else in the novel has
such genuine charm, lively intelligence, integrity, and a keen sense
of humour, which Dorothea utterly lacks. She is very like their
sharp-tongued, honest, passionate sister, who no longer had any
correspondence with them.

Admirers of George Eliot, sometimes quite unknown, sent
tangible offerings of gratitude—flowers, fruit, and, of course,
books. Mrs. Julia Cameron, who brought some of her famous
photographic portraits,[3] would gladly have added to her collection one of the elusive camera-shy George Eliot. Benjamin
Jowett, now Master of Balliol, in a letter to her, 14 August 1872,
wrote:

[1] *Letters*, v. 322.
[2] F. W. H. Myers, 'George Eliot', *Century Magazine*, 23 (Nov. 1881), 60.
[3] *Letters*, v. 133.

Some friends with whom I am staying are very desirous of sending you a box of game, and as they have not the pleasure of knowing you, I have been made their purveyor. Like all the world they have been reading Middlemarch and think, to use their own words, that 'it would be so nice if we could send Mrs. Lewes' some game.

Let me take the opportunity of congratulating you on the entire success of your last great work. It is a bond of conversation and friendship everywhere. We all of us have our wishes and interests about the future of the Garths. I must wish you also rest after such a great intellectual effort. For we cannot be always writing either in a small or in a large way, as I know by experience.

The 'Great Teacher' that readers discovered in *Middlemarch* brought George Eliot more letters than any other aspect of the book. Frederic Myers, a Fellow of Trinity College, Cambridge, wrote to her when it was finished, not expecting an answer, but only 'to give myself the pleasure and relief of thanking you for an enjoyment which has brightened the whole year'. Myers cared most for the scenes between Ladislaw and Dorothea, 'noble love-making', which is hardly ever described truly.

Life has come to such a pass,—now that there is no longer any God or any hereafter or anything in particular to aim at,—that it is only by coming into contact with some other person that one can be oneself. . . . And you seem now to be the only person who can make life appear potentially noble and interesting without starting from any assumptions. De Stendhal, perhaps, while himself detached from all illusions, has painted life in the same grand style. But he remains too much outside his characters, and though in his books nobleness seems possible it seems possible only as an aberration. And others who have shown more or less of the same power of rising into clear air,—Mme de Stael in *Corinne*, Mrs. Craven in *Fleurange*, George Sand in *Consuelo*—have all needed some fixed point to lean against before they could spread wings to soar. But one feels that you know the worst, and one thanks you in that you have not despaired of the republic.[1]

In January 1872 an unknown admirer named Elma Stuart sent from Dinan a book-slide that she had carved of oak for George Eliot. 'What for years, you have been to me, how you have comforted my sorrows, peopled my loneliness, added to my happiness, and bettered in every way my whole nature, you can never know: till the Great Day of Squaring comes', said the letter accompanying it.[2] Born Elvorilda Eliza Maria Fraser, Elma (as she understandably preferred to be called) was married in 1860 to J. G. G.

[1] F. W. H. Myers to GE, 8 Dec. 1872 (Yale).
[2] Mrs. Stuart's letter to GE, 29 Jan. 1872 (Yale).

Stuart, a lieutenant in the Black Watch, who died two or three years later, leaving her a scant pittance on which to live and educate her son Roland. At Dinan during the War she met some wood-carvers, refugees from Paris, who taught her something of their art. George Eliot, always susceptible to such sympathy as evidence of her 'place in other minds', thanked the unknown carver for 'this visible token of our spiritual companionship'. Lewes, glad of help in his endless effort to overcome George Eliot's diffidence, sent Mrs. Stuart a copy of Main's *Sayings* and the assurance that her letter had given him too 'a thrill of exquisite pleasure'.[1] The book-slide was followed by a mirror frame in walnut, an oak table, a writing board, and other specimens of her work, all elaborately carved with flowers, birds, leaves, and inscriptions linking her name with George Eliot's. Later came a shawl, a letter-case, slippers, gloves, handkerchiefs, a paper-weight, cologne, bonbons, and photographs of Roland, of herself, of her dogs Watch and Dora. In fervid letters Elma told how much George Eliot's work had meant to her, how she longed to be her servant, to kiss the hem of her garment, and so on. Though her own mother was still living, she adopted George Eliot as her 'spiritual mother'. In 1903 Elma was buried next to George Eliot beneath a stone describing herself as one 'whom for $8\frac{1}{2}$ blessed years George Eliot called by the sweet name of "Daughter".'

Elma was not her only 'spiritual daughter'. George Eliot had many other young women who confided their inner feelings to her and sought her counsel in their perplexities as if she were a mother. She often addressed Mrs. Pattison as 'Dear Figliuolina', 'God-daughter', or 'Daughter', and sometimes signed her letters 'Your affectionate Madre'. Edith Simcox also called her 'Mother', and a little later Alice Helps, the daughter of Lewes's old friend, adopted her in the same way.

The crescendo of fame that accompanied the publication of *Middlemarch* widened the circle of society in which George Eliot moved. She was now often invited to dinner. In December 1871 she dined with Frederick and Lady Charlotte Locker; besides their daughter Eleanor Locker and her governess, the only other guests were the Dean of Westminster, Arthur Stanley, and his wife Lady Augusta.[2] Dean Stanley, according to Locker, was under the impression that the Leweses had been married in Germany,

[1] *Letters*, v. 244–5.   [2] GHL Diary, 6 Dec. 1871.

and was somewhat taken aback when he later learned the truth.[1]
Marian, of course, knew nothing of that. She had never pretended;
she never desired to thrust herself into the company of conventional people. They sought her out. In his novel *Rose, Blanche,
and Violet* (1848) Lewes had written:

With what untiring perseverance do women in equivocal positions
manœuvre to obtain the presence of virtuous women at their houses!
. . . It is one of the most amusing scenes in the comedy of society to
witness the grateful attentions of a woman who is not 'received' to those
of her female acquaintance who shut their eyes to her real position, or
are ignorant of it.[2]

How ironic to see the author of this observation welcoming the
distinguished callers at the Priory! Many of the ladies received
there were interested in literature, music, art—indifferent to conventional taboos, or rebelling against them. George Eliot did not
manœuvre to bring them.

At Mrs. Benzon's one afternoon in March 1871 Lady Castletown asked Lewes 'to gratify her ambition of being introduced to
Polly, and then introduced her daughter Mrs. Wingfield, who said
she had recently become our neighbour'.[3] The following Sunday
they appeared at the Priory. Besides old friends, the group that
day included Lord Houghton, Lady Ashburton, Mr. and Mrs.
Godfrey Lushington, and Dr. and Mrs. Eustace Smith. On another
occasion Locker introduced Mrs. W. A. Tollemache, who promptly invited the Leweses to dinner.[4] There they met her sister-in-law
Mrs. Cowper-Temple, who confided to Lewes that 'she had copied
passages from *Romola* into her New Testament' and asked to be
allowed to call. She came the next Sunday, bringing her husband,
later Baron Mount-Temple, who had held several important posts
in the government. John Blackwood gave a letter of introduction
to a Mrs. Chetwynd, who, he said, 'is anxious to throw herself
at your feet'.[5] Though he spoke jocosely, this devotional attitude
was growing prevalent among the serious young worshippers of
George Eliot's genius. Since the days of their Italian travels Lewes
had sometimes called her 'Madonna', and their friends were
amused that two such staunch unbelievers should live in a house
called the Priory. Dickens, for example, would write: 'On Sunday

---

[1] F. Locker-Lampson, *My Confidences* (1896), p. 307.
[2] *Rose, Blanche, and Violet* (3 vols., 1848), II. 198–9.
[3] GHL Diary, 29 Mar. 1871.
[4] GHL Diary, 28 Feb. 1872. The Wingfields had a house at 8 Maida Vale.
[5] *Letters*, V. 269.

I hope to attend service at the Priory.'[1] The solemnity that came
to invest these gatherings was not initiated by George Eliot. If
none but lofty subjects were discussed with the succession of
visitors beside her, it was because they came prepared to hear
them. The Hon. Mrs. Henry Frederick Ponsonby, a grand-
daughter of Earl Grey, formerly Maid of Honour to Queen
Victoria, and now wife of the Queen's Private Secretary, describes
her introduction on 16 March 1873:

> George Howard (afterwards 9th Earl of Carlisle) offered to take me to
> St. John's Wood to see George Eliot, after asking her leave to do so,
> and one memorable Sunday I went off in a hansom and arrived at the
> Priory in the afternoon. It really was ridiculous to feel so shy and speech-
> less; I suppose I had put her on such a towering pinnacle that I was
> overpowered by the idea that it was positively George Eliot I was
> speaking to; certainly no Emperor or King in my Court days had ever
> been approached with such awe; it makes me laugh now to think of the
> involuntary deep curtsey I greeted her with—rather to George Howard's
> astonishment.

Mrs. Ponsonby, who was forty-one and had lived all her life in
Court circles, was no schoolgirl to be overawed by a famous name.
Like the rest, she felt some charismatic force that no acting, no
stage management could possibly explain. Deep sincerity under-
lay it, and genuine human interest.

> When I was allowed to see her alone, which happened at last pretty
> soon, I thought that to speak to her of all that was lying deepest in
> one's heart and mind without reserve, and to be received in the kindest
> and most sympathetic way, was a rare delight. I felt compelled, if I had
> not felt inclined, to be perfectly true, to be not only veracious but true,
> and I was met in the same spirit.[2]

All Mrs. Ponsonby's religious experience was later poured out in
a twenty-four-page letter to George Eliot, who, she felt, was 'in
possession of some secret' which made it possible for her to combine with sympathy for modern scientific thought 'a warmth of
approval for moral greatness and beauty and purity in the high
ideals you would set before us'.[3]

Marian's genius had carried her far since she wrote to Cara
Bray that women who are satisfied with light and easily broken
ties 'do *not* act as I have done—they obtain what they desire and

---

[1] Charles Dickens to GHL, 21 Mar. 1870.
[2] Magdalen Ponsonby, *Mary Ponsonby* (1927), pp. 89–90.
[3] Mary Ponsonby to GE, [Oct. 1874] (Yale).

are still invited to dinner'.[1] Such ties could never satisfy her. She had lived openly with Lewes from the beginning. Now she refused more invitations than she accepted, and turned away many who sought admittance to the Priory. She was like the famous scientist Meunier in her story 'The Lifted Veil', to whom 'elegant women pretended to listen, and whose acquaintance was boasted of by noblemen ambitious of brains'.[2]

[1] *Letters*, II. 214.   [2] Cabinet ed., p. 332.

CHAPTER XIV

DANIEL DERONDA

⁂

ARRIVING in Homburg 21 September 1872, the Leweses took the first floor of a house at 14 Obere Promenade, well furnished and only £2 a week, and put themselves at once on a regime, drinking the waters and taking the baths. After a week's rest, Marian wrote the finale of *Middlemarch*, which she duly read to George. He sent it off to Blackwood on 2 October. By the 8th the proof had been received, corrected, and returned to Edinburgh. Her great work was finished. Lewes's part, not in inspiring the novel, but in counselling and sustaining the morbidly diffident author throughout the long period of its creation, deserves the highest praise.

On the first day in Homburg, Lewes met Mrs. Wingfield, who came round at once with her mother, the Baroness Castletown, to call on Marian. Lady Castletown was a cheerful Irishwoman, daughter of a clergyman in Armagh. In 1869 after a long career in the Army, her husband, John Wilson Fitzpatrick, illegitimate son of the Earl of Upper Ossory, had succeeded to his father's Irish estates and had been created a peer of the United Kingdom as the Baron Castletown. They had come to the Priory a number of times since Mrs. Benzon presented them to George Eliot. When the Leweses returned the call the next morning, Lady Castletown introduced them to another of her daughters, Lady Murray, and her husband, the Honourable Sir Charles Murray. Murray, Minister to the Court of Portugal, who was more than thirty years his wife's senior, told Lewes of having spent three evenings with Goethe in 1830. They all welcomed the Leweses heartily to Homburg, driving with them through the pine forests, dining with them at the Hessischer Hof, and accompanying them to the concerts. At the Kursaal two or three times they watched the gambling. Lewes noticed 'a young man with one white lock in front take out napoleons by the handful from his paletot pocket, walk excitedly away after each loss, but return in time for the next play; when all the gold was gone he began to stake 1000 frs. notes in the same way and lost four before he gained once'.[1] George Eliot wrote to John Blackwood:

There is very little dramatic 'Stoff' to be picked up by watching or listening. The saddest thing to be witnessed is the play of Miss Leigh, Byron's grand-niece, who is only 26 years old, and is completely in the grasp of this mean, money-raking demon. It made me cry to see her young fresh face among the hags and brutally stupid men around her.[2]

She had lost £500, Lewes noted, and looked feverish and excited. 'Painful sight!'[3] But George Eliot was mistaken about the paucity of dramatic *Stoff*. This scene at the Kursaal proved to be the germ of her next novel, *Daniel Deronda*.

The Castletowns introduced several of their friends. One was Mrs. Richard Greville, a redoubtable elocutionist, who with the slightest urging would recite poems like Tennyson's 'May Queen'. Another, the Countess von Usedom, daughter of a former Governor of Bombay, was the wife of the Director of the Royal Museum at Berlin, 'a rattling, noisy, energetic woman only tolerable on account of her lovely daughter the Countess Hildegarde—a girl of 19, six foot two! with an exquisite face'. Hildegarde played *Tristan und Isolde* and *Lohengrin* to them for two hours and 'talked with enthusiasm about Wagner', 'whose music', Lewes wrote, 'remains a language we do not understand'.[4] He found friends of his own, too. S. D. Williams, Jr., the Birmingham manufacturer, an old friend of the Leweses, who had given them the bulldog Ben, was also there; he called several times and walked about with them. A less agreeable acquaintance, Alfred Wigan, the actor, just retired from the London stage, was making a long stay at Homburg with his wife and son. To avoid them, Lewes wrote, 'we employed the strategy of a Von Moltke', and after vaguely postponing their proffered hospitalities, he had finally to decline them point blank as 'among the impossibilities'.[5]

In her usual way Marian was soon receiving confidences from Lady Castletown, who 'gave a curious sketch of her early life',[6] and from Mrs. Wingfield, whose eccentric husband the Hon. Lewis Strange Wingfield—traveller, actor, writer, painter—was not easy to live with; she 'poured forth confidences to Polly', while Lewes promenaded in the corridor of the Kursaal in 'deeply

[1] GHL Diary, 1 Oct. 1872.   [2] *Letters*, v. 314.
[3] GHL Diary, 26 Sept. 1872.
[4] GHL Diary, 9 Oct. 1872; *Letters*, v. 317.
[5] *Letters*, v. 316.   [6] GHL Diary, 6 Oct. 1872.

interesting talk' with her mother.[1] Consciously or not, George Eliot was collecting materials for *Daniel Deronda*.

The English society depicted in her earlier novels was relatively stable; change in class or rank was rare. In the forty years since the Reform Bill life had changed radically. The railway had penetrated to the remotest regions; the telegraph provided them instant communication; the Suez Canal had shrunk the globe. Men moved around it at speeds undreamt of, amassing riches at home and abroad. The Lehmanns and Benzons in the steel industry were examples within George Eliot's view. *Daniel Deronda*, her only novel of contemporary life, reflects these changes. As Henry James said, it 'is full of the world'. It shows not only the stately halls of Brackenshaw Castle and Topping Abbey, the drawing-rooms in Park Lane and Grosvenor Square, but touches the international scene as well—Frankfurt, Hamburg, Mainz, Vienna, Prague, Genoa, Trieste, St. Petersburg, Beirut, Palestine, even New York, where Mirah lived for a time. Its social range is equally wide. Aristocrats mingle with parvenus; adventurers make vast fortunes and lose them. The operations of Mr. Lassmann in Grapnell & Co., which fails for a million, parallel the roulette table at Leubronn. The gamblers there were of 'very distant varieties of European type: Livonian and Spanish, Graeco-Italian and miscellaneous German, English aristocratic and English plebeian. Here certainly was a striking admission of human equality.'[2] This was the world that Dickens glanced at in *Our Mutual Friend*, Trollope in *The Way We Live Now* (which George Eliot read in 1874), and Henry James in *The Portrait of a Lady*. None of them caught it more faithfully than George Eliot. All these novels analyse a society dominated by the pursuit of wealth.

George Eliot had made her fortune, too. After the success of *Middlemarch* she had more money than she needed. Her income in 1872 was over £3,000 and in 1873 nearly £5,000—more than half of it from investments. As Blackwood's sizable cheques came into Lewes's account, John Cross, who had taken charge of their affairs, invested the money in a varied list of stocks and bonds of railways and public utilities, many of them American;[3] under his watchful care her capital increased rapidly. In their days of poverty Marian seemed utterly indifferent to clothes; now she began to

---

[1] GHL Diary, 9 Oct. 1872.   [2] *Daniel Deronda*, ch. 1.
[3] GHL Diary, 17 Jan. 1873. Lists of the shares and accounts of the income are found in GHL's Diary and (after 1878) in GE's.

show a quite normal feminine interest in them. Mrs. Pattison took her to Jay's to choose a mantle,[1] and Elma Stuart was constantly advising her about undergarments, which Edith Simcox got made for her. Even Mrs. Pullet would have approved of the lace for her caps. At Homburg, Lady Castletown went with her 'hunting the furriers for an Astrachan jacket', which they found at a shop in Frankfurt, with a muff to match—'much to our delight'.[2] Alice Helps got her a cloak lined with squirrel.[3] George began to buy her modest pieces of jewellery—a necklace, a brooch—for New Year's gifts, and to dress himself up with elegant waistcoats and a fur-lined coat of his own. A new Broadwood piano, on which the best musician could be asked to play without apology, appeared in the drawing-room at the Priory; there was a new mirror, a Persian rug, and a new dinner service. Finally, at the end of 1873, the Leweses indulged in that ultimate badge of Victorian status: they set up their own carriage, a beautiful new landau by Morgan, complete with a fine fur rug. Henceforth they went to the Saturday concerts at St. James's Hall in proper style.[4]

The amount of Marian's charitable contributions increased as well. She had never forgotten how much she owed to the Brays. From Rosehill they had moved in 1857 to Ivy Cottage, and four years later to even smaller quarters in Barr's Hill Terrace. They had fallen on very hard times. Mindful of their reduced circumstances, Marian wrote to Cara on 28 March 1861:

I suppose I must lose my memory altogether before I could forget all the tenderness, forbearance, and generous belief that made the unvarying character of your friendship towards me when we used to be a great deal together. I think I was not insensible to these things at any time, but experience deepens our insight into the past, and we feel we never understood or appreciated it thoroughly while it was the present. . . . So that if ever you can let me be in any way a sharer and helper in trouble as far as our parted lives and duties make that possible, you will be adding something more to what you have already given of trust and kindness.[5]

A house that Charles had built near the Crystal Palace at Sydenham proved an unfortunate speculation. After Marian spoke to

---

[1] GHL Diary, 22 Apr. 1874.   [2] GHL Diary, 12–13 Oct. 1872.
[3] *Letters*, VI. 32.
[4] Macaulay on setting up his brougham, 16 Jan. 1851, was 'pleased and proud, and thinking how unjustly poor Pepys was abused for noting in his diary the satisfaction it gave him to ride in his own coach. This is the first time I ever had a carriage of my own, except when in office' (Journal).
[5] GE to Mrs. Bray, 28 Mar. 1861 (Edinburgh Public Library).

her about it in 1868, Cara wrote: 'The kind look in your face when
you offered to help us in any money difficulty that might arise this
year is a warm, pleasant thing to think of.'[1] And Marian replied:
'But please remember that what I said refers to *any* Christmas,
or any time in the calendar, which finds us all above-ground.'[2]
It was not easy to get Cara to accept any money. In 1873 Marian
urged her to write a little story for children to inculcate kindness
to animals—a cause close to Mrs. Bray's heart—and sent £50,
not as ' " pay ", since there is no pay for good work ',[3] but as money
already devoted to that cause. It took some persuasion to make
her cash the cheque.

Marian's niece Emily Clarke was always remembered. To
Bertie Lewes in Natal she sent £50 towards a piano and £25 for his
eldest child, whom he had tactfully named for her. Gertrude
Lewes and her sister Octavia Hill were given sums of money to
distribute among deserving cases they knew. When a fund was
being raised to purchase an annuity for Octavia so that she could
give up teaching and devote all her time to her great work of
housing reform, George Eliot contributed £200.[4] Small gifts went
each year to the Women's Hospital, the Women's College, and
sometimes Girton College. The Comte Fund never got more than
£5 a year, which scarcely qualifies George Eliot as a pillar of
Positivism. When Harrison's faction split off from Congreve's in
1878, she contributed equally to both.

Another charitable act concerned her earliest friend Maria
Lewis. In the summer of 1874, learning (probably from Cara
Bray) that she was living in straitened circumstances at Leamington, Marian wrote to her, enclosing a cheque for £10. 'Your substantial token of remembrance comes opportunely', Maria replied
in her old formal style.

What divergence there has been in our different careers! As 'George
Eliot' I have traced you as far as possible and with an interest which
few could feel; not many knew you as intimately as I once did, tho'
we have been necessarily separated for so long. My heart has ever
yearned after you, and pleasant is it truly in the evening of life to find
the old love still existing.[5]

The largest item in Lewes's account was for Agnes and her
brood. To the end he was mindful of his responsibility to her, and

---

[1] Mrs. Bray to GE, n.d. (Berg Collection, NYPL).
[2] *Letters*, IV. 490.
[3] *Letters*, V. 390. In her will GE left Mrs. Bray an annuity of £100.
[4] *Letters*, VI. 31.   [5] Maria Lewis to GE, 22 Sept. 1874 (Yale).

Marian, who now provided the money, concurred. Since his life with Marian began, Agnes had never had less than £100 a year from him—often more, when she had run into debt. In 1874 Lewes gave her £154, in 1875, £175. 15*s*., and in 1876, £166. 13*s*. In addition he made gifts to her children. Edmund received £101. 3*s*. in 1875, possibly towards setting him up as a dentist in Kensington. Gifts of £10 or £20 or £25 are noted occasionally for Rose or Ethel or Mildred; in 1876 Mildred was given a Latin dictionary.

After less than a month 'the fatigue of acquaintances'—even in the peerage—drove the Leweses from Homburg. They fled to Stuttgart and Karlsruhe for 'ten days of delicious autumnal weather and quietude' before returning home the last day of October 1872. 'We have an affinity for what the world calls "dull places"', Marian wrote to Mrs. Cross, 'and always prosper best in them.'[1] The Sunday afternoons at the Priory began at once. Pressure to be invited to them increased with her fame. 'Lords and Ladies, poets and cabinet ministers, artists and men of science, crowd upon us', Lewes told Main.[2] He rebuked a young American disciple of Spencer for giving a letter of introduction to an acquaintance.[3] Though he could not refuse to admit Mrs. S. M. Downes, a literary young lady, who came armed with one from Emerson,[4] he had reason to regret it when she published in the New York *Tribune* a detailed account of her visit under the head-line: 'George Eliot. One of her Receptions. Face—Figure—Manner—Voice—Dress.' Her appraising Yankee eye saw George Eliot as 'a slender, tallish woman, with an oval face, abundant hair, doubtless once fair, now almost gray, and questioning light eyes'. She wore a 'high-bodiced black velvet dress' with simple sleeves and lace at the throat under a cameo surrounded by pearls, and lace also on top of her head. She moved her head and hands, Mrs. Downes thought, more than most Englishwomen. If she 'preferred standing as she talked' that day, it may have been to terminate the interview, from which Lewes, 'drawing closer not to lose one of her words', soon extricated her.[5]

Coming home one Friday afternoon Lewes found Mrs. Simpson, who had called to bring Polly a photograph, and 'gave her

---

[1] *Letters*, v. 318.   [2] Ibid. 275.   [3] Ibid. 453.
[4] R. W. Emerson to GE, 21 Nov. 1873 (Newnham College).
[5] New York *Tribune*, 25 Mar. 1876, p. 7d.

a "bit of my mind".[1] Marian wrote apologetically to the lady that she 'would have been less surprised at Mr. Lewes's outburst' if she knew how often he had seen her 'overdone by week-day appointments—the "boiling over" of receptions beyond the rim of Sunday'.[2] Friday afternoon was usually saved for Georgie Burne-Jones, who found slight chance for conversation on Sundays, when the visitors were taken up one by one for a few minutes with George Eliot.

The solution was escape to some country retreat where they could work quietly, find delightful long walks starting right at their door, see no one, and answer only the few letters that Charles sifted out to forward from the Priory. Marian never ceased to long for the rural scenes of her childhood. When her brother Isaac's eldest daughter, Edith, defied the family ban by calling on her famous aunt with her husband, Vicar of St. Nicholas, Birmingham, and sent her pictures of the house, Marian wrote:

Many thanks for the photographs which I am delighted to have. Dear old Griff still smiles at me with a face which is more like than unlike its former self, and I seem to feel the air through the window of the attic above the drawing room, from which when a little girl, I often looked towards the distant view of the Coton 'College'—thinking the view rather sublime.[3]

For three or four years the Leweses searched indefatigably for a house, looking at dozens of them in all the home counties and as far afield as Oxford and the Isle of Wight. They cherished an impossible ideal: a little country house with 'the cab-stand before and the desert behind', where they could have long days of sweet semi-solitude, away from all other houses but within reach of every convenience.[4] Among conveniences one must list the dentist. While they were spending Christmas week with the Cross family at Weybridge in 1872, severe toothache added to a cold made Polly so miserable that they came home on 28 December to consult Paget, now Sir James Paget. Afterwards, he took them up to Lady Paget to see a superb Russian wolfhound given him by the Prince of Wales. When the infection continued, Paget advised removal of the tooth.[5] Marian went to the dentist Mr. Wonfor at once, and for many weeks continued to visit him.

They avoided as many engagements as possible. Though Marian occasionally accompanied him to dinner parties, Lewes more often

---

[1] GHL Diary, 28 Feb. 1873.   [2] *Letters*, V. 382.   [3] *Letters*, VI. 45–6.
[4] *Letters*, V, 461, 446.   [5] GHL Diary, 21 Jan. 1873.

went alone. He dined at the Nortons' to meet Emerson, whom he described as 'very sweet, simple; young, healthy looking for his age—over 70'.[1] During that winter the Sunday afternoon guests overflowed the drawing-room of the Priory. Like Mrs. Burne-Jones, some of the older friends preferred to come for lunch or dinner or a quiet talk at the end of a day. A few of the lists noted in Lewes's Diary suggest the character of the Sunday gatherings:

22 March 1873. To lunch: Roundell, Sanderson, Clifford, Hodgson. Called: Mrs. Sellar, Johnnie Cross, Grant Duff, Darwin, Joachim, Lady Castletown, Mrs. Wingfield, the George Howards, Kinglake, Stuart Glennie, Mad. Novikoff, Mrs. Orr, Mrs. and Miss Clough, Du Maurier, Fred and Mrs. Chapman, Mrs. Eustace Smith.

6 April 1873. Charles to lunch. Called: Mr. and Mrs. Litchfield, H. Sidgwick, Johnnie Cross, Mrs. Sellar, Lady Colville, Fürstenberg, Oscar Liebreich, Rudolf and Mrs. Lehmann, Mrs. Clough, Barbara, Miss Lumsden, Prof. and Mrs. Robertson, Mr. and Mrs. Creighton, Sir H. Maine, Palgrave.

18 May 1873. Johnnie and Eleanor Cross to lunch. Called: Woolner, Lord and Lady Houghton, Lady Colville, Mrs. Strachey, Mlle Souvestre and friend, Mr. and Mrs. Harrison, Crompton, Forman, Col. Fielden, Mrs. Wingfield, Barbara, Mrs. Orr, Lady Castletown, Mr. and Mrs. Du Maurier, McLennan, Sanderson.

Lewes contributed the unfailing *bonhomie* that fused their widely disparate interests, keeping a watchful eye on Polly to see that no individual monopolized her conversation. According to Fred Myers, she showed 'an almost pathetic anxiety to give of her best —to establish a genuine human relation between herself and her interlocutor—to utter words which should remain as an active influence for good'. He told how her deeply lined face and massive features were at these moments transformed with an inward beauty, as the thin hands entwined themselves in their eagerness, the earnest figure bowed forward to speak and hear, and the deep gaze moved from one face to another with a grave appeal. 'But it was the voice which best revealed her, a voice whose subdued intensity and tremulous richness seemed to environ her uttered words with the mystery of a world of feeling that must remain untold.'[2]

Myers, a Fellow of Trinity College, invited the Leweses to Cambridge in May 1873. His invitation to R. C. Jebb to meet her

---

[1] GHL Diary, 17 Apr. 1873.
[2] *Century Magazine*, 23 (Nov. 1881), 62.

at supper after the boat-races was conveyed in a Pindaric ode, culimating in the lines:

> For men say that there is a woman now,
> Man-named, anonymous, known of all, George Eliot, wiser than the
>   wise,
> Her too, methinks, my subtle net shall bear within the academic wall:
> Her too in season thou must see. . . .

Besides Mrs. Henry Huth and her daughter, Myers's other guests were mostly Trinity men—Sidgwick, Edmund Gurney, Alfred Lyttleton, Hallam Tennyson, 'young Balfour' (probably Gerald), and Henry Jackson. Jebb talked with George Eliot about Pater's recently published *Studies in the History of the Renaissance*, which he thought misrepresented 'the great lineaments of the great creative works' so that their very creators would not recognize them. 'Her face lit up in a moment, and she said, "It is such a comfort and a strength to hear you say that." ' When Jebb asked how Sophocles had influenced her, he was startled to hear her say, 'In the delineation of the great primitive emotions', which was an impression he had written down privately long before.[1] One recalls how she startled Emerson in 1849 with her remark about Rousseau's *Confessions*.

Myers's description of his conversation with George Eliot walking in the Fellows' Garden on a rainy evening, is often quoted:

she, stirred somewhat beyond her wont, and taking as her text the three words which have been used so often as the inspiring trumpet-calls of men,—the words, *God, Immortality, Duty*,—pronounced, with terrible earnestness, how inconceivable was the *first*, how unbelievable the *second*, and yet how peremptory and absolute the *third*. Never, perhaps, have sterner accents affirmed the sovereignty of impersonal and unrecompensing Law. I listened, and night fell; her grave, majestic countenance turned toward me like a sibyl's in the gloom; it was as though she withdrew from my grasp, one by one, the two scrolls of promise, and left me the third scroll only, awful with inevitable fates. And when we stood at length and parted, amid that columnar circuit of the forest-trees, beneath the last twilight of starless skies, I seemed to be gazing, like Titus at Jerusalem, on vacant seats and empty halls,—on a sanctuary with no Presence to hallow it, and heaven left lonely of a God.[2]

---

[1] C. L. Jebb, *Sir Richard Claverhouse Jebb* (Cambridge, 1907), p. 154.

[2] *Century Magazine*, 23 (Nov. 1881), 62–3. Bertrand Russell in his *Autobiography* (1967), p. 87, says that Julian Sturgis, when he took him into the Fellows' Garden at Trinity, said: 'Oh yes! This is where George Eliot told F. W. H. Myers that there is no God, and yet we must be good; and Myers decided that there is a God and yet we need not be good.'

Those intent on demonstrating George Eliot's melancholy usually end here in quoting this over-dramatized account. But Myers continues: 'This was the severer aspect of her teaching. How gentle, how inspiring a tone it could assume when it was called upon to convey not impulse only, but consolation, I must quote a few words to show.' He then gives part of a letter that George Eliot wrote to a friend in the first anguish of bereavement—probably Edmund Gurney, whose brother and three sisters drowned in the Nile in 1875. Speaking of the idea of a future life, she said that 'to know what the last parting is seems needful to give the utmost sanctity of tenderness to our relations with each other'. This was the argument of 'The Legend of Jubal', written after Thornie died. She looked on death as 'a close, real experience, like the approach of autumn or winter'.[1]

The Cambridge visit was followed by a week-end in June 1873 with Benjamin Jowett at Balliol College, Oxford. There the guests were somewhat older; they included C. S. C. Bowen; Mr. and Mrs. Charles Roundell; Lady Julia Rich; Mark Pattison; W. H. Thompson, the Master of Trinity College, Cambridge; the Marquis of Tavistock; H. J. S. Smith; A. G. Vernon Harcourt; W. P. Warburton, the Inspector of Schools; the Max Müllers; F. W. Walker, Master of St. Paul's School; and George Rolleston, the physiologist. Jowett wrote of George Eliot:

She has the cleverest head I have every known, and is the gentlest, kindest, and best of women. She throws an interesting light on every subject on which she speaks. She seems to me just right about philosophy, quite clear of materialism, women's rights, idealism, etc. . . . Her voice was low and soft, yet penetrating, and she spoke with an earnestness and force of conviction which compelled attention.

In his notebook Jowett added:

She talked charmingly, with a grace and beauty that I shall always remember. She gives the impression of great philosophical power. She wanted to have an ethical system founded upon altruism; and argued that there was no such thing as doing any action because it was right or reasonable, but only because it accorded with one's better feelings towards others. She seems however to admit that there might be such a form of thought given by teaching, and acknowledged that practical moral philosophy should not be confined to one form. Her idea of existence seemed to be 'doing good to others'. She would never condemn any one for acquiescing in the popular religion. Life was so

[1] *Letters*, VI. 64.

complex, your own path was so uncertain in places, that you could not condemn others. She did not object to remaining within an established religion with the view of elevating and purifying it.[1]

The Leweses stayed only two days with Jowett,[2] going on to spend a few days with the Crosses at Weybridge before returning to the Priory.

On 2 June 1873 they found a charming old house called Black-brook, near Bickley, Kent, which delighted George Eliot. It was let until September. But they signed a year's lease on it and went abroad until it should be available. Their casual plan was to go from Paris to Aix-les-Bains and then through the Savoie to Geneva, where Marian wanted to see again her old friends the D'Alberts. But the heat was intense. After a week at Fontainebleau they turned eastwards to Plombières-les-Bains; there, quartered in a chalet annexed to the Grands-Hôtels, having a garden to themselves and a balcony with a superb view of the Vosges, they drank the waters and took the baths. Polly throve on the regime. 'No place ever did the Mutter more good in a short time', Lewes wrote to Charles.[3] He fared less well, troubled with an infected ear. They went on to Luxeuil for a week, and then by way of Frankfurt back to Homburg on 2 August. Lewes had examined the Kurlist to make sure that no acquaintances were there. The first day Captain Maxse appeared; within a week, Lady Castletown arrived and spent two hours 'talking of the Wingfield story'. The weather soon turned cold and rainy. On 15 August they turned homewards, reaching the Priory on the 23rd.

They gathered their books and, taking their three servants, set out for Bickley on 5 September. The day was cold and gloomy. Their spirits were considerably dampened to find the house

---

[1] E. Abbott and L. Campbell, *Benjamin Jowett* (3rd ed., 2 vols., N.Y., 1897), II. 144–5, 108.

[2] The statement that GE had tea in Charles Reade's rooms in Magdalen College is probably apocryphal. Neither she nor GHL ever mentions meeting him, nor is it likely that Jowett would have taken her there. The story was communicated to Malcolm Elwin by David Hunter-Blair (1853–1939), later Abbot of Fort Augustus monastery and Chamberlain of Sword and Cloak to Pope Pius IX; he was in his first year at Magdalen during GE's visit. The latter part of his story, about watching from Reade's window as Jowett and his guest walked past, is the most credible part. Reade may have seen the Leweses during their visit in 1878, when Jowett went with them to evening service at Magdalen. (Malcolm Elwin, *Charles Reade*, 1931, p. 265.)

[3] *Letters*, V. 424.

almost bare. The comfortable furniture, which they thought belonged to it, had been removed by the previous tenants, and what remained was broken or dilapidated. None of the few things they sent had been delivered from the railway. Though they were in lovely country, secluded, but within easy reach of all conveniences, with a beautiful lawn, tall trees, and a fine kitchen garden, before the first day was over they resolved to get released from their year's engagement. Again, they saw few visitors. Mrs. Congreve came for a day; their 'tall nephew' Johnny Cross came over for dinner; and Charles and Gertrude spent a week-end with them. Here Elma Stuart had her first face-to-face meeting with her 'spiritual mother' when she came to lunch on 3 October. Sir John Lubbock, the banker and scientist, whose wife first told the Leweses about the house, lived not far away at Beckenham. Lady Lubbock and her two daughters called promptly, brought grapes and game, took the Leweses driving about the country, and had them to lunch at High Elms, where Sir John, a noted entomologist, showed them his bees, which he could handle like flies. Charles Darwin lived only a few miles further at Downe, where the Leweses also went to lunch. Even that could not reconcile them to Blackbrook. The owner, Mr. Hamilton, surrendered the lease without difficulty, and on the last day of October they were back at the Priory.

One of Lewes's first errands in town concerned Agnes. Thornton Hunt had died on 25 June 1873, leaving an estate of under £1,000. But Agnes held an insurance policy on his life. When Lewes took her to inquire about it, they learned that it could not be paid without Kate Hunt's signature. Kate made no objection, however, and the money was paid on 3 November.

The Sunday afternoons were soon in full swing. On 23 November John Fiske, Spencer's American disciple, who had been introduced to Lewes in Trübner's shop, was among the guests. Fiske was captivated by Lewes's manners, 'in spite of his homely and meagre and puny physique. I don't wonder that he captivated George Eliot.' Fiske's first impression of her was favourable; he wrote to his wife:

Well, what do I think of her? She is not a 'fright' by any means. She is a plain-looking woman, but I think not especially homely. I see no reason why her photograph should not be circulated about. She is *much* better looking than George Sand. She isn't a blooming beauty, of course; you don't expect that at fifty-two;[1] but her features are regular

[1] GE had just had her 54th birthday.

her nose is very good, her eyes are a rich blue and very expressive, her mouth is very large, but it is pleasant in expression. Her hair is light and profuse, and she wears a lovely lace cap over it—and looks simple, frank, cordial, and matronly, and seems ever so proud of Lewes, and ever so fond of him. I call her a good, honest, genuine, motherly woman with no nonsense about her. She seemed glad to see me. She said when my Myth-book came to her—I sent her a copy last summer, as you know—she was sitting on the floor fixing a rug, or something of the sort, and she got so absorbed in my book that she sat on the *floor* all the afternoon, till Lewes came in and routed her up!. . .

I never saw such a woman. There is nothing a bit masculine about her; she is thoroughly feminine and looks and acts as if she were made for nothing but to mother babies. But she has a power of *stating* an argument equal to any man; equal to any man do I say? I have never seen any man, except Herbert Spencer, who could state a case equal to her. I found her thoroughly acquainted with the whole literature of the Homeric question; and she seems to have read all of Homer in Greek, too, and could meet me everywhere. She didn't talk like a blue-stocking—as if she were aware she had got hold of a big topic—but like a plain woman, who talked of Homer as simply as she would of flat-irons. She showed an amazing knowledge of the subject. . . .

I never before saw such a clear-headed woman. She thinks just like a man, and can put her thoughts into clear and forcible language at a moment's notice. And her knowledge is quite amazing. I have often heard of learned women, whose learning, I have usually found, is a mighty flimsy affair. But to meet a woman who can meet you like a man, on such a question as that of Homer's poems, knowing the ins and outs of the question, and not *putting on any airs*, but talking sincerely of the thing as a subject which has deeply interested her—this is, indeed, quite a new experience.

On the whole, I enjoyed Mr. and Mrs. Lewes immensely today; and I think Lewes a happy man in having such a simple-hearted, honest, and keenly sympathetic wife. I call them a wonderful couple. Spencer thinks she is the greatest woman that has lived on the earth—the female Shakespeare, so to speak; and I imagine he is not *far* from right. My only sorrow is that the afternoon was not quite long enough; but I shall go there again.

Mrs. Lewes calls it Casaubon, i.e., Că-sáw-bŏn, with the accent on second syllable. But she says a good many people of that name in England call themselves Cás-aŭ-bŏn, with accent on first syllable.

Remember that Lewes is just the age of Mr. Stoughton and George Eliot just the age of my mother—a queer coincidence. . . .[1]

On New Year's Day 1874 George Eliot summed up her blessings: The old year had brought constant enjoyment of life, love poured

---

[1] *Letters of John Fiske*, ed. Ethel Fiske Fisk (N.Y., 1940), pp. 277–9.

forth to her from distant hearts, and in her own home 'that finish to domestic comfort which only faithful, kind servants can give'. The children were prosperous and happy; 'we have abundant wealth for more than our actual needs; and our unspeakable joy in each other has no other alloy than the sense that it must one day end in parting'.[1] The parting worried many of her contemporaries too. Spiritualism was becoming a resource of many (even intelligent) people whose faith in religious revelation had declined. The Erasmus Darwins arranged with a professional medium named Williams to conduct a seance at their house on 16 January 1874, which the Leweses attended. The Charles Darwin family was there, the Litchfields, Hensleigh Wedgwood, Fred Myers, Galton, Mrs. Bowen, and others, seated about a large dining table. But Lewes, regarding the medium's insistence on complete darkness as unscientific, 'was troublesome and inclined to make jokes and not play the game fairly and sit in the dark in silence', wrote Mrs. Litchfield. After a few of the usual 'manifestations', he and George Eliot left in disgust.[2] She saw nothing to change her opinion that spiritualism was either 'degrading folly, imbecile in the estimate of evidence, or else impudent imposture'.[3]

The germ of *Daniel Deronda*, planted in September 1872 when George Eliot was watching Miss Leigh at the roulette table in Homburg, began to grow at once. She made notes on 'Gambling Superstitions' from an article in the *Cornhill*.[4] The Jewish elements, which careless readers used to think separable from Gwendolen's story, made part of her plan almost from the start. Soon after returning from Homburg, George Eliot was reading Pictet's *Origines des races aryennes*. Her interest in Jewish history, dating from the youthful attempt to compile a Chart of Ecclesiastical History, deepened as she translated Strauss and Spinoza. But her lively concern with the idea of Jewish nationalism sprang directly from her friendship with Emanuel Deutsch. Born in Silesia, Deutsch was educated by his uncle, a rabbi, and at the University of Berlin before coming to London in 1855 to work as a cataloguer of books in the British Museum. George Eliot first met him in 1866 at the Frederick Lehmanns', and the 'bright little man' was soon a frequent caller at the Priory. He had many radical ideas that

---

[1] *Letters*, VI. 3.
[2] *Emma Darwin: A Century of Family Letters* (2 vols., 1915), II. 216; GHL Diary, 16 Jan. 1874.
[3] *Letters*, V. 48–9.
[4] (R. A. Proctor), *Cornhill*, 25 (June 1872), 704–17.

shocked the orthodox, both Jewish and Christian. He used to maintain that in the first century there were plenty of young enthusiasts besides Jesus, Syrian moralists like Hillel, preaching a similar gospel.[1] When George Eliot first knew him, Deutsch was writing for the *Quarterly Review* his famous article on the Talmud. He sent her a proof, asking her criticism of

this young manifesto of the Deutsch-party (consisting at present of myself) that desires to explain the historical 'possibility' of so much that is really fine in Christianity, to bridge over one of the ghastliest gulfs in History, to restore to Humanity one of its finest and oldest vantage grounds, and to shame shrieking fanaticism and ignorance out of its existence by a few simple facts and adages.[2]

He began to come to the Priory about once a week in the evening to give George Eliot lessons in Hebrew, which her notebooks show she studied diligently.

Deutsch's enthusiasm for a Jewish national home developed during a visit to the Near East. His knowledge of the Amharic language brought him in 1868 an invitation to accompany the British Army on its campaign against Abyssinia, where it was hoped valuable manuscripts and other antiquities might be found. This invitation, like another from the Egyptian Foreign Minister Nubar Pasha to attend the opening of the Suez Canal, Deutsch declined. But they stirred in him a keen desire to travel in the East, and in the spring of 1869 he visited Palestine. His first letter was dated: 'The East: all my wild yearnings fulfilled at last!' With the lofty patriotism of his race 'he was himself astonished at the emotion that choked him when he found himself among his own people at the Wailing place in Jerusalem, and he could seldom speak of it afterwards without tears'.[3] The following year at Oxford, George Eliot heard his lecture on the Moabite Stone and Captain Charles Warren's account of his reconnaisance of Jerusalem and the Jordan Valley for the Palestine Exploration Fund. George Grove, who had started the Fund, wrote to George Eliot enthusiastically when *Daniel Deronda* was being published to say that it made him think of 'our dear Deutsch'.[4]

Soon after his return from Palestine, Deutsch began to suffer from the symptoms of a painful cancer. He submitted to several

---

[1] F. Harrison, *Autobiographical Memoirs* (2 vols., 1911), II. 109.
[2] Emanuel Deutsch to GE, 2 Oct. 1867 (British Museum).
[3] Emily Strangford, *Literary Remains of the Late Emanuel Deutsch, with a Brief Memoir* (N.Y., 1874), pp. x–xi.
[4] George Grove to GE, 27 Mar. [1876] (Yale).

operations without relief. Though keeping up his work at the British Museum, he shrank from most of his friends to endure his pain alone. A bachelor, he was taken into the home of the Reverend R. H. Haweis, the rather radical vicar of St. James, Marylebone. Mr. and Mrs. Haweis cared for him tenderly, giving him a sitting-room near the street door where the few friends he would see could call on him privately. Here George Eliot came several times. Sometimes she found him on the verge of despair. One of her letters to him, beginning 'Dear Rabbi', says: 'Remember, it has happened to many to be glad they did not commit suicide, though they once ran for the final leap, or as Mary Wollstonecraft did, wetted their garments well in the rain, hoping to sink the better when they plunged.'[1] The disease advanced relentlessly. In December 1872, wasted and in agony, Deutsch sailed again for Egypt, going up the Nile as far as Luxor. He grew steadily weaker. In April he was removed to hospital in Alexandria, where he died 12 May 1873, and was buried in the Jewish Cemetery. This sad event occurred just as George Eliot was planning her new novel; and memories of poor Deutsch are woven through her conception of the dying Mordecai. She makes Mordecai—like Deutsch—a great scholar,

a man steeped in poverty and obscurity, weakened by disease, consciously within the shadow of advancing death, but living an intense life in an invisible past and future, careless of his personal lot, except for its possibly making some obstruction to a conceived good which he would never share except as a brief inward vision.[2]

The news of Deutsch's death reached Marian shortly before she left for France. At Fontainebleau she and George 'went into the Park of the Chateau and sat down on the hay and on seats by the water discussing new projects for *novel and play* Deronda'.[3] The possibility of a dramatic form, mentioned several times, was

[1] *Letters*, v. 160–1. In *Daniel Deronda* (ch. 17) Mirah dips her cloak in the river when she is preparing to drown herself.

[2] *Daniel Deronda*, ch. 42. Israel Cohen (*TLS*, 23 Aug. 1947) denying a reviewer's conjecture that GE's enthusiasm for Jewish nationalism came from GHL, who had 'an Hebraic look about his face', advanced an equally unfounded assumption: 'In the course of a visit to Paris Lewes became acquainted rather intimately with Moses Hess', author of *Rome and Jerusalem* (1862). 'As Hess was passionately devoted to this idea, it can reasonably be presumed that he discussed the question with Lewes, who informed George Eliot about it on returning to London.' There is no evidence that Lewes ever saw Hess or knew his book.

[3] GHL Diary, 29 June 1873. GE told Helen Faucit that she thought of her while writing Klesmer's remarks on art and artists in ch. 23. T. Martin, *Helena Faucit* (1900), p. 338.

Lewes's idea, not hers, and was soon abandoned. Marian now began a closer study of Jewish matters. They were reading aloud Erckmann-Chatrian's *Le Juif polonais* and Kompert's *Geschichte einer Gasse*. At Frankfurt on the way home Lewes 'bought books —books on *Jewish subjects* for Polly's novel—and made inquiries'. They stayed till Friday so that she could go to the synagogue at sunset (as Deronda does in Chapter 32, where the inquiries in the bookshop are also described). At Homburg they 'walked through the moonlighted streets to the Synagogue'. The following Friday at Mainz, where Deronda receives his grandfather's papers, they rambled 'in the sweet light of sunset, found out the Synagogue and learnt the hours of service tomorrow', at which they were 'delighted with the singing—noted the rarity of the Jewish *type*—most of them might be German'.

One of Lewes's first errands after returning to London was 'to buy books for Polly on Judaism'.[1] Others were borrowed from the London Library. Her notebooks began to fill with extracts from such works as Milman's *History of the Jews*, Stanley's *Sinai and Palestine*, Grätz's *Geschichte der Juden*, Kompert's *Bömische Juden*, and Renan's *Histoire des langues sémitiques*. 'In the mornings', she wrote to Mrs. Pattison, 'my dwelling is among the tombs, farther back than the times of the Medici.'[2] In November she dropped the first hint to John Blackwood that she was 'slowly simmering towards another big book'.[3] According to the note on the order of her writings prefixed to her Journal (1861–77), her first 'Sketches towards Daniel Deronda' were made in January and February 1874.

In March 1874 Marian laid it all aside to collect a volume of poems, which, she told Blackwood, 'Mr. Lewes wishes me to get published in May'. There is no comment on his reason for choosing this time. Dated in the manuscript between 1865 and 1873, many of the poems had already appeared in magazines. The most interesting of the new ones are the 'Brother and Sister' sonnets (31 July 1869) and her most famous piece, 'O May I Join the Choir Invisible' (1867). The manuscript was sent to Edinburgh on 6 March 1874 and put at once into type. Though Blackwood welcomed it, of course, he wrote wistfully in sending the revise: 'if you have any lighter pieces written before the sense of what a great author should do for mankind came so strongly upon you,

---

[1] GHL Diary, 30 July, 8, 15, 16, 27 Aug. 1873.
[2] *Letters*, v. 461.   [3] *Letters*, v. 454.

I should like much to look at them'.[1] Perhaps he meant some less solemn verse for the pages of *Maga*. The volume was published early in May with the title *The Legend of Jubal, and Other Poems*. Presentation copies were sent to Caroline Bray 'with the author's compliments', to Anthony Trollope 'with the affectionate admiration and regard of George Eliot', to Main 'in memory of his helpful sympathy', and to Susanna Lewes 'from her affectionate sister George Eliot'.[2] When the bound manuscript was returned, George Eliot inscribed it: 'To my beloved Husband, George Henry Lewes, whose cherishing tenderness for twenty years has alone made my work possible to me', adding three lines from the title poem:

> And the last parting now began to send
> Diffusive dread through love and wedded bliss,
> Thrilling them into finer tenderness.

Lady Strangford, the friend of Deutsch who edited his *Literary Remains* (1873), also gave George Eliot information about Jewish matters. She had travelled widely in the Near East and written *Egyptian Sepulchres and Syrian Shrines*, of which a second edition was published in 1874. After the death of her husband, the eighth Viscount Strangford, in 1869, who was said to have been the original of Disraeli's *Coningsby*,[3] she took four years of hospital training as a nurse, and was active in the movement to provide trained nurses for the poor. In response to an inquiry of George Eliot, she wrote:

Since 1863 the 'Israelitish Alliance' (chiefly of Paris), shamed by the efforts of Christians to promote colonies and agricultural occupations in Palestine, have endeavoured to found a colony at Jaffa—and some other feeble efforts have been made of the same kind elsewhere.

Nothing had been done before 1863, she wrote, because the Rabbis inculcated the doctrine that all Jews who return to Palestine are saints, and that 'they and their descendants should be entirely supported by the alms of the faithful elsewhere'. They 'teach that it is *irreligious* of a Jew in Jerusalem to work, so to say', because then 'the faithful would be slower of sending the money for their support through the hands of the Rabbis'.[4] Lady Strangford's

---

[1] *Letters*, VI. 37.
[2] The first two are in the Berg Collection, NYPL; the third in the Parrish Collection, Princeton.
[3] J. W. Robertson Scott, *Story of the* Pall Mall Gazette (1950), p. 152.
[4] Emily Strangford to GE, 23 Apr. 1874 (Yale).

reply to another query shows George Eliot seriously considering a journey to the Near East to gather local colour for *Daniel Deronda*. Though spring was the fashionable time for tourists in Palestine, Lady Strangford declared autumn the best. She suggested that the Leweses leave England on 1 October, starting up the Nile the 20th to spend six or seven weeks on it, going by 'dahabieh' rather than steamer, then taking a house at Cairo or Ramleh or even at Thebes for the winter. Or they might go to Beirut in Syria; they could ride there from Jerusalem in five days. 'It would be grand to ascertain if Mr. Lewes *liked* travelling on a dromedary' —whose long, regular, swinging step she described enthusiastically.[1] But neither Lewes nor George Eliot was strong enough for such an adventure, or for the longer voyage to the West, which her American correspondents often urged on her to see 'the land of the Future'.[2]

They went instead on 2 June 1874 to a less exotic spot, the Cottage at Earlswood Common, near Redhill, Surrey, not fifteen miles from the Priory, taking their servants again and their own carriage. There for nearly four months they lived comfortably, undisturbed by Sunday callers. During long mornings of quiet work Marian got 'deep shafts sunk in my prose book', while Lewes worked away at the second volume of his *Problems of Life and Mind*. In the afternoon they would drive about the countryside or ramble on the Common or in Galton Park. They were constantly looking for a house which they could make their permanent refuge—at Weybridge, Reigate, Dorking, Burstow, Holmwood Common, Croydon, Penshurst—wherever they heard of one. Charles and Gertrude came twice for week-ends, once bringing little Blanche. Robert Lytton, now Lord Lytton, came to spend a day and night.[3] Mrs. Congreve and her sister Emily came for dinner one day, and Johnny Cross another. Elma Stuart, on the way to Scotland, brought her schoolboy son Roland, who was much impressed by George Eliot's voice—so low, and soft, and musical 'that once heard it could never be forgotten'—and her eyes with a 'magnetic power of looking down into your soul and of drawing you out and making you speak of yourself—at the same time giving you the impression that she was deeply interested in your doings and all that concerned you ... and the feeling that one could open one's heart to her and tell her *everything*, being

---

[1] Emily Strangford to GE, 30 May 1874 (Yale).
[2] *Letters*, VI. 319.   [3] GHL Diary, 21 Aug. 1874.

sure of being understood'.[1] It is not a long list of visitors during four months. 'I am flourishing now', George Eliot wrote to Blackwood in June, 'and am brewing my future big book with more or less (generally less) belief in the quality of the liquor which will be drawn off.'[2]

They left Earlswood Common at the end of September, and after a four-days' visit to Bullock-Hall at Six Mile Bottom, took a brief holiday—a week in Paris, then by way of Soissons, Reims, and Sedan to Brussels—returning to London on 19 October. Though they both had colds and sore throat, the very next day saw them on the train starting for Salisbury to seek a local habitation for characters George Eliot had already imagined. The names of some of them—Brackenshaw, Gascoigne, Vandernoodt—were chosen from a list in her notebook that includes names used in *Middlemarch*.[3] Now she needed definite topographical details for her Wanchester and Wessex.[4] They stayed three days at Salisbury. They walked twice through the village of Stratford to Old Sarum, once against wind so high they could scarcely stand, the next time in bright autumnal air. They drove out to Salisbury Plain and Stonehenge. But apparently Marian could not find just what she wanted. After a few days at home they set out again for Wiltshire on 28 October, this time to stay three days at Devizes, where Marian had visited Dr. Brabant in 1843. They drove first to Bowood, the seat of the Marquess of Lansdowne; the long avenue of beeches in the Park was in full autumnal glory. The next day, after walking about the Castle and New Park, they drove to Spye Park, Lacock Abbey, and round by Corsham Court, Baron Methuen's seat. The third day they took a carriage to Marlborough, where young Phil Burne-Jones was at school, but found that he was in bed in the infirmary, asleep and not to be seen. Over Roundaway Hill on the return, in spite of sleet and rain and driving winds, they had superb views. On the last day they drove through Savernake Forest to the railway. Marian now had a rich store of material to draw from for the background of *Daniel Deronda*. Lacock in particular gave her the details of Sir Hugo Mallinger's Topping Abbey.[5] Even with familiar scenes she

[1] *Letters from George Eliot to Elma Stuart*, ed. Roland Stuart (1901), p. 22.
[2] *Letters*, VI. 58.
[3] Folger Library M. a. 13, fol. 10.
[4] Hardy was publishing *Far from the Madding Crowd* in the *Cornhill* in 1874. Neither GE nor GHL ever refers to Hardy.
[5] For a good account of Lacock Abbey by H. Avray Tipping with excellent photographs see *Country Life*, 53 (3, 10, 17 Mar. 1923), 280–7, 314–21, 352–9.

liked to corroborate her memory: she and George drove one after-noon 'to Kew Bridge and walked along the river to Richmond, choosing a spot for the meeting of De Ronda and Mirah' in Chapter 17.[1]

Passion for correctness also led her again to consult Frederic Harrison about legal questions—the legitimization of a presump-tive heir to estates in tail and to a peerage. She had been looking into Joshua Williams's book on Real Property, but could not get the problem of resettlements clear.[2] A long correspondence en-sued. One Sunday afternoon she asked Leslie Stephen about scholarships in connection with Daniel's year at Cambridge. Stephen made inquiries the next time he was at Trinity and reported that the resignation of a scholarship, as she proposed it, would be impossible there.[3] Eventually George Eliot had Daniel fail to win the scholarship because he had spent so much time reading to Hans Meyrick, whose eyes were inflamed.[4] She turned also to Charles Lewes for advice on the choice of songs that Mirah sings.[5]

The summer in the country had proved fruitful. The book was slowly taking shape. On 11 November 1874 she wrote to Black-wood:

Don't despair of me. I am settled down now, and the thick slice of manuscript which had passed into the irrevocable before we left Earls-wood, had been read to my private critic and was immensely approved by him. I did not think it up to the mark myself, but he vows it is.[6]

Though Lewes did his best to hearten Marian, in her Journal she noted: 'as usual I am suffering much from doubt as to the worth of what I am doing and fear lest I may not be able to complete it so as to make it a contribution to literature and not a mere addi-tion to the heap of books. I am just now beginning the part about Deronda, at p. 234'—the first page of Chapter 16.[7]

Johnny Cross was full of ideas for pleasant diversions. On 9 November 1874, when Lewes had to be at a London Library meeting, he took Polly to the Lord Mayor's show. A week later he took both of them to the Bank of England, where the 'Album in which illustrious and royal visitors affixed their autographs to 1000 £ notes was shown, and then Polly had to affix *her* auto-

---

[1] GHL Diary, 2 Feb. 1875.   [2] *Letters*, VI. 110.
[3] Ibid. 140.   [4] Ch. 16.   [5] *Letters*, VI. 184.
[6] GE to J. Blackwood, 11 Nov. 1874 (NLS).
[7] GE Journal, 13 Jan. 1875.

graph.'[1] After giving them lunch at his office in the City, Johnny
took them to Woolwich Arsenal, which at the end of the day they
found 'fatiguing and not very interesting'. A few days later he
took them 'to the Tennis Court to see a celebrated player play
the game'. There were visits to the National Gallery and the South
Kensington Museum on successive days. They went twice to the
Russian Church—'strange weird and thrilling singing. The bass
voice like the reverberation of an organ', Lewes wrote.[2] More
than once Cross proposed a long expedition on a boat that he and
his brother-in-law Albert Druce had on the Thames, but she did
not feel well enough.

It is easy to be impatient with the frequent complaints of illness
that fill George Eliot's letters and journals. Some of her symptoms
were doubtless subjective, for they would vanish as soon as a book
was finished. Eye-strain probably contributed to the headaches;
until 1875, when Liebreich prescribed for her, she had no proper
glasses. The prolonged periods of pain she refers to as neuralgia
or face-ache came from decayed teeth and chronic infection of the
gums. But there was a more serious trouble. On 3 February 1874
she awoke before dawn with an excruciating pain in her left side
that lasted for five or six hours. Dr. Andrew Clark diagnosed it
as kidney stone. Marian doubtless recalled her father's similar
attack in 1836. Another sharp attack two days later was followed by
gradual recovery. On 2 March 1875 she had further violent attacks,
lasting several days, and there was another early in May. Until
the end of her life they recurred with increasing frequency. There
was no cure. Lewes nursed her tenderly. Opiates, hot baths, and
fomentations were the only treatment. Under the disability of this
recurring, agonizing pain, which she bore with surprising fortitude,
Daniel Deronda was written.

Blackwood was pressing her to let him see some of the manuscript. On 19 May 1875, after lunching at the Priory, he wrote to
Mrs. Blackwood: 'She is looking pale and a little languid, but
that was to be expected under the interesting circumstances, as
she delivered to me a volume of MS, which I am yearning to sit
down to.'[3] Her pallor and languor resulted from an attack of stone
the week before. Blackwood was enthusiastic about the opening
of the story, which he read until 3 in the morning. 'Daniel
Deronda is all right', he told Willie. 'It is splendid. It promises to

---

[1] GHL Diary, 17 Nov. 1874. A machine for testing coins is referred to in
'Shadows of the Coming Race', *Impressions of Theophrastus Such* (1879), p. 248.
[2] GHL Diary, 18, 19, 20 Nov. 1874.   [3] Chs. 1–18. *Letters*, VI. 143.

be a wonderful book.'[1] And he wrote a long detailed letter of admiration to the author, which made her very happy.

   The only escape from the stream of visitors was a hide-out in the country. At Rickmansworth, Lewes found a delightful house called the Elms, just opposite the Park. Again they closed the Priory and, taking all their servants, moved on 17 June 1875. Even here there was an occasional intrusion; Edith Simcox appeared one day without warning—a 'foolish visit' which she never repeated.[2] In the long quiet summer mornings the second and much of the third volume of *Daniel Deronda* were written. Since about 1870 Marian had been holding her writing on her knees, throwing herself backwards in her chair with a high support for her feet, to take advantage of her long-sightedness. But Dr. Liebreich disapproved of this posture and, when he gave her proper glasses, devised a sort of semi-couch on which she could write comfortably. After four or five hours of work, she would walk with George in the garden before lunch. In the afternoon they drove about the green lanes to Chenies or Harefield, Denham or Cassiobury, Watford or Amersham, getting down from time to time to walk about. Moor Park was one of their favourite haunts. In the evening they read aloud. Sometimes Polly would read him what she had written of *Deronda* and talk over her plans for the story. One September evening, after she had read him a new chapter, 'we walked in the garden discussing it under an unusually superb moonlight'.[3]

   Marian returned to London from Rickmansworth only once —28 July—to see the dentist, who pulled a tooth that had been tormenting her. Lewes went several times to see about the alterations under way at the Priory. They were both invited by Lady Airlie to a garden party to meet the Queen of Holland. Lewes, who went up alone, described it in a letter to Mary Cross:

> To my surprise I found that the Queen had expressed a special wish that I should be presented to her, so immediately on her arrival that ceremony took place. You must imagine a pale plain elderly woman of somewhat feeble and certainly unenchanting aspect—and opposite her stands—The Matchless! Then this dialogue ensues.

> *Queen.* Very glad to see you, Mr. Lewes. I saw you in 1871 at Florence. You were there were you not?

[1] J. Blackwood to W. Blackwood, 20 May 1875 (NLS).
[2] Simcox Autobiography, 24 Feb. 1885, fol. 132.
[3] GHL Diary, 14 Sept. 1875.

The M. I was, your Majesty. [He had not been, but knew better than to contradict royalty.]

Q. You were pointed out to me at the theatre, you and your wife. Lady Airlie (not having caught the word 'Florence' or because 'Weimar' was running in her head, we having been talking of it when the Q. arrived) 'Mr. Lewes says they were so very kind to him at Weimar.'

Q. (*with something like fretful impatience*) I don't want to hear about Weimar! (*loftily*) I have done with them. (*Family quarrel*)—So you like Weimar, Mr. Lewes? (*a touch of sarcasm in the tone*)

The M. Well, your Majesty, I was very happy there and much interested in everything.

Q. It's a very ugly place. You can't say it's beautiful!

The M. No, not beautiful—certainly not like Florence.

Q. Oh! Florence is charming. (*a pause*) I admire your writings—as to your wife's, all the world admires them. Here the Matchless bows, and begins to think 'when will this come to an end'. Lady Dillon and Jenny Lind were brought up to be presented, and this seemed an opening for escape, so I whispered to Mrs. Howard, 'May I consider the audience over?' 'Yes if you are bored.' 'I am.' 'Then come and talk with me.' Accordingly we slipped on to the lawn, and though I saw, I did not again approach her majesty.[1]

Lewes adds some details in his Diary:

It was a lovely sight—the gay dresses of the women dotted about the lawn, seated on persian rugs under trees etc. Jenny Lind begged I might be introduced to her and held my hand, pressing it fervently while she poured forth admiration of the Goethe, and explanations of why she had not liked to answer my letter to her until she could do it fully in person. As I have always felt an instinctive antipathy to her I did not respond to her warmth, and for the first time in her life I suppose she got no compliment.—The George Howards, Browning, Oscar Browning, Spencer, Sir H. Thompson, Hamilton Aïdé, Lyulph Stanley, Lady and Maude Stanley, Mrs. Lane Fox, Lord Stanhope etc. Lady Egerton of Tatton when I was introduced vowed she had dined with me at Mrs. Mildmay's—(she hadn't). Lady Clementina Mitford—quite a Gainsborough or Sir Joshua—charmed me with her beauty. Introduced also to Mrs. Tennant, who introduced me to her pretty daughter. Came away at 6.10 and got home to supper at 8.45.[2]

It would be surprising if on his way home Lewes had not stopped to see Agnes and the girls, who lived in the little house at 3 Campden Hill Terrace, not five minutes from Airlie Lodge.

---

[1] *Letters*, VI. 154–5.   [2] GHL Diary, 8 July 1875.

For some months letters from Bertie Lewes had given 'sad accounts' of his health. Like Thornie, as a boy he had had glandular disease—probably tubercular—but grew into a strong young man before he went out to Natal. In July when a letter arrived from him announcing the birth of his second child, a son whom he named George Herbert Lewes, Bertie had already died.[1] Charles wished to dash off at once to bring the widow and her two babies to England, but they dissuaded him; 'we couldn't think it right', said Lewes. He wrote to Eliza, sending money. In August, Charles and Gertrude, who was expecting another child, came to Rickmansworth for a long week-end, bringing little Blanche to cheer and delight her grandparents.[2] Their only other visitor that summer was the architect Basil Champneys, who since the death of Owen Jones, had undertaken to redecorate the Priory. He sent down wallpapers for them to consider, and came once himself to discuss the plans.

Returning to the Priory on 23 September, they found the drawing-room not yet papered and a horrible smell of paint everywhere. Toomey, the gardener, had discovered the key of George's cupboard and stolen his cigars. After one night they left the servants to contend with these problems and, putting the manuscript of *Deronda* in the bank, set off for a holiday in Wales. At Shrewsbury, Sir James Paget and his family were staying in the same hotel. When Lewes sent in his card, Paget 'at once came to us and dragged us to their room, which was *full* of young men and the family', with whom the Leweses spent a pleasant evening of singing and chat.[3] Their reading aloud included *Emma*, which they finished at Aberystwyth, Dickens's *Uncommercial Traveller*, Sterne's *Sentimental Journey*, and Turgenev's *Nouvelles Moscovites*, which included 'Le Juif', a short story of the Russian camp translated by Mérimée. The boisterous Welsh gales and incessant rain moderated during their three days at Llanberis, so that they caught a rare view of Snowden from the waterfall.

Returning home on 9 October, they were disgusted to find the drawing-room still in the hands of the paper-hangers. Nevertheless, they settled in to work. Mornings of writing were succeeded by afternoon sessions with Mr. Mummery, the dentist, who had much to do for both of them. Using nitrous oxide for the first time, he extracted two of Marian's canines, and she felt no un-

---

[1] At Durban, Natal, 29 June 1875.   [2] GHL Diary, 21–3 Aug. 1875.
[3] GHL Diary, 24 Sept. 1875.

pleasant after-effects. The two volumes of *Daniel Deronda* (Chapters 1–34) were sent to Edinburgh on 20 October and put at once into type. Blackwood, reading the proofs, renewed his letters of ecstatic appreciation. He anticipated Dr. Leavis in praising Gwendolen's 'running mental reflections after each few words she has said to Grandcourt . . . as far as I know a new device in reporting a conversation'.[1] Occasionally he would venture a trifling criticism. In the very first sentence, for example, he confessed to being halted by the *dynamic* quality of Gwendolen's glance; *dynamic* is 'a *dictionary* word to so many people', he said, and yet he could think of no other that would so fully convey the meaning.[2] When Mrs. Blackwood, who was also reading the proofs avidly, suggested that Primrose's knees were not likely to be broken by such a fall as she described in a *field*, George Eliot changed the scene (Chapter 7) to a rough pasture where coarse, tufted grass concealed some treacherous holes. Lewes, of course, read all the proofs. The newspapers were chattering about the novel with 'wild reports about the subject-matter', Marian wrote to Blackwood, '—among the rest, that it represents French life! But that is hardly more ridiculous than the supposition that after refusing to go to America I should undertake to describe society there', as some papers had declared.

Lewes was already negotiating the sale of foreign rights to *Daniel Deronda*. As early as June 1874 Porter and Coates of Philadelphia had offered £1,500 for advance sheets. When they renewed their offer in September 1875, they were competing with two other American houses. Harper's, who had behaved very fairly over *Middlemarch*, secured the book for £1,700 and published it simultaneously with the English edition in their new monthly magazine. For the German translation Lewes got £100, £40 for the Dutch translation, and £250 from Tauchnitz for the continental reprint. Simpson again persuaded the *Australasian* of Melbourne to pay £200 for serial rights. With Blackwood the arrangement was the same as for *Middlemarch*: 2s. for each 5s. part sold, a royalty of 40 per cent. It was agreed that February

[1] In ch. 11. *Letters*, VI. 182. Cf. F. R. Leavis, *The Great Tradition* (N.Y., 1948), pp. 102–3.
[2] *Letters*, VI. 183. Writing to Samuel Butler about 'hard words' in his *Life and Habit*, Eliza Savage said: 'I don't mind, for I have a dictionary which I bought two years ago as I wished to read *Daniel Deronda* in the original' (R. F. Rattray, *Samuel Butler* (1935), p. 103). Trollope confessed that 'there are sentences in *Daniel Deronda* which I have found myself compelled to read three times before I have been able to take home to myself all that the writer has intended' (*Autobiography*, ed. B. A. Booth (1947), p. 206).

would be the best month to launch the book. But opinion in George Street was divided on the interval between parts. Willie Blackwood and Simpson favoured two months to give readers more time to digest the story; John Blackwood, fearing that it would give the circulating libraries an opportunity to starve their supplies, thought one month enough. George Eliot and Lewes concurred, and *Daniel Deronda* was published in eight parts about the first of each month from February to September 1876.

In spite of ill health George Eliot wrote more rapidly as the end of the story drew near. Lewes, as always, shielded her from any unflattering comment. Before Willie Blackwood came to lunch, he wrote to warn him

against any mention of criticisms that may have appeared on Deronda. Mrs. Lewes is so easily discouraged and so ready to believe and exaggerate whatever is said against her books that I not only keep reviews from her but do not even talk of them to her. When people sometimes speak indignantly of objections that others have made they little know how it depresses her, and therefore whenever the subject is approached I step in if I can to stop their mouths.[1]

Luckily Willie was able to bring cheerful news of the advance sale of Book I, which had been favourably reviewed the first day in *The Times*. To John Blackwood Lewes wrote: 'I take good care that nothing comes to her ears or eyes that would sound or read like objection, being so well aware of how she would lay hold of it as proof of her forebodings being justified. And I don't let her see even the enthusiastic criticisms, for many reasons.'[2] John, long schooled in this strategy, told Willie privately: 'I think Lewes fidgets her in his anxiety both about her and her work and himself. She says she never reads any review, but she certainly hears plentifully all that is said or written in London on the subject of Deronda. She remarked that it was hard upon her that people should be angry with her for not doing what they expected with her characters. . . .'[3] Marian appreciated George's vigilance and expressed her gratitude by inscribing the bound manuscript of *Daniel Deronda* 'To my dear Husband, George Henry Lewes', adding the last twelve lines of Shakespeare's 29th Sonnet, ending:

> For thy sweet love rememb'red such wealth brings
> That then I scorn to change my state with kings.

[1] *Letters*, VI. 218.　　[2] *Letters*, VI. 219.　　[3] *Letters*, VI. 253.

From the first, Blackwood recognized that the weakness of
Daniel Deronda lay in the Jewish part, which in the privacy of her
Journal George Eliot herself confessed seems 'likely to satisfy
nobody'.[1] Lewes too 'sometimes shared her doubts on whether
people would sufficiently sympathize with that element in the
story'. However, he saw no reason why she should not conquer
the popular prejudice. He wrote to Blackwood:

You are surprised at her knowledge of the Jews? But only learned
Rabbis are so profoundly versed in Jewish history and literature as she
is—and this will not only make a Rembrandtish background to her
dramatic presentation, but I suspect will rouse all the Jews of Europe
to a fervor of admiration for the great artist who can—without dis-
guising the ludicrous and ugly aspects—so marvellously present the
ideal side of that strange life. Lydgate in Middlemarch conquered all
the medical profession—and Mordecai will in like manner conquer all
the Jews. What a stupendous genius it is![2]

Marian was familiar enough with Blackwood's gentle reservations
to sense his disapproval of Mordecai when he explained that
'puzzling and thinking over that phase of the Tale has been the
cause of my not having written to you sooner'. Marian had thought
it likely that he would be doubtful.

Perhaps when the work is finished you will see its bearings better. The
effect that one strives after is an outline as strong as that of Balfour of
Burley for a much more complex character and a higher strain of ideas.
But such an effect is just the most difficult thing in art—to give new
elements—i.e. elements not already used up—in forms as vivid as those
of long familiar types. Doubtless the wider public of novel-readers must
feel more interest in Sidonia than in Mordecai. But then, I was not
born to paint Sidonia.[3]

'More's the pity,' Blackwood probably thought. When reading the
proof of Book VII, he wrote a postscript on his letter to her: 'I
must tell you I sent for a Hebrew Dictionary to look up the word
tephillin but to my shame I could not make out the letters and
the dunderhead of a German who compiled the book had not
given a relative table of English and Hebrew letters.'[4]

Book VIII took nearly two months to write, though she was
anxious to finish it and get away for a rest. She had few diversions.
She went to the Lyceum on 18 April 1876—Lewes's 59th birthday
—to see Henry Irving and Kate Bateman in Tennyson's *Queen*

Mary. 'All the interest and excitement of a First Night', Lewes noted. 'Play horribly acted throughout—not one of them able to *speak*.' She dined at Lady Portsmouth's on 18 May with a distinguished company, including Lord Carnarvon (who took her down); Lord and Lady Abercromby; Lord Ramsay; Lord O'Hagan, the Lord Chancellor of Ireland; Mountstuart Grant-Duff; J. C. Adams, the discoverer of Neptune; Meredith Townsend, proprietor of the *Spectator*; and two of the Earl of Portsmouth's daughters. One of them exclaimed to Lewes what a delight it was to see Polly's 'saintly face again'.

Polly felt very poorly the next day and determined not to run the risk of going to Oxford, where they had promised to spend the week-end with Jowett at Balliol. But on Saturday she was so much better that she agreed to go. George Howard, John Addington Symonds, and Courtenay Ilbert with their wives were the other guests. 'Supped at New Hall—part-singing by the Choir—very sweet', Lewes noted, and Marian returned on the Monday 'none the worse for the lionizing'.[1] Lord Houghton invited her to meet the King of the Belgians on 30 May, but, worn with anxiety and fatigue over the last pages of *Deronda*, she refused to go. Lord Houghton was much put out. King Leopold, who had wished particularly to see her, asked to have Lewes presented. Beginning with a compliment about the *Life of Goethe*, Lewes reported, 'he conversed a few minutes with me in French, English, and German, not saying anything significant, but also not saying anything silly. Very affable. Young, tall, and well looking, the star on his breast the only difference from other gentlemen.' There was such a crowd that it took Lewes twenty-five minutes to get down the stairs, and if he had not acted as his own link boy, he would have been hours getting the carriage. Polly was well out of it.

She was writing the final pages of *Daniel Deronda* when Blackwood called with his son Jack on 6 June, and stayed for lunch. She did not see them, but stayed in her room writing till half-past four. Blackwood explained to Willie that she

was not visible, being in the agonies of the wind up and suffering from face-ache. We had, however, a most pleasant lunch with Lewes and Miss Helps, daughter of Arthur Helps, who was there. Lewes said his wife was writing with tears in her eyes, and I do not wonder at it. That portion of the proof which I received to-day certainly made me weep. There is a simplicity and power about it that has not been reached in my time.[2]

[1] GHL Diary, 20 May 1876; *Letters*, VI. 256.   [2] *Letters*, VI. 261.

Lewes was equally susceptible. In his Diary the next day he wrote: 'Polly read me last chapter but one of Deronda [Daniel's final interview with Gwendolen], and with hot eyes and a sense of having been beaten all over I walked out with her in the Park.' On 8 June the book was 'finished at last' and sent to Edinburgh. After packing, they drove round to Arlington Street to call on Blackwood, whom they found at lunch with Mrs. Oliphant, Major Lockhart, and Miss Blackwood. He came out to the carriage to speak to Marian, who would not come in. 'It troubled me to see her sitting pale and tired in her carriage at the door', he wrote to Lewes. 'No wonder she felt tired and unwilling for company, but I earnestly hope that the change across the Channel is already beginning to tell for good.'[1]

They lingered a few days in Paris, sitting in the Tuileries Gardens to read the final pages of proof on 12 June 1876, and went on to Aix-les-Bains. They were both ill. After a week, they paused at Chambéry long enough to visit Rousseau's house (they were reading the *Confessions* aloud), passed through Geneva without a word to the D'Alberts, and tried for a week to regain health at Lausanne and Vevey. They were still miserable, Polly with a return of her renal symptoms. When able to travel, they went on through Zurich to Ragatz.[2] There on a regime, taking long walks, Polly soon recovered her colour and appetite. In the woods for a few mornings she gave Lewes lessons in Hebrew, 'wakening the echoes with our laughter sometimes at my blunders and attempts at Israelitish eloquence'. It is doubtful if he ever progressed to the proficiency indicated by Espinasse's story that Lewes studied Hebrew, 'not that he might be able to read the Old Testament in the original, but that they might talk to each other without being understood by the polyglot landlords and waiters of Continental hotels!'[3] After five weeks in the eastern valleys of Switzerland, they stayed for a little in the Black Forest on their way back to London. They were at the Priory again on 1 September 1876, 'both the better for our journey', Marian told Blackwood, 'and I consider myself in as good case as I can ever reasonably expect. We can't be made young again and must not be surprised that infirmities recur in spite of mineral waters and air 3000 feet above sea-level.'[4] To Barbara Bodichon she added grimly, 'Death is the only physician, the shadow of his valley the only journeying that will cure us of age and the gathering fatigue of years.'[1]

Among the letters awaiting George Eliot was a gratifying one from Dr. Hermann Adler, Rabbi of the Bayswater Synagogue, expressing his 'warm appreciation of the fidelity with which some of the best traits of the Jewish character' were depicted in *Daniel Deronda* and enclosing his review of the first parts of it in the *Jewish Messenger*.[2] Soon she received a letter from Haim Guedalla, one of the heads of the Jewish community, thanking her 'for having represented us in so favourable a light and in so attractive and scholarly a manner before the world'.[3] He enclosed a pamphlet on Turkish finance written the previous November, in which he contemplated 'a vision of Syria again in the hands of the Jews', and his Hebrew translation of the club scene in Chapter 42, cut from a paper in Lemberg. George Eliot sent a hearty letter of acknowledgement, but his immediate request to publish it in the *Jewish Chronicle* she refused:

I have a repugnance to anything like an introduction of my own personality to the public which only an urgent sense of duty could overcome. But over and above this feeling I have a conviction founded on dispassionate judgment, that any influence I may have as an author would be injured by the presentation of myself in print through any other medium than that of my books. False statements are frequently made both in British and American newspapers about my history and opinions, but I shall never break silence in an effort at contradiction until I perceive that some one else is being injured by those falsities in any way that my protest can hinder.

It is my function as an artist to act (if possible) for good on the emotions and conceptions of my fellow-men. But, as you are aware, when anyone who can be called a public person makes a casual speech or writes a letter that gets into print, his words are copied, served up in a work of commentary, misinterpreted, misquoted, and made matter of gossip for the emptiest minds. By giving occasion for more of this frivolous (if not vitiating) kind of comment than already exists in sickening abundance, I should be stepping out of my proper function and acting for what I think an evil result.[4]

Other letters followed: from Abram Samuel Isaacs, an American Jew at the Theological Seminary in Breslau, assuring her that *Deronda* had had an elevating effect on the minds of his people; from Abraham Benisch, editor of the *Jewish Chronicle*, with a

[1] *Letters*, VI. 280.   [2] H. Adler to GE, 23 June 1876 (Yale).
[3] H. Guedalla to GE, 25 Sept. 1876 (Yale).   [4] *Letters*, VI. 289.

'generously appreciative' review of the book;[1] and from Harriet Beecher Stowe, the veteran novelist of oppressed people. To Mrs. Stowe she explained her motive in detail:

As to the Jewish element in 'Deronda', I expected from first to last in writing it, that it would create much stronger resistance and even repulsion than it has actually met with. But precisely because I felt that the usual attitude of Christians towards Jews is—I hardly know whether to say more impious or more stupid when viewed in the light of their professed principles, I therefore felt urged to treat Jews with such sympathy and understanding as my nature and knowledge could attain to. Moreover, not only towards the Jews, but towards all oriental peoples with whom we English come in contact, a spirit of arrogance and contemptuous dictatorialness is observable which has become a national disgrace to us. There is nothing I should care more to do, if it were possible, than to rouse the imagination of men and women to a vision of human claims in those races of their fellow-men who most differ from them in customs and beliefs. But towards the Hebrews we western people who have been reared in Christianity, have a peculiar debt and, whether we acknowledge it or not, a peculiar thoroughness of fellowship in religious and moral sentiment. Can anything be more disgusting than to hear people called 'educated' making small jokes about eating ham, and showing themselves empty of any real knowledge as to the relation of their own social and religious life to the history of the people they think themselves witty in insulting? They hardly know that Christ was a Jew. And I find men educated at Rugby supposing that Christ spoke Greek. . . .

Yes, I expected more aversion than I have found. But I was happily independent in material things and felt no temptation to accommodate my writing to any standard except that of trying to do my best in what seemed to me most needful to be done, and I sum up with the writer of the Book of Maccabees—'if I have done well, and as befits the subject, it is what I desired, but if I have done ill, it is what I could attain unto'.[2]

This frank avowal of didacticism contradicts George Eliot's basic tenet that fiction should represent real life, 'never lapse from the picture to the diagram'.[3] This is fiction with a purpose. It was not just prejudice that turned readers against it, but her failure to achieve creative realization. As William Cory said, 'It does not go into my blood.'[4] To the pioneers of what was to become the Zionist Movement, however, *Daniel Deronda* formed a momentous

---

[1] *Letters*, VI. 316–17.   [2] *Letters*, VI. 301–2.
[3] *Letters*, IV. 300.
[4] *Extracts from the Letters and Journals of William Cory*, ed. F. W. Cornish (Oxford, 1897), p. 420.

landmark. Twenty years before Theodor Herzl's *Der Judenstadt* George Eliot projected a heroic vision which, according to the *Encyclopaedia Britannica*, 'gave the Jewish national spirit the strongest stimulus it had experienced since the appearance of Sabbatai Zevi' in 1666.[1] Ingenious efforts to connect George Eliot's influence with the Balfour Declaration of 1917 remain hypothetical; though the 'young Balfour' whom she met at Cambridge in 1873 was not Arthur, but one of his brothers, she met Arthur when she visited the Sidgwicks there in 1877.

A good deal has been written about the so-called 'originals' of *Daniel Deronda*. A recent writer declared that the youthful Lewes of the 1830s—'an intense, restless young man in search of a creed—has obviously provided Eliot with the basis for her creation of Deronda'.[2] Leslie Stephen fancied that she drew some features of her hero from handsome young Edmund Gurney, another of the Trinity men she met in 1873,[3] Beatrice Webb thought Octavia Hill's friend Edward Bond the original.[4] Herzl's diary for 1895 recounts a conversation in which Colonel Albert Goldsmid told him, 'I am Deronda.' Goldsmid was born a Christian in India, the son of baptized Jews; but, when a lieutenant in the Bengal Fusiliers, he decided 'to return to my ancestral stock' and went over to Judaism. 'My family was indignant. My wife was also a Christian of Jewish origin. I eloped with her, contracted first a free marriage in Scotland; then she had to turn Jewess, and we were married in synagogue.'[5] His family's indignation might parallel that of Daniel's mother, who hated Judaism; for her no better candidate has been proposed than Mrs. Isaac D'Israeli![6] But with the mild young Daniel there could hardly be a stronger contrast than the second-generation Army man Colonel Goldsmid, of whose conversion George Eliot had never heard. His elder daughter, the Dowager Baroness Swaythling, wrote in 1949 that her father's connection with Deronda 'was just a romance and has no

---

[1] 'Zionism', *Encyclopaedia Britannica* (11th ed., 1911), XXVIII. 987. In the 14th ed. (1928) this article by L[ucien] W[olf], reprinted with the signature 'L. W.; X.', deletes this sentence and substitutes: *Daniel Deronda* 'was a striking illustration of the sympathy with which Jewish national aspirations were regarded by cultivated western minds'. Under 'George Eliot' the 11th ed. made no mention of the Jewish element in *Daniel Deronda*; in the 14th, an unsigned article calls it 'a strong intellectual plea against anti-Jewish prejudice', but does not allude to Zionism.
[2] Hannah Goldberg, *Notes and Queries*, 202 (Aug. 1957), 356–8.
[3] Leslie Stephen, *George Eliot* (1902), p. 191.
[4] B. Webb, *My Apprenticeship* (1926), pp. 264–5.
[5] *The Herzl Diaries*, ed. M. Lowenthal (1956), p. 82.
[6] Mudge and Sears, *A George Eliot Dictionary* (1924), pp. 105–6.

real foundation in fact'.[1] Certainly the Colonel's lady bore no resemblance to the devout Mirah. Deronda was imagined.

Mirah is often said to have been drawn from Mme Bodichon's protégé, Phoebe Sarah Marks. Miss Marks herself, who against the opposition of her family married a Christian, Professor W. E. Ayrton, could see no likeness, and Mme Bodichon declared that Mirah's story was written before George Eliot saw her.[2] The heroine of Byron's *Sardanapalus*, Myrrha, a pious, loyal, patriotic Greek slave exiled in Nineveh, offers a tempting literary source. But George Eliot named her Mirah (pronounced My-ra) after a sister of the fifteenth-century chronicler Rabbi Joseph ben Joshua ha-Cohen ben Meir.[3]

For her conception of Mordecai, Deutsch obviously provided the principal impetus. But the character was immediately connected with Kohn or Cohn, the consumptive watch-maker whom Lewes had known in his youth as a member of the Philosophers Club that met in Red Lion Square, which Lewes had described in his article on Spinoza in the *Fortnightly*.[4] Lewes repeatedly declared that no resemblance existed between the dreamy prophet Mordecai and Cohn, a 'keen dialectitian and a highly impressive man, but without any specifically Jewish enthusiasm'. According to George Eliot, Cohn's 'type was rather that of Spinoza, whose metaphysical system attracted his subtle intellect, and in relation to Judaism Spinoza was in contrast to my conception of Mordecai'.[5] Asher Isaac Myers, to whom she wrote this, considered Mordecai 'an unconscious photograph' of Abraham Benisch, whom she never saw. Hunters of originals run easily to the prophetic.

For the formidable musician Julius Klesmer, Franz Liszt has been generally accepted as the model since 1885, when Lord Acton asserted positively that he 'became Klesmer'.[6] When George Eliot knew Liszt at Weimar in his forty-third year, it was his sweetness, tenderness, benignity that impressed her. None of these qualities can be seen in the irascible Klesmer, nor do his massive square countenance and 'grand features' resemble in the slightest Liszt's long Dantesque face. Klesmer is 'the German, the Sclave, and the Semite', whose Jewishness forms an important part of the novel's structure. Liszt, born a Hungarian Catholic, was, after some scandalous decades with the countesses, recon-

[1] In a letter to S. Levy, 4 Nov. 1949 (Yale).
[2] Evelyn Sharp, *Hertha Ayrton* (1926), p. 38.
[3] Notebook, Pforzheimer Library: MS. 711, p. 60.
[4] *Fortnightly*, 4 (Apr. 1866), 386–7.   [5] *Letters*, VII. 96.
[6] 'George Eliot's Life', *Nineteenth Century*, 17 (Mar. 1885), 483.

ciled to the Church; taking minor orders in 1865, he appeared, ton-
sured and in clerical garb, as the Abbé Liszt. George Eliot describes
Klesmer specifically as 'not yet a Liszt, understood to be adored
by ladies of all European countries with the exception of Lapland'.[1]

But she did meet at Weimar the musician from whom the conception of Klesmer grew. Anton Rubinstein, then twenty-four
years old, fits precisely her description of 'the German, the Sclave,
and the Semite'. His mother was a German Jewess, his father, a
Russian, and like Klesmer he grew up knowing 'penury, ay even to
hunger' in a tiny house 'on the outskirts of Bohemia; and in the
figurative Bohemia too he had had large acquaintance with the
variety and romance which belong to small incomes'.[2] Rubinstein
had Klesmer's massive features and the thick mane of hair, which
he threw backward when he played in conscious imitation of his
hero, 'the king of musicians, Liszt'. Brusqueness is the trait in
which they resemble each other most closely. His writings bristle
with tart comments matching in acerbity anything said by 'the
terrible Klesmer'. When Rubinstein came to London early in May
1876, Mrs. Frederick Lehmann invited the Leweses to dine with
him. Marian, though ill and struggling with the last book of
Deronda, broke her rule to go. 'We shall so like to renew our
acquaintance with Klesmer, whom we met at Weimar in '54!'
Lewes wrote to Mrs. Lehmann.[3] When Rubinstein returned to
London in 1877, George Eliot was suffering from another attack
of kidney stone. Lewes went alone to meet him at the Felix
Moscheles' party,[4] where duets were sung from Rubinstein's sacred
opera *The Maccabees*, illustrated by *tableaux-vivants*. George Eliot
was doubtless gratified to think that *Daniel Deronda* had helped
create the patriotic interest in Jewish history that prompted the
choice of this programme.

By 1876 society had pretty much overlooked George Eliot's
equivocal marital position. Rumour had it that the first Mrs.
Lewes was insane, or a hopeless drunkard, or that her death had
lately made it possible to legalize George Eliot's marriage. None
of these was true. Agnes Lewes was living quietly as before in
Kensington with her son Edmund, a successful dentist, who never
married, and her daughters Rose and Ethel and Mildred. Rose
became a governess, greatly beloved by her young pupils. Both

[1] Ch. 22.   [2] Ch. 39.
[3] GHL to Mrs. F. Lehmann, [8 May 1876] (Yale).
[4] GHL Diary, 10 May 1877. See also G. S. Haight, 'George Eliot's Klesmer', in
Imagined Worlds, ed. M. Mack (1968), pp. 205-14.

PLATE XII

AGNES JERVIS LEWES AND HER DAUGHTER ROSE
c. 1888

of the younger sisters emigrated to California, where Ethel married John Welsh and Mildred a man named Elliott, in Ventura County. Agnes, cheerful and impenitent, lived on till 1902, receiving her regular allowance from Lewes and, later, from Charles, and then from his widow. The money came, of course, from royalties on George Eliot's novels. Lewes's total earnings after 1855 barely equalled what she earned from *Daniel Deronda* alone.[1]

The publication of this last of her novels marked the zenith of George Eliot's fame. She was regarded as the greatest living English novelist. From high and low came marks of appreciation. Theodore Martin, who was writing the *Life of the Prince Consort*, asked Blackwood to tell George Eliot how devoted the Queen was to her works, especially *Adam Bede*.[2] After the death of her Private Secretary, Sir Arthur Helps, Lewes wrote to his daughter Alice a letter of sympathy, which both he and Marian signed. The bottom of the page has been torn away, and a note in Alice's hand explains: 'The double autograph of G. H. Lewes and G. Eliot asked for by the Queen on seeing the letter.'[3] Poor working women in the American provinces wrote George Eliot long letters; aspiring authors sent her their books. A young lady in New York, Marian told William Blackwood, expressed

much gratitude for being saved, by reading Daniel Deronda, from marrying a man whom she could not love, but whom she was disposed to accept for the sake of his wealth, but she is so far from being absorbed by this momentous personal matter that she goes on to be still more effusive about the 'enjoyment and instruction' she has had from the Jewish elements in the book, and thinks the scene on the Bridge the best in the book—'flashing through one with a sort of electric sympathy' etc. Tell your uncle that America is the quarter of the world for 'appreciative butter'.[4]

Almost the only place where the curious could see George Eliot was at the Pop Concerts at St. James's Hall. Nearly every Saturday afternoon during the season eyes were turned on her as she followed Lewes down the aisle, 'walking slowly, bending a little forward, looking a little preoccupied, but with the dawn of a smile, as of expected enjoyment, on her long, pale face'.[5] Half a dozen sketches made of her during the concerts are known, most of them

[1] These figures are drawn from GHL's 'Literary Receipts' in the Berg Collection, NYPL, and from the accounts in GE's Diary. See *Letters*, VII. 358–83.

[2] *Letters*, VI. 137.

[3] *Letters*, VI. 129. A copy of the 1880 ed. of *Romola* presented to Disraeli by the Queen is at Hughenden Manor.   [4] *Letters*, VI. 396–7.

[5] Lucy Clifford, 'A Remembrance of George Eliot', *Nineteenth Century*, 74 (July 1913), 110.

crudely and hastily done. One by Mrs. Alma-Tadema is in the National Portrait Gallery. A better likeness was sketched by the Princess Louise on her programme at a concert for the Music School of the Blind, 16 March 1877. The best of them was drawn by a professional painter Lowes Dickinson, who annoyed Lewes by persisting in spite of his disapproving stares. During the intervals the Leweses often went to the green-room to chat with the musicians, many of whom were their friends. There one day after a fine performance of Schubert's trio, Norman Neruda 'kissed Polly's hand and then the two kissed each other'[1]—a display of emotion stirred by the music, to which (like Maggie Tulliver) she was always susceptible. Once when she and George were leaving the Hall, an elderly lady approached her and 'begged to be allowed *to kiss her hand*. This done, another younger lady did the same, declaring herself "one of the many thousands"'.[2] After an exciting concert at the Academy of Music a young lady helped Polly on with her cloak and kissed her hand and then her cheek. Polly said, 'Forgive me, but I do not recollect you.' She replied, 'Oh! it is too good of you to let me. If you speak to me I shall cry.'[3] In Paris a strange lady, recognizing George Eliot at the Théâtre Français, introduced herself and her husband.[4] Many similar episodes are recorded. Not all of them involve women. A young American at a concert, told by his companion that they were seated near George Eliot, was so excited by the proximity that he wrote to express his 'gratitude for the many hours of mental gratification which I have owed to your pen'.[5] A man in London dreamt that she was desperately ill, and, being haunted continually by the dream, asked Lewes to dispel his anxiety by having someone merely put 'Dream wrong' on the self-addressed postcard he enclosed and send it 'to a young man to whom Mrs. Lewes is as much an object of reverent affection as any one could be'.[6]

Scores of letters from unknown admirers poured into the Priory from all over the world. A Dutch girl in Utrecht sent an eight-page effusion beginning:

Dear Miss Evans,
If I were a german girl I would add: 'much adored', but we Dutch are not überschwänglich in affectionate expressions, as we are too much fulfilled with respect for those who awake our best soul . . . since I

---

[1] GHL Diary, 12 Feb. 1876.   [2] *Letters*, VI. 27–8.
[3] GHL Diary, 20 Mar. 1878.   [4] GHL Diary, 7 Oct. 1874.
[5] James F. Colman to GE, 22 Jan. 1874 (Yale).
[6] Leonard A. Montefiore to GHL, 17 Oct. [1877] (Yale).

finished with reading Middlemarch I could not resist something within me that draws me nearer to you. . . . You must have experienced much —you must much have felt. There are cries of the heart that awake an echo in every maiden's soul.[1]

Some of the letters were anonymous, written only to relieve the emotions of the sender. Melusina Fay Peirce, wife of the American philosopher Charles Sanders Peirce, in reply to her first letter had received a long, thoughtful letter of advice from George Eliot.[2] In 1869 she wrote again without signing her name:

Dearest—
  You will not be bored by another love letter—a little one? It is three whole years since I wrote to you before, and you sent me such a grave, kind, precious little answer. O how wise thou art! Where didst thou learn it all? . . . You wrote it for me, dearest, and often it has shamed me and spurred me on. . . .
  Don't answer this, dearest. I don't require you to think of me as anything more than the evening breeze that sometimes kisses your cheek. I *love* you, you are so love-worthy. And once in a long time I *love* to say so to you. But I would not burden you with the weight of a rose leaf.[3]

George Eliot's extraordinary attraction for women is seen throughout her life. It appears in her relation with her teacher Miss Lewis, with Sara Hennell, Barbara Bodichon, Bessie Parkes, and later with Mrs. Congreve, Mrs. Lehmann, Mrs. Burne-Jones, Mrs. Pattison, Mrs. Ponsonby, and many others. It is most consciously documented in the devotion of Elma Stuart, who even exhibited to Lewes 'the handkerchief with which she had wiped the tears from Polly's eyes, and henceforth has preserved as a *relic*'.[4]
  But for this kind of worship none of George Eliot's 'spiritual daughters' surpassed Edith Jemima Simcox. They first met on 13 December 1872 when, because she was reviewing *Middlemarch* for the *Academy*, Edith was invited to lunch at the Priory. The 'loud and insusceptible' Anthony Trollope[5] was also there, so that she had little chance for private talk. But Lewes immediately recognized Edith as a most discriminating young ally in his battle against diffidence, and welcomed her calls. The strange story of her life has been well told by Professor K. A. McKenzie in *Edith*

[1] Jeanne Buskes to GE, 26 Dec. 1874 (Yale).
[2] GE to Mrs. C. S. Peirce, 14 Sept. 1866 (Yale).
[3] Mrs. C. S. Peirce to GE, 21 Aug. 1869 (Yale).
[4] GHL Diary, 18 Feb. 1875.
[5] *Letters*, VI. 260.

Simcox and George Eliot (1961). Twenty-five years younger than George Eliot, she was quite as learned in her way: thoroughly grounded in Latin and Greek, speaking French fluently enough to make extemporaneous speeches, and considering the compilation of a German–English dictionary. She wrote articles of extraordinary distinction on art, literature, history, biography, philosophy, folklore, mythology, economics, education, women's suffrage, housing for the poor, trades unions, the employment of women, and many other subjects. Three books show the variety of her interests: *Natural Law: An Essay in Ethics* (1877), a courageous effort to formulate a moral code for a world deprived of its old faith; *Episodes in the Lives of Men, Women, and Lovers* (1882), a collection of sketches not unlike Pater's *Imaginary Portraits* (1887)—with some of the same sexual ambiguity; and *Primitive Civilizations* (1894), a fragment of an ambitious plan for a complete history of appropriation or ownership. With her friend Mary Hamilton she conducted a successful shirt-making company in Soho to employ women under decent working conditions. She took an active part in the trades union movement, serving several times as English representative at the International Labour Congress on the Continent. She was one of the first members elected to the London School Board, and worked indefatigably to provide sound compulsory education for all children, free from control of the Church.

Though small and slight, weighing about 7 stone (less than 100 pounds), Edith was astonishingly vigorous, walking many miles about London every day in any weather. Her way led frequently to the Priory. At first in George Eliot's presence she was shy and reticent. But by March 1873 she had undergone what she called her 'conversion'—to belief in George Eliot, the 'Madonna', whose letters to her were signed 'Your Loving Mother'. With warm pressure of the hand, 'glances of ineffable love', impulsive dropping to the floor to kiss her feet, Edith worshipped her Goddess.[1] Lewes, who was almost always present at their meetings, shared half-humorously in this hyperbolic devotion to Polly which, Edith admitted, 'was more welcome to him than to her'. He could not have suspected the pathological depth of her obsession. At home she recorded all her repressed passion with minute detail in a journal—*acta diurna amoris*—oddly entitled 'Autobiography of a Shirt Maker'. There the ardent words she dared not speak flame out: 'My Sweet Darling', 'My own beautiful Love',

[1] Cf. *Spanish Gypsy* (1868), p. 340; Cabinet ed. p. 362.

'Dearest, Dearest', she wrote. 'Day by day let me begin and end by looking to Her for guidance and rebuke, . . . make a dread rule to myself out of the vow that every night what has been done ill or left undone shall be confessed on my knees to my Darling and my God'.[1] To Edith they were one and the same. In the copy of her *Natural Law* inscribed to 'Marian Evans Lewes | January 21. 1877' the last sentence reads: 'Heaven and hell are names or visions; the earth is ours—here a hell of sensibility and hardened cruelty, there a heaven of love and wisdom, with a tender smile upon her gracious lips, and yearning prophecy in the melting depths of her unfathomable eyes.' Edith changed the final point to a comma and added: 'To whom | with idolatrous love | this book is dedicated.'[2] At their next meeting George Eliot treated this ardent homage with what Edith calls 'eloquent silence'.[3]

As Professor McKenzie says,[4] if the goddess found the incense not unpleasing, the woman was sometimes embarrassed by the fondling. She sympathized with women and liked to have them come to her in their troubles, but the friendship of men meant much more to her. Years before she had come to the same understanding with Mrs. Congreve, whom Edith never met during the eight years they were both seeing George Eliot. After her death they became good friends. Edith then learnt from Mrs. Congreve

with a sort of pleasure that she had loved my Darling lover-wise too —too much to repeat much of her words, but she told me how on seeing her again after an interval her heart was palpitating so violently that to avoid a painful breaking down she forced herself into a calm that seemed cold: she tried to talk in common fashion. Mr. Lewes was there, and then—the Darling, my sweet Darling rushed out of the room in tears. Mr. Lewes signed to Mrs. Congreve not to follow her and with a breaking heart she sat through his call. . . . After a while she, the dearest, spoke of it and then it could all be told. I said, were you not very happy to think that she could care so much for your love?[5]

Of the hundreds of letters that George Eliot wrote to them not one has survived. Excerpts from many of those to Mrs. Congreve were published by Cross in the *Life*. But he knew that it would be useless to ask even to see those to Edith Simcox. They were

---

[1] Simcox Autobiography, 24 Apr. 1881, fol. 93.
[2] Dr. Williams's Library: 1019. H. 11.
[3] Simcox Autobiography, 5 June 1880.
[4] K. A. McKenzie, *Edith Simcox and George Eliot* (1961), p. 91.
[5] Simcox Autobiography, 18 Jan. 1881, fol. 88. The episode probably occurred at Lucerne, 12 July 1859.

probably cremated with her.[1] The letters to Mrs. Congreve were destroyed after 1960 by her over-zealous nieces, children of the first marriage ever celebrated in the Church of Humanity, but unmindful of its motto, 'Live openly'. The destruction of their letters was a doubtful service to the memory of either 'lover', since it left their relation with George Eliot open to even darker speculation than the text might warrant.

The Victorians' conception of love between those of the same sex cannot be understood fairly by an age steeped in Freud. Where they saw only pure friendship, the modern reader assumes perversion. Henry James in *The Bostonians* dissects the twisted strands of 'one of those friendships between women which are so common in New England' with no apparent horror of what the schoolgirl today labels Lesbianism. Meredith in *Diana of the Crossways* innocently describes a scene between Diana and Lady Dunstane (chapter 36) that makes the modern reader uncomfortable. Even *In Memoriam*, for some, now has a troubling overtone. In reading Edith Simcox's record of her wild passion for George Eliot, we must guard against interpretations that could never have entered the writer's mind. What sinister significance we might see in her cheerful remark to William Bell Scott about one of her neighbour's pretty children: 'I want much to cut off the little girl's head to have the curls to play with'![2] This 'murderous confession', as she calls it, may have covered a dangerous impulse in the mild, unrequited little woman, weeping silently behind her spectacles in the British Museum. But she lived sixty-seven years full of active, useful work without violating the social mores. In reading her private account of George Eliot we should, as Geoffrey Tillotson suggests, allow for the intermingling of fantasy with fact.[3]

Some of the Leweses' interest in these morbidly passionate women may be attributed to their concern with psychology. Gwendolen Harleth, whose intricate character George Eliot was creating when she first knew Edith, has a similar physical aversion to men. Though Grandcourt is made frightful enough to justify it in his case, her rejection of Rex's love suggests a latent homosexual streak. Gwendolen confesses to having been jealous of her stepfather, and sleeps in her mother's bed till the day of her marriage. Traits like these obviously fascinate the novelist, George Eliot.

---

[1] Edith Simcox at one time planned to have her ashes 'scattered over Her grave'. *Autobiography*, 20 Feb. 1885.

[2] Edith Simcox to W. B. Scott, 25 July 1874 (Mrs. G. M. Troxell).

[3] 'Novelist Worship', *Sunday Times*, 4 June 1961.

But in her own life Lewes's love left no room for such a passion as Edith's. There was nothing masculine about her. Jowett declared that '*Elle était plus femme,* and had more feminine qualities, than almost anybody whom I have ever known.'[1]

While looking through some of John Blackwood's letters in October 1876, George Eliot was struck with how much she had owed to his encouragement through the years, and she wrote to tell him how grateful she was. She said—'pretty much that she could not have gone on without me', John declared. He was deeply touched.

Tears came into my eyes, and I read the passage at once to my wife who was sitting beside me when I received the letter. I look upon such expressions coming from you, as the very highest compliment that a man holding the position I do could receive, and I shall keep the letter for my children as a memorial that their father was good for something in his day. You are too good about my poor letters which I always felt to be too meagre and too few but I do look back upon our correspondence with pride and pleasure. Each letter from you is a treat and last summer, being pressed for your autograph, I turned over a number of your letters, but in each there was a feeling of something that I could not part with or deface by cutting off the signature so my friend went without an autograph.[2]

Like several of her letters that he put aside specially, this has vanished. In it she must have mentioned her dislike of biographers, who, as soon as a man is dead, rake through his desk and print every insignificant memorandum 'for the gossiping amusement of people too idle to re-read his books'.[3] Blackwood tried to comfort her:

That one who has risen so high as you have should be the subject of idle gossip is almost inevitable. It is a thing for which the public have a depraved appetite and I say 'idle' not evil as I do not think it is intentionally mischievous but why are great authors not to enjoy the privacy of common life? I do not know whether living gossips or posthumous memoir writers make me most savage. It is but little of such idle trash that I hear as no one would venture to speak to me of you with ought but praise and of that I do hear ample store.[4]

The ten-years' lease on George Eliot's earlier novels had almost run out; Blackwood offered her the sum of £4,000 for another

[1] E. Abbott and L. Campbell, *Benjamin Jowett* (3rd ed., N.Y., 1897), II. 181.
[2] *Letters*, VI. 294–5.   [3] *Letters*, VI. 23.   [4] *Letters*, VI. 295.

ten-years' lease on all of them, including *Romola*, which had reverted to George Eliot's control in 1870. 'We have a long career of successive triumphs to look back upon and I hope there is much yet before us', he wrote.[1] After duly considering the proposal with Lewes, she decided that a royalty on books sold was the most satisfactory arrangement for all—'not that we are in any way dissatisfied with the sum you propose,' Lewes wrote, 'but that we would rather be relieved from the sense that the arrangement might turn out disadvantageous to you; and also that we should like to have free command over editions and prices'.[2] It was a sound choice. The Cabinet edition, as it was called, brought her £4,330 in royalties during the next eight years alone.

After the publication of *Daniel Deronda* the Leweses' social life grew quieter. The Sunday afternoons—perhaps by design—were less crowded; a few of the 'swells', whose names Lewes delighted to note, disappear from the lists. In September 1876 when Marian's niece Emily Clarke came up from Brighton for a four-day visit, they took her to the Indian Museum, the Zoo, the National Portrait Gallery, the South Kensington Museum, and the Opera. On 27 September she went with them to see *Dan'l Druce, Blacksmith*, a play by W. S. Gilbert based on *Silas Marner*. Forbes-Robertson, playing Geoffrey Wynyard, made his first notable personal success in it. But Lewes thought it 'Wretched stuff, poorly acted.' Poor Emily may have had a more charitable opinion, for she had grown very deaf. Lewes soon sent her an ear trumpet.

Nearly every Sunday Johnny Cross called, often with one of his sisters. One Sunday afternoon in October he was their only guest.[3] The Leweses went to Six Mile Bottom to visit Henry Bullock-Hall and meet his new wife. Edmond Scherer, the Henry Sidgwicks, George Murray, the Professor of Anatomy, and Dr. George Paget, the Regius Professor of Physics at Cambridge, were among the other guests. One day after lunch they drove to Newmarket to visit the stables and saw Kisber, 'a beautiful creature', who had won both the Derby and the Grand Prix. The trainer, Lewes reported, 'treated Polly with great deference, always styling her My Lady and [was] much struck by her having pointed out a defect in the build of Kisber'.[4]

[1] *Letters*, VI. 297.   [2] *Letters*, VI. 303.
[3] GHL Diary, 8 Oct. 1876.
[4] Ibid. 5 Oct. 1876. Bullock-Hall's obituary of GE in the *Daily News* says that 'she drew attention to the fine points of the horse'.

Johnny Cross had been constantly on the look-out for a house that would suit them. At the end of November he met them at Waterloo Station and took them to see one called the Heights at Witley. The day was transcendently beautiful and made everything look glorious. The Leweses were enchanted with the house and grounds. The Surrey countryside was charming. They had come to know and love it well during the five months at Shottermill, while George Eliot was writing *Middlemarch*. Weybridge was not far away, and they returned there to spend the night with Mrs. Cross, having a good walk before dinner. After breakfast they took another delightful walk on St. George's Hill and looked in on Johnny's sister Anna and her husband Albert Druce. When they got home to the Priory, Lewes wrote to the agent about the Heights. Johnny came the next Sunday and arranged to meet Lewes with his solicitor. Having heard the report of the surveyor, Lewes agreed to bid up to £5,000 for the house, for which £8,000 was asked; then, after lunching with Johnny at Lloyd's, he walked to the Gaiety Theatre to meet Polly and see *Madame attend Monsieur*. Two days later word came from Johnny that they had secured Witley Heights. At last they had a country house of their own.

CHAPTER XV

WIDOW AND WIFE

※

THE HEIGHTS at Witley was a large red-brick house, half covered by vines, with high-gabled, red-tiled roofs and ample chimneys. Standing in eight or nine acres of ground—garden, field, and wood —it looked down a gentle slope across the valley towards Haslemere to the south, with Hindhead to the right and to the left Blackdown, where the Tennysons lived. The railway station was only five minutes away and London little more than an hour. Next door at the Pines lived the son of their old friend and physician Sir Henry Holland, through whom they had heard about the house. They lunched with Lady Holland and her children when they went down to inspect their purchase.[1] They were sadly disappointed to find the kitchen impossible, the 'wretched butler's pantry' small and ill-lit, and the plumbing totally inadequate.[2] Two weeks later they returned with the architect Elijah Hoole, who drew up two plans: complete alterations would cost £640, and partial improvements, enough to make the house habitable, £375. For a while the Leweses were tempted to give up altogether and sell the house, but decided to make the minimum improvements and try a camp-like life there for the summer.

The Christmas holidays they spent with the Cross family at Weybridge. During the greater part of the time Marian was too unwell to enjoy the pleasures these delightful younger friends prepared for her. Back in London, Mr. and Mrs. George Trevelyan had them to dinner with the Harrisons, the Grenfells, and others; Trevelyan, a brother of Lady Holland, gave them news of Witley.[3] In February a sudden attack of rheumatic gout immobilized Lewes for three weeks, and Polly had a return of her old kidney ailment. They recovered in time for a dinner at Mrs. Benzon's, where they met Browning, Leighton, both the Fred and Rudolf

---

[1] GHL Diary, 18 Jan. 1877.　　　[2] GE to Elijah Hoole, 2 Feb. 1877.
[3] GHL Diary, 24 Jan. 1877.

Lehmanns, the Schlesingers, Clara Schumann and her daughter, and Joachim, who played for them.[1] A few days later Leighton gave an afternoon music party where, not only Joachim, but Petri, Piatti, and Agnes Zimmermann played and Henschel sang. Here Lady Airlie's sister, Lady Gwendolen Herbert, with aristocratic disregard of etiquette asked to be introduced to Lewes and sat beside him during most of the concert, while Polly talked with Burne-Jones and Mrs. Ponsonby.[2] That same evening they went to the concert for the blind at which Joachim and Petri repeated the duet they had played at Leighton's. On this evening the Princess Louise made her sketch of George Eliot.

They were seeing a good deal of Tennyson in the spring of 1877. They met him with Hallam in the Park on Saturday morning, 24 March, and took a long walk with him. The next day he brought both Hallam and Lionel with him to the Priory to call on George Eliot, and on Monday had Lewes to lunch at his house with Locker and Hamilton Aïdé. He agreed to come the following Friday to read at the Priory. Marian went to Bumpus's to buy a complete edition of Tennyson's poems in preparation, while George wrote notes inviting a score of friends. Tennyson read with gusto, going on till midnight, when Hallam stopped him.[3]

The Princess Louise, Marchioness of Lorne, the first member of the royal family to marry a subject of the sovereign, was a talented sculptor, and was genuinely interested in higher education for women. Determined to know George Eliot, whom she had watched from her box at the Saturday concerts, she asked George Goschen, the banker and Liberal politician, to invite the Leweses to a dinner that he was giving in her honour on 15 May 1877. In a letter Lewes wrote that the Princess

had told Mrs. Ponsonby with great glee that she was going to meet us; and showed her pleasure in a very unusual way, for instead of Madonna being presented to her she asked, immediately on arriving, to be presented to Madonna, and at once sat down beside her and entered into friendly chat. After dinner they had a long talk—very agreeable. We went from the Goschens' to a music party and didn't get home till 1. Bright took her down to dinner and charmed her.[4]

May was the month of Richard Wagner's concerts in the Albert Hall. Though Lewes was not fond of the music, he was especially

---

[1] GHL Diary, 11 Mar. 1877.   [2] GHL Diary, 16 Mar. 1877.
[3] J. Lehmann, *Ancestors and Friends* (1962), p. 172.
[4] *Letters*, VI. 374.

concerned with the series because Mme Wagner had arrived with a
letter of introduction to him from her father, Franz Liszt. On
6 May, the first Sunday, she came to the Priory to be presented to
George Eliot, and gave them seats in her box for the opening
concert, at which Wagner conducted. During the next few weeks
they met the Wagners a dozen times at parties as well as at the
rehearsals and concerts. At one of these, where she was sitting
beside Lewes and Wagner beside George Eliot, with the Burne-
Joneses, William Morris, and Leighton close by, a young lady
with Richard Grosvenor in the row behind wondered why (except
for Leighton, who was an Adonis) 'genius was so terribly homely.
George Eliot wore a monstrous cross between a hat and a cap, and
her dress [to this critical youthful eye] was not beautiful; but
her face lighted up wonderfully when she spoke, and she seemed to
find much to talk about to Wagner in the intervals.'[1] At one
rehearsal, Mary Gladstone also 'watched George Eliot's repulsively ugly face'.[2] After another, Mme Wagner came back to the
Priory for lunch and went with the Leweses to Burne-Jones's
studio. George Eliot had written to him: 'She is, I think, a rare
person, worthy to see the best things.'[3] At the Dannreuthers' the
Leweses dined with the Wagners—'no one else present, until the
evening, when a small party assembled to hear Wagner read his
Parzival, which he did with great spirit and like a fine actor'.[4]

In the midst of all this dissipation they took a week-end with
Jowett at Oxford. At a dinner-party for sixteen the first night young
Adolphus G. C. Liddell, a barrister, grew restless during a long
after-dinner discussion between his host and Sir Charles Trevelyan
over Schliemann's excavation of the Homeric sites.

I was determined to have a talk with 'George Eliot', so taking advantage of the male hesitation in leaving the dining-room, I bolted
upstairs, not looking back till I had landed myself beside her. She has
a noble face of the equine type, with fine grey eyes, not large but deep-
set thoughtful and kind. She asked if I was a north countryman, saying
that my stature agreed with my being a Northumbrian, who were all
tall men. I felt flattered, but was afraid of showing my weakness before
such an analyst. She then asked for a specimen of the dialect, which I
gave her. The talk next passed to circuit, which she said must be interesting from the opportunity of hearing such a variety of cases, and seeing
so many types of humanity. I answered that there was too much same-

---

[1] Lady Gray to GSH, 28 Jan. 1934.
[2] *Mary Gladstone (Mrs. Drew). Her Diaries and Letters*, ed. Lucy Masterman
(2nd ed. [1930]), p. 124.
[3] *Letters*, VI. 368.   [4] GHL Diary, 17 May 1877.

ness about the cases, and then went on to tell her how from my habit
of sketching in Court I was struck with the constant reproduction of
similar types of face and figure. She said that the forms of Nature were
really few. I remarked how similarity of form was often accompanied
by similarity of voice, movement and character.

We then got on to the effect of a peculiarity of speech in conversation,
and the part it played in arresting the attention. She said that some men's
talk always seemed worth listening to, while others, who really talked
better, could obtain no hearing, and that one reason why Scotsmen's
talk often seemed more intellectual, was in a great measure due to the
effect of their dialect in arresting attention, giving Carlyle as an example.
She remembered a ludicrous effect in the conversation of the late Lord
Lytton, who was deaf, and who would go on murmuring for a time, and
then suddenly burst out for a sentence or two in a very loud key. The
English always dropped their voices at the end of a sentence, and were
much averse to any other form of talk than a *tête-à-tête*, and in illustration she pointed out all the various persons *tête-à-têting* around us.
Frenchmen had none of the English shyness, which did not arise from
superior mental endowments, but from a peculiar sensibility to outward
surroundings, which an Englishman had not. A Frenchman in conversation almost always reproduced in words the scene before him, or
remarked upon it, even to its most trivial details.

I continued that I had not met many good talkers, but thought
Professor Owen the best I had heard. She said he was a particularly
charming talker, and excelled greatly in narrative and description. We
talked a good deal about the Professor, and she asked if I was the son of
a Mrs. Liddell,[1] whom she remembered Owen mentioning as a beautiful
woman. This shows she must have a good memory, as it must have been
said a long time ago. In talking about the Professor, I remarked what a
good reader he was and how (illustrating what she had said a few
moments before), his Lancashire accent helped him. She said that Tennyson's reading was greatly improved by his Lincolnshire pronunciation,
which had the good effect of making his vowels very sonorous, the
reverse of which was the usual defect of English reading. I quoted
'mouthing out his hollow oes and aes', as to what Tennyson's own
notion of good reading was, which she seemed to think apposite.

She then spoke of the difference of Owen's son to his father. I said
he was a complete contrast. She said that often was the case, and was
going on to talk of the connection between parents and children, when
her husband came up with Mr. Spottiswoode, and I thought I ought to
retire. I felt that she had been very good-natured to talk so much to an
'ordinary mortal', and to look so kindly out of her grey eyes. Spottiswoode began to talk to her of a Frenchman who had solved theoretically the problem of turning up and down motion into circular, the
usual method in vogue being only an approximation to the theoretically

---

[1] Liddell's mother was born Frederica Elizabeth Lane-Fox.

perfect way. I could only hear now and then scraps of the talk. They got on to 'spiral vortices', and then 'imaginary geometry', after which I understood not one word. George Eliot said she supposed that this science consisted in a system of reasoning from abstractions still purer than the ordinary geometrical ones.[1]

Dinner the next night, again for sixteen, probably produced conversation of the same quality. On the Monday, Lewes smoked a cigar with Mark Pattison before they left for London.

While their servants were moving to Witley on 31 May 1877, the Leweses spent five days with the Sidgwicks at Cambridge. There, too, their stay was 'one uninterrupted excitement—guests at breakfast, lunch, and dinner', Lewes wrote.[2] Among those he mentions are Eustace and Arthur Balfour, James Stuart, R. C. Jebb, Michael Foster, C. V. Stanford, Lord Edmund Fitzmaurice, Coutts Trotter, B. H. Kennedy, J. Hughlings Jackson, F. W. H. Myers, and Sidney Colvin. They visited Girton and Newnham, went to Trinity Chapel on Sunday afternoon, and through the Fitzwilliam Museum before they left on Monday. One of the older students at Girton, Frances Müller, an active feminist, had invited George Eliot to come there to meet some of her friends. This caused a certain unpleasantness in the students' relations with the austere Mistress of Girton, Miss Bernard, who felt that such invitations should come from her rather than undergraduates. But it did not prevent George Eliot's visit.

At the Heights they found the usual annoyances. The furniture came three days later than it was promised; the water-pipes refused to work properly; the mattings all had to be relaid; 'our own bedroom', George Eliot wrote, 'looks rather as if we had been distrained for rent'.[3] The grocer called only once a fortnight. Johnny Cross was asked to arrange with the fishmonger at Waterloo Station to send them 'the fish of the day' on Wednesdays and Saturdays. But in the splendid June weather the lovely walks and drives they took every day, exploring the new neighbourhood, were enjoyed 'so much better than Society! (with a big S)'.[4] They intended to spend the summer like hermits, seeing no one—an obvious impossibility. Within a few days the Witley clergyman had called. Lady Holland and her family at the Pines, and Birket Foster, the artist, their neighbour on the other side, were cordial.

[1] A. G. C. Liddell, *Notes from the Life of an Ordinary Mortal* (1911), pp. 156–8.
[2] GHL Diary, 2 June 1877.
[3] *Letters*, VI. 400.   [4] Ibid. 386.

John Blackwood soon came down to spend the day and found George Eliot 'looking well and full of happiness'. He pronounced the view from the terrace at the Heights perhaps finer than that from Richmond Hill. 'I said something should be born here', he told Willie, 'and the answer was in the nature of assent.'[1] Tennyson wrote that he was coming to Aldworth in July and was hoping to see them.[2] The Henry Cromptons came from Churt to call. The Harrisons, who were staying at his family's home Sutton Place, north of Guildford, drove over for lunch. Another day they had the Congreves, who were visiting Mrs. Geddes at Guildford. There were visits by the Edmund Gurneys and the Allinghams. They saw Jowett several times, who was staying with the Hollands. Spencer, coming to spend the day, was driven to Hind Head. Elma Stuart and Alice Helps came down at different times for lunch. Susanna Lewes and her son Vivian came. Charles spent two weekends with them, though Gertrude could not travel so far; her third daughter Elinor was born 24 June.

The friend coming most frequently was their 'dear nephew' Johnny Cross, who made the journey from Weybridge cheerfully to see them. One day he 'brought an apparatus for *Lawn Tennis* and fixed it. Then initiated Polly at the game, and we played till we perspired freely.'[3] Thereafter, both the Leweses played quite regularly. They were in love with the Heights. The healthful exercise and quiet life were most beneficial. In spite of a few days of pain from kidney stone, Polly had grown well and strong during the last two months—'wonderfully well'.[4] When she left on 25 October, earlier than she wished because the workmen were to begin the alterations, she was 'conscious of more health and strength than I have known for several years'.[5]

Their reading at Witley included a few old favourites—*The Heart of Midlothian*, *The Legend of Montrose*, *Sir Charles Grandison*, and *Les Trois Mousquetaires*. Lewes's Diary also mentions a number of recent novels—Trollope's *The American Senator*, Reade's *A Woman Hater*, Turgenev's *Les Terres vierges*, Zola's *L'Assommoir*, and *The Pilot and His Wife* by the Norwegian novelist Jonas Lie— Cobbett's works, Tennyson's dramas and *The Idylls of the King*, Daudet, Sainte-Beuve, and Mme D'Agoult's *Mémoires* (probably suggested by the Wagners' visit). There is one bare reference to Edith Simcox's *Natural Law*. She was not invited to the Heights; no letter acknowledged the dedication.

[1] *Letters*, VI. 390. [2] Tennyson to GHL, 27 June 1877.
[3] GHL Diary, 28 Aug. 1877. [4] *Letters*, VI. 437. [5] *Letters*, VI. 419.

Though no new literary work by George Eliot was born during this peaceful summer at Witley, an old one was brought into print. Frederic Harrison, having told her about how Dr. Congreve used her poem 'O May I Join the Choir Invisible' at his New Year's Day service, wrote on 12 June 1877 to ask 'if you can give us anything further, either in prose or in verse, for public or for private use, by way of collect, hymn, or litany—something I mean to give form to our ideas of sympathy and confidence in Humanity?'

Indeed I have often longed that we could have your full estimate of the scheme of the Polity, now it is complete in its English form. I mean especially your judgment of a Religion of Humanity as a possible rallying point for mankind in the future. That you differ very much from the form which Comte has given it in such sharp lines, I know, or suppose that I know. But where you differ, wherein, how far; when you agree, how far—this is what we all want to know, those who accept Comte's ritual in different degrees, and those who reject it but converge to the general idea of Humanity, as the ultimate centre of life and of thought. Your readers are perpetually asking themselves the question—what is your real mind on this subject, and they answer it in different ways. Why, I keep asking myself, should you not quickly answer them, not by way of poetry, but by philosophy; and having asked myself the question so often, I now ask you—though I have no right to expect an answer.

There are some things that Art cannot do, and one is, to tell us what to believe; and there are many who will never be satisfied till they know what you have to say.[1]

George Eliot replied that to contribute to such a liturgy 'would hardly lie within my powers'. But Harrison's belief in her ability to serve as an organ of feelings 'which have not yet found their due expression' reminded her of 'A Symposium':

I wasted some time three years ago in writing (what I do not mean to print) a poetic dialogue embodying or rather shadowing very imperfectly the actual contest of ideas. Perhaps what you have written to me may promote and influence a different kind of presentation. At any rate, all the words of your letter will be borne in mind and will enter into my motives.[2]

This was not quite what Harrison wanted; he was hoping for 'a direct estimate of the main idea of the Religion of Humanity as a possible thing. I see the world running off upon the details of Comte's ritual, and the dominant principle is being forgotten by

---

[1] Brotherton Library, Leeds.   [2] *Letters*, VI. 388.

it, and overlaid by Positivists. And then, I ask, why should you so long abandon Religion for Art.'[1]

Harrison came to spend the day with them on 31 July. They discussed the question and his impending schism from Congreve, whose sacerdotal pretensions were growing unbearable. When George Eliot returned to the Priory, she got out the manuscript of 'A Symposium', which had grown from impressions of her talks with the young Trinity men during her first visit to Cambridge, renamed it 'A College Breakfast-Party', and sent it off to John Blackwood to have two proofs printed for her convenience in revision.[2] At her request Blackwood read the poem. She was not surprised when he declared himself somewhat 'puzzled' by it; it was clearly no sort of fare for *Maga*. Lewes undertook to arrange for its publication, eventually disposing of it for £250 to *Macmillan's Magazine*, where it appeared in July 1878. Macmillan had been trying to persuade her to write the life of Shakespeare for the new English Men of Letters series that John Morley was editing, but she wisely refused.

While the servants were reopening the Priory, the Leweses went again to visit the Bullock-Halls at Six Mile Bottom, where they again played tennis, when the rain permitted. In their own garden in London there was not room for the game. But their ever-thoughtful 'nephew' Johnny Cross sent them a badminton set. They tried it first out of doors; finding the wind too strong, they transferred the game, temporarily, to the drawing-room. There the Sunday afternoon receptions were soon under way again. On 7 November Edith Simcox called, tense with anxiety to learn how the passionate colophon to her *Natural Law* had affected her Madonna. She got nothing but teasing for her dislike of men. 'Clearly she has nothing to say to me about the book', Edith wrote in her Autobiography, 'and it is hardly for me to open the subject now.' But on a rainy Sunday ten days later, when, going early, she found the Leweses alone, George Eliot responded to the hint that she was perhaps dissatisfied with the book and, 'as by an effort of recollection', gave her opinion in detail: the book was 'perfectly reverent' in its treatment of religion; she used the words 'sound and wholesome'; she thought it 'likely to be useful', and so on; but again she made no reference to the dedication. Though there was nothing to flatter an author's vanity in

[1] F. Harrison to GE, 15 June 1877 (Brotherton Library, Leeds).
[2] One with a few corrections is in the Parrish Collection, Princeton.

these cool remarks, poor Edith's misery was lifted. Soon Frederick Locker and his daughter came in and then Myers. Edith withdrew and 'walked back through the pelting rain with inward sunshine'.[1]

Christmas of 1877 saw no cheerful interlude at Weybridge, for Mrs. Cross lay gravely ill with what proved to be the beginning of an incurable malady. Lewes impulsively proposed to Georgie that they celebrate Christmas with the Burne-Joneses, but Marian vetoed the plan: 'We are dull old persons, and your two sweet young ones ought . . . to have a group of young creatures to be joyful with.'[2] When the day came, she was laid up with a cold and they took their sober merry-making quietly at home. On Boxing Day, however, Charles and Gertrude brought all three of the grandchildren for lunch at the Priory. Elinor, the youngest, had been christened on 3 November at Hampstead. Besides Dr. Thomas Sadler, minister of the Rosslyn Unitarian Chapel, who performed the ceremony, the child's father and grandfather were the only men amidst George Eliot, Gertrude's mother, three sisters, and two other friends.

Another religious ceremony took them to Westminster Abbey for the marriage of Eleanor Locker to Tennyson's younger son Lionel. Henry VII's Chapel was crowded, Lewes wrote. 'Many of our friends and acquaintances there. The ceremony very touching and interesting.' One wonders whether his thoughts may not have turned back thirty-seven years to his own wedding at St. Margaret's, not a hundred yards away. As they were leaving the Abbey, Lewes 'saw a lady gazing very devoutly at Polly and then quietly as if unobserved stroke the back of her cloak and person. Du Maurier afterwards told us that Mrs. Kendall was in high spirits at having "touched George Eliot". Now the lady I saw was *not* Mrs. Kendall—so that there were two who had the same inspiration.'[3] Locker had not made it clear that they were invited to go into the Jerusalem Chamber for the reception and sign the book, as she would gladly have done, but he sent her a piece of the bridecake.

They saw Tennyson several times after the wedding. He came with Hallam to the Priory, Sunday, 31 March 1878, and invited Lewes to lunch on Tuesday, after which he smoked a cigar while Tennyson read him 'a new poem—very fine'. On 5 April Lewes met him at Lord Houghton's tea, and on the 8th he and Marian lunched at the Tennysons with Mrs. Vernon Lushington and

[1] Simcox Autobiography, 17 Nov. 1877.
[2] *Letters*, VI. 430.   [3] GHL Diary, 28 Feb. 1878.

James Knowles, the founder of the *Nineteenth Century*. On the 12th, after a musical party at the Grosvenor Gallery, they dined with the Tennysons to meet Lord Acton and Annie Thackeray with her young husband Richmond Ritchie. A large party, including the Cowper-Temples, Sir Garnet Wolseley, and Lord and Lady Monteagle, came in later to hear the poet read 'Boadicea', 'Maud', and 'The Revenge'. Mary Gladstone was there, not at all pleased with Mrs. Ritchie ('oh how affected she was') but happy to find Lord Acton, 'really drunk with delight over his dinner, seated next to George Eliot'.[1]

John Cross gave a dinner for Lewes at the Devonshire Club on 10 April, where he met Henry James, then settled in Bolton Street. James wrote of the evening: 'I sat next to Lewes, who is personally repulsive, but most clever and entertaining. He is rather too much of a professional *raconteur*—he told a lot of stories; but he recounts very well—chiefly in French.' As soon as they were introduced Lewes recalled James's queer first visit to the Priory in 1869, when Thornie lay writhing on the floor. Invited to come again, James went on 28 April. He described the visit in a letter to his brother William:

The Leweses were very urbane and friendly, and I think I shall have the right *dorénavant* to consider myself a Sunday *habitué*. The great G. E. herself is both sweet and superior, and has a delightful expression in her large, long, pale, equine face. I had my turn at sitting beside her and being conversed with in a low, but most harmonious tone; and bating a tendency to *aborder* only the highest themes, I have no fault to find with her.[2]

Lewes annoyed James by introducing him to Spencer as an American.

The Leweses attended many musical parties during this season. Mme Ignaz Moscheles, the widow of the composer, gave one on 29 March 1878, where Mary Gladstone, her opinion softened by closer acquaintance, observed them:

Found myself in a tiny room stuffed with musical celebrities and in the twinkling of an eye found myself on a sofa talking amicably with George Eliot, and very soon listening to Henschel's singing. . . . Meanwhile my neighbour, with her great strong face (a mixture of Savonarola and Dante), impressed me deeply with the gentleness and earnestness of her manner, both in speaking and listening. There is something a little like

---

[1] *Mary Gladstone*, pp. 136–7.
[2] *Letters of Henry James*, ed. P. Lubbock (2 vols., 1920), I. 61.

affectation sometimes, but I don't expect it's it. Mr. Lewes was rather obtrusively enthusiastic, I thought, and is a comic sight with his long disheveled hair.[1]

There were other music parties given by Leighton, Lady Claud Hamilton, the Pagets, the Lindsays, Lord Carnarvon, and one by Henschel himself.

At the concerts George Eliot and Lewes were a cynosure. On 16 February 1878 at St. James's Hall the Princess Christian of Schleswig-Holstein (the Princess Helena, Queen Victoria's fourth daughter) sent to say that she desired Lewes to be presented to her. He went to the royal box and talked briefly with her 'about Polly's works and the music'.[2] A month later she sent for him again. In this conversation he had a little contention with the Princess when she maintained that Santley sang German songs better than Henschel.[3] She did not ask to meet George Eliot as the Princess Louise had. Not to be outdone by her sister, the Queen's eldest daughter, the Princess Royal, the Crown Princess of Germany, had the Goschens invite the Leweses to a dinner they gave for her and the Crown Prince on 31 May. Lewes said that there were '22 at dinner and a number of swells and celebrities afterwards'. He lists Dean Stanley, the Bishop of Peterborough, the Lyon Playfairs, J. A. Froude, Trollope, A. W. Kinglake, Sir Garnet and Lady Wolseley, Lord and Lady Ripon, Lord Bridport, John Morley, Mrs. Ponsonby, and others. Lyon Playfair, who took Marian down to dinner, declared that she did not find out his name till the end. 'Then she became gushing, and said she had lost the evening, and asked me to go and see her often. However, we had spoken a good deal, and she was quite as clever and agreeable as I expected to find her from her novels.'[4] But, according to George Eliot, when Playfair was introduced, he claimed to have a common friend in Elma Stuart and made himself particularly agreeable.[5] He did not talk with Lewes, who had known him at Dr. Arnott's in the 1840s. Lewes's Diary reported:

Prince and Princess very gracious, and talked a great deal to Polly, reproaching her for not having let them know when we were in Berlin and both begging when they said 'goodbye' that the next time we came we would let them know. I told her about her 'English laxity in religion' —much to her amusement. She said she knew it. It was her friendship

---

[1] *Mary Gladstone*, pp. 134–5.   [2] GHL Diary, 16 Feb. 1878.
[3] GHL Diary, 16 Mar. 1878.
[4] T. Wemyss Reid, *Memoirs and Correspondence of Lyon Playfair* (1899), p. 276.
[5] *Letters*, VII. 39.

for Strauss. I sat next to Mrs. Ponsonby and Froude at dinner. Very
gay. Home at 12—knocked up.[1]

Social acceptance could hardly go further.

Buying furniture for the Heights, where the alterations were
finished, occupied a good deal of their last weeks in town. They
went to shops in Guildford as well as London, called at William
Morris's establishment to choose patterns and at Doulton's for
china. They went to auction sales. William Bell Scott describes
their call on him—the first time George Eliot had been in his house
—when they had just bought a billiard table, 'not, as Lewes explained in a doubtful accent, to play himself, but for guests on a
rainy day'. She was much interested in Scott's fine new house.
He and Lewes recalled complacently how far they had come from
those old days in the 1830s when they used to talk all night in his
little room up two stairs off Hampstead Road. Lewes 'is nearly
the only man among all my friends', Scott wrote, 'who has never
ceased to advance'.[2]

Their annual visit to Jowett at Balliol was less happy than
usual. It was the Whitsun holiday, and with the congestion at
the railway station they were two hours late and lost their portmanteau, which did not reach Oxford till 5 the next day.[3] There
were the usual dinners of big-wigs each evening. On Sunday,
Lewes called on the Pattisons in the morning and returned again
with Polly in the afternoon. Though Jowett urged them to stay
over for lunch on Monday, when the Empress Eugénie was coming,
they had had their fill of society and longed for quiet. Lewes was
suffering from agonizing cramps every night—a symptom of
serious illness.

At Witley on 21 June they settled into the Heights with relief.
Nothing had been spared to make it comfortable. The books
were soon arranged, the pictures hung, the new cottage for the
coachman approved. They strolled together in their wood, cutting
foxgloves, sometimes taking the new puppy along. They sat in the
arbour or summer-house, 'neatly matted and arranged', reading
The Times. They played a little tennis on the lawn. Their first guest
was Johnny Cross, who came to lunch on Sunday, 14 July. The
Congreves and Mrs. Geddes, whose husband had just returned to
India, came the following week for dinner.[4] But they were not

---

[1] GHL Diary, 31 May 1878.   [2] Autobiographical Notes, II. 247, 244.
[3] GHL Diary, 9 June 1878.   [4] GHL Diary. 23 July 1878.

seeking company. Polly was working every morning on *Theo-phrastus Such*, and Lewes, though he rallied his spirits to cheer her on when she read chapters to him, felt increasingly miserable with headache and serious irritation of the bowels. Cramps woke him before dawn. He took to rising as early as five o'clock to walk for relief, usually accompanied by his anxious Polly.

Edith Simcox was invited down for the day on 10 August—their 'first visitor', Lewes disingenuously told her. 'The only draw-back', she wrote in her Autobiography, 'is that he is unwell; his face made me rather unhappy by the looks of ill-health without a shade of ill-temper, which beautifies it in a melancholy kind of way.' Old Fanny Kemble had remarked cruelly to Henry James in London that Lewes looked as if 'he had been gnawed by the rats—and left'.[1] Edith

thought the country was very worthy of its happiness in harbouring her. She told me about Browning and his wife's Portuguese sonnets, and she said once more that she wished my letters could be printed in the same veiled way—'the Newest Héloïse'. . . . I am quite happy about her, con-tented to live, to strive, and if one's ambitions are to fail, still to strive for duty rather than success, to aim at the good and not be selfishly pained when one does not reach it. Only, for her sake, I should like to do somewhat that she might be glad to have inspired.[2]

Tom Trollope and his second wife—a sister of Ellen Ternan—came for two nights in August. After lunch they all 'went to Tennyson, who took us to the spring and then read two of his new poems'.[3] In the evening, the Du Mauriers, who had taken the Manor House for a month, came to dinner at the Heights; they sang together in the merry old way, and told stories till 11 o'clock. Even on his worst days Lewes always had a story to tell. The buoyancy of his spirits concealed the gravity of his illness from his closest friends. Cross recalled how one day at the Heights between bouts of pain he sang through 'the great portion of the tenor part in the *Barber of Seville*—George Eliot playing his accompani-ment, and both of them thoroughly enjoying the fun'.[4] But the intervals between pains were growing briefer. Charles and Gertrude sent little Blanche down with a nurse to visit her grand-parents at Witley, and came themselves for a week-end in Sep-tember. There was also occasional visiting with the neighbours—the Hollands, the Trevelyans, Birket Foster, and Edmund Evans,

[1] Leon Edel, *Henry James. The Conquest of London* (1962), p. 352.
[2] Simcox Autobiography, 11 Aug. 1878.
[3] GHL Diary, 22 Aug. 1878.
[4] Cross, III. 334.

the engraver and colour printer, who was married to Foster's niece. One day they drove Mr. and Mrs. Evans and their young friend Kate Greenaway to Dunsfold Mill and on the way home stopped at the Evanses to see Miss Greenaway's drawings.

In October the Leweses left the Heights for a few days to visit the Bullock-Halls at Six Mile Bottom. A number of Cambridge men were there—Munro and Sedley Taylor and Oscar Browning. But the great attraction this time was Turgenev. Lewes had known him on the Continent in student days, and Turgenev came to the Priory during his London visits. There was no literary man whose society Marian enjoyed so thoroughly and unrestrainedly. His conversation was delightful. She sat next him at the races at New-market[1] and heard him discuss the difference between Russian and English sport. At dinner, when Lewes proposed the health of Turgenev as 'the greatest living novelist' he parried the compliment by transferring it sincerely to George Eliot.[2] To Henry James's father, who wrote fulsomely about his son's admiration, Turgenev had modestly replied that he 'considered himself in a second or even third place, when compared with Dickens, George Eliot, or George Sand'.[3] Of these only George Eliot was still living.

The most frequent caller at the Heights was Mrs. Richard Greville, who lived near by and popped in without warning. She was a somewhat ridiculous person, 'crazy, stage-struck, scatter-brained, . . . on the whole the greatest fool I have ever known', Henry James said.[4] Lewes once got her to recite George Eliot's 'Armgart'. But her favourite piece was 'The Revenge', Tennyson's melodramatic ballad of the Armada. Mrs. Greville was the only other guest at Aldworth when Lewes went over to lunch with Tennyson (Polly was unwell) and read his yet-unfinished drama *Becket*, on which he wanted Lewes's professional opinion. Lewes had 'some serious doubts which I did not express, and some doubts which I did'[5]—suggestions which may have been useful when Henry Irving adapted the play to the stage. Once Mrs. Greville brought Sir Frederick Pollock and his wife to call at the Heights. On 19 October she came with a new novel called *The Europeans*, which its author, Henry James, had sent her, and on 1 November, a 'dreadful drenching afternoon', she arrived, again without

---

[1] GHL Diary, 22 Oct. 1878.
[2] Oscar Browning, *Life of George Eliot* (1890), p. 129.
[3] Leon Edel, *Henry James* (1962), p. 172.
[4] *Letters of Henry James*, I. 71.   [5] GHL Diary 12 Aug. 1878.

warning, accompanied by James himself. His visit was almost as devastating as the first one in 1869. Seeing 'our bland, benign, commiserating hostess beside the fire in a chill desert of a room where the master of the house guarded the opposite hearthstone', James felt that they liked to have us come 'mainly from a prevision of how they should more devoutly like it when we departed'. He could recall nothing George Eliot said except that she suffered from the cold weather. Since there was no preparation for tea, 'a conceivable feature of the hour', they soon took leave. Lewes accompanied them to the door. But as James was about to step into the carriage, Lewes signed him to wait. Going to the drawing-room, he returned with the two volumes of *The Europeans*, which he wanted to return to Mrs. Greville before leaving Witley. 'Ah, those books—take them away, please, away, away!' James fills several pages of *The Middle Years*[1] with impressions of the bruise this episode inflicted on his ego, already sore from his brother William's disappointment with the book. His assumption that the Leweses did not connect it with him and had not read it was wrong. They had. But they failed to realize James's projected vision of the occasion, in which George Eliot should recognize that he too was doing 'her sort of work'. For him 'to have caught our celebrities sitting in that queer bleak way wouldn't have bullied me in the least if it hadn't been the center of such a circle of gorgeous creation'—George Eliot's novels. Focused on his own feelings, James's mind failed to sense the tragic misery on that sad hearthstone.

Ten days later the Leweses left Witley, and while their servants opened the Priory, went to stay at the Gloucester Hotel in Brighton. There Emily Clarke came to dine with them, and they took her to the Chinese Museum in the Pavilion and looked into the Aquarium. Besides these mild pastimes and a call on the Peter Taylors, they did nothing but stroll on the Marine Parade. Lewes had been suffering for a week from what he thought to be piles. Sir James Paget, whom he consulted on returning to London, pronounced it, not piles, but 'a thickening of the mucous membrane'. A period of agony ensued. Paget, who came each day and surely foresaw the outcome, comforted Marian with his calm assurance that 'the actual trouble will soon be allayed'. On 20 November Lewes made the final entry in his Diary: 'Awoke very quiet. Paget came before breakfast. The storm has passed I think. Got up to lunch.' The next morning he wrote his last letter,

[1] *The Middle Years* (1917), pp. 80–4.

a note to John Blackwood to be enclosed with the manuscript of *Theophrastus Such*, which, he said, is 'the work of the last few months, and is *not* a story'. Soon his worst symptoms recurred, and Marian was writing to Barbara Bodichon, 'I have a deep sense of change within, and of a permanently closer companionship with death.'[1]

Each day Edith Simcox rang at the gate to inquire, and sent up little notes, which came down still in the maid's hand with word that 'Mr. Charles would write'. On 29 November Johnny Cross, summoned by a note from Marian, left his mother's death-bed to join Charles at his father's. Lewes talked about Polly's investments and asked them to give his cigars to Willie Cross, who was a great smoker. On the 30th Brett the maid told Edith, 'He is very ill—there are no hopes.' Edith wrote:

I could not leave the place, and walked up and down, and almost immediately a carriage like a doctor's drove up fast and two men got out. I hastened after them and they entered the gate; the other carriages followed, and the two with their four sleek horses stood a few paces back. The coachmen talked and laughed, cabs and coal carts and men and women on foot passed by as I stood behind the carriages, watching the gate down the fogbound road. Then, in about twenty minutes the two figures came in sight. I strode towards them and as they stood speaking together, I asked, Was there no hope? A tall man, probably Sir James Paget, answered kindly: 'None; he is dying—dying quickly.'[2]

At a quarter to six 'the dear little man'[3] was dead.

Harrison and Du Maurier heard the news the next afternoon, when they came for a Sunday call. Charles, who had stayed constantly at the Priory since before his father's death, announced it in letters to some of the closest friends, but the newspapers did not publish it till Tuesday, 3 December, the day before the funeral. At the ceremony in the chapel at Highgate Cemetery, Charles and Johnny Cross were the chief mourners. According to Frederick Locker only about a dozen people, mostly 'out-and-out rationalists', were there to hear Dr. Sadler half-apologize 'for suggesting the possible immortality of some of our souls'.[4] It is an ill-natured exaggeration. The Burne-Joneses and the Harrisons were there, and Spencer, who usually avoided funerals, went with Charles. Edith Simcox, stunned by the loss of her 'fellow-worshiper', did

---

[1] *Letters*, VII. 84.
[2] Simcox Autobiography, 30 Nov. 1878.
[3] Eleanor Cross used the phrase to Edith Simcox. Autobiography, 19 Jan. 1879.
[4] F. Locker-Lampson, *My Confidences*, p. 316.

not learn of it till the next day, like many of his old friends. G. J. Holyoake wrote to Spencer:

I never felt a pang before at being absent from a grave. Lewes's friendship for me made my life brighter in the evil days. I had an affection for him. I did not imagine he had died in London or I should have been an outside mourner. Lewes was my first friend in opinion. I wish you would tell Mrs. Lewes how sorry I am for her and how much I regarded him.[1]

We do not know whether Agnes Lewes went to the funeral. Marian did not go. For a week after his death she stayed in the room she had moved to during his last days, seeing no one but Charles and her maid Brett. To some of the neighbours Mrs. Dowling, the cook, spoke indiscreetly of her mistress's self-control 'breaking down entirely—her screams heard through the house'. The story reached the trembling ears of Edith, who 'gave a hint to Brett to give the other servants a hint not to be too communicative. ...I think she quite understood.'[2] All day long Charles was busy, writing letters or copying drafts that Marian wrote, telling her friends that 'it would be a very long time before it will be possible to her again to see even the nearest and dearest, the oldest, most intimate friends'.[3] She must be left, Charles said, 'to choose her own way and her own time of struggling back to life'.[2]

For a week Marian stayed in her room alone, struggling with the fact of 'the last parting'. For help she turned to the poets, reading *In Memoriam* over and over and copying long sections of it into her Diary, which opens with a line from *King John*: 'Here I and sorrow sit.'[4] In the first edition of Donne's *Poems*, which Barbara Bodichon had given her, she marked—among others—the lines

> For love, all love of other sights controules,
> And makes one little roome an every where.[5]

From Izaak Walton's 'Life of Donne' she copied a sentence on Mrs. Donne: 'She being now removed by death, a commensurable

[1] G. J. Holyoake to H. Spencer, 5 Dec. 1878 (Yale). Holyoake bought a place at the head of GHL's grave, where he was buried in 1906. His bearded bust watches benignly over his friends' graves.
[2] Simcox Autobiography, 13 Jan. 1879.
[3] CLL to Mrs. Mark Pattison, 10 Dec. 1878.
[4] *King John*, III. i. 73.
[5] John Donne, *Poems* (1633), p. 165.

grief took as full [a] possession of him as joy had done.' But the luxury of grief was an indulgence her intellect had long rejected. Many of her poems had dwelt on the acceptance of death. In a dialogue between 'Self and Life', written just before Lewes's last illness to be included in the Cabinet edition of her poems, she wrote

> Half man's truth must hidden lie
> If unlit by sorrow's eye.[1]

For years she had been declaring that the dead lived on 'In minds made better by their presence'.[2] Again her own works scourged her.

She came downstairs determined to finish the last volume of George's *Problems of Life and Mind* as He would have done. In her Diary she copied another passage from *King John*:

> Kneeling before this ruin of sweet life,
> And breathing to his breathless excellence
> The incense of a vow, a holy vow,
> Never to taste the pleasures of the world,
> Never to be infected with delight
> Nor conversant with ease and idleness
> Till—[3]

obviously, till she had published His book. Day after day she sat in the study reading through the mass of rough manuscript and notes with increasing anxiety lest it should be unworthy of Him. He was no longer there beside her to dispel her doubt with cheerful assurance. She had no one to lean upon. She could hardly bear to see even good, patient Charles, who was sorting the scores of letters that came to the Priory from all over the world and acknowledging those he could. When Georgie Burne-Jones and her two children called on New Year's Day bringing a pot of white lilies, she could not see them. Feeling wretchedly ill with 'la mort dans l'âme', she ploughed doggedly on through the manuscript, correcting, amplifying, abridging. Not till she had finished a complete second reading of it on 5 January did she first walk out into the frosty sunshine of the garden. Two days later she wrote what is apparently her first letter since Lewes's death:

Dearest Barbara

I bless you for all your goodness to me, but I am a bruised creature, and shrink even from the tenderest touch. As soon as I feel able to see anybody I will see *you*. Please give my love to Bessie and thank her for

---

[1] p. 274.   [2] p. 301.   [3] *King John*, IV. ii. 65–71.

me—I mean, for her sweet letter. It was a long while before I read any letters, but tell her I shall read hers again and again.

> Your loving but half dead
> Marian.[1]

Soon her thoughts inevitably turned to her own manuscript *Impressions of Theophrastus Such*. She was troubled about holding type for it so long, and suggested to John Blackwood on 13 January that if she were to read the proof, the sheets could be struck off and laid by for the future. 'Only two days before he died', Marian added, 'he asked me to let him see the specimen page (I had told him of it the morning it came—five days before), looked closely at it and said with a satisfied expression, "O how nice!"'[2] But till she had finished the *Problems* she could not look at the proofs. 'Head miserable and heart bruised', she kept at the uncongenial task, finishing Problem I on 22 January. Then after transcribing the stanzas from Section 13 of *In Memoriam*,

> Tears of a widower, when he sees
>   A late-lost form that sleep reveals,
>   And moves his doubtful arms, and feels
> Her place is empty, fall like these;
>
> Which weep a loss for ever new,
>   A void where heart on heart reposed;
>   And where warm hands have prest and closed,
> Silence, till I be silent too,

she read Lewes's Journals and 'lived with him all day'.

It was a bitter winter. Fierce blizzards blanketed the whole of Europe in snow. The water-pipes at the Priory froze and burst. Marian, who had always suffered from the cold, now felt only the cold at her heart. To Georgie Burne-Jones she wrote: 'Do not believe that your love is lost upon me, dear. . . . The world's winter is going, I hope, but my ever-lasting winter has set in. You know that, and will be patient with me.'[3] Johnny Cross, whose mother had died ten days after Lewes, was assiduous in inquiries. One January afternoon Edith Simcox

had rung the bell at the Priory and was looking vacantly eastward when I saw a tall reddish-bearded man coming up. I stared without moving, and when he had come within two or three paces he made some sign of recognition, and I knew it was Johnny. I had thought we should never meet so again. It was an intensely painful moment; there is

[1] *Letters*, VII. 93.   [2] Ibid. 93–4.   [3] Ibid. 100–1.

nothing much more pathetic than a look of set gravity on a habitually cheerful face. We went in together, and I asked him to question Brett. She had been out that morning in the garden for a little and felt the better. Johnny said 'Give her our love.' I listened and came away without speaking, but was faintly pleased at the strange chance that brought us there together, because I thought, servant-like, Brett would tell her of the fact, and I hoped it would please her to think of our meeting as friends.[1]

As they walked across Regent's Park together, he said that George Eliot's isolation might be the only possibility now, but it would be fatal if prolonged too far. He looked forward to the end of it, and wrote to tell her so. 'Dearest Nephew', Marian replied on 22 January. 'Some time, if I live, I shall be able to see you—perhaps sooner than any one else. But not yet. Life seems to get harder instead of easier.'[2]

A week later severe pain in the hip sent her to bed. Sir James Paget came several times and prescribed palliatives. The attacks continued intermittently for nearly a month. With headache, nausea, and acute pain her work on the manuscript was desultory. She fainted more and more 'under the anxiety of finding no satisfactory arrangement of parts in Problem III'.[3] Barbara Bodichon urged her to come for a visit in the country, but Marian felt unfit to undertake any sort of journey. 'I have never yet been outside the gate', she wrote. 'Even if I were otherwise able, I could not bear to go out of sight of the things he used and looked on.'[4]

Following up the word that she would see him 'some time', Cross pressed for a day. She replied:

Sunday. [30 January 1879]

Dearest Nephew

When I said 'some time' I meant still a distant time. I want to live a little while that I may do certain things for his sake. So I take care of my diet, and try to keep up my strength, and I work as much as I can to save my mind from imbecility. But that is all at present. I can go through anything that is mere business. But what used to be joy, is joy no longer, and what is pain is easier because he has not to bear it. . . .

You will not mention to anyone that I wrote about seeing you. I know your thoughtful care. But if you feel prompted to say anything, write it to me.

Always yours affectionately and gratefully

M. E. L.[5]

[1] Simcox Autobiography, 6 Jan. 1879.　　　[2] *Letters*, VII. 97.
[3] GE Diary, 11 Feb. 1879.　　[4] *Letters*, VII. 101.　　[5] *Letters*, VII. 99.

He wrote a week later, and Marian answered at once:

February 7. 79

Dearest Nephew

I do need your affection. Every sign of care for me from the beings I respect and love is a help to me. And I did *not* mean that I should prefer you or my dear nieces not to call. Only I fear it takes up valuable time to make this out of the way round.

In a week or two I think I shall want to see you. Sometimes even now I have a longing, but it is immediately counteracted by a fear. The perpetual mourner—the grief that can never be healed—is innocently enough felt to be wearisome by the rest of the world. And my sense of desolation increases. Each day seems a new beginning—a new acquaintance with grief.

I have written this just on receiving your kind answer. Love to them all at home.

Your affectionate Aunt
M. E. L.[1]

The next day she ordered the carriage for the first time and drove out along the Kilburn Road. The break was made. She was returning to life. In her Diary for Sunday, 23 February she wrote: 'Saw Johnnie for the first time. . . . Herbert Spencer called —did not see him.' The drives were repeated whenever she felt well enough. Going through Maida Vale into the Kilburn Road until she was beyond the ranks of hideous houses, she would get down and walk the lanes in the spring air 'in perfect privacy among the fields and budding hedgerows'.[2] Through this mild exercise she began to gather a little strength. But, she told Barbara, 'I am incredibly thin.'[3] In July she weighed 7 stone 5½ [103½] pounds.

Instead of waiting to solve Problem III, for which Lewes had collected a mass of chaotic notes, Marian resolved to issue Problem I 'The Study of Psychology', separately, leaving the other three for another volume. Trübner came to discuss the printing on 16 March; the book was soon in type with a notice that it was 'published separately in obedience to an implied wish of the Author, and has been printed from his manuscript with no other alterations than such as it is felt certain that he would have sanctioned'. With that duty done, Marian noted in her Diary on 20 March: 'Moved into our Bedroom' and, the next morning: 'Felt beaten with sadness.' She looked over George's photographs and prints, arranged his books and periodicals in the bookroom

---

[1] *Letters*, VII. 101–2. [2] *Letters*, VII. 131. [3] *Letters*, VII. 113.

closet, put away his microscope and other scientific apparatus. The 'things he used and looked on' were no longer in sight.

Now, turning to her own book, Marian quickly read the proof and returned it to Edinburgh. The manuscript bears no title. The one she had in mind was 'Characters and Characteristics, or Impressions of Theophrastus Such. Edited by George Eliot.'[1] She wrote to Blackwood: 'The first two words are truthfully descriptive, but they have been much used, and the book is sure to be called "Theophrastus Such"'. The eighteen essays it contains, all written at Witley during that last sad summer, are connected only through the fictitious narrator, a device she had first used in 1846–7 in her contributions to the Coventry *Herald*, 'Poetry and Prose from the Notebook of an Eccentric'. If *Theophrastus Such* proved effective, she said, 'the form would lend itself to a "Second Series", supposing I lived and kept my faculties'.[2] The opening essay, 'Looking Inward', sketches the character of Such: a bachelor with 'a permanent longing for approbation, sympathy, and love'. Friends of both sexes confide in him all their triumphs and griefs, but withdraw at the least sign of hearing *his* experiences; so he turns to the garrulousness of paper to tell his impressions posthumously. 'Looking Backward', describing his background as the son of a country parson in the Midlands, is a masterly summary of the social and political atmosphere of England through a century past. A number of essays are 'characters' in the Theophrastian sense: 'A Too-deferential Man'; 'A Man Surprised at His Own Originality'; a man of temper; a man whose mistakes are excused because he is 'so young'; a woman whose powerful imagination reports everything falsely; a man whose Liberal politics and interest in the public welfare come merely from concern for his cotton business; a 'half-breed' financier, who intended to use his wealth to reform society, but (not unlike Mr. Benzon, who died in 1873) grows 'richer even than he dreamed of being, has a little palace in London, and entertains with splendour the half-aristocratic, professional, and artistic society which he is proud to think select'.[3] Six of the remaining essays treat aspects of writing: originality; literary controversy; burlesque; plagiarism; 'too-ready' writing; and the vanity of 'small-authorship'. Others are conventional moral essays like that on 'Affectation and Conceit' in Marian's earliest notebook. One attacks society's tendency

---

[1] *Letters*, VII. 111, 119.   [2] *Letters*, VII. 126.
[3] 'A Half-Breed', *Impressions of Theophrastus Such* (1879), p. 167; Cabinet ed., p. 137.

to pity the disgrace of a notorious swindler because he was 'a thoroughly *moral* man'—that is, 'an excellent family man'; he kept no mistress and was 'so charitable around his place at Tiptop'.[1] 'Shadows of the Coming Race', whose title glances back to Bulwer Lytton's fantasy, considers a future when all work will be done by machines, which will supersede humanity. Samuel Butler was sure that George Eliot cribbed that chapter from his *Erewhon* (1872). Though there is no reference to Butler's book anywhere in her papers or Lewes's, the idea had probably been discussed with friends like Spencer while Lewes was writing the section on 'Animal Automatism' in *Problems*.[2] In the final essay 'The Modern Hep! Hep! Hep!', George Eliot returns to the problem of the Jews, basing their claim to Palestine partly on a dubious analogy with the Anglo-Saxons' conquest of the ancient Britons, and making so eloquent a plea for sympathy that the chapter was translated at once into German by Emil Lehmann and widely circulated.

On 2 January 1879 Marian received a letter from Dr. Michael Foster, volunteering to help her with any physiological points that might arise in her work on Lewes's manuscript. Lewes had visited him at Cambridge in 1875 and worked for a day or two in his laboratory; they met also at conferences and at the dinners of the Physiological Society. Lewes had held Foster in high esteem. His letter set her ruminating on the establishment of some sort of foundation to give young students the training that Lewes had had to get by his own (often-mistaken) efforts; in acknowledging Foster's letter she expressed her interest. Henry Sidgwick came to London to discuss the plan with her on 9 March, and Dr. Foster a few days later. They drew up the terms of the George Henry Lewes Studentship in Physiology and selected as trustees Francis Balfour, W. T. T. Dyer, Huxley, Pye Smith, and Sidgwick. Marian made over to them the sum of £5,000. C. S. Roy was the first student elected; Sir Charles Sherrington and many other distinguished physiologists have since described themselves in their books as 'George Henry Lewes Student'.

These arrangements could not be made while Marian remained in seclusion. Sir James Paget, Dr. Clark, and Brett, the principal link between Marian and the many callers at 21 North Bank, all urged her to see people. Necessity soon forced her out. There were

[1] 'Moral Swindlers', p. 283; Cabinet ed., p. 232.
[2] *Problems of Life and Mind*, III (1877), 307–409. See *The Correspondence of Samuel Butler with his Sister May*, ed. D. F. Howard (Berkeley, 1962), p. 86.

legal matters to attend to. Lewes's will, made in 1859, leaving his copyrights to his three sons and all his other property to 'Mary Ann Evans, spinster', was proved on 16 December 1878 by oath of Mary Ann Evans, spinster, the sole executrix, to whom administration was granted.[1] His estate was valued at under £2,000. But Marian's securities—more than £30,000—her bank account, and both her houses were in Lewes's name. Before funds could be conveyed for the Studentship, they had to be transferred to Mary Ann Evans, spinster; then by deed she took the added name of Lewes, and with another transfer got possession of her own property. Charles Lewes and John Cross were the witnesses in these transactions. Consulting with her about investments on 6 March, Johnny advised the sale of some of her American holdings. She drove the next day to the lawyer C. H. Warren in Bloomsbury Square for the proper documents and then on into the City to record the change of ownership at the office of the American Consul. Soon Johnny was back with a register of all Marian's investments, neatly written out. With his advice she authorized the sale of San Francisco Bank, Continental Gas, and other American securities to the amount of £5,000 to be invested in London and Northwestern debentures. Charles took her will to the lawyer's, where she went and signed it on 18 March. Johnny came in the same day bringing her the account of sales and purchase of stock. She now saw him frequently.

Once the break was made, she began to see her old friends one by one. Mrs. Congreve came on 19 March, Mrs. Burne-Jones on the 22nd, Spencer—and Johnny—on Sunday the 30th, Elma Stuart on 8 April. On the 12th, the day before Easter—without invitation—came Edith Simcox. Edith had been bleeding her heart out since Lewes's death; every few days she would inquire at the Priory, where Brett or Mrs. Dowling reported on their mistress, and she made longer journeys to pump Gertrude Lewes at Hampstead and Eleanor Cross at Weybridge. Little went on at 21 North Bank that Edith did not hear about. Sleet and rain, falling heavily, did not deter her.

Brett exclaimed at my being out such a day and said—Would I come in for a little? I said—O no! and then she, Perhaps I was too wet to

[1] The publication of GHL's will 'in which he leaves *all* his property to Marian Evans (*one* thousand pounds) positively disturbed my peace', Fanny Houghton wrote to Isaac Evans, 28 Jan. 1881. 'I could not sleep for thinking of it—for, of course, she was the source of the household expenses . . . his poor legacy was a farce; besides, her name ought not to have been mentioned. The sons should have been made executors.' (Mrs. Michael Womersley.)

stop now, but Mrs. Lewes had said she would like to see me the next time I came. . . . She went to ask Mrs. Lewes if I should come in; presently, the answer came, she would be glad to see me.

I came in with my veil down; she received me almost as usual, and but for the veil, which she made me take off, would have received me with a kiss of welcome.

They talked about the cold weather, the working men's clubs and coffee palaces; 'had I seen much of them?'

She had in her hands some of his Ms. and proof and said she would leave me for a moment to put it in a place of safety. I tried to force back the tears, and stooped as she came back to move the footstool out of her way. She called me a thoughtful child. . . . She said she had seen no one but men about the Studentship, Mrs. Congreve, and Elma. She spoke about the foundation and the volume she was bringing out, and when she found I knew of both, she touched my cheek almost playfully and asked me how I came to know so much. Before this I had risen to go, fearing to weary her, but instead she made me sit down on her footstool, and she took my hand in hers. I told her how I had met Charlie and that Eleanor Cross had been to see me and given me news of her from Johnny. She said the latter told her he had seen me—and he praised me for unselfishness—said I never seemed to think of myself.

She spoke, to my delight, freely and often of her husband, and said at first she had an intense repulsion from every one—it seemed wicked —but she could hardly bear even Charlie—who was as good as a son could be, but so different [i.e. from George]. . . . She spoke of the servants, of the comfort of human kindness without companionship when any nearer sympathy would be intolerable. Nothing could be further from morbid sensibility than her whole manner and words. She said she did not know how she could have lived if she had not had his Ms. and the Studentship to think about. . . . She had always identified herself with his Mss. so that he said she found more fault with them than she would if they had belonged to any one else, and now she had a dread of any light words that might be said in forgetfulness of the unfinished state of the work:—which was foolish, since he would not have cared—he was the only man who really delighted in adverse criticism, in a fair spirit, as a means of reaching truth. . . . I was inexpressibly thankful to find that one might speak freely of the dear one.[1]

On 23 April, when Anne Thackeray Ritchie called, she spoke of the recent death of her husband's friend William Kingdon Clifford, the brilliant young Professor of Mathematics at University College, London. Clifford, one of the men at Trinity College, Cambridge, who were influenced by the new theories of Spencer and Lewes, had reviewed the first volume of the *Problems*. He was a regular

[1] Simcox Autobiography, 12 Apr. 1879.

Sunday visitor at the Priory, and after his marriage to Lucy
Lane in 1875, they were both welcomed there. When he died of
tuberculosis on 3 March 1879, leaving his wife and two children
unprovided for, George Eliot promptly sent £10 to the fund his
friends collected for her, and wrote offering to go and see Lucy or
asking her to call at the Priory any week-day afternoon. Coming
on 25 April, Lucy found Mme Belloc with George Eliot.

Presently, when she had gone, Mrs. Lewes made a little sign that took
me from the arm-chair on her right to a grey cushioned footstool by her
side. She took off my hat, and so we sat, she talking and I listening.
Now and then she put her wonderful hands on my hair, they sent a
thrill through me—the memory does: even yet.[1]

Mrs. Clifford returned several times that spring. Once George
Eliot talked about Swinburne. She 'considered *Bothwell* the finest
of his long poems, and its second act a wonderful thing'. Speaking
of his prose, she alluded to his attack on her in his *Note on
Charlotte Brontë* (1877). This performance, written deliberately
'to undermine the reputation of George Eliot' with such vulgar
invective as calling her 'an Amazon thrown sprawling over the
crupper of her spavined and spur-galled Pegasus', dismayed even
his warmest friends.[2] It was certainly one of the criticisms that
Lewes kept from her. But after his death she had obviously read it;
speaking of it to Mrs. Clifford, she became—though she never
raised the low tone of her voice—almost vehement. 'He suggested',
she exclaimed, and angrily doubled the fist that rested on her knee,
'that I'd taken some things in *The Mill on the Floss* from a story
by Mrs. Gaskell called *The Children of the Moor*'—that is, *The
Moorland Cottage*, which George Eliot had never seen.[3]

Herbert Spencer, a zealous controversialist in his own affairs,
showed little sympathy for hers when he called on 20 April,
'asking advice about his Autobiography'. Lewes's nephew Vivian
came the following day, asking for £100 'to save him from reducing
his capital'. She gave him £50 on the spot, but he returned the
cheque the next morning with a note 'confessing his error'. In
the same post came a letter from Mme Belloc, 'asking me to lend
her £500'. Marian could not cope with demands like these. George

---

[1] Lucy Clifford 'A Remembrance of George Eliot', *Nineteenth Century*, 74
(July 1913), 116.
[2] E. Gosse, *Life of Swinburne*, Bonchurch ed. (1927), p. 215.
[3] Cf. Yvonne ffrench's assertion that Maggie Browne 'was the direct begetter
of Maggie Tulliver, and George Eliot . . . made no attempt to disguise the fact
of her debt to Mrs. Gaskell'. *From Jane Austen to Joseph Conrad*, ed. R. C
Rathburn and M. Steinmann, Jr. (Minneapolis, 1958), p. 136.

had always handled them for her. She told Charles about Vivian, but dared not speak to him about Mme Belloc. She sent off a note to John Cross at his office beginning: 'Dearest N., I am in dreadful need of your counsel. Pray come to me when you can—morning, afternoon, or evening. I shall dismiss anyone else.' She signed it 'Your much worried Aunt'. That very evening Johnny came. She wrote a note to Mme Belloc declining.

From this time forward Marian saw Johnny constantly. She needed much more than advice about business matters. Most of all she needed the sympathy of one man who shared her feelings and interests. Merely to keep her mind from her sorrow, she had begun in April to reread the *Iliad*. Johnny, in a similar mood since his mother's death, had begun—though he knew little Italian— to read Dante's *Inferno* with the help of Carlyle's translation. When he told Marian, she exclaimed:

'Oh I must read that with you.' And so it was [Cross wrote]. In the following twelve months we read through the *Inferno* and the *Purgatorio* together—not in a *dilettante* way, but with minute and careful examination of the construction of every sentence. The prodigious stimulus of such a teacher (*cotanto maestro*) made the reading a real labour of love. . . . The divine poet took us into a new world. It was a renovation of life.[1]

Since the death of Herbert Lewes his widow Eliza kept up her correspondence with his family, who contributed at least £200 a year for her support. They thought she should keep her children Marian and George in Natal until they were about twelve years old, when they would come to England for education. As soon as the news of Lewes's death reached her, Eliza wrote to George Eliot, and before any reply could reach her, sent another letter announcing that she and the children had embarked for England on a sailing vessel. They arrived in London on 28 April. Charles took them to stay with him in Hampstead; the next day George Eliot drove there to meet them and brought them back to the Priory for lunch. It was pleasant to find that the children, if uncivilized, were quite beautiful. Marian took her first shopping trip to buy toys for them. But she enjoyed Charlie's children much more than the little 'Africans'. When Mrs. Clifford came to call one day,

the maid-servant let me in with a queer little smile on her face that I understood on entering the room, for there was George Eliot with a ring of chairs round her, just as on the Sunday afternoons of old; but

[1] Cross, III. 359.

instead of philosophers, poets, and other Victorian giants sitting on them, there were dolls; and through an open window—it was early springtime—came the sound of merry voices.

'Charles's children are in the garden,' she explained, smiling, but with a sad little shake of her head, 'they've brought their children to see me', nodding to the dolls.[1]

Eliza was disappointed with her famous new-found family. She had fancied that she would be asked to live at the Priory, and George Eliot had to send 'a painful letter' at once to set her right.[2] Six-year-old Marian went every day to kindergarten with her well-brought-up little cousins, while her mother reconciled herself as best she could 'to our non-colonial inferiority'. Eliza begins 'to think better of the Kafirs', Charles wrote to the Mutter, 'because she finds our common men so much ruder!'[3] George Eliot sent monthly cheques for Eliza's allowance, which were never enough to satisfy her; she had some dim notion of borrowing money on the strength of her family connection. 'Don't take a tone of dissuasion about her going back to Natal or remaining', George Eliot advised Charlie.[4]

Marian had delayed her departure for Witley until the Africans should have arrived. During her last week or two in town she drove several times to Highgate. A plain granite slab now covered the grave, inscribed:

GEORGE HENRY LEWES.

BORN 18ᵀᴴ APRIL 1817.

DIED 30ᵀᴴ NOVEMBER 1878.

Marian saw the gardener and ordered ivy and jessamine planted about the stone. On 16 May a cryptic entry in her Diary, 'Crisis', is followed by another visit to the cemetery. In addition to Dante, she was reading George's *Life of Goethe* 'with great admiration and delight'. *Impressions of Theophrastus Such* and *The Study of Psychology* both came to her on 19 May. She had added a few touches to Lewes's work. Where his manuscript in the section on remorse read: 'He forever sees the Eumenides in pursuit', Marian substituted: 'Wordsworth has depicted a remorse of this kind'— and quoted five good lines from *The Excursion*.[5]

[1] *Nineteenth Century*, 74 (July 1913), 116.
[2] GE Diary, 29 Apr. 1879.
[3] *Letters*, VII. 169–70.
[4] *Letters*, VII. 185.
[5] *Problems*, IV (1879), 150. (MS.: Yale); *The Excursion*, III. 850–5.

She went down to Witley on 22 May, a lovely, mild day. Though we know she saw Johnny often there, her Diary rarely mentions his name. She notes that she 'Touched the piano for the first time' on 27 May, with the ominous allusion to Lewes the next day: '*His presence came again*',—perhaps drawn by the familiar strains. Cross's note says: 'At the end of May I induced her to play on the piano at Witley for the first time; and she played regularly after that whenever I was there, which was generally once or twice a-week, as I was living at Weybridge, within easy distance.'[1] As the dove flies it is a good sixteen miles from Weybridge to Witley, but railway service was incomparably better in those days. He came on 2 June bringing his sister Mary and his nephew 'Alky' Hall, now nine years old. But most of his visits were private and unrecorded. To John Blackwood, who had sent her a copy of *The Ethics of George Eliot*, a little book by John Crombie Brown, for many years proof-reader at 45 George Street, Marian wrote that she 'had only cut a very little way into the volume when a friend came and carried it off'.[2] The same day she wrote to Georgie Burne-Jones that no one is 'permanently here except my servants, but Sir James Paget has been down to see me, I have a very comfortable country practitioner to watch over me from day to day, and there is a devoted friend who is backwards and forwards continually to see that I lack nothing'.[3] When the time came for Charlie's holiday, she assured him that 'any business at the Bank or with Mr. Warren, Mr. Cross will easily attend to, and he will order anything for me from town'.[4]

Paget had prescribed a pint of champagne for her every day. In a new *solitude à deux* in the summer house at Witley she and Johnny studied the *Divine Comedy*. With her soft, low voice, *soave e piane*, Marian read him those wonderful words,

> Nessun maggior dolore,
> Che ricordarsi del tempo felice
> Nella miseria.[5]

In August there came a day when in that book they read no more. Johnny declared that he wanted to be more than a friend to Marian. She probably dismissed it as impossible. After the laconic entry in her Diary for 21 August, 'Decisive conversation' (which obviously has no relation to 'Balance at Banker's £718' that follows), the few references to Johnny are more formal. Eleanor

---

[1] Cross, III. 360. [2] *Letters*, VII. 173. [3] *Letters*, VII. 174.
[4] *Letters*, VII. 185. [5] *Inferno*, V. 120–2.

Cross 'and her *brother*' came to call; when Barbara Bodichon stayed at the Heights for some days, '*Mr. Cross* came to dinner with us'; and the 'Tears, tears', that follow are hardly accounted for by Barbara's departure. On 8 October we find, 'Joy came in the evening'. Is Joy a unique abbreviation for Johnny or a term of endearment? The next entry is also equivocal: 'Choice of Hercules.' Was she reading in Xenophon the story of Hercules's decision between Pleasure and Virtue? Or was she making a similar choice of her own? Alone all day Sunday, 12 October, she studied Hebrew and Plato's *Republic*. But on the 14th, when reading the *Purgatorio*, she was surely not alone. That morning she wrote to Elma Stuart:

I am learning to encourage the hopefulness (for my friends) of which my Husband always set me the example. He never was tempted to fore-cast the fashion of uncertain ills, and liked to keep in mind that the year brings in its hand much unexpected good as well as ill to us mortals. ... My health is wonderfully better, and, by dint of being better taken note of *medically*, I am really stronger than I was eighteen months ago.[1]

This mild optimism scarcely prepares us for the revelation of her letter to Johnny two days later, written like all the others on mourn-ing paper with black border a quarter of an inch wide:

The Heights, Witley
Nr. Godalming
Thursday

Best loved and loving one—the sun it shines so cold, so cold, when there are no eyes to look love on me. I cannot bear to sadden one moment when we are together, but wenn Du bist nicht da I have often a bad time. It *is* a solemn time, dearest. And why should I complain if it is a painful time? What I call my pain is almost a joy seen in the wide array of the world's cruel suffering. Thou seest I am grumbling today—got a chill yesterday and have a headache. All which, as a wise doctor would say, is not of the least consequence, my dear Madam.

Through everything else, dear tender one, there is the blessing of trusting in thy goodness. Thou dost not know anything of verbs in Hiphil and Hophal or the history of metaphysics or the position of Kepler in science, but thou knowest best things of another sort, such as belong to the manly heart—secrets of lovingness and rectitude. O I am flattering. Consider what thou wast a little time ago in panta-loons and back hair.

Triumph over me. After all, I have *not* the second copy of the deed. What I took for it was only Foster's original draft and my copy of it. The article [on Lewes] by Sully in the New Quarterly is very well done.

[1] *Letters*, VII. 210–11.

I shall think of thee this afternoon getting health at Lawn Tennis, and I shall reckon on having a letter by tomorrow's post.

Why should I compliment myself at the end of my letter and say that I am faithful, loving, more anxious for thy life than mine? I will run no risks of being 'inexact'—so I will only say 'varium et mutabile semper' but at this particular moment thy tender

Beatrice.[1]

She was not fitted to stand alone.

When the manuscript of *Theophrastus* came to her from Edinburgh, richly bound in red morocco, she put it on the shelf beside the others without any dedicatory inscription such as the rest all bear. John Blackwood had undertaken the arrangements for foreign rights to the book, which George had always done for her. About the time it was published, Blackwood suffered a heart attack. Though he rallied enough to go to St. Andrews for the summer, he could no longer play golf. His charming letters to George Eliot continued, however, bringing her news of the gratifying success of *Theophrastus*, of which over 6,000 copies were sold in the first four months, and over 15,000 within two years. As he had done with *Adam Bede*, Blackwood generously increased her share of the profits. At the end of September 1879 he had another attack. Marian wrote:

I do not like to think that you are scant of breath in the clear sunshine. I am melancholy enough under it, but my health is better, and I try to get along from day to day without carrying about a sorrowful face I am sure Mrs. Blackwood is anxious about you, and when you say that you are not so well, I always think of her. Be a good, good patient, and cherish your life wisely for her sake.[2]

She wrote to him again on 28 October. But before the letter arrived, he was sinking rapidly; he died the 29th. 'I wish so much I could have given him your loving message', Willie wrote. 'About the last business talk I had with him he spoke much of you.'[3] For Marian it was the end of an epoch. 'He will be a heavy loss to me', she told Charles Lewes. 'He has been bound up with what I most cared for in my life for more than twenty years and his good qualities have made many things easy to me that without him would often have been difficult.'[4] She had lost another of those she had leaned upon.

---

[1] *Letters*, VII. 211–12.   [2] *Letters*, VII. 206–7.
[3] *Letters*, VII. 220.   [4] *Letters*, VII. 217.

PLATE XIII

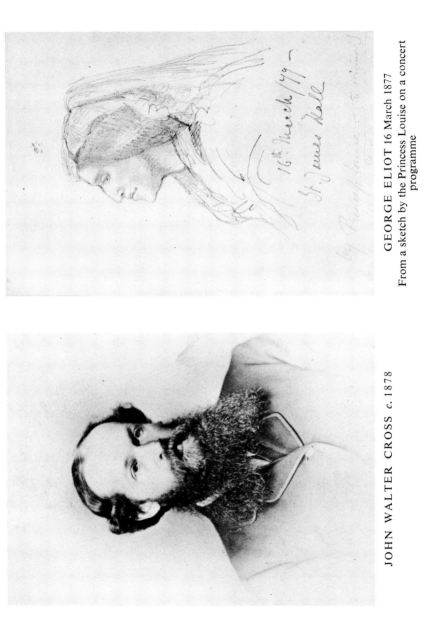

GEORGE ELIOT 16 March 1877
From a sketch by the Princess Louise on a concert
programme

JOHN WALTER CROSS c. 1878

While the servants opened the Priory, Marian spent a night at Weybridge, and on 1 November she was at home again in the familiar rooms. There she and Johnny could see each other almost every evening. 'Besides Dante', he wrote, 'we read at this time a great many of Sainte-Beuve's *Causeries*, and much of Chaucer, Shakspeare, and Wordsworth.'[1] An enlarged photograph of George looked calmly down at them above the fire-place in the study, where she had hung it before going to Witley. To Elma Stuart, who (in Italy for the winter) was busying herself about getting a bust of Lewes made, Marian wrote:

Any portrait or bust of Him that others considered good I should be glad to have placed in any public institution. But for *myself* I would rather have neither portrait nor bust. My inward representation even of comparatively indifferent faces is so vivid as to make portraits of them unsatisfactory to me. And I am bitterly repenting now that I was led into buying Mayall's enlarged copy of the photograph you mention. It is smoothed down and altered, and each time I look at it I feel its *un*likeness more. *Himself as he was* is what I see inwardly, and I am afraid of outward images lest they should corrupt the inward. It is painful to me to write this after all the generous effort you have given to the subject, but it would be a sort of treachery not to tell you that it would be repugnant to me to have the bust and that I could not *myself* present it to any public institution. Perhaps you will think this an almost blameworthy strangeness in me. But it is unalterable.[2]

When she went to Highgate, Marian was disappointed with the ivy and the position of the grave. She drove more often 'in the Kilburn Road and walked up the old lane, ruminating in the sweet air. A lovely autumnal day.'[3] Her sixtieth birthday, 22 November, was passed without comment, even in a letter to Sara Hennell, which ended with the melancholy reflection: 'People are very good to me, and I am exceptionally blessed in many ways, but more blessed are the dead who rest from their labours, and have not to dread a barren useless survival.' Edith Simcox, who was in the drawing-room the next day when Johnny arrived, wrote: 'I could have kissed him, for he kissed her hand when he came in.'[4] On 25 November Marian recorded 'Another turning point.' She went again to the cemetery on the 28th; on the 29th she wrote:

Reckoning by the days of the week, it was this day last year my loneliness began. I spent the day in my room where I passed through the

[1] Cross, III. 360.   [2] *Letters*, VII. 233.
[3] GE Diary, 7 Nov. 1879.   [4] Simcox Autobiography, 23 Nov. 1879.

first three months. I read his letters, and packed them together, to be buried with me. Perhaps that will happen before next November.

Mrs. Hans Sotheby called,[1] bringing her the text of Emily Brontë's poem; into the Diary Marian copied all eight stanzas:

> Cold in the earth—and the deep snow piled above thee,
>   Far, far removed, cold in the dreary grave!
> Have I forgot, my only love, to love thee,
>   Severed at last by Time's all severing wave?
>
>   .   .   .   .
>
> Cold in the earth—and fifteen wild Decembers
>   From those brown hills have melted into Spring.
> Faithful indeed is the spirit that remembers
>   After such years of change and suffering!
>
> Sweet love of youth, forgive, if I forget thee
>   While the world's tide is bearing me along;
> Other desires and other hopes beset me,
>   Hopes which obscure but cannot do thee wrong!

Friends called freely now—Spencer (to say good-bye before going to Egypt), the Burne-Joneses, Mrs. Congreve, Edith Simcox, Pigott, the Harrisons, William Blackwood, Leslie Stephen, the Darwins, Jowett, Frederick Locker with Mrs. Alfred Tennyson, Albert Druce with Anna. Christmas Day Marian spent alone, finishing at noon a letter on mourning paper to Johnny, who went for the holiday with his sister Emily Otter at Wragby, Lincolnshire.

December 24. 79

Bester Mann!

I received the card you kindly posted for me at the Station—your kindness was the chief impression I got from its hieroglyphics. I imagined Mary and you dining cozily after your journey and having a glorious walk in the sunshine today.

My time has been well filled. The grandchildren came with their mamma to lunch and I managed to amuse them till four. Then came Dr. Congreve and Lady Strangford, and yesterday I had Mr. Sully and Burne Jones—the last bringing me beautiful photographs which I may keep as long as I like, so your imagination may be enlarged with them whenever you feel inclined for self-culture, sweetness and light.

Tomorrow I shall be alone all day smelling the servants' goose and

----

[1] GE Diary, 18 Dec. 1879. Her copy of the poem is at Yale.

hoping that a fraction of this world's inhabitants are enjoying themselves.

More news follows, of Elma Stuart's gout and Lady Strangford's efforts for the Bulgarians.

Charles is coming to dine with me on Monday, but I suppose that I shall hardly have any company before then, except a stray person glad to escape from 'the bosom of his (or her) family'. I am quite contented, being out of pain and not (that I know of) annoying anybody.

If you return to town in time to dine with me on Tuesday, will you do me that honour? Or perhaps you will prefer Wednesday?

Give my love to any creature who wants that small alms and believe me to remain

Your obliged ex-shareholder of A and C Gaslight and Coke.[1]

Christmasday. It is now mid-day and I am still owing all my light to candles. The fog is dense and one thinks of cab accidents. You are well off to be out of London.[2]

On Boxing Day Edith Simcox found Marian alone, cutting a new book. She forgot at first to return Edith's kiss. She spoke of Lady Strangford and her Bulgarians, whom Marian thought less good than the Turks. She defended Disraeli vigorously—was 'disgusted with the venom of the Liberal speeches from Gladstone downwards'; Dizzy was ambitious and no fool, 'and so he must care for a place in history, and how could he expect to win that by doing harm?' Even Louis Napoleon, whom she used to hate, Marian now defended; he had done 'one bad action as a means, and then meant to do good ones'. When Edith's hyperbolic devotion, 'lapsed into some of the fond folly which always provokes her', Marian checked it and said

she did not like for me to call her 'Mother'. . . . she knew it was her fault, she had begun, she was apt to be rash and commit herself in one mood to what was irksome to her in another. Not with her own mother, but her associations otherwise with the name were as of a task, and it was a fact that her feeling for me was *not* at all a mother's—any other name she didn't mind; she had much more 'respect and admiration' for me now than when she knew me first, but etc.—she hoped I was not hurt.[3]

Edith sat up late writing 'a short reassurance' that she was not.

---

[1] Cross had just sold her shares in this company, which had been paying her £132 a year.
[2] *Letters*, VII. 234–5.   [3] Simcox Autobiography, 26 Dec. 1879.

Jowett sent a charming New Year's letter, urging George Eliot to go on writing; 'you must not throw this precious trust away'.[1] But even such pleasant correspondence Marian was finding a heavy burden. She now had to read scores of letters—which George would have disposed of without even showing her— business letters, mad letters signed 'Dolores' or enclosing inter- minable 'Revelations', appeals for good causes—saving St. Mark's, or spelling reform—'affectionate letters from strangers'. On Sunday afternoons, when visitors were again filling the draw- ing-room, she missed George even more, though the faithful Charles helped in his quiet, practical way, and Johnny was often there. Trübner one day introduced the American writer Bret Harte, recently appointed Consul at Glasgow, who wrote:

I was very pleasantly disappointed in her appearance, having heard so much of the plainness of her features. And I found them only strong, intellectual, and *noble*—indeed, I have seldom seen a grander face! I have read somewhere that she looked like a horse—a great mistake, as, although her face is long and narrow, it is only as Dante's was. It expresses elevation of thought, kindness, power and *humour*. . . . Mrs. Lewes's eyes are grey and sympathetic, but neither large nor beautiful. Her face lights up when she smiles and shows her large white teeth, and all thought of heaviness vanishes. She reminds you continually of a man—a bright, gentle, lovable, philosophical man— without being a bit *masculine*. . . . She said many fine things to me about my work, and asked me to come again to see her, which was a better compliment, as she has since Lewes's death received no one.[2]

He returned several times, once bringing her an inscribed copy of his latest book, *The Twins of Table Mountain*.

There were no concerts or music parties for Marian that season. But the piano at the Priory was kept tuned, and she played regularly for Johnny. She went out to exhibitions—to the Old Masters, the South Kensington Museum, the Grosvenor Gallery, the British Museum, and to Dulwich—With whom? Edith Simcox wondered, noting ruefully, 'she has a spring of vitality within which makes her winter less barren than my prime'.[3] From a long week-end at Weybridge, Marian came back on Tuesday, 30 March to preside at Maud Lewes's sixth birthday party. The 'Africans' had emi- grated as far as Brighton, to everyone's relief, and did not have to be invited to the luncheon at the Priory.

---

[1] B. Jowett to GE, 30 Dec. 1879 (Brotherton Library, Leeds).
[2] *Letters of Bret Harte*, ed. G. B. Harte (Boston, 1926), p. 168.
[3] Simcox Autobiography, 1 Feb. 1880.

Edith had perhaps her most revealing interview with George Eliot on 9 March 1880:

I got there a little before 5; she had just come in from her drive and came down after a few minutes. She was looking well.

Soon Mrs. E. R. Lankester and her daughter, who lived close by in North Bank, were announced; Marian had invited them for any afternoon. The conversation turned on whether the approaching marriage of a certain Miss Bevington could prove consoling, or whether it was too late, and Marian remarked that Edith considered such consolation 'a gambling speculation'. When the Lankesters left, Marian asked Edith to wait a little longer. Reopening the conversation, Edith said it was hard that after seven years she had not made clear what she meant by 'a gambling speculation'. Marian

moved to a low chair opposite the fire to warm her feet and I ventured to kneel by her side. She was a little tired by the discussion and said I had taken it up too seriously, she only spoke in play. I said it was ungrateful to complain of one thing she had said when all the rest had been full of consolation. She answered, Nay she had given up all thought of consoling me. I kissed her again and again and murmured broken words of love. She bade me not exaggerate. I said I didn't—nor could, and then scolded her for not being satisfied with letting me love her as I did—as in present reality—and proposing instead that I should save my love for some imaginary he. She said—expressly what she has often before implied to my distress—that the love of men and women for each other must always be more and better than any other and bade me not wish to be wiser than 'God who made me'—in pious phrase.

I hung over her caressingly and she bade me not think too much of her; she knew all her own frailty and if I went on, she would have to confess some of it to me. Then she said—perhaps it would shock me —she had never all her life cared very much for women—it must seem monstrous to me. I said I had always known it. She went on to say, what I also knew, that she cared for the womanly ideal, sympathised with women and liked for them to come to her in their troubles, but while feeling near to them in one way, she felt far off in another; the friendship and intimacy of men was more to her.

Then she tried to add what I had already imagined in explanation, that when she was young, girls and women seemed to look on her as somehow 'uncanny' while men were always kind. I kissed her again, and said I did not mind—if she did not mind having holes kissed in her cheek. She said I gave her a very beautiful affection.—and then again she called me a silly child, and I asked if she would never say anything kind to me. I asked her to kiss me. Let a trembling lover tell of the intense consciousness of the first deliberate touch of the dear one's lips. I returned the kiss to the lips that gave it and started to go—she waved me a farewell.[1]

Sir James Paget called on 9 April at Marian's invitation and had a long talk with her. She told him that for the third time John Cross had asked her to marry him; she may have spoken of the disparity in age (Johnny had turned forty on 12 March 1880), of her precarious health, of the effect on her 'influence'. Paget discounted all these objections. He probably mentioned the example of Annie Thackeray, who in 1877 married Richmond Ritchie, hardly more than an undergraduate, eighteen years younger than she. On the day of their marriage Marian had written:

I saw him at Cambridge and felt that the nearly 20 years' difference between them was bridged hopefully by his solidity and gravity. This is one of several instances that I have known of lately, showing that young men with even brilliant advantages will often choose as their life's companion a woman whose attractions are wholly of the spiritual order.[2]

Paget knew Marian thoroughly. On his advice she told Johnny when he came that evening that she would marry him. Her Diary says simply, 'My marriage decided.'

There was no time to be lost. The next morning they went to see 4 Cheyne Walk, a fine old house overlooking the river, where they would live except for summers at the Heights. A month was all too short for getting clothes made. Marian had long since abandoned her widow's cap, the bill for which (7s. 6d.) Edith's bird-like eye saw lying open on the chimney-piece two weeks after Lewes's death. With the easy malice of the young and beautiful, Mrs. Lionel Tennyson afterwards declared that 'George Eliot had been seen at all the fashionable milliners and dressmakers in London, choosing her trousseau. Whatever money and taste could do to make her look not too unsuitable a bride for a man of forty had been done.'[3] The Cross clan, who were genuinely fond of her, rallied loyally, and her 'dear nieces' assured their new 'sister' of affection. 'You can hardly think how sweet the name Sister is to me, that I have not been called by for so many, many years',

[1] Simcox Autobiography, 9 Mar. 1880.
[2] *Letters*, VI. 398.
[3] Lady Jebb, *With Dearest Love to All* (1960), p. 163.

Marian wrote. 'Yet I quail a little in facing what has to be gone through—the hurting of many whom I care for.'[1]

Did her mind turn back to that earlier day when she quailed at telling Sara and Cara that she was going to live with George? She breathed no word of her plans to Maria Congreve, who lunched with her as usual. Calling on Elma Stuart, she denied any intention of rejection in asking her 'to serve me only through serving others'. But she inquired 'whether your love and trust in me will suffice to satisfy you that, when I act in a way which is thoroughly unexpected there are reasons which justify my action, though the reasons may not be evident to you?'[2] A similar vague preparation was given to Mrs. Burne-Jones, on whom she called on 23 April 1880.

She came to say good-bye before going abroad, and after first sitting with Edward in the studio came down and talked with me. Her manner was even gentler and more affectionate than usual, and she looked so unfit to do battle with daily life, that in spite of all her power a protecting feeling towards her rose in my heart. She seemed loth to go, and as if there was something that she would have said, yet did not. I have always remembered, though, the weariness she expressed of the way in which wisdom was attributed to her. 'I am so tired of being set on a pedestal and expected to vent wisdom.'[3]

To Barbara Bodichon, Marian wrote only that 'I have changed my plans and am going abroad for a little while. But I shall write to you again before long and tell you more.'[4]

After a consultation at Weybridge, where she went on 24 April for the week-end, Marian wrote to John's brother-in-law Albert Druce to ask if he 'would be willing to come and take me from my house to the church and "give me away"'.[5] She hadn't had the courage to tell Charles, who called with news of his promotion to Principal Clerk at the Post Office, but made Johnny do it. Dear Charles, trump that he was, hurried at once to the Priory, and they had a long interview, in which he showed 'perfectly beautiful feeling'.[5] Devoted as he was to the Mutter, Charles must secretly have welcomed the marriage for the help it promised him in looking after her many problems. He knew that his father would only have wished her to be happy.

At St. George's, Hanover Square, at 10.15, Thursday, 6 May 1880, it was Charles who gave her away. He was the only one

[1] *Letters*, VII. 259.
[2] *Letters*, VII. 262–3.
[3] *Memorials of Edward Burne-Jones*, II. 103–4.
[4] *Letters*, VII. 265.
[5] *Letters*, VII. 266.

of her 'family' present; Gertrude and the children were on holiday at Broadstairs. All the Crosses were there with the Druces and Bullock-Hall. After the ceremony Mr. and Mrs. John Walter Cross went back to the Priory to sign their wills, which their solicitors witnessed, and started for Dover. They spent the night at the Lord Warden, where she and George had slept when they returned to England in 1855.

The day before her wedding Marian had written to William Blackwood, Mme Bodichon, Mrs. Bray, Mrs. Burne-Jones, and Mrs. Congreve. Blackwood replied with proper sentiments. Cara Bray at once sent warm and sincere wishes: 'It is a comfort to know that you have now one to protect and cherish you; and hence we are prophesying no end of good and great work and even happiness—for many years after we have slipped away. Our blessing will follow you through this new phase of your life.'[1] Marian had told Mrs. Congreve simply that a 'great momentous change is going to take place', and that Charles would call on Saturday to tell her what he could of it. To poor Charles, whom she herself had dared not tell the news, Marian delegated the task of breaking it to her most emotional friends, Mrs. Congreve, Mrs. Stuart, and Edith Simcox.

Edith received it very calmly, telling Charles that she was not surprised. At their last meeting Marian had taken her breath away by saying that she was going, not to Witley, but abroad for two or three months. Edith wrote at once, enclosing her note with another to John Cross—both letters 'finely felt', Marian remarked, as she read them aloud in their sunshiny apartment at the Hôtel Vouillemont in Paris.[2] Elma Stuart, too, accepted the news calmly. Her devotion was only a sentimental indulgence far less intense than Edith's obsession. She too wrote at once to Johnny, whom she did not know, and got in return a polite note from him and a long, impersonal letter from Marian signed, not 'Your loving Mother', but 'M. A. Cross'.[3]

From Maria Congreve no word came. In spite of two reminders Charles was unusually reticent about his interview with her. It had been painful on both sides. Mrs. Congreve was the oldest of these women who loved Marian 'passionately', or, as Edith put it, 'lover-wise', and she was deeply hurt at not having been told. Furthermore, she held a firm belief in the Comtian dogma of

---

[1] *Letters*, VII. 275.
[2] *Letters*, VII. 274.   [3] *Letters*, VII. 276, 282.

'perpetual widowhood'. Writing to console her, Dr. Congreve, on holiday at Alassio, said: 'The world will taunt Positivism with it.'[1] Yet, he added in other letters, 'I have long doubted whether we should get any real great service from her. . . . She has never given anything but intellectual support, the support contained, that is, in the fact that so powerful an intellect adopts the doctrine—the central idea of our system, the Religion of Humanity, and that no weakness can take from us.'[2] Nearly three weeks passed before Mrs. Congreve could bring herself to write 'a loving but brief letter' to Marian, who excused her failure to tell of the 'once undreamed-of change' on the flimsy ground that Mrs. Congreve had been absorbed with her sister, whose husband had recently died.[3]

There was nothing morbid in Mrs. Burne-Jones's affection for George Eliot. But she too felt hurt by the lack of candour. Marian had written to her on 5 May:

Dearest Georgie

Fate laid me low with influenza last week, a fact only important just now because it has filled the present week with an oppressive crowd of details and made me simply unable to write to you until this eleventh hour.

A great momentous change is taking place in my life—a sort of miracle in which I could never have believed, and under which I still sit amazed. If it alters your conception of me so thoroughly that you must from henceforth regard me as a new person, a stranger to you, I shall not take it hardly, for I myself a little while ago should have said that this thing could not be.

I am going to be married to Mr. Cross whom you may sometimes have seen here. He has been a devoted friend for years, much loved and trusted by Mr. Lewes, and now that I am alone, he sees his only longed for happiness in dedicating his life to me. This will make no difference in my care for my lost one's family either during or after my life. Mr. Cross has a sufficient fortune of his own.

Explanations of these crises, which seem sudden though they are slowly dimly prepared, are impossible. I can only ask you and your husband to imagine and interpret according to your deep experience and loving kindness.

We are going away tomorrow and shall be abroad two or three months. In August we shall be at Witley according to actual intentions. But this house will not again be my home. When in London we shall inhabit 4 Cheyne Walk, Chelsea.

---

[1] Bodleian: MS. Eng. let. e. 56.
[2] Bodleian: MS. Eng. let. e. 67, fols. 122–3.   [3] *Letters*, VII. 296.

Good bye, dear ones. Always, in all changes either with you or me, I shall be your deeply attached friend,

M. E. L.

Excuse any word that seems the wrong one—any apparent brusqueness or neglect. I have been terribly pressed.[1]

At midnight the day of the wedding Georgie replied without salutation:

I have been away with the exception of one clear day until this afternoon, when I returned and found your letter—for which I thank you with all my heart—and I cannot sleep till it is answered. Dear friend, I love you—let that be all—I love you, and you are *you* to me 'in all changes'—from the first hour I knew you until now you have never turned but one face upon me, and I do not expect to lose you now. I am the old loving

Georgie.[2]

Still stung by the sense of betrayal, she kept the note for six weeks before sending it with the following letter:

The Grange
June 16: 1880

Dear Friend,

You will see by the enclosed that I answered your letter at once and that I was grateful for it—but when my answer was written I put it aside, hoping to find more and brighter words to send. Forgive it if they have not come yet, and let me send those first ones—anything rather than you should think my silence a want of respect or feeling—I would rather you were displeased with what I say than that.

Give me time—this was the one 'change' I was unprepared for—but that is my own fault—I have no right to impute to my friends what they do not claim. Forgive what would be an unforgivable liberty of speech if you had not said anything on the subject to me or if you had not also looked closely into my life. Edward joins me in love, and I am always

Your loving
Georgie.[3]

On Barbara Bodichon's sympathy Marian knew that she could rely. To her she wrote in much the same phrases, asking her at the end, 'Please tell Bessie for me, with my love to her.' By a strange fatality, in her haste and excitement Marian tucked this letter away in her drawer; there it lay till Charles Lewes was sent to search for it seven weeks later. But great-hearted Barbara did not

---

[1] *Letters*, VII. 269–70.   [2] *Letters*, VII. 272.   [3] *Letters*, VII. 299.

wait for a letter. As soon as she read the news, spread in large type in the newspapers, she wrote to Marian:

My dear I hope and I think you will be happy. Tell Johnny Cross I should have done exactly what he has done if you would have let me and I had been a man.

You see I know all love is so different that I do not see it unnatural to love in new ways—not to be unfaithful to any memory. If I knew Mr. Lewes he would be glad as I am that you have a new friend.

I was glad to hear you were going to Italy but I did not guess this. My love to your friend if you will.

Your loving
Barbara.[1]

Marian's greatest joy came with a stiff, meagre note from her brother Isaac. His wife Sarah had written a sympathetic letter after Lewes's death, in acknowledging which Marian wrote, 'Give my love to my Brother.'[2] But Isaac, sternly righteous, remained unmoved, maintaining the icy silence begun in 1857, when he ordered Mr. Holbeche, the family solicitor, to ascertain the facts of her 'marriage' to Lewes. Mr. Holbeche, as joint trustee of her father's bequest, had now been duly informed of her marriage to Cross. Only then did Isaac unbend:

Griff | Nuneaton
May 17, 1880

My dear Sister

I have much pleasure in availing myself of the present opportunity to break the long silence which has existed between us, by offering our united and sincere congratulations to you and Mr. Cross, upon the happy event of which Mr. Holbeche has informed me. My wife joins me in sincerely hoping it will afford you much happiness and comfort. She and the younger branches unite with me in kind love and every good wish. Believe me

Your affectionate brother
Isaac P. Evans.[3]

Marian replied from Milan, 26 May:

My dear Brother

Your letter was forwarded to me here, and it was a great joy to me to have your kind words of sympathy, for our long silence has never broken the affection for you which began when we were little ones. My Husband too was much pleased to read your letter. I have known

---

[1] *Letters*, VII. 273.   [2] *Letters*, VII. 105.   [3] *Letters*, VII. 280.

his family for nine years, and they have received me amongst them very lovingly. He is of a most solid, well tried character and has had a great deal of experience. The only point to be regretted in our marriage is that I am much older than he, but his affection has made him choose this lot of caring for me rather than any other of the various lots open to him.

After some complimentary remarks about his children—Frederick, now Rector of Bedworth, and Edith, 'a noble-looking woman', she gave her addresses at Witley and Chelsea.

I hope that your own health is quite good now and that you are able to enjoy the active life which I know you are fond of.
Always your affectionate Sister
Mary Ann Cross.[1]

No comment from her half-sister Fanny Houghton has been found. Charles was still making his rounds explaining the Mutter's unexpected marriage. 'If you can see Mrs. Pattison', she wrote from Grenoble, 'I should like you to tell her that I have been wondering for nearly a year that I did not hear from her.'[2] Annie Thackeray Ritchie in a letter to her young husband described Charles's visit to her on 23 May:

He gave her away, and looks upon Mr. Cross as an elder brother. . . . He is generous about the marriage. He says he owes everything to her, his Gertrude included, and that his father had no grain of jealousy in him, and only would have wished her happy, and that she was of such a delicate fastidious nature that she couldn't be satisfied with anything but an ideal tête-à-tête. George Eliot said to him if she hadn't been human with feelings and failings like other people, how could she have written her books?

He talked about his own mother in confidence, but his eyes all filled up with tears over George Eliot, and altogether it was the strangest page of life I ever skimmed over. She is an honest woman, and goes in with all her might for what she is about. She did not confide in Herbert Spencer.[3]

Charlie's report of Spencer's sympathy was more than Marian expected. So was the letter that came from Jowett: 'You know that you are a very celebrated person', he wrote, 'and therefore the world will talk a little about you, but they will not talk long and what they say does not much signify. It would be foolish to give

[1] *Letters*, VII. 287.   [2] *Letters*, VII. 282.
[3] *Letters of Anne Thackeray Ritchie*, ed. Hester Ritchie (1924), p. 181.

up actual affection for the sake of what people say.'[1] It was sound advice. Some of her radical friends like Mrs. Peter Taylor, who had stood loyally by her through a quarter-century of marriage outside the law, were more shocked by her lapse into convention. They underestimated her essential conservatism. After her few years of rebellion Marian—like Wordsworth—reverted quickly to traditional ways, which her equivocal position made her particularly anxious to follow in other respects. Her union with Lewes was made openly and deliberately, not in defiance of the marriage laws, but in obedience to a higher personal morality that could brook no deceit. No marriage could have been more constant. To marriage with Cross no impediment existed; so it was quite natural that she should marry him in the conventional way. They were as religious, perhaps, as many couples married in Church, though neither of them would have subscribed to the Thirty-nine Articles. Dr. Congreve wrote to his wife: 'I suppose her peculiar position made her wish a marriage at St. George's,—else that is rather a queer step. Is he more of a believer than she?'[2] Many others speculated about her motives. Malicious stories were gossiped about. One cannot doubt Cross's devotion to Marian or her affection for him. An English gentleman, educated at Rugby, tall, handsome, athletic, a good talker, a successful banker—his obvious virtues were those her father would have admired.

During their wedding journey the air of the Continent had its usual salubrious effect on Marian. From the moment she set foot on the quay at Calais till the day she returned to Witley 'she was never ill—never even unwell', Cross said. 'She began at once to look many years younger'.[3] At Paris they altered their original plan to go to Italy by the Corniche and went instead through Grenoble and Mount Cenis, the route that she and Lewes took on their first Italian journey. At the Grande Chartreuse her one regret, she wrote to Charles, was 'that the Pater had not seen it. I would give up my own life willingly if he could have the happiness instead of me. But marriage has seemed to restore me to my old self. I was getting hard, and if I had decided differently I think I should have become very selfish.'[4] They travelled slowly through northern Italy, spending a week at Milan and reaching Venice just a month after their wedding. There they settled down

---

[1] *Letters*, VII. 289.
[2] Bodleian: MS. Eng. let. e. 56.
[3] Cross, III. 417.
[4] *Letters*, VII. 283.

at the Hôtel de l'Europe for a long stay, taking all their meals in their rooms. Visits to the galleries and churches were interspersed with pleasant longer turns in their gondola. At the Lido one day Johnny wanted to have a swim. Though the June air was agreeably warm, a plunge in the cold water was deemed inadvisable.[1]

On 16 June at the end of their second week in Venice Johnny fell suddenly ill. In referring to the episode in *George Eliot's Life* he attributes it to heat and lack of exercise:

We thought too little of the heat, and rather laughed at English people's dread of the sun. But the mode of life at Venice has its peculiar dangers. It is one thing to enjoy heat when leading an active life, getting plenty of exercise in riding or rowing in the evenings; it is another thing to spend all one's days in a gondola—a delicious, dreamy existence,—going from one church to another—from palaces to picture galleries—sight-seeing of the most exhaustively interesting kind—traversing constantly the *piccoli rei*, which are nothing more than drains, and with bedroom-windows always open on the great drain of the Grand Canal. The effect of this continual bad air, and the complete and sudden deprivation of all bodily exercise, made me thoroughly ill.[2]

From this account one might assume that Johnny had got some acute intestinal infection. But the facts point otherwise. It is now clear that the illness he suffered at this time was a sudden mental derangement. He jumped from his balcony into the Grand Canal. The gondoliers quickly pulled him out. Dr. Giacomo Ricchetti, the leading medical man, who was called, brought in Dr. Cesare Vigna in consultation. They prescribed chloral to calm the patient. Marian, terrified, telegraphed to his brother Willie Cross, who arrived on the evening of the 18th. Five days later Johnny was well enough to be moved to Verona, whence by easy stages they took him to Innsbruck and Munich and on 8 July to Wildbad. There Willie left them. A fortnight later they followed him home.[3]

Though the surviving letters tell no more about the episode, family tradition confirms the belief that Cross's illness was an acute mental depression. Mme Bodichon confided to Edith Simcox that she had been told it was not the first of its kind in his life. 'If this were so', Edith wrote in her Autobiography, 'and of course She [George Eliot] knew it, it throws a flood of light

---

[1] *Letters*, VII. 298.   [2] Cross, III. 407–8.
[3] GE Diary, 1880. Lord Acton's note reads: 'At Venice she thought him mad, and she never recovered the dreadful depression that followed. Sent for Ricchetti, told him that Cross had a mad brother. Told her fears. Just then, heard that he had jumped into the Canal.' (Cambridge University Library: MS. 5109, item 1571.)

upon the relation and on Her previous enthusiasm of admiration for one who led so cheerily a busy, useful life in spite of such impending cloud.'[1] There is no evidence that the malady ever recurred. Cross died in 1924 at the age of eighty-four.

Back at Witley they were soon entertaining visitors in the normal way. John's sisters came from Weybridge; Lady Holland came to tea and invited Johnny to play tennis with the younger members of her family; Charles and Gertrude came once or twice to spend the night. In August there was a round of visits to Cross's married sisters—to the Druces at Sevenoaks, the Otters at Wragby, and the Bullock-Halls at Six Mile Bottom. At the Halls the Jebbs came to dinner, happy to find the Sidgwicks there too, for, Mrs. Jebb wrote to her sister, the Crosses 'might have been too much for us in their new felicity'.

George Eliot, old as she is, and ugly, really looked very sweet and winning in spite of both. She was dressed in a short dark soft satin walking dress with a lace wrap half shading the body, a costume most artistically designed to show her slenderness, yet hiding the squareness of age. . . . In the evening she made me feel sad for her. There was not a person in the drawing-room, Mr. Cross included, whose mother she might not have been, and I thought she herself felt depressed at the knowledge that nothing could make her young again; to her we were all young of a later generation. She adores her husband, and it seemed to me it hurt her a little to have him talk so much to me. It made her, in her pain, slightly irritated and snappish, which I did not mind, feeling that what troubled her was beyond remedy. He may forget the twenty years difference between them, but she never can. . . .

If Marian was watching her Johnny, one wonders whether Mrs. Jebb was not casting a rather jaundiced eye across the table at her own husband, absorbed, as men always were, in George Eliot's fascinating conversation. Mrs. Jebb's letter continues:

If ever she did wrong in her life, I am afraid she will suffer enough now to make atonement. Not that Mr. Cross is apparently not devoted to her, but such a marriage is against nature. . . . She has always cared much more for men than for women, and has cultivated every art to make herself attractive, feeling bitterly all the time what a struggle it was, without beauty, whose influence she exaggerates as do all ugly people.[2]

Johnny went occasionally to Weybridge to play tennis, and before the summer was over he began to lay out a tennis court at

[1] Simcox Autobiography, 5 Feb. 1882.
[2] Lady Jebb, *With Dearest Love to All* (1960), pp. 163-4.

the Heights. 'He has turned woodman lately,' Marian wrote to Barbara, 'and has been cutting away some of the too abundant fir trees which made an ugly mass and line against the sky. I think you will find the clearance an improvement.'[1] She told Cara Bray how 'he cuts down a thickish tree in half an hour, with a special axe which he bought on purpose to make a desirable clearance in our little forest'.[2] And to his sister Anna she boasted about 'how well he looks and how stalwart he has become.'[3] Alas, the same could not be said of Marian. In mid September her old renal malady returned with severe pains. On 29 September Johnny took her to Brighton for ten days, but she returned feeling no better. She was taken very ill in the night of 17 October; only an opiate relieved her the next day. Dr. Andrew Clark came down from London to see her on 22 October. A week later she began to feel herself recovering. She was weak and thin.

Johnny had been going up to town several days a week to oversee the preparation of 4 Cheyne Walk and the removal of books and furniture from the Priory. In her Diary Marian takes no notice of her sixty-first birthday: 'Fine frosty day. Having finished Spencer's *Sociology* we began Max Müller's *Lectures on the Science of Language*.' She was sorting over relics and papers, wondering whether to burn them. 'I hate the thought that what we have looked at with eyes full of living memory should be tossed about and made lumber of, or (if it be writing) read with hard curiosity', she wrote to Cara. 'I am continually considering whether I have saved as much as possible from this desecrating fate.'[4]

On 29 November they left Witley to stay at Bailey's Hotel in Gloucester Road while the last touches were put on the new house. Even at this busy time the readings went on: Tennyson's new volume (*Ballads and Other Poems*), *Hermann und Dorothea*, and Comte's *Discours préliminaire* (in Bridge's translation) are mentioned. Cross was increasingly impressed with the persistency and the depth of her concentration. 'She could keep her mind on the stretch hour after hour: the body might give way, but the brain remained unwearied.'[5] They moved into 4 Cheyne Walk on 3 December. The next day they first appeared together at the Saturday Pop Concert in St. James's Hall—doubtless the focus of more eyes than ever.

Johnny, who had worked hard arranging everything, had a bad

---

[1] *Letters*, VII. 332.   [2] Ibid. 340.   [3] Ibid. 339.
[4] Ibid. 341.   [5] Cross, III. 422.

cold, which lasted most of a week. Marian now began to write to a few of her old friends, asking them to call—Spencer, the Congreves, and Edith Simcox—but did not go out much except to the Concerts. 'I am quite flourishing again in my rickety fashion, a mended piece of antique furniture', she wrote, when inviting Mme Belloc.[1] She refused an invitation from Mrs. Lionel Tennyson to private theatricals because they had taken a box for *Agamemnon*, given in Greek by Oxford undergraduates at St. George's Hall, 17 December. Marian came home from it 'fired with the old words', and planning to read through the Greek dramatists again with Johnny. On Saturday, as usual, they were in their seats at the concert; after dinner that evening she played through on the piano some of the music they had heard.

Spencer came on Sunday afternoon, 19 December, and had a long, pleasant talk with her. He 'thought her looking worn, but she did not seem otherwise unwell'.[2] After he left, Edith came— by appointment; she had not seen George Eliot since April.

She was alone when I arrived. I was too shy to ask for any special greeting—only kissed her again and again as she sat. Mr. Cross came in soon and I noticed his countenance was transfigured, a calm look of pure *beatitude* had succeeded the ordinary good nature.—Poor fellow! She was complaining of a slight sore throat; when he came in and touched her hand, said she felt the reverse of better. I only stayed half an hour therefore; she said Do not go, but I gave as a reason that she should not tire her throat and then she asked me to come in again and tell them the news. He came down to the door with me and I only asked after his health. She had spoken before of being quite well and I thought it was only a passing cold—she thought it was caught at the Agamemnon.[3]

Marian sat down to write a letter to Mrs. Strachey about her sister Lady Colville, whose husband had died: 'One great comfort I believe she has—that of a sister's affection.' We must turn to Cross to finish the story: 'Here the letter is broken off. The pen which had carried delight and comfort to so many minds and hearts, here made its last mark. The spring, which had broadened out into so wide a river of speech, ceased to flow.'[4]

The sore throat of which she had complained got worse during the night. The first thing Monday morning Cross went to Dr. Clark,

---

[1] *Letters*, VII. 348.
[2] David Duncan, *Herbert Spencer* (1908), p. 214.
[3] Simcox Autobiography, 23 Dec. 1880.
[4] Cross III. 438. On GE's coffin he inscribed the lines from the *Inferno* (I. 79–80): 'Quella fonte / Che spande di parlar si largo fiume.'

who gave him the name of an old pupil of his, George Mackenzie, who lived near by. He diagnosed it as acute laryngitis and was not in the least anxious about her, since neither pulse nor temperature was very high. On Tuesday she was decidedly better, the pulse down to about 90. But she had a disturbed night with great pain over her right kidney. Wednesday morning Mackenzie found her pulse much faster and her strength wonderfully reduced. Cross describes the rest in a letter to Elma Stuart the next day:

Dr. Andrew Clark meantime had written that he would be here at 6. Mr. Mackenzie came again at 2 and found her still weak but she was drowsy and he said sleep was the best of medicines for her. After taking some cold beef tea jelly and an egg beaten up with brandy she dozed again, and I listened to her breathing, hoping it was curing sleep—but it was death coming on.

When Dr. Clark came he found her lying on her back, her shoulders raised, eyes closed, her face of an ashen grey, lips slightly livid, arms extended on the coverlet. Her breathing was frequent but quiet, her pulse small and irregular, her hand cold and clammy. 'With the stethoscope a loud to-and-fro friction was heard.'[1] He said at once that the heart was struck and that he feared she had no power of resistance. She had just time to whisper to Johnny, 'Tell them I have great pain in the left side', before she lost consciousness.[2] She 'passed away quite painlessly at 10 last night', he wrote. 'And I am left alone in this new House we meant to be so happy in.'[3]

In notifying Spencer of her death, Cross alluded to the possibility of burial in Westminster Abbey. Spencer, in Hastings, telegraphed to Dean Stanley, who replied that he would need 'strong representations' before making such a decision. Charles Bowen and Sidgwick collected signatures; Burne-Jones solicited Leighton and others; Spencer sent telegrams to a number of his friends, asking them to urge the Dean to admit George Eliot to the Poets' Corner. John Tyndall wrote to Stanley on Christmas Day:

It was, I am told, the expressed wish of George Eliot to be buried in Westminster Abbey, and it has been hinted to me that I ought to aid in furthering the realization of this wish. Well, I can only say, that if you consent to give her shelter, the verdict of the future will be that

---

[1] *Lancet*, 1 Jan. 1881, p. 26. This long clinical account, obviously contributed by Dr. Clark, also gives briefer comments on GE's attacks of kidney stone since 1873.
[2] Cross, III. 439.   [3] 23 Dec. 1880. *Letters*, VII. 351.

Dean Stanley has enshrined a woman whose achievements were without parallel in the previous history of womankind.[1]

Huxley, on the other hand, though no champion of the Establishment, felt that the proposal was certain to be bitterly opposed, perhaps with the raking up of past histories, as happened (with less provocation) in the case of John Stuart Mill. The Abbey, he argued, is not a Pantheon, but a Christian Church.

George Eliot is known not only as a great writer, but as a person whose life and opinions were in notorious antagonism to Christian practice in regard to marriage, and Christian theory in regard to dogma. How am I to tell the Dean . . . to do that which, if I were in his place, I should most emphatically refuse to do? . . . One cannot eat one's cake and have it too.[2]

John Morley agreed with him. If Browning, Tennyson, and other prominent friends were solicited in the same way, as they probably were, their replies have been discreetly lost. Cross soon saw that it would be unwise to press the issue.

He chose instead a plot in the unconsecrated portion of Highgate Cemetery near Lewes's grave, which it touched at one corner. The cold rain and snow that fell all day on 29 December, whipped by bitter wind, did not prevent a great throng from attending George Eliot's funeral. Slush lay on the ground, and the floor of the chapel was red with mud. The chief mourners, Cross, Charles Lewes, Isaac Evans—reunited with his sister at last in death—and his son the Reverend Frederick Rawlins Evans, Cross's brother Willy, his three brothers-in-law Albert Druce, Henry Bullock-Hall, and Francis Otter, gathered at Cheyne Walk for the long drive in mourning coaches behind the hearse to Highgate. A score of close friends were in other carriages: Spencer, Congreve, Pigott, Robert Browning, Burton, Harrison, Gurney, George Howard, Locker, Roland Stuart, Vivian Lewes, Kegan Paul, William Blackwood, Joseph Langford, the family lawyers, and Cross's business partner. They were joined by many private coaches along the way. Among the distinguished men the newspapers noticed were Sir Theodore Martin, Tyndall, Colvin, Oscar Browning, Beesly, Du Maurier, Millais, Lyulph Stanley, Hamilton Aïdé, Thomas Woolner, Ralston, Lehmann, Edmund Yates, Sir Garnet Wolseley, Lord Arthur Russell, Sir Henry Thompson,

---

[1] J. Tyndall to Dean Stanley, 25 Dec. 1880 (Yale).
[2] *Life and Letters of T. H. Huxley*, ed. L. Huxley (2 vols., 1902), II. 19. Huxley's first draught is in the Imperial College of Science, London (7. 247).

T. H. Huxley, Lionel Tennyson, Sir Lewis Pelly, Sir Henry Maine, George Goschen, John Morley, Sir Charles Dilke, and Sir John Lubbock. Though the newspapers list only Miss Alice Helps and Lady Colville among those present, from other accounts we know that there were as many women as men at the ceremony.

Edith Simcox has left the most detailed description of the day:

This morning at 10 when the wreath I had ordered—white flowers bordered with laurel leaves—came, I drove with it to Cheyne Walk, giving it silently to the silent cook. Then, instinct guiding—it seemed to guide one right all day—I went to Highgate, stopping on the way to get some violets—I was not sure for what purpose. In the cemetery I found the new grave was in the place I had feebly coveted, nearer the path than his and one step further south. Then I laid my violets at the head of Mr. Lewes's solitary grave and left the already gathering crowd to ask which way the entrance would be. Then I drifted towards the chapel, standing first for a while under the colonnade where a child asked me 'Was it the late George Eliot's wife was going to be buried?'—I think I said Yes. Then I waited on the skirts of the group gathered in the porch between the church and chapel sanctuaries. Then some one claimed a passage through the thickening crowd and I followed in his wake and found myself without effort in a sort of vestibule past the door which kept back the crowd. Mrs. Lankester was next the chapel —I cannot forget that she offered me her place. I took it and presently every one else was made to stand back. Then the solemn procession passed me. The coffin bearers paused in the very doorway, I pressed a kiss upon the pall and trembled violently as I stood motionless else, in the still silence with nothing to mar the realization of that intense moment's awe. Then—it was hard to tell the invited mourners from the other waiting friends—men many of whose faces I knew—and so I passed among them into the chapel, entering a forward pew. White wreaths lay thick upon the velvet pall—it was not painful to think of her last sleep so guarded. I saw her husband's face, pale and still; he forced himself aloof from the unbearable world in sight.

Dr. Thomas Sadler conducted the service, as he had Lewes's, using most of the order of the Prayer Book with discreet Unitarian omissions. Edith was surprised to find it 'so like our own'. At the end of his intelligent address,[1] the coffin, covered with white flowers, which concealed the inscription giving her birth-date as 1820 instead of 1819, was borne across the road to the grave. Edith, who had gone ahead, watched the interment from a vantage point between George Eliot's grave and Lewes's:

As we left the chapel Miss Helps put her arm in mine, but I left her at

[1] The full text is given in the *Daily News*, 30 Dec. 1880, p. 2.

the door, to make my way alone across the road to the other part where
the grave was. I shook hands silently with Mrs. Anderson and waited
at the corner where the hearse stopped and the coffin was brought up
again. Again I followed near, on the skirts of the procession, a man—
Champneys I thought—had a white wreath he wished to lay upon the
coffin, and as he pressed forward those behind bore me on, till I was
standing between his grave and hers and heard the last words said:
the grave was deep and narrow—the flowers filled all the level space.
I turned away with the first—Charles Lewes pressed my hand as we
gave the last look. Then I turned up the hill and walked through rain
by a road unknown before to Hampstead and a station. Then through
the twilight I cried and moaned aloud.

Her grief was no more poignant than that of poor John Cross—
George Eliot's widow, they were soon calling him in the clubs—
who wandered alone through the lovely rooms in Cheyne Walk,
looking across the Thames to the muddy bank at Battersea.

APPENDIX I

GEORGE ELIOT'S SCHOOL NOTEBOOK

✳

THIS Notebook, the earliest known George Eliot manuscript, was discovered in 1943 in a bookshop at Chippenham, Wiltshire, by J. H. P. Pafford, Goldsmiths' Librarian of the University of London. Through his interest it was added to the George Eliot collection at Yale in 1961. With the permission of Mrs. Ouvry and the Librarian of the Beinecke Library it is here published for the first time.

It consists of sixty-six leaves, the paper watermarked 1830, bound in boards. On the first page in large, ornate script is written 'Marianne Evans', a spelling of her name which probably reflects her recent introduction to French. The first fifty-six pages are filled mostly with rules and illustrative problems in arithmetic. The next three leaves have been torn out. On pages 57–9 appears an essay on 'Affectation and Conceit'. This ends what will be called the A opening.

Reversing the book and opening from the other end (the B opening), one finds again within the front cover, carefully written —(in imitation of Miss Rebecca Franklin's 'beautiful calligraphy'?) —'Marianne Evans. March 16th 1834.' In the B opening the first thirty pages are filled with poems copied from various sources. The story 'Edward Neville' fills pages 31–7; pages 38–64 are blank. On p. 65 are scribbled a few trial lines of doggerel verse. A sketch of a tombstone with urn and willow is found on p. 86, and on p. 88 there is a small pencil sketch of a cottage and tree with the lines,

> Give me a Cottage on some Cambrian wold
> Far from the haunts of men.

The text is given exactly as it was written with deleted words enclosed in angular brackets.

[AFFECTATION AND CONCEIT]

A small very small portion of the many reasons why affectation is not only a folly distressing to the more sensible and humble part of mankind, but one of the most contemptible weaknesses of the human species—

Affectation taken in the proper sense of the word is nothing ⟨but gre⟩ less than a species of deceit and hypocrisy it is an assumption of some merit which we do not really possess and therefore a distinct thing from vanity or conceit, though always an accompaniment of that latter folly, since they who pride themselves upon gaining the admiration & envy of the world at large though impressed with a false notion of their own charms or worth, still endeavour generally to impose more upon their wondering worshippers by practising artificially those graces which despite their own conceit, conscience informs they do not possess naturally—But if the affected man or woman could be persuaded how seldom they can contrive to blind even the silliest of their species, if they could see how ⟨readily⟩ easily their disguise is penetrated it is to be hoped they would be as disgusted with their own conduct as those are, upon whom they practise it—I perceive that Mrs. Spectator has very much in my opinion confounded the two follies affection & conceit— Now I consider them certainly as different vices, though as I remarked above they are seldom if ever separate—The conceited man is vain of some superiority over his fellows, which he is falsely conscious of possessing, and reposing himself in this comfortable assurance, considers himself quite at liberty to impose upon ⟨the inferior⟩ mankind by aping some odd or eccentric manner or style, eagerly desiring to be the admired and envied one of the ⟨comp⟩ society ⟨to which he may belong⟩ in which he may move—Adulation and praise is his food and without a constant daily supply of this unwholesome nourishment, he cannot be said to live; when then he perceives that what he has flattered himself has procured him this necessary dish, begins to tire or cease to please his audience, he of necessity turns to some other art by which to call up the dying embers of their praise & wonder and consequently not possessing the requisite charm naturaly, has recourse to the deceit of affectation, and affects that, which ⟨is not⟩ notwithstanding his own good opinion of himself, he cannot but perceive he is still deficient in.—

Thus women guilty of this foible, are those who set great store by their personal charms these in their youth they consider sufficient to ⟨create⟩ secure the admiration and worship of the whole world and safe in this belief they flutter, on the flattered of the one sex, the envy of the other; and they are happy while thus admired and envied, their whole minds being in one confusion & whirl of excitement & vanity; They study no ⟨arts⟩ graces of mind or intellect their whole thoughts are how they shall best maintain their empire over their surrounding inferiors, and the right fit of a dress or bonnet will occupy their minds for hours together: still so conscious are they of the power of their personal attractions that in youth they do not generally as yet, exert themselves to affect ⟨any⟩ much beyond a fancied superiority: They are conceited not affected but when that youth departs alas how often do we find the conceited ⟨& a⟩ woman one mass of nothing but affectation, real genuine affectation—She is so used to admiration that she finds it impossible to live without it, and as the ⟨gambler⟩ drunkard turns to ⟨th⟩ his wine to drown his cares, she the former beauty, finding all that before naturally attracted gone, flies to artificial means, in order she vainly hopes and believes to secure still her usual meed of adulation —She affects a youthful walk, & a youthful manner, upon all occasions, and at the age of fifty may often be seen clothed in the girlish fashion of sixteen totally forgetting that her once rounded neck and shoulders which at the latter age, ⟨are⟩ were properly uncovered, are now pointed & scraggy and would be much better ⟨cov⟩ hidden from sight by a more matronly ⟨dress⟩ habiliment—

How often too are we compelled to witness the vice (for surely it is a vice) of affectation ⟨too,⟩ in the nobler sex, ay even in those whose strong sense ought to enable them to bear up above such contemptible weaknesses, if it is so despicable in women oh how far more contemptible is it in man—how often even in men of sense do we discover an itching inclination to be commended, and lay traps for a little incense even from those whose opinion they cannot be said to value—Few I fear are safe against this weakness in some degree, the best way to cure ourselves of this desire of applause, is to take care to cast away the love of it upon all occasions, that are not in themselves praiseworthy, among such may be ranked, all graces in our persons, dress, or bodily deportment, which things will be far more winning and attractive if we think not of them, but lose their force in proportion to our endeavour to *make* them such—

[EDWARD NEVILLE]

It was on a bright and sunny morning⟨towards the⟩end of the Autumn of the year 16 ⟨49⟩ ⟨53⟩ 50 that a stranger mounted on a fine black horse ⟨appr⟩ descended the hill which leads into the small but picturesque town of Chepstow. Both horse and rider appeared to have ⟨ridden⟩ travelled far for besides their both being covered with dust, the poor animal bore the marks of the spur in his reeking sides, and notwithstanding the impetuosity with which his master still urged him on, he seemed almost unable to proceed even at a foot pace—The Riders age might have been about six an twenty he was tall and well proportioned and bore in his very handsome countenance the marks of a determined and haughty character—His dress ⟨might⟩ was such as ⟨was⟩ at that time was worn by yeomen or better kind of farmers, but ⟨simple⟩ humble as it was it could by no means conceal ⟨that⟩ the rank of the wearer ⟨was far above what his apparel appeared to be⟩ which by his air and manner bore evident marks of being far above what a glance at his ⟨low⟩ simple apparel might at first seem to ———

As he approached the bridge which crosses the river Wye at the entrance to the town, he ceased to urge his weary beast and dropping the bridle on his neck allowed him to proceed at his own pace, ⟨the tide was at its highest spring and the rel⟩ while he seemed as he gazed on the beautiful ⟨scene⟩ prospect before him to unbend the stern rigidity of his ⟨pale⟩ fine features, and a tear ⟨stood fo⟩ started to his eye; it was indeed a scene of beauty; the tide was at its highest spring, before him on its opposite bank rose the majestic walls of the Castle then in its ⟨greatest⟩ prime. (tho' now still more beautiful in its ruins) and founded upon the solid rocks, ⟨before him were the a ma at on his right hand at some distance tho' almost hidden by the foliage of the woods he could discern⟩ but it was not at these near objects the traveller gazed with such intensity; at some little distance on his right, almost embosomed in the rich foliage of the woods ⟨tho⟩ he could discern the ⟨gables⟩ stately ⟨buildings⟩ walls of Piercefield House, and it was while fixing his ⟨proud⟩ proud eye of this object, that ferocity and sternness vanished from his countenance and a deep sigh burst from his heart: "Well done my brave and trusty Ronald said he addressing his horse & patting him, thou hast served me this day better than thou has ever before done, though never yet, hast thou been lacking in thy service to thy master, but I will urge thee no more. Now thy trusty feet have brought me where I had ⟨never⟩ scarcely ever dared hope I might again come—Welcome welcome to my eyes the scene of my happiest days, and yet in what a manner have I returned to thee, an outcast from ⟨societ the⟩ society I used to shine in an alien from my family a deserter, and a regicide; as he pronounced the last word a bitter smile curled his lip and dashing the tear from his eye, in a moment resumed his former reckless demeanor he crossed the bridge and without entering the town turned at once up the road which led to the Castle—Here he demanded of the porter permission to proceed to the apartments of Henry Marten ⟨the⟩ at that time a prisoner, confined in the Eastern Tower; and having obtained it he delivered the horse into the charge ⟨of one of the⟩ a servant ⟨s⟩ who was lounging in the courtyard, and ⟨in⟩ was in a few minutes was ⟨in the⟩ conducted to the prisoners presence: Henry Marten ⟨was on account of his having been one of the first to sign the execution of the unfortunate Charles was⟩ was the son of an ⟨Sir Char a knight⟩ a gentleman ⟨who had made a conspicuous figure in the⟩ possessing considerable property and influence in the county of Berks —. He had intended his son for the Church and in consequence had ⟨ear⟩ given him an excellent education, and early sent him to colledge; ⟨but⟩ Henry Marten besides all these advantages possessed great talent which unfortunately he turned to unlawful ends His character was licentious in the extreme and hating the profession he was intended for, he early in life married a rich widow, and gave gave [*sic*] up his gown From being careless on [t]he religious subject he soon began to grow opposed to them and joined with several public characters of the time in openly denying the truths of revelation —His temper was ungovernable and his hatred of royalty was only second to his detestation of religion—When the temper of the times enabled him to disclose his sentiments without restraint he added disdain ⟨to hatred of⟩ and insult to dislike of the King and eventually with his own hand signed the warrant for that unhappy monarchs execution: for which act he was brought to trial ⟨and⟩ on the charge of treason: he however escaped the just punishment of his crime by pleading a misnomer, he having been called in the Indictment Henry Marten whereas his real name was Harry He was however found guilty and confined for life in the Castle of Chepstow to which I have now introduced my reader: He was at this time about seventy years of age, but ⟨years not⟩ tho the years which had rolled over his head had bleached his locks and bent his form, there still remained the same keen eagle eye and unbending fierceness of expression which in his youth had made the feeble-minded quail before him—Such was the person into whose presence the stranger was ushered: Marten ⟨started as he entered⟩ was deeply engaged in reading as he entered and for ⟨an⟩ an instant did not raise his eyes from the volume over which he leant, but when the stranger addressed him by the name of "Uncle" he started and rising hurriedly from his seat exclaimed: Edward is it possible. what evil genius brings you here *now*? ⟨What have⟩ Why in that dress, speak what has happened. My ⟨own wi⟩ horse and my *will* have brought me here said the young man, is not that answer sufficient: I am come to you for shelter and if you cannot afford it I must seek it elsewhere. And how am I a prisoner to afford you shelter Edward Neville I *must* I *will know* what has brought you here, are you aware of the risk you run if your relationship to me be discovered, I hope said he bending on his newphew a keen and searching look that you are not such a boy as to be drawn hither by a fair form & a bright eye. Uncle said the young man, from you only would I brook such questions, but do not provoke me too far. I have served you through many dangers, I would serve you thro' more if you needed them, for you are my nearest living relative but breathe not one word of *her* in my presence, no, stay he rejoined as the old man was about to interrupt him; I will tell you all that has befallen me since we last parted, but not another word on the subject you have broached, or we part for ever—Tell me then exclaimed Marten Why you are here now, and in that dress, have you deserted that you no longer appear in the uniform a brave soldier should never blush to wear either in war or piece: What news of Saltmarsh? and the rest of you[r] noble friends

& companions in arms: Saltmarsh replied Edward with a bitter smile is well in health, ay and as far as I know in all that concerns *him alone*. as for the rest I know not where one of them now is, I left them scattered far and wide over the country, ⟨some of them are taken prisoner and among them my beloved friend Fane —⟩ fugitives they themselves know not where — ⟨Is he⟩ How continued Marten impatiently have you all deserted your noble commander, and for what reason, what am I to understand Neville by this—Simply this Uncle. Saltmarsh is a traitor, —Marten started ⟨as if⟩ abruptly from his seat and gazing with a ⟨terrified glance⟩ terrified & upon his newphew exclaimed; A traitor? Edward Neville what do you mean by uttering such a word of one of the noblest best of men—Patience dear Uncle calm your wrath and you shall know all—⟨He has betrayed us⟩ I wrote you the account of our last engagement on the side⟨s⟩ of Faldon Hill. therefore you are aware of the defeat we then suffered, Many of the bravest of us fell in that sad and I must add ill arranged encounter, had Cromwell been with us I am convinced that we should not now have to bewail that day: we all inwardly blamed Saltmarsh for his impetuosity in attacking a party so ⟨m⟩ greatly our superior in number, but there was none no not one who outwardly either by word or act showed the slightest indignation or anger. We were all true to our leader and would have defended him to the last drop of our blood: little did we then think what would so soon follow—Immediately after our defeat I was commissioned to bear the news of it to the Protector. he heard me to the end with his usual calmness, but a cloud had gathered on his brow. Neville he said I am sorry for this, ⟨but I can clearly see⟩ for as you say it has cost me some of my bravest men it was ill judged in Saltmarsh to hazard and engagement with Lord Evandales's party without ⟨me⟩ first apprising me of it: but the deed is done and cannot be helped. I will make you the bearer of a letter to your leader, and inform him what I think of this, and for the future I trust he will be less hasty or I must appoint another commander to your troop: ⟨the King's⟩ Charles party are gaining ground upon us, and another such loss would be a serious thing for our cause —And ⟨whos⟩ How said Marten interrupting him, how did Saltmarsh receive the Protectors letter how did his impatient temper brook his generals resentment—You may well ask me I can tell you in few words, he tore the paper in a thousand fragments stamped on it in his rage, and ordering his horse without one moments reflection galloped away he knew not where for he was absent two whole days and we began to fear he had fallen into the hands of the opposite party, and so he had as we soon found to our cost, he had gone immediately on the height of his resentment to be against the Protector, to Lord Feversham, and telling them he had renounced the Protectors cause, and intended to join the Kings: ⟨standard⟩ Hold exclaimed Marten, why will you torture my ears with the name of King. Well Uncle then Charles' standard & was ready to betray to them all the retreats of ⟨that⟩ his former generals

troops who were scattered about the ⟨m⟩ recesses of the mountains—
Accordingly the next day we were surprised in an unguarded moment
most of us taken prisoner after a desperate resistance on our parts and
the rest compelled to fly they knew not where: for they even now on
the chase after us: I borrowed this suit of a poor farmer ⟨to⟩ whom I
had some time ago obliged by loans of money when he was in distress
and he now helped me in *my* need: ⟨as the⟩ five hundred pounds are
set upon my head, for Fevershams resenttment to me has been great
ever since I compelled him to surrender his arms after the affair at
Ballybridge—And how in the name of heaven could you with such
dreadful peril behind you think of flying ⟨here⟩ to me: Why did you
not flee to the coast and endeavour to get across to France, any where
but here, it is completely rushing into the lion's mouth: of course their
first pursuit will be to this town in search of you: I think not Uncle
for I guess they would never suppose me so mad as to come here, and
therefore I stand a much better chance of escape for a few days, and
then when they grow wearied in the ⟨pu⟩ first heat of the chace I will
cross the seas for a few months until I may return in safety, for affairs
cannot continue in this state long—God grant it may happen as you
say Edward but at any rate in this castle you must not stay or you will
excite the suspicion of its inmates, it being a thing so unusual for me to
have a visitor ⟨for so⟩ to remain longer than at the most a day—Neither
must you be seen abroad in the town, for there are many still living who
might recognise you ⟨at any rate⟩ tho' time has altered you greatly
from what you were when you last left me a tall raw stripling of 18—
however you must run no risk—I do not mean to do so replied Edward. ⟨there is a cave near here where I ha⟩ but it grows late Uncle and
for this night I think I may venture to sleep at old Hughes's Inn, I am
sure I shall pass but as a stranger and tomorrow I shall inform them
it is my intention to leave, but I will see you again ere I do—Farewell
Edward then for the present I conjure you by all the love I bear you
for your own and your dead mothers sake be careful and not too reckless——

Edward Neville was the only son of ⟨the⟩ a favourite sister of Henry
Marten who ⟨died in giving him birth his father had been the staunch
friend of his⟩ had early in life married a a staunch friend of her brother's
Sir Hugh Neville whose political opinions and sentiments being the
same has Martens had ripened a youthful intimacy into the strongest
bonds of friendship: but not many months did Julia Neville enjoy the
society of her beloved husband he fell in battle within a year after their
marriage and his loss so shattered the constitution of his bereaved wife
that not long after the brith of her son Edward she ⟨fell⟩ declined slowly
into the grave: Edward was immediately taken into the family of his
Uncle who having no children of His own, and possessing but little
love for his wife, whom fortune alone had induced him to marry,
lavished all the love his stern ⟨comp⟩ heart could hold upon his young

newphew—It might indeed truly be said that Edward was the only being who Marten ⟨could be said to re⟩ ever seemed to regard with affection, ⟨when he was to⟩ he had him constantly with him whether at home or abroad and when ⟨taken⟩ sentenced for his treason to endless confinement, he begged and obtained permission ⟨to carry his⟩ for his newphew then in his eighth year to accompany him to Chepstow Castle —In this manner young Edward spent his childhood and early youth, educated by his Uncle in all his own political opinions and predjudices, he early imbibed a hatred of Kingly power, and an impatience of control. he could not brook a reprimand from his greatest superior, His Uncle alone possessed ⟨the lea⟩ any influence over him—His temper was by nature impetuous and ungovernable and during his residence in his Uncles prison, from which he was allowed egress whenever he thought proper, he could not be said to have formed one tie of friendship, or contracted ⟨any⟩ much intimacy with any one—⟨But though he had⟩ he was too vain to associate with any beneath him, and too proud to render to any of his superiors the homage which is generally necessary to secure the favour of the great—But though unconnected by the ties of friendship with any of the neighbouring inhabitants of the scene of his early days, Edward had contrived to form a tie ⟨of⟩ much closer and lasting import; he had given his hearts best affections to one well worthy of possessing them for young Neville tho ⟨pass guilty⟩ pround impetuous and rash, was nobleminded and warmhearted he would have scorned to do an unjust action or in any way to act deceitfully. he was candid open and brave, and tho' stern and harsh to others to Mary Mordaunt he was gentle tender and kind—⟨He ch She was He was⟩ She was the daughter [of] Sir Verner Mordaunt ⟨at tha⟩ who had for many years resided in the beautiful mansion of Piercefield, and Marten having obtained permission to visit the neighbouring families occasionly when invited by them, had ⟨often⟩ always in his visits to Sir Verner been accompanied by his young newphew: Mary was three years younger than Edward, and a mutual intimacy had sprung up between them which as they grew up ripened into a much warmer sentiment—Whilst in his early boyhood Edward had been accustomed to see Mary almost daily as he had always some little present to convey to hear, either for her dog or her birds which furnished an excuse for his frequently visiting Piercefield—While in their childhood this was not objected to on the part of the elder Mordaunts but when Edward reached his eighteenth year and Mary her 15th it was deemed advisable they should be separated. Sir Verner was firmly attached to royalty, and ⟨only admitted⟩ directly opposed to Marten's principles, but being a humane & kindhearted man he admitted Marten to his table, thinking thereby to contribute as much as possible ⟨to⟩ in softening the rigors of his confinement, and as they never broached political subjects together, they had contrived to pass the time they spent in each other's society with pleasure and concord—⟨but on Edward⟩ and indeed could not but

indulge in the hope that Marten had seen his error and repented of it
and one day at dinner ventured to ask how he would behave could the
whole former scene of events in which he had played so conspicuous
& fatal a part be acted over again—Marten immediately replied without
hesitation, that he would ⟨have⟩ do again in every particular exactly as
he *had* done before—his host was so ardignant at this reply that he never
would see him after and Marten received his final dismissal from Piercefield. his newphew of course was concluded in this mandate. for the
parents of Mary were glad of some pretext for removing him from her
society

Here the story breaks off, though thirty-six blank pages follow in
the notebook. Perhaps invention faltered. The wavering of the date
from 1649 to 1653 to 1650 suggests some perplexity on the part
of the young author. The story is apparently laid before the
defeat of Charles II at Worcester in 1651, when Cromwell was
Commander-in-Chief, though not yet Protector, and Henry
Marten, still a Member of Parliament, was defending its rights
strongly against Cromwell's growing power. It was not till the
Restoration in 1660 that Marten surrendered as a regicide, and
he was not confined to Chepstow Castle till 1665, fifteen years
after Mary Anne's tale begins. This anachronism, which the author
of *Romola* would never have tolerated, is partly explained by her
source, a book entitled *An Historical Tour in Monmouthshire* by
William Coxe, Rector of Bemerton and Stourton, illustrated with
views by Sir Richard Hoare, Bart., London, 1801. From this
splendidly printed quarto she took all the descriptions of Chepstow
and Piercefield House and the details about Henry Marten. Coxe
speaks of his imprisonment as beginning 'after the Restoration',
but gives no date, and though the epitaph quoted says that he
died in 1680, chronology did not much concern the young
romancer. A few phrases suggest how she used her source. Coxe's
'majestic ruins of Chepstow castle' (p. 399) is touched up to 'the
majestic walls of the Castle, then in its prime (tho' now still more
beautiful in its ruins)'. On the same page she found the fine word
'picturesque', along with the forbidding information that Marten
was confined in 'the Eastern tower'. When she placed Mary
Mordaunt's house at some little distance on Neville's right,
'almost embosomed in the rich foliage of the woods', she was

obviously looking at Hoare's romantic engraving and reading
Coxe's description of the 'rich groves of Piercefield' (p. 358).

From William Coxe (1747–1828), who spent most of his life
as tutor for young noblemen and published among other works
The Memoirs of Sir Robert Walpole, *The Memoirs of the Duke of
Marlborough*, *Memoirs of the Bourbon Kings of Spain*, and a
History of the House of Austria, we should hardly expect a sympathetic portrait of Henry Marten. The anecdotes he collected
from Anthony à Wood, Clarendon, and the rest are infused with
an abhorrence of regicides quite naturally shared by a daughter of
Robert Evans. To a less prejudiced historian Marten might seem
a better man than Coxe allows; he deserves some acknowledgement for the way he asserted the rights of Parliament against King
and Protector alike. The profligate manners his Puritan detractors
make so much of were no worse than those of many aristocratic
gentlemen in both political parties—a good deal less vicious than
those of loyal friends of the Merry Monarch like Rochester and
Buckingham. Mary Anne followed her authority closely. Coxe
writes that Henry Marten, son of Sir Henry Marten of Longworth,
Berkshire,

possessed good talents, which he greatly improved by classical attainments; his temper, however, was volatile and capricious, and he was
too much inclined to pleasure, to pay due attention to his intended
profession [the law]. But he was relieved from the necessity of application by espousing a rich widow, whom he afterwards treated with
great indifference and neglect. The dissoluteness of his life and immorality of his conduct led Marten to reject that pure religion which
enjoins the controul of the passions. Hence he united with [James] Har-
rington, [Algernon] Sydney, [Sir John] Wildman, [Henry] Nevill, and
others, who supposed themselves more enlightened than the rest of
mankind, and denied the truth of revelation. The same licentiousness of
opinion which delivered him from the restraints of religion, influenced
his sentiments on politics . . . and [he] joined the party adverse to the
court. When the temper of the times enabled him to disclose his sentiments with less restraint, Marten added disdain and insult to hatred
of royalty (pp. 378–80).

Many of these phrases are echoed by Mary Anne.

In Coxe she also found the names of most of the other characters.
That of Edward Neville stands, not in connection with Henry
Marten, but at the head of a long pedigree of the barons of Aber-
gavenny (p. 180), recording the death of Edward Neville in 1476.
Saltmarsh, whom Coxe mentions as a friend of Marten, was a
Puritan clergyman, the author of virulent pamphlets attacking

King and Church; but he died in 1647, before the story begins. The beloved Mary Mordaunt has an actual namesake, a niece of Lord Peterborough, living with her husband at Piercefield House in 1752, whom Coxe describes as 'a lady of great beauty and accomplishments, but without fortune' (p. 392). If she was a century too late for our hero, the original Edward Neville was at least three hundred years too early for her. The name of Mordaunt was doubtless endeared to Mary Anne by Mordaunt Merton, the hero of Scott's *The Pirate*; and Lord Evandale she lifted bodily from *Old Mortality*.

APPENDIX II

EDWARD CASAUBON AND MARK PATTISON

❋

THE earliest allusion I have found to the alleged resemblance of Mr. Casaubon to Mark Pattison is in the *Autobiography* of Mrs. Oliphant, who at Oxford in February 1879 met Pattison, 'a man who is supposed to be the Casaubon of *Middlemarch*—at least his wife considers herself the model of Dorothea. He is a curious wizened little man, but a great light, I believe. He wrote a life of the great scholar Isaac Casaubon' (1899, p. 277). Pattison's obituary in the *Academy* (9 Aug. 1884, p. 94) by Henry Nettleship says:

There have been those who judging from a very imperfect knowledge of a few facts, and from the name of the book by which he is best known, have fancied that George Eliot had the Rector's studious habits in mind to a certain extent when she drew the character of Mr. Casaubon in *Middlemarch*. There was, however, nothing in common between the serious scholar at Lincoln and the mere pedant frittering away his life in useless trivialities; nor was George Eliot, Mark Pattison's friend, at all likely to draw a caricature of one she loved and valued.

Then with a glance at Rhoda Broughton's *Belinda* Nettleship adds:

It was reserved for a vulgar and frivolous spirit to dare, in a more recent and inferior novel, such foolish insult to good taste.

Mrs. Pattison's second husband Sir Charles Dilke in a manuscript 'Memoir of E. F. S. Dilke', later prefixed to her *The Book of the Spiritual Life* (1905), declared: 'To those who know, Emilia Strong was no more Dorothea Brooke than Pattison was Casaubon; but it is the case that the religious side of Dorothea Brooke was taken by George Eliot from the letters of Mrs. Pattison.' Like Dorothea, he says, Mrs. Pattison knew many passages of Jeremy Taylor and Pascal by heart and prayed and fasted when she was at school.

But just what was 'the religious side of Dorothea'? A single sentence in the first chapter of *Middlemarch* refers to her girlish notions of praying at the bedside of sick labourers, her 'strange whims of fasting like a Papist, and of sitting up at night to read old theological books'. The comparison to St. Theresa in the Prelude involves not mysticism, but the opportunity for practical work as the reformer of a religious order. Dorothea in the 19th century, finding no epic life of 'far-resonant action' like that, must turn instead to plans for cottages and devotion to Casaubon's barren scholarship; his fancied learning, not his clerical function, attracted her. Dorothea's asceticism was not Anglo-Catholic like Mrs. Pattison's, but Puritanical, springing from Evangelicalism before the Oxford Tracts began. The only time she lay all night on the floor, she was impelled, not by penance, but by a paroxysm of sexual jealousy, which George Eliot had no need to study in the letters of her 'Dear Goddaughter'. Mary Ann Evans was quoting Jeremy Taylor when Mrs. Pattison was less than a year old. As for Pascal, the *Pensées* were the first prize she won at school and she had learnt many of them by heart before Mrs. Pattison was born.

Sir Charles Dilke also says that 'Dorothea's defence of her marriage to Casaubon, and Casaubon's account of his marriage to Dorothea' are given in *Middlemarch* 'almost in Mark Pattison's words'. It is not quite clear which pages in the novel he is referring to in either case. If he was comparing Mr. Casaubon's letter of proposal in Chapter 5 with one that Pattison wrote to Emilia Strong, it has not been seen.

In *Mark Pattison and the Idea of a University* (1967) Mr. John Sparrow finds a close likeness to Mr. Casaubon in Pattison's personal appearance and in the nature of his studies. The great *Isaac Casaubon*, published four years after *Middlemarch*, bears not the slightest resemblance to Casaubon's preposterous Key to All Mythologies, which was never finished. As for personal appearance, Pattison had a reddish beard and moustache, hair with little trace of grey even in his latest years, a long, hooked nose, and prominent bright eyes. George Eliot's Casaubon had iron-grey (not 'sandy') hair, no beard or moustache, a pale, sallow face, two white moles with hairs on them, and tired, blinking eyes in deep eye-sockets that made him look to Dorothea like the portraits of Locke.

Nor were their habits similar. Casaubon led a completely sedentary life. Though he had a trout stream at Lowick, he never fished. He did not smoke. Pattison, like his wife, smoked constantly. He was a noted fisherman, a strenuous walker, kept good horses, and from boyhood used to follow the hounds.

No evidence is advanced to support Mr. Sparrow's insinuation that Mrs. Pattison 'may have sanctioned or actually encouraged' George Eliot to caricature her husband as Casaubon. For a discussion of their relations see *Notes and Queries*, 213 (May 1968).

INDEX

'camping' at Witley, 504; learns tennis from Cross, 505; refuses to write liturgy for Religion of Humanity, 506, or Shakespeare for EML series, 507; plays badminton at Priory, 507; silent about Edith's dedication of *Natural Law*, 507; at christening of Elinor Lewes, 508; vetoes Christmas with Burne-Joneses, 508. **1878** at Lionel Tennyson's wedding, 508; strangers 'touch' GE, 508; desc. by Mary Gladstone, 509–10; dines at Goschens with the Crown Princess of Germany, 510; buys furniture for Witley, 511; calls on W. B. Scott, 511; visits Jowett, 511; writes *Theophrastus Such*, 511–12; alarmed by GHL's illness, 512; Turgenev toasts GE as 'greatest living novelist', 513; Mrs. Greville brings James to call, 514; GHL sends *Theophrastus* to JB, 514; not at GHL's funeral, reads *In Memoriam* and Donne's *Poems*, 516; completes GHL's *Problems*, 517; sees no one but CLL, 518. **1879** refuses to see Cross, 519; renal attacks, 519; sees Cross, but not Spencer, 520; 'incredibly thin', 520; pub. GHL's *The Study of Psychology*, 520; reads proof of *Theophrastus*, 521; establishes GHL Studentship at Cambridge, 522–3; executor of GHL's will, 523; sees Edith, 524; sends for Cross, 526; sees Bertie's wife and children, 526–7; visits Highgate Cemetery, 527; finishes pub. of GHL's *Problems*, 527; at Witley sees Cross frequently, 528; 'Decisive conversation', 528; love letters to Cross, 529; saddened by death of JB, 530; 60th birthday, 531; wants neither portrait nor bust of GHL, 531; spends anniversary of his death reading his letters, 532. **1880** receives friends again, 532; asks Edith not to call her 'Mother', 533; desc. by Bret Harte, 534; visits museums with Cross, 534; at Maud Lewes's 6th birthday

party, 534; desc. by Lucy Clifford, 535–6; tells Edith she never cared much for women, 535; consults Paget about marrying Cross, 536; Cross takes 4 Cheyne Walk, 536; welcomed by Cross family, 537; married at St. George's, Hanover Sq., 537; CLL gives her away, 537, and breaks news, 538; Isaac breaks silence, 541–2; Jowett's advice, 542–3; looks younger on wedding journey, 543; at Venice Cross jumps into Canal, 544; telegraphs for Willie Cross, 544; returns to Witley, 544; desc. by Mrs. Jebb, 545; recurrent renal attacks, 546; moves into 4 Cheyne Walk, 546; at Pop Concert, 546; at *Agamemnon*, 547; sees Spencer, the Congreves, Edith, 547; dies, 548; burial in the Abbey discussed, 548–9; funeral at Highgate, 549–50.

Portraits, by Mrs. Bray (1842), 45, facing 72; by Sara Hennell from Deville's cast of head (1844), facing 52; by D'Albert Durade, facing 72, 77; photograph by Mayall (1858), 102, etched (1884) by Rajon for frontispiece of Cross, Vol. II, but not used, facing 116; by Laurence (1860), frontispiece, 338, facing 340; by Burton (1865), facing 340, 377–8; by the Princess Louise (1877), 492, 501, facing 530.

Reading, 7, 13–15, 20, 22–5, 29, 35–6, 39–40, 47, 59, 65, 77, 173–4, 225, 246, 258, 271, 305, 342, 344–5, 349, 361, 381, 383, 399, 400, 404, 428, 430–1, 448, 472, 480, 505, 514, 526–7, 531, 546–7.

Unpublished works, 'Affectation and Conceit', 12, 553–4; ['Edward Neville'], 15–18, 206, 554–62; tr. Spinoza, *Ethics*, 200.

Projected Works, 'Chart of Ecclesiastical History', 24, 469; 'The Clerical Tutor', 249; 'The Idea of a Future Life', 141; 'Savello', 375; art. on Sir Walter Scott, 188; poems: 'Der arme Heinrich', 'The Burning of the Crucifix', 'But